PRACTICING TEXAS POLITICS

Enhanced 17e

Lyle C. Brown Baylor University

Joyce A. Langenegger Blinn College

Sonia R. García St. Mary's University

Robert E. Biles Sam Houston State University

Ryan T. Rynbrandt Collin College

Veronica Vega Reyna Austin Community College

Juan Carlos Huerta Texas A&M University—Corpus Christi

 CENGAGE

Australia • Brazil • Mexico • Singapore • United Kingdom • United States

Practicing Texas Politics,
Enhanced Seventeenth Edition

Lyle C. Brown
Joyce A. Langenegger
Sonia R. García
Robert E. Biles
Ryan T. Rynbrandt
Veronica Vega Reyna
Juan Carlos Huerta

Product Director: Laura Ross

Product Manager: Richard Lena

Product Assistant: Haley Gaudreau

Marketing Manager: Valerie Hartman

Content Manager: Dan Saabye

IP Analyst: Deanna Ettinger

IP Project Manager: Kelli Besse

Production Service and Compositor:
SPi Global

Art Director: Sarah Cole

Text and Cover Designer: Sarah Cole

Cover Image: Hero Images/Media Bakery -
AP Images/Nick Wagner

For product information and technology assistance, contact us at **Cengage Customer & Sales Support, 1-800-354-9706 or support.cengage.com.**

For permission to use material from this text or product, submit all requests online at **www.cengage.com/permissions**.

Library of Congress Control Number: 2019941094

Student Edition:
ISBN: 978-0-357-13246-3

Loose-leaf Edition:
ISBN: 978-0-357-13251-7

Cengage
200 Pier 4 Boulevard
Suite 400
Boston, MA 02210
USA

Cengage is a leading provider of customized learning solutions with employees residing in nearly 40 different countries and sales in more than 125 countries around the world. Find your local representative at **www.cengage.com**.

Cengage products are represented in Canada by Nelson Education, Ltd.

To learn more about Cengage platforms and services, register or access your online learning solution, or purchase materials for your course, visit **www.cengage.com**.

Printed in the United States of America
Print Number: 01   Print Year: 2019

Brief Contents

Detailed Contents

State Learning Outcomes

Practicing Texas Politics helps you meet the State Learning Outcomes for *GOVT 2306:*

1. Explain the origin and development of the Texas constitution.

2. Demonstrate an understanding of state and local political systems and their relationship with the federal government.

3. Describe separation of powers and checks and balances in both theory and practice in Texas.

4. Demonstrate knowledge of the legislative, executive, and judicial branches of Texas government.

5. Evaluate the role of public opinion, interest groups, and political parties in Texas.

6. Analyze the state and local election process.

7. Describe the rights and responsibilities of citizens.

8. Analyze issues, policies, and political culture of Texas.

Chapter in *Practicing Texas Politics*	GOVT 2306 State Learning Outcomes (SLO) that are specifically addressed in the chapter
1: The Environment of Texas Politics	SLO 8 Analyze issues, policies, and political culture of Texas.
	With some attention to
	SLO 1 Explain the origin and development of the Texas constitution.
	SLO 2 Demonstrate an understanding of state and local political systems and their relationship with the federal government.
	SLO 3 Describe separation of powers and checks and balances in both theory and practice in Texas.
	SLO 4 Demonstrate knowledge of the legislative, executive, and judicial branches of Texas government.
	SLO 7 Describe the rights and responsibilities of citizens.
2: Federalism and the Texas Constitution	SLO 1 Explain the origin and development of the Texas constitution.
	SLO 2 Demonstrate an understanding of state and local political systems and their relationship with the federal government.
	SLO 3 Describe separation of powers and checks and balances in both theory and practice in Texas.
	SLO 4 Demonstrate knowledge of the legislative, executive, and judicial branches of Texas government.
	SLO 7 Describe the rights and responsibilities of citizens.

(*Continued*)

Chapter in *Practicing Texas Politics*	GOVT 2306 State Learning Outcomes (SLO) that are specifically addressed in the chapter	
3: Local Governments	SLO 2	Demonstrate an understanding of state and local political systems and their relationship with the federal government.
	SLO 6	Analyze the state and local election process.
	SLO 7	Describe the rights and responsibilities of citizens.
	SLO 8	Analyze issues, policies, and political culture of Texas.
4: Political Parties	SLO 2	Demonstrate an understanding of state and local political systems and their relationship with the federal government.
	SLO 5	Evaluate the role of public opinion, interest groups, and political parties in Texas.
	SLO 6	Analyze the state and local election process.
	SLO 8	Analyze issues, policies, and political culture of Texas.
5: Campaigns and Elections	SLO 2	Demonstrate an understanding of state and local political systems and their relationship with the federal government.
	SLO 5	Evaluate the role of public opinion, interest groups, and political parties in Texas.
	SLO 6	Analyze the state and local election process.
	SLO 7	Describe the rights and responsibilities of citizens.
	SLO 8	Analyze issues, policies, and political culture of Texas.
6: The Media and Politics	SLO 5	Evaluate the role of public opinion, interest groups, and political parties in Texas.
	SLO 8	Analyze issues, policies, and political culture of Texas.
7: The Politics of Interest Groups	SLO 5	Evaluate the role of public opinion, interest groups, and political parties in Texas.
	SLO 8	Analyze issues, policies, and political culture of Texas.
8: The Legislative Branch	SLO 3	Describe separation of powers and checks and balances in both theory and practice in Texas.
	SLO 4	Demonstrate knowledge of the legislative, executive, and judicial branches of Texas government.
	SLO 8	Analyze issues, policies, and political culture of Texas.
9: The Executive Branch	SLO 3	Describe separation of powers and checks and balances in both theory and practice in Texas.
	SLO 4	Demonstrate knowledge of the legislative, executive, and judicial branches of Texas government.
	SLO 8	Analyze issues, policies, and political culture of Texas.
10: The Judicial Branch	SLO 3	Describe separation of powers and checks and balances in both theory and practice in Texas.
	SLO 4	Demonstrate knowledge of the legislative, executive, and judicial branches of Texas government.
	SLO 7	Describe the rights and responsibilities of citizens.
	SLO 8	Analyze issues, policies, and political culture of Texas.
11: Finance and Fiscal Policy	SLO 2	Demonstrate an understanding of state and local political systems and their relationship with the federal government.
	SLO 3	Describe separation of powers and checks and balances in both theory and practice in Texas.

Chapter in *Practicing Texas Politics*	GOVT 2306 State Learning Outcomes (SLO) that are specifically addressed in the chapter	
12: Public Policy and Administration	SLO 8	Analyze issues, policies, and political culture of Texas.
13: The Criminal Justice System	SLO 2	Demonstrate an understanding of state and local political systems and their relationship with the federal government.
	SLO 4	Demonstrate knowledge of the legislative, executive, and judicial branches of Texas government.
	SLO 7	Describe the rights and responsibilities of citizens.
	SLO 8	Analyze issues, policies, and political culture of Texas.

A Letter to Instructors

Dear Texas Government Instructor:

Texas politics is a dynamic enterprise. As Texas moves from being a majority-minority state to becoming a majority-Latino state, the changing demographics will alter election outcomes and public policy decisions. An economy that fluctuates with the rise and fall of oil and gas prices results in a surplus of funds in one legislative session and a scarcity in the next session. Reliance on money from the federal government, especially for funding social-welfare programs, regularly brings state officials into conflict with federal authorities and conditions placed on use of those funds. Limited water resources and a decaying infrastructure require innovative government solutions before these problems erode the state's economic success and growth. Government officials play an active role in negotiating and resolving policy issues in the context of an ever-changing demographic, economic, and ideological environment. Students in our classrooms will be the ones who select policymakers and policies to deal with a multiplicity of concerns that face the Lone Star State in the 21st century. Understanding their government and appreciating its dynamism is critical to our students' future role as active, informed citizens.

- *Practicing Texas Politics* analyzes **the practices and policies** of the Lone Star State by giving students a realistic introduction to how public policymaking is conducted in Texas. The state's individualistic and traditionalistic political culture, together with the role of Texas's rapidly changing demographics, are referenced throughout to aid students in placing policy decisions in a historical and cultural context. Students are introduced to current policymakers, their decisions, and the impact of the resulting policies. Roles of political parties, special interest groups, voters, and the media in influencing public policy are also explored. Policymaking and process are integrated within each chapter throughout the book with a special emphasis on public education, higher education, social services, and infrastructure needs both from a budgetary perspective in Chapter 11, "Finance and Fiscal Policy," and as policy issues in Chapter 12, "Public Policy and Administration."

- Through **learning outcomes, learning checks, and other pedagogical features**, students are given an organizational structure that helps them learn, understand, and remember the material.

New to This Edition

In this edition, we have continued to focus on aligning our narrative with the **state learning outcomes** for GOVT 2306. New to this edition, we have introduced a strategy for addressing the skills-based **core objectives** required of the discipline, as defined by the Undergraduate Education Advisory Committee (UEAC) of the Texas Higher Education Coordinating Board (THECB).

- The enhanced edition has been designed to support students' development of these core objectives, with the expansion of core objective questions that prompt students to engage in critical thinking, develop communication skills, evaluate social responsibility, and reflect on their own sense of personal responsibility.

- **The role of the emerging Latino majority** in reshaping Texas politics is addressed in several areas, including political party dominance, representation in all branches of state government, the media, and public policy.
- **"Keeping Current: The Impact on Texas"** analyzes the outcome and effect of both the national and state 2016 and 2018 elections on aspects of Texas politics and the 86th legislative session.
- The text has been updated to include the effects of **recent court decisions** such as *South Dakota v. Wayfair, Inc.*, and other changes in laws and procedures.
- Updates highlighting **new laws enacted by the 86th regular session** are included.
- **All images are now numbered,** which will enhance navigation in the electronic version of the book.

MindTap

As an instructor, MindTap is here to simplify your workload, organize, and immediately grade your students' assignments, and allow you to customize your course as you see fit. Through deep-seated integration with your Learning Management System, grades are easily exported and analytics are pulled with just the click of a button. MindTap provides you with a platform for easily adding current events, videos, and RSS feeds from national or local news sources.

Our goal, first and foremost, is to help you engage your students in the dynamic process of politics and develop them into active, informed participants in their democracy. We have attempted to present a realistic and up-to-date picture of how Texas politics is practiced in all branches and at both local and state levels of government. We welcome your feedback on any material or feature in this book.

Sincerely,

The *Practicing Texas Politics* Author Team

A Letter to Students

Dear Student:

Welcome to Texas government. Whether you're a native-born Texan or a newly arrived Texan, you can feel the energy of change all around you. You live in a state that no longer has a majority population from any race or ethnic group and in a few short years will have a majority Latino population. Despite the economic downturn that affected the rest of the world, you're in a state that consistently created more new jobs than any other state for most of the last decade. By 2019, the Texas economy more closely resembled the US economy in job creation and unemployment rates. Even with the erratic nature of the energy sector and related job losses, the number of new Texans continued to increase. Four of the 11 largest metropolitan areas in the nation are in Texas: Houston, San Antonio, Dallas-Ft. Worth, and Austin. All were projected to experience significant population growth through 2019 and beyond. This same state, however, has the most uninsured children in the nation, the highest dropout rate in the country, and one of the greatest gaps in earnings between the wealthy and the poor in the United States. A decaying transportation infrastructure and depleted water resources will require multibillion-dollar solutions. And who will solve these problems? You, the future voters and taxpayers of Texas, will have that responsibility. That's why you need to understand your role and how the system works so you can keep Texas the vibrant state we all want it to be. Helping you become an effective participant in that system is why we wrote *Practicing Texas Politics*.

In this book, you'll be introduced to today's important policymakers and learn what we all have a right to expect of them. You'll meet students just like you, who have chosen to get involved and make a difference at their colleges and universities, in their communities, and in this state. You'll learn about ways you can become involved through internships and other programs, as well as by voting and through political campaigns. You'll see how Texas compares to other states, and you'll be exposed to the diversity and uniqueness of the Lone Star State—home to the only State Tweeter Laureate in the nation (Supreme Court Justice Don Willett), a host of musicians from Los Lonely Boys to Chingo Bling to Willie Nelson, and four former U.S. presidents (Dwight Eisenhower, Lyndon Johnson, George H. W. Bush, and George W. Bush). You'll come to understand what this state could be in the future and how you can shape the outcome.

- Updated **"Students in Action"** features in each chapter help you make a personal connection to the content. The features highlight how Texas students like you have participated in the community or provide information on internships and other opportunities for interested students.

- **"Point/Counterpoint"** examines a key controversial issue in Texas politics from both sides of the controversy and asks you to take a stand on each issue.

- **"Learning Checks"** provide a few factual questions at the end of major sections for you to use in checking your knowledge. Answers are provided at the end of the chapter.

- **"How Do We Compare?"** boxes compare Texas with other states.

- A **Marginal Glossary** allows you to access terms as they are needed for easier understanding of the text.

- **End-of-chapter materials** include a conclusion that wraps up the chapter and offers final thoughts for you to consider, a chapter summary organized by learning outcome, Key Terms, and Learning Check answers.

- **Skills-based, core objective** questions with all images ask you to engage in critical thinking, develop communication skills, evaluate social responsibility, and reflect on your personal responsibility by thinking about your political opinion and beliefs on a variety of important issues in this state.

- **Charts, graphs, and maps** are used to give you a visual image for understanding concepts.

- **Keeping Current: The Impact on Texas** provides insight into what recent state and national elections and legislative decisions mean for the Lone Star State.

- **Social media icons** mark explanations of the ways social media is influencing government, affecting political campaigns, and transforming the media.

The Benefits of Using Mindtap as a Student

As a student, the benefits of using MindTap with this book are endless. With automatically graded practice quizzes and activities, an easily navigated learning path, and an interactive eBook, you will be able to test yourself in and outside of the classroom. Accessibility of current events coupled with interactive media makes the content fun and engaging. On your computer, phone, or tablet, MindTap is there when you need it, giving you easy access to flashcards, quizzes, readings, and assignments.

You will guide Texas through the 21st century. It is our hope that when you understand how to get involved in Texas politics, you will choose to do so. And that once you are involved, you will use your vote and influence to create the kind of Texas in which you want to live. It is to you, the students of Texas, that we dedicate this book.

Sincerely,

The *Practicing Texas Politics* Author Team

Resources

Students

Access your *Practicing Texas Politics* resources by visiting **www.cengage.com**.

If you purchased MindTap access with your book, click on "Register a Product" and then enter your access code.

Cengage Unlimited

Cengage Unlimited is the first-of-its-kind digital subscription that empowers students to learn more for less. One student subscription includes total access to every Cengage online textbook, platform, career and college success centers, and more—in one place. Learn across courses and disciplines with confidence that you won't pay more to access more. Available now in bookstores and online.

*Available only in select markets. Details at **www.cengage.com/unlimited**.

Instructors

Access your *Practicing Texas Politics* resources via **www.cengage.com/login**.

Log in using your Cengage Learning single sign-on user name and password, or create a new instructor account by clicking on **"New Faculty User"** and following the instructions.

MindTap for *Practicing Texas Politics*
ISBN for Instant Access Code: 9780357132494
MindTap for *Practicing Texas Politics* is a highly personalized, fully online learning experience built upon Cengage content and correlating to a core set of learning outcomes. MindTap guides students through the course curriculum via an innovative Learning Path Navigator where they will complete reading assignments, challenge themselves with focus activities, and engage with interactive quizzes. Through a variety of gradable activities, MindTap provides students with opportunities to check themselves for where they need extra help, as well as allowing faculty to measure and assess student progress. Integration with programs like YouTube and Google Drive allows instructors to add and remove content of their choosing with ease, keeping their course current while tracking local and global events through RSS feeds. The product can be used fully online with its interactive eBook for *Practicing Texas Politics,* Enhanced 17e, or in conjunction with the printed text.

MindTap Resource Center

Thousands of primary and secondary sources at your fingertips!

Access to Gale's authoritative library reference content is now available in every Political Science MindTap. Gale, part of Cengage, has been providing research and education resources for libraries for over 60 years.

Instructors have the option to choose from thousands of primary and secondary sources, images, and videos to enhance their MindTap course with the click of a button. This capability can replace a separate reader and conveniently keeps all course materials in one place. The selections are curated by experts, designed specifically for introductory courses, and can be accessed through MindTap's *Activity Builder* feature.

Instructor Companion Website for *Practicing Texas Politics* —for instructors only

ISBN: 9780357132470

This Instructor Companion Website is an all-in-one multimedia online resource for class preparation, presentation, and testing. Accessible through **Cengage.com/login** with your faculty account, you will find the following available for download: book-specific Microsoft® PowerPoint® presentations, a Test Bank compatible with multiple learning management systems, and an Instructor Manual.

The Test Bank, offered in Blackboard, Moodle, Desire2Learn, Canvas, and Angel formats, contains Learning Objective–specific and core competency–specific multiple-choice, critical thinking short answer questions, and essay questions for each chapter. Import the test bank into your LMS to edit and manage questions and to create tests.

The Instructor's Manual contains chapter-specific learning objectives, an outline, key terms with definitions, and a chapter summary. Additionally, the Instructor's Manual features a critical thinking question, lecture launching suggestion, and an in-class activity for each learning objective.

Microsoft® PowerPoint® presentations are ready-to-use, visual outlines of each chapter. These presentations are easily customized for your lectures. Access the Instructor Companion Website at www.cengage.com/login.

Cognero for *Practicing Texas Politics,* Enhanced 17e—for instructors only

ISBN: 9780357132524

Cengage Learning Testing Powered by Cognero is a flexible, online system that allows you to author, edit, and manage test bank content from multiple Cengage solutions; create multiple test versions in an instant; and deliver tests from your LMS, your classroom, or wherever you want. The test bank for *Practicing Texas Politics,* Enhanced 17e, contains Learning Objective–specific and core competency–specific multiple-choice, critical-thinking short answer, and essay questions for each chapter.

Practicing Texas Politics on Twitter

https://twitter.com/PracTexPol

Follow the *Practicing Texas Politics* author team's Twitter feed @PracTexPol for the latest news and updates that affect politics in the Lone Star State. Twitter feed also regularly posts tips for studying and thriving in college and engaging in active and informed citizenship.

Acknowledgments

We are indebted to many personal friends, government officials and their staffs, political activists, lawyers, and journalists who have stimulated our thinking. Likewise, we owe much to librarians and archivists who located hard-to-obtain facts and photos. We also appreciate the professional assistance rendered by the editorial, production, and marketing staff of Cengage Learning. Without the benefit of their publishing experience, this textbook and its ancillaries would be of much less value to students and instructors.

Of course, expressions of appreciation are due to spouses, family members, and others important to us who helped to produce this new edition of our book and have learned to cope with the irregular working hours of authors struggling to meet deadlines. We are especially grateful to the many students who assisted us in writing *Practicing Texas Politics*, especially those who willingly gave of their time and expertise in the production of the *Students in Action* feature, as well as those who assisted us by providing input to some of our early drafts. We give special thanks for the assistance and support of Macaella Gray, Lane Fraiser, Denise Alba-Ellington, and Nathaniel Torres of Austin Community College; and, Maria "Lupita" Partida of St. Mary's University.

We would also like to thank Jeffrey Goldings, for authoring this edition's Instructor's Manual and PowerPoint, and author Eric Miller of Blinn College and John Osterman of San Jacinto College, for authoring this edition's Test Bank. Our hope is that through the efforts of all, this book will help Texas students better understand the practice of Texas politics and their role as participants.

Reviewers

We would also like to thank the instructors who have contributed their valuable feedback through reviews of this text:

New Reviewers

Eric T Lundin
Lone Star College—Kingwood

Neal Tannahilll
Houston Community College

Jamey Crane
Houston Community College

Reisha Beaty
Houston Community College

Jennifer Bachan
Houston Community College

Daniel Allen
Hardin-Simmons University

Alicia Andreatta
Angelina College

Dorris Robinson
Texas Southern University

Vida Davoudi
Lone Star College—Kingwood

Previous Edition Reviewers

Margaret Richardson
San Antonio College

Kevin T. Holton
South Texas College

Olivia Wilson
Angelina College

Dr. Ashley D. Ross
Texas A&M University Galveston Campus

Prof. David E. Birch
Lone Star College—Tomball

Mario Marcel Salas
Northwest Vista College

Brian R. Farmer
Amarillo College

Billy Hathorn
Laredo Community College

Amy S. Glenn
Northeast Lakeview College

Jim Startin
University of Texas at San Antonio

Sandra Creech
Temple College

Patrizio Amezcua
San Jacinto College—North

Debra St. John
Collin College—Preston Ridge Campus

Evelyn Ballard
Houston Community College—Southeast College

Aaron Knight
Houston Community College—Northeast College

About the Authors

Lyle C. Brown is professor emeritus of political science at Baylor University, where he served as departmental director of graduate studies and director of Baylor's Foreign Service Program. His international academic experience includes teaching at Mexico City College (now University of the Americas) and postgraduate study at the Instituto Tecnológico de Monterrey in Mexico. He received his M.A. from the University of Oklahoma and Ph.D. from the University of Texas at Austin. Dr. Brown served as president of the Southwestern Council of Latin American Studies. His writing experience includes coediting *Religion in Latin American Life and Literature* and authoring numerous articles.

Joyce Langenegger teaches government at Blinn College and is the college's Executive Director of Academic Success. She received M.A. and J.D. degrees from Baylor University, and an M.A. and Ph.D. from Fielding Graduate University. Dr. Langenegger has been named to "Who's Who Among America's Teachers" and received a NISOD Award for Teaching Excellence, Teacher of the Year for Blinn College-Bryan, and "Most Valuable Player" award from San Jacinto College for her work as a professor and administrator at that institution. She is a frequent workshop presenter on innovative teaching strategies. Before beginning her teaching career, she practiced law in Houston.

Sonia R. García is a professor of political science, coordinator of the women's studies program, and a pre-law advisor at St. Mary's University in San Antonio. She has also served as chair and graduate director of the political science department. Dr. García received her master's degree from the University of Arizona and her Ph.D. from the University of California, Santa Barbara. She has published articles on Latina politics and is a co-author of *Mexican Americans and the Law: El Pueblo Unido Jamás Será Vencido* and lead author of *Políticas: Latina Public Officials in Texas*. Her involvement includes leadership development for various Latino/a-based organizations.

Robert E. Biles, professor emeritus and former chair of political science at Sam Houston State University, has taught college students about Texas politics in Texas, Colombia, and Ecuador. He received his M.A. and Ph.D. from The Johns Hopkins University-School of Advanced International Studies. Dr. Biles is the author of numerous books and articles. His involvement in politics includes serving as a school board member, county party chair, county election supervisor, and staff member of the U.S. Senate Foreign Relations Committee. He has advised state agencies and held leadership positions in statewide lobbying groups and professional organizations. Dr. Biles has received four Fulbright grants, as well as awards for his research, teaching, and administrative service.

Ryan T. Rynbrandt is a professor of political science and former director of the Honors Institute at Collin College in Plano, Texas, where he teaches courses in American government and Texas Government. Professor Rynbrandt leads campus initiatives that help students improve academic and life skills, develop mental and emotional resilience, and increase civic engagement. His research and writing examines the role of the pursuit of happiness in American political history, culture, and public policy. He earned his master's degree from the University of Michigan in Ann Arbor, where he received multiple teaching awards and served as president of the Graduate Association of Political Scientists. He has been active in politics at the local, state, and national levels.

Veronica Vega Reyna is associate professor of government and assistant dean of Social and Behavioral Sciences for Austin Community College. She has been faculty advisor to a civil rights organization at ACC. Professor Reyna earned her M.A. in Political Science from St. Mary's University in San Antonio, where she taught as adjunct faculty. Her political involvement has included interning for Congressman Ciro Rodriguez, working as a union organizer, and volunteering in various Texas campaigns. She has also taught Texas politics at colleges and universities in San Antonio.

Juan Carlos Huerta is a professor of political science at Texas A&M University—Corpus Christi. He earned his M.A. and Ph.D. in political science from the University of Houston. Dr. Huerta is active in promoting teaching and learning in political science and has served as president of the Political Science Education Organized Section of the American Political Science Association and the Southwestern Political Science Association. He is the founding president of the Learning Communities Association. His research and writing examines political representation, public opinion, Latino/a politics, political science education, and learning communities.

Career Opportunities: Political Science

Introduction

It is no secret that college graduates are facing one of the toughest job markets in the past 50 years. Despite this challenge, those with a college degree have done much better than those without since the 2008 recession. One of the most important decisions a student has to make is the choice of a major; many consider future job possibilities when making that call. A political science degree is incredibly useful for a successful career in many different fields, from law to policy advocate, pollster to humanitarian worker. Employer surveys reveal that the skills that most employers value in successful employees—critical thinking, analytical reasoning, and clarity of verbal and written communication—are precisely the tools that political science courses should develop. This brief guide is intended to help spark ideas for what kinds of careers you might pursue with a political science degree and the types of activities you can engage in now to help you secure one of those positions after graduation.

Careers in Political Science

Law and Criminal Justice

Do you find that your favorite parts of your political science classes are those that deal with the Constitution, the legal system, and the courts? Then a career in law and criminal justice might be right for you. Traditional jobs in the field range from attorney or judge to police or parole officer. Since 9/11, there has also been tremendous growth in the area of homeland security, which includes jobs in mission support, immigration, travel security, as well as prevention and response.

Public Administration

The many offices of the federal and state governments combined represent one of the largest employers in the United States. Flip to the chapter on the executive branch of this textbook and consider that each state department and agency you see looks to political science majors for future employees. At the federal level, a partial list of such agencies would include the Department of Education, the Department of Health and Human Services, and the Federal Trade Commission. Texas offers similar opportunities including the Texas Education Agency and the Health and Human Services Commission. There are also thousands of staffers who work for members of Congress or the Congressional Budget Office, and at the state level for legislators and the Legislative Budget Board. Many of these staffers were political science majors in college. This does not even begin to account for the multitude of similar jobs in local governments that you might consider as well.

Campaigns, Elections, and Polling

Are campaigns and elections the most exciting part of political science for you? Then you might consider a career in the growing industry based around political campaigns. From volunteering and interning to consulting, marketing, and fundraising, there are many opportunities for those who enjoy the competitive and high-stakes electoral arena. For those looking for careers that combine political knowledge with statistical skills, there are careers in public opinion polling. Pollsters work for independent national organizations, such as Gallup and YouGov, or as part of news operations and campaigns. For those who are interested in survey methodology, there are also a wide variety of nonpolitical career opportunities in marketing and survey design.

Interest Groups, International and Nongovernmental Organizations

Is there a cause that you are especially passionate about? If so, there is a good chance that there are interest groups out there that are working hard to see some progress made on similar issues. Many of the positions that one might find in for-profit companies also exist in their nonprofit interest group and nongovernmental organization counterparts, including lobbying and high-level strategizing. Do not forget that there are also quite a few major international organizations, such as the United Nations, the World Health Organization, and the International Monetary Fund, where a degree in political science could be put to good use. While competition for those jobs tends to be fierce, your interest and knowledge about politics and policy will give you an advantage.

Foreign Service

Does a career in diplomacy and foreign affairs, complete with the opportunity to live and work abroad, sound exciting to you? Tens of thousands of people work for the U.S. State Department, in Washington D.C. and in consulates and embassies around the world. They represent the diplomatic interests of the United States abroad. Entrance into the Foreign Service follows a very specific process, starting with the Foreign Service Officers Test—an exam given three times a year that includes sections on American government, history, economics, and world affairs. Being a political science major is a significant help in taking the FSOT.

Graduate School

While not a career, graduate school may be the appropriate next step for you after completing your undergraduate degree. Following the academic route, being awarded a Ph.D. or Master's degree in political science could open additional doors to a career in academia, as well as many of the professions mentioned earlier. If a career as a researcher in political science interests you, you should speak with your advisors about continuing your education.

Preparing While Still on Campus

Internships

One of the most useful steps you can take while still on campus is to visit your college's career center in regard to an internship in your field of interest. Not only does it give you a chance to experience life in the political science realm, it can lead to job opportunities down the road and add experience to your resume.

Skills

In addition to your political science classes, there are a few skills that will prove useful as a complement to your degree:

Writing: Like anything else, writing improves with practice. Writing is one of those skills that is applicable regardless of where your career might take you. Virtually every occupation relies on an ability to write clearly, concisely, and persuasively.

Public Speaking: An oft-quoted 1977 survey showed that public speaking was the most commonly cited fear among respondents. And yet oral communication is a vital tool in the modern economy. You can practice this skill in a formal class setting or through extracurricular activities that get you in front of a group.

Quantitative Analysis: As the Internet aids in the collection of massive amounts of information, the nation is facing a drastic shortage of people with basic statistical skills to interpret and use this data. A political science degree can go hand-in-hand with courses in introductory statistics.

Foreign Language: One skill that often helps a student or future employee stand out in a crowded job market is the ability to communicate in a language other than English. Solidify or set the foundation for your verbal and written foreign language communication skills while in school.

Student Leadership

One attribute that many employers look for is "leadership potential" which can be quite tricky to indicate on a resume or cover letter. What can help is a demonstrated record of involvement in clubs and organizations, preferably in a leadership role. While many people think immediately of student government, most student clubs allow you the opportunity to demonstrate your leadership skills.

Conclusion

Hopefully, reading this section has sparked some ideas on potential future careers. As a next step, visit your college's career placement office, which is a great place to further explore what you have read here. You might also visit your college's alumni office to connect with graduates who are working in your field of interest. Political science opens the door to a lot of exciting careers. Have fun exploring the possibilities!

The Environment of Texas Politics

1

Learning Objectives

1.1 Analyze how political culture has shaped Texas's politics, government, and public policy.

1.2 Describe the relationship between the social history of Texas and the political characteristics of the state's diverse population.

1.3 Discuss the political implications of Texas's size in both geography and population, along with the geographic distribution of its residents.

1.4 Describe the industries that formed the historic basis for the Texas economy, the diversification of the modern Texas economy, and the implications for Texas politics.

1.5 Identify five major policy challenges Texas faces in the 21st century.

IMAGE 1.1 Governor Abbott uses social media to attract business to Texas

Gov. Greg Abbott
@GovAbbott

⚙ 👤 Follow

#Texas is the land of opportunity. Our economy is diverse and our workforce strong. bit.ly/1X41Zzu

#1 best state for business 11 years in a row

12th largest economy in the world

2.4 million small business job creators

54 Fortune 500 companies

TEXAS

work-ready job force of 13 million

#1 state for private sector jobs added

RETWEETS 138   LIKES 134

8:00 AM - 4 Feb 2016

Source: Twitter

— Competency Connection —
⚙ **CRITICAL THINKING** ⚙

How can the Texas government most effectively work to continue the state's success and address its challenges?

I have said that Texas is a state of mind, but I think it is more than that. It is a mystique closely approximating a religion. And this is true to the extent that people either passionately love Texas or passionately hate it and, as in other religions, few people dare to inspect it for fear of losing their bearings in mystery or paradox. But I think there will be little quarrel with my feeling that Texas is one thing. For all its enormous range of space, climate, and physical appearance, and for all the internal squabbles, contentions, and strivings, Texas has a tight cohesiveness perhaps stronger than any other section of America. Rich, poor, Panhandle, Gulf, city, country, Texas is the obsession, the proper study and the passionate possession of all Texans.

—*John Steinbeck, 1962*

⊡ Everything Is Changing in Texas

They say everything is bigger in Texas. Even the stereotypes are big—big trucks, big belt buckles, big hair—but if that's all you know about the Lone Star State, you don't know today's Texas. Perhaps the biggest things about Texas are the changes it has seen and the diversity that has resulted. It's the land of Willie Nelson, for certain; but it's also the land of Selena Gomez, Beyoncé Knowles, Chingo Bling, Leon Bridges, Chamillionaire, The Mars Volta, Kacey Musgraves, Post Malone, and Mitch Grassi. It's still the land of cattle barons and oil tycoons; but it's also the land of high-tech pioneers, international traders, defense contractors, manufacturers, and service providers. Texas's stunning growth in recent decades has brought massive transformation and breathtaking variety in its people, economy, and politics.

If you live here, these transformations and the way our political system handles them have a significant impact on your life. Better understanding Texas and its political system will help you navigate these changes and contribute to the development of a better government. If you don't live here, pay attention anyway; the Texas experience is a preview of the changes facing the United States as a whole. The Lone Star State's successes and failures in negotiating these changes and balancing diverse interests will provide lessons for the rest of the nation. And you'll probably end up moving here anyway—everyone else seems to be. Since 2005, Texas has welcomed nearly twice the number of new arrivals as any other state. In the past few decades, tens of millions have told their place of origin what David Crockett allegedly told the people of his Kentucky district: "You may all go to hell, and I'll go to Texas." Because of the sheer size of Texas, what happens here also has an impact on the direction of the United States as a whole.[1] In 2019, the U.S. Census Bureau ranked Texas second largest among the 50 states, with a population approaching 29 million. That places the Lone Star State between California with its 39.5 million residents and Florida with more than 21 million.

Substantial changes and diverse interests put democratic institutions of government to the test. The increased population of the Lone Star State includes over 21 million men and women of voting age (18 years or older).[2]

Our analysis of the politics of Texas's state and local governments will help you understand political action and prepare you to be an active and informed participant in the political life of the state and its counties, cities, and special districts. As Texas Congresswoman Barbara Jordan once said, "The stakes are too high for government to be a spectator sport." It's time to suit up and play. To help you play effectively, we will introduce you to the playing field (government, political culture, land, and economy of the state), the players (citizens, activists, politicians, public employees, and opinion leaders), and the rules of the game (constitution, laws, and political processes).

★ Texas Politics and Political Culture

LO 1.1 Analyze how political culture has shaped Texas's politics, government, and public policy.

There has never been full agreement in democratic societies about the proper size and role of government. Views on that question vary widely and are held deeply. Yet aside from a handful of anarchists, there *is* agreement that society needs rules, or public policies, by which to live. Making, implementing, and enforcing these policies is the job of **government**. The government of the state of Texas is modeled on that of the United States, with the power to make policy divided among legislative, executive, and judicial branches. Each branch has its own powers, and each has some ability to limit or check the power of the others. The state government also delegates some policymaking power to local governments, including counties, cities, and special districts. As a result, **public policies** take different forms.

Government, Politics, and Public Policy in Texas

Many policies are laws passed by the legislature, approved by the governor, implemented by an executive department, and interpreted by the courts. Others are constitutional amendments proposed by the legislature and ratified by the voters of Texas. Some policies derive from rules promulgated by state agencies and ordinances passed by local governments. What all of these efforts share in common is that they are attempts to meet a public need or reach a public goal. Government tries to meet public needs by allocating resources. For example, state or local government may formulate, adopt, and implement a public policy, such as raising taxes to pay for more police protection or better streets and highways. Government tries to meet public goals by using policy to encourage or discourage specific behaviors. The state can encourage some behaviors using incentives—for example, establishing scholarships or student loan programs to encourage getting an education. It can discourage other conduct with punishments, such as imposing prison time for selling drugs. In addition, the government can encourage or

government
A public institution with authority to formulate, adopt, implement, and enforce public policies for a society.

public policy
What government does to or for its citizens to meet a public need or goal as determined by a legislative body or other authorized officials.

discourage behaviors through public relations and information campaigns, such as the famous "Don't Mess with Texas" campaign against littering.

In the political realm, you may think of public policy as the product and government as the factory in which policy is made. If that's the case, then **politics** is the process that produces public policy. In fact, the government has at times been compared to a sausage factory—even if you like the product it produces, the process isn't always very pleasant to watch. The politics of policymaking often involves conflict among government officials, political parties, interest groups, media figures, citizens, noncitizen residents, and other groups that seek to influence how policies in Texas are enacted and implemented. Conflict over power and resources can encourage the worst behavior in people, and opportunities for corruption and greed abound. Yet politics also requires cooperation and can inspire noble and courageous action. In sum, politics is the moving force by which government produces public policy, which in turn determines whether and how we use the power of the state to address our challenges and take advantage of our opportunities.

Types of Political Culture

We may not all agree on the proper role of government or what makes good public policy. Yet when certain widely shared values, attitudes, traditions, habits, and general behavioral patterns develop over time, they shape the politics and public policy of a particular region. We call this **political culture**. According to political scientist Daniel Elazar (1934–1999), "Culture patterns give each state its particular character and help determine the tone of its fundamental relationship, as a state, to the nation."[3] Based on the settlers in the original colonies, Elazar identified three distinct cultures that exist in the United States: moralistic, individualistic, and traditionalistic.

In the moralistic culture that originated in Puritan New England, citizens view government as a public service. They expect government to improve conditions for the people through economic regulation and to advance the public good to create a just society. Citizens see it as their duty to become active in governmental decision making through participation in politics and government, and they hold the government accountable to their high expectations.

The individualistic culture grew out of the focus on individual opportunity, especially in business, in the mid-Atlantic colonies. The business community advanced the individualistic culture, often viewing government as an adversary that taxed and regulated them; therefore, they wanted to limit its size and scope. Individualistic culture believes government activity, because it restricts individual economic freedom, is mostly negative and should be limited. Today, the individualistic culture is dominant in a majority of the midwestern and western states.

The traditionalistic culture grew out of the Old South and is rooted in feudal-like notions of society and government that developed in the context of the slave states, where property and income were unequally dispersed. Governmental policymaking fell to a few powerful families or influential social groups

politics
The process of policymaking that involves conflict and cooperation between political parties and other groups that seek to elect government officials or to influence those officials when they make public policy.

political culture
Widely shared attitudes, habits, and general behavior patterns that develop over time and affect the political life of a state or region.

who designed policies to preserve their place of dominance in the social order. The poor and minorities were often disenfranchised. In the traditionalistic culture, government is a vehicle for maintaining the status quo and its hierarchy. This culture has often developed one-party systems, which tend to strengthen those who are already powerful. Today, the traditionalistic culture remains dominant throughout the South.

Texas Political Culture

Texas exudes pride in its own uniqueness. The state's distinctive historical, geographical, and cultural identity has created a political culture that influences the Lone Star State's government, politics, and policy. As with all states, this culture is a mix of moralistic, individualistic, and traditionalistic subcultures. Although elements of each subculture exist in Texas, individualists and traditionalists have historically dominated the state and controlled the political system.

Texas Moralism The moralistic subculture in Texas has historically been the domain of those who lack power, yet moralists have helped shape Texas through numerous movements to use government for the betterment of society. The Radical Republicans of the post–Civil War era sought to use government to end a white supremacist political system and achieve racial equality. Radical Republican Governor E. J. Davis's aggressive use of state government power in an effort to protect African American political participation made him many enemies in the white power structure that regained control of the government when Reconstruction ended. Reaction to his administration resulted in the decentralized, weak government established by the 1876 Texas Constitution, which is still in operation today.

In the late 19th and early 20th centuries, **progressive** groups like the Farmers' Alliance, the Populist Party, and the Socialist Party surged in popularity in Texas as they challenged government to control the damaging effects of rising corporate capitalism.[4] Throughout the 1800s and into the early 1900s, a powerful Temperance movement in Texas sought to use government to end the sale and consumption of alcohol. From the earliest days of the civil rights struggle, **African Americans** and **Latinos** in Texas engaged in organized political activism to change the traditionalistic political structure of the state.

For most of its history, Texas has been a one-party-dominant state, one of the key identifiers of a traditionalistic political culture. Yet, within this traditionalistic environment, challenges occurred, whether the dominant party was Democratic or Republican. Individualists argued for policies that favored individual economic opportunity, and moralists sought greater government involvement to improve the lives of middle- and low-income Americans.

Texas Individualism Daniel Elazar asserted that the political culture of Texas is strongly individualistic, in that those in positions of power have tended to believe that government should maintain a stable society but intervene as little as possible in the lives of people.

progressive
Favoring and working for progress in conditions facing the majority of society or in government.

African American
A racial classification applied to Americans of African ancestry. The term is commonly applied on the basis of skin color, omitting white Americans whose ancestors immigrated from Africa and including black Americans whose ancestors immigrated from the Caribbean, Latin America, and Europe.

Latino
An ethnic classification of Americans of Latin American origin. When applied to females, the term is Latina. We will use this term throughout the book in addition to the term "Hispanic," which refers to people who trace their ancestry to Spain and other Spanish-speaking countries.

An important source of Texas's individualism is the mostly English-speaking, **Anglo** settlers who came to Texas in search of individual economic opportunity, either directly from the mid-Atlantic states or via the Midwest. In the early 19th century, a growing number of white colonists from the United States entered Texas individually or because they were recruited by *empresarios*, such as Stephen F. Austin. These settlers, without significant government backing or restraint, established farms and communities and persevered through extreme hardships.[5]

The power of Texas individualists is reflected in the government structure they helped create and continue to dominate. Compared with other heavily populated states, Texas has a limited government with restricted powers: a legislature that meets biennially, with low salaries that can be increased only after approval by Texas voters; a governor who has limited budgetary, appointment, and removal powers; and an elected judiciary. Per capita government spending for social services and public education is consistently among the lowest in the nation. Power at the local level is dispersed across more than 5,000 governments—counties, cities, school districts, and other special districts. The public perception of government and elected officials remains negative, although this viewpoint appears more directed to the federal government. Polls in 2018 indicated that only 1 percent of Texans trusted the government in Washington, D.C., to do the right thing all the time, and only 10 percent trusted it do to the right thing most of the time. State government, on the other hand, received the trust of twice as many Texans.[6]

Texas Traditionalism The dominance of traditionalistic culture in Texas also can be traced to the early 19th century and the immigration of Southern plantation owners. The plantation system thrived in East Texas, and cotton was king. Before Texas joined the Confederacy, much of its wealth was concentrated in a few families. Although slave owners represented only a quarter of the state's population and one-third of its farmers, these slave owners held 60 to 70 percent of the wealth and controlled state politics.[7] After the Civil War (1861–1865), **Jim Crow laws** limited African Americans' access to public services. In the late 19th and early 20th centuries, poll taxes and all-white primaries further restricted voting rights.

Today, many Texans are the descendants of migrants from traditionalistic states of the Old South, where conservatism, elitism (upper-class rule), and one-party politics were entrenched. Although urbanization and industrialization, together with an influx of people from other states and countries, are changing Texas, the traditionalistic influence of the Old South lingers. Prior to the 2018 midterm elections, participation in politics and voter turnout were consistently low. Turnout averaged less than 50 percent for presidential elections and was consistently below 30 percent for gubernatorial elections. Elazar noted that many Texans inherited Southern racist attitudes, which for a century after the Civil War were reflected in state laws that discriminated against African Americans and other minority groups. Though Texas has in recent years removed more symbols of the confederacy than any other state, it still has the second highest number of confederate memorials. These symbols and monuments continue to cause controversy.[8]

The traditionalistic influence of Mexico is also discernible among Texans of Mexican ancestry, who were affected by a political culture featuring the elitist **patrón** (protective political boss) **system** that dominates certain areas of South

Anglo
As commonly used in Texas, the term is not restricted to persons of Anglo-Saxon lineage but includes those of European ancestry more generally. Traditionally, the term applies to all whites except Latinos.

Jim Crow laws
Discriminatory laws that segregated African Americans and denied them access to public services for many decades after the Civil War.

patrón system
A type of boss rule that has dominated areas of South Texas and Mexico.

Texas. For more than four decades, however, the old political order of that region has been challenged—and, in many instances, defeated—by new generations of Mexican Americans. Compared with other areas of the state, however, voter turnout remains much lower in counties along the Mexican border.

The individualistic culture can be seen in the state's economic conservatism and deference to the power of wealthy businessmen and corporations. Texas has a climate favorable to business owners. It remains one of the few states without a personal or corporate income tax and has adopted **right-to-work laws**, which hinder the formation and operation of labor unions. City councils have drawn criticism for publicly financing corporate ventures or providing businesses with property tax abatements. The City of Arlington drew attention for its use of local tax dollars and **eminent domain** to remove people from their homes to make way for Jerry Jones's Dallas Cowboys (now AT&T) stadium. The traditionalistic-individualistic political culture of Texas is reflected in the important role powerful individuals and families continue to play in local and state politics and their influence on public policies.

A Changing Culture?

Since the mid-1970s Texas has experienced massive population influx from other areas of the nation and from other countries, many with more heavily moralistic political cultures. This in-migration raises an important question: How long will

IMAGE 1.2 Texas State Capitol Building

Courtesy of the Texas House of Representatives

— Competency Connection —
◉ **SOCIAL RESPONSIBILITY** ◉

In what ways is Texas's political culture (moralism, individualism, and traditionalism) reflected in politics, policies, and the people's attitudes about, and expectations of, government today?

right-to-work laws
Laws that limit the power of workers to bargain collectively and form and operate labor unions, increasing the power of employers relative to their employees.

eminent domain
The power of the government to take private property for public uses, so long as just compensation is paid.

the historical dominance of individualism and traditionalism continue to be the primary influences on Texas's style of politics and government? Will population changes shift the state toward the moralistic culture? Texas's political culture, inherited largely from the 19th century, faces the transformative power of widespread urbanization, industrialization, education, communication, and population shifts. Change is inevitable, but the direction, scope, and impact of the change remain to be seen.

✪ The People

LO 1.2 Describe the relationship between the social history of Texas and the political characteristics of the state's diverse population.

> *I am forced to conclude that God made Texas on his day off, for pure entertainment, just to prove that all that diversity could be crammed into one section of earth by a really top hand.*
>
> —*Mary Lasswell*

Texas is amazingly diverse in racial, ethnic, and cultural terms. According to the U.S. Census Bureau, more than one-half of all Texans are either African American or Latino. The remainder are predominantly Anglos (non-Hispanic whites), with a small but rapidly growing **Asian American** population and approximately 287,000 **Native Americans**. More than one-third of all Texans speak a language other than English at home. In 2012, the Houston metropolitan area replaced New York City as the most ethnically diverse city in the country. The historical changes that brought about this diversity were not always free of conflict.

Texans Throughout History: From Conflict Toward Cooperation

The politics of democracy is about forging a path for diverse groups with sometimes opposing interests to live together peaceably. One of the remarkable facets of Texas is that, though racial and ethnic tensions still exist, most members of its diverse population live together peacefully. Historically, peaceful coexistence was difficult. Texans have a reputation for toughness, and that reputation was formed over hundreds of years of surviving an often unforgiving terrain, made harsher by a social atmosphere that historian and political scientist Cal Jillson has called "breathtakingly violent."[9]

The First Texans Few specifics are known about the people who inhabited what would become the Lone Star State for more than 10,000 years before Spanish explorers planted the first of Texas's six flags here in the 1500s. When Spaniards arrived, the land was inhabited by more than 50 Native American tribes and nations. Population estimates vary widely, ranging from 50,000 to perhaps

Asian American
An ethnic classification for persons whose ancestry originates in the Far East, Southeast Asia, or the Indian subcontinent.

Native American
A term commonly used for those whose ancestors were living in the Americas before the arrival of Europeans and Africans. Another commonly used term in the United States is "American Indian."

a million people. In East Texas, the Caddo lived in organized villages with a complex political system. The state's name comes from the word *tejas*, meaning "friendly," which was the tribal name for a group of Indians within the Caddo Confederacy. The Comanche were arguably the most important tribe in shaping Texas history. Excellent horsemen and valiant warriors, they maintained a successful resistance to the northward expansion of Spaniards and Mexicans and to the westward expansion of Anglos.[10] Native American tribes were not unified. For example, the Tonkawa of Central Texas often allied with Anglos in fights against the Comanches and the Wichitas, another important South Plains tribe.

European Colonization Accurate estimates of the Native American population are not available, but whatever the true size, their numbers declined rapidly after European contact in the 16th century. With Spanish explorers and their African slaves came diseases that decimated native communities. Though sometimes peaceful, early contact also included the taking of slaves, torture, and even cannibalism.[11] Spain and France claimed Texas, but neither country actively ruled all of the territory. Their activities involved exploring, surveying, and fighting. Spanish activities included farming and livestock herding. Missions and towns were established around present-day Nacogdoches and San Antonio, and in a few places along the Rio Grande, but the area remained sparsely populated through the Mexican War of Independence (1810–1821). In 1824, three years after Mexico overthrew Spanish rule, the area that is now Texas became part of a federal republic for the first time.

Mexican Texas Around the time of Mexican independence, Anglo American settlers began coming to the Mexican province of *Tejas* in greater numbers. Although the first non-Spanish-speaking immigrants to Texas were largely of English ancestry, some were Scots, Irish, or Welsh descendants. Others were French, Scandinavian, and Eastern European, with a few Italians, Greeks, and other European nationalities. The arrival of Anglo settlers sped the decline of the Native American population, which had already been reduced to 20,000 to 30,000 people. Violence between the native population and immigrant whites was constant and pervasive. Despite the Mexican government's authorization of Stephen F. Austin to offer free land to settlers willing to work it, Mexican officials were concerned about the immigrants. Many Anglo newcomers resisted the constitution and laws of Mexico that established Catholicism as the state religion and abolished slavery. (See Chapter 2, "Federalism and the Texas Constitution," for more discussion of the historical context).

When General Antonio López de Santa Anna was elected president of Mexico in 1833, most Texans did not expect him to repudiate the principles of the federal democratic republic he was elected to serve. When he did so, one result was the Texas Revolution, with its famous battles at Goliad, the Alamo, and San Jacinto. A great deal of blood was shed to establish the independent Republic of Texas in 1836.

The Republic of Texas The elected presidents of the Republic, Sam Houston (twice) and Mirabeau B. Lamar, and the Texas Congress struggled to establish Texas as an independent nation, even as many in the government sought to join the United States. The burdens of establishing and maintaining an army and navy, operating a postal system, printing paper money, administering justice, and providing other governmental services were made difficult by conflicts within and without the Republic's borders.

Anglo-Indian warfare continued because of increased immigration from the United States and because some Texian Anglo leaders pursued policies of removal and extermination. Fighting was so fierce that two decades after independence, one observer in 1856 estimated the state's Native American population at only 12,000, with most having been killed or driven from the state.[12] While many Tejanos had fought for Texas's independence, Cal Jillson notes that "some Texas leaders sought to equate Indians and Mexicans and urge the expulsion or extermination of both."[13] From the time of Texas independence until 1890, immigration from Mexico all but ceased. Latinos remained concentrated in settlements such as San Antonio that were founded during the 18th century and within Central and South Texas. Conflicts, in some cases violent, among Anglo Texans, Native Americans, and Latino Texans, identified as Tejanos, continued into Texas's statehood, which came about in 1845, less than a decade after its independence.

The Lone Star State In South Texas, Latinos comprised a majority of the population despite the increased number of Anglo arrivals after the Mexican-American War of 1846–1848 (which followed admission of Texas into the Union). Anglo immigration dominated much of the rest of the state. Before the Civil War, more than one-half of the state's Anglo residents had migrated from Alabama, Arkansas, Georgia, Kentucky, Louisiana, Mississippi, Missouri, and Tennessee. Many of these new immigrants were slaveholders, so it was no surprise that the Republic of Texas legalized slavery and entered the federal Union as a slave state. By 1847, African Americans accounted for one-fourth of the state's population, and most were slaves.

Yet slavery was not universally accepted in Texas. Some estimates suggest as many as 24,000 German immigrants and descendants settled in the Hill Country of Central Texas by 1860. Most opposed slavery on principle, whereas others simply had no need for slaves. As a result, 14 counties in the region voted 40 percent or greater against secession in 1861. Despite Sam Houston's opposition, the secessionists won and Texas joined the Confederate States of America in February of that year. In the ordinance of secession and in an official explanation of the causes of secession issued the following day, Texas leaders repeatedly cited northern attacks on the institution of slavery, along with the alleged failure of the federal government to protect Anglo Texans against Mexican and Indian banditry and other grievances.[14]

The Civil War and Reconstruction Though Texas experienced less fighting than other southern states in the Civil War, ravages of combat were felt. In addition to battles with Union troops, Central Texas was scarred by what has been called "a civil war within a Civil War," as hundreds of opposing Union and Confederate sympathizers died in armed confrontations. The Confederacy lost the war, and Texas was brought back into the Union through Reconstruction, a period in which the U.S. government sought to protect African Americans and to remake the political and economic structures of southern states.

Governor Edmund J. Davis's heavy-handed tactics used to enfranchise freed slaves during Radical Reconstruction temporarily made political participation safe for freed slaves but disenfranchised many Anglo citizens who had supported the Confederacy. This change even led to a small wave of freedmen migration into Texas.

The Great State of Texas Texas was fully readmitted to the United States in 1870, but civil strife continued. Although Anglo migration into the state declined during the Civil War and Reconstruction, it resumed by the 1870s. Westward settlement further displaced Native Americans and converted the prairies into cattle and sheep ranches. A combination of Anglo in-migration and African American out-migration reduced the percentage of African Americans in the population from 31 percent in 1870 to 13 percent by 1950.

Those African Americans who remained in Texas faced great difficulty. Slavery was replaced for many by a different form of servitude in the form of sharecropping, in which they farmed land as tenants for a portion of the crops grown. De jure segregation, or segregation by law (also known as Jim Crow laws), resulted in denial of adequate education, scarcity of economic opportunities, and incidents of racial violence. Texas saw almost 340 lynchings of African Americans between the end of Reconstruction and World War II.[15]

Early in the 20th century, waves of immigrants escaping the Mexican Revolution and its aftermath fed the American need for seasonal laborers. Many Latinos worked for Anglo farmers and ranchers. The Great Depression and resulting competition for work greatly increased anti-immigrant sentiment and policy in Texas. Violence sometimes erupted as a result.[16]

After World War II, many Latinos left agriculture and sought manufacturing jobs in cities. Most of them experienced improvements in wages and working conditions as unskilled or semiskilled laborers. Nevertheless, a growing number of Latinos entered managerial, sales, and clerical professions. Many Texans joined Latino and African-American civil rights groups in the fight for equality.[17] In the 1960s, the federal government began to enforce the desegregation decisions of the U.S. Supreme Court, and Texan President Lyndon Johnson signed a series of new anti-discrimination civil rights laws. Public schools, workplaces, and some neighborhoods, especially in urban areas, were integrated.

Integration has reduced, but not eliminated, intergroup tension in Texas. Dramatic incidents of racial tension in the Lone Star State still occasionally garner national news. Major protests in Dallas, Austin, and Houston followed the 2014 unrest in Ferguson, Missouri, after police shot Michael Brown, an unarmed, 18-year-old African-American. In 2015, the public outcry over a video of a white police officer's physically rough treatment of a young African-American woman in McKinney and the death of Sandra Bland in police custody in Prairie View (near Houston) spread nationwide. Such incidents—along with statistics demonstrating continued discrimination in housing, employment, and criminal justice—illustrate that conflict and inequality still exist in the Lone Star State.

Yet historical minority groups have made major strides in education, employment, and political representation in recent decades. In increasing numbers, Texans work, live, socialize, date, and marry across racial, ethnic, and religious lines. Evidence shows that young people use more social media than other groups and that persons who use social media websites like Facebook or Twitter have more racially and ethnically diverse social networks. The Post-Millennial Generation is the most racially and ethnically diverse generation in American history and is poised to become the largest generation in the United States. This generation is coming of age as Texas moves from a majority-minority state, with no racial or ethnic majority, toward a majority Latino state.[18]

The U.S. Census Bureau projected racial/ethnic categories in Texas for 2018 at the following percentages:

White/Anglo	42.0
Hispanic/Latino	39.4
Black/African American	12.7
Asian	5.0
American Indian or Alaskan Native	1.0
Native Hawaiian or other Pacific Islander	0.1
Two or more races	2.0

Totals exceed 100 percent because some people report in more than one racial or ethnic category.

Texans Today

Texas ranks among the most racially and ethnically diverse states in the nation. There really is no such thing as a "typical Texan." Five groups comprise the major racial and ethnic groups in the state: Native American, Asian American, African American, Latino, and Anglo.

Native Americans Although some counties (Cherokee, Comanche, Nacogdoches), cities and towns (Caddo Mills, Lipan, Waxahachie), and other places have Native American names, by 2018, Texas Native Americans numbered about 287,000. Most Native Americans live and work in towns and cities, with only a few remaining on reservations. Approximately one-half of the 1,291 members of the Alabama-Coushatta tribe reside on a 4,351-acre East Texas reservation. On the U.S.–Mexican border near Eagle Pass, a few hundred members of the Kickapoo tribe are allowed by the governments of Mexico and the United States to move freely between Texas and the Mexican state of Coahuila. At the far western boundary of the state, the once poor 1,700-member Tigua tribe inhabits a reservation near El Paso.

As of mid-2019 all three tribes operated casino-like facilities. The Kickapoo have done so continuously since 1996, transforming their 850-member tribe from poverty to a middle-class lifestyle. The Tigua and Alabama-Coushatta tribes gained federal recognition later than the Kickapoo. At that time, Texas applied all state laws to Native American tribes, including those regarding gambling. Though both tribes opened very successful casino-like facilities, a federal judge ordered them shut down in 2002. Since then the Tigua and Alabama-Coushatta have organized politically to gain gaming rights on their reservations. They have made substantial campaign contributions, used the courts, and engaged in lobbying activity. In 2015, the National Indian Gaming Commission and the U.S. Department of the Interior declared that they would allow certain types of casino-like facility gambling on both the Tigua and Alabama-Coushatta reservations. Despite repeated attempts by Texas Attorney General Ken Paxton to shut down the facilities, both tribes used some forms of gambling to generate tens of millions of dollars a year. A federal judge again ruled against the tribes in March 2019, declaring them to be in violation of state law and ordering them to halt their operations. In 2019, Texas State Representative Joe Deshotel submitted a bill to amend the Texas Constitution to allow casino gambling with six casino licenses across six coastal counties. The amendment would have used casino profits to subsidize the state's windstorm insurance system but the bill did not pass.[19]

Asian Americans The Lone Star State is home to one of the largest Asian American populations (over 1.4 million) in the nation. Texas has long received immigrants from Asia. In recent years, immigration from the region has increased, while immigration from Latin American countries has declined. Census data indicate that the Asian population of Texas is diverse, with the largest groups claiming ancestry from Vietnam or the Indian subcontinent, but with substantial populations of East Asian or Filipino heritage. Vietnamese-born Hubert Vo (D-Houston) became the first Vietnamese American elected to the Texas House of Representatives in 2004 and has been reelected seven times. He was joined in the House by Taiwanese American Angie Chen Button in 2008, and by Chinese American Gene Wu in 2012.

Most Asian Americans live in the state's largest urban centers. Fort Bend County near Houston has the greatest percentage of Asian Americans in the state at 20 percent. More than one-half of Texas's first-generation Asian Americans entered this country with college degrees or completed their degrees after arrival.[20] The intensity with which the state's young Asian Americans focus on education is revealed by enrollment data at major Texas universities. Although Asian Americans account for less than 4 percent of the total population of the state, they comprised 19 percent of the undergraduate enrollment at the University of Texas at Austin and 33 percent of the enrollment at the University of Texas at Dallas in the fall 2018 semester.

African Americans By 2018, Texas was home to approximately 3.6 million African Americans, approximately 12.7 percent of the state's population. The African American population has continued to grow, but more slowly than other ethnic groups. Today, Texas has the second highest number of African Americans in the nation, after New York. Most African American Texans reside in southeast, north central, and northeast Texas. More than one-half of the state's African Americans reside in and near major urban areas. In recent years, a significant number of people seeking employment and a higher standard of living have immigrated from the African continent to the United States and settled in Texas. Although African Americans do not constitute a majority in any Texas county or large city, according to the 2010 census, the city of Beaumont had the highest percentage of African Americans at more than 47 percent.

From the years following Reconstruction until 1958 (when Hattie White was elected to the Houston School Board), no African American held elective office in the state. In recent decades, the political influence of African American Texans has increased in local, state, and national government. In 1972, Barbara Jordan became the first African American since Reconstruction to represent Texas in Congress; and in 1992, Morris Overstreet became the first African American to win a statewide office when he was elected to the Texas Court of Criminal Appeals. The 2018 election saw some remarkable victories for African American candidates in Texas. All 19 African American women who ran for judge in Harris County won. Dallas Democrat and former NFL star Collin Allred's victory over GOP incumbent House Rules Committee Chair Pete Sessions increased the number of Texas African Americans in Congress to six. The Democrats' new majority in the U.S. House of Representatives also meant that Eddie Bernice Johnson became the first African American from Texas to chair a standing committee in the U.S. House.

Latinos Texas has received immigrants from Central America, South America, and the Caribbean, but more than 88 percent of Texas Latinos are of Mexican origin. By 2016, Texas ranked second in the nation behind California in the number of Latino residents with over 10.4 million and second in the nation behind New Mexico in percentage of Latino residents with approximately 39 percent of the state's population. The majority of the population in 51 Texas counties is Latino. In eight counties in the Rio Grande Valley and along the border, more than 90 percent of the population is Latino. More than one-half of all newborns in the state are Latinos. Based on current population trends, some demographers suggest that by 2022 Latinos will be the largest population group.[21] Though poverty rates are significantly higher for Latinos than Anglos, Texas's Spanish-surnamed residents are gaining economic strength, and the number of Latino-owned businesses is growing rapidly.

As Latinos continue to be the fastest-growing ethnic group in Texas (in terms of numbers), their political influence is increasing. Between 1846 and 1961, only 19 Latino politicians were elected to the Texas legislature. Since 1961, however, Latinos have won election to many local, state, and national positions. In 1984, Raul Gonzalez became the first Latino in a statewide office when he won election to the Texas Supreme Court. Though group solidarity among Latino voters is lower than other groups and they do not always support Latino candidates, organizations such as the League of United Latin American Citizens (LULAC) and the Southwest Voter Registration Education Project have worked to increase voter registration and turnout in recent years. By 2017, Texas had more than 2,700 Latino elected officials, by far the largest number of any state and more than 41 percent of all Latino elected officials in the country.[22] Henry Gonzalez was the first Texas Latino elected to the U.S. House in 1963, and in 2011, Ted Cruz became the first elected to the U.S. Senate. In 2016, Cruz was a major contender for the Republican Party's presidential nomination. Texans reelected him to the Senate in 2018 and sent the state's first two Latinas, Sylvia Garcia and Veronica Escobar, to the U.S. House of Representatives. George P. Bush, whose mother was born in Mexico, identifies as Hispanic and won elections for Commissioner of the General Land Office in 2014 and 2018. Of the 29 officials elected on a statewide basis, as of 2019, three were Latino. Julián Castro, the former San Antonio mayor and former secretary of Housing and Urban Development in the Obama administration, has announced that he will run for the Democratic Party's presidential nomination in 2020.

Anglos According to the 2000 census, more than 52 percent of Texas's population was composed of "non-Hispanic whites," a category including people of European ancestry but also those of Middle Eastern and North African heritage. That percentage dropped to less than 50 percent in 2004, when Texas joined Hawaii, New Mexico, and California as majority-minority states. By 2018, the Anglo population of Texas was just over 12 million, or about 42 percent of the state's population. Projections indicate that the percentage of Anglos in the

IMAGE 1.3 Henry R. Muñoz III, co-founder of the Latino Victory Project, actress and political activist Eva Longoria, and Rep. Joaquín Castro, D-Texas, at an event launching The Latino Victory Project, a Latino political action committee.

AP Images/Charles Dharapak

— Competency Connection —
⚖ PERSONAL RESPONSIBILITY ⚖

In an increasingly diverse political landscape, how might you contribute to the representation of your community's interests?

state will continue to decrease and the percentage of other racial/ethnic groups will continue to increase.

Poverty rates among Texas Anglos remain dramatically lower than other groups, and incomes remain significantly higher. The poverty rate for Texas Anglos was 7 percent in 2017, compared to 17 percent for African Americans and 18 percent for Latinos. In 2016, African American and Latino households had median annual incomes below $45,000 whereas Anglo and Asian households averaged $94,000 to $101,800.[23] Anglos own almost two-thirds of all businesses in Texas. They also continue to hold most local, state, and national political offices in the Lone Star State.

Implications of Racial and Ethnic Diversity The changing demographics of Texas lead many to speculate that the partisan makeup of Texas will soon change. "Demographics Is Destiny," as the saying goes. Many point to Democratic Senate candidate Beto O'Rourke's nearly successful challenge to an incumbent Republican in 2018 as evidence that Texas will soon become a Democratic state. In that election, O'Rourke won 84 percent of the state's African American votes, 74 percent of Latinos, and 66 percent of Asian/Pacific Islanders.[24]

Yet the ascendance of Democrats over Republicans in Texas is not a foregone conclusion. Many Texas Latinos are ineligible to vote; and among those who are eligible, voting rates have been consistently low. Though registration and turnout by people of color increased in 2016 and 2018, it remains to be seen whether this will continue or is an isolated reaction to a president viewed by many as hostile to minority groups. Moreover, Texas Republicans have historically done better among Latino voters than Republicans at the national level and are making efforts to continue that trend.

Religious Diversity

Texas is becoming less religious overall and more diverse in terms of religious identification, with implications for politics and policy. The number of Texans claiming no religious affiliation is growing; yet at 18 percent of the state's population, that percentage is still among the lowest in the nation. Nationally, 22 percent of the population claims no religious affiliation. By most measures of religiosity, the percentage of the population claiming a religious affiliation, attending a weekly worship service, and holding religious beliefs, Texas ranks among the 10 most religious states. The Lone Star State still has some claim to the title of "Buckle of the Bible Belt."[25]

Texans are becoming increasingly diverse in their religious identification. About 31 percent of Texans identify with one of the many denominations of evangelical Protestantism. Yet almost 25 percent of Texans are Catholic, and about one in five identifies with either a mainline or historically black Protestant denomination. Although Mormons, Jehovah's Witnesses, Muslims, Hindus, Jews, Buddhists, and other minority religions only comprise 6 percent of the Texas population combined, membership in these groups is growing, both in number and as a percentage of the population. In fact, Texas has a larger population and a higher percentage of many of these religious groups than the national average.[26]

Because Texas's population is so large, small percentages disguise how large the membership is. Although representing only 1 percent of the Texas population, almost a half million Muslims live in the state. Most Texans respect religious freedom; however, increasing diversity sometimes sparks intergroup tensions. Fear of terrorism by radical Islamic groups fueled much debate in the 2016 election and sparked a near doubling of anti-Muslim incidents in the United States by 2018. During that time, Texas saw armed protests against Muslim organizations; incidents of threats, vandalism, and arson at Islamic mosques; and religiously motivated acts of violence against Muslims.[27] According to one poll in 2017, an estimated 45 percent of Texans supported barring non-American Muslims from entering the United States, but an estimated 47 percent opposed such a ban.[28]

These changes in the religious make-up of the state have broad political ramifications. White evangelical Christians tend more toward political conservatism and the Republican Party, but religious groups that favor political liberalism and the Democratic Party are growing as a proportion of the state's population. Religion also has an impact on people's views on a wide variety of public policies; and religious beliefs affect policy debates, from abortion to gay rights to economic justice to the death penalty.

> ### ✔ 1.2 Learning Check
>
> 1. How has the size and political power of Texas's Latino population changed in recent decades?
> 2. How has religious identification in Texas changed in recent years?
>
> *Answers at the end of this chapter.*

❖ The Land and Population Distribution

LO 1.3 Discuss the political implications of Texas's size in both geography and population, along with the geographic distribution of its residents.

Texas's politics and public policy have always been shaped by the state's size. With more than 267,000 square miles of territory, Texas is second only to Alaska (570,640 square miles) in area and is as large as the combined areas of Florida, Georgia, Alabama, Mississippi, and Tennessee. Connecting the more than 1,200 incorporated cities in Texas requires approximately 314,000 miles of roadways, including more than 80,000 miles of major highways constructed and maintained under the supervision of the Texas Department of Transportation. The state government is also responsible for more than 6,200 traffic signals, 1,000 dynamic message signs, and programs to prevent and respond to accidents and damage to roads and bridges.[29] Texas's massive size has an impact on political campaigns as well. Running for statewide office—and in some instances for district-level office—requires a significant investment of financial resources. Despite the rise of **social media** as an inexpensive and effective campaigning and organizing tool, traveling the state for rallies and fundraisers while targeting 18 media markets with advertisements is an expensive undertaking that requires extensive fundraising.

Texas is large both physically and in population. In every decade since 1850, Texas's population has grown more rapidly than the overall population of the United States. According to the federal census estimate of 2018, Texas's

social media
Websites and computer applications that allow users to engage in social networking and create online communities. Social media provide platforms for sharing information and ideas through discussion forums, videos, photos, documents, audio clips, and the like.

population totaled **28,701,845**—a stunning increase of 38 percent from 2000. (The population estimate for the United States in 2018 was 327,167,434—an increase of approximately 6 percent from 2000.) Texas also has had five of the fastest-growing metropolitan areas in the nation since the turn of the century. By 2018, the top three fastest-growing cities with populations of at least 50,000 and seven of the top 13 fastest-growing were in Texas.[30]

Urbanization

Although many outside the state may still associate Texas with lonesome cowboys on vast ranges, the great majority of the state's population growth has occurred in urban areas and metropolitan areas which are composed of one or more large cities and their surrounding suburban communities. Texas was 80 percent rural at the beginning of the 20th century, but today more than 85 percent of the state's population is urban. The state's four most populous counties (Harris, Dallas, Bexar, and Tarrant) have a combined population of almost 11 million people, larger than the population of 44 of the 50 states. The Texas Demographic Center projects that nearly 95 percent of the state's 2010–2050 population growth will be in its 82 metropolitan counties.[31] Most of these population concentrations are within the Texas Triangle, roughly outlined by segments of interstate highways 35, 45, and 10.

The Lone Star State's Metropolitan Statistical Areas (those with populations over 50,000) contain more than 88 percent of the state's population but are located in fewer than 20 percent of the state's 254 counties. It is politically significant that these 48 counties potentially account for about four of every five votes cast in statewide elections. Thus, governmental decision makers are primarily accountable to people living in one-fifth of the state's counties. Metropolitan Statistical Areas contain both urban (inner city) and suburban areas. Urban voters are consistently more supportive of the Democratic Party, except in Fort Worth, while suburban voters tend more toward the Republican Party. Since metropolitan voters, as a whole, are rarely of one mind at the polls; they do not tend to overwhelm rural voters by taking opposing positions on all policy issues.

Suburbanization and Gentrification

Between 1980 and the present, Texas suburbs (relatively small municipalities, usually outside the boundary limits of a central city) experienced explosive growth and spread into rural areas. The early history of suburbanization was marked by racial segregation, with Anglos in more affluent suburbs and historical minority groups in the inner city and less affluent suburbs. Government policies were used purposefully to ensure residential segregation. The federal government used **redlining** to restrict lending in low-income neighborhoods. Because historical minority groups are disproportionately included in lower socioeconomic groups, this practice barred lending to many minority borrowers. Additionally, the federal government used interstate highway designs and **urban renewal** projects to isolate and eliminate minority neighborhoods. Local policies like **exclusionary zoning** and federal policies requiring **racial covenants** prevented

redlining
A discriminatory rating system used by federal agencies to evaluate the risks associated with loans made to borrowers in specific urban neighborhoods. Today, the term also refers to the same practice among private businesses like banks and real estate companies.

urban renewal
The relocation of businesses and people, the demolition of structures, and the use of eminent domain to take private property for development projects.

exclusionary zoning
The use of local government zoning ordinances to exclude certain groups of people from a given community.

racial covenants
Agreements written into real estate documents by property owners, subdivision developers, or real estate operators in a given neighborhood, binding property owners not to sell, lease, or rent property to specified groups because of race, creed, or color.

🏛 HOW DO WE COMPARE...

In Population?

2018 Population Estimates as Reported
by the U.S. Bureau of the Census

Most Populous U.S. States	Population	U.S. States Bordering Texas	Population
California	39,557,405	Louisiana	4,659,978
Texas	**28,701,845**	Oklahoma	3,943,079
Florida	21,299,325	Arkansas	3,013,825
New York	19,542,209	New Mexico	2,095,428

Competency Connection
☼ CRITICAL THINKING ☼

How does a large and rapidly growing population create both opportunities and challenges for Texas?

minorities from renting or buying homes in more affluent suburbs. Even when laws and court decisions moved official policies away from racially discriminatory practices, economic inequality, the phenomenon of white flight, and the practice of some realtors' and lenders' steering their clients into segregated neighborhoods limited integration. Today, de facto racial segregation (segregation by fact rather than by law) remains, especially in suburban areas, though to a lesser extent than in the past.[32]

Texas has seen large demographic movements from rural to urban areas and from large cities to the suburbs and back. Although the shift from rural to urban areas and the growth of exurbs (extra-urban areas beyond suburbs) have continued into the 21st century, a repopulation of inner cities has revitalized numerous downtown neighborhoods and attracted new residents. In a process called **gentrification**, middle-class and affluent people move into struggling inner city areas, investing in property improvement and new businesses. Gentrification can be controversial, as lower-income residents are often displaced by increases in rent and property values, and locally owned small businesses are frequently unable to compete with new competition from incoming businesses.[33]

Rural Texas

Though Texas is primarily metropolitan, small-town Texas is still a reality for the more than 14 percent of Texans who live in rural areas, which cover 84 percent of the state's total land area. In rural Texas, a variety of challenges complicate the charms of small town life. Hospital closures and the difficulty of recruiting doctors have increased the difficulty of accessing health care in rural communities. Aging roads, water systems, and other public infrastructure continue to age

gentrification
A relocation of middle-class or affluent people into deteriorating urban areas, often displacing low-income residents.

and crumble as the cost of upgrades, repairs, and maintenance falls most heavily on local taxpayers. The same funding shortages have led to school closures and cutbacks in important educational services, including those for the increasing number of homeless rural students. The threat of natural disasters in the form of floods, fires, droughts, and tornadoes make farming a risky business, which many young people choose to avoid.

Farming and ranching communities tend to change slowly. Texas's least-populated county (Loving County) has remained at a population between 33 and 285 since 1900 (134 in 2018). Yet some rural areas in the Lone Star State experienced rapid population growth and development as a result of the resurgence in oil and natural gas production that reached a fever pitch after 2010. These boomtowns saw explosive increases in employment, investment, and tax revenue as drilling operations moved in. But booms also bring challenges to small communities in the form of environmental damage, crime and drugs, traffic, and soaring housing costs. Many such towns saw equally rapid economic decline following the rapid drop in oil prices that began in 2014.

Well drillers began moving out and cutting jobs at an alarming rate. As oil money and customers disappeared, hotels, restaurants, and retailers across the state struggled to stay in business. Unemployment rose dramatically in such towns. Sales tax revenues plummeted. Although some new residents remained, hoping for a reversal of fortune and an increase in oil prices, many joined the exodus.

In late 2015, the Obama administration and the U.S. Congress lifted 40 years of restrictions on crude oil exports. New foreign demand drove massive increases in production. By 2019, the **Permian Basin** in West Texas was producing twice as much oil as it had in 2014. A second boom hit many small towns in the region. Though many former boom towns on the Eagle Ford and Barnett Shale continued to languish, production revived to a lesser extent in those regions as well. While most such towns haven't experienced a "second boom," they have seen an economic resurgence.[34]

The Regions of Texas

Because of the state's vast size and geographic diversity, many Texans have developed a concept of five areas—North, South, East, West, and Central Texas—as five potentially separate states. In fact, the United States congressional resolution by which Texas was admitted to the Union in 1845 specifies that up to four states "in addition to said state of Texas" may be formed out of its territory and that each "shall be entitled to admission to the Union." Over the years, various plans for carving Texas into five states have been proposed to the Texas legislature. Few Texans have taken these plans seriously. The Texas Comptroller's office identifies 13 separate economic regions in Texas. For simplicity, we condense these 13 regions to 6 (Figure 1.1).

The West Texas Plains Agriculture is the economic bedrock of the West Texas Plains, from sheep, goat, and cattle production in its southern portions to the cotton, grain sorghum, and feedlot cattle in the north. The area depends heavily on the continually depleting and environmentally sensitive Ogallala Aquifer.

Permian Basin
Also known as the West Texas Basin, this sedimentary basin in western Texas and southeastern New Mexico is known for its rich deposits of petroleum and natural gas.

FIGURE 1.1 The Six Regions of Texas

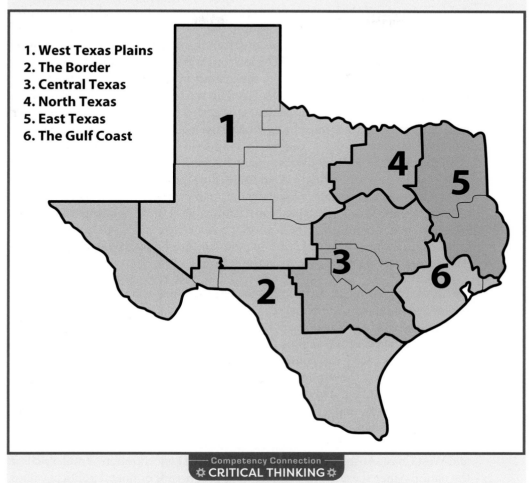

1. **West Texas Plains**
2. **The Border**
3. **Central Texas**
4. **North Texas**
5. **East Texas**
6. **The Gulf Coast**

Competency Connection
☼ **CRITICAL THINKING** ☼

How does Texas's large geographic size affect its politics and governance?
How do the state's regions differ in culture, politics, and economy?

Formed almost 10 million years ago during the Pliocene epoch, the Ogallala Aquifer underlies eight states in the Great Plains, including the High Plains of Texas. Heavy agricultural demands are depleting the aquifer more rapidly than it is being replenished. Careful management of this underground water-bearing rock formation will be crucial to the region's future. South of the Cap Rock Escarpment, oil production forms the economic base of cities like Odessa and Midland, and the recent boom in oil production in the Permian Basin has lifted the local economy.

From the Panhandle to Odessa, West Texas is known for social, economic, and political conservatism. Dominated by white evangelical Christians, agriculture, and oil, West Texas is fertile soil for the Republican Party. Democrats have little electoral success here even in the larger cities of Lubbock and Amarillo.

The Border South and Southwest Texas border Mexico. Like the West Texas Plains, the western border region has also benefited economically from the Permian Basin oil boom. The region produces citrus fruits and vegetables, but increasingly international trade is vital to the region's economy, which can thus be sensitive to swings in the Mexican economy. In 1994, the **North American Free Trade Agreement (NAFTA)** lowered trade barriers among Mexico, the United States, and Canada. In 2018, the Trump administration renegotiated the agreement and moved to replace NAFTA with the United States–Mexico–Canada Agreement (USMCA). The agreement is intended to reduce the U.S. trade deficit with both countries, but must be ratified by the legislature of each country before it is actually adopted.

From El Paso to Brownsville, many Texans near the border have close ties with Mexico and are strongly linked to it through family, friends, media, and trade. Spanish is the primary language for many here, and the Catholic Church is a major part of everyday life. Many Latinos tend to show strong support for government intervention in the economy, an extensive social safety net, and progressive taxation. The large Latino population thus helps the Democratic Party gain substantial electoral success in the region.

Central Texas Waco, Austin, and San Antonio are all in Central Texas. The region is dominated by universities and colleges, the high-tech sector, state government, tourism, and major military bases. It is also home to the German Hill Country, an agricultural region that holds onto its Central European cultural identity and its social and political conservatism.

Despite being the capital of a conservative state, Austin is politically and socially liberal and self-avowedly "weird." With a boom in the high-tech industry, a major university, and a thriving art and music scene, Austin has experienced rapid growth and in-migration from all over the country and the world. In particular, there has been an influx of highly educated former residents of the Northeast and West Coast. Austin also has the second highest concentration of millennials in the nation. Since these groups tend to hold progressive or liberal political values, the Democratic Party does well in Austin, and also in San Antonio, though surrounding areas tend toward Republican conservatism.

North Texas Observers say Dallas is where the East begins, and Fort Worth is where the West begins. The metropolitan area that contains these cities, known popularly as the Metroplex, has seen decades of explosive growth and economic development as national and international corporations continue to move their headquarters to these cities. Although Fort Worth residents still embrace their cowboy past, Dallasites seem to prefer diving headlong into the future. Both cities have become modern centers for high-tech industries, financial services, defense contractors, and food processing.

Democrats sometimes find electoral success in the urban centers of the Metroplex, but the suburban and rural parts of the region are conservative Republican strongholds. With many large corporations and wealthy residents, the Dallas–Fort Worth area (often referred to as DFW) is also a major source of

North American Free Trade Agreement (NAFTA)
An agreement among Mexico, the United States, and Canada designed to expand trade by eliminating tariffs among the three nations.

funding for the Republican Party, with a sizeable number of the biggest political donors in the country living in the area.[35]

East Texas Cotton production has been a constant in East Texas since its settlement by Anglo colonists, but recent years have been difficult for cotton farmers. In the past decade, the area's economy has also felt the impacts of both boom and bust in oil and gas production, and production is again on the rise. Forestry and logging, along with the production of wood and paper products, in the area known as the Piney Woods, cattle and poultry farming, and some manufacturing have helped fill the gap while other economic diversification continues. Even so, wages and employment remain lower than the state average, while the poverty rate continues to exceed the state average.

The westernmost extension of the Deep South, East Texas can seem a world apart, as references to life "behind the Pine Curtain" suggest. The area remains racially segregated and dominated by evangelical Christianity and powerful families with deep historical roots in the area. It is now firmly a part of the Republican "Solid South."

The Gulf Coast The coast of the Gulf of Mexico stretches from the Louisiana border to the Rio Grande. Shipping and fishing are naturally important to the economy, but so are manufacturing and the presence of major corporate headquarters. Petrochemicals remain fundamental to the region's economy. It has thus been sensitive to oil booms and busts, including the recent fluctuations in fracking activity and in oil prices. The region is anchored by Houston, the state's largest city. In 2014, with fracking at its height, Houston's local economy was adding 100,000 jobs per year, far better than the nation as a whole. From 2015 through 2017, low oil and gas prices slowed job growth and unemployment rates exceeded the national rate. But the city has continued to diversify its economy to help weather booms and busts. And despite the devastation of Hurricane Harvey, post-storm reconstruction became an economic net positive for Houston in late 2017 and helped with the city's continuing economic rebound.[36]

The Beaumont-Port Arthur area has the highest concentration of union members in Texas. As a result of Houston's ethnic diversity and high levels of union membership in Beaumont-Port Arthur, Democrats have some electoral wins in the region. Suburban and rural parts of the Gulf Coast remain reliably Republican, however.

✪ The Economy

LO 1.4 Describe the industries that formed the historic basis for the Texas economy, the diversification of the modern Texas economy, and the implications for Texas politics.

The Lone Star State's economic success has relied heavily on four land-based industries. These days, the Texas economy is vastly more diverse and includes a variety of 21st century industries.

✔ **1.3 Learning Check**

1. What is the impact of the Lone Star State's size on Texas's politics?

2. True or False: All the regions of Texas are economically dependent on the same industries, and thus are nearly identical in culture and politics.

Answers at the end of this chapter.

The Texas Economy Through History

Much of Texas's early history was dominated by cattle, cotton, timber, and minerals (oil and gas). These four industries remain important sectors of the Texas economy and culture.

Cattle Plentiful land and minimal government interference encouraged huge cattle empires in Texas, established by politically powerful entrepreneurs such as Richard King and Mifflin Kenedy. During the 25 years after the Civil War, approximately 35,000 men drove nearly 10 million cattle and 1 million horses north to Kansas railheads. By the late 1880s, when the railroads were built closer to Texas ranches, the cattle drives ended. In time, newly emerging industries diluted the economic impact of the beef business. Although the severe drought that began in 2011 forced a reduction in the number of cattle in the state, Texas still leads the nation in cattle production. The inventory of approximately 12.5 million cattle is twice as many as that of Nebraska, the next largest cattle-producing state. Texas also leads the nation in production of sheep, goats, wool, and mohair.

Cotton Although popular culture romanticizes 19th-century cowboys and cattle drives, cotton formed the backbone of the state's economy in that era, particularly in East and Central Texas where soil and weather conditions resemble those in the Old South. Before the Civil War, slaves performed much of the field labor as cotton production spread. During that war, revenue from the export of Texas cotton (mostly shipped from Mexico to Europe) aided the Confederacy. As more frontier land was settled, cotton production moved westward and increased in volume.

Today, the Lone Star State produces almost a quarter of the nation's cotton and leads the country in exported cotton. Although cotton is grown throughout the state, the High Plains region of West Texas accounts for approximately 60 percent of the state's annual cotton yield. During the 2011 drought, cotton production in West Texas fell from a 10-year average of about 4.5 million bales per year to fewer than 1.5 million bales. This reduction represented a financial loss of more than one-third of the U.S. cotton crop. By 2014 continuing drought, hail, and blowing sand reduced the Texas cotton yield by 50 percent. Since then, some areas of Texas have gotten too little rain, but others have had too much, leading to devastating flooding and crippling storms. The return of rain also coincided with a glut in global supply and the elimination of federal price subsidies for the crop. Most recently, President Trump's trade war led China to enact retaliatory tariffs on U.S. cotton exports. The partial shutdown of the federal government in December 2018 and January 2019 also meant delays in taxpayer-funded subsidies aimed at helping farmers hurt by the trade war.

Timber East Texas includes the densely wooded Piney Woods and the Big Thicket areas that were largely uninhabited until the 1800s. As the population grew, new towns and railroad lines increased demand for timber. By the mid-1800s, more than 200 sawmills were in operation from East to Central Texas. In the early 1900s, the timber industry was the state's largest employer, manufacturer, and revenue generator.[37]

The economic impact of timber declined in the 1920s, as clear-cutting by some logging companies and those exploring for oil depleted timber supply in many parts of East Texas. In 1933, the Texas legislature authorized the federal government to purchase more than 600,000 acres in East Texas for four national forests (Angelina, Davy Crockett, Sabine, and Sam Houston). In addition, the timber industry began to implement reseeding and sustainable logging practices. At the end of the 20th century, Texas was the nation's 10th largest timber producer, generating more than $12.9 billion annually.

The 2011 drought resulted in the loss of between 100 and 500 million trees throughout the state. Texas Forest Service officials estimated that more than 166,000 acres of trees in East Texas needed to be replanted, at a cost of $57 million. An additional 1.5 million trees on more than 16,200 acres were destroyed in a catastrophic wildfire in Bastrop County in late 2011, leading one Texas Parks and Wildlife Department official to predict that it would take more than half a century to recover fully from the loss. Precipitation increased in 2015 and by 2016 most areas in Texas were recovering from extreme drought.[38] Continued rain and demand for timber in the housing, construction, and oil and gas industries fueled a Texas timber recovery. The impacts of protective timber tariffs on the industry are still unclear. Timber prices increased by 60 percent over two years, making lumber more profitable. But increased prices and the trade war with China have reduced exports and contributed to the major increase in construction costs triggered by retaliatory tariffs. This means dampened demand and increased incentives for buyers to seek out foreign sources of timber.[39]

Oil and Gas In 1901, when the Spindletop Field was developed, petroleum ushered in the industry that dominated the state's economy for nearly a century. During the next 50 years, drilling, refining, and delivering oil and gas brought industrial employment on a grand scale to rural Texas. Several major oil companies were created, such as Humble (now ExxonMobil Corporation), Magnolia Petroleum Company, Sun Oil Company, Gulf Oil Corporation, and the Texas Company (Gulf Oil Corporation and the Texas Company [Texaco] now are a part of Chevron). This domination by a single industry resulted in the rise of some of the most politically powerful businesses and individuals in Texas history. In 1919, the Texas legislature gave the Railroad Commission of Texas limited regulatory jurisdiction over the state's oil and natural gas industry.[40] Since oil and gas producers were so economically and politically powerful in Texas, the Commission quickly gained a reputation less for regulating the industry than for supporting and promoting it. At its peak in the early 1980s, the Texas oil and gas industry employed half a million workers, who earned more than $11 billion annually. Oil and natural gas production and related industries accounted for almost one-third of the state's economy. That peak ended in an oil price crash that reached full swing in 1986 and ushered in an economic recession for the state. Over the next two decades, fluctuating prices reduced revenue and led Texas's leaders to seek diversification of the state's economy.

Discovery of major natural gas deposits in South, Central, and North Texas in the early 21st century, along with the newly profitable drilling method of **hydraulic fracturing**, launched another oil boom that helped insulate the state's

hydraulic fracturing
Also known as "fracking," this method of extracting oil and natural gas involves forcing open fissures in subterranean rocks by introducing liquid at high pressure.

economy from the global recession that began in 2008, but oil prices dropped from over $100 a barrel in June of 2014 to $35 a barrel in early 2016.[41] The downturn in prices made it difficult for many drillers to continue operating. Though a few shale patches remained profitable, across the country 110 companies filed for bankruptcy by the end of that year.[42] Texas's monthly tax revenue from oil and natural gas production dropped 82 percent, from $583 million in August 2014 to $107 million in March 2016. But soaring production in the Permian Basin and new U.S. Geological Survey estimates of massive reserves of recoverable oil in that region started a second boom. By November 2018, revenue had rebounded to almost $530 million.[43] Revenues from taxes on oil and gas help the Texas government fill its Rainy Day Fund, complete highway construction and maintenance, invest in higher education through the Permanent University Fund, and fund the State Water Plans.

Texas still accounts for approximately 40 percent of oil production and 23 percent of natural gas production in the United States. If it were its own country, Texas would be the fourth largest oil and gas producer in the world. Most oil and gas jobs pay relatively high wages and salaries, but can be insecure. Employment in the industry rises and falls rapidly based on swings in oil prices and other factors. In the past decade, the number of jobs changed frequently, bouncing around between a high of 306,300 in December 2014 and a low of 192,000 in September 2016.[44] Despite dramatic booms and busts in petrochemical industry revenue and jobs, because of the diversification of the state's economy, such cycles do not have the same impact on Texas's revenues or its overall economy as they once did. The oil and gas industry now accounts for less than 3 percent of the state's jobs. Although industry officials continue to be politically powerful in Texas, they are not expected to regain their former level of political dominance.[45] Meanwhile, awareness is growing that fossil fuels (including oil, gas, and coal) burned for industrial purposes and in automobiles, trucks, buses, and airplanes are the world's principal source of air pollution, contributing to significant human health problems.[46] As a result, Texas is placing increased emphasis on new industries and opportunities, including the production of alternative energy, such as wind and solar power.

New Economic Directions

The devastation of plunging oil prices in the 1980s demonstrated the dangers of reliance on a single industry. Texas's business and government leaders subsequently pursued a restructuring and diversification of the state's economy. Texans launched new industries that have quickly spread across the state, bolstering the Texas economy and playing an important role in the national economy. In 2006, for the first time, more *Fortune* 500 companies were headquartered in Texas than in any other state. In 2018, however, New York ranked first with 58 and Texas ranked third (behind California) with 48.[47] Texans today are employed in a variety of enterprises. In 2018, the state added jobs in 10 of its 11 major nonagricultural industries, including professional and business services, trade, transportation and utilities, leisure and hospitality, education and health services, mining and logging, construction, manufacturing, government, financial activities, and other services. The diversity of the Texas economy, its employer-friendly taxation and regulation policies, and other factors combined to help Texas weather the Great Recession better than most states. In 2018, Texas accounted for one of every seven jobs created in the United States. Continuing this success will require effective public policies, an educated and productive labor force, an adequate supply of capital, and sound business management practices.

Energy Thirty-seven of the 48 *Fortune* 500 companies headquartered in Texas in 2018 were energy related. Texas is the country's leading producer not only of oil and gas but also lignite coal. In addition to the economic benefits of the fracking boom, environmental and health concerns have also accompanied this recovery method. These concerns have caused many people to switch to alternative fuels. In Texas, growth of renewable energy sources outpaced the growth of coal, natural gas, and other energy sources until the peak of the fracking boom. Renewables made up only 1 percent of Texas's energy supply in 2001. That percentage rose to more than 10 percent in 2013; but by 2018, usage had reduced to 2.5 percent.[48]

The overwhelming share of Texas's renewable energy comes from wind power, largely produced on West Texas wind farms. With 17 percent of its electricity generated by wind, Texas leads the nation in generation capacity from wind power and is well positioned to produce even more.[49] The Lone Star State also has abundant yearly sunshine. Though the solar industry has received little support from the Texas Legislature, local governments have increasingly turned to solar to meet their energy needs. Private sector demand has also spurred the industry's development.[50] By 2018, Texas ranked seventh among the states in solar energy production. Though solar accounts for only 1 percent of energy production in Texas, a recent study by Rice University researchers concluded that Texas has enough sun and wind combined to operate without coal. All that is required is further construction of solar and wind farms, wise use of the Texas power grid and battery storage, and natural gas power plants for when wind slackens. Texas also generates a small amount of energy from geothermal and hydroelectric plants.[51]

Texas already ranks second in the nation for employment in the renewable energy industry. Anticipating the need for workers, 12 statewide Texas colleges created the Texas Renewable Energy Education Coalition, aimed at offering degrees, certificates, professional development, and technical training. Today, students in Texas can enroll in renewable energy programs and classes in wind and solar power at Texas Tech University, Texas A&M University, West Texas A&M University, the University of Texas at Austin, the University of Texas at San Antonio, the University of Houston, Texas State Technical College, and community colleges in Austin, Houston, Dallas County, and Tarrant County.

High Technology The term *high technology* applies to research, development, manufacturing, and marketing of a seemingly endless line of electronic products, such as computers, smartphones, drones, and medical equipment.[52] High-technology businesses employ just over 7 percent of Texas's labor force and comprise almost 9 percent of the state's economy. Most high-tech jobs in

Texas are in the fields of IT and software services, engineering, R&D and testing, telecommunications, Internet services, and tech manufacturing. As Texas lacks the startup culture of Silicon Valley, the field is dominated by large firms, such as Motorola, Dell, Hewlett-Packard, Texas Instruments, and Applied Materials. In December 2018, Apple announced a major expansion of its operations in Austin. The tech giant intends to invest over $1 billion in a new campus there.[53]

Salaries and wages in the Texas high-tech sector, averaging over $106,000 per year, are almost double the average wages for the rest of the state. The vast majority of these jobs are centered in the state's major cities.[54] During the first decade of the 21st century in cities such as Houston, Dallas, and Austin, jobs in semiconductor, computer, and circuit board manufacturing actually declined. Several high-tech companies left Texas in pursuit of lower labor costs; predictable regulations; and access to markets, incentives, and a skilled workforce. This trend later reversed with an increasing number of companies and workers flowing to Texas from places like California. By 2018, more than 774,000 Texans held high-tech jobs; and Texas ranked second only to California in the size of its high-tech workforce.[55]

The Texas government has sought to expand not only the high-tech industry in Texas but has also worked to develop **biotechnology** and the life sciences, which comprise a multibillion-dollar industry producing new medicines and vaccines, chemicals, and other products designed to benefit medical science, human health, and agricultural production. In the past two decades, biotech-related jobs have increased four times faster than the overall increase in employment in Texas. Home to more than 5,000 biotechnology firms, manufacturing companies, industry consortia, and research university facilities, Texas employs approximately 100,000 workers in the biotech sector at an average annual salary of over $84,500.[56]

Four areas of particular focus in Texas are biodefense and pandemic preparedness, personalized medicine, regenerative medicine, and vaccines. With nearly 24,000 clinical trials underway in the state, the Texas biotech industry spends approximately $5.3 billion in research and development projects. More than $2.1 billion of that is spent at 10 of the state's research universities and colleges. The Texas A&M Center for Innovation in Advanced Development and Manufacturing, established in 2012 to lead the nation's biosecurity research efforts, is a public-private partnership likely worth $1.5 to $2 billion. An initial federal grant of more than $175 million is the largest sum of federal money awarded to Texas since NASA (near Houston) in the 1960s.

biotechnology
Also known as biotech, this is the use and/or manipulation of biological processes and microorganisms to perform industrial or manufacturing processes or create consumer goods.

Services Employing one-fourth of all Texas workers, service industries continue to provide new jobs more rapidly than all other sectors. Service businesses include health-care providers (hospitals and nursing homes); personal services (hotels, restaurants, and recreational enterprises, such as water parks and video arcades); and commercial services (printers, advertising agencies, data processing companies, equipment rental companies, and consultants). Other service providers include education, investment brokers, insurance and real estate agencies, banks and credit unions, and merchandising enterprises. Many high school and college students work in the service sector as restaurant waitstaff, retail store sales associates, and other customer service jobs.

Most service jobs come with few or no benefits and pay lower wages and salaries than manufacturing firms that produce goods. Thus, the late journalist Molly Ivins warned that "the dream that we can transform ourselves into a service economy and let all the widget-makers go to hell or Taiwan is bullstuff. The service sector creates jobs all right, but they're the lowest paying jobs in the system. You can't afford a house frying burgers at McDonald's, even if you're a two-fryer family."[57]

Agriculture Texas ranks second in the nation in agricultural production (behind California) and sixth in agricultural exports. It leads the country in total acreage of agricultural land and numbers of farms and ranches, the number of women and minority-owned farm operations, value of farm real estate, and production of beef, sheep, hay, goats, cotton, and mohair. Other important cash crops include corn, sorghum grain, rice, cottonseed, peanuts, soybeans, pecans, and fresh market vegetables and citrus. Gross income from the products of Texas agriculture amounts to about $22 billion annually, making agriculture the second largest industry in the state. One in seven Texans are employed in agriculture-related jobs.[58] Most agricultural commodities are shipped abroad or to other parts of the United States without being processed in Texas. Consequently, Texas needs industrial development for the processing of food and fiber to derive maximum economic benefit from its agricultural products.

Over the past eight decades, the number of farms and ranches in Texas has decreased from more than 500,000 to fewer than 250,000. This reduction largely reflects the use of labor-saving farm machinery and chemicals. Small family farms are also being rapidly replaced by large agribusinesses or sold for real estate development. When farm commodity prices are low (because of overproduction and weak market demand) or when crops are poor (as a result of drought), many farmers end the year deeply in debt. Some must sell their land—usually to larger farm operators and sometimes to corporations. Wealthy individuals may purchase agricultural property (especially ranchland) as a status symbol—even though their land generates little or no income. Agricultural property ownership qualifies for various exemptions and reductions in local, state, and federal taxes. In addition, much farm and ranchland near expanding cities is lost to urban

IMAGE 1.4 Texas leads the nation in energy production capacity from wind farms and continues to develop its solar energy potential.

Richard Ellis/The Image Bank/Getty Images

— Competency Connection —
☼ **CRITICAL THINKING** ☼

What industries are essential to sustain and continue to develop the Texas economy in the 21st century?

sprawl, becoming roads, shopping malls, or subdivisions. Once a major force, small farmers are seeing their political influence wane in Texas as corporate farms gain in economic resources and connections with the political elite.

Trade By reducing and ultimately eliminating tariffs during the 15-year period from 1993 to 2008, the North American Free Trade Agreement (NAFTA) stimulated U.S. trade with Canada and Mexico. Because more than 60 percent of U.S. exports to Mexico are produced in or transported through Texas from other states, expanding foreign trade produces jobs for Texans, profits for the state's businesses, and revenue for state and local governments. Under NAFTA, the U.S. exports more services than it imports from Canada and Mexico.[59]

Conversely, the nation imports more goods than it exports to its partner nations. Texas's garment industry and some fruit and vegetable producers have been adversely affected by NAFTA, especially in border counties. In addition, increased trucking on highways between Mexico and Canada contributes to air pollution and causes traffic problems that make road travel slower and more dangerous. Under NAFTA, exports from **maquiladoras** are not taxed and beginning wages for Mexican workers may be less than a dollar per hour. Work at these facilities can be dangerous, with increasing reports of serious work-related injuries, illnesses from working with dangerous materials, and mental health problems from a stressful work environment.[60]

A more prosperous and stable Mexico usually means more trade and fewer jobless workers migrating to the United States, but a succession of crises in Mexico starting in 2006 raised serious questions concerning NAFTA's future. In that year, Mexico's voters selected Felipe Calderón as president. With encouragement and assistance from the U.S. government, he began a military assault on criminal drug cartels, but violence over the next few years reached record levels. In January 2012, the Mexican government reported that 47,515 people had been killed in drug-related violence since President Calderón's election, with others estimating as many as 80,000 deaths.[61]

In July 2012, Enrique Peña Nieto was elected to serve as Mexico's president. While he made some changes in violence-prevention programs and security reorganization, his approach to organized crime strongly resembled that of Calderón, and despite some gains, high levels of violence continued. Availability of guns in border states like Texas plays a role in the ongoing struggle, as 70 percent of the guns used in Mexico's drug war come from U.S. sources near the border.[62] Despite violence in Mexico, Texas border cities have lower crime rates than many other parts of Texas.[63]

In July 2018, Mexican voters selected leftist Andrés Manuel López Obrador as president. López Obrador promised peace and an end to the drug war by recalling soldiers, pardoning nonviolent drug offenders and increasing social programs. Despite the fact that this would be the first major departure from American preferences for dealing with drugs in decades, and that López Obrador has in the past been critical of President Trump, the new president has worked cooperatively with the United States on trade reforms. In December 2018, the leaders of the two countries joined Canada's prime minister in signing the United States–Mexico–Canada Agreement (USMCA), which would replace NAFTA. The new agreement makes major changes to NAFTA, particularly in the areas of auto manufacturing, dairy products, safety standards, intellectual property, and pharmaceuticals.

maquiladoras
Industrial plants on the Mexican side of the border which are partnered with American companies. Such plants typically use low-cost labor to assemble imported parts for a wide range of consumer goods and then export these goods back to the United States or to other countries.

President Trump has declared that the United States will withdraw from NAFTA if the legislatures of the three countries fail to ratify the agreement.[64]

Mexico is far from Texas's only trading partner, as Texas leads the nation in exports. The state does business with countries all over the globe, even some that are controversial. Texas politicians debated increasing trade relations with communist Cuba. In 2014, the Obama administration began opening relations with Cuba. The next year, Governor Abbott took a three-day trip to Cuba to explore economic opportunities for Texas industries. Travel to and trade with the island nation increased until 2017, when President Trump reinstated travel and trade restrictions. Though many Texas politicians, including Comptroller Glen Hegar, have touted the benefits of opening to Cuba and Texas has continued trade, the U.S. has largely stayed out of the country's continuing political reforms. Still, many Texas businesses are preparing for increased Cuban trade.[65]

> ✓ **1.4 Learning Check**

> 1. What four industries were important to the Texas economy in the past?
> 2. Which economic sector is currently creating the most jobs for Texans?

> *Answers at the end of this chapter.*

✪ Meeting New Challenges

LO 1.5 Identify five major policy challenges Texas faces in the 21st century.

Clearly, Texas has experienced rapid and dramatic change in recent decades, and though change provides opportunities, it also brings challenges. The continued success of the state will depend heavily on public policy decisions concerning immigration, protection of the ecological system and water supply, restructuring and financing of the state's public schools and institutions of higher education, and addressing poverty and social problems.

Immigration: Federal and State Problems

Since Texas became part of the United States, immigration has been the source of many controversies: how to control the flow of immigrants, the length of time a nonresident may remain within U.S. territory, the type of labor nonresidents may perform, and other issues. Some immigrants are undocumented and enter the United States in violation of federal immigration law or overstay legal visas. Most come for work or to escape dangerous situations in their homeland. In recent years, Texas has seen a decrease in immigration from Mexico, but an increase in immigration from Central America.[66]

The impact of immigration on the Texas economy is complex. Because Texas relies largely on consumption and property taxes to fund state and local government services, even **undocumented immigrants** pay state taxes when they buy goods and services or rent or buy property. Yet, many Texas citizens question whether undocumented immigrants pay enough to cover the social services they sometimes use. In 2017, AngelouEconomics (an Austin-based consulting firm) undertook the most recent major analysis and concluded that undocumented immigrants produced more in-state revenue, $2.7 billion, than the $2 billion they cost in state services.[67] This confirms the findings of The Perryman Group in Waco the previous year and the state comptroller's analysis a decade prior. However, the comptroller's report also concluded that undocumented immigrants cost local governments about $1.44 billion in health-care and law enforcement costs not reimbursed by

undocumented immigrant
A person who enters the United States in violation of federal immigration law and thus lacks proper documentation and identification.

the state. The costs and benefits of having an estimated 1.7 million undocumented immigrants are not distributed evenly among the Texas population. Employers in construction, agriculture, hospitality, and tourism benefit from an inexpensive supply of labor; and the consumers who buy their products and services benefit from the resulting lower prices. Those who hire undocumented domestic workers at low wages also benefit. American workers without high school diplomas lose out in competition for low-wage unskilled jobs and the accompanying depressed wages.

Texas politicians often face the difficult task of balancing constituents' demands for increased border security against the demands of a growing Latino constituency and a politically active business community pushing for immigration reforms. Despite increasing anti-immigrant sentiments nationally in the 1990s, in June 2001, a substantial bipartisan majority in the Texas legislature passed and Governor Perry signed the Texas DREAM Act. This law allows undocumented immigrants brought to Texas as children by their parents to pay in-state tuition at public colleges and universities if they graduated from high school or received a GED in the state. Available to those who have at least three years of residency and are seeking legal residency, this provision has benefited almost 25,000 Texas students. Two high-profile anti-immigration bills failed to pass the 84th Texas Legislature in 2015: one repealing the Texas DREAM Act and the other ending sanctuary cities (municipalities that decline to support aggressive prosecution of undocumented immigrants in Texas).[68] Republican legislators reintroduced both bills during the 85th Texas Legislature in 2017. The attempt to repeal the DREAM Act failed again, due in part to opposition from the business community. The sanctuary cities bill, known as "SB4," passed, and Governor Abbott signed it after much heated and emotional debate. The city of El Cenizo and Maverick County immediately sued to prevent implementation of the law. In March 2018, a panel of three U.S. Courts of Appeals justices ruled in favor of most provisions of the bill, allowing the state to enforce SB4 while the appeals process plays out. The law allows law enforcement to question the immigration status of those they detain or arrest and requires local governments, including public colleges and universities, to cooperate with federal immigration officers.[69]

Recent Texas executive officials have also attempted to limit immigration and to challenge benefits for undocumented immigrants. After President Barack Obama issued an executive order directing the U.S. Department of Homeland Security to expand the Deferred Action for Children Arrivals (DACA) program and to establish the Deferred Action for Parental Accountability (DAPA) program in 2014, then Attorney General Greg Abbott filed a lawsuit to block implementation. DACA provided two-year work permits and exemption from deportation to undocumented immigrants in Texas who were under the age of 16 at their time of arrival, had no criminal record, and met several other requirements. DAPA was initiated to provide temporary protection against deportation to undocumented immigrants whose children were citizens or lawful residents of the United States and who presented no criminal or terroristic threat to the country. In 2016, in a 4-4 split, the U.S. Supreme Court upheld the lower court's injunction blocking the expansion of the program. In 2017, President Trump rescinded DACA altogether, but the next year, the U.S. Court of Appeals upheld lower court rulings that DACA must remain in place.[70]

Texas is also often at the center of controversy over state and federal efforts to prevent unauthorized attempts to cross the U.S. border with Mexico. Following the terrorist attacks of September 11, 2001, Congress passed the Enhanced Border Security and Visa Entry Reform Act of 2002, which President George W. Bush signed into law. In addition to provisions regarding terrorist organizations, this act also concerns the tracking of international students at U.S. educational institutions and the issuance of visas. In 2006, President Bush signed the Secure Fence Act authorizing, among other barriers, more than 700 miles of fencing along the almost 2,000-mile-long U.S.–Mexico border from California to Texas to combat illegal immigration. Building the fence is an expensive undertaking, with some segments costing $6.5 million per mile. As of 2019, only about 115 miles of fencing had been completed along Texas's 1,254-mile border.[71] During his campaign for the presidency, Donald Trump promised to build a border wall and make Mexico pay for it. The Mexican government has steadfastly refused to do so. In late 2018, President Trump refused to sign any bill funding the government if it did not include $5.6 billion from U.S. taxpayers for the wall. Congressional Democrats objected, and the longest government shutdown in U.S history ensued. Unable to strike a deal for full funding of the wall, President Trump followed through on a threat to declare a national emergency. The move, intended to facilitate the use of U.S. military troops and funds to seize land along the border and build a wall met with immediate lawsuits and a Congressional resolution to end the emergency declaration. Trump vetoed the resolution and his administration continues to defend the declaration in the federal court system.[72]

Physical barriers like a wall are not the only attempts made to prevent border crossings. The same year that Texas sued to block President Obama's DACA expansion, Governor Rick Perry sent 1,000 National Guard troops to the border. The number of troops dropped to 100 by July 2015. Later in 2015, newly elected Governor Abbott extended their deployment, ordered more boat patrols on the Rio Grande, and increased air surveillance.[73] In 2018, Abbott increased the number of troops to 1,145. In October of that year, he praised President Trump's announcement that the United States would send as many as 15,000 active duty troops to the border to prevent a caravan of thousands of Central American migrants from entering the United States. The first soldiers of what promised to be the largest domestic deployment in modern history arrived in Texas on November 1, just days before the midterm election. Only about 5,800 troops were actually deployed, 2,800 of whom were stationed in Texas. Because of the 1878 *Posse Comitatus* Act, these troops cannot actively engage in border patrol activities. Instead, they have assisted in setting up wire barriers and in transporting and protecting border agents. What was left of the migrant "caravan" by the end of the year arrived at the California border rather than Texas. By that time, the federal deployment of troops had already cost an estimated $300 million dollars. At the same time, the Texas government was spending $800 million per year on border security for a total approaching $2 billion since Governor Perry's initial deployment of the guard.[74]

In 2018, Texas also became the center of national attention regarding the treatment of those caught crossing the border without authorization. In April of that year, President Trump's attorney general, Jeff Sessions, ordered a "zero tolerance" policy to deter families from entering the United States illegally. Over the next two months, more than 2,500 immigrant children were separated from their families. Outrage about the psychological toll on the children and the conditions in which they were held spread nationwide, sparking widespread political

📋 STUDENTS IN ACTION

From Mexico to Texas

Diana Quiñonez was born and raised in Mazatlán, Sinaloa, Mexico. Her father enjoyed a good job, making enough money for his wife to stay home and raise their four children. Their peaceful life fell apart when Diana was seven years old and the high levels of violence in the city hit home. When her father's co-workers began disappearing and the Quiñonez family was attacked, they hurriedly gathered their savings and what few possessions they could carry and fled to the Dallas area, where a few family members gave them shelter and helped them begin a new life.

A New Start

With only a few changes of clothing, no job prospects, and no facility with English, Diana's family struggled to learn the language and adjust to a new culture. With sponsorship from her grandfather, an American citizen, they immediately applied for citizenship. More than 10 years later, they are still wading through the bureaucratic forms and procedures.

After graduating from high school, Diana began her college studies at Collin College in Plano, near Dallas. Having been involved with the League of United Latin American Citizens (LULAC) since seventh grade, she joined the Collin chapter and deepened her civic engagement, volunteering, and community service. Her peers elected her president of the campus organization, and she created events to help those with limited English language skills navigate the college experience. The school now repeats these events annually. Serving others through work on violence prevention, women's rights, minority empowerment, voter registration, and other causes opened her eyes to what she really wanted to do with her life. Though her family encouraged her to pursue engineering like her brother, Diana geared her studies and activities toward community outreach and earned a full scholarship to Texas A&M University-Commerce, where she is finishing her bachelor's degree in bilingual education, maintains a near 4.0 GPA, and consistently makes the

Diana Quiñonez

Interview with Diana Quiñonez, January 10, 2019.

Dean's List. She has continued her civic engagement by working for LULAC's national president, traveling to Washington, D.C., to talk to elected leaders about the DREAM Act, and block-walking for her favorite local, state, and national political candidates.

Diana strives to convey that most immigrants are in the United States to work hard and benefit their community. She believes that everyone should have equal opportunity to make the most of his or her life regardless of place of birth. Diana encourages civic engagement among other young people, because she sees the importance of having their voices heard in decisions at all levels of government that affect their lives. "I wish I could vote," she says. "People don't think that it matters, but I believe that it does."

Competency Connection
⚖ PERSONAL RESPONSIBILITY ⚖

How might you use your skills and talents to make a difference in your community?

mobilization to end the policy. Texas Attorney General Ken Paxton supported the Trump policy. But Governor Abbott along with members of the Texas delegation to the U.S. Congress, Speaker of the Texas House Joe Straus, and a variety of other Texas politicians sought policy changes to end family separation. In June, President Trump issued an executive order ending the separation of families. With a confused bureaucratic reunification process, many families remained separated for months following the order. By 2019, the number of unaccompanied migrant children in Texas shelters (over 8,500) reached its highest point ever, comprising 60 percent of the nation's institutionalized minors.[75] So long as families seek to escape poverty and violence at home and so long as jobs and safety are available in Texas, the state will continue to deal with those who wish to move there.

Water

After a devastating drought in the 1950s, the Texas legislature created the Texas Water Development Board (TWDB) in 1957 and mandated statewide water planning. Since then, the TWDB and the Texas Board of Water Engineers have prepared and adopted nine state water plans, including the most recent, entitled *Water for Texas 2012*. TWDB chair Edward Vaughn explained that the message of the plan is simple: "During serious drought conditions, Texas does not and will not have enough water to meet the needs of its people, its businesses, and its agricultural enterprises." This plan makes recommendations for the development, management, and conservation of water resources and for better preparation for and response to drought conditions.

With the state's population expected to double by the middle of the 21st century, and a strong economy increasing business activity, assuring all Texans adequate water will be a formidable challenge. Texas's water supply was severely depleted by the drought that began in 2011. From that time until 2016, the use of water per fracking well increased 770 percent resulting in the pumping of an estimated 45 billion gallons in Texas.[76] In 2012, the Office of the Comptroller issued a report, "The Impact of the 2011 Drought and Beyond," which projected that demand for water will rise by 22 percent by 2060, while the state's current dependable water supply will meet only about 65 percent of that projected demand. Since 2011, Texas voters have ratified constitutional amendments authorizing loans to local governments for water, wastewater, and flood control projects. By 2019, the TWDB was providing approximately $27.6 billion in loan and grant programs for the planning, acquisition, design, and construction of water-related infrastructure and other water quality improvements across the state.[77]

Increased precipitation beginning in 2015 has refilled many lakes and rivers. By early 2019, monitored water supply reservoirs in Texas were near 90 percent full. Stream flow was above normal across the state. Still, increased groundwater use for fracking (particularly on the Ogallala Aquifer), agriculture, and a growing population kept groundwater levels in most areas below normal. The increased rain and snow has mostly been the result of a strong El Niño weather pattern (a cyclical event in the Pacific Ocean that only occurs every two to seven years) along with numerous and severe tropical storms in the Gulf of Mexico. Texas cannot rely on increased precipitation from El Niño and must continue to prepare for future droughts and water shortages.

 POINT/COUNTERPOINT

Should Texas expand regulations to protect the environment?

THE ISSUE As part of its strategy of attracting industry to the state, the Texas government keeps regulation of industry to a minimum. The state regularly challenges federal environmental regulations in court.

FOR	AGAINST
1. Texas is among the top five states in release of virtually every category of toxic and carcinogenic waste and pollution into the environment, with severe consequences for human and animal health.[78]	1. Regulation increases operating costs for businesses and can result in lower employment and higher prices for consumers.
2. Many studies show little or no economic damage to states resulting from environmental regulation. Businesses often overstate the costs of regulation and ignore the economic benefits of reduced health-care costs and an improved housing market.	2. Environmental agencies frequently underreport the negative effect of regulations because they rely on a partial or direct analysis that looks only at the direct effect of a regulation on the affected industry and not at the indirect effect of a regulation on the economy as a whole, other industries, and consumer behavior.[79]
3. Strict regulations spur innovation and technological advancement as industries develop cleaner and more energy-efficient ways of doing business and more sustainable ways of producing and delivering energy.	3. Many businesses seek to locate their operations where the cost of doing business is low. Texas's limited regulations bring economic activity and employment to the state, which has contributed to a state economy that is stronger than the national economy.

Source: This "Point/Counterpoint" is based in part on William Fulton, "Do Environmental Regulations Hurt the Economy?" *Governing*, March 2010, http://www.governing.com/columns/eco-engines/Do-Environmental-Regulations-Hurt.html.

Competency Connection
🗨 COMMUNICATION SKILLS 🗨

How might you communicate your views about the proper balance between economic growth and environmental protection to your elected representatives?

Education

With a public school student population that compares in size to the total population of Colorado, the future of the Texas economy and the quality of its workforce depend heavily on the quality of education. Texas faces significant challenges in this regard. More than 60 percent of public school students are classified as economically disadvantaged and more than 17 percent are English-language learners.[80] In a recent study that included 13 measures of chances for student success, 12 measures of K-12 achievement, and 8 measures of school finance, *Education Week* awarded Texas a C- and ranked the state's public school system 41st among the 50 states.[81] College educators complain many students are poorly prepared for higher education, and employers express concern about a marked decline in reading and writing skills among young Texans.

Funding education is a major controversy in Texas politics. The state cut $5.4 billion in funding for public schools in 2011 to balance the state budget. The budget reduction resulted in the elimination of more than 10,000 teaching positions and almost 1,000 support staff jobs. More than 600 school districts filed suit against the state. Approximately 90 percent of the reduced funding was restored by the 83rd and 84th Legislatures, and in 2016, the Texas Supreme Court ruled that the system satisfied minimal constitutional requirements, but also recommended "transformational, top-to-bottom reforms." (For a discussion of this issue, see Chapter 11, "Finance and Fiscal Policy.") As of 2018, Texas ranked 37th among the 50 states in spending per student, but the state was still spending 6.3 percent less per student than it was in 2010. With the federal government's share of public education funding dropping as well, local property taxes have increased to fill the gap.[82] Texas also ranked 34th in average teacher salary. In 2019, Governor Abbott signed an $11.6 billion school finance bill into law. The law increases per-student funding, gave raises to teachers, funded pre-kindergarten programs and more. The law also included about $5.1 billion devoted to reducing local property taxes.[83]

Teachers are the key element in any educational system, but from year to year, the Lone Star State confronts shortages of certified personnel to instruct its K-12 students. Although estimates of the severity of the teacher shortage vary, the Texas Education Agency reports that over 10 percent of the state's 358,000 teachers quit teaching each year.[84] The report indicates that even though some educators retire, most leave the profession for reasons that include inadequate pay and benefits, low prestige, conflicts with parents, and increasing time-consuming chores that often must be done at night and on weekends. Contributing to their decision to seek other careers is stress over classroom problems affected by the poverty and troubled home lives of many students. Additionally, teachers complain of burdensome government-mandated assessment and accountability measures.

Poverty and Social Problems

The Lone Star State has alarming numbers of children living in poverty. Births to unwed teenagers, juvenile arrests, and violent acts committed by and against teenagers and preadolescents also signal some of the social dysfunctionality associated with poverty. By 2018, Texas had achieved its lowest poverty rate in a decade. Still, approximately one of every five children in Texas was living in poverty, the 14th highest child poverty rate of any state. Estimates of the number of homeless people (including many children) vary widely, but at least 20,000—and perhaps more than 30,000—Texans cannot provide themselves with shelter in a house or apartment. Voting can be a challenge for people without a permanent address or valid photo identification. Voting rates are low for those below the federal poverty level, and just under 15 percent of Texans fit that category. Citizens who do not vote or participate in political campaigns have less access to elected officials.[85]

Health care is also a major issue for Texas. Of the 50 states, Texas has the highest percentage and largest number of uninsured residents. In 2018, 4.7 million, or 19 percent of non-elderly, Texans were without health insurance. After implementation of the federal Affordable Care Act (also known as Obamacare) began in 2010, the state's uninsured rate dropped from nearly 25 percent of the non-elderly uninsured to 16.6 percent of the non-elderly uninsured in 2016. Texas, however, continues to refuse federal funds to expand Medicaid coverage for adults under Obamacare and thus lags behind other states in increasing the number of people insured. Further, the Trump administration shortened the ACA enrollment period, dramatically reduced funding for ACA enrollment assistance, removed subsidies that helped recipients pay for insurance, and repealed the law's mandate that all individuals be insured or face a fine. As a result, in 2017 the uninsured rate in Texas began rising again for the first time since 2010.[86]

Some Texans argue that any public assistance for the poor is too much and encourages dependence instead of self-reliance. Others advocate for increased government spending for social service programs, noting that government support increases spending in impoverished communities, keeping local businesses open. Between these extremes are Texans who support a limited role for government in meeting human needs but who call for nongovernmental organizations to play a more active role in dealing with social problems. Texas voters, however, tend to support candidates for public office who promise lower taxes, less government spending, fewer public employees, and a reduction or elimination of social services. As a result, the Lone Star State continues to rank near the bottom of the 50 states in governmental responses to poverty and social problems.

✓ 1.5 Learning Check

1. True or False: If current trends persist, demand for water will rise by 10 percent by 2060, and the state's current dependable water supply will meet that projected demand.

2. True or False: Texas has the highest rate and largest number of uninsured people in the nation.

Answers at the end of this chapter.

✪ KEEPING CURRENT
2016–2018 Elections

In the months before Election Day 2016, many predicted major change in Texas politics. Record-breaking turnout for early voting suggested Texas might break its patterns of low participation and Republican dominance. Republican Donald Trump's anti-immigrant rhetoric inspired unusually high registration and early voting turnout among Democratic-leaning Texas Latinos. For the first time in many years Texas looked like a battleground state, with national campaigns investing money and energy in efforts to court its voters.

Despite predictions, the results showed little change in Texas. There was no significant rise in voter turnout rate and Republicans once again won Texas's electoral votes and all statewide races.

Two years later, opposition to the Trump administration had inspired even greater activism and organization among Texas Democrats, particularly among female, minority, and young voters. Democratic Senate candidate Beto O'Rourke gained an enthusiastic following both in Texas and nationally. Again, many predicted high turnout and a "blue wave" of Democratic victories in the state. This time, turnout was exceptionally high. In 2018, turnout hit almost 55 percent, more than 20 percentage points higher than the 2014 midterm elections. While the increased turnout did not result in a "blue wave," Democrats did make some major gains, gaining 12 seats in the state legislature and a majority on half of Texas's Courts of Appeals. Though Republicans won all statewide races, they did so by much smaller margins of victory than in the past, indicating that Texas is much closer to being a battleground state than it has been in decades.

CONCLUSION

With changing demographic, economic, social, and environmental conditions in the Lone Star State, Texas policymakers face several challenges. The diversity of the state both demographically and geographically presents myriad opportunities and problems. Because of its business-friendly policies, the state has been successful in attracting new industries. Recent downturns in the oil and gas industry, in particular, have weakened the state's economy. Even when the Lone Star State's economy flourishes, however, many Texans live in poverty. Both ordinary citizens and public officials must realize that their ability to cope with public problems now and in the years ahead depends largely on how well homes and schools prepare young Texans to meet the crises and demands of an ever-changing state, nation, and world.

CHAPTER SUMMARY

LO 1.1 Analyze how political culture has shaped Texas's politics, government, and public policy. The political culture of Texas is dominated by the individualistic and traditionalistic subcultures. The individualistic culture is rooted in the search for individual opportunity of the state's early settlers and is reflected in its constitutionally weak government and low spending on public programs. The traditionalistic culture grew out of the Old South, where policies were designed to preserve the social order of a landed aristocracy, and the poor and minorities were often disenfranchised (not allowed to vote). With an increasingly diverse population, some areas in Texas may be shifting toward an increase in the moralistic subculture, which favors government intervention to improve society.

LO 1.2 Describe the relationship between the social history of Texas and the political characteristics of the state's diverse population. Texas has a population of almost 29 million. Over 80 percent of all Texans live in the state's most highly urbanized counties. Texas's past was riddled with intergroup conflict, but the state has increasingly moved toward integration and cooperation. The three largest groups today are Anglos, Latinos (the fastest-growing group by number), and African Americans. Texas has a small but growing population of Asian Americans and approximately 287,000 Native Americans.

LO 1.3 Discuss the political implications of Texas's size in both geography and population, along with the geographic distribution of its residents. With more than 267,000 square miles of territory and almost 29 million people, Texas ranks second in both size and population among the 50 states. Infrastructure is therefore a major government issue. The cost of political campaigns in such a geographically large state and the necessary fundraising are major political issues. Rapid population growth presents a variety of opportunities and challenges for the political system. Each of the six major regions in Texas is different in its economic and political climate.

LO 1.4 Describe the industries that formed the historic basis for the Texas economy, the diversification of the modern Texas economy, and the implications for Texas politics. The Texas economy historically relied on cattle, cotton, timber, and oil and gas. Although each is still important, the Texas economy is now very diverse and includes many businesses that work in renewable energy sources, high technology, the service sector, a variety of forms of agriculture, and international trade. Service jobs make up the bulk of the increase in employment, but most such jobs pay little and offer few benefits. Diversification has decreased the political dominance of the four historical industries and helped stabilize the Texas economy.

LO 1.5 Identify five major policy challenges Texas faces in the 21st century. Challenges that face Texas include the need to respond to international immigration, manage the state's water supply, protect the environment, develop more effective educational programs, and deal with poverty and social problems. Each of these areas affects the lives of real people. Addressing these issues will cost taxpayers money. The future of Texas depends on Texans' abilities to resolve problems and capitalize on human resources.

KEY TERMS

African American, p. 5
Anglo, p. 6
Asian American, p. 8
biotechnology, p. 28
eminent domain, p. 7
exclusionary zoning, p. 18
gentrification, p. 19
government, p. 3
hydraulic fracturing, p. 25

Jim Crow laws, p. 6
Latino, p. 5
maquiladora, p. 30
Native American, p. 8
North American Free Trade
    Agreement (NAFTA), p. 22
patrón system, p. 6
Permian Basin, p. 20
political culture, p. 4

politics, p. 4
progressive, p. 5
public policy, p. 3
racial covenants, p. 18
redlining, p. 18
right-to-work laws, p. 7
social media, p. 17
undocumented immigrant, p. 31
urban renewal, p. 18

LEARNING CHECK ANSWERS

✓ 1.1 **1.** True. Public policy aims to address a public need by allocating resources or meet a public goal by encouraging, discouraging, or modifying behavior.

2. Texas has historically been dominated by the individualistic culture and the traditionalistic culture.

✓ 1.2 **1.** The Latino population is the fastest growing in the state in terms of size. This has led to increasing political influence for Texas Latinos at the local, state, and national level.

2. Texas is becoming less religious overall and more diverse in terms of religious identification.

✓ 1.3 **1.** Texas's large size makes infrastructure a major budget item for the state government and increases the cost of running for many offices, making campaign fundraising very important.

2. False. Each region of Texas has a distinctive economic base, social system, and political culture.

✓ 1.4 **1.** Cattle, cotton, timber, and oil and gas were most important to the Texas economy in the past.

2. The service sector is currently creating the most jobs for Texans.

✓ 1.5 **1.** False. Demand for water will rise by 22 percent by 2060, and the state's current dependable water supply will meet only about 65 percent of that projected demand.

2. True. Texas has a greater percentage and larger number of citizens without health insurance than any other state.

Federalism and the Texas Constitution

2

Learning Objectives

2.1 Analyze federalism and the powers of the state in a constitutional context.

2.2 Explain the origins and development of the state constitution.

2.3 Analyze the amendment process, focusing on recent constitutional amendment elections as well as attempts to revise the Texas Constitution.

2.4 Explain and analyze the basic sections of the Texas Constitution.

IMAGE 2.1 Pro-Trump Activists and Masked Anti-Trump protesters at Pro-Trump Rally at the State Capitol, March 3, 2018

Visions of America, LLC / Alamy Stock Photo

Competency Connection
⚖ PERSONAL RESPONSIBILITY ⚖

How important is it for your to be politically engaged and convey your political views?

The Texas Constitution, adopted in 1876, serves as the Lone Star State's fundamental law. This document outlines the structure of Texas's state government, authorizes the creation of counties and cities, and establishes basic rules for governing. It has been amended frequently over the course of more than 14 decades. Lawyers, newspaper editors, political scientists, government officials, and others who consult the state constitution tend to criticize it for being too long and for lacking organization. Yet despite criticism, Texans have expressed strong opposition to, or complete lack of interest in, proposals for wholesale constitutional revision.

The Texas Constitution is the primary source of the state government's policymaking power. The other major source of its power is membership in the federal Union. Sometimes, tensions between the federal government and Texas may erupt, as when both former Governor Rick Perry and Governor Greg Abbott challenged the passage and implementation of the Affordable Health Care Act (Obamacare). Within the federal system, state constitutions are subject to the U.S. Constitution.

⬧ The American Federal Structure

LO 2.1 Analyze federalism and the powers of the state in a constitutional context.

Federalism can be defined as a structure of government characterized by the division of powers between a national government and associated regional governments. The heart of the American federal system lies in the relationship between the U.S. government (with Washington, D.C., as the national capital) and the governments of the 50 states. Since 1789, the U.S. Constitution has prescribed a federal system of government for the nation, and since 1846, the state of Texas has been a part of that system.

Political scientist David Walker emphasizes the important role that states play in federalism: "The states' strategically crucial role in the administration, financing, and planning of intergovernmental programs and regulations—both federal and their own—and their perennial key position in practically all areas of local governance have made them the pivotal middlemen in the realm of functional federalism."[1] At the same time, the distribution of governmental power between national and state governments remains a constant tension within federalism. In a chapter titled "Why States Matter," Rick Perry (the longest-serving governor in Texas history) asserts: "the very essence of America stems from a limited, decentralized government."[2] Yet, federal laws and court decisions often grant substantial power to the national government. American federalism has survived more than two centuries of stresses and strains. Among the most serious threats were the Civil War from 1861 to 1865, which almost destroyed the Union, and economic crises, such as the Great Depression, which followed the stock market crash of 1929.

Follow *Practicing Texas Politics* on Twitter **@PracTexPol**

Distribution of Constitutional Powers

Division of powers and functions between the national government and the state governments was originally accomplished by listing the powers of the national government in the U.S. Constitution and by adding the **Tenth Amendment**. The latter asserts that "the powers not delegated to the United States by the Constitution, nor prohibited by it to the States, are reserved to the States, respectively, or to the People." Although the Tenth Amendment may seem to endow the states with powers comparable to those delegated to the national government, Article VI of the U.S. Constitution contains the following clarification: "This Constitution, and the laws of the United States which shall be made in pursuance thereof; and all treaties made, or which shall be made, under the authority of the United States, shall be the supreme law of the land; and the judges in every State shall be bound thereby, anything in the Constitution or laws of any State to the contrary notwithstanding." Referred to as the **national supremacy clause**, this article emphasizes that the U.S. Constitution and acts of Congress, as well as U.S. treaties, must prevail over state constitutions and laws enacted by state legislatures.

Powers of the National Government Article I, Section 8, of the U.S. Constitution lists powers that are specifically delegated to the national government. Included are powers to regulate interstate and foreign commerce, borrow and coin money, establish post offices and post roads, declare war, raise and support armies, provide and maintain a navy, levy and collect taxes, and establish uniform rules of naturalization. Added to these **delegated powers** is a clause that gives the national government the power "to make all laws which shall be necessary and proper for carrying into execution the foregoing powers, and all other powers vested by this Constitution in the government of the United States, or in any department or officer thereof." Since 1789, Congress and the federal courts have used the "necessary and proper" clause as a grant of **implied powers** to expand the national government's authority.[3] Another way in which the federal government has expanded its powers is through the commerce clause in Article I, Section 8 of the U.S. Constitution. For instance, the U.S. Supreme Court, in a case originating in Texas, gave significant leeway to Congress under the commerce clause to legislate in matters traditionally reserved for the states. In this case, the Court allowed Congress to set a minimum wage for employees of local governments.[4]

Guarantees to the States The U.S. Constitution provides all states with an imposing list of **constitutional guarantees**, which include the following:

- A state may be neither divided nor combined with another state without the consent of Congress and the state legislatures involved. (Texas, however, did retain power to divide itself into as many as five states under the terms of its annexation to the United States.)

- Each state is guaranteed a republican form of government (that is, a representative government with elected lawmakers).

Tenth Amendment
The Tenth Amendment to the U.S. Constitution declares that "the powers not delegated by the Constitution, nor prohibited by it to the States, are reserved to the States, respectively, or to the people."

national supremacy clause
Article VI of the U.S. Constitution states, "This Constitution, and the laws of the United States which shall be made in pursuance thereof; and all treaties made, or which shall be made, under the authority of the United States, shall be the supreme law of the land."

delegated powers
Specific powers entrusted to the national government by Article I, Section 8 of the U.S. Constitution (for example, regulate interstate commerce, borrow money, and declare war).

implied powers
Powers inferred by the constitutional authority of the U.S. Congress "to make all laws which shall be necessary and proper for carrying into execution the foregoing [delegated] powers, and all other powers vested by this Constitution in the government of the United States, or in any department or officer thereof."

- Each state is guaranteed two senators in the U.S. Senate and at least one member in the U.S. House of Representatives.

- All states participate in presidential elections through the electoral college. Each state has a number of electoral college votes equal to the total number of U.S. senators and U.S. representatives from that state. (Through 2020, Texas has 38 electoral college votes.)

- All states participate equally in approving or rejecting proposed amendments to the U.S. Constitution. Approval requires ratification either by three-fourths of the state legislatures (used for all but the Twenty-First Amendment, which repealed Prohibition) or by conventions called in three-fourths of the states.

- Each state is entitled to protection by the U.S. government against invasion and domestic violence, although Texas has its own Army National Guard, Air National Guard, and State Guard units. For more information on the state's military forces, see Chapter 9, "The Executive Branch."

- Texas is assured that trials by federal courts for crimes committed in Texas will be conducted in Texas.

Another constitutional guarantee provided to the states is the authority to propose constitutional amendments to the U.S. Constitution. Such action requires two-thirds of the state legislatures to call a national constitutional convention. Specifically, state legislatures must submit an application to Congress to call for a national convention of the states. This procedure, which has never been used, received considerable attention in 2016 when Texas Governor Greg Abbott called on states to convene a constitutional convention to propose several amendments as a means to restore states' rights.[5] In May 2017, the Texas Legislature became the 11th state in the country to pass a resolution calling for a national convention.

Limitations on the States As members of the federal Union, Texas and other states are constrained by limitations imposed by Article I, Section 10, of the U.S. Constitution. For example, they may not enter into treaties, alliances, or confederations or, without the consent of Congress, make compacts or agreements with other states or foreign governments. Furthermore, states are forbidden to levy import duties (taxes) on another state's products. From the outcome of the Civil War and the U.S. Supreme Court's landmark ruling in *Texas v. White*, 74 U.S. 700 (1869), Texans learned that states cannot secede from the Union. In the *White* case, the Court ruled that the national Constitution "looks to an indestructible union, composed of indestructible states." In subsequent cases, the U.S. Supreme Court further restricted state power. For instance, a state legislature cannot limit the number of terms for members of the state's congressional delegation. The U.S. Supreme Court held that term limits for members of Congress could be constitutionally imposed only if authorized by an amendment to the U.S. Constitution.[6]

Other provisions in the U.S. Constitution prohibit states from denying anyone the right to vote because of race, gender, failure to pay a poll tax (a tax paid for the privilege of voting), or age (if the person is 18 years of age or older). The Fourteenth Amendment forbids states from denying to any persons

constitutional guarantees
Rights and protections assured under the U.S. Constitution. For example, among the guarantees to members of the Union include protection against invasion and domestic uprisings, territorial integrity, a republican form of government, and representation by two senators and at least one representative for each state.

the equal protection of the laws. For example, in a 1950 Supreme Court case (prior to the Thelma White case highlighted in the "Students in Action" segment), segregation on the basis of race at the University of Texas Law School was held to be in violation of the Fourteenth Amendment's equal protection clause. Although the state had established "a separate but equal law school" for African Americans at the time, the Court held that it was grossly unequal to the University of Texas Law School. Therefore, the equal protection clause required Heman Sweatt's (the plaintiff of the case) admission to the University of Texas. This ruling opened the door to other qualified African Americans' admission to the law school.[7]

The Fourteenth Amendment also provides that no state may deprive persons of life, liberty, or property without due process of law. These protections include those rights covered in the U.S. Constitution's Bill of Rights. This expansion to the states has occurred primarily through a series of cases heard by the U.S. Supreme Court. Using a principle known as the incorporation theory, the U.S. Supreme Court through a series of cases has applied portions of the Bill of Rights to the states by virtue of the Fourteenth Amendment's due process clause. In effect, states are obligated to provide most of the protections covered in the Bill of Rights. For example, state and local law enforcement officers are required to inform anyone taken into custody of his or her right to remain silent (Fifth Amendment's right against self-incrimination) and the right to an attorney (Sixth Amendment's right to assistance of counsel). To ensure these protections, Congress has enforcement powers under the Fourteenth Amendment.

📋 STUDENTS IN ACTION

Thelma White Case Forced College Integration

"In his court order no. 1616 issued July 25, 1955, Judge Robert E. Thomason prohibited Texas Western College from denying Thelma White 'or any member of the class of persons she represents, the right or privilege of matriculating or registering … because of their race or color.'"

—Veronica Herrera and Alan A. Johnson

How it all began
On March 30, 1955, Thelma White filed suit in a U.S. District Court challenging the denial of her admission to Texas Western College (TWC; now University of Texas at El Paso [UTEP]). When she applied to TWC, officials rejected her application because of her race. The college was forced to obey the state's segregation law. Black students could attend only two public colleges in Texas: Prairie View A&M or Texas Southern University, both in the Houston area and a considerable distance from El Paso.

Winning her case
While waiting for her lawsuit to go to court, White enrolled at New Mexico A&M (later New Mexico State University), where she continued her education. Before the case went to judgment, the University of Texas System decided that TWC could admit black students. [U.S. District] Judge R. E. Thomason [for the Western District of Texas] ruled that the state laws requiring segregation violated the U.S. Constitution, that White must be admitted, and that the entire University of Texas System, along with all other public universities, must admit black students to their undergraduate programs. Before this case, law and medical schools, as well as several

graduate programs, had been opened to blacks, but all undergraduate schools had remained closed.

Fighting for educational rights

White felt that she and other black students were being denied their educational rights. TWC admitted White and 12 other black students for the 1955 fall semester. White's victory opened the door for the students, although she remained at New Mexico A&M. The next year several more black students came to TWC.

Leaving a legacy

White's legacy lives on at UTEP to this day. In her memory, UTEP founded the Thelma White Network for Community and Academic Development. The network's single purpose is to assist black students with social and academic development at UTEP. Today, African American students are enrolled in virtually every academic program at UTEP, a fact made possible by White and her pioneering efforts to change the educational system in El Paso.

Edited excerpt from Veronica Herrera and Alan A. Johnson, "Thelma White Case Forced College Integration," *Borderlands* 14 (Spring 1996); abridged and reprinted by permission

Shown above are seven of the Negro Freshman students as they come out of freshman orientation September 9. They are, from left to right: William Milner, Marcellus Fulmore, John English, Mable Butler, Clarence Stevens, Margaret Jackson, and Sandra Campbell.

The University of Texas at El Paso

White's victory opened the door for African American students attending, what would ultimately become, the UT El Paso campus.

of the authors (Note: the original text and terminology were retained.) *Borderlands* is a collection of student-written articles on the history and culture of the El Paso–Juárez–Las Cruces border region. It is published annually by El Paso Community College. The website for this publication is http://epcc .libguides.com/borderlands.

— Competency Connection —
◉ **SOCIAL RESPONSIBILITY** ◉

What are your initial impressions regarding the student who believed so strongly in equality for African Americans? How essential is the 14th Amendment in our U.S. Constitution to our values of equality? How strongly do you support these values, and to what extent are you be willing to take action like Thelma White in this story?

Interstate Relations and State Immunities

Two provisions of the U.S. Constitution specifically affect relations between the states and between citizens of one state and another state. These provisions are Article IV and the Eleventh Amendment. Article IV of the U.S. Constitution provides that "citizens of each state shall be entitled to all privileges and immunities of citizens in the several states." This means that citizens of Texas who visit another state are entitled to all the **privileges and immunities** of citizens of that state. It does not mean, however, that such visiting Texans are entitled to all the privileges and immunities to which they are entitled in their home state. More than 200 years ago, the U.S. Supreme Court broadly defined "privileges and immunities" as follows: protection by government, enjoyment of life and liberty, right to acquire and possess property, right to leave and enter any state, and right to the use of courts. For some advocates of gun rights, this clause extends to the right to keep and bear arms.

Article IV also states that "full faith and credit shall be given in each State to the public acts, records, and judicial proceedings of every other State." The **full faith and credit clause** means that any legislative enactment, state constitution, deed, will, marriage, divorce, or civil court judgment of one state must be officially recognized and honored in every other state. This clause does not apply to criminal cases. For example, a person convicted in Texas for a crime committed in Texas is not punished in another state to which he or she has fled. Instead, such cases are handled through extradition, whereby the fugitive would be returned to the Lone Star State at the request of the governor of Texas. Furthermore, for some felonies, the U.S. Congress has made it a federal offense to flee from one state to another for the purpose of avoiding arrest.

A controversy regarding the full faith and credit clause revolved around whether states must recognize same-sex marriages. In 1996, during President Bill Clinton's administration, Congress passed the Defense of Marriage Act (DOMA), prohibiting the national government from recognizing same-sex marriages and allowing states or political subdivisions (such as cities) to deny any marriage between persons of the same sex recognized in another state. In 2003, the Texas legislature passed a law prohibiting the state or any agency or political subdivision (such as a county or city) from recognizing a same-sex marriage or civil union formed in Texas or elsewhere. Then, in November 2005, Texas joined 15 other states in adopting a state constitutional amendment that banned same-sex marriage and defined marriage as "only the union of one man and one woman."[8] According to the National Conference of State Legislatures, 33 states had similar bans, either in their constitutions or by statutory law by 2015.

Although several challenges to the constitutionality of these state laws were presented to the U.S. Supreme Court, the Court was reluctant to review any such cases until 2012. In the 2013 case, *United States v. Windsor*, the U.S. Supreme Court struck down a provision of the Defense of Marriage Act that denied more than 1,000 federal benefits for same-sex married couples. The court concluded that the provision deprived same-sex couples of rights and responsibilities protected by the due process clause of the Fifth Amendment and treated them differently in violation of equal protection principles.[9] Although the decision applied to federal laws and directives affecting legally recognized same-sex marriages performed in 17 states at the time, it left unclear whether states had to recognize same-sex marriages legally sanctioned in other states. In exercising its state's rights, Texas chose to refuse national directives in this area of law. For instance, the Texas National Guard initially refused to provide federal spousal benefits for same-sex couples despite a mandate by the U.S. Department of Defense.

privileges and immunities
Article IV of the U.S. Constitution guarantees that "citizens of each state shall be entitled to the privileges and immunities of citizens of the several states." According to the U.S. Supreme Court, this provision means that citizens are guaranteed protection by government, enjoyment of life and liberty, the right to acquire and possess property, the right to leave and enter any state, and the right to use state courts.

full faith and credit clause
Most government actions of another state must be officially recognized by public officials in Texas.

At least three federal lawsuits were filed as challenges to Texas's ban on same-sex marriage, claiming that the law subjected gay couples to unequal treatment in violation of the U.S. Constitution. In February 2014, U.S. District Judge Orlando L. García of the Western District in San Antonio struck down the Texas ban, ruling it did not have a "legitimate government purpose." Then the U.S. Supreme Court agreed to hear a case which directly challenged the marriage restrictions in Kentucky, Michigan, Tennessee, and Ohio. Kentucky's law was similar to the Texas law in declaring marriage to involve "one man and one woman." The U.S. Supreme Court ultimately ruled in a 5-4 decision that the Fourteenth Amendment guarantees all couples the right to marry, regardless of sexual orientation, and that states must recognize same-sex marriages performed in other states.[10] Same-sex marriage bans in Texas and 12 other states were effectively struck down. Thus, same-sex marriages are now legal in all 50 states. Further expanding these rights, in a unanimous decision in the case of *V.L. v. E.L.*, 577 U.S. ___ (2016), the Court upheld the principle of full faith and credit, when the Court forced the state of Alabama to recognize parental rights granted to a same-sex ex-partner by a Georgia court.

The Eleventh Amendment also affects relations between citizens of one state and the government of another state. It provides, in part, that "The Judicial power of the United States shall not be construed to extend to any suit in law or equity, commenced or prosecuted against one of the United States by citizens of another state." U.S. Supreme Court rulings have ensured that a state may not be sued by its own citizens, or those of another state, without the defendant state's consent, nor can state employees sue the state for violating federal law.[11] This law, otherwise known as sovereign immunity, gives a tremendous shield to state governments. Yet this power is not absolute. For example, in 1993, several families whose children were eligible for Medicaid sued the state of Texas for its failure to provide these programs. The District Court ordered the state to correct the problem. A consent decree was issued (an agreement of both parties to avoid further litigation). When the District Court ordered enforcement of the decree, the state appealed to the Fifth Circuit Court of Appeals arguing that the decree had many more requirements than the Medicaid law. The plaintiffs appealed to the U.S. Supreme Court, which held that the decree should be enforced even if it went beyond federal law. The Supreme Court ultimately held that this was not a sovereign immunity case because the suit was not against the state but against state officials who had acted in violation of federal law. The Eleventh Amendment does not prohibit enforcement of a consent decree; enforcement by the federal courts is permitted to ensure observance of federal law.[12]

State Powers

Nowhere in the U.S. Constitution is there a list of state powers. As mentioned, the Tenth Amendment simply states that all powers not specifically delegated to the national government, nor prohibited to the states, are reserved to the states or to the people. The **reserved powers** of the states are, therefore, undefined and often very difficult to specify, especially when the powers

reserved powers
Reserved powers are derived from the Tenth Amendment of the U.S. Constitution. Although not spelled out in the U.S. Constitution, these reserved powers to the states include police power, taxing power, proprietary power, and power of eminent domain.

are concurrent with those of the national government, such as the taxing power. Political scientists, however, view reserved powers in several broad categories:

- Police power: protection of the health, morals, safety, and convenience of citizens, and provision for the general welfare
- Taxing power: raising revenue to pay salaries of state employees, meet other costs of government, and repay borrowed money
- Proprietary power: public ownership of property, such as airports, energy-producing utilities, and parks
- Power of eminent domain: taking private property at a fair price for various kinds of public projects, such as highway construction

Needless to say, states today have broad powers, responsibilities, and duties. They are, for example, responsible for the nation's public elections—national, state, and local—because there are no nationally operated election facilities. State courts conduct most trials (both criminal and civil). States operate public schools (elementary and secondary) and public institutions of higher education (colleges and universities), and they maintain most of the country's prisons.

One broad state power that has raised controversy is the power of eminent domain. Customarily, government entities have used the power of eminent domain to appropriate private property for public projects, such as highways, parks, and schools, as long as the property owners are paid a just compensation. In 2005, the U.S. Supreme Court expanded this power under the Fifth Amendment, allowing local governments to seize private homes for private development; the Supreme Court, however, left the door open for states to set their own rules.[13] Then-Governor Rick Perry responded by calling a special legislative session in the summer of that year. As a result, statutory limits were imposed on government entities condemning private property where the primary purpose is for economic development. Exceptions were made, however, for public projects and to protect the city of Arlington's plan to build the Cowboys Stadium (now known as the AT&T Stadium), home of the Dallas Cowboys National Football League team. To ensure constitutional protection of private property rights against abuses by governments, an amendment to the Texas Constitution was proposed and adopted in 2009. This amendment, however, does not bar energy companies from condemning private property for the construction of oil and gas pipelines. The pipeline owner must assure the Texas Railroad Commission that other companies will be able to use the pipeline. In doing so, the pipeline becomes a "common carrier" that benefits the general public and not private individuals or companies. Controversy in East Texas surrounded the construction of the Keystone Pipeline, owned by TransCanada, a Canadian company. The northern portion of the pipeline was eventually approved by President Trump after he took office in 2016 despite environmental concerns. The southern portion from Cushing, Oklahoma, to Houston has been in operation since 2014. The Trans-Pecos pipeline, an intrastate pipeline intended to transport natural gas from the Ft. Stockton area in West Texas to Mexico, is even more controversial. The gas pipeline encountered growing resistance from landowners and conservationists for the potential damage to ranching, public safety, and Big Bend National Park.

Nonetheless, in May 2016, the Federal Energy Regulatory Commission approved construction and the pipeline has been in operation since 2017.[14]

Although most state powers are recognizable, identifying a clear boundary line between state and national powers often remains complicated. Once again, the U.S. Supreme Court has played a critical role in defining this balance of power. Take, for example, the constitutional provision of interstate commerce in the U.S. Constitution. Not until *United States v. Lopez* (1995), a case that originated in Texas, did the U.S. Supreme Court indicate that the U.S. Congress had exceeded its powers to regulate interstate commerce when it attempted to ban guns in public schools to address the increasing violence on school grounds. Operation of public schools has traditionally been considered a power of state and local governments, and the Supreme Court has used the *Lopez* case in later cases to rein in the federal government's power.[15] States have also become more willing to make claims of state sovereignty over federal authority in these cases.

The Supreme Court has limited state sovereignty with regard to the use of a class of products—specifically, marijuana for medical treatment of terminally ill patients. In *Gonzales v. Raich*, the Court struck down a California initiative that made an exception to the illegalization of marijuana. It ruled that Congress has the sole power to regulate local and state activities that substantially affect interstate commerce.[16] Although the California measure would have protected noncommercial cultivation and use of marijuana that did not cross state lines, the federal government contended that it would handicap enforcement of federal drug laws. In this regard, the Court ruled that the federal government is primarily responsible for regulating narcotics and other controlled substances. While the official position of the White House during the Obama administration was that it "steadfastly oppose[d] legalization of marijuana," the federal government did not fully enforce the U.S. restriction on marijuana in states that had decriminalized marijuana for either medicinal or recreational use. As of 2018 California and 30 other states, plus Washington, DC, have legalized the medical use of marijuana. As many as 10 states, such as Colorado, Washington, Alaska, and Oregon, including the District of Columbia, have legalized small amounts of marijuana for recreational use. In effect, these states have ignored a limited area of federal law.[17] In 2015, Texas joined 15 states that allow limited use of cannabis oil to treat certain illnesses.

Through 2017, Texas had led (or been part of) close to 50 lawsuits against the federal government and the Obama administration in a continuing fight for states' rights and a broad interpretation of state power under the Tenth Amendment. Many of these suits were led by Governor Greg Abbott, when he served as the state's Attorney General (2003–2015). Some of the legal challenges were filed under Abbott's successor, Attorney General Ken Paxton. The suits covered a variety of issues, including several challenges dealing with environmental standards and climate change, as well as funding for women's health programs and health-care reform. Among these cases (which have been largely funded by taxpayer money), Texas had lost 12 cases and won seven (mainly around environmental regulations) as of January 2017, with other cases pending.[18] One area of law where Texas has both won and lost involves the Patient Protection and Affordable Care Act of 2010 (also known as Obamacare). Texas was one of 26 states led by Republican attorneys general and governors to challenge the constitutionality of this federal law. Contested provisions included congressional mandates requiring states to expand coverage and eligibility for Medicaid programs, as well as requirements that individuals purchase health insurance or face a penalty.

The U.S. Supreme Court ultimately heard *National Federation of Independent Business v. Sebelius*, concluding that it was within the Congress's taxing power to impose a penalty on individuals who failed to obtain health insurance. Nevertheless, the Court ruled that Congress could not withdraw existing Medicaid funding from states that failed to comply with the expanded coverage requirements for adults.[19] In response, Texas remained one of several states that did not expand Medicaid coverage. In a subsequent challenge to the Affordable Care Act, originating in the state of Virginia, the Supreme Court in 2015 refused to limit federal subsidies (in the form of tax credits) for eligible low-income individuals who obtained insurance through a federally administered health-care exchange. Health-care exchanges are online portals where insurance companies offer different health insurance plans to consumers. By forcing competition between the companies, federal government officials hoped insurers would lower health care premiums. The condition for federal subsidies was initially created as an incentive to encourage states to operate health care exchanges specifically designed for their residents. Texas and 35 other states chose not to establish state-run exchanges. The Court ultimately concluded that eligible residents of these states would also receive federal subsidies even though they purchased insurance through the federal exchange.[20] At the time, observers speculated that nearly one million Texans stood to lose these subsidies if the Supreme Court had decided differently. Litigation challenging the federal law continues. In December 2018, for instance, a federal district judge in Texas struck it down as being unconstitutional because Congress had repealed the individual mandate requirement, which imposed a tax penalty on consumers without coverage, making the federal law obsolete.

In another area of law, Texas and 24 other states sued the federal government in 2014 granting temporary relief from deportation for more than four million undocumented immigrant parents of children who were U.S. citizens (known as DAPA). A federal district court said that the Department of Homeland Security under the Obama Administration had exceeded its administrative authority. A panel of three appellate justices on the U.S. Fifth Circuit Court of Appeals affirmed the lower court's decision, striking down Obama's immigration plan in November 2015. Under pressure from the White House, the U.S. Supreme Court agreed to hear the case. In June of 2016, the U.S. Supreme Court was evenly divided on the immigration program. Without a majority opinion to overturn the lower court's decision, the immigration plan was blocked from going into effect.[21] In May 2018, Attorney General Paxton led a coalition of 10 states to end the immigration program, DACA (Deferred Action for Childhood Arrivals) that grants lawful presence and work permits to roughly 700,000 (known as Dreamers) if they were under 17 when they arrived and if they arrived by 2007. The lawsuit, supported by President Trump, was still pending as of December 2018.

Federal-State Relations: An Evolving Process

Since the establishment of the American federal system, states have operated within a constitutional context modified to meet changing conditions. At the same time, the framers of the U.S. Constitution sought to provide a workable balance of power between national and state governments that would sustain the nation indefinitely. This balance of power between federal and state governments has evolved over the years, with certain periods reflecting an expansion or decline of the federal government, while also affecting Texas's resistance to national control over state power. In certain areas of policy, such as regulating the legalized use of medicinal and recreational marijuana, as mentioned earlier, the federal government under the Obama administration has left enforcement to state and local authorities. President Trump's administration has not taken action on the issue, and he stated during his presidential campaign that enforcement of marijuana laws was a state issue.

From 1865 until about 1930, Congress exercised power to regulate railroads and interstate commerce within and among states. In addition, with the onset of the Great Depression of the 1930s, the federal government extended its jurisdiction to areas traditionally within the realm of state and local governments, such as regulating the workplace. For example, expansion of federal law extended to worker safety, minimum wages, and maximum hours. This expansion occurred principally through broad interpretation of the interstate commerce clause by the U.S. Supreme Court, which, in a series of cases, expanded the national government's power to include these matters.

Grants of money to the states from the federal government have also been used to influence state policymaking. The number and size of **federal grants-in-aid** grew while Congress gave states more financial assistance. As federally initiated programs multiplied, the national government's influence on state policymaking widened, and the states' control lessened in many areas. However, beginning in the 1980s and continuing through the presidential administration of George W. Bush, state and local governments gained more freedom to spend federal funds as they chose. In some areas, however, such as public assistance programs, they were granted less money to spend.

Decline in national control over state governments has often been identified as another development in federal-state relations called devolution. The underlying concept of devolution is to bring about a reduction in the size and influence of the national government by reducing federal taxes and expenditures and by shifting many federal responsibilities to the states. Because one feature of devolution involves sharp reductions in federal aid, states are compelled to assume important new responsibilities with substantially less revenue to finance them. Texas and other states have been forced to assume more responsibility for formulating and funding their own programs in education, highways, mental health, public assistance (welfare), and other areas. In some cases, federal programs are shared. States must match federal monies to benefit from a program, such as the Children's Health Insurance Program (CHIP), or risk losing the funds. (See Chapter 11, "Finance and Fiscal Policy," for a discussion of CHIP funding.)

An important feature of devolution is Congress's use of **block grants** to distribute money to state and local governments. Block grants are fixed sums of

federal grants-in-aid
Money appropriated by the U.S. Congress to help states and local governments provide needed facilities and services.

block grant
Congressional grant of money that allows the state considerable flexibility in spending for a program, such as providing welfare services.

✚ POINT/COUNTERPOINT

Should Texas Support the Affordable Care Act?

THE ISSUE In 2010, under the Obama administration, Congress passed the Patient Protection and Affordable Care Act, providing increased access to health care coverage for more people. Opponents and proponents of the law continued to debate the merits of the newly enacted law even after the U.S. Supreme Court upheld it twice. Opponents, such as former Governor Rick Perry and Governor Greg Abbott, argue that this law represents an overstepping of federal authority; whereas proponents argue that health care is an absolute necessity for all Texans. Whether to dismantle the law was a major issue for both Democrat and Republican candidates during the 2016 presidential election and 2018 mid-term election. And, specifically, whether to expand Medicaid in Texas has been contentious.

FOR	AGAINST
1. Expanding Medicaid would provide necessary health care for the state's low-income adults. This expansion is cost-effective for Texas because the federal government will cover 100 percent in the first few years and 90 percent thereafter.	1. The act is an intrusion on state sovereignty in an area of policy that has traditionally been a state power.
2. Texas will lose billions of dollars in federal funding if it opts out of the Medicaid expansion.	2. Even though the federal government will provide almost all of the funding for expanding Medicaid in the first few years, no guarantee exists that this level of funding will continue. If federal spending is reduced, the burden would shift to the states.
3. When fewer people are covered under health insurance, state and local governments will spend more on uncompensated medical care.	3. The law increases taxes and imposes a burden on the Texas economy.

— Competency Connection —
◆ COMMUNICATION SKILLS ◆

Should the federal government have the authority to require states to expand Medicaid coverage? Why or why not? How does this issue impact federal-state relations? How would you convey your views?

money awarded according to an automatic formula determined by Congress. Thus, states that receive block grants have greater flexibility in spending. Welfare policy is an excellent case. The country's welfare programs became primarily a federal responsibility during the Great Depression and the administration of Franklin D. Roosevelt (1933–1945). Other federal responses to unemployment and poverty included such programs as food stamps and medical assistance for the poor as part of President Lyndon B. Johnson's Great Society. The Clinton administration (1993–2001) and a Republican-controlled Congress, however, eventually forced states to assume more responsibility for welfare programs and supplied federal funding in the form of block grants.[22] President George W. Bush continued these trends and added a new twist to devolution by giving federal financial assistance to faith-based organizations that provide social services to the poor.

Despite the focus on devolution from 2001 to 2009, federal laws such as the No Child Left Behind Act of 2001 suggested that the Republican Congress and Republican President George W. Bush's administration aggressively pursued policies that once again expanded the federal government's role. No Child Left Behind, which among other mandates required participating states to administer accountability tests (selected by the state) in public schools, expanded the national government's reach into a traditional area of state and local responsibility.

In 2015, the Congress and the Obama administration revisited No Child Left Behind, passing the Every Child Succeeds Act which restored authority for school performance and accountability to local districts and the states. The law still requires testing in grades three through eight, but it allows local and state control for setting goals, establishing school ratings, and determining remedial measures. After several years of federal control, the law signals the return of authority over education policy to state and local officials.[23]

As mentioned, Texas has challenged federal authority primarily through lawsuits. Less frequently, Texas has also refused some federal funds. Typically, more than one-third of the Lone Star State's biennial budget is funded by the federal government. Yet state officials have at times refused funding for unemployment benefits, Medicaid expansion, and public school funding, arguing that these funds required the adoption of national standards for state-run programs. State legislative actions or bills proposed in recent legislative sessions are part of the State Sovereignty Movement. This movement, which began gaining momentum in 2009, claims sovereignty under the Tenth Amendment against all powers not otherwise enumerated or granted to the federal government in the U.S. Constitution. Similar unsuccessful bills were proposed in the Texas House in recent legislative sessions. Senator Brandon Creighton (R-Conroe), who has primarily led this movement in the legislature, for instance, introduced SCR1 during the 84th legislative session. This resolution, which did not have the force and effect of law, reaffirmed state sovereignty and called for a new relationship between the state of Texas and the federal government. It passed the Senate, but was not voted on by the House.[24] For some observers, these actions symbolize the increasing polarization of national–state politics.

During his 2012 and 2016 unsuccessful presidential bids, former Governor Perry positioned himself as a champion of states' rights and described the fight to defend the Tenth Amendment as the "battle for the soul of America." In *Fed Up! Our Fight to Save America from Washington*, Perry states that "the spirit and intent of the Tenth Amendment … is under assault and has been for some time. The result is that today we face unprecedented federal intrusion into numerous facets of our lives."[25] Talk of secession was even more pertinent in 2011 during the 150th anniversary of Texas's attempted secession from the Union at the onset of the Civil War. In a similar vein, Governor Greg Abbott, as mentioned earlier, called for a national constitutional convention in 2016. Among Abbott's nine recommendations are a constitutional amendment prohibiting "Congress from regulating activity that occurs wholly within one state" and allowing "a two-thirds majority of the states to override a federal law or regulation."[26] Governor Abbot outlined his proposal in his book, *Broken Not Unbowed: The Fight to Fix a Broken America*. As mentioned earlier, his call for a national convention has gained some momentum.

✔ **2.1 Learning Check**

1. True or False: The Tenth Amendment specifically identifies states' powers.

2. Does devolution give states more or less freedom to make decisions?

Answers at the end of this chapter.

The Texas Constitution: Politics of Policymaking

LO 2.2 Explain the origins and development of the state constitution.

As already mentioned, the current Texas Constitution is the main source of power for the Texas state government. Surviving for more than 140 years, this constitution establishes the state's government, defines governing powers and imposes limitations, and identifies Texans' civil liberties and civil rights. Political scientists and legal scholars generally believe that a constitution should indicate the process by which problems will be solved, both in the present and in the future, and should not attempt to solve specific problems. Presumably, if this principle is followed, later generations will not need to adopt numerous amendments. In many areas, however, the Texas Constitution mandates specific policies in great detail, which has required frequent amendments.

The preamble to the Texas Constitution states, "Humbly invoking the blessings of Almighty God, the people of the state of Texas do ordain and establish this Constitution." These words begin the 28,600-word document that became Texas's seventh constitution in 1876. By the start of 2019, that same document had been changed by no fewer than 498 amendments and contained about 87,000 words.

The constitution's framers spelled out policymaking powers and limitations in minute detail. This specificity, in turn, made frequent amendments inevitable as constitutional provisions were altered to fit changing times and conditions. For more than a century, the length of the Texas Constitution has increased through an accumulation of amendments, most of which are essentially statutory (resembling laws made by the legislature). The resulting document more closely resembles a code of laws than a fundamental instrument of government. To fully understand the present-day Texas Constitution, we will examine the historical factors surrounding its adoption, as well as previous historical periods and constitutions.

Historical Developments

The Texas Constitution provides the legal basis on which the state functions as an integral part of the federal Union. In addition, the document is a product of history and an expression of the dominant political philosophy of Texans living at the time of its adoption.

In general, constitution drafters have been pragmatic people performing an important task. Despite the idealistic sentiment commonly attached to constitutions in the United States, the art of drafting and amending them is essentially political in nature. In other words, these documents reflect the drafters' views and political interests, as well as the political environment of their time. With the passing of years, the Texas Constitution reflects the political ideas of new generations of people who amend or change it.

The constitutional history of Texas began with promulgation of the Constitution of Coahuila y Tejas within the Mexican federal system in 1827 and the Constitution of the Texas Republic in 1836. Texas has since been governed under its state constitutions of 1845, 1861, 1866, 1869, and 1876. Each of these seven constitutions has reflected the political situation that existed when the specific document was drafted.[27] In this section, we will see the political process at work as we examine the origins of these constitutions and note the efforts to revise and amend the current Texas Constitution.

The First Six Texas Constitutions In 1824, three years after Mexico gained independence from Spain, Mexican liberals established a republic with a federal constitution. Within that federal system, the former Spanish provinces of Coahuila and Tejas became a single Mexican state that adopted its own constitution. Thus, the Constitution of Coahuila y Tejas, promulgated in 1827, marked Texas's first experience with a state constitution.

Political unrest among Anglo Texans, who had settled in Mexico's northeastern area, arose almost immediately. Factors that led Texians (as Texans called themselves at the time) to declare independence from Mexico included, among others, their desire for unrestricted trade with the United States, Anglo attitudes of racial superiority, anger over Mexico's abolition of slavery, increasing numbers of immigrant settlers, insufficient Anglo representation in the 12-member Coahuila y Tejas legislature, and Mexico's failure to provide greater access to government in the English language.[28]

On March 2, 1836, at Washington-on-the-Brazos (between present-day Brenham and Navasota), a delegate convention of 59 Texans and Tejanos issued a declaration of independence from Mexico. Mexicans in Texas who also wanted independence and who fought for a free Texas state referred to themselves as Tejanos. Three Tejanos in particular served as delegates at the convention: Lorenzo de Zavala (representing Harrisburg [now a part of Houston]), Francisco Ruiz, and José Antonio Navarro (both representing Béxar). The delegates drafted the Constitution of the Republic of Texas, modeled largely after the U.S. Constitution.

During this same period, in an effort to retain Mexican sovereignty, General Antonio López de Santa Anna defeated the Texians (many of whom were not even from Texas) and some Tejanos in San Antonio in the siege of the Alamo, which ended on March 6, 1836. Shortly afterward, Sam Houston's troops, including a company of Tejanos who were recruited by Captain Juan N. Seguín, crushed the Mexican forces in the Battle of San Jacinto on April 21, 1836. Part of Texas's unique history in the United States is its existence as an independent nation for close to 10 years.

After Houston's victory over Santa Anna, Texas voters elected Houston as president of their new republic; they also voted to seek admission to the Union. Not until 1845, however, was annexation authorized by a joint resolution of the U.S. Congress. Earlier attempts to become part of the United States by treaty had failed. Texas's status as a slave state, as well as concerns that annexation would lead to war with Mexico, stalled the earlier efforts. Texas president Anson Jones ultimately called a constitutional convention whose delegates drew up a new state

HOW DO WE COMPARE...

In State Constitutions?

Year of Adoption, Length of State Constitutions, and Number of Amendments (2017)

Most Populous U.S. States	Year of Adoption	Approximate No. of Words and Number of Amendments	U.S. States Bordering Texas	Year of Adoption	Approximate No. of Words and Number of Amendments
California	1879	67,000 (535)	Arkansas	1874	59,000 (106)
Florida	1968	57,000 (126)	Louisiana	1974	70,000 (190)
New York	1894	44,000 (229)	New Mexico	1911	33,000 (170)
Texas	**1876**	87,000 (498)	Oklahoma	1907	82,000 (198)

Source: The Book of States, 2018, http://knowledgecenter.csg.org/kc/content/book-states-2018-chapter-1-state-constitutions.

—— Competency Connection ——
⚙ **CRITICAL THINKING** ⚙

Analyze this chart. What are your initial impressions regarding the number of words and number of amendments in the Texas Constitution in comparison to other state constitutions? In what way has adding amendments influenced the development of the Texas Constitution?

constitution and agreed to accept the invitation to join the Union. In October 1845, after Texas voters ratified both actions of the constitutional convention, Texas obtained its third constitution and on December 29 became the 28th member of the United States.

These events, however, set the stage for war between Mexico and the United States (1846–1848), especially with regard to where the boundary lines between the two countries would be drawn. For some historians, U.S. expansionist politicians and business interests actively sought this war. When the Treaty of Guadalupe Hidalgo between Mexico and the United States was signed in 1848, Mexico lost more than half its territory and recognized the Rio Grande as Texas's southern boundary. Negotiations also addressed the rights of Mexicans left behind in Texas, many of whom owned land in the region. Under the treaty, Mexicans had one year to choose to return to Mexico or to remain in the newly annexed part of the United States; it also guaranteed Mexicans all the rights of citizenship. For all intents and purposes, these residents became the first Mexican Americans of Texas and the United States. Many Mexican Americans, however, were soon deprived of most of their rights, especially their property rights.

The Texas Constitution of 1845 lasted until the Civil War began. When Texas voted to secede from the Union in 1861, it joined with other southern states to form the Confederate States of America. At the time, secessionists argued that the U.S. Constitution created a compact among the states, and that each state had a right to secede. During this period, Texas adopted its Constitution of 1861, with the aim of making as few changes as possible in government structure and

IMAGE 2.2 The Tejano Monument on the Texas Capitol grounds, erected in 2012, symbolizes official recognition by the state of contributions by Tejanos in the state's development.

Marjorie Kamys Cotera/Bob Daemmrich Photography/Alamy Stock Photo

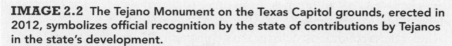

Competency Connection
☼ **CRITICAL THINKING** ☼

Reflect on this photo. What are your impressions of the Tejano Monument and the images it represents especially in the development of our state's history?

powers. The new constitution included changes necessary to equip the government for separation from the United States, as well as the maintenance of slavery. After the Confederacy's defeat, however, the Constitution of 1866 was drafted amid a different set of conditions during Reconstruction. For this constitution, the framers sought to restore Texas to the Union with minimal changes in existing social, economic, and political institutions. Although the Constitution of 1866 was based on the Constitution of 1845, it nevertheless recognized the rights of former slaves to sue in the state's courts, to enter into contracts, to obtain and transfer property, and to testify in court actions involving black citizens (but not in court actions involving white citizens). Although the Constitution of 1866 protected the personal property of African American Texans, it did not permit them to vote, hold public office, or serve as jurors.

The relatively uncomplicated reinstatement of Texas into the Union ended abruptly when the Radical Republicans gained control of the U.S. Congress after the election of November 1866. Refusing to seat Texas's two senators and three representatives, Congress set aside the state's reconstructed government, enfranchised former slaves, disenfranchised anyone who had participated in or supported the Confederacy, and imposed military rule across the state. U.S. Army officers replaced civil authorities. As in other southern states, Texas functioned under a military government.

Under these conditions, delegates to a constitutional convention met in intermittent sessions from June 1868 to February 1869 and drafted yet another state constitution. Among other provisions, the new constitution centralized more power in state government, provided compulsory school attendance, and guaranteed a full range of rights for former slaves. This document was ratified in 1869. Then, with elections supervised by federal soldiers, Radical Republicans gained control of the Texas legislature. At the same time, Edmund Jackson Davis (commonly identified as E. J. Davis), a former Union army general, was elected as the first Republican governor of Texas. Some historians (such as Charles William Ramsdell and T. R. Fehrenbach) described the Davis administration (January 1870–January 1874) as one of the most corrupt in Texas history.[29] In recent years, however, revisionist historians (such as Patrick G. Williams, Carl H. Moneyhon, and Barry A. Crouch) have made more positive assessments of Davis and his administration.[30]

White Texans during the Davis administration tended to react negatively and with hostility to the freedom of former black slaves and to the political influence, albeit quite limited, that these freedmen exercised when they became voters. Violence and lawlessness were serious problems at the time; thus, Governor Davis imposed martial law in some places and used police methods to enforce his decrees. Opponents of the Davis administration claimed that it was characterized by extravagant public spending, property tax increases to the point of confiscation, gifts of public funds to private interests, intimidation of newspaper editors, and control of voter registration by the military. In addition, hundreds of appointments to various state and local offices were filled with Davis's supporters.

Although the Constitution of 1869 is associated with the Reconstruction era and the unpopular (with most whites) administration of Governor Davis, the machinery of government created by this document was quite modern. The new fundamental law called for annual sessions of the legislature, a four-year term for the governor and other executive officers, and gubernatorial appointment (rather than popular election) of judges. It abolished county courts and raised the salaries of government officials. These changes centralized more governmental power in Austin and weakened local government.

During the Davis administration, Democrats gained control of the legislature in 1872. In December 1873, Governor Davis (with 42,633 votes) was badly defeated by Democrat Richard Coke from Waco (with 85,549 votes). When Davis refused to leave his office on the ground floor of the Capitol, Democratic lawmakers and Governor-elect Coke are reported to have climbed ladders to the Capitol's second story where the legislature convened. When President Ulysses S. Grant refused to send troops to protect him, Davis left the Capitol under protest in January 1874. In that same year, Democrats wrested control of the state courts from Republicans. The next step was to rewrite the Texas Constitution.

Drafting the Constitution of 1876 In the summer of 1875, Texans elected 75 Democrats and 15 Republicans (six of whom were African Americans) as delegates to a constitutional convention; however, only 83 attended the gathering

IMAGE 2.3 Some of the Constitutional Convention delegates of 1875.

Texas State Library and Archives Commission

— Competency Connection —
⚙ CRITICAL THINKING ⚙

How does Texas's constitutional history during the 1875 Constitutional Convention continue to influence the state's present-day constitution and government?

in Austin. The majority of the delegates were not native Texans. More than 40 percent of the delegates were members of the **Texas Grange** (the Patrons of Husbandry), a farmers' organization committed to strict economy in government (reduced spending) and limited governmental powers. Its slogan of "retrenchment and reform" became a major goal of the convention.[31] So strong was the spirit of strict economy among delegates that they refused to hire a stenographer or to allow publication of the convention proceedings. As a result, no official record was ever made of the convention that gave Texas its most enduring constitution.

In their zeal to undo policies of the Davis administration, delegates on occasion overreacted. Striking at Reconstruction measures that had given Governor Davis control over voter registration, the overwrought delegates inserted a statement providing that "no law shall ever be enacted requiring a registration of voters of this state." Within two decades, however, the statement had been amended to permit voter registration laws.

As they continued to dismantle the machinery of the Davis administration, delegates restricted powers of the three branches of state government. They reduced the governor's salary, powers, and term (from four years to two); made all executive offices (except that of secretary of state) elective for two-year terms;

Texas Grange
A farmers' organization, also known as the Patrons of Husbandry, committed to low levels of government spending and limited governmental powers; a major influence on the Constitution of 1876.

and tied the hands of legislators with biennial (once every two years) sessions, low salaries, and limited legislative powers. All judgeships became popularly elected for relatively short terms of office. Justice of the peace courts, county courts, and district courts—all with popularly elected judges—were established. In addition, public services were trimmed to the bone. Framers of the new constitution limited the public debt and severely curbed the legislature's taxing and spending powers. They also inserted specific policy provisions. For example, they reinstated racially segregated public education and repealed the compulsory school attendance law, restored precinct elections, and allowed only taxpayers to vote on local bond issues.

Texas's proposed constitution was put to a popular vote in 1876 and was approved by a more than two-to-one majority. Although Texans in the state's largest cities—Houston, Dallas, San Antonio, and Galveston—voted against it, the much larger rural population voted for approval.

Distrust of Government and Its Legacy Sharing in the prevailing popular distrust of, and hostility toward, government, framers of the Texas Constitution of 1876 sought with a vengeance to limit, and thus control, policymaking by placing many restrictions in the state's fundamental law. The general consensus of the time held that a state government could exercise only those powers listed in the state constitution. Therefore, instead of being permitted to exercise powers not denied by the U.S. Constitution, Texas lawmakers are limited to powers spelled out in the state's constitution. In addition, the 19th-century Texas Constitution (even with amendments) provides only limited powers for the governor's office in the 21st century. It is considered one of the weakest gubernatorial offices in the nation. (See Chapter 9, "The Executive Branch," for a discussion of the governor's office.)

Today: After More Than a Century of Usage

The structural disarray and confusion of the Constitution of 1876 compound the disadvantages of its excessive length and detail. Unlike the Texas Constitution, the U.S. Constitution has only 4,400 words and merely 27 constitutional amendments. With all its shortcomings, the **Texas Constitution of 1876** has lasted for more than 140 years. In actuality, it is quite common that state constitutions are lengthy documents, given the nature of state and local responsibilities. For one observer, the virtues of the Texas constitution are "its democratic impulses of restraining power and empowering voters." It is a "document of history as much as it is a charter of governance."[32]

Filling the Texas Constitution with many details and creating a state government with restricted powers would inevitably lead to constitutional amendments and frequent alterations. In fact, many substantive changes in Texas government require an amendment. For example, an amendment is needed to change the way the state pays bills, to abolish certain unneeded state and county offices, or to authorize a bond issue pledging state revenues. Urbanization, industrialization, technological innovations, population growth, demands for programs and services, and countless social changes contribute to pressures for frequent constitutional change.

Texas Constitution of 1876
The lengthy, much-amended state constitution, a product of the post-Reconstruction era that remains in effect today.

Most amendments apply to matters that should be resolved by statutes enacted by the Texas legislature. Instead, an often uninformed and usually apathetic electorate must decide the fate of many complex policy issues. In this context, special interests represented by well-financed lobbyists and the media often play influential roles in constitutional policymaking. They are also likely to influence the success or defeat of proposed amendments.

Then-Governor Rick Perry, for instance, played a pivotal role in advocating for specific constitutional amendment proposals. As the most visible policymaker in Texas, his public support or nonsupport of key propositions swayed voters. In 2005, for example, he supported Proposition 2, which signified a new direction in the substantive nature of constitutional amendment proposals on the ballot. The controversial nature of Proposition 2, which sought to ban same-sex marriage, produced unprecedented media coverage and interest group activity. As mentioned previously, the amendment proposal defined marriage as consisting only of the "union of one man and one woman." It also prohibited the state and all political subdivisions from "creating or recognizing any legal status identical or similar to marriage." The measure overwhelmingly passed with 76 percent of the voters (more than 1.7 million) supporting it and 24 percent (more than 500,000) opposing it.[33]

Constitutional Amendment Elections Often, Texas voters are expected to evaluate numerous constitutional amendments. (Table 2.1 provides data on amendments proposed and adopted from 1876 through 2017.) Of the 680 constitutional amendment proposals presented to voters, 498 have been approved and 182 have been defeated. According to the Texas Legislative Council, 70 percent of the proposals were approved from 1876 to 2001. From 2003 to 2015, voters were presented with 86 constitutional amendment proposals, with as many as 22 in 2003, and voters approved 94 percent of these proposals. So, unless there is strong and vocal opposition, constitutional amendment proposals are increasingly likely to be approved. One underlying theme among recent constitutional amendment elections relates to public finance. For instance, some constitutional amendments that have been approved provide property tax exemptions for different types of homeowners, such as surviving spouses of military personnel killed in action or deceased disabled veterans. One increased the residence homestead exemptions for taxes supporting public schools. Another dedicated a portion of sales tax revenue toward the state highway fund to build roads. Other constitutional amendments have centered on the legislative process, most notably a 2007 amendment that requires state legislators to cast a recorded final vote on all substantive bills or constitutional amendment proposals and have it posted on the Internet for public review.

Some of the more noteworthy constitutional amendments in recent years have had an impact on colleges and universities. For instance, in 2009, a proposal that received special attention by graduate students and faculty at state universities allowed Texas's public "emerging research universities" (including the University of Houston, University of Texas at El Paso, Texas Tech, and Texas State University) to compete for research money from the state's National

TABLE 2.1 Texas Constitution of 1876: Amendments Proposed and Adopted, 1879–2017

Year Proposed	Number Proposed	Number Adopted	Year Proposed	Number Proposed	Number Adopted
1879	1	1	1951	7	3
1881	2	0	1953	11	11
1883	5	5	1955	9	9
1887	6	0	1957	12	10
1889	2	2	1959	4	4
1891	5	5	1961	14	10
1893	2	2	1963	7	4
1895	2	1	1965	27	20
1897	5	1	1967	20	13
1899	1	0	1969	16	9
1901	1	1	1971	18	12
1903	3	3	1973	9	6
1905	3	2	1975	12	3
1907	9	1	1977	15	11
1909	4	4	1978	1	1
1911	5	4	1979	12	9
1913	8	0	1981	10	8
1915	7	0	1982	3	3
1917	3	3	1983	19	16
1919	13	3	1985	17	17
1921	5	1	1986	1	1
1923	2	1	1987	28	20
1925	4	4	1989	21	19
1927	8	4	1990	1	1
1929	7	5	1991	15	12
1931	9	9	1993	19	14
1933	12	4	1995	14	11
1935	13	10	1997	15	13
1937	7	6	1999	17	13
1939	4	3	2001	20	20
1941	5	1	2003	22	22
1943	3	3	2005	9	7
1945	8	7	2007	17	17
1947	9	9	2009	11	11
1949	10	2	2011	10	7
			2013	9	9

Year Proposed	Number Proposed	Number Adopted	Year Proposed	Number Proposed	Number Adopted
			2014	1	1
			2015	7	7
			2017	7	7
			Totals	**680**	**498**

Source: Research Division, Texas Legislative Council, Amendments to the Texas Constitution Since 1876, *http://www.tlc.state .tx.us/pubsconamend/constamend1876.pdf.*

── Competency Connection ──
⚙ **CRITICAL THINKING** ⚙

Examine this table. What are your initial impressions of the number of constitutional amendments proposed by the Texas legislature and approved by the voters? Should voters be deciding so many constitutional amendments, especially when you consider the nature of some of these proposals?

Research University Fund. The objective was to raise the status of these schools to what are referred to as "Tier One" research institutions.[34] As of 2018, only two of Texas's public institutions (the University of Texas at Austin and Texas A&M University) and one private institution (Rice University) were ranked as Tier One by all ranking authorities. (See Chapter 12, "Public Policy and Administration," for a discussion of higher education.) Another proposal that affected college students dealt with authorizing the Texas Higher Education Coordinating Board to expand the state's ability to create bonds for the College Access Loan program in 2009. This program provides low-interest loans to college students, irrespective of financial need. Private colleges and universities strongly supported this proposal because of the high cost of their tuition. The proposition came as lawmakers were making cuts in educational funding sources for students, specifically the Texas Grants Program and the Texas Equalization Program. (See Chapter 11, "Finance and Fiscal Policy," for a discussion of higher education funding.)

Some proposals have received strong support from the governor's office. For instance, in 2013, a proposal that received strong backing from former Governor Perry, as well as former House Speaker Joe Straus, allowed the state legislature to pull $2 billion from the "rainy day" fund (the state's savings account) for specially created accounts to make low-interest loans for water infrastructure and conservation projects.[35] Organizations, such as H2O4Texas.org and stateimpact. npr.org of Texas (a collaboration of local public radio stations), at the time, integrated social media sites to inform voters about the proposal and water issues.[36] Facebook pages, such as txwaterprop6yes.org, were created to gain support for the proposal.

In the November 2015 constitutional amendment election, seven proposals were presented to the voters and approved, ranging from lowering property taxes for homeowners to increasing spending on highways. Most notable was a proposal establishing a right to hunt, fish, and harvest wildlife, which was strongly supported by Governor Abbott. In an editorial opinion piece, he stated:

> Texans have long lived off the bounty of the land and we know how to conserve our natural resources for future generations. It's so incredibly important that we protect our connection with the land. We need to act now so no special-interest group can come in and try to strip away your rights.[37]

Another proposal repealed a requirement that statewide elected officials physically reside in Austin, with the governor as the only exception. According to the House Research Organization, supporters maintained that the requirement was instituted initially during the 1870s when travelling to Austin took several days and it was necessary for public officials to physically be in Austin. Given the reliance on technology, supporters argued that the law was outdated. Opponents, in contrast, argued that statewide officials are full-time elected officials, and their presence is essential and expected in the capitol.[38] Of the seven constitutional amendments in 2017, the one that received the most attention was whether the list of professional sports teams should be expanded to allow charitable raffles. Voters had already approved a constitutional amendment in 2015 allowing specific professional sports team charitable foundations to conduct charitable raffles at home games. This amendment, which ultimately passed, raised concerns among opponents that expanding the number of eligible professional sports teams would encourage gambling in Texas.[39] As noted above, all proposals passed, resulting in almost 500 amendments to the state's constitution.

✓ 2.2 Learning Check

1. How many different constitutions has Texas had throughout its history?
2. True or False: Texas's present-day constitution has been amended just under 100 times.

Answers at the end of this chapter.

⬛ Constitutional Amendments and Revision

LO 2.3 Analyze the amendment process, focusing on recent constitutional amendment elections as well as attempts to revise the Texas Constitution.

constitutional amendment process
Process for changing the Texas Constitution in which an amendment is proposed by a two-thirds vote of each chamber of the legislature and approved by a simple majority of voters in a general or special election.

Each of the 50 American state constitutions provides the means for changing the powers and functions of government. Without a provision for change, few constitutions would survive long. A revision may produce a totally new constitution to replace an old one. Also, courts may alter constitutions by interpreting the wording of these documents in new and different ways. Finally, constitutions may be changed by formal amendment, which is the chief method by which the Texas Constitution has been altered.

Because Texas's registered voters have an opportunity to vote on one or more proposed amendments every two years—and sometimes each year—an understanding of the steps in the **constitutional amendment process** is important.

Article XVII, Section 1, provides a relatively simple procedure for amending the Texas Constitution. The basic steps in that process follow:

- A joint resolution proposing an amendment is introduced in the House or in the Senate during a regular session or during a special session called by the governor.

- Two-thirds of the members in each chamber must adopt the resolution.

- The secretary of state prepares an explanatory statement that briefly describes the proposed amendment, and the attorney general approves this statement.

- The explanatory statement is published twice in Texas newspapers that print official state notices.

- A copy of the proposed amendment is posted in each county courthouse at least 30 days before the election.

- The voters must approve the proposed amendment by a simple majority vote in a regular or special election.

- The governor, who has no veto power in the process, proclaims the amendment.

For a constitutional amendment to be considered by Texas voters, the legislature must adopt a joint resolution by a two-thirds vote in each chamber. Hundreds of constitutional amendment resolutions are considered every legislative session.

The Texas legislature decides whether a proposed amendment will be submitted to the voters in a **constitutional amendment election**, typically in November of an odd-numbered year. In some cases, a proposed amendment will be presented to voters in a special election scheduled for an earlier date. For instance, of the 17 amendments proposed in 2007, only one was presented to voters in May; the other proposals were presented in November of that same year. In 2014, voters were presented with (and approved) one proposal in the general election in November, diverting money from the "rainy day" fund to the State Highway Fund to pay for road construction and maintenance.

Part of the problem with frequent constitutional amendment elections is the typically low voter turnout in odd-numbered years, when no statewide offices are up for election. Generally, most constitutional amendment proposals are approved by a relatively small percentage of the voting population. The complex subject matter of most amendments is one explanation why voter interest and turnout is low. Constitutional amendment elections turnout is typically less than 10 percent. Turnout in 2011 was at an all-time low (less than 5 percent) and rose just slightly to 6 percent in 2013. Voter turnout for 2015 and 2017 proved to be equally low, with 8 percent and 6 percent, respectively. The 2013 constitutional election was also the first statewide election for which the voter photo ID law was implemented. (For more on the voter ID law, see Chapter 5, "Campaigns and Elections.")

Unlike voters in other states, Texans do not have the power of **initiative** at the state level; however, this power is exercised under some local governments. (See Chapter 3, "Local Governments," for a discussion of how these powers work

constitutional amendment election
Election, typically in November of an odd-numbered year, in which voters are asked to approve one or more proposed constitutional amendments. An amendment must receive a majority of the popular vote to be approved.

initiative
A citizen-drafted measure proposed by a specific number or percentage of qualified voters that becomes law if approved by popular vote. In Texas, this process occurs only at the local level, not at the state level.

locally.) If adopted, the initiative process would bypass the legislature and allow individual Texans or interest groups to gather the signatures required to submit proposed constitutional amendments and statutes (ordinary laws) for direct popular vote. According to the *Book of States*, as of 2019 there were 18 states with some form of constitutional amendment procedure by initiative.[40] In recent years, no serious legislative efforts for amending the Texas Constitution to authorize the initiative process at the state level have emerged.

Constitutional Revision

Attempts to revise Texas's Constitution of 1876 began soon after its adoption. A legislative resolution calling for a constitutional revision convention was introduced in 1887 and was followed by others. Limited success came in 1969, when an amendment removed 56 obsolete constitutional provisions.

The only comprehensive movement to achieve wholesale **constitutional revision** began in 1971. In that year, the 62nd Legislature adopted a joint resolution proposing an amendment authorizing the appointment of a study commission and naming the members of the 63rd Legislature as delegates to a constitutional convention. Except for the state Bill of Rights, any part of the Texas Constitution of 1876 could be changed or deleted. Submitted to the voters in 1972 as a proposed constitutional amendment, the resolution was approved by a margin of more than half a million votes (1,549,982 in favor to 985,282 against).

A six-member committee (composed of the governor, the lieutenant governor, the speaker of the House, the attorney general, the chief justice of the Texas Supreme Court, and the presiding judge of the Court of Criminal Appeals) selected 37 persons to serve as members of the Constitutional Revision Commission. The commission prepared a draft constitution on the basis of opinions and information gathered at public hearings conducted throughout the state and from various authorities on constitutional revision. One-fourth the length of the present constitution, the completed draft was submitted to the legislature on November 1, 1973.

On January 8, 1974, all 181 members of both chambers of the Texas legislature met in Austin at a **constitutional revision convention**. Previous Texas constitutions had been drafted by convention delegates popularly elected for that purpose. When the finished document was put to a vote, the result was 118 for and 62 against, three votes short of the two-thirds majority of the total membership needed for final approval. (Approval required a total of at least 121 votes.) Attempts to reach compromises on controversial issues proved futile.

The Constitutional Convention of 1974 provided perhaps the best demonstration of the politics surrounding Texas's constitution making. First, the convention was hampered by a lack of positive political leadership. Then-Governor Dolph Briscoe maintained a hands-off policy throughout the convention. Former Lieutenant Governor Bill Hobby similarly failed to provide needed political leadership, and the retiring speaker of the House, Price Daniel Jr., pursued a nonintervention course. Other members of the legislature were distracted by their need to campaign for reelection.

constitutional revision
Extensive or complete rewriting of a constitution.

constitutional revision convention
A body of delegates who meet to make extensive changes in a constitution or to draft a new constitution.

The primary reason that the convention failed to agree on a proposed constitution was the phantom "nonissue" of a right-to-work provision (which means people cannot be denied employment based on whether or not they are members of a labor union or labor organization). A statutory ban on union shop labor contracts was already in effect. Adding this prohibition to the constitution would not have strengthened the legal hand of employers to any significant degree. Nevertheless, conservative, antilabor forces insisted on this provision, and a prolabor minority vigorously opposed it. The controversy aroused much emotion and at times produced loud and bitter name-calling among delegates on the floor and spectators in the galleries.[41] Stung by widespread public criticism of the 1974 convention's failure to produce a proposed constitution for public approval or rejection, the 64th Legislature resolved to submit a proposal to Texas voters. In 1975, both houses of the legislature agreed on a constitutional revision resolution comprising 10 articles in eight sections to be submitted to the Texas electorate in November of that year. The content of the articles was essentially the same as that of the final resolution of the unsuccessful 1974 convention.

The revision proposed in 1975 represented years of work by men and women well informed about constitution making. Recognized constitutional authorities evaluated the concise and orderly document as one of the best drafted state constitutions ever submitted to American voters. Although new and innovative in many respects, the proposal did not discard all of the old provisions. In addition to retaining the Bill of Rights, the proposed constitution incorporated such basic principles as limited government, separation of powers, and bicameralism (a two-house legislature).

Nevertheless, Texas voters demonstrated a strong preference for the status quo by rejecting each proposition. In the end, voters in 250 of the state's 254 counties rejected all eight proposals. A mere 23 percent of the estimated 5.9 million registered voters cast ballots, meaning that only about 10 percent of the state's voting-age population participated in this important referendum. When asked to explain the resounding defeat of the eight propositions, Bill Hobby, then lieutenant governor, responded, "There's not enough of the body left for an autopsy."

More Revision Attempts

After the revision debacle of 1975, two decades passed before the next attempt to revise the constitution. In 1995, Senator John Montford (D-Lubbock) drafted a streamlined constitution that incorporated many of the concepts contained in the failed 1975 proposal. Montford's plan also called for a voter referendum every 30 years (without requiring legislative approval) on the question of calling a constitutional revision convention. But Montford resigned from the Texas Senate to become chancellor of the Texas Tech University System in 1996. With such issues as tax changes, welfare reform, and educational finance pressing for attention, the 75th Legislature did not seriously consider constitutional revision in 1997.

In 1998, Senator Bill Ratliff (R-Mount Pleasant) and Representative Rob Junell (D-San Angelo) launched another attempt to revise the constitution.[42] With assistance from Angelo State University students and others, they prepared a complete rewrite of the much-amended 1876 document. Subsequently, they introduced a draft for consideration by the 76th Legislature in 1999. It failed to muster enough support for serious consideration in committee and never received a floor vote in either legislative chamber.[43] This proposal would have cut the then 80,000-word document to approximately 19,000 words. Significant changes included expanding the powers of the governor, repealing the current partisan election method of selecting state judges, and increasing salaries of the House speaker and the lieutenant governor.

One proposal that the legislature may consider in future sessions was created by a bipartisan team led by Roy Walthall (a retired instructor at McLennan Community College in Waco). In 2010, the team set out to reorganize the constitution. Rather than make substantive changes, which would provoke political opposition, their proposal included changes to make the document more readable and usable. The team claimed that they did not change the content or legal meaning. According to Walthall, the bulk of their work was rearranging many of the existing provisions into more logical sections. The governor would have to appoint a commission to study the reorganized constitution, and it could take several legislative sessions before the constitutional proposal would be presented to the state's voters. If approved, a new state constitution would enable Texas to join the other 49 states that have updated their constitutions since the beginning of the 20th century.

During the 21st century, the legislature has ignored or delayed the issue of constitutional revision. A series of budget crises, redistricting issues, and school funding has dominated the legislative agenda. As a result, large-scale constitutional reform remains an unaddressed problem. However, certain individuals in the legislature want to keep the subject on the agenda. In previous legislative sessions, Representative Charles Anderson (R-Waco) has introduced a resolution asking the leadership in the legislature to create a joint study committee to examine a nonsubstantive reorganization of the state constitution similar to Walthall's proposal. In 2011, the request was never brought up for a vote in the legislature. During the 2013 legislative session, Anderson introduced a similar resolution, HCR 88. It was referred to the House Committee on Government Efficiency and Reform, where it received a public hearing and Walthall provided testimony. Anderson's concurrent resolution, however, never reached the House floor as the session was coming to a close.[44]

Then, during the 84th legislative session, a similar concurrent resolution, HCR 37, was referred to the House committee on State Affairs. The committee report was sent to the Major State Calendars Committee, but the resolution never reached the House floor.[45] Since then, constitutional revision attempts have not gained momentum. Today, the Texas Constitution, despite its flaws, remains the "supreme law of the State of Texas."

Piecemeal Revision

Because extensive constitutional reform has proved futile, Texas legislators have sought to achieve some measure of government reform by other means, including legislative enactments and piecemeal constitutional amendments. In 1977, for example, the 65th Legislature enacted into law two parts of the 1975 propositions defeated at the polls. One established a procedure for reviewing state administrative agencies; the other created a planning agency within the Office of the Governor. In 1979, the 66th Legislature proposed six amendments designed to implement parts of the constitutional revision package rejected in 1975. Three were adopted by the voters and added to the Texas Constitution. They accomplished the following:

- Established a single property tax appraisal district in each county (discussed in Chapter 3, "Local Governments")
- Gave criminal appellate jurisdiction to 14 courts of appeals that formerly had exercised civil jurisdiction only
- Allowed the governor restricted removal power over appointed statewide officials[46]

Proposals for important constitutional changes have been unsuccessful in the House and the Senate. For example, during the regular session of the 77th Legislature in 2001, Representative Rob Junell (D-San Angelo) submitted a proposal that was considered and approved by the House Select Committee on Constitutional Revision. Among other items, the proposal would have changed the terms of office for state senators and House members. It also would have created a Texas Salary Commission to set salaries for elected and appointed officials of the executive, judicial, and legislative branches. This proposal, however, was never brought up for a floor vote in the legislature.[47]

To modernize the Texas Constitution, one constitutional amendment (adopted in 1999) authorized elimination of certain "duplicative, executed, obsolete, archaic and ineffective provisions of the Texas Constitution." Among resulting deletions were references to the abolished poll tax and the governor's authority "to protect the frontier from hostile incursions by Indians." In November 2007, voters also eliminated the constitutional county office of inspector of hides and animals, which had been created in the 1880s. Nevertheless, the Texas Constitution still has problems.

✓ 2.3 Learning Check

1. When was the last time voters were presented with a wholesale constitutional revision proposal from the state legislature?
2. True or False: Amending the Texas Constitution requires two-thirds of the members of each chamber of the state legislature voting for a proposed amendment and three-fourths of the voters approving it in a constitutional amendment election.

Answers at the end of this chapter.

◨ The Texas Constitution: A Summary

LO 2.4 Explain and analyze the basic sections of the Texas Constitution.

Chiefly because of its length (over 200 pages), complete printed copies of the Texas Constitution are not readily available to the public. Until publication of its Millennium Edition (2000–2001), the *Texas Almanac* was the most widely used source for the text of this document. That edition and subsequent editions, however, now refer persons seeking the text of the Texas Constitution to the Internet.

Although *Practicing Texas Politics* does not include the entire text of the Texas Constitution, each chapter looks to Texas's basic law for its content. The rest of this chapter presents a brief synopsis of the document's 17 articles.[48]

The Bill of Rights

We begin by examining Article I, the Texas Constitution's Bill of Rights. The **Texas Bill of Rights** is similar to the one found in the U.S. Constitution. Composed of 30 sections, it guarantees protections for people and their property against arbitrary actions by state and local governments. Included among these rights are freedom of speech, press, religion, assembly, and petition; the rights of accused and convicted criminals and victims of crime; and equal rights for women. Article I also includes philosophical observations that have no direct force of law.

Constitutional Rights Against Arbitrary Governmental Actions

Eleven of Article I's sections provide protections for people and property against arbitrary governmental actions. Guarantees, such as freedom of speech, press, religion, assembly, and petition, are included. The right to keep and bear arms, prohibitions against the taking of property by government action without just compensation, and protection of contracts are also incorporated. Most of these rights found in the Texas Constitution are also protected under the U.S. Constitution. Thus, with their basic rights guaranteed in both national and state constitutions, Texans, like people in other states, have a double safeguard against arbitrary governmental actions.

One of these constitutional rights, protected for Texans by both state and federal constitutions, centers on freedom of religion. A constitutional right to freedom of religion is essentially the same in both the Texas Constitution and the U.S. Constitution, yet when one examines the actual wording, it is different. The Texas Bill of Rights, Section 6, states, "All men have a natural and indefeasible right to worship Almighty God according to the dictates of their own conscience. No man shall be compelled to attend, erect or support any place of worship, or to maintain any ministry against his consent … and no preference shall ever be given to any religious society or mode of worship." Under the U.S. Constitution, the First Amendment (as applied to the states under the Fourteenth Amendment) provides that states "shall make no law respecting an establishment of religion, or prohibiting the free exercise thereof."

Cases on religious freedom stemming from the U.S. Constitution have gone from Texas all the way to the U.S. Supreme Court. Included among these are two cases that yielded different results: one centered on student-led prayer before a school football game; the other involved a Ten Commandments monument placed on the Texas state Capitol grounds. The U.S. Supreme Court, interpreting the establishment clause of the U.S. Constitution to require a separation of church and state, struck down school prayer before public school football games, contending that the message conveyed amounted to an endorsement of religion on school grounds.[49] In contrast, the U.S. Supreme Court upheld the Ten Commandments display, concluding that it is a historical monument among other historical monuments on state grounds.[50]

Rights of Criminals and Victims

Thirteen sections of the Texas Constitution's Bill of Rights relate to the rights of persons accused of crimes and to the rights of individuals who have been convicted of crimes. For example, one section

Texas Bill of Rights
Article I of the Texas Constitution guarantees protections for people and their property against arbitrary actions by state and local governments. Protected rights include freedom of speech, press, religion, assembly, and petition.

concerns the right to release on bail, another prohibits unreasonable searches and seizures, and a third declares that "the right to trial by jury shall remain inviolate." These provisions relate closely to similar language in the national Bill of Rights.

The Texas Constitution is even more protective of certain rights than is the U.S. Constitution. An additional set of rights added by constitutional amendment in 1989 protects crime victims. This provision was developed in the early 1980s in response to findings of a presidential task force that explored the inequality of rights for crime victims. In general, the state constitution now gives victims rights to restitution, information about the accused (conviction, sentence, release, etc.), protection from the accused throughout the criminal justice process, and respect for the victim's privacy.

Equal Rights for Women Another example of the Texas Constitution's providing more protection than the U.S. Constitution relates to equal rights for women. Attempts nationwide to add a proposed Equal Rights Amendment (ERA) to the U.S. Constitution failed between 1972 and 1982 (even though the amendment was approved by the Texas legislature). Nevertheless, the **Texas Equal Legal Rights Amendment (ELRA)** was added to Article I, Section 3, of the Texas Constitution in 1972. It states: "Equality under the law shall not be denied or abridged because of sex, race, color, creed, or national origin." This constitutional amendment was proposed and adopted after several unsuccessful attempts dating back to the 1950s.[51] Interestingly, despite the ELRA, the Texas Constitution still has a provision that states, "All free men have equal rights."

Additional Protections Additional protections in the Texas Constitution include prohibitions against imprisonment for debt, outlawry (putting a convicted person outside the protection of the law), and the punishment of transportation (punishing a convicted citizen by banishment from the state). Monopolies are prohibited by a provision of the Texas Bill of Rights but not by the U.S. Constitution, although federal statutory law does prohibit monopolies. Some of these protections have been added through constitutional amendments. For instance, in 1993, taxpayers were provided constitutional protection by prohibiting the establishment of a state income tax without voter approval. In 2009, property homeowners were provided additional protection from the government's taking private property for the primary purpose of economic development. As mentioned earlier, since 2015, Texans have had the constitutional protection to hunt, fish, and harvest wildlife.

Interpretation of the Texas Constitution by the Texas Supreme Court has also provided additional rights, such as the court's interpretation of Article VII, Section 1 (titled Education), which requires the state legislature to provide support and maintenance for "an efficient system of free public schools." In 1989, the high court first held that the state legislature had a constitutional requirement to create a more equitable public school finance system. The Texas Supreme Court revisited school finance in 2005 and declared the school finance system unconstitutional. Rather than focusing on the system's continued and persistent inequities, however, the court focused on whether the state-imposed property tax cap amounted to a statewide property tax, which the Texas Constitution forbids.

Texas Equal Legal Rights Amendment (ELRA) Added to Article I, Section 3, of the Texas Constitution, it guarantees that "equality under the law shall not be denied or abridged because of sex, race, color, creed, or national origin."

(Property taxes can be collected only at the local level.) Because more than 80 percent of all school districts had reached this cap and state funding had continued to decline, the court held that school boards had effectively lost control of tax rates. Equally important, the Court rejected the claim that more money in the system was necessary to comply with the Texas Constitution's requirement to provide for the "general diffusion of knowledge."[52] Challenges to school funding in the courts continued. In 2015, district court judge John Dietz considered more evidence in the case after the 84th Legislature restored $3.7 billion (out of the $5.4 billion) of the cuts made to school funding in 2011. He ruled that the school finance system was still unconstitutional. Then, the Texas Supreme Court heard oral arguments in an appeal in September 2015. The Texas Supreme Court overturned the lower court's decision in May 2016 when it held that the state's funding system met "minimum constitutional standards" despite being "a Band-Aid on top of Band-Aid" reform effort.[53] (For more on school finance, see Chapter 11, "Finance and Fiscal Policy.")

Philosophical Observations Three sections of the Texas Bill of Rights contain philosophical observations that have no direct force of law. Still stinging from what they saw as the "bondage" years of Reconstruction, the angry delegates to the constitutional convention of 1875 began their work by inserting this statement: "Texas is a free and independent state, subject only to the Constitution of the United States." They also asserted that all political power resides with the people and is legitimately exercised only on their behalf and that the people may at any time "alter, reform, or abolish their government." To guard against the possibility that any of the rights guaranteed in the other 28 sections would be eliminated or altered by the government, Section 29 proclaims that "everything in this 'Bill of Rights' is excepted out of the general powers of government, and shall forever remain inviolate."

The Powers of Government and Separation of Powers

Holding fast to the principle of limited government and a balance of power, the framers of the Constitution of 1876 firmly embedded in the state's fundamental law the familiar doctrine of **separation of powers**. In Article II, they assigned the lawmaking, law-enforcing, and law-adjudicating powers of government to three separate branches, identified as the legislative, executive, and judicial departments, respectively.

Article III is titled "Legislative Department." Legislative powers are vested in a bicameral legislature, composed of the House of Representatives with 150 members and the Senate with 31 members. A patchwork of more than 60 sections, this article provides vivid testimony of the many decades of amendments directly affecting the legislative branch. For example, in 1936, an amendment added a section granting the Texas legislature the authority to levy taxes to fund a retirement system for public school, college, and university teachers. Today, public school teachers and personnel employed by public universities and community colleges benefit from pension programs provided by the state.

separation of powers
The assignment of lawmaking, law-enforcing, and law-interpreting functions to separate branches of government.

Article IV, "Executive Department," states unequivocally that the governor "shall be the Chief Executive Officer of the State" but then shares executive power with four other popularly elected officers independent of the governor: the lieutenant governor, the attorney general, the comptroller of public accounts, and the commissioner of the General Land Office. (A state treasurer was originally included in this list, but a constitutional amendment abolished the office.) With this and other provisions for division of executive power, some observers consider the Texas governor no more than first among equals in the executive branch of state government.

Through Article V, "Judicial Department," Texas joins Oklahoma as one of only two states in the country with a bifurcated court system that includes two courts of final appeal: one for civil cases (the Supreme Court of Texas) and one for criminal cases (the Court of Criminal Appeals). Below these two supreme appellate courts are the courts authorized by the Texas Constitution: intermediate appellate courts (14 courts of appeal) and more than 1,500 courts of original jurisdiction (trial courts), including district courts, county courts, and justice of the peace courts. The legislature is allowed to create any other courts it deems necessary and has therefore created county courts-at-law and probate courts by statute.

Suffrage

Article VI, titled "**Suffrage**" (the right to vote), is one of the shortest articles in the Texas Constitution. Before 1870, states had the definitive power to conduct elections. Since that time, amendments to the U.S. Constitution, acts of Congress such as the Voting Rights Act of 1965, and U.S. Supreme Court rulings have vastly diminished this power. In addition, amendments to the Voting Rights Act of 1975 require Texas to provide bilingual ballots. For more than 35 years, Texas had to receive federal preclearance for any changes to voting laws or district boundary lines for elected officials. In 2013, however, mandatory preclearance was eliminated when the U.S. Supreme Court found the requirement unconstitutional in a separate case originating in Alabama, *Shelby County v. Holder* (2013).[54] During this time, a lawsuit was filed against the state under Section 2 of the Voting Rights Act challenging one of the strictest ever photo voter ID laws approved by the 82nd Legislature (2011) from going into effect, claiming that the law discriminated against minority voters. Rather than wait for a court decision, then-Attorney General Gregg Abbott interpreted the *Shelby* decision to allow the immediate implementation of the voter ID photo requirement beginning with the constitutional amendment election in 2013. Litigation led the Texas Legislature to ultimately revise the photo ID law to allow voters without one of the acceptable forms of ID to sign an affidavit confirming their identity and provide acceptable documents verifying their identity, such as utility bills. In April 2018, a panel on the 5th Circuit Court of Appeals upheld the revised law as constitutionally acceptable, despite concerns among many that it disproportionately discriminates against racial and ethnic minorities.[55]

Within the scope of current federal parameters, the Texas Constitution establishes qualifications for voters, provides for citizen voter registration, and governs the conduct of elections. In response to federal-level changes, this article has been

Suffrage
The right to vote.

IMAGE 2.4 Governor Greg Abbott speaks at a campaign rally with U.S. President Trump for Senator Ted Cruz in Houston, October 2018.

Bloomberg/Getty Images

Competency Connection
✿ **CRITICAL THINKING** ✿

How important do you think it is for our Texas governor to participate in a campaign rally with the President in support of one of our U.S. Senator's re-election campaign? What are the implications for federal-state relations?

amended to abolish the payment of a poll tax or any form of property qualification for voting in the state's elections and to change the minimum voting age from 21 to 18.

Local Governments

The most disorganized part of the Texas Constitution concerns units of **local government**: counties, municipalities (cities), school districts, and other special districts. Although Article IX is titled "Counties," provisions concerning county government are scattered through four other articles. Moreover, the basic structure of county government is defined not in Article IX on counties but in Article V on the judiciary. Article XI on municipalities is equally disorganized and inadequate. Only four of the sections of this article relate exclusively to municipal government. Other sections concern county government, taxation, public indebtedness, and forced sale of public property.

Along with counties and municipalities, the original text of the Constitution of 1876 referred to school districts but not to other types of special districts.

local government
Counties, municipalities, school districts, and other special districts that provide a range of services, including rural roads, city streets, public education, and protection of persons and property.

Authorization for special districts, however, crept into the Texas Constitution with a 1904 amendment that authorized the borrowing of money for water development and road construction by a county "or any defined district." Since then, special districts have been created to provide myriad services, such as drainage, conservation, urban renewal, public housing, hospitals, and airports.

Other Articles

The nine remaining articles also reflect a strong devotion to constitutional minutiae: Education, Taxation and Revenue, Railroads, Private Corporations, Spanish and Mexican Land Titles, Public Lands and Land Office, Impeachment, General Provisions, and Mode of Amendment. The shortest is Article XIII, "Spanish and Mexican Land Titles." The entire text was deleted by amendment in 1969 because its provisions were deemed obsolete. The longest article is Article XVI, "General Provisions." Among other provisions, it prohibits the bribing of public officials and authorizes the legislature to regulate the manufacture and sale of intoxicants.

> ✓ **2.4 Learning Check**
>
> 1. True or False: The Texas Constitution contains constitutional rights not found in the U.S. Constitution.
> 2. Article II of the Texas Constitution assigns powers to which branches of government?
>
> *Answers at the end of this chapter.*

CONCLUSION

As a member of the United States, Texas is provided with certain constitutional guarantees as well as limitations on its powers. The U.S. Constitution plays a significant role in defining federal-state relations. This balance of power between the federal government and the state government is constantly evolving. The Texas government derives most of its powers from the Texas Constitution. Understanding Texas's constitutional history explains to a large degree the characteristics of its present-day constitution. Amending the Texas Constitution occurs frequently through constitutional amendment elections, but recent attempts to revise the constitution have not been successful. As a result, the structure of the Constitution of 1876 remains essentially unchanged.

CHAPTER SUMMARY

LO 2.1 Analyze federalism and the powers of the state in a constitutional context.
The American federal system features a division of powers between a national government and 50 state governments. As a member of the Union, Texas has certain constitutional guarantees and limitations. Several constitutional provisions in the U.S. Constitution affect interstate relations and state immunity. Controversy may arise when uniformity in certain areas of policy among the states does not exist. Powers not delegated (nor implied, as interpreted by federal courts) to the federal government are reserved to the states or to the people under the Tenth Amendment. These state powers have largely formed around several broad categories, and identifying a clear boundary between state and national powers (or responsibilities) is often complicated. Striking a balance of power between the national and state governments is constantly shifting and evolving over time.

LO 2.2 Explain the origins and development of the state constitution. Today's Texas Constitution is the country's second longest and, by 2018, had 498 amendments. Most amendments are statutory in nature, so the document resembles a code of laws. Texas has had seven constitutions, each reflecting the political situation that existed when the specific document was drafted. The Constitution of 1876 has endured, despite its excessive length, confusion, and statutory detail.

LO 2.3 Analyze the amendment process, focusing on recent constitutional amendment elections, as well as attempts to revise the Texas Constitution. Changing the Texas Constitution requires an amendment proposed by a two-thirds majority vote of the members in each legislative chamber and approved by a simple majority of the state's voters in a general or special election. Despite efforts to conduct a wholesale revision of the Texas Constitution, only piecemeal revisions have occurred.

LO 2.4 Explain and analyze the basic sections of the Texas Constitution. The Texas Constitution is the fundamental law that sets forth the powers and limitations of the state's government. It is composed of 17 articles. Included are the Bill of Rights, an article on suffrage, articles on the three branches of state government, and provisions concerning the powers of state and local governments.

KEY TERMS

block grant, p. 53

constitutional amendment
    election, p. 67

constitutional amendment
    process, p. 66

constitutional guarantees, p. 44

constitutional revision
    convention, p. 68

constitutional revision, p. 68

delegated powers, p. 44

federal grants-in-aid, p. 53

full faith and credit clause, p. 48

implied powers, p. 44

initiative, p. 67

local government, p. 76

national supremacy clause, p. 44

privileges and immunities, p. 48

reserved powers, p. 49

separation of powers, p. 74

suffrage, p. 75

Tenth Amendment, p. 44

Texas Bill of Rights, p. 72

Texas Constitution of 1876, p. 62

Texas Equal Legal Rights
    Amendment (ELRA), p. 73

Texas Grange, p. 61

LEARNING CHECK ANSWERS

2.1 **1.** False. The Tenth Amendment does not specifically identify the powers of the states.

2. Devolution gives the states more freedom to make decisions, especially with funding.

2.2 **1.** Texas has had seven constitutions throughout its history.

2. False. Our present-day Texas Constitution has been amended almost 500 times.

1. November 1975 was the last time that voters were presented with a whole-sale constitutional revision proposal from the state legislature; more recent attempts have failed.

2. False. Amending the Texas Constitution requires two-thirds of the members of each chamber of the state legislature to vote for a proposed amendment but only a simple majority of the voters to approve it in a constitutional amendment election.

 1. True. The Texas Constitution does contain additional constitutional rights, such as the Equal Legal Rights Amendment, not found in the U.S. Constitution.

2. The Texas Constitution assigns power to the legislative, executive, and judicial branches.

3 Local Governments

Learning Objectives

3.1 Explain the relationships that exist between a local government and all other governments, including local, state, and national governments.

3.2 Describe the forms of municipal government organization.

3.3 Identify the rules and social issues that shape local government outcomes.

3.4 Analyze the structure and responsibilities of counties.

3.5 Explain the functions of special districts and their importance to the greater community.

3.6 Discuss the ways that local governments deal with metropolitan-wide and regional issues.

IMAGE 3.1 City councils reach out to citizens in a variety of ways, including social media and, often, detailed websites providing a wealth of information.

Source: City of San Antonio

Competency Connection
☼ CRITICAL THINKING ☼

What information from your city would be of value to you? Why?

When most Texans think about government, they think about the national or state government, but not about the many local governments. Yet of all three levels of government, local government has the greatest impact on citizens' daily lives. Most people drive every day on city streets or county roads, drink water provided by the city or a special district, attend schools run by the local school district, play in a city or county park, eat in restaurants inspected by city health officials, and live in houses or apartments that required city permits and inspections to build. Many citizens' contacts with local governments are positive. Potholes are filled, trash is picked up regularly, baseball fields are groomed for games—but other experiences are less positive. Streets and freeways are increasingly congested, many schools are overcrowded, and the property taxes to support them seem high.

Commonly, the sharpest divisions in Texas local government are between central cities, suburbs, and small town/rural Texas. In urban areas, local governments face a growing list of demands for more and better traditional services (such as streets and safety) and newer services (such as skate parks, public housing, and pre-kindergarten). Many needs, such as transportation and hospital access, cross government boundaries. Central cities and their suburbs often fight over what kinds of services are needed and who will pay for them. Suburbanites, for example, tend to prefer more freeways, while central city residents often want more public transportation. Many rural Texans prefer that government provide only the most minimal services, regulate little, and collect few taxes. But even they want roads maintained, a good education for their kids, and safety for their families and businesses.

A common problem facing almost all local governments in both rural and urban Texas is that there is not enough money to satisfy all the demands citizens make. Tax revenue doesn't grow as fast as demands, and the state and national governments have been relatively stingy. The result is that local governments have had to limit services and go heavily into debt. In 2018, Texas school districts owed $84 billion for which they will have to pay $49 billion in interest for a total of $133 billion. Cities were second in debt, with a total of $112 billion. The state government was third at $93 billion, with counties owing $20 billion in principal and interest.

To confront problems successfully and make local governments more responsive to our needs and wishes, we have to understand how these governments are organized and work. Local government comes in many forms. Texas has municipalities (more than 1,200 city and town governments), counties (254), and special districts (more than 3,200). The special district that most students know best is the school district, but there are also special districts for water, hospitals, conservation, housing, and a multitude of other services. Each local government covers a certain geographic area and has legal authority to carry out one or more government functions. Most collect revenue such as taxes or fees, spend money while providing services, and are controlled by officials ultimately responsible to voters. These local, or **grassroots**, governments affect our lives directly.

Follow *Practicing Texas Politics* on Twitter **@PracTexPol**

grassroots
Local (as in grassroots government or grassroots politics).

⬕ Local Politics in Context

LO 3.1 Explain the relationships that exist between a local government
and all other governments, including local, state, and national
governments.

Local government and politics are greatly affected by the context within which
they operate—the federal system. In Texas and elsewhere, local governments
were created by the state, and what they do is often shaped by the actions of other
governments—national, state, and local.

Local Governments and Federalism

In the 19th century, two opposing views emerged concerning the powers of local
governments. **Dillon's Rule**, named after federal judge John F. Dillon and still
followed in most states (including Texas), dictates that local governments have
only those powers granted by the state government, those powers implied in the
state grant, and those powers indispensable to their functioning.[1] The opposing
Cooley Doctrine, named after Michigan judge Thomas M. Cooley and followed
in 10 states, says "Local Government is a matter of absolute right; and the state
may not take it away."[2]

   Texas's local governments, like those of other states, are at the bottom rung of
the governmental ladder, which makes them politically and legally weaker than
the state and federal governments. In addition, Texas is among those states that
more strictly follow Dillon's Rule.[3] Cities, counties, and special district governments are creatures of the State of Texas. They are created through state laws
and the Texas Constitution, and they make decisions permitted or required by
the state. Local governments may receive part of their money from the state or
national government, and they must obey the laws and constitutions of both.
States often complain about unfunded mandates (requirements placed on states
by the federal government without federal money to pay the costs). Local governments face mandates from both the national and state governments. Some
of these mandates are funded by the higher levels of government, but some are
not. Examples of mandates at the local level are as diverse as improving the quality of the air, meeting state jail standards, providing access for the disabled, and
prohibiting cities from banning plastic grocery bags.

   Local and state government rely on federal assistance and grants for different
needs. In times of natural disaster, states often turn to the national government for
assistance. From 1953 to 2014, Texas led the nation in the number of Fire Management Assistance Grant Declarations (235) and Major Disaster Declarations (88)
and ranked fourth in the number of Emergency Declarations (13) issued by the
federal government.[4] Not all the state's requests have been approved, however. In
the years 2011–2013, Texas requested and was denied more than $583 million
in federal grants to fund projects to assist with natural disaster recovery efforts.
Although many requests for money to cover the cost of replacing damaged

Dillon's Rule
A legal principle, still
followed in the majority
of states including Texas,
that local governments
have only those powers
granted by their state
government.

infrastructure and providing emergency responders were approved, some appeals for assistance were denied: for example, from Bastrop County for $139 million after the 2011 fire that destroyed 3,400 acres of timber and 1,600 homes; from Austin for $84 million for affordable housing lost in a 2013 flood; and from the city of West for $9 million after the 2013 fertilizer plant explosion. In 2018, a year after Hurricane Harvey, Houston had received $13.8 billion in federal assistance, but the small amounts received by individuals and the slowness of the payouts caused widespread complaints.

At the local level, federalism is more than just dealing with the state and national governments. Local governments have to deal with each other as well. Texas has almost 5,000 local governments. Bexar County (home of San Antonio) has 64 local governments, Dallas County has 60, and Travis County (Austin) has 124. The territories of local governments often overlap. Your home, for example, may be within a county, a municipality, a school district, a community college district, and a hospital district—all of which collect taxes, provide services, and hold elections.

Local governments generally treat each other as friends but occasionally act as adversaries. For example, the city of Houston and Harris County worked together, as well as with state and national officials, to respond to Hurricanes Katrina, Rita, Ike, and Harvey. On the other hand, in 2014, the small border city La Villa shut off the local school district's water in a dispute over rates, and in 2018, the Texas Supreme Court decided a dispute between Nueces and San Patricio Counties over which could tax piers in Corpus Christi Bay.[5] Clearly, federalism and the resulting relationships between and among governments, (**intergovernmental relations**), are important to how local governments work. (For more on federalism, see Chapter 2, "Federalism and the Texas Constitution.")

Grassroots Challenges

When studying local governments, it is important to keep in mind the challenges these governments face daily. About 85 percent of all Texans reside in cities and towns, and residents have concerns they want addressed: fear of crime; decaying infrastructures, such as streets, roads, and bridges; controversies over public schools; and threats of terrorism. Residents' concerns can be addressed in part through communication between government and citizens.

One way to help anxious citizens communicate with their government is to provide easy access to information. To enhance government-citizen communication a law passed by the 84th Legislature (2015) requires school districts with 10,000 students or more, municipalities with a population of 50,000 or more, and counties with a population of 125,000 residents or more to video record their public meetings and post these events online. Coauthored by Representative Terry Canales (D-Edinburg), this legislation pushes for government officials to be more responsive to their constituents and provide transparency. Representative Canales stated that most people are unable to attend their local school board, city council,

intergovernmental relations
Relationships between and among different governments that are on the same or different levels.

or commissioners court meetings; therefore, they are unaware of what transpires in the meetings until much later.[6] The law requires that videos be made available online no more than seven days after the meeting and remain online for at least two years. Videos may be uploaded to any Internet site, including social networking sites. For example, the city of Victoria posts its city council meetings on YouTube. McAllen Independent School District, the city of McAllen, and Hidalgo County are a few of the local governments that made recordings of their meetings available online prior to enactment of Representative Canales's bill. Whether availability of information results in a more engaged citizenry has not yet been determined.

Texas cities are also becoming increasingly diverse, with many African American and Latino Texans seeking access to public services and local power structures long dominated by Anglos. Making sure that all communities receive equal access to public services is a key challenge for grassroots-level policymakers, community activists, and political scientists. Opportunities to participate in local politics begin with registering and then voting in local elections. (See Chapter 5, "Campaigns and Elections," for voter qualifications and registration requirements under Texas law.) Some citizens will decide to run for city council, county commissioners court, school board, or another local policymaking body. Additional opportunities to be politically active include homeowners' associations, neighborhood associations, community or issue-oriented organizations, voter registration drives, and election campaigns of candidates seeking local offices. By gaining influence in city halls, county courthouses, and special district offices, individuals and groups may address grassroots problems through the democratic process.

Grassroots government faces the challenge of widespread voter apathy. Frequently, fewer than 10 percent of a community's qualified voters participate in a local election. The good news is that voter interest increases when people understand that they can solve grassroots problems in Texas through political participation.

✓ 3.1 Learning Check

1. Do local governments have more flexibility to make their own decisions under Dillon's Rule or the Cooley Doctrine? Which one does Texas follow?

2. Are intergovernmental relations marked by conflict, cooperation, or both?

Answers at the end of this chapter.

✪ Municipal Governments

LO 3.2 Describe the forms of municipal government organization.

Perhaps no level of government influences the daily lives of citizens more than **municipal (city) government**. Whether taxing residents, arresting criminals, collecting garbage, providing public libraries, or repairing streets, municipalities determine how millions of Texans live. Knowing how and why public policies are made at city hall requires an understanding of the organizational and legal framework within which municipalities function.

Legal Status of Municipalities

City government powers are outlined and restricted by municipal charters, state and national constitutions, and statutes (laws). Texas has two legal classifications of cities: **general-law cities** and **home-rule cities**. A community with a

municipal (city) government
A local government for an incorporated community established by law as a city.

general-law city
A municipality with a charter prescribed by the legislature.

home-rule city
A municipality with a locally drafted charter.

population of 201 or more may become a general-law city by adopting a charter prescribed by a general law enacted by the Texas legislature.[7] A city of more than 5,000 people may be incorporated as a home-rule city, with a locally drafted charter adopted, amended, or repealed by majority vote in a citywide election. Once chartered, a general-law city does not automatically become a home-rule city just because its population increases to greater than 5,000. Citizens must vote to become a home-rule city, but that status does not change even if the municipality's population decreases to 5,000 or fewer.

Texas has almost 900 general-law cities, most of which are fairly small in population. Although some of the about 350 home-rule cities are small, most larger cities tend to have home-rule charters. The principal advantage of home-rule cities is greater flexibility in determining their organizational structure and how they operate. Citizens draft, adopt, and revise their city's charter through citywide elections. The charter establishes the powers of municipal officers; sets salaries and terms of offices for council members and mayors; and spells out procedures for passing, repealing, or amending **ordinances** (city laws).

The ordinance-making power of Texas municipalities is not unlimited. Under Dillon's Rule, the state creates and can limit local government authority. For example, in November 2014, Denton, located north of Dallas–Fort Worth, passed an ordinance banning hydraulic fracturing (fracking) within city limits. Seeking to prevent environmental problems, a majority of Denton voters made their city the first in Texas to ban fracking. However, in May 2015, the Texas legislature responded to oil and gas industry lobbying by passing a law prohibiting cities from regulating underground oil and gas operations, which includes fracking.[8] This began a period of increased limitations on local governments by state leaders who had long championed local government decision-making over, particularly, federal mandates. (For a discussion of how much authority the state legislature should have over city ordinances, see this chapter's Point/Counterpoint feature.)

Home-rule cities may exercise three powers not held by the state government or general-law cities: recall, initiative, and referendum. **Recall** provides a process for removing elected officials through a popular vote. In May 2016, a recall election was held in Crystal City, a small community in South Texas located about 50 miles north of the Mexican border, after federal agents arrested the mayor, two city council members, and the city manager on bribery and kickback charges. Subsequent indictments against these officials listed over $18,000 in bribes. Another council member was arrested on human smuggling charges. After the city clerk rejected a citizen-initiated recall petition saying there were not enough signatures, five Crystal City residents filed a lawsuit asking to force approval of the petition. In February 2016, State District Judge Amado Abascal ordered the clerk to verify the signatures, and if valid, move forward with the election. Under court order, the mayor (who had previously resigned) and two of the indicted council members attended a city council meeting, along with the sole unindicted council member, to order a recall election for May 2016.[9] In that election, voters removed the mayor, the mayor pro-tempore, and a councilman. In recent years, recall elections in Texas have become more common, even though they can cost a community many thousands of dollars.[10]

ordinance
A local law enacted by a city council or approved by popular vote in a referendum or initiative election.

recall
A process for removing elected officials through a popular vote. In Texas, this power is available only for home-rule cities.

An **initiative** is a citizen-drafted measure proposed by a specified number or percentage of qualified voters. If approved by popular vote, an initiative becomes law without city council approval, whereas a **referendum** approves or repeals an existing ordinance. Ballot referenda and initiatives require voter approval and, depending on city charter provisions, may be binding or nonbinding on municipal governments.

Initiatives and referenda can be contentious. For example, in 2014, the Houston City Council enacted the Houston Equal Rights Ordinance (HERO) banning discrimination in a number of areas, including sexual orientation and gender identity. Controversy arose because the ordinance would allow transgender people to use facilities such as restrooms consistent with their gender identity rather than their biological sex. It quickly became known as the "bathroom bill." Opponents raised a petition calling for a vote to repeal the ordinance. The petition was rejected by the city because of a number of legal issues, but in July 2015, the Texas Supreme Court granted a writ of mandamus requiring the city to repeal the ordinance or place it on the ballot. In November, voters rejected the ordinance by a vote of of 61 percent to 39 percent. A proposed statewide bathroom bill requiring use of facilities consistent with the sex listed on one's birth certificate failed in the 2017 legislature. In 2019, the state's top three leaders rejected trying again.[11]

Across the nation, conflict has arisen over how to regulate ridesharing services such as Uber and Lyft. In 2016, a political action committee supported by the two companies obtained 65,000 signatures calling for a referendum to prevent an Austin ordinance from going into effect. The ordinance required fingerprint-based background checks for ridesharing drivers, a process similar to that used for taxi drivers. Proponents of fingerprinting argued that it was necessary for public safety. Opponents maintained that it was an unnecessary and costly regulatory barrier.[12] Uber and Lyft spent nearly $9 million on the campaign, the most expensive referendum campaign in the city's history. In May 2016, Austin voters defeated Proposition 1, allowing the city council ordinance to take effect. Days after the election, Lyft and Uber pulled out of Austin, and local companies quickly filled the gap. Uber and Lyft immediately lobbied the legislature to pass statewide regulations preempting local regulations. Many legislators saw the issue in terms of liberal Austin vs. free enterprise. The legislature passed a bill giving the state the power to regulate ridesharing and requiring a background check without fingerprints. Both companies were back in Austin, a year after leaving.

Red-light cameras have produced controversy, lawsuits, and occasional repeal votes since they came to Texas in 2003. They were used by some cities to reduce the number of accidents (and, according to critics, produce more revenue). In 2015, a suit to block a vote was rejected by the courts, and Arlington voters repealed use of the cameras. In 2019, the legislature effectively banned the cameras.

initiative

A citizen-drafted measure proposed by a specific number or percentage of qualified voters, which becomes law if approved by popular vote. In Texas, this process occurs only in home-rule cities.

referendum

A process by which issues are referred to the voters to accept or reject. Voters may also petition for a vote to repeal an existing ordinance. In Texas, this process occurs at the local level in home-rule cities. At the state level, state constitutional amendments and bonds secured by taxes must be approved by the voters.

Forms of Municipal Government

The four principal forms of municipal government used in the United States and Texas—strong mayor-council, weak mayor-council, council-manager, and commission—have many variations. The council-manager form prevails in almost

90 percent of Texas's home-rule cities, and variations of the two mayor-council systems operate in many general-law cities. Citizens often ask, "How do you explain the structure of municipal government in my town? None of the four models accurately depicts our government." The answer lies in home-rule flexibility. Various combinations of the forms discussed in the following sections are permissible under a home-rule charter, depending on community preference, as long as they do not conflict with state law. Informal practice also may make defining a city's form difficult. For example, the council-manager form may work like a strong mayor-council form if the mayor has a strong personality and the city manager is timid.

Strong Mayor-Council Among larger American cities, the **strong mayor-council form** continues as the predominant governmental structure. Among the nation's 10 largest cities, Dallas, San Antonio, Phoenix (Arizona), and San Jose (California), operate with a structure (council-manager) other than some variation of the strong mayor-council system. In New York City, Los Angeles, Chicago, and Philadelphia, the mayor is the chief administrator and the political head of the city. Of Texas's 25 largest cities, however, only Houston and Pasadena still have the strong mayor-council form of government. Many people see the strong mayor-council system as the best form for large cities because it allows strong leadership and is more likely than the council-manager form to be responsive to the full range of the community. In the early 20th century, however, the strong mayor-council form began to fall out of favor in many places, including Texas, because of its association with the corrupt political party machines that once dominated some cities. Now most of Texas's home-rule cities have chosen the council-manager form.

In Texas, cities operating with the strong mayor-council form have the following characteristics:

- A council traditionally elected from single-member districts, although many now have a mix of at-large and single-member district elections

- A mayor elected at large (by the whole city), with the power to appoint and remove department heads

- Budgetary power (for example, preparation and execution of a plan for raising and spending city money) exercised by the mayor, subject to council approval before the budget may be implemented

- A mayor with the power to veto council actions

Houston's variation of the strong mayor-council form features a powerful mayor aided by a strong appointed chief of staff and an elected controller with budgetary powers (Figure 3.1). Most Houston mayors have delegated administrative details to the chief of staff, leaving the mayor free to focus on the larger picture. Duties of the chief of staff, however, vary widely depending on the mayor currently in office.

Weak Mayor-Council As the term **weak mayor-council form** implies, this model of local government gives the mayor limited administrative powers. The

strong mayor-council form
A type of municipal government with a separately elected legislative body (council) and an executive head (mayor) elected in a citywide election with veto, appointment, and removal powers.

weak mayor-council form
A type of municipal government with a separately elected mayor and council, but the mayor shares appointive and removal powers with the council, which can override the mayor's veto.

FIGURE 3.1 Strong Mayor-Council Form of Municipal Government: City of Houston

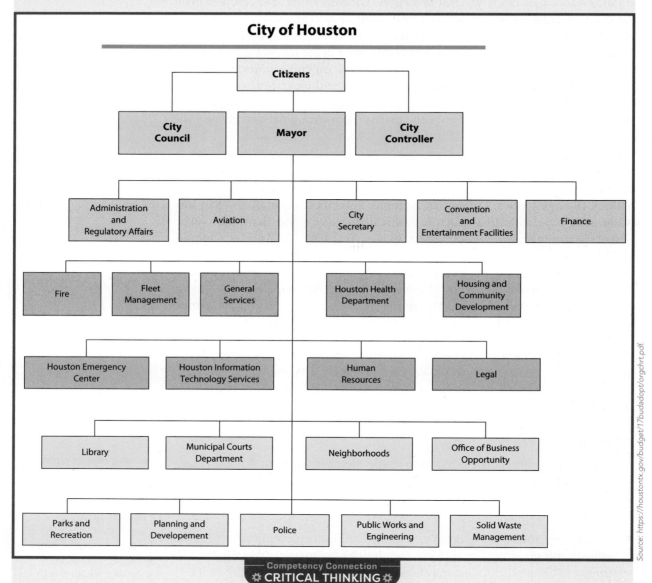

Source: https://houstontx.gov/budget/17budadopt/orgchrt.pdf.

— Competency Connection —
☼ **CRITICAL THINKING** ☼

What are the differences between strong mayor-council and weak mayor-council forms of government?

mayor's position is weak because the office shares appointive and removal powers over municipal government personnel with the city council. Instead of being a chief executive, the mayor is merely one of several elected officials responsible to the electorate. In popular elections, voters choose members of the city council, some department heads, and other municipal officials. The city council has the power to override the mayor's veto.

The current trend is away from the weak mayor-council form. None of the largest cities in Texas has this form, though some small general-law and home-rule cities in Texas and other parts of the country use it. For example, Conroe, a city with a population of more than 85,000 in Montgomery County (north of Houston), describes itself on its website as having a mayor-council form of government. The mayor's powers are limited, and the city administrator manages city departments on a day-to-day basis. The mayor, however, maintains enough status to serve as a political leader.

Council-Manager When the cities of Amarillo and Terrell adopted the **council-manager form** in 1913, a new era in Texas municipal administration began. Today, most of Texas's almost 350 home-rule cities follow the council-manager form (sometimes termed the commission-manager form).

Figure 3.2 illustrates how this form is used in San Antonio. The council-manager form has the following characteristics:

- A mayor, elected at large, who is the presiding member of the council but who generally has few formal administrative powers
- City council or commission members elected at large or in single-member districts to make general policy for the city
- A city manager who is appointed by the council (and can be removed by the council) and who is responsible for carrying out council decisions and managing the city's departments

Under the council-manager form, the mayor and city council make decisions after debate on policy issues, such as taxation, budgeting, annexation, and services. The city manager's actual role varies considerably; however, most city managers exert strong influence. City councils generally rely on their managers for the preparation of annual budgets and policy recommendations. Once a policy is made, the city manager's office directs an appropriate department to implement it. Typically, city councils hire professionally trained managers. Successful applicants usually possess graduate degrees in public administration and can earn competitive salaries. In 2018, city managers for Texas's five largest cities earned $309,000 to $475,000 annually, plus bonuses. San Antonio paid its city manager $475,000, the highest salary in Texas, plus benefits. Obviously, a delicate relationship exists between appointed managers and elected council members. In theory, the council-manager system has a weak mayor and attempts to separate policy-making from administration. Councils and mayors are not supposed to "micro-manage" departments. However, in practice, elected leaders sometimes experience difficulties in determining where to draw the line between administrative oversight and meddling in departmental affairs.

A common weakness of the council-manager form of government is the lack of a leader to whom citizens can bring demands and concerns. The mayor is weak; the city council is composed of a number of members (anywhere from 4 to 16 individuals, with an average of 7, among the 25 largest cities in Texas); and the city manager is supposed to "stay out of politics." Thus, council-manager cities tend to respond more to elite and **middle-class** concerns than to those of

council-manager form
A system of municipal government in which an elected city council hires a manager to coordinate budgetary matters and supervise administrative departments.

middle class
Social scientists identify the middle class as those people with white-collar occupations (such as professionals and small business owners).

Source: https://www.sanantonio.gov/Manager/Organizational-Chart.

FIGURE 3.2 Council-Manager Form of Government: City of San Antonio (2018)

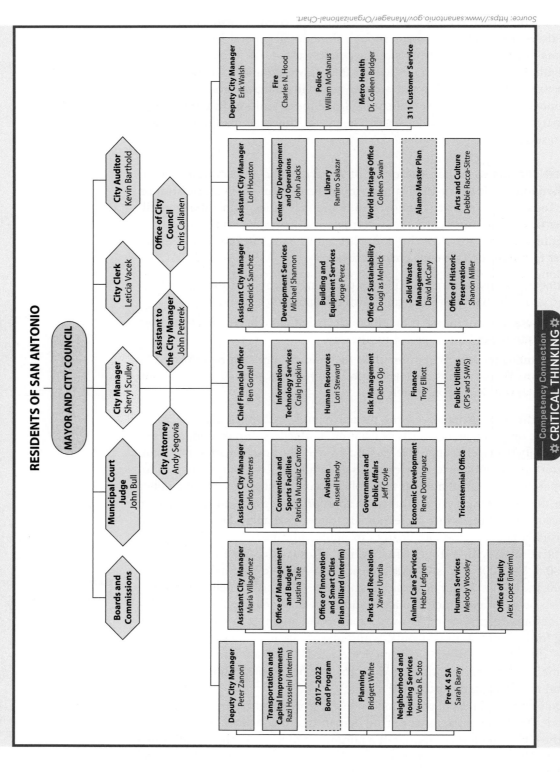

--- Competency Connection ---
✿ CRITICAL THINKING ✿

What advantages does the city manager have in this form of government over the mayor? What concerns would citizens have about this form of government and why?

the **working class** and ethnic minorities. (The business elite and the middle class have more organizations and leaders who have access to city government and know how to work the system.) Few council-manager cities have mayors who regularly provide strong political and policy leadership. One of these exceptions is San Antonio, where mayors, due to tradition and personality, generally are strong leaders. The council-manager form seems to work well in cities where most people are of the same ethnic group and social class and thus share many common goals. Few central cities fit this description, but many suburbs do.[13]

Commission Today, none of Texas's cities operates under a pure **commission form** of municipal government. First approved by the Texas legislature for Galveston after a hurricane demolished the city in 1900, this form lacks a single executive, relying instead on elected commissioners that form a policy-making board.

In the pure commission form known as the Galveston Plan, each department (for example, public safety, finance, public works, welfare, or legal) is the responsibility of a single commissioner. Most students of municipal government criticize this form's dispersed administrative structure and lack of a chief executive. No home-rule city in Texas uses the commission form, and general-law cities are prohibited from using the Galveston Plan. Therefore, the few Texas municipalities that have a variation of the commission form operate more like the mayor-council form and designate a city secretary or another official to coordinate departmental work.

> ✔ **3.2 Learning Check**
>
> 1. Name the two legal classifications of cities in Texas and indicate which has more flexibility in deciding its form and the way it operates.
> 2. Which form of municipal government is most common in Texas's larger home-rule cities?
>
> *Answers at the end of this chapter.*

▣ Municipal Politics

LO 3.3 Identify the rules and social issues that shape local government outcomes.

Election rules and socioeconomic change make a difference in who wins and what policies are more likely to be adopted. This section examines several election rules that affect local politics. It then looks at social changes that affect the nature of local politics in Texas.

Rules Make a Difference

Under Texas law, home-rule cities have the option to allow partisan elections in which a candidate's political party affiliation is included on the ballot.[14] Nonetheless, all city and special district elections in Texas are **nonpartisan elections**. That is, candidates are listed on the ballot without party labels in order to reduce the role of political parties in local politics. This rule has been effective in most local Texas governments, where political parties play little to no role. However, they do become involved in a few areas, particularly the Houston and Dallas metropolitan areas.

working class
Social scientists identify the working class as those people with blue-collar (manual) occupations.

commission form
A type of municipal government in which each elected commissioner is a member of the city's policymaking body and heads an administrative department (e.g., public safety with police and fire divisions).

nonpartisan election
An election in which candidates are not identified on the ballot by party label.

Nonpartisan elections have at least two negative consequences. First, without political parties to stir up excitement, voter turnout tends to be low compared with state and national elections. Studies of voting patterns in the United States suggest that voters are racially polarized (that is, people tend to vote for candidates of their own race or ethnicity).[15] Because those who do vote are more likely to be Anglos and middle class, the representation of ethnic minorities and the working class is reduced. San Antonio, for example, has a majority Latino population, but the greater Anglo voter turnout has meant that most San Antonio mayors have been Anglo. Recent exceptions have been Mexican American candidates who appealed to both Anglos and Latinos (Henry Cisneros, Edward Garza, and Julián Castro). In 2014, Ivy Taylor became the city's first African American mayor by appointment and then was elected with a coalition of Anglos and African Americans. She was defeated in 2017 by Ron Nirenberg (of Eastern European Jewish and Asian background), who ran as the more progressive candidate. A second problem is that nonpartisan elections tend to be more personal and less issue-oriented. Without a party for a guide, voters focus on personalities, not issues. In smaller communities, local elections are often decided by who has more friends and neighbors.

The two most common ways of organizing municipal elections are the **at-large election**, in which council members are elected on a citywide basis, and the **single-member district election**, in which voters cast a ballot only for a candidate who resides within their district. Texas municipalities have long used at-large elections. However, this system was challenged because it tended to overrepresent the majority Anglo population and underrepresent ethnic minorities. In at-large elections, the city's majority ethnic group, in terms of voting, tends to be the majority in each electoral contest. This electoral structure works to the disadvantage of ethnic minorities.

Throughout the country, representative bodies whose members are elected from districts (such as the state legislature, city councils, county commissioners court, and school boards) must **redistrict** (redraw their district boundary lines) after every 10-year census. If at-large or cumulative voting (described below) is used, redistricting is not necessary. After the 2010 census, Texas's city councils had to redraw districts to reflect shifts in population within cities and between districts. The process will be repeated after the 2020 census.

In 1975, because of its long history of racial discrimination, all Texas governments were placed under a provision of the federal Voting Rights Act that required governments to receive clearance from the U.S. attorney general or the Federal District Court for the District of Columbia for rule changes in voting. However, the Supreme Court case of *Shelby v. Holder* (2013) altered preclearance. The Court ruled as unconstitutional Section 4 of the Voting Rights Act, making preclearance much less likely. Section 5 still allows preclearance, but a new lawsuit would be required. The city of Pasadena, which is two-thirds Latino, has long been dominated by its minority Anglo population, which received the majority of city spending but felt threatened by increasing Latino council membership. Without the threat of federal preclearance, the city changed the council from

at-large election
Members of a policymaking body, such as a city council, are elected on a citywide basis rather than from single-member districts.

single-member district election
Voters in an area (commonly called a district, ward, or precinct) elect one representative to serve on a policymaking body (e.g., city council, county commissioners court, state House and Senate).

redistricting
Redrawing of boundaries after the federal decennial census to create districts with approximately equal population (e.g., legislative, congressional, commissioners court, and city council districts in Texas).

eight district seats to six district and two at-large, which made continued Anglo dominance likely. In 2015, five Anglos and three Latinos were elected. In 2017, in a suit filed by Latino leaders, a Houston federal district judge threw out the at-large seats and ordered the 2017 elections to be held with eight district seats. Because of low turnout, Latinos continued to be a minority on the council but believed that the all-district system would reward get-out-the-vote efforts. The election and term-limiting of the former mayor led to a unanimous council decision to drop the city's appeal of the order, accept being under federal preclearance until 2023, and pay plaintiffs' court costs ($1.1 million).

In recent decades, the major controversy over redistricting at the local level has been the issue of the representation of Texas's major ethnic groups—particularly Latinos, who were the main source of the state's population growth in the 2010 census and since. Expansion of the Latino population in urban areas has increased the number of Latino opportunity districts. These districts are drawn to include a large enough population of Latinos to give a Latino candidate a good chance of winning.[16] Low Latino turnout, however, has limited the number of Latino council members elected. (For a discussion of minority opportunity districts, see Chapter 5, "Campaigns and Elections.")

Dividing a city into single-member districts tends to create some districts with a majority of historically excluded ethnic minorities, thereby increasing the chance of electing a Latino, African American, or Asian American candidate to the city council. Prompted by lawsuits and ethnic conflict, all but one of Texas's 10 largest cities have adopted single-member districts or a mixed system of at-large and single-member districts. Only Plano (near Dallas) continues to elect all council members on an at-large basis. Houston, for example, has five council members elected at large (citywide) and eleven elected from single-member districts. Increased use of single-member districts has led to more ethnically and racially diverse city councils.[17] Low voter turnout by an ethnic group, however, can reduce the effect of single-member districts.

As of 2018, to increase minority representation, 50 Texas local governments, including 34 school districts and 16 cities, used **cumulative voting**. In this election system, voters cast a number of votes equal to the positions available and may cast them for one or more candidates in any combination. For example, if eight candidates vie for four positions on the city council, a voter may cast two votes for Candidate A, two votes for Candidate B, and no votes for the other candidates. By the same token, a voter may cast all four votes for Candidate A. In the end, the candidates with the most votes are elected to fill the four positions.

Where racial minority voters are a numerical minority, cumulative voting increases the chances that they will have some representation. The largest government entity in the state to use cumulative voting is the Amarillo Independent School District, which adopted the system in 1999 in response to a federal Voting Rights Act lawsuit. The district was 30 percent minority but had no minority board members for two decades. With the adoption of cumulative voting, African American and Latino board members were elected. In 2019, the seven-member board included one African American and one Latino member.

cumulative voting
When multiple seats are contested in an at-large election, voters cast one or more of the specified number of votes for one or more candidates in any combination. It is designed to increase representation of historically underrepresented ethnic minority groups.

Home-rule cities may also determine whether to institute **term limits** for their elected officials. Beginning in the 1990s, many cities (including San Antonio and Houston) amended their charters to institute term limits for their mayor and city council members. Houston adopted a limit of three, two-year terms for its mayor. When popularly elected officials are denied the opportunity to seek reelection, city officials frequently discuss overturning term-limit ordinances. Gaining support to eliminate term limits has proved difficult. A more successful compromise has been to increase the number of terms or to lengthen the terms of office for elected officials. In 2008, San Antonio changed its limits from two to four terms, with two-year terms for its mayor and city council members. This move was expected to make it easier for Latino city council members to build the support necessary to run for mayor. Houston extended terms of office for all city officeholders to two, four-year terms in 2015, although a lawsuit was filed to invalidate the election. The plaintiff argued the wording on the ballot "to limit the length for all terms of elective office to four years" caused voters to believe they were limiting officeholders to a single four-year term.[18] In March 2016, a state district judge ruled in the city's favor, stating that the language was not "invalid." The case has been appealed. Andy Taylor, a Brenham-based elections lawyer, believes the appellate court will find the language to be misleading and deceptive. Both supporters and opponents feel strongly about term limits. This issue is not restricted to local governments in Texas. U.S. Term Limits (USTL) is a national, nonprofit organization that lobbies for term limits at the local, state, and national levels of government.

Socioeconomic and Demographic Changes

It should be clear that election rules make a difference in who is elected. Historical, social, and economic factors make a difference as well. Texas's increasing levels of urbanization, education, and economic development have made the state more economically, culturally, and politically diverse (or more pluralist). Local politics reflect these changes. Many Texas city governments were long dominated by elite business organizations, such as the Dallas Citizens Council and the San Antonio Good Government League. But greater pluralism and changes in election rules have given a say to a wider range of Texans determining how their local governments function. Racial and ethnic conflict remains a problem in Texas, but communities are working to resolve their issues, albeit in differing ways and to different degrees. Growth in the population's size, increased amounts of citizen organization, and higher levels of personal income tend to increase demands on local government and produce higher public spending.

Houston has long been Texas's most diverse local political system. It has a strong business community, many labor union members, an African American community with almost a century's experience in fighting for its views and interests, a growing and increasingly organized Latino community, an expanding Asian American community that is becoming more active, and an activist gay community. Multiethnic coalitions have been the norm in Houston's mayoral

term limit
A restriction on the number of terms officials can serve in a public office.

races for decades; and nonbusiness interests have significant, if variable, access to city hall. In 2015, Houston elected its second African American mayor, former state representative Sylvester Turner.

Dallas has long had serious black–white racial tensions. Although these conflicts have not been resolved, changes in election rules have increased the number of racial minorities on the city council. In 1995, Dallas's Ron Kirk became the first African American in modern times elected mayor of a major Texas city.

▣ POINT/COUNTERPOINT

Should the State of Texas have more control over city government decisions?

THE ISSUE The 2015 legislature considered more than 1,600 different bills affecting the authority of cities. The 2017 and 2019 legislatures continued to reduce local decision-making, generally by giving the state government authority in an area and thus preempting local decisions. Among the bills considered were attempts to bar sanctuary cities, ban red light cameras, limit cities' taxing and borrowing power, reduce cities' annexation authority, and prohibit local regulation of fracking, knives, tree removal, small honey operations, plastic bags, and straws. The Texas Municipal League called it a "philosophical attack on local control."

FOR	AGAINST
1. For efficiency and economy, laws that regulate businesses should be consistent throughout the state. A patchwork of regulations that vary across local governments is costly for business owners.	1. Different communities have different needs. Allowing local governments to address these differences is more appropriate than applying the same regulatory scheme statewide.
2. Some city ordinances, such as prohibitions against fracking, interfere with individuals' property rights because they effectively destroy the right to exploit one's property for financial gain.	2. Texas law provides that if a government takes someone's property, the property owner must be compensated. Therefore, if an ordinance destroys someone's property, the property owner should be paid for the loss.
3. Texas is being "Californiazed" by local officials with unnecessary regulations that ban plastic bags, fracking, and tree-cutting. Because local governments are exercising too much power, state government must step in to restore order and protect individual rights.	3. When problems develop, local officials are more accessible to average citizens than state agencies and state elected officials. Limiting local control gives too much influence to powerful business interests in the resolution of these issues.

Sources: Mike Ward, "Mayors to Lawmakers: Don't Mess with Taxes," *Houston Chronicle*, February 17, 2015; "TMC Legislative Update No. 23," *Texas Municipal League*, June 5, 2015, http://www.tml.org/p/LU2015-23.pdf; and "Expressly Preempting Local Oil and Gas Regulations," *Major Issues of the 84th Legislature* (Austin: House Research Organization, September 22, 2015), http://www.hro.house .state.tx.us/pdf/focus/major84.pdf.

Competency Connection
◉ SOCIAL RESPONSIBILITY ◉

If you were in the Texas legislature, would you support increasing the state's authority over local governments?

In 1991, Austin elected its first Latino mayor, Gus Garcia; in 1998, Laredo elected its first Latina mayor, Betty Flores; and in 2009, San Antonio elected Julián Castro, the youngest mayor (at age 34) of a major U.S. city. Castro was reelected twice, but in 2014 he was appointed by President Obama to head the U.S. Department of Housing and Urban Development. He was replaced by the city's first African American mayor, Ivy Taylor. In 2016, he received strong consideration as a vice presidential running mate with the Democratic presidential nominee Hillary Clinton, and in 2019, he began a bid for president.

In both 2013 and 2017, Texas had the largest number of Latino elected officials in the nation (over 40 percent of the total in 2017), with most at the local level.[19] Since the 1970s, South Texas's majority Latino population has elected Latino (and some non-Latino) leaders at all levels. In the rest of the state, central cities and some near-in suburbs tend to have a majority of Latinos, African Americans, and Asian Americans, which gives these groups more electoral clout. Suburbs farther from the center tend to be predominantly Anglo and often heavily middle class, which produces more middle-class Anglo leaders. In Texas, as throughout the United States, an increasing number of ethnic and racial minority populations are moving to the suburbs. Clearly, the face of local government has changed as a result of increased use of single-member districts; greater pluralism in the state; and the growing number, organization, and political activity of minority Texans.

Municipal Services

Most citizens and city officials believe city government's major job is to provide basic services that affect people's day-to-day lives: police and fire protection, streets, water, sewer and sanitation, and perhaps parks and recreation. These basic services tend to be cities' largest expenditures, though the amounts spent vary from city to city. Municipalities also regulate important aspects of Texans' lives, notably zoning (regulating the use of land by separating commercial and industrial areas), construction, food service, and sanitation.

A financial concern for many local governments in the state, especially cities, is increased liability for employee pensions and other retirement benefits. Firefighters, police, and other municipal employees can participate in defined-benefits pension plans. While they are working, employees contribute a portion of their salaries to the pension plan. Each year, the city funds an amount equal to a percentage of the department's payroll to the plan. When an individual city worker retires or becomes disabled, the retirement plan is obligated to make monthly payments for the remainder of the former employee's life regardless of the city's financial condition. Over the years, cities have negotiated lower salaries with employee groups in exchange for better retirement benefits. For example, although the average salary for Houston firefighters is 143rd in the nation, some of the department's retirees receive monthly pension benefits that exceed the monthly pay they would receive if they were working.[20]

In the 2015 Houston mayoral election, dire predictions regarding the city's economic future because of its pension obligations were a major campaign issue.

The city contributed more than $350 million to its three pension funds in 2015, almost twice its spending for libraries, trash pickup, and parks combined.[21] The city reported a $3.2 billion gap between pension assets and future liabilities, an amount equal to more than its entire city budget.[22] The concern is that as more city revenue is dedicated to funding pensions, less will be available to provide city services.

This problem is not unique to Houston. There are at least 93 pension funds in the state. Scarce financial resources available to local governments, pressures from employees and citizens, growing health costs, longer life expectancies, and frequent over-optimism have created similar problems across the country. When Moody's listed the 15 cities with the largest unfunded pension gaps, four Texas cities made the list: Dallas second, Houston fourth, Austin ninth, and San Antonio twelfth.[23]

To resolve the issue in Houston, Mayor Turner negotiated a plan requiring city employees to contribute more to their pension funds and accept benefit cuts in exchange for an infusion of money to maintain the pension funds. The city agreed to limitations to ensure its continued support of the funds. The city had to persuade the 2017 legislature to pass a bill authorizing the deal and then win approval of a $1 billion bond by city voters later that year.[24] Firefighters, who had opposed the compromise, filed suit and supported a successful 2018 charter amendment to grant firefighters pay parity with police. Conflict over implementation of pay parity and a suit against the amendment continued into 2019.

Over time, many Texas cities have added libraries, airports, hospitals, community development, and housing to their list of services. Scarce resources (particularly money) of local governments increase competition between traditional services and newer services demanded by citizens or the state and national governments, such as protecting the homeless, providing elder services, offering job training, fighting air pollution, and preventing delinquency. These competing demands for municipal spending often result in controversy requiring elected officials to make difficult decisions.

Municipal Government Revenue

Most city governments in Texas and the nation face a serious financial dilemma: they barely have enough money to provide basic services; thus, they must reject or shortchange new services. Cities' two largest tax sources—sales and property taxes—are limited by state law. These taxes produce inadequate increases in revenue as the population grows. Moreover, Texas voters are increasingly hostile to higher property taxes. Adding to the problem are low levels of state assistance to Texas cities as compared to those of many other states. As a result, Texas cities are relying more heavily on fees (such as liquor licenses, franchise fees for cable television companies, and water rates) and are going into debt. Per capita local government debt in Texas was the second highest in the nation in 2018. Only Nevada's was higher. (Texas state government, by comparison, was tenth lowest.)[25]

The revenue of Texas governments at all levels has long been tied to the ups and downs of the oil and gas industry. Between 2008 and 2014, local

📋 STUDENTS IN ACTION

Service in the Community

"Working within the community provided an experience in government that I could not have learned in a classroom. It truly exposes the individual needs of those within the community and gives you the sense that you can actually make a difference."

—Kaitlin Piraro

Community centers provide neighborhood children with a safe place to engage in fun activities.

Kaitlin Piraro worked for the City of Austin part-time at the Dittmar Recreation Center from the spring of 2011 through fall 2012. As a counselor, she worked one-on-one with children aged 5 to 11 in the recreation center's after-school program. Her primary responsibility was to keep the youth, who were from local neighborhoods, focused on positive after-school activities. Kaitlin soon volunteered to work on the teen art project at the center. She provided specific classes for the students in art, cooking, sculpture, painting, and film. She found that introducing new projects to the students was rewarding, and they were excited to be involved in interactive learning. Selected art projects were shown at galleries in Austin. At the end of the semester, Kaitlin worked with others at the center to create an awards ceremony to recognize the students' hard work. She learned how to work with young students, coordinate projects, and communicate with parents and others in the community.

This experience opened Kaitlin's eyes to local bureaucracy, how it works, and how it helps communities. Her hope is to someday work again with city government. She believes that opportunities to work in community projects, as a volunteer, intern, or paid employee, are a great way to learn firsthand about government. Her advice to other students is to explore all possible community projects, so that they can give back and learn more about the needs of their community.

— Competency Connection —
⊛ SOCIAL RESPONSIBILITY ⊛

If you could intern with a city department or program in your community, which would you select and why?

governments in Texas benefited from a flourishing oil and gas market. The major revenue sources for local government, property and sales tax receipts, grew in counties and municipalities with oil and gas development. In 2014, the price of West Texas Intermediate crude oil (the benchmark in oil pricing) reached $108 per barrel. When OPEC (the Organization of Petroleum Exporting Countries) decided to increase oil production in that year, the price of oil began to plummet. In 2016, the price hit a low of $26 per barrel. Cities and counties where oil drilling had surged experienced a decrease in property and sales tax revenue and an increase in unemployment. The state government's revenue declined as well, decreasing the ability to assist local governments.[26] In 2018, the average closing price of West Texas Intermediate was $65, and prices were expected to remain low.[27] Local government revenues recovered somewhat but remained precarious.

With less revenue, municipalities try to reduce costs. Conservatives argue for privatization, that is, hiring private companies to provide services such as issuing building permits and budget planning. Liberals point out the serious problems in state efforts to privatize prisons, Medicaid, and Child Protective Services. Research indicates that the profit motive works well "if the task is clear-cut and it's possible to define concrete goals and reward those who meet them."[28] But if the objectives are complex and diffuse, as is often the case in public services, it is difficult to align profit and public goals. Thus, privatization has a mixed record, sometimes saving local governments money and sometimes reducing the quality of service.

Taxes The state of Texas permits municipalities to levy taxes based on the value of property (**property tax**). The tax rate is generally expressed in terms of the amount of tax per $100 of the property's value. This rate varies greatly from one city to another. In 2014 (the most recent year for comprehensive

IMAGE 3.2 Denton residents object to the state law that denies cities the right to ban fracking.

Tribune Content Agency LLC/Alamy Stock Photo

— Competency Connection —
⚖ PERSONAL RESPONSIBILITY ⚖

Should you protest? What would you protest? And how can you make your protest more effective?

property tax
A tax that property owners pay according to the value of real estate and other tangible property. At the local level, property owners pay this tax to the city, the county, the school district, and often other special districts.

data), rates varied from 5 cents per $100 valuation to $1.45, with an average of 52 cents.[29] A problem with property taxes is that poorer cities with low property values must charge a high rate to provide minimum services. In the Dallas area, for example, in 2014, Highland Park (near downtown Dallas) had an annual median family income of $193,000 and set a property tax rate of 22 cents per $100 in valuation. Wylie (north of Dallas) had an annual median family income of $83,000 and set its tax rate at 88 cents per $100 in valuation.

The other major source of city tax revenue is the optional 1.25 to 2 percent sales tax that is collected along with the state sales tax. Local governments are in competition for sales tax dollars. The sum of city, county, and special district government sales taxes cannot exceed 2 percent. For example, a city might assess 1 percent; the county, 0.5 percent; and a special district, 0.5 percent. In order to prevent going over the cap of 2 percent, state law sets up the order in which sales taxes are required to be collected. First to collect is the city, second is the county, and third are the special districts. Further, voters must approve the imposition of a local sales tax within their jurisdiction. An additional problem is that sales tax revenues fluctuate with the local economy, making it difficult to plan how much money will be available. The hotel occupancy tax is another significant source of revenue for cities with tourism; professional sports teams; major sports events, such as the NFL Super Bowl or Grand Prix racing; or international festivals like South by Southwest Music, Film, and Interactive Festival (SXSW).

Fees Lacking adequate tax revenues to meet the demands placed on them, Texas municipalities have come to rely more heavily on fees (charges for services and payments required by an agency upon those subject to its regulation). Cities levy fees for such things as beer and liquor licenses and building permits. They collect traffic fines and may charge franchise fees based on gross receipts of public utilities (for example, telephone and cable television companies). Texas municipalities are authorized to own and operate water, electric, and gas utility systems that may generate a profit for the city. Charges also are levied for such services as sewage treatment, garbage collection, hospital care, and use of city recreation facilities. These user fees may allow a city to provide certain services with only a small subsidy from its general revenue fund or perhaps no subsidy at all.

Bonds and Certificates of Obligation Taxes and fees normally produce enough revenue to allow Texas cities to cover day-to-day operating expenses. Money for capital improvements (such as construction of city buildings or parks) and emergencies (such as flood or hurricane damage) often must be borrowed. This money is obtained through the sale of municipal **bonds**, which may be redeemed over periods of 1 to 30 years. The Texas Constitution allows cities to issue bonds, but any bond issue to be repaid from taxes must be approved by the voters. In November 2018, there were 98 bond elections in Texas, with voters approving 88. For example, citizens approved seven bond

bond
A mechanism by which governments borrow money.

issues in Austin worth $925 million, one for the Fort Bend Independent School District for $993 million, and three in Collin County totaling $750 million. During the recent recession, local governments made more use of certificates of obligation, which do not require voter approval and typically reach maturity in 15 to 20 years. The certificates traditionally have been used for smaller amounts and short-term financing.

To increase their borrowing power, some local governments now issue capital appreciation bonds that require no repayment for years. Borrowers pay one lump sum, including principal and accrued interest, on maturity. The amount borrowed only counts against debt limitations in the year of repayment, an issue especially important to school districts because of limitations on the amount of money they can borrow. Capital appreciation bonds have many critics. Because of the length of time between the date of borrowing and the date of repayment, taxpayers who authorized the issuance of the bonds will have little or no obligation to repay them. Additionally, these bonds frequently have much higher interest rates than current-interest bonds (in which interest is paid regularly over time).

Property Taxes and Tax Exemptions Property owners pay taxes on the value of their homes, businesses, and land to the city as well as to the county, the school district, and often other special districts. When property values or tax rates go up, the total tax bill goes up as well. To offset the burden of higher taxes resulting from reappraisals of property values, local governments (including cities) may grant homeowners up to a 20 percent homestead exemption on the assessed value of their homes. Cities may also provide an additional homestead exemption for disabled veterans and their surviving spouses, for homeowners 65 years of age or older, or for other reasons, such as adding pollution controls.

Cities, counties, and community college districts may also freeze property taxes for senior citizens and the disabled. Property tax caps (or ceilings) can be implemented by city council action or by voter approval. The dilemma is that cities can help their disadvantaged citizens, but doing so costs the city revenue. In 2015, exemptions cost Texas cities an estimated $44.41 billion in revenue. As baby boomers reach retirement age, exemptions and property tax caps will reduce revenue even further. Ranked from lowest to highest, the Lone Star State has one of the highest property tax rates in the nation (47th out of 50 in 2015).[30]

The Bottom Line Because of pressure against increasing property tax rates, municipal governments sometimes refrain from increased spending, cut services or programs, or find new revenue sources. Typically, city councils are forced to opt for one or more of the following actions:

- Create new fees or raise fees on services such as garbage collection
- Impose hiring and wage freezes for municipal employees
- Cut services (such as emergency rooms) that are especially important for inner-city populations

tax increment reinvestment zone (TIRZ)
Also called a Tax Increment Finance District (TIF). An area in which municipal tax incentives are offered to encourage businesses to locate in and contribute to the development of a blighted urban area. Commercial and residential property taxes may be frozen.

✔ 3.3 Learning Check

1. What are two methods to increase the number of elected officials who are members of historical racial or ethnic minority groups?

2. What are the two largest tax sources that provide revenue to local governments? Do these taxes usually provide enough revenue for local governments to meet the demands placed on them?

Answers at the end of this chapter.

- Contract with private firms for service delivery
- Improve productivity, especially by investing in technology

Generating Revenue for Economic Development

State and federal appropriations to assist cities are shrinking, especially for economic development. Inner cities face the challenge of dilapidated housing, abandoned buildings, and poorly maintained infrastructure (such as sewers and streets). This neglect blights neighborhoods and contributes to social problems, such as crime and strained racial relations. Texas cities do have the local option of a half-cent sales tax for infrastructure upgrades, such as repaving streets and improving sewage disposal. The increased sales tax, however, must stay within the 2 percent limit the state imposes on local governments. Following a national trend, some Texas cities are trying to spur development by attracting businesses through tax incentives. The Texas legislature authorizes cities to create **tax increment reinvestment zones (TIRZs)**, often called tax increment finance (TIF) districts. A TIRZ uses tax breaks such as freezing taxes to attract private investment in blighted areas needing development. Cities using TIRZs/TIFs include Houston, Dallas, Fort Worth, Austin, San Antonio, El Paso, Waco, Arlington, and Wichita Falls. Whether such plans work is controversial. Many observers argue that companies attracted by tax breaks often make minimal actual investments and leave as soon as they realize a profit from tax subsidies. Yet, because TIRZs sometimes work, many cities starved for resources are willing to take the gamble.

🏛 HOW DO WE COMPARE...

in Local Debt?

Local Debt Per Capita

Most Populous U.S. States	Per Capita Debt	U.S. States Bordering Texas	Per Capita Debt
California	$7,793	Arkansas	$3,402
Florida	$4,486	Louisiana	$3,687
New York	$7,134	New Mexico	$3,699
Texas	**$8,101**	Oklahoma	$2,537

Source: "Comparison of State and Local Government Spending in the United States," *US Government Spending,* https://www.usgovernmentspending.com/compare_state_spending_2018dH0D. Amounts are projections.

— Competency Connection —
⊛ SOCIAL RESPONSIBILITY ⊛

Should the state provide more funding to local governments to lower local debt?

✪ Counties

LO 3.4 Analyze the structure and responsibilities of counties.

Texas **counties** present an interesting set of contradictions. These local entities are technically an arm of the state, created to serve its needs, but both county officials and county residents see them as locally controlled governments and resent what some view as state interference. Counties collect taxes on both urban and rural property but focus more on the needs of rural residents and people living in unincorporated suburbs, who do not have city governments to provide services. This 19th-century form of government serves 21st-century Texans.

Texas is divided into 254 counties, the most of any state in the nation. The basic form of Texas counties is set by the state constitution, though their activities are heavily shaped by whether they are in rural or metropolitan areas. As an agent of the state, each county issues state automobile licenses, enforces state laws, registers voters, conducts elections, collects certain state taxes, and helps administer justice. In conjunction with state and federal governments, the county conducts health and welfare programs, maintains records of vital statistics (such as births and deaths), issues various licenses, collects fees, and provides a host of other public services. Yet state supervision of county operations is minimal. Rural counties generally try to keep taxes low and provide minimal services. They are reluctant to take on new responsibilities, such as regulating septic systems and residential development. In metropolitan areas, however, counties have been forced by citizen demands—and sometimes by the state—to take on varied urban tasks, such as providing ballparks and recreation centers, hospitals, libraries, airports, and museums.[31]

Politics in Texas's larger counties is changing. Outer suburbs and rural and small town areas in much of the state remain Republican, while Democrats are gaining in central cities and close-in suburbs. Since 2006, Dallas County has tended to be Democratic with a major victory in 2018. In Harris County (Houston), both parties were competitive (depending on turnout) in 2008–2016, but in 2018, Democrat Lina Hidalgo ousted longtime Republican county judge Ed Emmett, as Democrats won all seven countywide races. Seventeen African American women were elected as judges. At the same time, in Nueces County (Corpus Christi), a Latina, Barbara Canales, became the first woman and the first Democrat in a decade to win the county judge race, giving the Democrats a majority on the commissioners court.

Structure and Operation

As required by the state constitution, all Texas counties have the same basic governmental structure, despite wide demographic and economic differences between rural and urban counties. (Contrast Figure 3.3, Harris County, the most populous Texas county with more than 4.5 million residents in 2017, with Figure 3.4, Loving County, the least populous with 74 residents in that year.)

county
Texas is divided into 254 counties that serve as an administrative arm of the state and provide important services at the local level, especially in rural areas.

FIGURE 3.3 Harris County Government (County Seat: Houston).

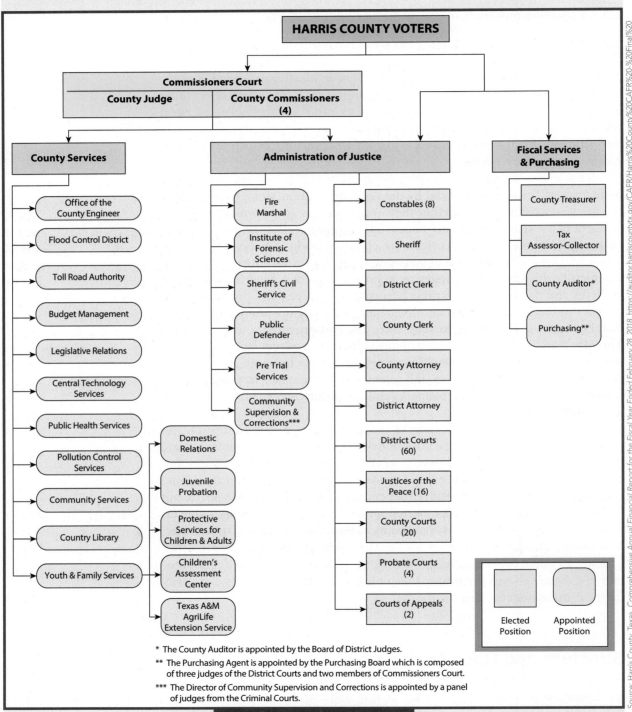

Source: Harris County, Texas, Comprehensive Annual Financial Report for the Fiscal Year Ended February 28, 2018, https://auditor.harriscountytx.gov/CAFR/Harris%20County%20CAFR%20-%20Final%20 FY%202018.pdf.

Competency Connection

★ PERSONAL RESPONSIBILITY ★

Do most citizens know the role of their county commissioners court? Why is it important for more citizens to understand its role?

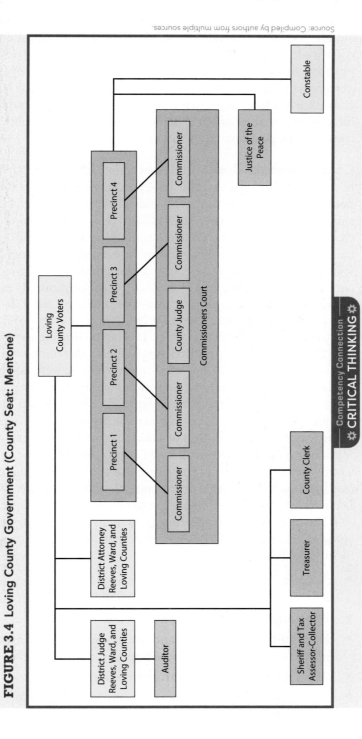

FIGURE 3.4 Loving County Government (County Seat: Mentone)

Source: Compiled by authors from multiple sources.

Competency Connection
☼ CRITICAL THINKING ☼

How does a county's population size change the job of the county commissioners court? Compare Figure 3.3 (Harris County) to Figure 3.4 (Loving County).

The Texas Constitution provides for the election of four county commissioners, county and district attorneys, a county sheriff, a county clerk, a district clerk, a county tax assessor-collector, a county treasurer, and constables, as well as judicial officers, including justices of the peace and a county judge. All elected county officials are chosen in partisan elections and serve four-year terms. In practice, Texas counties are usually highly decentralized, or fragmented. No one person has formal authority to supervise or coordinate the county's elected officials, each of whom tends to think of the office as a personal fiefdom and resents interference by other officials. Sometimes, however, the political leadership of the county judge produces cooperation.

Commissioners Court All elected county officials make policies for their area of responsibility, but the major policymaking body is called the **commissioners court**. Its members are the county judge, who presides, and four elected commissioners. The latter serve staggered four-year terms, so two commissioners are elected every two years. Each commissioner is elected by voters residing in a commissioner precinct; thus commissioners are elected from single-member districts. Boundary lines for a county's four commissioner precincts are set by its commissioners court. Precincts must be of substantially equal population as mandated by the "one-person, one-vote" ruling of the U.S. Supreme Court in *Avery v. Midland County* 390 U.S. 474 (1968).

Counties must redistrict every 10 years, following the federal census. After the 2010 census, county redistricting battles centered on political party power in Dallas County, and racial and ethnic representation were major sources of conflict in Harris County (Houston), Galveston County, and Travis County (Austin). In Dallas County, the Democratic-controlled commissioners court added another Democratic seat, and the Republican majority on Harris County's commissioners court was sued over dilution of Latino votes. The Galveston County plan was rejected by the U.S. Department of Justice for diluting minority votes. Bexar County's (San Antonio) redistricting was less controversial than usual and was overshadowed by the battle over congressional redistricting. (See Chapter 8, "The Legislative Branch," for a discussion of congressional redistricting.)

The term *commissioners court* is actually a misnomer because its functions are administrative and legislative rather than judicial. The court's major functions include the following:

- Adopting the county budget and setting tax rates, which are the commissioners court's greatest sources of power and influence over other county officials
- Providing a courthouse, jails, and other buildings
- Maintaining county roads and bridges, which is often viewed by rural residents as the major county function
- Administering county health and welfare programs
- Administering and financing elections (general and special elections for the nation, state, and county)

Beyond these functions, a county is free to decide whether to take on other programs authorized, but not required, by the state.

commissioners court
A Texas county's policymaking body, with five members: the county judge, who presides, and four commissioners representing single-member precincts.

In metropolitan areas, large numbers of people live in unincorporated communities with no city government to provide services, such as police protection and water. Within those communities, the county, special districts, and volunteer fire departments provide some basic services. In rural areas, counties take on few new tasks, and residents are generally happy not to be hassled by too much government. In rural counties, commissioners generally are responsible for roads and bridges in their own precinct. In other, particularly urban, counties, a county engineer may be responsible for all county roads.

County Judge The **county judge** holds the most prominent job in county government and generally is the most influential county leader. This county officer presides over the commissioners court, has administrative responsibility for most county agencies not headed by another elected official, and in some counties, presides over court cases, but does not need to be a lawyer. Much of the county judge's power or influence comes from leadership skills, playing a lead role in budgeting, and, commonly, higher social status background. The judge has essentially no formal authority over other elected county officials.

County Attorney and District Attorney The **county attorney** represents the state in civil and criminal cases and advises county officials on legal questions. Nearly 50 counties in Texas do not elect a county attorney because a resident district attorney performs those duties. Other counties elect a county attorney but share the services of a **district attorney** with one or more neighboring counties. Where there are both a county and a district attorney, the district attorney generally specializes in the district court cases, and the county attorney handles lesser matters in county and justice of the peace courts. District attorneys tend to be important figures in the criminal justice system because of the leadership they provide to local law enforcement and the discretion they exercise in deciding whether to prosecute cases. The legal advice of the county or district attorney carries considerable weight with other county officials.

If a vacancy occurs during a county attorney's term of office, this vacancy is filled by the commissioners court. Although local voters choose the district attorney, the governor fills a vacancy that occurs between elections. In 2014, then-Governor Rick Perry was indicted by a Travis County grand jury for abuse of office involving his alleged attempts to force the resignation of Travis County District Attorney Rosemary Lehmberg. A unique responsibility of the Travis County District Attorney's office was overseeing the Public Integrity Unit that was charged with the duty to investigate possible corruption of state-level officials. Complainants insisted that Perry sought Democrat Lehmberg's resignation after she pled guilty to driving while intoxicated, so he could replace her with a Republican district attorney who would be friendlier to Perry's appointees and other Republican elected officials.[32] The 84th Legislature (2015) transferred investigatory authority of most public corruption cases to the Texas Rangers and gave prosecutorial authority to the district attorney for the home county of the accused. In 2016, the Texas Court of Criminal Appeals dismissed charges against Perry for abuse of power.

county judge
An official popularly elected to preside over the county commissioners court, perform some administrative duties, and in smaller counties, hear civil and criminal cases.

county attorney
An official elected to represent the county in civil and criminal cases, unless a resident district attorney performs some of these functions.

district attorney
An official elected to serve one or more counties who prosecutes criminal cases, gives advisory opinions, and represents the county in civil cases.

County Sheriff The **county sheriff**, as chief law enforcement officer, is charged with keeping the peace in the county. In this capacity, the sheriff appoints deputies and oversees the county jail and its prisoners. In practice, the sheriff's office commonly focuses on crime in unincorporated areas and leaves law enforcement in cities primarily to the municipal police. In a county with a population of fewer than 10,000, the sheriff may also serve as tax assessor-collector, unless that county's electorate votes to separate the two offices. In a few rural counties, the sheriff may be the county's most influential leader.

Law Enforcement and Judges Counties have a number of officials associated with the justice system, ranging from a few in sparsely populated Loving County to many in heavily populated Harris County. The judicial role of the constitutional county judge varies. In counties with a small population, the county judge may exercise important judicial functions, such as handling probate matters, small civil cases, and serious misdemeanors. In counties with a large population, county judges are so involved in their political, administrative, and legislative roles that they have little time for judicial functions. Instead, **statutory county courts** have often been established with lawyers for judges and more formal procedures. In addition to the sheriff, and county and district attorneys discussed above, there are the district clerk, justices of the peace, and constables. The **district clerk** maintains records for the district courts.

Each county has from one to eight justice of the peace precincts. The number is decided by the commissioners court, which may also abolish courts (often to save money), as happened in Brazos and McLennan Counties in 2014 and Bexar County in 2016. **Justices of the peace** (commonly called JPs) handle minor civil and criminal cases, including small claims court cases. Statewide, JPs hear a large volume of legal actions, with traffic cases representing a substantial part of their work. In some counties, they also serve as coroner (to determine cause of death in certain cases) and as a magistrate (to set bail for arrested persons). Similar to the constitutional county court judge, they do not have to be lawyers but are required to take some legal training. **Constables** assist the justice court by serving subpoenas and other court documents and maintaining order in JP courts as the court's bailiff. They and their deputies are peace officers and may carry out security and investigative responsibilities. They are an important part of law enforcement, particularly for rural areas of the county. The commissioners court of a county may abolish the office of constable. Like other county officials, the judges, justices of the peace, district clerks, and constables are elected in partisan elections for four-year terms.

Constables are often responsible for enforcing school truancy laws. In 2015, the Legislature passed a "Failure to Attend" law changing truancy from a criminal to a civil offense. Before this, Texas and Wyoming had been the only states that sent juvenile truants to adult criminal court. Texas referred over 100,000 juveniles each year for missing school, 36,000 of whom were in Dallas County. The U.S. Department of Justice began an investigation in 2015 (still ongoing in 2018) to determine if students' due process rights had been violated.[33] Because of a 2017 change in the law, the number of students affected dropped by half, and the number of Dallas County truancy courts was reduced.

county sheriff
A citizen popularly elected as the county's chief law enforcement officer; the sheriff is also responsible for maintaining the county jail.

statutory county court
Court created by the legislature at the request of a county; may have civil or criminal jurisdiction or both, depending on the legislation creating it.

district clerk
A citizen elected to maintain records for the district courts.

Justice of the peace
A judge elected from a justice of the peace precinct who handles minor civil and criminal cases, including small claims court.

Constable
An official elected to assist the justice of the peace by serving papers and in some cases carrying out security and investigative responsibilities.

County Clerk and County Tax Assessor-Collector A **county clerk** keeps records and handles various paperwork chores for both the county court and the commissioners court. In addition, the county clerk files legal documents (such as deeds, mortgages, and contracts) in the county's public records and maintains the county's vital statistics (birth, death, and marriage records). The county clerk may also administer elections, but counties with larger populations often have an administrator of elections.

One of the responsibilities of Texas's county clerks is to issue marriage licenses. In June 2015, the Supreme Court ruled in *Obergefell v. Hodges* that same-sex marriage was legal in all 50 states. County clerks across Texas had to purchase computer software and update application forms to be able to issue marriage licenses to all couples, regardless of sexual orientation. Attorney General Ken Paxton made a statement after the Court's decision that county clerks with religious convictions against gay marriage could disregard the U.S. Supreme Court's ruling. Paxton didn't authorize clerks to refuse service to same-sex couples but said that an employee not opposed could issue the license. For a time, tiny Irion County was the only county in the nation refusing to issue marriage licenses to same-sex couples. The noncompliant county clerk was elected county judge in 2018.

A county office that has seen its role decline over time is the **county tax assessor-collector**. The title is partially a misnomer. Since 1982, the countywide **tax appraisal district** has assessed (or determined) property values in each county. The tax assessor-collector, on the other hand, collects county taxes and fees and certain state fees, including the license tag fees for motor vehicles and fees for handicapped parking permits. The office also commonly handles voter registration, whereas some counties have an elections administrator.

Treasurer and Auditor The **county treasurer** receives and pays out all county funds authorized by the commissioners court. If the office is eliminated by constitutional amendment, the county commissioners assign treasurer duties to another county office. When voters allowed Tarrant and Bexar Counties to eliminate the office, these counties authorized the county auditor to deal with responsibilities that were once held by the county treasurer. A county of 10,000 or more people must have a **county auditor**, appointed by the county's district court judges. The auditing function involves checking the account books and records of officials who handle county funds. Some observers worry that allowing the county auditor to perform both jobs of auditor and treasurer eliminates necessary checks and balances in county government.[34]

County Finance

Increasing demands for services impose an ever-expanding need for money. Just as the structure of county governments is frozen in the Texas Constitution and law, so is the county's power to tax and, to a lesser extent, to spend. Financial problems became even more serious for most counties during the Great Recession, which affected the economy from 2007 to 2016. Although financial problems lessened as the economy improved, low oil prices from 2014 to 2018 placed renewed financial pressure on counties.

county clerk
An official elected to perform clerical chores for the county courts and commissioners court, keep public records, maintain vital statistics, and administer public elections, if the county does not have an administrator of elections.

county tax assessor-collector
This elected official no longer assesses property for taxation but does collect taxes and fees and commonly handles voter registration.

tax appraisal district
The district appraises all real estate and commercial property for taxation by units of local government within a county.

county treasurer
An elected official who receives and pays out county money as directed by the commissioners court.

county auditor
A person appointed by the district judge or judges to check the financial books and records of other officials who handle county money.

Taxation The Texas Constitution authorizes county governments to collect taxes on property, and that is usually their most important revenue source. Although occupations may also be taxed, no county implements that provision. Each year the commissioners court sets the county tax rate. Under a 2019 law, if a city or county's property tax rate will increase revenue by 3.5 percent or more, there must be a citizen vote to approve. The previous "roll back" limit was 8 percent, which remains in effect for community college and hospital districts. Counties may also add 0.5 to 1.5 cents onto the state sales tax, which is 6.25 cents on the dollar. (Remember, however, that the add-on by all local governments may not exceed 2 cents on the dollar.) Fewer than half of Texas counties (primarily those with relatively small populations) impose a sales tax, and most set the rate at 0.5 cents.

Revenues From Nontax Sources Counties receive small amounts of money from various sources that add up to an important part of their total revenue. All counties may impose fees on the sale of liquor, and they share in state revenue from liquor sales, various motor vehicle taxes and fees, and traffic fines. Like other local governments, counties are eligible for federal grants-in-aid; but over the long term, this source continues to shrink. With voter approval, a county may borrow money through sale of bonds to pay for capital projects, such as a new jail or sports stadium. The Texas Constitution limits county indebtedness to 35 percent of a county's total assessed property value.

Tax Incentives and Subsidies Like cities, a commissioners court may grant tax abatements (reductions or suspensions) on taxable property, reimbursements (return of taxes paid), or tax increment financing (TIF; the use of future gains in property value to finance current development projects) to attract or retain businesses. For instance, in 2003, Bexar County offered a $22 million tax abatement for a Toyota factory to be built to produce pickup trucks in San Antonio. The offer was part of a complex incentive package put together by state, county, city, and other officials that totaled an estimated $133 million in tax breaks and infrastructure spending. The plant went into operation in 2006, creating more than 2,000 high-paying jobs and contributing to economic development in the region. From 2008 to 2010, the plant suffered from the national economic downturn, but by 2011, it had returned to full production and had expanded operations through 2018.[35]

The Bottom Line Despite various revenue sources, Texas counties, like other units of local government, are pressured to increase property taxes or to balance their budgets by eliminating or reducing programs and services. Although administrative costs and demands for expanded public services continue to increase, sources of county revenue are not expanding as quickly as demand.

Expenditures The state restricts county expenditures in certain areas and mandates spending in others, yet patterns of spending vary considerably from county to county. The greatest variation is between rural and metropolitan counties. Hospitals and health care, public safety, and roads are the largest expenditures for Texas counties overall. This expenditure pattern holds for Texas's largest counties, which also spend smaller, but still significant, amounts on urban amenities (such as parks) and social services (such as housing and welfare). Rural counties tend to spend a large portion of their budget on public safety and roads but little on social services and urban amenities. Many counties spend little on health care and hospitals because they have shifted the costs to a hospital district (a special district).

Although the county judge, auditor, or budget officer prepares the budget, the commissioners court is responsible for final adoption of an annual spending plan. Preparation of the budget generally enhances the commissioners court's power within county government. Counties do not have complete control over their spending because state and federal rules mandate certain county services and regulatory activities. Examples include social services, legal assistance and medical care for poor people, and mental health programs. Over the last decade, counties have made a major effort to pressure the legislature to limit unfunded mandates. An unfunded mandate is a requirement imposed on local governments by the state or a governing agency without providing funding to execute the requirement. Almost all counties have passed resolutions calling for a state constitutional amendment to ban mandates. Through 2019, the Texas legislature had not proposed such an amendment.

County jails must follow regulations imposed by the state legislature and the Texas Commission on Jail Standards. In 2015, the legislature passed HB 549, requiring two face-to-face visitation periods per week for each county inmate. Fiscal notes to the proposed bill warned that some counties might incur significant costs. The Commission on Jail Standards is responsible for establishing rules and procedures for the face-to-face visits. County jails "that have substantially invested in standing or under construction facilities" are exempted from complying with these in-person visitation requirements. Travis County had been exempt from the requirement because they spent a significant amount of money on a video system for inmate visits. Two of the facilities, however, used a Skype-like video-based system furnished by a private contractor, who made money from those who used the system. For that reason, the Commission indicated it might disapprove Travis County's exemption. To avoid controversy, the Travis County Commissioners Court approved a measure in September 2015 that reinstated face-to-face visits, which began in April 2016. Additional software, personnel, and physical space were required to accommodate in-person visits.[36] Thus, these additional expenditures constituted an unfunded mandate.

County Government Reform

Texas counties experience various problems: rigid structure and duties fixed in the state constitution and statutes, inefficiency related to too many elected officials and the lack of merit systems (hiring and promoting based on competence rather than who they know), and too little money. Counties with larger populations may establish merit employment systems, and half of those eligible have done so. One often-suggested reform is county home rule to give counties more ability to organize and operate in accordance with local needs and wishes. Research suggests that although county home rule better meets community demands, it also tends to expand county spending.

Different states allow varying degrees of county home rule. Texas is among the states that are most strongly opposed to home rule.[37] Until 1969, Texas actually had a home-rule provision for counties in the constitution, but it was too difficult to implement. Reviving a workable version today would be hard to achieve. Many (probably most) county officials prefer the present system, as do many people served by counties outside of the metropolitan areas.

Border Counties

The population of counties near the Rio Grande has grown markedly because of immigration and NAFTA (the North American Free Trade Agreement), now US–Mexico–Canada Agreement (USMCA). Unfortunately, population growth has outstripped economic growth, and the traditionally impoverished region now has even more poor people. Many of the poor live in **colonias** (depressed housing settlements, often without running water or sewage systems). Current estimates identify about 2,300 colonias in Texas, where as many as 500,000 Texans live in substandard conditions.

colonia
A low-income community, typically located in South Texas and especially in counties bordering Mexico, that lacks running water, sewer lines, and other essential services.

IMAGE 3.3 Colonias lack infrastructure or utilities.

Lisa Wiltse/Corbis

— Competency Connection —
✿ **CRITICAL THINKING** ✿

How should county governments along the border improve the conditions of colonias? Why?

Minimal efforts have been made to deal with problems of the colonias. Security and public safety are a major concern for their residents. Hidalgo County has more colonias than any county in Texas or elsewhere in the United States.[38] The county's colonia residents petitioned for streetlights for several decades. Nearly 85 percent of these neighborhoods lacked streetlights. Without lighting, children were vulnerable when playing outside after sunset; furthermore, this problem increased vandalism and theft. In 2007, legislation gave the county needed authority to install streetlights, but it did not set up a process for collecting fees. In 2015, House Bill 3002, passed without Governor Greg Abbott's signature, allowed Hidalgo County to collect fees to pay for streetlights in colonias. In 2016, streetlights were installed in eight of Hidalgo County's 1,000-plus colonias, increasing safety and evening activity.

Another major issue for colonias is drainage. Extreme storms have devastated some areas in the Rio Grande Valley, particularly in colonias where drainage facilities are lacking and there is nowhere for water to go. Front yards of homes turn into lakes and a breeding ground for mosquitoes, other insects, and vermin. Colonias have to wait for counties to bring in pumps after a flood, which can take a long time. Activists pushed for a 2015 study by the Texas General Land Office of 400 colonias that had a documented history of flooding. They put together a design for a drainage system specific to the needs of colonias. Spanish Palms, located in Hidalgo County, used the newly designed drainage system and connected it to the county's drainage ditch, which allowed water to empty out of the colonia. Activists urged other colonia residents to build drainage systems, specifically designed for their community, the way Spanish Palms did; but funding has lagged. The 2017 legislature cut several programs that benefit the colonias, and Governor Abbott vetoed another. Advocates for border counties fear that the area's serious infrastructure, educational, and medical needs will continue to be neglected.

In recent years, the flow of undocumented immigrants, combined with the continuing violence by drug gangs on the Mexican side of the border, has created great controversy. The national government has responsibility for border security, but Texas has supplemented the federal effort, spending over $2.4 billion from 2008 to 2019. By the end of 2018, Texas had over 1,000 Department of Public Safety (DPS) personnel and 1,100 national guard troops on the border. Sheriffs and police departments have received federal and state money to increase their own capabilities. Although violence in Mexico occasionally spills over the Rio Grande, the Texas side remains relatively safe. In spite of great growth in population (usually accompanied by higher crime rates), border cities have lower crime rates than Houston, San Antonio, and Austin. Anecdotal evidence suggests, however, that safety in some rural areas has significantly declined.[39]

The national government's decision to build a physical wall along major portions of the border has created problems. Walls divide communities, separate families, and cause environmental dislocation. Experts tend to believe that other measures would be more effective in impeding border crossing. Since the 2016 presidential campaign, completion of the border wall has been a major issue. Polls consistently indicate that the majority of border residents oppose completing the wall, as do Texans as a whole, although by smaller margins.

> ### ✓ 3.4 Learning Check
>
> 1. True or False: Local residents of each county can determine the structure of their own county government.
> 2. What is the major policymaking body in each Texas county?
>
> *Answers at the end of this chapter.*

✪ Special Districts

LO 3.5 Explain the functions of special districts and their importance to the greater community.

Among local governmental units, the least known and least understood are special district governments, yet they represent the fastest-growing form of government. They fall into two categories: school districts and noneducation special districts. Created by an act of the legislature or, in some cases, by local ordinance (for example, establishing a public housing authority), a **special district** usually has one function and serves a specific group of people in a particular geographic area. Districts can cover more than one county.

Public School Districts

Citizen concerns over public education cause local school systems to occupy center stage among special district governments. More than 1,100 Texas **independent school districts (ISDs)**, created by the legislature, are governed by popularly elected, nonsalaried boards of trustees. The school board selects the superintendent, who by law and practice makes most major decisions about the district's educational programs and who tends to influence other decisions as well. It is the superintendent who is responsible for leading the school district. Major functions of the superintendent include preparing a budget for approval by the board, day-to-day operations, and acting as chief communicator with legislators, media, parents, and others. Board members, generally made up of local businesspeople and professionals, tend to focus on money issues, such as taxes, budgets, salaries, and textbook selection. School board elections are generally low-turnout, friends-and-neighbors affairs. When these elections become heated, it is generally because of sharp divisions within the community over volatile cultural issues, such as sex education or prayer in the schools, racial and ethnic conflict, emphasis on athletic programs (especially football), or differences over taxing and spending decisions.

Texas has traditionally had a highly centralized educational system in which the Texas Education Agency placed significant limitations on local district decisions. Since 1995, however, school boards have been given increased local autonomy over some decisions. National influence has been far more limited and targeted than that of the state. Federal involvement has focused on improving the situation of groups historically neglected or discriminated against in Texas education. Districts must comply with federal regulations in areas such as racial and gender nondiscrimination and treatment of students with disabilities. Money is also a source of influence. In academic year 2016–2017, school districts raised an average of 51 percent of their revenue locally (primarily from property taxes); the state contributed 39 percent; and the federal government added 10 percent.[40] Federal aid has particularly targeted the children of the poor and language minorities. Thus, school districts make local educational policy in the context of substantial limits, mandates, and influences from the state and federal governments.

special district
A unit of local government that performs a particular service, such as providing schools, hospitals, or housing, for a particular geographic area.

independent school district (ISD)
Created by the legislature, an independent school district raises tax revenue to support its public schools. Voters within the district elect a board that hires a superintendent, determines salary schedules, selects textbooks, and sets the district's property tax rate.

This shared control of public education has been highlighted in recent years by increased state, and now federal, requirements for accountability testing of students. Districts have been forced to spend more time and money on preparing students for standardized tests. Supporters say that testing has improved student performance and made local schools more accountable. Critics charge that although students are now better at taking tests, they learn less in other areas.

A second challenge for local education is the increasing ethnic and economic diversity of Texas's schoolchildren. For two decades, traditional minorities have been a majority in Texas schools, and for a decade, a majority of Texas students have come from economically disadvantaged families. Meeting their needs is important not only for the children but for the economic health of the entire state.

A third challenge facing Texas education is school finance, which actually has two faces: equity (the quality or ideal of being just, fair, and impartial) and amount (how much should be spent). In 1987, a state district court (later affirmed by the Texas Supreme Court) held that the state's system for school finance violated the Texas Constitution. The basic problem was that poor districts, relying on property taxes, had to tax at a high rate to provide minimum expenditures per pupil. Wealthier districts, on the other hand, could spend much more with significantly lower tax rates. The issue continues today.

The other school finance issue is the conflict between the increased need for services and the slow growth of funding. Clearly, demands on the schools to do more (and therefore to spend more) have increased. Yet the two major sources of funding for school districts (state appropriations and the property tax) have expanded more slowly than demand. The proportion of education funding provided by the state has remained at 40 percent or below, and property tax revenue tends to grow slowly and to fluctuate. In the face of the Great Recession, the 2011 legislature (for the first time in 60 years) reduced the actual amount appropriated for schools. The results were more than 10,000 teacher and staff layoffs, larger classes, and cuts in such programs as arts, athletics, and field trips. Although most of this funding was restored by the 83rd Legislature in 2013 and the 84th Legislature in 2015, school enrollment had increased so that the available dollars per student was less.

The property tax is the only local source of tax revenue for Texas public schools. Unlike other local governments, school districts cannot use the sales tax for revenue. Not surprisingly, school districts receive more than 50 percent of property taxes collected in the state. State laws exempt part of a property's value from taxation for a number of groups, including those living in their own home (homestead exemption), those 65 or older, disabled veterans, and nonprofit organizations. In 2019, school districts were expected to lose $14 billion to exemptions, 31 percent of what they could have collected.[41]

In 2019, legislators increased school funding and sought to slow the growth of property taxes. They increased the state portion of school funding from 38 to 45 percent with $6.5 billion aimed in part to increase teacher salaries. Another $5.1 billion was to lower property taxes. Previously, the state attempted to limit school property tax increases by requiring voter approval of increases over 4 percent. From 2009 to 2018, however, voters approved the increase in 82 percent of the 434 school districts holding a "rollback election."[42] With new funding, it was hoped that school districts could lower tax rates an average of 21 cents per $100 valuation through 2021. Beginning that year, the state would limit school property taxes. While the increased funding was widely welcomed, many worried whether the increases would be sustained over time. For more detailed discussions of education policy and finance, see Chapter 11, "Finance and Fiscal Policy" and Chapter 12, "Public Policy and Administration."

Junior or Community College Districts

Another example of a special district is the **junior college or community college district**, which offers two-year academic programs beyond high school, as well as various technical and vocational programs. The latter two may be part of the regular degree and certificate programs or special nondegree training programs to meet local worker and employer needs. Each district is governed by an elected board that has the power to set property tax rates within limits established by the state legislature, issue bonds (subject to voter approval), and adopt an annual budget. There are 50 districts, and many have multiple campuses. For example, in 2018 Austin Community College (ACC) had 11 campuses (with a twelfth under construction) throughout Austin and the surrounding area. ACC's Hays Campus is in partnership with Texas State University, which allows students to pay community college tuition rates for the first two years of a bachelor's degree program, then transfer to Texas State. Students who are in their first year at ACC Hays are given an option to live in Texas State dormitories. In addition to the community college districts, the Texas State University System has three two-year colleges–all located in southeast Texas: Beaumont, Port Arthur, and Orange–and the Texas State Technical College System (TSTC) has ten campuses across the state. Unlike community colleges, neither the Texas State two-year schools nor the TSTC campuses receive financial support from local property taxes. Together, Texas's community colleges enroll more than 740,000 students, which is approximately equal to the enrollment of the state's public and private universities. (See Figure 3.5 for the locations of these districts.)

Community colleges, like state universities and technical colleges, are funded by state appropriations, student tuition and fees, and small amounts of federal aid and private donations. Where they differ from public universities is the support that community colleges receive from property taxes raised by the local district. Because of these funds, community colleges are able to charge lower tuition rates than four-year schools. As a result of the Great Recession, however, community college enrollment increased markedly, while revenues from local taxes and state appropriations slowed. In response, the two-year schools raised tuition, and some considered limiting enrollment. Tuition costs remain below that of universities. Community colleges reached their highest enrollments in 2011 and experienced a decline in enrollment through 2017, while the number of students attending the state's universities increased. In 2018, community college enrollment still exceeded that of public universities.

Research has consistently documented the positive influence of these schools on their local communities. Studies by both the state comptroller and the Texas

junior college or community college district
Establishes one or more two-year colleges that offer both academic and vocational programs.

Association of Community Colleges found that community colleges stimulate their local economies and are critical to a region's economic development. Community colleges are also positively associated with improvements in health and reductions in crime, welfare costs, and unemployment.[43]

Noneducation Special Districts

Texas has almost 2,300 **noneducation special districts** handling a multitude of problems—water supply, sewage, parks, housing, irrigation, and fire protection, to name a few. Among reasons that Texas has so many special districts, three stand out. First, many local needs—such as mass transit, hospitals, and flood protection—cut across the boundaries of cities and counties. Second, in

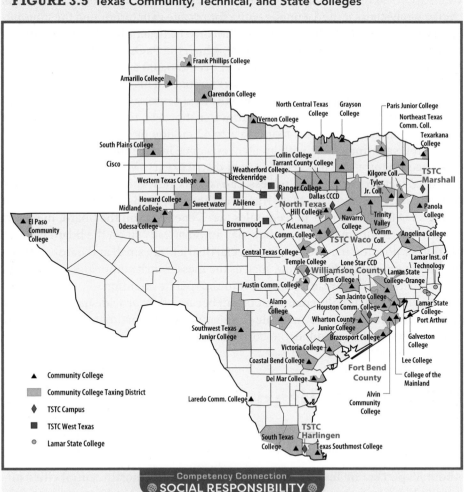

FIGURE 3.5 Texas Community, Technical, and State Colleges

- ▲ Community College
- ▢ Community College Taxing District
- ◆ TSTC Campus
- ■ TSTC West Texas
- ● Lamar State College

Competency Connection
◉ **SOCIAL RESPONSIBILITY** ◉

How will tuition increases affect student access to and success in higher education?

noneducation special districts
Special districts, other than school districts or community college districts, such as fire prevention or municipal utility districts, that are units of local government and may cover part of a county, a whole county, or areas in two or more counties.

other cases, restrictive state constitutional provisions or the unwillingness of local government leaders make it difficult for existing governments to take on new tasks. Finally, in some cases, individuals create special districts to make money for themselves. For example, real estate entrepreneurs in the Houston area have often developed subdivisions in unincorporated areas through the creation of municipal utility districts (MUDs). The developer is reimbursed for infrastructure (roads and water and sewage systems) construction costs with bond proceeds. Homeowner property taxes are used to repay bondholders. Therefore, the developer is reimbursed for initial investment costs and homeowners ultimately repay these amounts through, often, high property taxes.

Oilman T. Boone Pickens illustrates one way in which special districts can be manipulated for private gain. In 2007, Pickens created a public water district on eight acres outside of Amarillo. He sold the land to five employees. Two of them, the couple who managed his ranch (and the only residents of the eight acres), voted approval of the district. The water district met serious political and legal challenges because it used a public entity for private gain, promoted the unpopular taking of land for rights-of-way, and involved extraction of large amounts of water from the troubled Ogallala Aquifer, which the Panhandle's agriculture and cities depend upon. In 2011, Pickens sold over 200,000 acres of water rights for $103 million to a West Texas–based water supplier. This deal gave nearly half a million West Texans access to water into the next century. Water experts and legislators are increasingly concerned with water shortage, particularly because the state's population is projected to increase to 42 million by 2060, so private efforts to control water may meet with greater resistance in the future.[44]

The structure and powers of special districts vary. Most are governed by a board, collect property taxes and fees, can issue bonds, and spend money to provide one or more services. Mass transit authorities, such as Houston's Metro or Dallas's DART, rely on a 1 percent sales tax. Depending on the board, members may be elected or appointed, or they may automatically sit on the board because of another position they hold. Most special districts are small and hardly noticed by the general public. Only a few, such as the mass transit authorities in the state's largest metropolitan areas, receive continuing public attention.

Special districts will remain important because they provide many necessary services. Because they are invisible to most voters, unfortunately, they are the local government most subject to corruption and abuse of power.

✓ **3.5 Learning Check**

1. What are the two categories of special districts in Texas?
2. Why are special districts so important?

Answers at the end of this chapter.

✛ Metropolitan Areas

LO 3.6 Discuss the ways that local governments deal with metropolitan-wide and regional issues.

About 88 percent of Texans live in metropolitan areas, mostly central cities surrounded by growing suburbs. People living in a metropolitan area share many problems, such as traffic congestion, crime, pollution, and lack of access to health care. Yet having so many different governments makes effectively addressing problems affecting the whole area difficult. The situation is made worse by differences between central city residents and suburbanites. Most people who live in central cities need and use public facilities, such as bus and rail lines, parks, and public hospitals, whereas many suburban residents have less interest in public services, particularly public transportation. Class and ethnic differences also divide metropolitan communities, especially the central city from the suburbs.

One way to deal with area-wide problems is **metro government** (consolidation of local governments into one "umbrella" government for the entire metropolitan area). Examples include Miami–Dade County, Florida; Louisville–Jefferson County, Kentucky; and Nashville–Davidson County, Tennessee. In 2013, state Representative Lyle Larson (R-San Antonio) proposed two bills to allow San Antonio and Bexar County governments to consolidate. Bexar County Judge Nelson Wolff and two county commissioners supported consolidation, arguing it was cost effective. Former San Antonio Mayor Julián Castro opposed consolidation. His concerns were twofold: increased government spending and slowed emergency response times for city residents. Both bills died in committee. Larson filed similar proposals in 2015 and subsequently withdrew them from consideration. Instead of consolidation, Texans are likely to continue to rely on councils of governments and annexation.

Councils of Governments

Looking beyond city limits, county lines, and special district boundaries requires expertise from planners who think regionally. In the 1960s, the Texas legislature created the first of 24 regional planning bodies known as **councils of governments (COGs)** or, in some areas, planning/development commissions/councils (Figure 3.6).

COGs are voluntary associations of local governments. Staff employees perform regional planning activities and provide services requested by member governments or directed by federal and state mandates. Their expertise is particularly useful in implementing state and federally funded programs. Membership may be necessary or helpful in obtaining state or federal grants. COGs also provide a forum where local government leaders can share information with each other and coordinate their efforts.

Municipal Annexation

To assist cities grappling with suburban sprawl, the 1963 legislature gave Texas cities **extraterritorial jurisdiction (ETJ)**, or limited authority outside their city boundaries. Within its ETJ, a home-rule city could regulate aspects of development and make an area part of the city (**annex**) contiguous unincorporated areas without a vote by those who live there. (Incorporated areas could not be annexed without consent of their residents.) In fiscal year 2018, 51 cities annexed and one deannexed territory. How far out an ETJ goes (from one-half mile to five miles) increases with the city's population size, which gives central cities an advantage over the suburbs. Development regulation under ETJ raised mild controversy, but annexation produced major conflicts.

metro government
Consolidation of units of local government within an urban area under a single authority.

council of governments (COGs)
A regional planning body composed of governmental units (for example, cities, counties, special districts); functions include review and comment on proposals by local governments for obtaining state and federal grants.

extraterritorial jurisdiction (ETJ)
The limited authority a city has outside its boundaries. The larger the city's population size, the larger the reach of its ETJ.

annex
To make an outlying area part of a city. Now, this must be done by vote or petition of those to be annexed.

FIGURE 3.6 Texas Councils of Governments

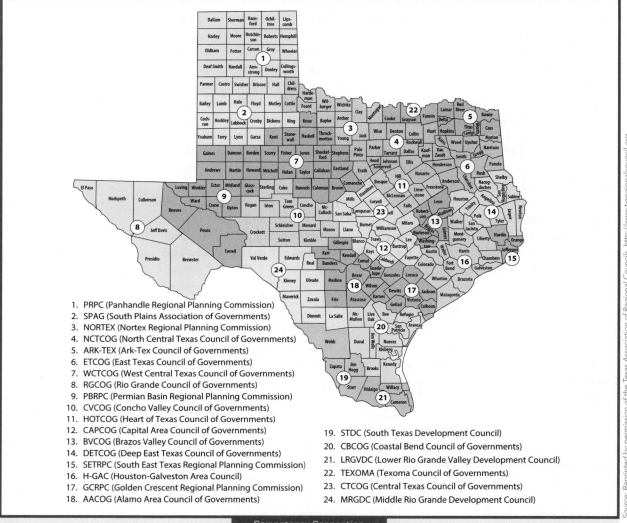

1. PRPC (Panhandle Regional Planning Commission)
2. SPAG (South Plains Association of Governments)
3. NORTEX (Nortex Regional Planning Commission)
4. NCTCOG (North Central Texas Council of Governments)
5. ARK-TEX (Ark-Tex Council of Governments)
6. ETCOG (East Texas Council of Governments)
7. WCTCOG (West Central Texas Council of Governments)
8. RGCOG (Rio Grande Council of Governments)
9. PBRPC (Permian Basin Regional Planning Commission)
10. CVCOG (Concho Valley Council of Governments)
11. HOTCOG (Heart of Texas Council of Governments)
12. CAPCOG (Capital Area Council of Governments)
13. BVCOG (Brazos Valley Council of Governments)
14. DETCOG (Deep East Texas Council of Governments)
15. SETRPC (South East Texas Regional Planning Commission)
16. H-GAC (Houston-Galveston Area Council)
17. GCRPC (Golden Crescent Regional Planning Commission)
18. AACOG (Alamo Area Council of Governments)
19. STDC (South Texas Development Council)
20. CBCOG (Coastal Bend Council of Governments)
21. LRGVDC (Lower Rio Grande Valley Development Council)
22. TEXOMA (Texoma Council of Governments)
23. CTCOG (Central Texas Council of Governments)
24. MRGDC (Middle Rio Grande Development Council)

Source: Reprinted by permission of the Texas Association of Regional Councils, http://www.txregionalcouncil.org.

— Competency Connection —
✿ **CRITICAL THINKING** ✿

Why does Texas have so many levels of government? Are COGs really necessary?

Texas cities, particularly central cities, strongly support ETJ. In most states, central cities are surrounded by incorporated suburbs and cannot expand. Because of ETJ, however, Texas's central cities tend to be much larger in physical size than cities in other states. By capturing part of the revenue growth of Texas's expanding metropolitan areas, they are also financially healthier than those in many other states. The approach to annexation varies. Houston tends to wait until areas develop and can provide tax revenue, whereas cities in the Dallas–Fort Worth area tend to annex undeveloped land and oversee its development. San Antonio has considered limited annexation in which residents of an annexed area would gain the right to vote for city council and be subject to city zoning ordinances but not be taxed or receive city services.

Attitudes of people living in a city's ETJ vary. Communities with few urban services (such as police, fire, and sewer) are often happy to be annexed. However, established communities generally object strenuously to being "gobbled up" without their permission. Examples from the Houston area include Clear Lake City, Kingwood, and The Woodlands (which avoided annexation by Houston or Conroe). The annexing city is required to provide the same level of service to annexed areas that it provides to the rest of the city, but some communities complain that they had better services before annexation.

After years of unsuccessful lobbying by suburban opponents to annexation, the 2017 and 2019 legislatures made unilateral annexation unlikely. In 2019, the legislature allowed annexation only under four circumstances: (1) on request of the landowner; (2) of an area with less than 200 people by petition; (3) of an area with over 200 residents by election; and (4) certain narrowly-defined situations (such as a city-owned airport or navigable stream). With the changes, annexation is likely only for communities wanting city services or undeveloped areas. The major cities worry about problems with regional planning and revenue. Opponents of annexation emphasize freedom, property rights, and maintaining their communities.[45] Likely losers are suburban poor and ethnic minority communities.

> ✔ **3.6 Learning Check**
>
> 1. What were the two primary ways that Texas dealt with problems in metropolitan areas?
> 2. Which groups want to be annexed? Which do not?
>
> *Answers at the end of this chapter.*

CONCLUSION

Local governments deliver a substantial number of government services directly to their residents. The success of these governments depends heavily on the actions and cooperation of other local governments and the two levels above them (state and national). What local governments do is largely shaped by three forces: formal rules (such as laws, the way governments are organized, and election rules), socioeconomic forces (such as economic power and ethnic/racial cooperation and conflict), and the efforts of individuals and groups. Texas has three kinds of local government (municipalities, counties, and special districts) with differences in structure and behavior both within each type and among types. Understanding the basic forces at work in local government helps those who want to make a difference apply the general principles of government organization and citizen participation to the issues affecting their own community.

CHAPTER SUMMARY

LO 3.1 Explain the relationships that exist between a local government and all other governments, including local, state, and national governments. Local governments are part of the federal system and thus are affected by decisions made by state, national, and other local governments. Under Texas law and its constitution, local governments are largely limited to what is required or permitted by the state. Although local governments provide the most direct contact between residents and their government, voter apathy at this level remains a problem. This situation is unfortunate because local governments are important to most Texans' day-to-day lives. Election rules for local governments and the way they are organized make a difference in who is elected and who benefits from government.

LO 3.2 Describe the forms of municipal government organization. Texas has two legal classifications of municipalities: general-law cities and home-rule cities. Large municipalities have home-rule charters that spell out the structures and powers of individual cities, whereas a smaller municipality is prescribed a charter by the legislature. Texas law allows four forms of municipal government: strong mayor-council, weak mayor-council, council-manager, and commission.

LO 3.3 Identify the rules and social issues that shape local government outcomes. Elections for cities and special districts are nonpartisan, and most are organized as either at-large or single-member districts. The increased use of single-member districts; greater pluralism; and the growing number, organization, and political activity of minority Texans are changing the face of local governments. Formal rules and socioeconomic change help shape the way government works, including who wins and who loses. City governments focus primarily on delivering basic services—police and fire protection, streets, water, sewer and sanitation, and often parks and recreation. They also regulate important aspects of our lives, such as construction and food service sanitation. The two major sources of revenue for cities are property taxes and the sales tax. Counties rely primarily on property taxes. Both cities and counties are having a difficult time as they face increasing demands for services from their citizens, the state, and the national government. As a result, local governments are utilizing fees and taking on debt because of limited revenue sources.

LO 3.4 Analyze the structure and responsibilities of counties. County governments have fragmented organizational structures and powers restricted by the Texas Constitution. Counties must provide an array of services, conduct elections, and enforce state laws. Actual governmental activities vary greatly between metropolitan and rural counties. Various county officials are policymakers, but the major policymaker is the commissioners court, composed of the county judge (who generally leads) and four elected commissioners.

LO 3.5 Explain the functions of special districts and their importance to the greater community. The many special district governments are separate legal entities providing services that include public schools, community colleges, and noneducation special districts for services like mass transit. Although they are important for the multitude of services they provide, many voters are unaware of this form of government. A lack of public awareness allows smaller and more obscure districts to be subject to fraud and manipulation.

LO 3.6 Discuss the ways that local governments deal with metropolitan-wide and regional issues. Dealing with metropolitan-wide problems is a difficult task. To do so, Texas relies heavily on councils of governments that are designed to increase cooperation. Annexation remains a controversial process and is now largely voluntary and much less likely to be used.

KEY TERMS

annex, p. 119
at-large election, p. 92
bond, p. 100
colonia, p. 112
commission form, p. 91
commissioners court, p. 106
constable, p. 108
council of governments (COGs),
    p. 119
council-manager form, p. 89
county, p. 103
county attorney, p. 107
county auditor, p. 109
county clerk, p. 109
county judge, p. 107
county sheriff, p. 108
county tax assessor-collector, p. 109
county treasurer, p. 109

cumulative voting, p. 93
Dillon's Rule, p. 82
district attorney, p. 107
district clerk, p. 108
extraterritorial jurisdiction (ETJ),
    p. 119
general-law city, p. 84
grassroots, p. 81
home-rule city, p. 84
independent school district (ISD),
    p. 114
initiative, p. 86
intergovernmental relations, p. 83
junior college or community college
    district, p. 116
justices of the peace, p. 108
metro government, p. 119
middle class, p. 89

municipal (city) government, p. 84
noneducation special districts, p. 117
nonpartisan election, p. 91
ordinance, p. 85
property tax, p. 99
recall, p. 85
redistricting, p. 92
referendum, p. 86
single-member district election, p. 92
special district, p. 114
statutory county court, p. 108
strong mayor-council form, p. 87
tax appraisal district, p. 109
tax increment reinvestment zone
    (TIRZ), p. 102
term limit, p. 94
weak mayor-council form, p. 87
working class, p. 91

LEARNING CHECK ANSWERS

✓ 3.1

1. Local governments have the greatest flexibility under the Cooley Doctrine. Under Dillon's Rule, which is followed closely in Texas, local governments can do only those activities permitted by the state.

2. The relations among the three levels of government and among the various local governments are marked by both cooperation and conflict.

✓ 3.2

1. The two legal classifications of cities in Texas are general-law and home-rule cities. A home-rule city has more flexibility because it establishes its own charter, which specifies its form and operation. A general-law city adopts a charter set in law by the Texas legislature.

2. The council-manager form of municipal government is most common in Texas's larger home-rule cities, although the strong mayor-council form is most common in the U.S.'s largest cities.

✓ 3.3

1. Single-member districts and cumulative voting are most likely to increase the representation of minorities in government. Redistricting may help or hurt, depending on how lines are drawn.

2. Most revenue of local governments comes from property taxes and sales taxes, but these two sources are frequently inadequate to meet the demands.

✓ 3.4 **1.** False. The structure of county governments is determined by the state constitution.

2. The major policymaking body in each Texas county is the commissioners court.

✓ 3.5 **1.** The two categories of special districts in Texas are school districts and non-education districts.

2. Many local needs cut across boundaries of cities and counties; and limitations in the state constitution and the unwillingness of some officials to act make it difficult to take on new tasks. Special districts can take on these responsibilities.

✓ 3.6 **1.** The two primary ways Texas dealt with problems in metropolitan areas were through councils of government and annexation, which is now weakened.

2. Unincorporated communities lacking services, such as police and sewers, often want to be annexed. Established communities with existing services generally oppose annexation.

4 Political Parties

Learning Objectives

4.1 Evaluate the role of political parties in Texas.

4.2 Compare and contrast the different political ideologies found in the Lone Star State.

4.3 Identify electoral trends in Texas, including realignments, third parties, and independent candidates.

4.4 Trace the evolution of political parties in Texas.

4.5 Describe the political party system in Texas.

IMAGE 4.1 Texas Senator Ted Cruz (R) joins President Trump at a bill signing ceremony.

NICHOLAS KAMM/AFP/Getty Images

Competency Connection
★ PERSONAL RESPONSIBILITY ★

Do we have a responsibility to identify with a political party, or is it more responsible to identify as an independent?

For the past two decades, the Republican Party has dominated Texas elections and politics. No Democratic candidate has been elected to a statewide office since 1998. In addition, every Republican presidential nominee has carried the Lone Star State since 1980. Political commentators often refer to red states as those in which the Republican Party is dominant and blue states as those in which the Democratic Party prevails. Although Texas is a red state, the percentage of the state's population that is Latino is growing, and Latinos tend to vote Democratic. Thus, Democrats believe that they have an opportunity to become competitive. This chapter examines the features of political parties in Texas, their evolution, recent electoral trends, voting coalitions, and changing demographics.

⬢ Role of Political Parties

LO 4.1   Evaluate the role of political parties in Texas.

Although neither the U.S. Constitution nor the Texas Constitution mentions political parties, these organizations are an integral part of the American governmental process. A **political party** can be defined as a combination of people and interests whose primary purpose is to gain control of government by winning elections. Whereas interest groups tend to focus on influencing governmental policies, political parties are chiefly concerned with the recruitment, nomination, and election of citizens to governmental office. (For a discussion of interest groups, see Chapter 7, "The Politics of Interest Groups.") In Texas, as throughout the United States, the Democratic and Republican parties are the two leading political parties. State election laws have contributed to the continuity of the two-party system. These laws make the process of getting on the ballot complex for third parties. They also require that the winner of the general election, held in November of even-numbered years to elect officeholders, is the candidate who receives the most votes (a plurality). Third-party candidates have little chance of winning an election by defeating the two major-party nominees.

Nations that have a multiparty system (more than two parties that win elections) typically have a proportional representation (PR) system. PR systems allocate seats to parties based on the percentage of the vote received by a party during the election. In a simplified system, a party that receives 12 percent of the vote in an election for instance, wins 12 percent of legislative seats. In the PR system, parties that receive a smaller percentage of the vote can still win seats, whereas a small percentage of the vote will not win any seats in our two-party plurality system.

⬢ Political Ideology

LO 4.2   Compare and contrast the different political ideologies found in the Lone Star State.

Today's politics in the Lone Star State reflect Texas's political history. Traditions, determined by centuries of political experience and culture, influence current attitudes

Follow *Practicing Texas Politics* on Twitter **@PracTexPol**

political party
An organization with the purpose of controlling government by recruiting, nominating, and electing candidates to public office. Those who share the same beliefs and values often identify with a specific political party.

✓ **4.1 Learning Check**

1. True or False: Political parties are specifically mentioned in the U.S. Constitution.
2. Which type of electoral system is likely to lead to a multiparty system?

Answers at the end of this chapter.

toward parties, candidates, and issues. Nevertheless, Texans' changing demands and expectations have led to political parties changing to reflect new expectations and issues. Political parties cannot remain static and survive, nor can politicians win elections unless they are in step with the opinions of a large percentage of voters.

Since the 1930s, the terms *liberal* and *conservative* have meant more to many Texas voters than have the actual names of political parties. Liberal and conservative are difficult to define because each label has varying shades of meaning for different people. Whereas the Republican Party tends to be dominated by right-wing social conservatives, the Democratic Party is influenced (but not dominated) by left-wing liberals. The origins of the terms *left* and *right* to refer to political affiliation can be traced back to the time of the French Revolution, when monarchists sat to the right side of the president in the French National Assembly and supporters of a republic sat to his left. Ideology, in contemporary American politics, is largely defined by the preferred role of government.

Conservatism

Conservatism today has a belief in a minimal role of government in regulating the economy and business. In addition, conservatism is typically associated with an emphasis on traditional social values. While conservatives generally advocate a minimal role for government on economic matters, they tend to favor a more active role for government on social issues. **Conservatives**, therefore, are generally opposed to government-managed or government-subsidized programs, such as assistance to poor families with dependent children, unemployment insurance, the Affordable Care Act ("Obamacare"), and environmental regulations. Nevertheless, conservatives support a more active role for government with regard to restriction of reproductive rights for women and opposition to same-sex marriage.[1]

Conservatives are divided between fiscal conservatives and social conservatives. Today's fiscal conservatives give the highest priority to reduced taxing and spending. Social conservatives (such as those associated with the Christian Coalition or Christian Citizens) stress the importance of family values, including opposition to abortion and homosexuality. They support school vouchers that would provide government-funded assistance to parents who choose to send their children to private schools, especially church-affiliated schools.[2] Teaching of creationism and intelligent design in public schools is also favored by social conservatives.[3]

In the 2014 Republican run-off primary for lieutenant governor, state Senator Dan Patrick (social conservative) easily defeated incumbent David Dewhurst (fiscal conservative) largely by drawing upon the support of social conservatives. Patrick received endorsements from the *Texas Conservative Review*, the Texas Coalition of Christian Candidates, and several prominent Tea Party-affiliated organizations.

Libertarianism

Those who believe in a minimal role for government in economic matters and social issues are known as **libertarians**. A libertarian would oppose a government-mandated minimum wage as an intrusion in economic matters and would also

conservative
A person who advocates minimal intervention by government in economic matters and who gives a high priority to reducing taxes and curbing public spending, while supporting a more active role for government in traditional social issues.

libertarian
A person who advocates minimal government intervention in both economic and social issues.

oppose laws making marijuana possession illegal because those laws are an unnecessary intrusion into private lives. Texas has a registered Libertarian Party and libertarians also comprise a faction in the Republican Party. Former Republican U.S. Congressman from Texas, Ron Paul, is associated with the libertarian wing of the Republican Party.

In 2009, some conservatives within the Republican Party formed the Tea Party movement. Taking their name from the Boston Tea Party, an event that led to the American Revolution, Tea Party activists have argued that the size and scope of government have grown out of control. Starting in the 2010 Republican Primary and in subsequent primaries, Tea Party-backed Republicans have defeated several mainstream Republican candidates, and helped elect Ted Cruz to the U.S. Senate. Tea Party-backed Republicans are noted for being more conservative than mainstream Republicans. This success has pushed the Republican Party in a more conservative direction and made the Tea Party a strong faction in the Texas Republican Party. Analyses of the Tea Party indicate it had a libertarian economic ideology, focused on such fiscal issues as government debt reduction, less spending, and tax cuts.[4]

Liberalism

Liberals favor an active role for government regulation in economic areas. They claim that government is obligated to aid the unemployed and to alleviate poverty (especially for the benefit of children). In addition, liberals favor government action to protect the environment and to guarantee equal rights for minorities, women, and LGBTQIA (lesbian, gay, bisexual, transgender, questioning, intersex, and allied) people. Liberalism seeks a limited role for government involvement with regard to other social issues, especially those related to morality or religion. Liberals are more likely to oppose prayer in public schools, government subsidies for religious institutions, and church involvement in secular politics. Many Texas Democrats have a **neoliberal** ideology. This position incorporates a philosophy of less government regulation of business and the economy while adopting a more liberal view of greater government involvement in social programs.[5]

✪ Electoral Trends

LO 4.3   Identify electoral trends in Texas, including realignments, third parties, and independent candidates.

During the past 40 years, competition between Texas's Democratic and Republican parties has brought more women, Latinos, and African Americans into the state's political system. As a result, party politics has become more competitive and tied to national trends. Compared with the politics of earlier years, Texas politics today is more partisan (party centered). However, both the Democratic and the Republican parties experience internal feuding (factionalism) among competing groups.

liberal
A person who advocates government support in social and economic matters and who favors political reforms that extend democracy, achieve a more equitable distribution of wealth, and protect individual freedoms and rights. Liberals tend to favor less government regulation in the private lives of individuals.

neoliberal
A political ideology that advocates less government regulation of business and supports governmental involvement in social programs.

✓ **4.2 Learning Check**

1. How do social conservatives and fiscal conservatives differ?
2. What role for government do liberals support with regard to intervention in the economy?

Answers at the end of this chapter.

Political scientists assert that the rising tide of Republican electoral victories throughout the 1990s and into the 21st century, in Texas and across the South, demonstrates that there was a regional **realignment** among white voters (Latinos and African Americans tend to remain Democratic Party supporters).[6] Realignments indicate that there has been a major change in the support of political parties. The change in Texas from a solidly Democratic state to a solidly Republican state is evidence of a regional realignment. A **dealignment** occurs when voters no longer identify with a political party.

Republican candidates carried Texas in 13 of the 17 presidential elections between 1952 and 2016, including all of the last 10 elections in that period. Republican candidates also won eight of 10 gubernatorial elections between 1978 and 2018. As Republican dominance of statewide elections increased, so did intraparty competition. Republican strongholds are in West Texas including the Panhandle–South Plains; some small towns and rural areas in East Texas; and the suburbs of Dallas, Fort Worth, Houston, San Antonio, and Austin. With the exception of Democratic El Paso, West Texas Republicanism is predominant from the Permian Basin (Midland–Odessa) through the Davis Mountains and the Hill Country. This West Texas region, like the Panhandle–South Plains area to the north, is populated primarily by conservative farmers and ranchers, as well as people connected with the oil and gas industry in Midland–Odessa and other parts of the Permian Basin.

Although the Democratic Party has been unsuccessful in statewide election contests in recent years, it still controls many county offices. Democratic voting strength is concentrated in El Paso, South Texas, the Golden Triangle (Beaumont, Port Arthur, and Orange), and portions of the diverse Central Texas region. In addition, the Democratic Party continues to receive support from Latinos and especially African Americans. Fewer Texans (primarily Anglos) choose to remain "yellow-dog Democrats." This term has been applied to people whose party loyalty is said to be so strong that they would vote for a yellow dog if it were a Democratic candidate for public office. **Straight-ticket voting** for all Democratic candidates in the urban counties (such as Harris and Dallas) led to an increase in Democratic victories. In response, a law was passed during the 2017 legislative session to eliminate straight-ticket voting after the 2018 general election.

Third Parties

Americans commonly apply the term **third party** (or minor party) to any political party other than the Democratic or Republican Party. Throughout the United States, third parties have never enjoyed the same success as the two principal parties. A major party's success is measured by its ability to win elections. By this measure, minor parties are unsuccessful. Instead, third parties' successes can be better measured by their ability to make the public aware of their issues, persuade the major parties to adopt those issues, or force the major parties to bring those issues into a coalition. When judged by these measures, third parties in Texas have enjoyed modest success. Lacking the financial resources of the two major parties to purchase expensive airtime on a television or radio station, third

realignment
Occurs when there is a major change in the support of political parties.

dealignment
Occurs when citizens have no allegiance to a political party and become independent voters.

straight-ticket voting
Voting for all the candidates of one party.

third party
A party other than the Democratic Party or the Republican Party. Sometimes called a "minor party" because of limited membership and voter support.

IMAGE 4.2 Libertarian Party of Texas Tweets

Libertarian Party TX
@LPTexas

➕ Follow

You are witnessing history, first the RNC, then the DNC in death throes. It's time to exit. #libertarian #LibertyNow #tlot

RETWEETS   LIKES
12   21

7:26 PM - 18 Jul 2016

↩   🔁 12   ♥ 21   •••

Source: Twitter

— Competency Connection —
◉ **SOCIAL RESPONSIBILITY** ◉

What are political issues that the major parties are not addressing that could provide an opening for a third party to increase its vote share?

parties and third-party candidates have often relied on social media (for example, Facebook or Twitter) to share their messages. The screenshot shown in Image 4.1 of the Libertarian Party of Texas's Twitter page is an example of a political tweet and the use of hashtags to generate attention for the party at little to no financial cost.

During the 1890s, the Populist Party successfully promoted agricultural issues and displaced the Republicans as the "second" party in Texas.[7] In the 1970s, La Raza Unida Party fielded and elected candidates to local offices in South Texas (principally Crystal City, Zavala County, and school board offices) and forced the Democratic Party to begin to address Mexican American (Latino) concerns.[8] Mexican Americans were, and continue to be, the largest Latino national origin group in Texas. The dominant conservative faction of the Democratic Party had not been particularly concerned with Mexican American issues. La Raza Unida took votes away from the Democrats in the early 1970s and pressed the Democratic party to become more moderate and address Mexican American concerns.

During the past 30 years, the Libertarian Party (a party that advocates minimizing government involvement at all levels while maximizing individual freedom and rights) has nominated candidates for national, state, and local offices throughout Texas. In 1988, the Libertarian Party nominated former Texas congressman and longtime advocate of limited government Ron Paul for president. When Paul ran for president in 2008 and 2012, he maintained his advocacy of limited government. In those two presidential campaigns, however, he did so as a candidate for the Republican nomination. For the 2016 general election, Libertarian Party Railroad Commission candidate Mark Miller received numerous newspaper endorsements.

The Green Party has advocated environmental protection and government reform policies. In 2000, Green Party presidential candidate Ralph Nader received 2.2 percent of the popular vote in Texas. Two years later, the Green Party fielded candidates for U.S. senator, governor, lieutenant governor, attorney general, comptroller, land commissioner, agriculture commissioner, railroad commissioner, and several statewide judgeships and congressional seats. However, Green candidates (like Libertarians) won no elections and rarely received more than 3 percent of the vote. In 2018, the Green Party did not have a gubernatorial candidate and the Libertarians chose Mark Tippets as their nominee. Tippets received 1.69 percent of the vote.

Independents

The term **independent** applies to candidates who have no party affiliation. Their success is less likely because they usually lack a ready-made campaign organization and fundraising abilities. In addition, they have difficulty in gaining ballot access. For instance, the Texas Election Code requires independent candidates to file by gathering signatures on a petition. The number of signatures required for a statewide office is "one percent of the total vote received by all candidates for governor in the most recent gubernatorial general election."[9] Based on this criterion, to qualify for statewide ballot access in 2016, an independent candidate was required to gather 49,798 signatures from registered voters who had not voted in either the Democratic or Republican primary elections or the primary runoff elections and who had not signed another candidate's petition for that office that year.

independent
A candidate who runs in a general election without party endorsement or selection.

🏛 HOW DO WE COMPARE...

Which Party Controls the Statehouses in 2019?

Most Populous U.S. States	Governor/Senate/House	U.S. States Bordering Texas	Governor/Senate/House
California	Democrat/Democrat/Democrat	Arkansas	Republican/Republican/Republican
Florida	Republican/Republican/Republican	Louisiana	Democrat/Republican/Republican
New York	Democrat/Democrat/Democrat	New Mexico	Democrat/Democrat/Democrat
Texas	**Republican/Republican/Republican**	Oklahoma	Republican/Republican/Republican

Source: http://www.ncsl.org/Portals/1/Documents/Elections/Legis_Control_112118_26973.pdf.

Competency Connection
⚙ CRITICAL THINKING ⚙

What criteria would you use to assess if it is better to have one party control a statehouse instead of having divided control?

In 1859, Sam Houston was elected governor of Texas as an independent candidate. No one has succeeded in winning the governorship without affiliation with one of the two major political parties since that election. In 2006, songwriter, author, and humorist Richard S. "Kinky" Friedman and former state comptroller Carole Keeton Rylander Strayhorn ran for governor as independents. Despite Friedman's celebrity and Strayhorn's previous electoral success on a statewide basis as a Republican, their election experience was the same as that of most independent candidates: they lost. Still, in the general election, Strayhorn received slightly more than 18 percent of the vote, and Friedman garnered a little more than 14 percent. Democratic gubernatorial candidate Chris Bell got 30 percent, and Governor Rick Perry, the Republican candidate, was reelected with a plurality of 39 percent.

★ An Overview of Texas Political History

LO 4.4   Trace the evolution of political parties in Texas.

How did the current political parties in Texas get to the point where they are today? Parties evolve over time in response to political issues. From the time political parties developed in Texas through the 1960s, the Lone Star State was dominated primarily by one political party: the Democratic Party. In the late 1970s and 1980s, Texas moved toward a competitive two-party structure. By 2002, however, the state had become a one-party state with the Republican Party in control and this remains the case today.

1840s to 1870s: The Origin of the Party System

Before Texas's admission into the Union in 1845, its political parties had not fully developed. Political factions during the years that Texas was an independent republic tended to coalesce around personalities. The two dominant factions were the pro-(Sam) Houston and the anti-Houston groups (Houston was opposed to secession). Even after the Lone Star State's admission into the Union, these two factions remained. By the 1850s, the pro-Houston faction began referring to itself as the Jackson Democrats (Unionists), whereas the anti-Houston faction called themselves the Calhoun Democrats (after South Carolina senator John C. Calhoun, a states' rights and proslavery advocate). In the course of the Civil War, after Texas seceded from the Union, Anglo Texans became firmly aligned with the Democratic Party and Republicans (party of Abraham Lincoln) were viewed as a disloyal minority and, in a few cases, were even shot or hanged.

During the period of Reconstruction (1865–1873) that followed the Civil War, the Republican Party controlled Texas politics. The Reconstruction Acts passed by the U.S. Congress purged all officeholders with a Confederate past.

Congress also disenfranchised all Southerners who had ever held a state or federal office before secession and who later supported the Confederacy. Republican governor Edmund J. Davis, a former Union army general, was elected in 1869 during this period of Radical Reconstruction. The Davis administration quickly became unpopular with Texas's Anglo majority. During his tenure in office, Davis took control of voter registration and appointed more than 8,000 public officials. From Texas Supreme Court justices to state police to city officials, Davis placed Republicans (including some African Americans) in office throughout the state. Opposed by former Confederates, Davis's administration was condemned by most Anglo Texans for corruption, graft, and high taxation.[10] After Davis's defeat for reelection in 1873 by a newly enfranchised electorate, Texas voters did not elect another Republican governor for more than 100 years.

1870s to 1970s: A One-Party Dominant System

From the end of Reconstruction until the 1970s, Texas and other former Confederate states had a one-party identity in which the Democratic Party was dominant. During those years (when a gubernatorial term in Texas was two years), Democratic candidates won 52 consecutive gubernatorial elections, and Democratic presidential nominees carried the state in all but three of the 25 presidential elections.

In the latter part of the 19th century, Democrats faced a greater challenge from the Populist Party than they did from Republicans. The Populist (or People's) Party formed in Texas as an agrarian-based party, winning local elections throughout the state. From 1892 to 1898, its gubernatorial nominees received more votes than did Republicans. Although its ideas remained influential in Texas (for example, protection of common people by government regulation of railroads and banks), the Populist Party became less important after 1898. In large measure, the Populist Party declined because the Democratic Party adopted Populist issues, such as government regulation of railroads and banks. The Department of Banking, for example, was established in 1905 by the state legislature to provide bank supervision.[11] Rural Texans continued to be active in politics, but most farmers and others who had been Populists shifted their support to Democratic candidates.[12]

In the early 20th century, the Democratic Party strengthened its control over state politics. Having adopted Populist issues, Democratic candidates faced no opposition from Populist candidates. During the next five decades, two factions emerged within the Democratic Party: conservatives and liberals. Fighting between these two factions was often as fierce as between two separate political parties. For example, conservative Democrats were considered probusiness and pushed for right-to-work laws (laws that weakened labor unions), whereas liberals were associated with New Deal policies (and the Roosevelt Administration), including support for organized labor.[13] By the late 1940s and early 1950s, Republican presidential candidates began enjoying greater support from the Texas electorate. With the backing of conservative Democratic governor Alan Shivers, Republican presidential nominee Dwight D. Eisenhower successfully carried Texas in 1952 and 1956. In addition, in 1961, Texas Republican John Tower, a political science professor at Midwestern State University in Wichita Falls, won election to the U.S. Senate. Tower won a special election to fill the vacancy created when Lyndon Johnson left the Senate to become vice president (later president) of the United States. Johnson was the Majority Leader in the U.S. Senate and a legendary, powerful, political leader. Tower was the first Republican to win statewide office in Texas since 1869, and he won successive elections until his retirement in 1984.

During the 1960s, Texas Latinos and African Americans became more active in Texas politics and began to have an impact on the Democratic Party. In particular, they had the potential to strengthen the liberal faction of the party. Viva Kennedy Clubs were created in Texas as Latinos (primarily Mexican Americans) worked to elect John Kennedy as President during his 1960 election campaign. The overwhelming Latino support (estimates of 85 percent) helped Kennedy win Texas and the presidency.[14] During the late 1960s and early 1970s, the La Raza Unida Party, as mentioned earlier, emerged in South Texas and won some local races, defeating Democratic candidates.[15]

1970s to 1990s: An Emerging Two-Party System

Mexican American (Latino) political activism continued into the 1970s and began to have an impact on the Democratic Party, in particular, the liberal faction of the party. In 1972, Ramsey Muñiz was nominated as La Raza Unida Party's (LRUP) gubernatorial candidate. Muñiz won 6 percent of the vote and denied the winner of the election, Democrat Dolph Briscoe, a majority of votes. Briscoe's election marked the first time in the 20th century that the winner of a gubernatorial election did not win a majority of votes. The final statewide general election contested by LRUP was in 1978.

The year 1978 was a watershed year for Republican success in Texas elections. When William P. ("Bill") Clements was elected governor of the Lone Star State in 1978, he became the first Republican to hold that office since Reconstruction. In the 1980s, Republican voters elected growing numbers of candidates to the U.S. Congress, the Texas legislature, and county courthouse offices. Moreover, Republican-elected officials began to dominate local politics in suburban areas around the state (Table 4.1).

During the 1980s, Latinos, African Americans, female candidates, and candidates from the liberal faction began to have more success in the Democratic Party and won several statewide elections. In 1986, Democrat Raul Gonzalez was elected to the Texas Supreme Court, becoming the first Latino (Mexican American) to win a statewide election in Texas. Democrat Dan Morales was elected as Attorney General in 1990 and reelected in 1994. Democrat Ann Richards became the second female elected governor in 1990, defeating Clayton Williams for an open seat. Democrat Morris Overstreet was elected to the Court of Criminal Appeals, becoming the first African American to win a statewide office. The conservative Democratic faction was in decline.

The Republican Party continued to make substantial gains throughout the 1990s. The Republican victory of U.S. senatorial candidate Kay Bailey Hutchison in 1993 signaled a series of "firsts" for the Texas Republican Party: the first woman to represent Texas in the U.S. Senate and the first representation of Texas by two Republican U.S. senators since Reconstruction.

The election of 1994 was a preview of future elections. This election was the last one in which any Democrat won a statewide office. Republican George W. Bush defeated Ann Richards, and Rick Perry was reelected agriculture commissioner. Democrats won only four executive offices: lieutenant governor, attorney general, comptroller of public accounts, and commissioner of the general land office. All other positions were won by Republicans.

2000 to 2016: Republican Dominance

The realignment of conservative Anglo Texans was completed in the early 2000s. Conservative Anglo Democrats switched their allegiance to the Republican Party. Texas has long been dominated by conservatives. Historically, conservative Democrats had been in a party with liberal Democrats. Now with the conservative Democrats gone, the Democratic Party became more liberal than it had been compared to the party of the 1960s and 1970s.[16] Today's Republican Party is dominated by conservatives, many of whom identify with the Tea Party movement.[17]

In the closest presidential election of modern times, former Texas Governor George W. Bush defeated Democratic nominee Al Gore by four electoral votes (271 to 267) in 2000, even though Gore won the national popular vote. After controversial recounts and protracted court battles over Florida's 25 electoral votes, Bush was ultimately declared the victor in mid-December 2000 after a 5–4 ruling by the U.S. Supreme Court. Bush's election made lieutenant governor Rick Perry governor. For the third straight election, all statewide Republican candidates won.

🗒 STUDENTS IN ACTION

Party Politics and the Impact on Our Lives

Justin Guajardo, born and raised in Corpus Christi, Texas, attended Texas A&M University–Corpus Christi, majoring in political science. His interest in politics can be traced to middle school, where he enjoyed the stories of great civic leaders, politicians, and generals. Learning about laws and the positive or negative impact that they could have on people's everyday lives captivated him, and he particularly enjoyed learning about Franklin Delano Roosevelt, the Great Depression, and the New Deal. Justin

started identifying as a Democrat as a teenager. For years, his grandfather had told him about voting and what the political parties stood for. He would always tell him, "The Democratic Party cares about the working people—the common man who is just trying to live life to its best."

Justin is attracted to the Democratic Party because he believes it stands for people—no matter their age, cognitive ability, sexual orientation, race, or income level. He believes the party cares about

(Continued)

doing the most good that is possible for people. As a whole, the ideals and policies of the party line up almost perfectly with what Justin believes in. Justin says the party is accepting of change as it occurs; it recognizes that it is an important part of life and the progress of a nation.

Taking Action

Justin's involvement in politics began when he applied to the Mexican American Legislative Leadership Foundation, a subsidiary of the Mexican American Legislative Caucus in the Texas Legislature, to work in a legislative office as a policy analyst. He was assigned to State Representative Marisa Marquez, a Democrat from El Paso. While working in the office, Justin got to experience policymaking firsthand—from fighting for funding for schools on the Appropriations Committee to introducing the first medical marijuana bill in the history of Texas. One experience in particular that left a lasting impression on Justin was working on a bill to expand the legal functions of Colonia Self-Help Centers and casework. The Colonia Self-Help Center bill was aimed at allowing Colonia Self-Help Centers to increase the services they offered to their constituencies to help them work their way out of poverty.

Currently, Justin is working for the American Federation of Teachers as an educational representative and organizer. The American Federation of Teachers, a teacher's union, advocates for fair wages, working conditions, and treatment. This

Justin Guajardo

federation also advocates for children in the community. Justin does not consider himself merely a labor organizer; he considers himself to be a social justice advocate who cares about the well-being of students who are sometimes ignored by their school districts.

In the future, Justin intends to attend graduate school and to continue being active in his community as well as championing social justice causes.

Competency Connection
☼ CRITICAL THINKING ☼

If you were an intern for a legislator like Justin was, what kind of bill would you like to work on that you think would most benefit your community?

In 2002, Democrats selected what was dubbed the "dream team" for the three highest statewide offices: Laredo businessman Tony Sanchez, Jr., a Latino, for governor; former Dallas mayor Ron Kirk, an African American, for U.S. senator; and former state comptroller John Sharp, an Anglo, for lieutenant governor. The expectation was that the multiracial Democratic ticket would encourage higher levels of voter participation by members of minority groups. Texas Democrats ran with a full slate of candidates for other statewide offices. On election night, however, the Republicans swept all statewide races. The 2002 election increased Republican control over the Texas Senate from a one-seat majority to a seven-seat majority (19 to 12). For the first time since Reconstruction, Republicans gained control of the Texas House of Representatives, winning 88 of 150 seats. The stage was set to elect a Republican speaker of the Texas House in the 78th regular legislative session in January 2003.

Because of redistricting efforts in 2003 that redrew districts to be more favorable to the election of Republicans, the Texas congressional delegation has been majority Republican since 2005. In addition to gaining a majority of Texas congressional seats in the 2004 general election, Republicans won all statewide elections, maintained control of the Texas Senate and the Texas House, and picked up approximately 200 more county- and district-level offices. Benefiting many of the Republican candidates was the fact that at the top of the ballot, President Bush carried the state with more than 61 percent of the popular vote, compared with Senator John Kerry's 38 percent. Bush's strong showing also benefited Republicans on the ballot running for other races down the ballot.

In the presidential election of 2008, Barack Obama became the second Democratic presidential candidate in history to be elected without winning Texas. Republican nominee John McCain carried the state with almost one million more popular votes than Obama (4,479,328 to 3,528,633). Although Obama did not win the state, Democrats could point to gains in several areas. The 2008 election marked the first presidential election in more than a quarter of a century in which the Democratic nominee carried at least four of the state's five most populous counties. One reason Obama fared so well in these counties was the support he received from Latino and African American voters. Democratic candidates also won a majority of countywide offices in Harris County for the first time in more than 20 years. In addition, for the third straight general election cycle, Democrats gained seats in the Texas House of Representatives.

In the 2010 Republican primary, incumbent Rick Perry's victory over U.S. Senator Kay Bailey Hutchison and Tea Party activist Debra Medina set up a general election showdown with popular three-term Houston mayor and former Texas Democratic Party chair Bill White. Many believed White to be the most viable Democratic gubernatorial nominee since Ann Richards in 1990. In the general election, however, White lost to Perry, receiving 42 percent of the vote to Perry's 55 percent.

In 2010, Republican candidates were once again elected to all statewide offices and gained additional seats in the Texas delegation to the U.S. House of Representatives. The Republican Party continued to maintain its majority in the Texas Senate (19 Republicans to 12 Democrats) and extended its majority in the Texas House of Representatives, winning 99 seats (to the Democrats' 51 seats). The Republican Party increased its membership in the Texas House of Representatives to 101 when two Democratic state representatives switched to the Republican Party after the November election.

In the presidential election of 2012, Barack Obama was reelected president without carrying the Lone Star State. Republican nominee Mitt Romney

TABLE 4.1 Number of Selected Republican Officeholders, 1974–2018

Year	U.S. Senate	Other Statewide Offices	U.S. House	Texas Senate	Texas House	S.B.O.E.*	Total
1974	1	0	2	3	16	—	22
1976	1	0	2	3	19	—	25
1978	1	1	4	4	22	—	32
1980	1	1	5	7	35	—	49
1982	1	0	5	5	36	—	47
1984	1	0	10	6	52	—	69
1986	1	1	10	6	56	—	74
1988	1	5	8	8	57	5	84
1990	1	6	8	8	57	5	85
1992	1	8	9	13	58	5	94
1994	2	13	11	14	61	8	109
1996	2	18	13	17	68	9	127
1998	2	27	13	16	72	9	137
2000	2	27	13	16	72	10	140
2002	2	27	15	19	88	10	161
2004	2	27	21	19	87	10	166**
2006	2	27	21	20	79	10	159***
2008	2	27	20	19	77	10	155***
2010	2	27	20	19	77	10	155***
2012	2	27	23	19	101	10	182***
2014	2	27	25	20	98	10	182***
2016	2	27	25	20	94	10	179***
2018	2	27	23	19	83	10	154***

*State Board of Education
**Data for 1974–2004 reprinted by permission of the Republican Party of Texas.
***Data for 2006–2018 were compiled by the authors.

— Competency Connection —
🔊 COMMUNICATION SKILLS 🔊

Looking at this data, when would you argue that Texas became a Republican state? Has Republican control of the state legislature peaked?

won Texas by 57 percent to Obama's 41 percent and received over 1.2 million votes more than the president (4,569,843 to 3,308,124). Although President Obama received fewer votes in 2012 than he had in 2008, he again carried four of the state's five most populous counties (Harris, Dallas, Bexar, and Travis)

(Figure 4.1). Following the 2012 general election, the Republican Party remained firmly in control of all three branches of state government.

In July 2013, Governor Rick Perry announced that he would not seek reelection in 2014. In December of that year, Texas Court of Criminal Appeals Judge Larry Meyers, a Republican member of that court since 1993, switched parties and filed as a Democrat in a special election for the Texas Supreme Court against Republican Justice Jeff Brown, who was appointed in 2013. Because Meyers was not required to resign from the Texas Court of Criminal Appeals to run unsuccessfully for the Texas Supreme Court, his switch gave Democrats their first incumbent statewide officeholder since 1998. Meyers's last term on the Court of

FIGURE 4.1 Texas Counties won by Hillary Clinton (in blue) and by Donald Trump (in red) in the 2016 Presidential Election

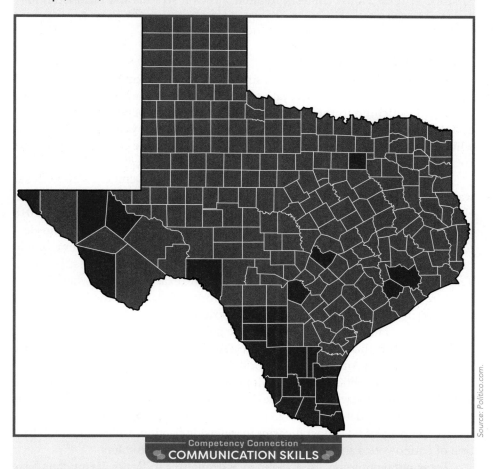

Source: Politico.com.

Competency Connection
COMMUNICATION SKILLS

Donald Trump continued the Republican winning streak in Texas presidential elections. Looking at the map, are there counties where Democrats may win in the future, or are Republicans likely to expand the counties they win?

Criminal Appeals expired at the end of December 2016, after he was defeated by Republican Mary Lou Keel in the November general election.

More than 4.7 million voters cast their ballots in the 2014 general election. This turnout represented approximately 35 percent of the 14 million registered voters at that time. Following the election, the Republican Party retained control of all three branches of government. Republican nominee Greg Abbott defeated Democratic nominee Wendy Davis by more than 950,000 votes (2,790,227 to 1,832,254). Abbott won 59 percent of the vote compared to Davis's 39 percent (the remaining 2 percent was split among the Libertarian Party, Green Party, and write-in candidates). Republicans held on to all 27 statewide offices (plus two U.S. Senate positions), with no candidate receiving less than 58 percent of the vote. Of the 36 U.S. congressional seats, Republicans won 25 positions and Democrats won 11. In legislative races, the Republican Party extended its margin of control in the Texas Senate by picking up a seat previously held by a Democrat and holding 20 out of 31 seats. In Texas House contests, Republicans won 98 seats and Democrats 52.

2016 and Beyond

What happened to the Democrats? A similar realignment pattern occurred across the southern states, with conservative white Democrats leaving the Democratic Party and switching to the Republican Party. The Democratic Party in Texas, and throughout the South, is the party supported by most voters who are liberal whites or members of historical minority groups. Thus, the changes in Texas are consistent with those that occurred in other southern states.

Results from the 2016 and 2018 elections have given Democrats hope. Texas was one of the few states that voted more Democratic in the 2016 presidential election compared to 2012. Beto O'Rourke gained national attention in his 2018 Senate race against Ted Cruz, losing by 2.5 percent. An analysis of the Latino electorate found that if voter mobilization efforts in Texas were effective, Texas would be as competitive as Florida in statewide contests.[18] A group named Battleground Texas aimed to register and mobilize voters to turn Texas into a state where Democrats are competitive.[19] Battleground Texas worked to support the Wendy Davis campaign in 2014. Results of Battleground Texas's efforts in 2014 were disappointing for Democrats as Wendy Davis lost the gubernatorial election by 20 percent. Analyses indicate that it they did not have a sufficient plan to register and mobilize Latino and African American voters or to reach persuadable white voters.[20]

According to political strategist Molly Beth Rogers, Democrats need to win at least 35 percent of the white vote to be competitive. Wendy Davis, 2014 Democratic gubernatorial candidate, received 25 percent of the white vote while Beto O'Rourke received 31 percent.[21] Democratic wins in statewide elections will require mobilization of Latino voters and an increase in support from white voters.

Texas public opinion survey evidence from 2017 indicates Democrats have a potential opportunity among younger Texans. Looking at the percentage of those who either identify as strong Democrats, not very strong Democrats, or leaning toward the Democrats (Figure 4.2) reveals that younger Texans are more likely to identify as Democrats than older Texans. This pattern endures when

FIGURE 4.2 Percent Identifying as Strong, Not Very Strong, and Lean Democrat by Age and Ethnicity

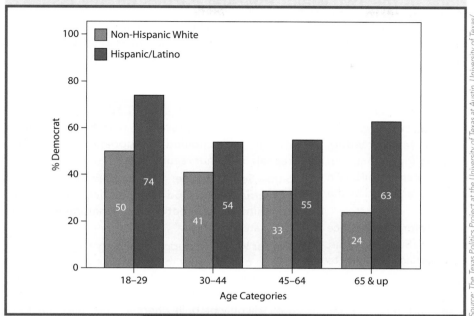

Source: The Texas Politics Project at the University of Texas at Austin. University of Texas/Texas Tribune Poll, February, June, and November 2017. https://texaspolitics.utexas.edu/polling-data-archive.

───── Competency Connection ─────
◉ **SOCIAL RESPONSIBILITY** ◉

Can you think of reasons why younger Texans are more likely to identify as Democrats? Are younger Texans likely to begin identifying as Republicans as they get older?

comparing Hispanics to non-Hispanic whites (survey uses the term Hispanic instead of Latino). Among 18–29-year-old whites, 50 percent identify as Democrats compared to 24 percent for whites 65 and older. A similar pattern emerges in the Hispanic population, except that the levels of identifying as a Democrat are much higher. As older Texans are replaced in the electorate by younger Texans, it is possible that the thresholds to be a competitive political party identified by Rogers may be met.

✚ Party Structure

LO 4.5 Describe the political party system in Texas.

American political parties exist on four levels: national, state, county, and precinct (the division of an area into smaller units within which voters cast their ballots at the same location). In part, these levels correspond to the organization of the U.S. federal system of government. Whereas a corporation is organized as

⊠ POINT/COUNTERPOINT

What Are the Positions of the Two Major Political Parties on Key Issues?

THE ISSUE The two major parties, as identified in their platforms, differ substantially on many social and economic issues. The following excerpts, taken from each party platform as adopted at their respective state conventions in 2016, illustrate several of these different points of view. The complete texts of the parties' platforms are available on their websites.

DEMOCRATIC PLATFORM

1. **Voting Rights Act:** "We support:…existing voter protection policies under the federal Voting Rights Act and the Texas Voting Rights Act, and restoration of the federal preclearance policies in the Voting Rights Act that were overturned by the U.S. Supreme Court."

2. **Same Sex Marriage:** "We therefore…denounce efforts to not comply with the U.S. Supreme Court decisions which guaranteed marriage equality to all couples."

3. **Border Wall:** "We therefore denounce efforts to build a border wall of any size and the unrealistic claims a foreign country will pay for a border wall."

4. **Campus Carry:** "We strongly support:…repealing campus carry policies for public university and community college campuses."

REPUBLICAN PLATFORM

1. **Voting Rights Act:** "We urge that the Voter Rights Act of 1965, codified and updated in 1973, be repealed and not reauthorized."

2. **Same Sex Marriage:** "We support the definition of marriage as a God-ordained, legal and moral commitment only between one natural man and one natural woman."

3. **Border Wall:** "We support building a high wall with a wide gate in order to prevent illicit border crossings without preventing legal border crossings as one part of a complete border security plan. The wall will only be built where it is deemed effective and cost-efficient."

4. **Campus Carry:** "We call for the elimination of all gun free zones."

Sources: 2016–2018 *Texas Democratic Party Platform*, https://docs.google.com/viewerng/viewer?url=http://texasdemocraticconvention .com/wp-content/uploads/2016/06/platform2016.pdf; *Republican Party of Texas*, 2016, http://3npv5lo075n4f1mrxbxvz8hv.wpengine .netdna-cdn.com/wp-content/uploads/2016/05/PERM-PLATFORM-as-Amended-by-Gen-Body-5.13.16.pdf.

Competency Connection
⋆ PERSONAL RESPONSIBILITY ⋆

We often hear that there is no difference between the Democrats and Republicans. After reading these platform excerpts, do you believe that statement is true? Why or why not?

---

stratarchy
A political system in which power is diffused among and within levels of party organization.

a hierarchy, with a chain of command that makes each level directly accountable to the level above it, a political party is organized as a **stratarchy**, in which power is diffused among and within levels of the party organization.[22] Each major party is loosely organized so that state and local party organizations are free to decide their positions on party and policy issues. State and local-level organizations operate within their own spheres of influence, separate from one another. Although these levels of the two major parties are encouraged to support national party policies, this effort is not always successful. As mandated by the Texas

Election Code, Texas's two major parties are alike in structure. Each has permanent and temporary organizational structures (Figure 4.1).

Temporary Party Organization

The **temporary party organization** consists of primaries and conventions. These events are temporary because they are not ongoing party activities. Through primaries, members of the major political parties participate in elections to select candidates for public office and local party officers. Primary election voting may involve a second, or runoff, primary. For a discussion of party primaries and runoff primaries, see Chapter 5, "Campaigns and Elections."

Conventions elect state-level and senate-district party officers and can be scheduled at precinct, county, state senatorial district, and state-levels. Each convention lasts a limited time, from less than an hour to one or two days. At the state level, conventions select party leaders chosen by delegates elected at the local level. Rules of the Texas Democratic and Republican parties mandate that party policy be determined at their conventions. These policy decisions are evidenced by resolutions, passed in both local and state conventions, and by party platforms adopted at the state conventions. A party's **platform** is a document that sets forth the party's position on current issues. In presidential election years, state-level conventions select delegates who attend a party's national convention. In addition, state delegates nominate a slate of electors to vote in the electoral college if their party's presidential candidate wins a plurality of the general election vote. At the national party convention, candidates are officially chosen to run for president and vice president of the United States. All Texas political conventions must be open to the media, according to state law.

Precinct Conventions **Precinct conventions** in Texas have traditionally occurred every even-numbered year on the first Tuesday in March, which is the day of the first primary. The state executive committees of each party establish rules governing the determination of the time and place for precinct conventions and whether the party will hold precinct conventions separate from county and senatorial district conventions. If a political party decides to conduct a separate precinct convention, this event serves as the lowest level of temporary political party organization. There, participants adopt resolutions and select delegates to a county (or district) convention. In recent years, only the Republican Party has chosen to conduct separate precinct conventions.

By state law, if a political party decides to conduct a precinct convention, any citizen who voted in the party primary or has completed an oath of affiliation with a political party is permitted to attend and participate in that party's precinct convention as a delegate (Figure 4.3). For the Republican Party, each county organization chooses the date and location of the precinct convention.[23] The main business of the Republican precinct convention is to elect delegates to the county or district convention (one for each 25 votes cast in the precinct for the most recent Republican gubernatorial nominee). Delegates to the Republican precinct convention are also allowed to submit and debate resolutions. These resolutions

temporary party organization
Primaries and conventions that function briefly to nominate candidates, pass resolutions, adopt a party platform, and select delegates to party conventions at higher levels.

platform
A document that sets forth a political party's position on public policy issues, such as income tax, school vouchers, or the environment.

precinct convention
A convention, held at the voting precinct level, to adopt resolutions and to select delegates and alternates to the party's county or senatorial district convention.

FIGURE 4.3 Texas Political Party Organization

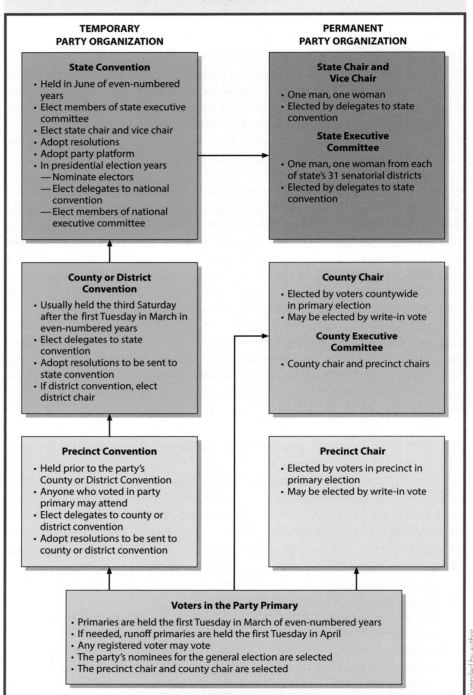

TEMPORARY PARTY ORGANIZATION

State Convention
- Held in June of even-numbered years
- Elect members of state executive committee
- Elect state chair and vice chair
- Adopt resolutions
- Adopt party platform
- In presidential election years
  — Nominate electors
  — Elect delegates to national convention
  — Elect members of national executive committee

County or District Convention
- Usually held the third Saturday after the first Tuesday in March in even-numbered years
- Elect delegates to state convention
- Adopt resolutions to be sent to state convention
- If district convention, elect district chair

Precinct Convention
- Held prior to the party's County or District Convention
- Anyone who voted in party primary may attend
- Elect delegates to county or district convention
- Adopt resolutions to be sent to county or district convention

PERMANENT PARTY ORGANIZATION

State Chair and Vice Chair
- One man, one woman
- Elected by delegates to state convention

State Executive Committee
- One man, one woman from each of state's 31 senatorial districts
- Elected by delegates to state convention

County Chair
- Elected by voters countywide in primary election
- May be elected by write-in vote

County Executive Committee
- County chair and precinct chairs

Precinct Chair
- Elected by voters in precinct in primary election
- May be elected by write-in vote

Voters in the Party Primary
- Primaries are held the first Tuesday in March of even-numbered years
- If needed, runoff primaries are held the first Tuesday in April
- Any registered voter may vote
- The party's nominees for the general election are selected
- The precinct chair and county chair are selected

Compiled by author.

— Competency Connection —
⚙ **SOCIAL RESPONSIBILITY** ⚙

Is participating in party politics an effective way to engage in local and state politics?

express the positions of precinct convention participants on any number of issues, ranging from immigration and abortion to the national debt. If adopted, a resolution will be submitted to a county or district convention for consideration.

Democratic Party precinct conventions are held the day of the county or senatorial district convention (for 2016, the date was March 19). The precinct convention is used to begin the process of selecting delegates to the state convention. Precincts with fewer voters are combined. Each precinct (or group of precincts) is allocated one state convention delegate and one alternate for each 175 votes for the Democratic gubernatorial candidate from the previous election (2014 election for 2016 precinct conventions).[24]

County and Senatorial District Conventions State law requires that **county conventions** and **senatorial district conventions** occur on the date selected by the party's state executive committee. These conventions are held after precinct conventions, and the main business of county and district conventions is to elect delegates to the state convention. Delegates attending a county or district convention also consider resolutions. These resolutions then go to the party's state convention for consideration.

Under the rules for each party, county and district conventions select delegates to their respective state conventions. Republicans may select one delegate to the state convention for every 300 votes cast in the county or district for the party's gubernatorial nominee in the most recent general election. Democrats may select one delegate to the state convention for every 175 votes cast in the county or district for the party's gubernatorial nominee in the most recent general election. In addition, in selecting delegates and alternates at all levels, rules of the Democratic Party require delegations to reasonably reflect the presidential preferences (in presidential years), to include young people and people with disabilities, and to reflect diversity in race, sex, gender identity, ethnicity, and sexual orientation.

State Conventions In accordance with the Texas Election Code, in even-numbered years, each political party must hold a biennial **state convention** to conduct party business. State conventions occur during a two-day period. Delegates conduct the following tasks:

- Certify to the secretary of state the names of party members nominated in the primaries for Texas elective offices (or by convention if no primary was held)[25]
- Write the rules that will govern the party
- Draft and adopt a party platform
- Adopt resolutions that express the official position of the party
- Select members of the party's state executive committee

In presidential election years, state convention delegates also perform the following three functions:

- Elect delegates to the national presidential nominating convention (the total number for Texas is calculated under national party rules)

county convention
A party meeting of delegates held in even-numbered years on a date and at a time and place prescribed by the party's state executive committee to adopt resolutions and to select delegates and alternates to the party's state convention.

senatorial district convention
Held in even-numbered years on a date and at a time and place prescribed by the party's state executive committee in counties that have more than one state senatorial district. Participants select delegates and alternates to the party's state convention.

state convention
Convenes every even-numbered year to make rules for a political party, adopt a party platform and resolutions, and select members of the state executive committee; in a presidential election year, it elects delegates to the national convention, names members to serve on the national committee, and elects potential electors to vote if the party's presidential candidate receives a plurality of the popular vote in the general election.

- Elect members from Texas to serve on the party's national committee
- Elect a slate of potential presidential electors to cast Texas's electoral votes if the party's ticket wins a plurality of the state's popular presidential vote

Texas casts 38 electoral votes. A state's electoral vote equals the number of its members in the U.S. Congress (two senators and, for Texas, 36 representatives apportioned according to the state's population based on the 2010 census). However, in accordance with Article II, Section 1 of the United States Constitution, "no Senator or Representative, or Person holding an Office of Trust or Profit under the United States, shall be appointed an Elector."

Both the Texas Democratic Party and Texas Republican Party used Facebook and Twitter to post minute-by-minute happenings at their respective state conventions in 2018. In addition, delegates to each party's convention used these forms of social media to communicate their experiences as they occurred.

IMAGE 4.3 Lillian Wang, Chair of the High School Democrats, tweeting about her participation at the Texas Democratic Convention.

Source: Twitter

— Competency Connection —
⚙ **CRITICAL THINKING** ⚙

How would politics in Texas be different if young adults were more active?

IMAGE 4.4 Texas Republican Party tweet thanking Senator Ted Cruz after his Texas Republican Party Convention speech.

Texas GOP ✓
@TexasGOP

+ Follow

Thank You, @tedcruz!!! We love you!

RETWEETS 410   LIKES 1,042

12:07 PM - 14 May 2016

↩   ⟳ 410   ♥ 1K   •••

Source: Twitter

— Competency Connection —
🗨 **COMMUNICATION SKILLS** 🗨

Are tweets more effective in mobilizing party supporters or in attracting new supporters to the party?

Selection of National Convention Delegates

Selection of delegates to a national party convention depends on the delegates' support of particular candidates for the party's presidential nomination. In a **presidential preference primary**, individual party members can vote directly for the presidential candidates of their choice. Delegates to the party's national convention are usually chosen according to the results of the primary vote. The respective national conventions nominate the parties' candidates for president and vice president.

In several states, such as Iowa, parties select delegates to a national convention in **caucuses**. Party members assemble in caucuses at the respective precinct, county, and state levels. Here, they choose national convention delegates who either are pledged to support a particular presidential candidate or are uncommitted.

presidential preference primary
A primary in which the voters indicate their preference for a person seeking nomination as the party's presidential candidate.

caucus
A meeting at which members of a political party assemble to select delegates and make other policy recommendations at the precinct, county, or state senatorial district, and state levels.

Democratic Selection Presidential candidates are awarded delegates to local and state conventions in proportion to the number of their supporters in attendance. National delegates are selected based on primary election results. These delegates are selected by state senatorial districts and on an at-large basis at the state convention. In recent years, Texas Democrats have combined the two delegate selection plans into a primary-caucus described as the "Texas Two-Step." Two-thirds of delegates were selected by primary election results and one-third were selected at caucuses held during precinct conventions. The Democratic National Committee adopted rules for 2016 that eliminated the Texas Two-Step for that year's presidential primaries.[26] In 2016, Texas sent 252 (out of a total of 4,764) delegates to the Democratic National Convention.[27] Almost 150 delegates were supporters of Hillary Clinton.

In addition, **superdelegates** (unpledged party and elected officials) are selected. Superdelegates are state party leaders and elected officials who are automatically seated at the party's national convention. Unlike other delegates to the national convention, they are not required to pledge their support for a particular candidate and may support any candidate for the party's presidential nomination.

Republican Selection The Republican Party selects national delegates proportionally from the results of the presidential preference primary for those

IMAGE 4.5 Governor Greg Abbott campaigning in 2018

— Competency Connection —
⬤ **COMMUNICATION SKILLS** ⬤

What kinds of communication skills are most effective in a political campaign?

Bloomberg/Getty Images

superdelegate
An unpledged party official or elected official who serves as a delegate to a party's national convention.

candidates who finish above 20 percent of the vote statewide. Three additional delegates are awarded in each Congressional district (there are 36 districts), and a candidate wins all three delegates if they clear 50 percent of the vote in the district. If no candidate exceeds 50 percent per district, the first place candidate receives two delegates and the second place finisher receives one.[28] Others are chosen on an at-large basis by the entire convention. A nominating committee selects all at-large delegates. State convention delegates approve all national delegates. In 2016, Texas sent 155 (out of a total of 2,472) delegates to the Republican National Convention.[29] Senator Ted Cruz won 104 delegates in the Texas Republican primary election and Donald J. Trump won 48.

Permanent Party Organization

Each major political party in the United States consists of thousands of virtually autonomous executive committees at the local, state, and national levels. These committees are given great latitude in their operating structures. For Democrats and Republicans alike, the executive committees across the nation are linked only nominally. At the highest level, each party has a national committee. In Texas, the precinct chairs, together with the county, district, and state executive committees, make up the permanent organization of the state parties. The role of the **permanent party organization** is to recruit candidates, devise strategies, raise funds, distribute candidate literature and information, register voters, and turn out voters on Election Day.

Precinct Chair In Texas, the basic party official is the **precinct chair**, who is elected to a two-year term by precinct voters in the party primaries. A party precinct chair's duties and responsibilities include registering and persuading voters within the precinct, distributing candidate literature and information, operating phone banks within the precinct on behalf of the party and its candidates, and getting people to the polls. A precinct chair is an unpaid party official who also arranges for the precinct convention (in the Republican Party) and serves on the county executive committee.

County and District Executive Committees A **county executive committee** comprises all the precinct chairs and the county chair, who are elected by county party members in the primaries. The county chair heads the party's countywide organization. County executive committees conduct primaries and arrange for county conventions. At the local level, the **county chair** is the key party official and serves as the party's chief strategist within that county. Duties of the county chair include recruiting local candidates for office, raising funds, establishing and staffing the party's campaign headquarters within the county, and serving as the local spokesperson for the party.

The **senatorial district executive committee** consists of precinct chairs who reside within the senatorial district. Senatorial district committees may be

permanent party organization
In Texas, the precinct chairs, county and senatorial district executive committees, and the state executive committee form the permanent organization of a political party.

precinct chair
The party official responsible for the interests and activities of a political party in a voting district.

county executive committee
Composed of a party's precinct chairs and the elected county chair.

county chair
Elected by county party members in the primaries, this key party official heads the county executive committee.

senatorial district executive committee
Composed of a party's precinct chairs who reside within a senatorial.

called upon to select a nominee for a vacancy in a districtwide office. Committee members also perform any other statutory or party responsibilities that may be required of them.

State Executive Committee For each major political party, the highest permanent party organization in the state is the **state executive committee**. As mandated by state law, an executive committee is composed of one man and one woman from each of the 31 state senatorial districts, plus a chair and a vice chair, one of whom must be a woman and the other a man. For both the Democratic and Republican Parties, a state executive committee with 64 members is elected at the party's state convention. At the same time, convention delegates choose the chair and vice chair at large. The party's state chair serves as its key strategist and chief spokesperson. In addition to the 64 statutory members of the party's state executive committee, party rules may allow "add-on" members. An add-on member may represent recognized statewide auxiliary organizations that have voting power within the party, such as women's groups (Texas Democratic Women, Texas Federation of Republican Women), racial groups (Texas Coalition of Black Democrats, Hispanic Caucus, Republican National Hispanic Assembly), House and Senate caucus chairs, youth groups (Texas Young Democrats, Texas College Republicans), and county chairs associations (Texas Democratic County Chairs Association and the Texas Republican County Chairmen's Association).

The party's state chair works with the party's state executive committee to recruit candidates for statewide and district offices, plan statewide strategies, and raise funds for the party at the state level. At its 2012 state convention, the Democratic Party chose the first Latino chair of a major political party in Texas when it selected Rio Grande Valley native and former court of appeals judge Gilberto Hinojosa as its state chair. Hinojosa was reelected state party chair in 2014 and 2018 at the Democratic state conventions in June of those years for four-year terms. The state executive committee of each party must also canvass (or count) statewide primary returns and certify the nomination of party candidates. It also conducts the state convention, promotes party unity and strength, maintains relations with the party's national committee, and raises some campaign money for party candidates (though most campaign funds are raised by the candidates themselves).

Political parties often place several nonbinding resolutions on the primary ballot for voters to decide upon. These proposals, identified as "ballot referenda" by Democrats and "propositions" by Republicans, are used to express party primary voters' opinions and have no legal effect. In 2016, the Texas Democratic Party placed six referenda on the Texas Democratic primary ballot.[30] A sample of them include:

- Voting Rights Act: Should the United States Congress pass the new Voting Rights Advancement Act to protect all American voters?

- Campus Carry: Should the Texas Legislature allow each public institution of higher education (not only private universities) to opt out of the ability to carry guns on campus?

state executive committee
Composed of a chair, vice chair, and two members from each senatorial district, this body is part of a party's permanent organization.

The 2016 Republican ballot had four propositions, including the following two:

- Texas should prohibit governmental entities from collecting dues for labor unions through deductions from public employee paychecks.

- Texas and its citizens should strongly assert 10th Amendment Rights guaranteed by the U.S. Constitution which states "The powers not delegated to the United States by the Constitution, nor prohibited by it to the States, are reserved to the States respectively, or to the people."[31]

All proposals were overwhelmingly approved by each party's primary voters.

> ✓ **4.5 Learning Check**
>
> 1. What role does a party's temporary organization have with the presidential nomination system?
> 2. True or False: A political party's state platform is approved at the state convention.
>
> *Answers at the end of this chapter.*

✪ KEEPING CURRENT

The Impact of the 2018 Election on Texas

The 2018 midterm election brought national attention to Texas as Beto O'Rourke mounted a strong challenge to incumbent Senator Ted Cruz. Cruz wound up winning reelection by 2.5 percent, a much narrower margin compared to past elections that saw Republicans winning by large margins. Several other statewide races all had close margins, though Governor Abbott easily defeated Democrat Lupe Valdez in the gubernatorial election. The Republican Party won all statewide elections and retained control of the state legislature. Democrats gained two seats in the Texas Senate, 12 seats in the Texas House, and two seats in the U.S. House. Republicans maintained their areas of strength throughout the state. Democrats continued to do best in South Texas, and the urban counties of El Paso, Bexar, Dallas, Travis, and Harris. Democrat O'Rourke also won in Nueces County and in reliably Republican Tarrant County. Democrats did particularly well in Harris County, winning control of the county government.

According to the 2018 election exit poll, 38 percent of Texas voters identified as Republicans and 34 percent as Democrats. Whites continued to be the most supportive of Republican candidates, while African Americans and Latinos remained supportive of Democrats.

The lingering question of when, or if, Texas will become a competitive two-party state remains under investigation. Donald Trump's nine-percentage point victory margin over Hillary Clinton was the smallest margin since Bill Clinton's five-point loss in 1996, and Democrats made gains in the 2018 midterms. Will 2020 be the year that Texas Democrats becomes competitive statewide, or will Republicans continue to dominate?

Sources: https://www.cnn.com/election/2018/exit-polls/texas/senate. "Is Texas finally turning blue? We looked at the electorate to find out," accessed January 31, 2019, https://www.washingtonpost.com/news/monkey-cage/wp/2018/12/18/are-texass-demographics-finally-turning-the-state-blue-we-looked-at-the-electorate-to-find-out/?noredirect=on&utm_term=.d13d704c4716

CONCLUSION

Historically, Texas politics has been characterized by prolonged periods of one-party domination—first the Democrats and later the Republicans. With changing demographic patterns, however, the nature of partisan politics in Texas and the struggle for control of public office by political parties continue to evolve. Shifts in voting alignments will change how both parties develop campaign strategies and target groups of voters.

CHAPTER SUMMARY

LO 4.1 Evaluate the role of political parties in Texas. Political parties are considered an integral part of the American governmental process and are defined as a combination of people and interests whose primary purpose is to gain control of government by winning elections. In Texas, and across the United States, the Democratic and Republican parties are the two leading parties, thus creating a two-party system. Nations that have two-party systems tend to have plurality electoral systems (the type used in the United States) while nations with multiparty systems typically have proportional representation systems.

LO 4.2 Compare and contrast the different political ideologies found in the Lone Star State. Texas voters and political parties represent various political ideologies, including conservatism and liberalism. Conservatives believe in a minimal role of government in regulating the economy and business, while emphasizing traditional social values and an active role for government on social issues. However, they are further divided between fiscal conservatives and social conservatives. Fiscal conservatives tend to give the highest priority to reduced taxing and spending. Social conservatives support greater government intervention in social issues (for example, laws against abortion and same-sex marriage) to support their family values. Liberals generally favor government regulation of the economy to achieve a more equitable distribution of wealth and favor a limited role for government in social issues. In Texas, many Democrats have a neoliberal ideology, which incorporates a philosophy of less government regulation of business and the economy while adopting a more liberal view of greater government involvement in social programs.

LO 4.3 Identify electoral trends in Texas, including realignments, third parties, and independent candidates. Beginning in the late 1970s, competition between Texas's Democratic and Republican parties has brought more women, Latinos, and African Americans into the state's political system. As a result, party politics has become increasingly competitive and tied to national trends. Compared with the politics of earlier years, Texas politics today is more partisan (party centered). However, both the Democratic and the Republican parties experience internal feuding (factionalism) among competing groups. Political scientists assert that the success of the Republican Party throughout the 1990s and into the 21st century demonstrates that many Texans who were previously Democrats have switched their political affiliation and loyalty to the Republican Party in a realignment of voters. A dealignment occurs when voters no longer identify with a political party. Minor (or third) parties and independents have never enjoyed the same success as the two principal parties. Their victories are generally limited to their ability to make the public aware of their issues or persuade the major parties to adopt those issues.

LO 4.4 Trace the evolution of political parties in Texas. Before Texas's admission into the Union in 1845, its political parties had not fully developed, and political factions tended to form around personalities. During the Civil War, as Texas seceded from the Union, politics became firmly aligned with the Democratic Party. However, during the period of Reconstruction (1865–1873) after the Civil War, the Republican Party controlled Texas politics. From the end of Reconstruction until the 1970s, Texas was dominated primarily by one political party: the Democratic Party. In the 1970s and 1980s, Texas moved toward a competitive two-party structure. By the 1990s and into the 21st century, the Lone Star State had seemingly become a one-party state with the Republican Party in control. As Texas voters become younger and more racially and ethnically diverse, the Democratic Party may become more competitive. Beto O'Rourke's 2018 Senate race and gains Democrats made in the legislature and U.S. House have raised the possibility that Texas could become a competitive state.

LO 4.5 Describe the party system in Texas. Political parties are organized as stratarchies in which power is diffused among and within levels of the party organization. The temporary party organization consists of primaries and conventions. Through primaries, members of the major political parties participate in elections to select candidates for public office and local party officers. Conventions elect state-level and senate-district party officers and are scheduled at precinct, county/state senatorial district, and state levels. At the state level, conventions also write party rules, adopt party platforms, and (in presidential election years) select delegates to national conventions and presidential electors.

KEY TERMS

caucus, p. 147
conservative, p. 127
county chair, p. 149
county convention, p. 145
county executive committee, p. 149
dealignment, p. 129
independent, p. 131
liberal, p. 128
libertarian, p. 127
neoliberal, p. 128

permanent party
    organization, p. 149
platform, p. 143
political party, p. 126
precinct chair, p. 149
precinct convention, p. 143
presidential preference primary,
    p. 147
realignment, p. 129
senatorial district convention, p. 145

senatorial district executive
    committee, p. 149
state convention, p. 145
state executive committee, p. 150
straight-ticket voting, p. 129
stratarchy, p. 142
superdelegate, p. 148
temporary party organization, p. 143
third party, p. 129

LEARNING CHECK ANSWERS

 4.1 **1.** False. Political parties are not mentioned in the U.S. Constitution, even though they are now considered essential in democracies.

2. Proportional electoral systems are more likely to lead to multiparty systems, whereas plurality systems are associated with two-party systems.

 4.2 **1.** Social conservatives emphasize traditional social issues like abortion and private school vouchers, while fiscal conservatives emphasize less government regulation of the economy, low taxes, and low government spending.

2. Liberals favor an active governmental intervention in the economy, such as minimum wage laws and environmental regulations.

 4.3 **1.** Conservative white Democrats realigned as Republicans during this era. This realignment occurred across the southern region of the United States and is referred to as a regional realignment.

2. The La Raza Unida Party affected the Democratic Party in the 1970s by making Democrats more responsive to Mexican American concerns.

4.4 1. False. The Democratic Party was uncompetitive in statewide elections throughout the 2000s.

2. In several urban counties, such as Harris and Bexar, strong support from African Americans and Latinos has led to Democratic Party victories in those counties.

4.5 1. The temporary party organization consists of primaries and conventions in which delegates for presidential candidates are selected.

2. True. A responsibility of a party's state convention is to approve the state party platform for the political party.

5 Campaigns and Elections

Learning Objectives

5.1 Analyze the components of a political campaign.

5.2 Describe the impact of Texas's changing demographics on politics.

5.3 Describe the evolving role of women in Texas politics.

5.4 Explain how the voting process promotes and inhibits voter participation.

5.5 Identify the differences among primary, general, and special elections.

IMAGE 5.1 Voters waiting in line to vote on Super Tuesday

Ron Jenkins/Getty Images

— Competency Connection —
⊛ **SOCIAL RESPONSIBILITY** ⊛

Voting is fundamental to democracy. How important is it, for the health of democracy, for eligible voters to participate in elections by voting?

The fundamental principle on which every representative democracy is based is citizen participation in the political process. Yet in Texas, even as the right to vote was extended to almost every citizen 18 years of age or older, voter turnout remains in the mid-40 percent range in presidential elections.[1] This chapter focuses on campaigns and the role that media and money play in our electoral system. Citizen participation through elections and the impact of that participation are additional subjects of our study.

✪ Political Campaigns

LO 5.1 Analyze the components of a political campaign.

Elections in Texas allow voters to decide whether state and local governments can borrow money by issuing bonds; make some public policy decisions; and choose officials to fill national, state, county, city, and special district offices. With so many electoral contests, citizens are frequently besieged by candidates seeking votes and asking for money to finance election campaigns. The democratic election process, however, gives Texans an opportunity to influence public policymaking by expressing preferences for candidates and issues when they vote.

Conducting Campaigns in the 21st Century

Campaigns are no longer limited to speeches by candidates on a courthouse lawn or from the rear platform of a campaign train. Today, prospective voters are more likely to be harried by a barrage of campaign publicity involving television and radio broadcasting, yard signs, bumper stickers, newspapers, and billboards. Moreover, voters may encounter door-to-door canvassers, receive political information in the U.S. mail, and be asked to answer telephone inquiries from professional pollsters or locally hired telephone bank callers. In recent years, the array of available social media tools has altered political campaigns in Texas and other states. Politicians set up Facebook and Instagram accounts, and some also have iPhone apps. Campaigns use Twitter to tweet about important events and decisions. To the dismay of some politicians, YouTube videos provide a permanent record of misstatements and misdeeds. Private and public lives of candidates remain open 24/7 for review and comment.

Despite increasing technological access to information about candidates and issues, a minority of Texans, and indeed other Americans, are actively concerned with politics. To many voters, character and political style have become more important than issues.

Importance of the Media Since the days of W. Lee "Pappy" O'Daniel, the media have played an important role in Texas politics. In the 1930s, O'Daniel gained fame as a radio host for Light Crust Flour and later his own Hillbilly Flour Company. On his weekly broadcast show, the slogan "Pass the biscuits, Pappy" made O'Daniel a household name throughout the state. In 1938, urged by his radio fans, O'Daniel ran for governor and attracted huge crowds. With a platform featuring the Ten Commandments and the Golden Rule, he won the election by a landslide.[2] In an attempt to duplicate O'Daniel's feat, Kinky Friedman (a singer, author, and humorist with a cult following) ran unsuccessfully as an **independent candidate** for governor in 2006, using TV appearances the way O'Daniel used the radio.

By the 1970s, television and radio ads had become a regular part of every gubernatorial and U.S. senatorial candidate's campaign budget. Radio became the medium of choice for many "middle-of-the-ballot" (statewide and regional candidates for offices other than governor or senator) and local candidates. The prohibitive cost of television time, with the exception of smaller media markets and local cable providers, forced the use of radio to communicate with large numbers of Texans. To visit every county personally during a primary campaign, a candidate would need to go into four counties per day, five days a week, from the filing deadline in January to the March primary (the usual month for party primaries). Such extensive travel would leave little time for speechmaking, fundraising, and other campaign activities. Although some candidates for statewide office, including 2018 Democratic senatorial candidate Beto O'Rourke, have traveled to each county in the state, none has won an election. Therefore, Texas campaigners must rely more heavily on television, radio, and social media exposure than do candidates in other states.

Most Texas voters learn about candidates through television commercials that range in length from 10 seconds for a **sound bite** (a brief statement of a candidate's campaign theme) to a full minute. Television advertisements allow candidates to structure their messages carefully and avoid the risk of a possible misstatement that might occur in a political debate. Therefore, the more money a candidate's campaign has, the less interest the candidate has in debating an opponent. Usually, the candidate who is the underdog (the one who is behind in the polls) wants to debate.

Candidates also rely increasingly on email and social media to communicate with voters. Email is inexpensive and easy to send; however, there is a risk of its being ignored or flagged as junk mail. Facebook, Instagram, Twitter, YouTube, and Snapchat are all used by candidates to reach voters. Campaigns should remain current when using social media, because different media attract different types of users. Candidates must be savvy and understand how to best use social media to reach potential supporters and mobilize their supporters to vote.

Issues with using social media include limited use and understanding of this type of media by the older (over 65) voting population. Additional complexities include access to smartphones and computers, hyperlinks to inappropriate websites, and "cybersquatting" (individuals other than the candidate's purchasing domain names similar to the candidate's name and then selling the domain name to the highest bidder). In Texas Senator Ted Cruz's quest for the Republican presidential nomination in 2016, his campaign did not own the domain name tedcruz.com. Instead, it was used by someone endorsing President Obama's immigration reform plan.[3]

independent candidate
A candidate who runs in a general election without party endorsement or selection.

sound bite
A brief statement intended to be easily quotable by the news media that is designed to convey a specific message that a campaign wishes to make.

Mudslide Campaigns Following gubernatorial candidate Ann Richards's victory over Jim Mattox in the Democratic runoff primary of April 1990, one journalist reported that Richards had "won by a mudslide." This expression suggests the reaction of many citizens who were disappointed, if not infuriated, by the candidates' generally low ethical level of campaigning and by their avoidance of critical public issues. Nevertheless, as character has become more important as a voting consideration, negative campaigning has become even more prominent.

IMAGE 5.2 Tweet from U.S. Senate Candidate Beto O'Rourke, Democrat, after visiting the Selena Statue in Corpus Christi during his 2018 campaign against Senator Ted Cruz, Republican. Senator Cruz won reelection in a race that drew national attention.

Source: Twitter, Inc.

Competency Connection
★ PERSONAL RESPONSIBILITY ★

While widely used in campaigns, social media has been criticized for the way false stories can be shared. Is it important for students to understand both positive and negative consequences of social media on politics?

The 2018 gubernatorial election also had its share of negative campaigning. Republican Governor Greg Abbott, in his reelection campaign against Democrat Lupe Valdez, former Dallas County sheriff, tweeted, "She can't even keep track of her gun," after reports surfaced that the pistol she was issued while sheriff could not be located. The Abbott campaign posted an online ad questioning Valdez's judgment and fitness to serve as governor if she was unable to keep track of her pistol. Valdez responded that she returned the pistol, but that it was misplaced during her transition out of office.

Already lagging behind Abbot in the polls, Valdez received days of negative coverage for the missing pistol. A few days after the report of the missing pistol, the office of the Dallas County Sheriff announced the pistol had been located in a property room. The pistol had been turned in but was not properly entered into inventory. The sheriff's office apologized for any hardship it had caused Valdez.[4]

Campaign Reform

Concern over the shortcomings of American election campaigns has given rise to organized efforts toward improvement at all levels of government. Reformers range from single citizens to members of the U.S. Congress and large lobby groups. Reform issues include eliminating negative campaigning, increasing free media access for candidates, and regulating campaign finance.

Eliminating Negative Campaigning More than 25 years ago, the Markle Commission on the Media and the Electorate concluded that candidates, the media, consultants, and the electorate were all blameworthy for the increase in negative campaigns. Candidates and consultants, wishing to win at any cost, employ negative advertising and make exaggerated claims. The media emphasize poll results and the horserace appearance of a contest, rather than basic issues and candidate personalities that relate to leadership potential. In addition, there is a concern that negative campaigns lower electoral participation by turning voters off to politics. Political science research on negative campaigning finds that some negative campaign messages that focus on irrelevant material, presented in an uncivil fashion, are the most likely to discourage voters. Negative messages addressing relevant topics, presented civilly, may lead to greater political participation.[5]

Increasing Free Media Access Certainly a candidate for statewide office in Texas cannot win without first communicating with a large percentage of the state's voting population. As noted previously, television is the most important, and the most expensive, communication tool. One group supporting media access reform is the Campaign Legal Center. Although initially they sought to increase requirements for broadcasters to make the air waves more available at no cost to political candidates, more recent efforts have focused on campaign finance reform and voting rights. As long as paid media advertising is a necessary part of political campaigns and media outlets generate a significant source of revenue from political campaigns, fundraising will remain important to electoral success.

By the early 21st century, many political campaigns used social networking resources to get their message out to a larger voter base at little or no cost using social media. Twitter, Facebook, and YouTube became commonly used tools for candidates to reach potential voters. In 2008, Barack Obama used cell phone text messaging as one means of announcing his vice presidential selection (U.S. Senator Joe Biden). That year, Obama also became the first presidential candidate to provide a free iPhone application (Obama '08). Users could get current updates about the campaign and network with other users. Relaying campaign information by phone also provided the Obama campaign with millions of cell phone numbers. These strategies have become common practice in campaigns. This shift, however, was not limited to presidential campaigns. Both the Republican and Democratic parties of Texas solicit email addresses and use Facebook and Twitter.

Nonetheless, there are drawbacks to social media. In 2018, most candidates for statewide office in Texas regularly used social media sites, such as Twitter, Facebook, Snapchat, Instagram, and YouTube, to reach potential voters and provide forums for comment and feedback. Because of the open nature of these media and the ability of the public to post comments, campaigns often set strict guidelines for posting comments on candidates' social media sites.

While social media is popular, candidates are also learning that past social media posts can be used against them. Opponents of Senator Ted Cruz's 2018 reelection posted a 2016 anti-Cruz tweet made by then-presidential candidate Donald Trump (when both were seeking nomination as the Republican presidential candidate) on a traveling billboard that made its way across Texas.

Campaign Finance

On more than one occasion, President Lyndon Johnson bluntly summarized the relationship between politics and finance: "Money makes the mare go." Although most political scientists would state this fact differently, it is obvious that candidates need money to pay the expenses of election campaigns. Unlike the federal government, however, Texas has few laws that limit political contributions. The laws that exist apply to some judicial races.

Texas's 2018 U.S. Senate campaign between Cruz and O'Rourke was the second most expensive campaign in the nation (after Florida), with a total of $138,562,773 spent on the election. Of that amount, $124,712,559 was spent by the candidates, and $13,850,214 was spent by outside groups supporting one of the candidates. Cruz's campaign raised $45,260,806 and O'Rourke's raised $78,979,726.[6]

Many Texans are qualified to hold public office, but relatively few can afford to pay their own campaign expenses (as 2014 lieutenant gubernatorial candidate David Dewhurst did). Others are unwilling to undertake fundraising drives designed to attract significant campaign contributions. Candidates need to raise large amounts of funds at local, state, and national levels. Successful Houston City Council candidates often require from $150,000 (for district races) to $300,000 (for at-large races), and mayoral candidates may need $2 million or more. In 2003, Houston businessman Bill White spent a record $8.6 million on his mayoral election, including $2.2 million of his own money. In 2015, in a seven-person race for mayor, candidates spent more than $13 million.

Some individuals and **political action committees (PACs**, which are organizations created to collect and distribute contributions to political campaigns) donate because they agree with a candidate's position on the issues. The motivations of others, however, may be questionable. Certainly, there is an appearance that money is influencing votes. However, it is very difficult to demonstrate that campaign contributions cause elected officials to vote in favor of the contributor. For example, the payday-loan industry has grown in Texas, and the state legislature has not updated laws to tighten regulations. Payday loans are high interest, high fee, short-term cash advances that individuals typically use to get money until the next paycheck. Individuals who take these out can find themselves

political action committee (PAC)
An organization created to collect and distribute contributions to political campaigns.

paying very high interest and fees as they attempt to pay off the loan. The Federal Trade Commission warns consumers about the risks of payday loans.[7] In 2014, the payday-loan industry donated $2.5 million to Texas legislative candidates. Did the money cause the legislature to not pass laws to regulate the payday-loan industry, or was the payday-loan industry helping to elect lawmakers that support free markets?[8]

Both federal and state laws have been enacted to regulate various aspects of campaign financing. Texas laws on the subject, however, are relatively weak and tend to emphasize reporting of contributions with few limits on the amounts of the donations. Federal laws, most prominently the Federal Election Campaign Act, are more restrictive, featuring both reporting requirements and limits on contributions to a candidate's political campaign by individuals and PACs.

In 1989, chicken magnate Lonnie "Bo" Pilgrim handed out $10,000 checks on the Texas Senate floor, leaving the "payable to" lines blank, as legislators debated reforming the state's workers' compensation laws. Many were surprised to find that Texas had no laws at that time prohibiting such an action. Two years later, the Texas legislature passed laws prohibiting political contributions to members of the legislature while they are in session; and in 1993, Texas voters approved a constitutional amendment establishing the **Texas Ethics Commission**.

Administration and enforcement of the Texas Election Code as it relates to campaign fundraising, expenditures, advertising, and ethics of government officials and state employees are responsibilities of the Texas Ethics Commission. Some key responsibilities include collecting and maintaining political fundraising and spending activity reports. Lobbyists are required to file reports of their activities (see Chapter 7, "The Politics of Interest Groups," for more information about lobbyists). State officials, including elected and appointed officials and the executive heads of state agencies, also file personal financial disclosure reports with the Commission. The power of the Commission is its authority to levy fines for violations, such as a candidate's failure to report campaign fundraising donations.[9]

Further restricting the amount of money that can be contributed to campaigns is another area of possible reform. However, success in this area has been fairly limited. In 2002, the U.S. Congress passed the long-awaited **Campaign Reform Act**, signed into law by President George W. Bush. This federal law prohibited **soft money** (money used to fund election activities that is not directly donated to a political campaign); increased the limits on individual **hard money** (or direct) contributions; and restricted corporations' and labor unions' ability to run "electioneering" ads that feature the names or likenesses of candidates close to Election Day.[10]

Plaintiffs, including former Texas Congressman Ron Paul (R-Lake Jackson) and others, challenged the constitutionality of this act. They claimed it was an unconstitutional restraint on freedom of speech. In a sharply divided decision, the U.S. Supreme Court upheld the constitutionality of the soft money ban in *McConnell v. FEC*, 540 U.S. 93 (2003). Seven years later, however, in a 5–4 decision, the U.S. Supreme Court in *Citizens United v. Federal Election Commission*, 558 U.S. 50 (2010), overturned a provision of the act that banned

Texas Ethics Commission
A state agency that enforces state standards for lobbyists and public officials, including registration of lobbyists and reporting of political campaign contributions.

Campaign Reform Act
Enacted by the U.S. Congress and signed by President George W. Bush in 2002, this law restricts donations of soft money and hard money for election campaigns, but its effect has been limited by federal court decisions.

soft money
Unregulated political donations made to national political parties or independent expenditures on behalf of a candidate that is used to fund election activities but are not directly donated to a political campaign.

hard money
Campaign money donated directly to candidates or political parties and restricted in amount by federal law.

unlimited **independent expenditures** made by corporations, unions, and nonprofit organizations in federal elections. This decision was widely criticized by Democrats and by some members of the Republican Party as judicial activism that would give corporations and unions unlimited power in federal elections.

That same year, a nine-judge federal appeals court unanimously ruled in *SpeechNow.org v. Federal Election Commission*, 599 F. 3rd 686 (2010) that campaign contribution limits on independent organizations using the funds only for independent expenditures are unconstitutional. The U.S. Supreme Court refused to hear this case on appeal, letting the lower court's decision stand. Decisions in these cases led to creation of **super PACs**, which are independent expenditure-only committees that may raise unlimited sums of money from corporations, unions, nonprofit organizations, and individuals. Super PACs are then able to spend unlimited sums to openly support or oppose political candidates. By February 2019, a total of 2,395 super PACs reported having spent more than $808 million on the 2018 election cycle.[11]

Although the *Citizens United* decision removed limits on how much money can be given to or spent by outside groups on behalf of federal candidates, it did not address limits on campaign contributions to candidates or committees by individual donors. In another sharply divided decision, the U.S. Supreme Court in *McCutcheon v. Federal Election Commission*, 572 U.S. ___ (2014) struck down the aggregate limits on the amount an individual may contribute during a two-year period to all federal candidates, parties, and political action committees combined. By a vote of 5-4, the Court ruled that the aggregate limit an individual could donate to candidates for federal office, political parties, and political action committees per election in an election cycle was unconstitutional under the First Amendment. The amount that can be donated to a specific candidate, political party, or PAC is limited, however. As with the *Citizens United* decision, several groups criticized this ruling as a further erosion of protections against undue influence in elections by a small portion of the electorate.

As noted above, the Lone Star State places few limitations on the amount of money contributors may donate to a candidate's political campaign. Texas's state campaign finance laws have focused on making contributor information more easily available to citizens. Restrictions on the amount of donations apply only to some judicial candidates. Individual contributions to judicial candidates are limited to $5,000 for candidates for the Supreme Court of Texas and the Texas Court of Criminal Appeals. This limitation applies to courts of appeals, district courts, and county courts if the population of the judicial district is more than one million. The limit is $2,500 for candidates if the population of the judicial district is from 250,000 to one million and $1,000 for candidates if the population of the judicial district is less than 250,000.[12] Treasurers of campaign committees and candidates are required to file periodically with the Texas Ethics Commission. With limited exceptions, these reports must be filed electronically. Sworn statements list all contributions received and expenditures made during designated reporting intervals. Candidates who fail to file these reports are subject to a fine.

In 2003, the Texas legislature passed a law requiring officials of cities with a population of more than 100,000 and trustees of school districts with enrollments

independent expenditures
Expenditures that pay for political campaign communications and expressly advocate the nomination, election, or defeat of a clearly identified candidate but are not given to, or made at the request of, the candidate's campaign.

super PAC
Independent expenditure–only committees that may raise unlimited sums of money from corporations, unions, nonprofit organizations, and individuals.

of 5,000 or more to disclose the sources of their income, as well as the value of their stocks and their real estate holdings. In addition, candidates for state political offices must identify the employers and the occupations of donors contributing $500 or more to their campaigns. Furthermore, they are required to publicly report cash on hand.[13] The law also prohibits state legislators from lobbying for clients before state agencies.

Recent court decisions and loopholes in disclosure laws have opened the door for **dark money**. This is political spending by nonprofit groups, with the money coming from anonymous sources because the nonprofits do not need to disclose the sources of their contributions. These groups claim to be social-welfare organizations, and their contributions go toward independent expenditures instead of candidates.[14] In 2013, then-Governor Rick Perry vetoed a bill that would have required nonprofit organizations spending $25,000 or more on political campaigns to publicly disclose contributors who donate more than $1,000. The Texas Ethics Commission adopted a rule in 2015 to require some disclosure of dark money contributors if they spend money on advertising within 30 days of an election.[15] Opponents of the disclosure have filed lawsuits in an attempt to defeat the regulation. In March of 2016, a U.S. District Judge dismissed a lawsuit that challenged the dark money rule as unconstitutional. Additional lawsuits against the rule are pending.[16]

Federal and state campaign finance laws have largely failed to regulate transfers of large amounts of money from donors to political campaigns in the form of campaign contributions. Rulings from the U.S. Supreme Court, equating campaign contributions and spending with free speech, have hindered legislation that the court will consider constitutional. In addition, donors wishing to make large contributions find legal means to evade the intent of existing laws.

dark money
Political spending by nonprofit groups, with the money coming from anonymous sources because the nonprofits do not need to disclose the sources of their contributions

✓ **5.1 Learning Check**

1. Why is Texas considered a media state for political campaigns (especially for statewide office)?

2. True or False: Texas has strict limits on how much individuals can donate to candidates for statewide office.

Answers at the end of this chapter.

✪ Racial and Ethnic Politics

LO 5.2 Describe the impact of Texas's changing demographics on politics.

Racial and ethnic factors strongly influence Texas politics and shape political campaigns. Fifty-six percent of Texas's total population is composed of Latinos (chiefly Mexican Americans), African Americans, and Asian Americans, making Texas a majority-minority state. Numerically, the state's historical ethnic and racial minorities wield enough voting strength to decide any statewide election and determine the outcomes of local contests in areas where their numbers are concentrated. African American and Latino voters are more likely to participate in Democratic primaries and vote for Democratic candidates in general elections.

Latinos

Early in the 21st century, candidates for elective office in Texas, and most other parts of the United States, recognized the potential of the Latino vote. Chapter 4, "Political Parties," has information about how the Kennedy campaign in 1960 mobilized Mexican American voters via Viva Kennedy Clubs and in the 1970s how the emergence of La Raza Unida Party also compelled Democrats to pay more attention to Latinos. Most Anglo candidates now use Spanish phrases in their speeches, advertise in Spanish-language media (television, radio, and newspapers), and voice their concern for issues important to the Latino community. During presidential elections, candidates from both major political parties included appearances in Latino communities and before national Latino organizations, such as the League of United Latin American Citizens (LULAC) and the National Council of La Raza, as a part of their campaign strategy. Such appearances recognize the political clout of Latinos in the Republican and Democratic presidential primaries, as well as in the general election.

Although Latinos played an important role in South Texas politics throughout the 20th century, not until the 1960s and early 1970s did they begin to have a major political impact at the state level. In the 1980s, Latino election strategy became more sophisticated as a new generation of Latinos sought public office and assumed leadership roles in political organizations.

Communities and counties with larger Latino populations, and electoral districts with majority Latino populations, are more likely to vote for Democrats. The Democratic Party argues that because the majority of Latinos are more likely to support Democratic candidates, increasing Latino voter turnout will elect more Democrats to office. Registering and turning out voters among the increasing Latino population is a focus for Democratic strategists who hope to turn Texas into a competitive state for Democrats again.

In 2002, Laredo businessman Tony Sanchez, Jr. became the first Latino candidate nominated for governor by a major party in Texas. Challenged for the Democratic nomination by former Texas attorney general Dan Morales, on March 1, 2002, the two men held the first Spanish-language gubernatorial campaign debate in U.S. history. Underscoring its strategy to attract more Latino voters, in 2012 the Democratic Party selected the first Latino state chair of a major political party in Texas when it chose Gilberto Hinojosa for that position. In 2018, Democrats Sylvia Garcia of Houston and Veronica Escobar of El Paso became the first Latinas elected to the U.S. House from Texas, while Lupe Valdez became the first Latina candidate for governor after winning the Democratic nomination.

By early 2019, a substantial number of Latinos held elected office, including the following:

- Two statewide positions (commissioner of the general land office and one supreme court justice)
- One U.S. senator
- Seven U.S. representative seats in Texas's congressional delegation
- Forty-four legislative seats in the Texas legislature
- More than 2,200 of the remaining elected positions in the state

With a growing, and Democratic-leaning, Latino population, why are Texas Democrats unsuccessful in statewide elections? Republicans have had success, yet this success has come despite growth of the Latino voting age population. Analysis of the 2016 election indicates that 77 percent of Texas Latinos supported Clinton and 18 percent supported Trump.[17] In the 2018 Senate race,

74 percent of Latinos indicated support for O'Rourke compared to 24 percent for Cruz.[18] Thus, Latinos are favoring Democratic candidates. From 2012 to 2016, Latino turnout increased by 30 percent while the population increased by 15 percent, indicating that the increase in Latino turnout is outpacing the increase in population growth.[19]

An analysis of the Texas electorate indicates that the long-awaited impact of Latinos (and African Americans, Asian Americans, and other people of color) may finally be emerging. Whites are disproportionately among the older population in Texas while Latinos comprise the largest percentage of younger Texan adults. Older whites have been the strongest supporters of Republican candidates. In each election, older whites become a smaller percentage of the electorate. As the Latino population continues to grow (and remains Democratic), this may be leading to an electorate that is more supportive of Democratic candidates. O'Rourke's strong showing, and Clinton's stronger showing than Obama in 2012, may be an indication of the changes coming to Texas.[20]

Senator Ted Cruz, Land Commissioner George P. Bush, and Supreme Court Justice Eva Guzman are statewide elected Republicans. There are two Latino Republican is in the state legislature. In 2012, the Republican National Committee launched the Growth and Opportunity Project, with a list of recommendations and strategies designed to expand the base of the party and win more elections. Among recommendations, this report encouraged the Republican Party to focus messaging, strategy, outreach, and budget efforts to gain new supporters and voters in the Latino community (as well as in other racial/demographic communities, including Pacific Islanders, African Americans, Asian Americans, Native Americans, women, and youth). Political observers have noted that the outreach envisioned in the project was not implemented by the Republican Party in the 2016 election.[21]

Nonetheless, the Republican Party has also pursued policies that are popular with many conservatives, such as legislation to repeal in-state tuition for undocumented immigrants at state institutions of higher education. The Republican Party thus has a number of activists and elected officials who wish to take a hard line on immigration-related legislation, such as President Trump's proposed border wall. However, anti-immigrant proposals carry the risk of alienating many in the Latino community and costing Republicans the support of Latinos.[22] Hispanic Republicans have noted that the proposals attacking the citizenship of Hispanics are perceived as anti-Hispanic and put support for the Republican Party at risk.[23]

The sheer size of the Latino population causes politicians to solicit their support because Latino voters can represent the margin of victory for a successful candidate. Lower levels of political activity than the population at large, however, both in registering to vote and in voting, limit an even greater impact of the Latino electorate. Nationally, nearly 20 percent of all Latinos in the United States live in Texas, and 39 percent of the Texas population is Latino. By 2020, Latinos are expected to outnumber Anglos in Texas (42 percent to 41 percent), and by 2040, Latinos will be a majority of the state population.[24] The mobilization and electoral preferences of Texas Latinos are the key to future elections.

IMAGE 5.3 Senator Cruz tweeted about his upcoming campaign events. Texas is a large state, and candidates have many places to visit as they seek to rally their supporters at campaign events.

Source: Twitter, Inc.

— Competency Connection —
🕮 **COMMUNICATION SKILLS** 🕮

What kind of communication techniques work best for political rallies? Are candidates able to provide much information about their issues? Do they need compelling visuals to communicate effectively?

African Americans

In April 1990, the Texas State Democratic Executive Committee filled a candidate vacancy by nominating Potter County court-at-law judge Morris Overstreet, an African American Democrat, for a seat on the Texas Court of Criminal Appeals. Because the Republican candidate, Louis Sturns, was also African American, this historic action guaranteed the state's voters would elect the first African American to statewide office in Texas. Overstreet won in 1990 and again in 1994. Governor George W. Bush appointed Republican Michael Williams to the Texas Railroad

Commission in 1999. Williams was elected to a six-year term in 2002 and again in 2008. He was appointed by Governor Perry as commissioner of education in 2012 and resigned in 2015.

Wallace Bernard Jefferson's appointment by Governor Perry to the Texas Supreme Court in 2001 made him the first African American to serve on that court. Jefferson and another African American, Dale Wainwright, were elected to the Texas Supreme Court in 2002 and reelected in 2008. Jefferson again made history in 2004 when Governor Perry appointed him as chief justice. In 2002, former Dallas mayor Ron Kirk became the first African American nominated by either major party in Texas as its candidate for U.S. senator. Although unsuccessful in the general election, Kirk's candidacy appeared to many political observers as an important breakthrough for African American politicians. Houston, Dallas, and San Antonio have all elected African Americans as mayors. In 2014, no African Americans from either party were candidates for statewide office and one was a candidate in 2016 and 2018.

Since the 1930s, most African American Texans have identified with the Democratic Party. After national civil rights legislation was adopted in the 1960s under the leadership of President Lyndon Johnson, a Texan, Democratic party identification of African Americans strengthened. In a 2018 Senate race survey, 86 percent of African Americans intended to vote for O'Rourke and 10 percent for Cruz.[25] African Americans make up 12 percent of the total population of Texas and more than 11 percent of the voting age population.[26] According to an analysis of U.S. Census data of estimated voter turnout by racial/ethnic group, African Americans had the highest voter turnout with slightly more than 63 percent in 2012.[27] Both in Texas and nationally, the 2012 presidential election was the first election in which African American turnout exceeded turnout of all other groups and was critical to the reelection of President Obama.[28] African American voters also contributed to Democratic Party gains in the 2018 midterms, especially in Harris County.

By early 2019, many African American Texans held elected office, including the following:

- Six U.S. representative seats in Texas's congressional delegation
- Seventeen seats in the Texas legislature
- More than 500 of the remaining elected positions in the state

---

✓ **5.2 Learning Check**

1. Which group is more supportive of the Democratic Party—Latinos or African Americans?
2. Why are Latinos considered to be an important group in Texas elections?

Answers at the end of this chapter.

⬟ Women in Politics

LO 5.3 Describe the evolving role of women in Texas politics.

Texas women did not begin to vote and hold public office for three-quarters of a century after Texas joined the Union. Until 1990, only four women had won a statewide office in Texas, including two-term governor Miriam A. ("Ma") Ferguson (1925–1927 and 1933–1935). Ferguson owed her office to supporters of her husband, Jim, who had been impeached and removed from the governorship in 1917. By 1990, Texas female voters outnumbered male voters, and Ann Richards was elected governor. After 1990, the number of women elected to statewide office increased dramatically.

In the early 1990s, Texas women served as mayors in about 150 of the state's towns and cities, including the top four in terms of population (Houston, Dallas, San Antonio, and El Paso). Mayor of Dallas Annette Strauss (1988–1991) was fond of greeting out-of-state visitors with this message: "Welcome to Texas, where men are men and women are mayors." In 2010, when Annise Parker was sworn in as mayor of Houston, she made history as the first openly gay mayor of a major U.S. city. Although Parker had been public about her sexual orientation during her previous elections as the city's comptroller and, before that, as a city council member, her November 2009 election as mayor of the nation's fourth-largest city received national media attention. As of 2019, of the five largest cities in Texas, only Fort Worth had a female mayor, Betsy Price. In 2018, Lina Hidalgo (Harris) and Barbara Canales (Nueces) won their elections for county judge.

The impact of women's voting power was also evident in several elections early in the 21st century, when women (U.S. Senator Kay Bailey Hutchison and state comptroller Carole Keeton Rylander Strayhorn) led all candidates on either ticket in votes received. In 2013, Governor Perry appointed Nandita Berry (originally from India) the 109th Texas secretary of state. The Democratic primary results in 2014 marked the first election in which female candidates held the top two positions on a party's ticket in Texas. The Democratic Party nominated Wendy Davis for governor and Leticia Van de Putte for lieutenant governor. For the 2016 general election, Democrats had three female candidates for statewide office (four, if one includes Hillary Clinton) and Republicans had three. Democrats fielded six statewide female candidates, and the Republicans had four.

Female candidates also succeeded in winning an increasing number of seats in legislative bodies. In 1971, no women served in Texas's congressional delegation, and only two served in the Texas legislature. As a result of the 2018 election, in 2019 the number of women in Texas's congressional delegation was six. The number of women in the Texas legislature was 41 (9 in the Senate and 32 in the House of Representatives), an increase of five compared to the 85th Legislature (2017). The expanded presence of women in public office is changing public policy. For example, increased punishment for family violence and for sexual abuse of children can be attributed in large part to the presence of women in policymaking positions. However, this has not been apparent in the area of reproductive rights or the availability of women's health services (for example, abortion clinics) in Texas.[29]

Despite their electoral victories in Texas and elsewhere across the nation, fewer women than men seek elective public office. Several reasons account for this situation, chief of which is difficulty in raising money to pay campaign expenses. Female candidates face numerous obstacles that may prevent them from seeking public office. Although women enjoy increasing freedom, they still shoulder more responsibilities for family and home than men do (even in two-career families). Some mothers feel obliged to care for children in the home until their children finish high school. Such parental obligations, together with age-old prejudices, deny women their rightful place in government. In addition, female candidates have been criticized for pursuing professional careers. In the 2014 gubernatorial election, Democratic candidate Wendy Davis was accused of "abandoning her children" because she left them with extended family while she attended Harvard

Law School in Massachusetts.[30] The 2018 election was a good one for women candidates, with Democrats doing particularly well in congressional and legislative contests. Republican women fared better in statewide races.[31]

✪ Voting

LO 5.4 Explain how the voting process promotes and inhibits voter participation.

The U.S. Supreme Court has declared the right to vote the "preservative" of all other rights.[32] For most Texans, voting is their principal political activity. For many, it is their only exercise in practicing Texas politics. Casting a ballot brings individuals and their government together for a moment and reminds people anew that they are part of a political system.

Obstacles to Voting

The right to vote has not always been as widespread in the United States as it is today. **Universal suffrage**, by which almost all citizens 18 years of age and older can vote, did not become a reality in Texas until the mid-1960s. Although most tactics to prevent people from voting have been abolished, their legacy remains.

Adopted after the Civil War (1861–1865), the Fourteenth and Fifteenth Amendments to the U.S. Constitution were intended to prevent denial of the right to vote based on race. For the next 100 years, however, African American citizens in Texas and other states of the former Confederacy, as well as many Latinos, were prevented from voting by one barrier after another—legal or otherwise. For example, the white-robed Ku Klux Klan and other lawless groups used terrorist tactics to keep African Americans from voting. Northeast Texas was the focus of the Klan's operations in the Lone Star State.[33] Disenfranchisement of African Americans began at the end of the Reconstruction era (1873 in Texas) via violence, intimidation, and harassment.[34]

Poll Tax Beginning in 1902, Texas required that citizens pay a special tax, called the **poll tax**, to become eligible to vote. The cost was $1.75 ($1.50, plus 25 cents that was optional with each county, and is about $45 in 2018). For the next 64 years, many Texans—especially low-income persons, including disproportionately large numbers of African Americans and Mexican Americans—failed to pay their poll tax during the designated four-month period from October 1 to January 31. This failure, in turn, disqualified them from voting during the following 12 months in party primaries and in any general or special election. As a result, African American voter participation declined from approximately 100,000 in the 1890s to about 5,000 in 1906. With ratification of the Twenty-Fourth Amendment to the U.S. Constitution in January 1964, the poll tax was abolished as a prerequisite for voting in national elections. Then, in *Harper v. Virginia State Board of Elections*, 383 U.S. 663 (1966), the U.S. Supreme Court invalidated all state laws that made payment of a poll tax a prerequisite for voting in state elections.

universal suffrage
Voting is open for virtually all persons 18 years of age or older.

poll tax
A tax levied in Texas from 1902 until voters amended the Texas Constitution in 1966 to eliminate it; failure to pay the annual tax (usually $1.75) made a citizen ineligible to vote in party primaries or in special and general elections.

All-White Primaries The so-called **white primary**, a product of political and legal maneuvering within the southern states, was designed to deny African Americans and some Latinos access to the Democratic primary.[35] Texas's White Primary law, passed in 1923, designated the Democratic Party primary to be a private party function, thus not protected by the Fourteenth and Fifteenth Amendments. The law allowed the Democratic Party to ban nonwhites from voting in the primary. Since the winner of the Democratic primary would win in the general election (because Texas was a one-party Democratic state), the white primary effectively disenfranchised nonwhite voters. In *Smith v. Allwright*, 321 U.S. 649 (1944), the U.S. Supreme Court overturned an earlier ruling that had allowed the white primary.[36] As a result of this action, the white primary was disallowed in 1944.

Literacy Tests Beginning in the 1870s, as a means to prevent African Americans from voting, some southern states (although not Texas) began requiring prospective voters to take a screening test that conditioned voting rights on a person's literacy. Individuals who could not pass these **literacy tests** were not allowed to vote. These tests consisted of difficult and abstract questions concerning a person's knowledge of the U.S. Constitution or understanding of issues supposedly related to citizenship. In no way, however, did these questions measure a citizen's ability to cast an informed vote. The federal Voting Rights Act of 1965 made literacy tests illegal.

Grandfather Clause Another device, not used in Texas but enacted by other southern states to deny suffrage to minorities, was the **grandfather clause**. Laws with this clause provided that persons who could exercise the right to vote before 1867, or their descendants, would be exempt from educational, property, or tax requirements for voting. Because African Americans had not been allowed to vote before adoption of the Fifteenth Amendment in 1870, grandfather clauses prevented African Americans from voting. The U.S. Supreme Court, in *Guinn v. United States*, 238 U.S. 317 (1915), declared the grandfather clause unconstitutional because it violated the equal voting rights guaranteed by the Fifteenth Amendment.

Diluting Minority Votes **Gerrymandering** is drawing the boundaries of a district, such as a state senatorial or representative district, to include or exclude certain groups of voters and thus affect election outcomes. While gerrymandering in and of itself is not discriminatory against minorities, there are situations where it has been used to dilute minority voting strength. Minority representatives have a difficult time getting elected from districts that do not have a large minority population. For example, Latino representatives are unlikely to be elected from districts with small Latino populations.[37] Thus, one method for minimizing the impact of a minority community is to spread out the population among several districts so there is not a majority of the minority population in any district (cracking or splintering), reducing the likelihood of a minority winning an election. Another tactic, packing, concentrates minority voters into a few districts with very large percentages of minorities. Thus, a minority population in a state may be large enough to elect several representatives if they are distributed

white primary
A nominating system designed to prevent African Americans and some Latinos from participating in Democratic primaries from 1923 to 1944.

literacy tests
Although not used in Texas as a prerequisite for voter registration, the test was designed and administered in ways intended to prevent African Americans and Latinos from voting.

grandfather clause
Although not used in Texas, the law exempted people from educational, property, or tax requirements for voting if they were qualified to vote before 1867 or were descendants of such persons.

gerrymandering
Drawing the boundaries of a district, such as a state senatorial or representative district, to include or exclude certain groups of voters and thus affect election outcomes.

more evenly across districts, instead of concentrated into a few districts. Although racial gerrymandering that discriminates against minority voters is disallowed, federal law allows **affirmative racial gerrymandering** that results in the creation of "majority-minority" districts (also called minority-opportunity districts) favoring election of more racial and ethnic minority candidates. These districts must be reasonable in their configuration and cannot be based solely on race. For a further discussion of gerrymandering, see Chapter 8, "The Legislative Branch."

Another way minority voting strength may be diluted is through the creation of **at-large districts**. At-large districts refer to elected representatives who are elected from an entire entity, such as a city. Thus, an at-large member of a city council is elected in a citywide election, instead of a single-member district. Under this scenario, the votes of a minority group can be diluted when combined with the votes of a majority group. Even though a minority group, such as Latinos or African Americans, can comprise a numerical majority, from a political power standpoint they are still considered minorities. Thus, in a city such as Corpus Christi, where Latinos are a numerical majority, they are still considered to be a minority group from a political perspective. Federal courts have declared at-large districts unconstitutional where representation of ethnic or racial minorities is diminished.[38] For a comparison of at-large and single-member districts in local elections, see Chapter 3, "Local Governments."

Federal Voting Rights Legislation The Voting Rights Act (VRA) of 1965 expanded the electorate and encouraged voting. This act has been renewed and amended by Congress four times, including in 2006, when it was extended until 2031. The law (together with federal court rulings) now does the following:

- Abolishes the use of all literacy tests in voter registrations
- Prohibits residency requirements of more than 30 days for voting in presidential elections
- Requires states to provide some form of absentee or **early voting**
- Allows individuals (as well as the U.S. Department of Justice) to sue in federal court to request that voting examiners be sent to a particular area
- Requires states and jurisdictions within a state with a significant percentage of residents whose primary language is one other than English to use bilingual ballots and other written election materials, as well as provide bilingual oral assistance. In Texas, this information must be provided in Spanish throughout the state and in Vietnamese and Chinese in Harris County and Houston.

In *Shelby County v. Holder*, 570 U.S. ___ (2013), the U.S. Supreme Court declared unconstitutional Section 4(b) of the Voting Rights Act (VRA) of 1965, which established a formula for determining which jurisdictions were required to obtain preclearance from the U.S. Department of Justice before making any alterations to their election laws. Preclearance meant that voting jurisdictions, including states, counties, and cities, that had a history of violating minority voting rights had to obtain approval before making changes for elections, such as drawing boundaries for state legislative districts. The State of Texas was among the governmental entities that had such a history.

affirmative racial gerrymandering
Drawing the boundaries of a district designed to favor representation by a member of a historical minority group (for example, African Americans) in a legislative chamber, city council, commissioners court, or other representative body.

at-large district
Elected representatives who are elected from an entire entity, and not a single-member district.

early voting
Conducted at the county courthouse and selected polling places before the designated primary, special, or general election day.

Writing for a 5-4 Court, Chief Justice John Roberts invalidated the provision because the coverage formula was based on 40-year-old data, making the formula no longer responsive to current needs and "an impermissible burden on the constitutional principles of federalism and equal sovereignty of the states." Governor Rick Perry called the ruling "a clear victory for federalism and the states." He noted, "Texas may now implement the will of the people without being subject to outdated and unnecessary oversight and the overreach of federal power." Greg Abbott, then serving as Attorney General of Texas, announced that "redistricting maps passed by the Legislature [could] also take effect without approval from the federal government."[39] In dissent, Supreme Court Justice Ruth Bader Ginsburg wrote, "Throwing out preclearance when it has worked and is continuing to work to stop discriminatory changes is like throwing away your umbrella in a rainstorm because you are not getting wet."[40] Other parts of the VRA are still in effect, including Section 2 which "… prohibits voting practices or procedures that discriminate on the basis of race, color, or membership in one of the language minority groups…."[41]

Democratization of the Ballot

In America, successive waves of democratization have removed obstacles to voting. In the second half of the twentieth century, the U.S. Congress enacted important voting rights laws to promote and protect voting nationwide.

The National Voter Registration Act (1993), or **motor-voter law**, permits registration by mail; at welfare, disability assistance, and motor vehicle licensing agencies; or at military recruitment centers. People can register to vote when they apply for, or renew, driver's licenses or when they visit a public assistance office. Motor vehicle offices and voter registration agencies are required to provide voter registration services to applicants. Using an appropriate state or federal voter registration form, Texas citizens can also apply for voter registration or update their voter registration data by mail, but not online. If citizens believe their voting rights have been violated, federal administrative and judicial agencies, such as the U.S. Department of Justice, are available for assistance.

Amendments to the U.S. Constitution have also expanded the American electorate. The Fifteenth Amendment (1870) prohibits the denial of voting rights because of race; the Nineteenth Amendment (1920) precludes denial of suffrage on the basis of gender; the Twenty-Fourth Amendment (1964) prohibits states from requiring payment of a poll tax or any other tax as a condition for voting; and the Twenty-Sixth Amendment (1971) forbids setting the minimum voting age above 18 years.

motor-voter law
Legislation requiring certain government offices (for example, motor vehicle licensing agencies) to offer voter registration applications to clients.

Two Trends in Suffrage From our overview of suffrage in Texas, two trends emerge. First, voting rights have steadily expanded to include virtually all persons, of both genders, who are 18 years of age or older. Second, there has been a movement toward uniformity of voting policies among the 50 states. However, democratization of the ballot has been pressed on the states largely by the U.S. Congress, by federal judges, and by presidents who have enforced voting laws and judicial orders.

Voter Turnout

Now that nearly all legal barriers to the ballot have been swept away, universal suffrage has not resulted in a corresponding increase in voter turnout, either nationally or in Texas. Frequently used definitions of **voter turnout** are the percentage of the voting-age population (adults 18 or older) or voting-eligible population (estimate of persons eligible to vote) casting ballots. Not all adults 18 or older are eligible to vote. In Texas, turnout is higher in presidential elections than in nonpresidential elections. Although this pattern reflects the national trend, electoral turnout in Texas tends to be significantly lower than in the nation as a whole. According to data from the *United States Election Project* (www.electproject.org), in the 2016 presidential election, turnout among the voting-eligible population in Texas was 51.4 percent, compared to the 60.1 percent national average. Texas had the second lowest turnout among the voting-eligible population in 2016, only ahead of Hawaii. Minnesota had the highest turnout among the voting-eligible population, with 74.7 percent in 2016. Researchers at the *United States Election Project* estimated that 13.3 percent of the Lone Star State's population was ineligible to vote in 2016 because of citizenship status. Another 0.2 percent of Texas's population was ineligible to vote because of their status as convicted felons who had not completed serving their sentences. The right to vote is restored upon the felon's completion of a prison sentence. Therefore, voter turnout in Texas fares better when the voting-eligible population (rather than voting-age population) is considered. A third way to measure voter turnout is by including only registered voters.

Voter turnout in state and local elections is usually lower than in presidential elections. For instance, the 2018 Texas midterm election yielded a 46.3 percent turnout of the voting-eligible population.[42] Turnout in the Texas 2014 midterm election was 28.3 percent. The higher turnout in 2018 is attributed to the Senate race (Cruz vs. O'Rourke) and the response to the Trump presidency. In local elections at the city or school district level, a turnout of 20 percent is relatively high. In 2017, registered voter turnout in the San Antonio mayoral election was 13.2 percent.[43] These figures illustrate one of the ironies in politics: People are less likely to participate at the level of government where they can potentially have the greatest influence. In an effort to increase turnout, cities such as El Paso and Corpus Christi moved their city elections from spring of odd years to the end of even-numbered years.

Practices associated with higher voter turnout, such as same-day or online voter registration and ballots by mail for all voters (as in, for example, Washington, Oregon, and California), are not used in Texas. Low citizen participation in elections has also been attributed to voter fatigue resulting from too many elections. Members of the Texas legislature determined that low voter turnout was caused by governmental entities holding too many elections. To cure "turnout burnout," the legislature passed a law that limits most elections to two uniform election dates each year: the second Saturday in May and the first Tuesday after the first Monday in November. However, this change has failed to yield a higher voter turnout. For instance, in 2017, statewide registered voter turnout was 5.8 percent in the constitutional amendment election on a date that coincided with a number of municipal elections (see Point/Counterpoint for a way to increase turnout).[44]

voter turnout
The percentage of voters (either voting age population, voting eligible population, or registered voters) casting a ballot in an election.

People decide to vote or not to vote in the same way they make most other decisions: on the basis of anticipated consequences. A strong impulse to vote may stem from interest in politics, peer pressure, self-interest, or a sense of duty toward country, state, local community, political party, or interest group. People also decide whether to vote based on costs measured in time, money, experience, information, job, and other resources, such as political efficacy and strength of party identification. Political science research has identified external political efficacy (that is the belief that elected officials respond to attempts to influence them) and strength of party identification as factors in explaining voter turnout. Those with high levels of political efficacy are more likely to vote, while those with low levels are less likely. Also, those who identify as strong Republicans or strong Democrats are more likely to vote than those with weaker attachments.[45]

Of all the socioeconomic influences on voting, education is by far the strongest. Statistics clearly indicate that as educational level rises, so does the likelihood of voting, assuming all other socioeconomic factors remain constant. Educated people usually have more income and leisure time for voting; moreover, education enhances one's ability to learn about political parties, candidates, and issues. Education also strengthens political efficacy. In addition, income strongly affects voter turnout. According to the U.S. Census Bureau, in 2017 Texas ranked 15th in the nation in poverty, with 14.7 percent of the population living below the poverty level. People of lower income often lack access to the polls, information about the candidates, or opportunities to learn about the system. Income levels and their impact on electoral turnout can be seen in the 2018 U.S. Senate election. For example, Starr County, with a median household income of $27,133, had a registered voter turnout of 32.57 percent. By contrast, Collin County, with a median income of $90,124, experienced a turnout of 61.38 percent of its registered voters.[46]

Although less important than education and income, gender and age also affect voting behavior. In the United States and Texas, women are slightly more likely to vote than men. Young people (ages 18–25) have the lowest voter turnout of any age group. Nevertheless, participation by young people has increased in the last 10 years. The highest voter turnout is among Americans, 60 years of age and older.[47]

Race and ethnicity also influence voting behavior. The section on "Racial and Ethnic Politics" in this chapter presented turnout data for Texas's African Americans and Latinos. Recall that African American turnout was the highest among racial and ethnic groups in the state in 2012. The higher turnout among people of color in Texas in the 2018 elections, compared to their turnout in the 2014 and 2016 elections, is credited with contributing to Democratic Party gains in 2018. Turnout in 2018 was close to the turnout for a presidential election, rather than a typical midterm election.[48]

A bill passed by the Texas legislature in 2011 that required voters to provide photo identification to cast a ballot failed to obtain Department of Justice preclearance in August 2012. Following the U.S. Supreme Court's decision in *Shelby County v. Holder*, Texas Attorney General Greg Abbott announced that the state's voter identification (ID) law that had been challenged by the U.S. Department of Justice "[would] take effect immediately" and tweeted about the decision.

IMAGE 5.4 Then Attorney General Greg Abbott celebrating the 2013 Supreme Court decision that allowed the voter identification law to take effect.

Greg Abbott ✓
@GregAbbott_TX

⚙ 👤+ Follow

Eric Holder can no longer deny #VoterID in #Texas after today's #SCOTUS decision. #txlege #tcot #txgop

RETWEETS
158

LIKES
55

8:02 AM - 25 Jun 2013

Source: Twitter, Inc.

Competency Connection
COMMUNICATION SKILLS

What do you think of the use of hashtags by politicians? Does it help them to communicate effectively?

Proponents argue that voter ID laws protect against voting fraud. This law, which went into effect in 2013, enhances the penalties for illegal voting from a third-degree felony to a second-degree felony. Attempted illegal voting is a state jail felony instead of a Class A misdemeanor. Acceptable forms of photo identification include a driver's license, passport, military ID card, concealed handgun license, or state-issued ID card from the Department of Public Safety. Student ID cards are not an acceptable form of photo identification. Opponents of the voter ID law argue that individuals without a driver's license, such as many who are elderly or poor, may not be able to vote because they lack documents (original or certified copy of birth certificate) required for getting the state issued ID card.[49]

In October 2014, shortly before early voting began, a U.S. District Court judge in Corpus Christi ruled the ID law unconstitutional in the case of *Veasey v. Abbott*, No. 14-41127. Because the election was imminent, the Fifth Circuit Court of Appeals and the U.S. Supreme Court allowed the general election to proceed with the voter ID law in effect.

On July 20, 2016, the full Fifth Circuit Court of Appeals ruled against Texas, declaring that voter ID law violated the Voting Rights Act because it has a discriminatory effect against black and Latino voters. On August 10, 2016, U.S. District Judge Nelva Gonzales Ramos (the judge who originally ruled against the Voter ID Law) signed an agreement between the civil rights plaintiffs, Texas, and the federal government that allows voters to cast a ballot without a photo ID if they have a "reasonable impediment" to acquiring one of the acceptable forms detailed in the law. In 2017, the Texas Legislature passed Senate Bill 5, which revised the photo ID law to include the changes agreed upon (and approved by Judge Ramos) between the plaintiffs, Texas, and the federal government. On April 27, 2018, a divided three-judge panel of the 5th Circuit Court of Appeals upheld Senate Bill 5, ruling that the opponents of the revised photo ID law did not prove it had a discriminatory effect. This ended the legal challenge against the photo ID law.[50]

Texas maintained that the voter ID law was necessary to prevent voter fraud and protect the integrity of elections. This law is supposed to prevent voter-impersonation fraud, whereby a person gives the name of another voter and then votes under that voter's name. Critics of the law note that the type of voter fraud that the voter ID bill is intended to prevent is very rare. An analysis of elections from 2000 to 2014, with 72 million votes cast, found only four cases of in-person voter-impersonation fraud, meaning the chance of in-person voter fraud is 1 in 18 million.[51]

STUDENTS IN ACTION

Fighting for the Right to Vote

In 2011, the Texas legislature passed one of the strictest requirements for voting, mandating valid photo identification. Because of court challenges, the law did not go into effect until 2013, however. The acceptable photo identifications are a Texas driver license issued by the Texas Department of Public Safety (DPS), Texas Election Identification Certificate issued by DPS, Texas personal identification card issued by DPS, Texas license to carry a handgun issued by DPS, United States military identification card containing the person's photograph, United States citizenship certificate containing the person's photograph, and the U.S. passport. The Texas Voter Identification law (Senate Bill 14) was quickly challenged as discriminatory against racial and ethnic minorities because they are less likely to have one of the valid types of photo identification. Not everyone has a Texas driver's license, and obtaining one of the valid photo identifications can be a cumbersome and expensive process.

MALDEF, the Mexican American Legal Defense and Education Fund, sought to identify individuals who would be affected by this new requirement. Twins Victoria and Nicole Rodriguez, who were high school students at the time, were approached by MALDEF and asked if they would be willing to provide testimony before a federal three-judge panel in Washington, D.C. The sisters represented a group of young people who did not have a driver's license or another form of acceptable identification in order

to vote. All they had was their high school identification cards. What follows is their experience.

Getting ready for D.C.
In March 2012, Nicole and Victoria Rodriguez were 18-year-old high school seniors when they were asked if they would meet with attorneys for MALDEF. At the deposition, the attorneys asked them various questions, such as why they did not possess a driver's license. The sisters explained that their family was low-income and that their parents would not be able to afford the added costs of car insurance if their daughters drove. Plus, the parents were always working, and they did not have time to take their daughters for the driving test. They pointed out that they voted for the first time in the Texas primary in 2012 using their voter registration cards. Since the law was being challenged in the courts, the sisters were not required to show any form of photo identification.

Testifying in D.C.
MALDEF attorneys decided that Victoria would provide the testimony that day in D.C. Victoria was asked only three questions: (1) what forms of ID did she have, (2) who provides her transportation, and (3) did she only use her high school ID to get by.

The court's decision and the aftermath
In August, the three-judge panel in the U.S. District Court of D.C. ultimately struck down the photo ID

requirement as discriminatory against minority voters. It failed to get federal preclearance as required by the Voting Rights Act. Nicole and Victoria were very excited to hear the news, and in the fall of 2012 when they were attending college at St. Mary's University in San Antonio, they voted in the presidential election, again without photo IDs.

Then in a separate case, *Shelby v. Holder*, a case originating in Alabama, the U.S. Supreme Court, on June 25, 2013, struck down the preclearance provision (Section 5) of the Voting Rights Act. What this decision meant for the voter ID law was that Texas was free to implement the law because the rulings against it had been based on Section 5 preclearance. Those rulings no longer applied since that part of the law was struck down.

Speaking at the rally

While the Supreme Court heard oral arguments for *Shelby v. Holder* in February 2013, there were several rallies outside the Supreme Court building. MALDEF attorneys, along with Nicole Rodriguez, went back to D.C. to speak at the rallies. Nicole found it both scary and exciting to share her experience there.

Since then

Nicole's and Victoria's high school student identification cards are not acceptable forms of identification for the Texas voter identification law, yet they were the only forms of photo identification they had. The student identification cards were acceptable for airport and train security, and security at the District of Columbia courthouse, yet were not acceptable for

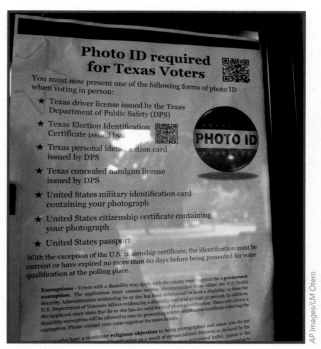

The list of acceptable forms of photo identification for voting.

Texas voter identification. The sisters are still attending St. Mary's and plan to graduate soon. They now each have a driver's license and voted in the Texas primary in 2016. The 5th Circuit Court of Appeals, in 2018, upheld the photo ID law.

Based on an interview with Nicole and Victoria Rodriguez on March 4, 2016, by Dr. Sonia García.

--- Competency Connection ---
✿ CRITICAL THINKING ✿

Student identification cards are not accepted for photo identification but drivers' licenses are accepted. Are drivers' licenses easy to obtain? Why or why not?

Administering Elections

In Texas, as in other states, determining voting procedures is essentially a state responsibility. The Texas Constitution authorizes the legislature to provide for the administration of elections. This term refers to the various individuals and officials who have a role in running, or administering, elections. State lawmakers, in turn, have made the secretary of state the chief elections officer for Texas but have left most details of administering elections to county officials. Thus, administration of elections in Texas is decentralized.

All election laws currently in effect in the Lone Star State are compiled into one body of law, the **Texas Election Code**.[52] In administering this legal code, however, state and party officials must protect voting rights guaranteed by federal law.

Qualifications for Voting To be eligible to vote in Texas, a person must meet the following qualifications:

- Be a native-born or naturalized citizen of the United States
- Be at least 18 years of age on Election Day
- Be a resident of the state and county for at least 30 days immediately preceding Election Day
- Be a resident of the area covered by the election on Election Day
- Be a registered voter for at least 30 days immediately preceding Election Day
- Not be a convicted felon (unless sentence, probation, and parole are completed)
- Not be declared mentally incompetent by a court of law[53]

Most adults who live in Texas meet the first four qualifications for voting, but registration is required before a person can vote. Anyone serving a jail sentence as a result of a misdemeanor conviction or not finally convicted of a felony is not disqualified from voting. The Texas Constitution, however, bars from voting anyone who is incarcerated, on parole, or on probation as a result of a felony conviction and anyone who is "mentally incompetent as determined by a court." A convicted felon may vote immediately after completing a sentence or following a full pardon. (For examples of misdemeanors and felonies, see Table 13.1 in Chapter 13, "The Criminal Justice System.") Voter registration is intended to determine in advance whether prospective voters meet all the qualifications prescribed by law. Most states, including Texas, use a permanent registration system. Under this plan, voters register once and remain registered unless they change their mailing address and fail to notify the voting registrar within three years or lose their eligibility to register in some other way.

Because the requirement of voter registration may deter voting, the Texas Election Code provides for voter registration centers in addition to those sites authorized by Congress under the motor-voter law. Thus, Texans may also register at local marriage license offices, in public high schools, with any volunteer deputy registrar, or in person at the office of the county voting registrar. Students away at college may choose to reregister using their college address as their residence if they want to vote locally. Otherwise, they must request an absentee ballot or be in their hometown during early voting or on Election Day if they wish to cast a ballot.

Between November 1 and November 15 of each odd-numbered year, the registrar mails to every registered voter in the county a registration certificate that is effective for the succeeding two voting years. Postal authorities may not forward a certificate mailed to the address indicated on the voter's application form to

Texas Election Code
The body of state law concerning parties, primaries, and elections.

another address; instead, the certificate must be returned to the registrar. This practice enables the county voting registrar to maintain an accurate list of names and mailing addresses of persons to whom voting certificates have been issued. Registration files are open for public inspection in the voting registrar's office, and a statewide registration file is available in Austin at the Elections Division of the Office of the Secretary of State.

Although voter registration certificates are issued after a person registers to vote, one can legally cast a ballot without a certificate by providing some form of identification (such as a driver's license) and signing an affidavit of registration at the polls. However, under the state's law requiring a voter to show a valid photo identification to cast a ballot, the voter's name on the photo identification must appear exactly as it appears on the elections department's registration list. If the name on the photo ID doesn't match exactly but is "substantially similar" to the name on the registration list, the voter will be permitted to cast a ballot as long as the voter signs an affidavit stating that he or she is the same person as the one on the list of registered voters.

Voting Early Opportunities to vote early in Texas are limited to in-person early voting, voting by mail, and facsimile machine voting (for military personnel and their dependents in hostile fire or combat zones). Texas law allows voters to vote "early"—that is, beginning 17 days preceding a scheduled election, beginning 12 days preceding a scheduled May election and runoff, and 10 days preceding runoffs in all other elections. Early voting ends, however, four days before any election or primary. In less populated rural counties, early voting occurs at the courthouse. In more populous urban areas, the county clerk's office accommodates voters by maintaining branch offices for early voting, including at malls, schools, college campuses, and mobile units. Polling places are generally open for early voting on weekdays during the regular business hours of the official responsible for conducting the election. According to figures from the Texas Secretary of State's office, almost 40 percent of registered voters voted early in the 2018 general election.

Registered voters who qualify may vote by mail during an early voting period. Voting by mail has been available for decades to elderly Texans and those with physical disabilities. Today, anyone meeting any of the following qualifications can vote by mail-in ballot:

- Will not be in his or her county of residence during the entire early voting period and on Election Day
- Is at least age 65
- Is, or will be, physically disabled on Election Day, including those who expect to be confined for childbirth on Election Day
- Is in jail (but not a convicted felon) during the early voting period and on Election Day
- Is in the military or is a dependent of military personnel and has resided in Texas[54]

IMAGE 5.5 Texas voter presenting valid photo identification in order to vote. Voters have additional options for identification if they do not have one of the forms of photo identification specified in the Photo ID Law.

— Competency Connection —
⚙ **CRITICAL THINKING** ⚙

Is voter impersonation fraud a threat to elections in Texas? Are there other threats to elections that photo identification will not prevent?

AP Images/Eric Gay

Voting Precincts The basic geographic area for conducting national, state, district, and county elections is the **voting precinct**. Each precinct usually contains between 100 and approximately 2,000 registered voters. Texas has more than 8,500 voting precincts, drawn by the 254 county commissioners courts (a county judge and four commissioners). Citizens vote at polling places within their voting precincts or, if voting precincts have been combined for an election, at a polling place convenient to voters in each of the combined voting precincts. Municipal and special district precincts must follow the boundary lines of county-designed voting precincts adjusted to their respective boundaries. Subject to this restriction, municipal and special district voting precincts are designated by the governing body of each city and special district, respectively.

Voting Centers While most Texas counties use voting precincts, Texas election law allows for the elimination of voting precincts and the establishment of countywide **voting centers**. Counties establish several voting centers, and registered voters in the county can vote at any one of the centers that is most convenient for them. Election workers electronically verify the voter's eligibility.[55] More than 50 counties, including Galveston, Collin, and Brazos, use voting centers.

voting precinct
The basic geographic area for conducting primaries and elections; Texas is divided into more than 8,500 voting precincts.

voting center
A countywide voting system that allows voters to vote, after being electronically verified, at any voting center in a county.

Election Officials Various county and political party officials have a role in administering federal, state, and county elections. Municipal elections and special district elections are the responsibility of their respective jurisdictions (see Chapter 3, "Local Governments"), although they may contract with the county to run elections. Whereas party officials conduct primary elections, the county clerk or **elections administrator** prepares general election and special election ballots based on certification of candidates by the appropriate authority (that is, the secretary of state for state and district candidates and the county clerk or elections administrator for county candidates). Some counties have officials whose sole responsibility is administering elections. In other counties, administering elections is one of many responsibilities of the tax assessor-collector or (if designated by the county commissioners court) the county clerk. There is also a county election commission, which consists of the county judge, county clerk or elections administrator, sheriff, and the chairs of the two major political parties. Commission responsibilities include selecting polling places, printing ballots, and providing supplies and voting equipment.

County commissioners' courts appoint one **election judge** and one alternate judge, each from different political parties, to administer elections in each precinct for a maximum term of two years. Furthermore, each county's commissioners court canvasses and certifies election results. The election judge selects as many clerks as will be needed to assist in conducting general and special elections in a precinct. Clerks must be selected from different political parties. In city

IMAGE 5.6 Waiting in line to vote

AP Images/Eric Gay

— Competency Connection —
⊛ **SOCIAL RESPONSIBILITY** ⊛

It is our civic responsibility to participate in elections. However, waiting in line to vote can discourage voting. Some states, such as Washington and Oregon, do their voting by mail. Would voting by mail in Texas be a way to increase participation in elections?

elections administrator
Person appointed to supervise voter registration and voting for a county.

election judge
Official appointed by the county commissioners court to administer an election in a voting precinct.

⬨ POINT/COUNTERPOINT

Should Texas switch to a Proportional Representation system?

THE ISSUE The Single-Member District Plurality (SMDP) system is widely used in the United States and Texas to elect members of Congress and state legislators. In this system, candidates compete in an electoral district, and the candidate receiving the most votes wins the election. Another type of system, utilized by democracies around the world, uses the percentage of the vote a party receives to determine how many seats a party wins in a legislature. Candidates do not run in single-member districts, instead if a legislature has 100 seats, and a party wins 33 percent of the vote, the party then wins 33 percent of the legislative seats. This system is known as proportional representation (PR).

FOR	AGAINST
1. PR more accurately translates votes cast into seats won. Parties win seats in legislatures based on the total votes they receive, while in a SMDP system, the party winning a majority of seats in a legislature may not have received a majority of votes.	1. PR can lead to fragmentation of the political party system and can make governing more difficult. On the other hand, SMDP creates a connection between constituents and their elected representative.
2. PR promotes representation by offering minor parties a chance to win seats, while SMDP discourages smaller political parties. A minor party receiving 10 percent of the vote can win seats in a PR system (while not winning any seats in SMDP).	2. Extremist parties can win seats in the legislature.
3. PR systems encourage voter turnout because voters' perception is that all votes can make a difference in the election outcome.	3. No party wins a majority, meaning a coalition of parties is necessary to govern. These coalition governments may be unstable if they do not have sufficient common policy preferences. In contrast, SMDP is more likely to produce a majority party in the legislature.
4. SMDP is susceptible to gerrymandering, while PR systems are not because they use multimember districts.	4. SMDP produces clear-cut choices for voters between the two main parties, whereas in PR there will likely be several main parties competing for votes.[56]
5. SMDP excludes minorities from fair representation. It is rare for racial/ethnic minority candidates to win in districts, unless a majority of voters are from the racial/ethnic minority group. Members of racial/minority groups have an improved chance of winning seats in PR systems.	

Competency Connection
⬨ SOCIAL RESPONSIBILITY ⬨

Do you recommend Texas switches to a PR system to increase political participation, improve representation, and eliminate gerrymandering? Why or why not?

elections, the city secretary appoints election judges, unless the city contracts with the county to administer an election.

Voting Systems In general elections, Texas uses three voting systems: paper ballot; optical scan (similar to a Scantron); and direct recording electronic (DRE), also known as a touch screen. In every county, the county commissioners court determines which system will be used. Each system has advantages and disadvantages in such matters as ballot and equipment costs, ease of use by voters, accuracy of counting, labor cost, and time required to count the votes. For example, paper ballots are relatively cheap and easy to use, but counting is a slow, laborious, and error-prone process. Some sparsely populated counties continue to use paper ballots, which must be counted by hand. Some optical scan and DRE systems automatically count each vote as the ballot is cast. Optical scan and DRE systems require mechanical and electronic voting equipment, which is expensive to purchase and store but can reduce election costs when many voters are involved. Under Texas law, anyone on a space flight on Election Day can vote by electronic ballot that is transmitted from the astronaut-voter's home county through NASA.

On general election ballot forms, a list of parties for straight party ticket voting appears first, followed by lists of candidates for national, state, district, and local offices, in that order. (Figure 5.1 shows a sample ballot used in a recent general election.) A list of all write-in candidates who have filed an appropriate declaration is posted in each polling place on the day of an election. Legislation passed in 2017 will eliminate straight ticket voting, starting with the 2020 general election.

In some instances, candidates for nomination or election to an office may request a recount of ballots if they believe vote tabulations were inaccurate. The Texas Election Code also provides detailed procedures for settling disputed elections.

Since the 1960s, several changes in voting procedures by both the federal and state governments have been made to encourage full, informed participation in elections. As a result of the 1975 extension of the federal Voting Rights Act, registration and election materials used in all Texas counties must be printed in both English and Spanish. As noted above, in Harris County and the City of Houston, materials in Chinese and Vietnamese must also be provided. Texas voters can also take voting guides, newspaper endorsements, and other printed material into the voting booth, although wireless communication devices such as cell phones and tablet computers are prohibited.[57] Disabled voters are ensured access to polling places and the opportunity to cast a secret ballot.

> ✔ **5.4 Learning Check**
>
> 1. Identify two methods formerly used in Texas to limit people's right to vote.
> 2. True or False: The only people who can vote early are those who will be away from their regular polling place on Election Day.
>
> *Answers at the end of this chapter.*

✪ Primary, General, and Special Elections

LO 5.5 Identify the differences among primary, general, and special elections.

The electoral process includes the nomination and election of candidates through primary, general, and special elections. This section will focus on state and county elections. Local elections are discussed in Chapter 3, "Local Governments."

FIGURE 5.1 Sample General Election Ballot for Nueces County, Texas

SAMPLE BALLOT

OFFICIAL BALLOT BOLETA OFICIAL
GENERAL ELECTION
ELECCIÓN GENERAL
NUECES COUNTY, TEXAS
CONDADO DE NUECES, TEXAS
November 08, 2016 – 08 de noviembre de 2106

Precinct Precinto 2-02

Instruction Text:
Please use a black or blue ink pen to mark your choices on the ballot. To vote for your choice in each contest, completely fill in the box provided to the left of your choice. To vote for a write-in candidate, completely fill in the box provided to the left of the words "Write-in" and write in the name of the candidate on the line provided.

Texto de Instrucción:
Por favor use solamente una pluma de tinta negra o azul. Llene completamente el espacio cuadrado a la izquierda de su selección. No haga marcas extraviadas. No use tintas que se pueden penetrar el papel. Para votar por un candidato por voto escrito, llene completamente el espacio cuadrado a la izquierda de las palabras "Voto Escrito" y escriba el nombre del candidato en la línea provista.

Correct
Incorrect

BALLOT LEGEND
(LYENDA de la BOLETA)

REP	Republican Party *(Partido Republicano)*
DEM	Democratic Party *(Partido Demócrata)*
LIB	Libertarian Party *(Partido Libertario)*
GRN	Green Party *(Partido Verde)*
IND	Independent *(Independiente)*

United States Representative, District 27
Representante de los Estados Unidos, Distrito Núm. 27
☐ Blake Farenthold REP
☐ Raul "Roy" Barrera DEM

Railroad Commissioner
Comisionado de Ferrocarriles
☐ Wayne Christian REP
☐ Grady Yarbrough DEM
☐ Mark Miller LIB
☐ Martina Salinas GRN

Justice, Supreme Court, Place 3
Juez, Corte Suprema, Lugar Núm. 3
☐ Debra Lehrmann REP
☐ Mike Westergren DEM
☐ Kathie Glass LIB
☐ Rodolfo Rivera Munoz GRN

Justice, Supreme Court, Place 5
Juez, Corte Suprema, Lugar Núm. 5
☐ Paul Green REP

Judge, Court of Criminal Appeals, Place 6
Juez, Corte de Apelaciones Criminales, Lugar Núm. 6
☐ Michael E. Keasler REP
☐ Robert Burns DEM
☐ Mark W. Bennett LIB

State Senator, District 20
Senador Estatal, Distrito Núm. 20
☐ Velma A. Arellano REP
☐ Juan "Chuy" Hinojosa DEM

State Representative, District 32
Representante Estatal, Distrito Núm. 32
☐ Todd Hunter REP

Justice, 13th Court of Appeals District, Place 3
Juez, Corte de Apelaciones, Distrito Nm. 13, Lugar Núm. 3
☐ Greg Perkes REP
☐ Leticia Hinojosa DEM

District Judge, 28th Judicial District

Justice of the Peace, Precinct No. 2, Place 1
Juez de Paz, Precinto Núm. 2, Lugar Núm. 1
☐ Jo Woolsey REP
☐ Alex Garcia DEM

Constable, Precinct No. 2
Condestable, Precinto Núm. 2
☐ Mitchell Clark REP

DEL MAR COLLEGE DISTRICT GENERAL ELECTION
DISTRITO DE DEL MAR COLLEGE ELECCIÓN GENERAL

Regent, At Large
Vote for none or one
Regente, En General
Vote por ninguno o uno
☐ Trey McCampbell
☐ Laurie Turner

DEL MAR COLLEGE DISTRICT BOND ELECTION
DISTRITO DEL DEL MAR COLLEGE ELECCIÓN DE BONOS

Proposition
The issuance of $139,000,000 of Bonds to

(Note: middle portion of ballot excluded here.)

President and Vice President
Presidente y Vice Presidente
☐ Donald J. Trump / Mike Pence REP
☐ Hillary Clinton / Tim Kaine DEM
☐ Gary Johnson / William Weld LIB
☐ Jill Stein / Ajamu Baraka GRN
☐ Write-in Voto Escrito

Judge, Court of Criminal Appeals, Place 5
Juez, Corte de Apelaciones Criminales, Lugar Núm. 5
☐ Scott Walker REP
☐ Betsy Johnson DEM
☐ William Bryan Strange, III LIB
☐ Judith Sanders-Castro GRN

☐ Jim Kaelin REP
☐ Larry Olivarez DEM

Tax Assessor-Collector
Asesor-Colector de Impuesto
☐ Kevin Kieschnick REP

County Commissioner, Precinct No. 3
Comisionado del Condado, Precinto Núm. 3
☐ John Marez DEM

Vote for none or one
Alcalde
Vote por ninguno o uno
☐ Dan McQueen
☐ Nelda Martinez

SAMPLE BALLOT

http://www.co.nueces.tx.us/countyclerk/elections/clerks/sample_ballots/002-02.pdf

Competency Connection
PERSONAL RESPONSIBILITY

Straight ticket voting will be eliminated beginning with the 2020 general election. Do voters have a personal responsibility to learn about each race and candidate, or is voting for a party a responsible action because there are too many candidates for voters to learn about?

primary
An election conducted within the party to nominate candidates who will run for public office in a subsequent general election.

general election
Held in November of even-numbered years to elect county, state, and federal officials from among candidates nominated in primaries or (for minor parties) in nominating conventions.

A clear distinction must be made between party primaries and general elections. **Primaries** are party functions that allow party members to select nominees to run against the candidates of opposing parties in a general election for national, state, and county offices. **General elections** determine which candidates will fill government offices. These electoral contests are public and are conducted, financed, and administered by state, county, and municipal governments as well as by special districts. This distinction between party primaries and general elections is valid, even though the U.S. Supreme Court has ruled that primaries are of such importance in the selection of general election candidates that they are subject to government regulation.

Thus, even though the state regulates and largely finances primaries, they serve only as a means for political parties to nominate candidates. The general election ballot also includes the names of independent candidates, space for write-in candidates, and names of candidates nominated by party convention because the law does not require nomination by direct primary.

Primaries

Political parties conduct primaries to select their nominees for public office. In Texas, party primaries are held in even-numbered years. Presidential primaries occur every four years and provide a means for Democrats and Republicans to select delegates to their parties' national conventions, where candidates for president and vice president are nominated. Other primaries occur every two years, when party members go to the polls to choose candidates for the U.S. Congress and for many state, district, and county offices. If a political party's candidate receives more than 20 percent of the total gubernatorial vote, the party must use primaries to select its nominees in the following even-numbered year. Political parties may use primaries for selecting their nominees "… if the party's nominee for governor in the most recent gubernatorial election received at least two percent but less than 20 percent of the total number of votes received by all candidates for governor."[58] Even minor parties that reach this threshold, along with those that fail to do so, use conventions to select their nominees.

Development of Direct Primaries A unique product of American political ingenuity, the **direct primary** was designed to provide a nominating method that would avoid domination by party bosses and allow wider participation by party members. This form of nomination permits party members to choose their candidates directly at the polls. For each office (except president and vice president of the United States and some local officials), party members select by popular vote the person they wish to be their party's candidate in the general election, in which candidates of all parties compete. In Texas, an absolute majority of the vote (more than 50 percent) is required for nomination. If the primary fails to produce such a majority, a **runoff primary** is held the fourth Tuesday in May to allow party members to choose a candidate from the first primary's top two vote-getters.

Four basic forms of the direct primary have evolved in America. Most states use some form of **closed primary**, which requires voters to declare a party affiliation when registering to vote. They must show party identification when voting in a primary election and can vote only in the party primary for which they are registered. Other states use an **open primary**, which does not require party identification of voters. At the polls, voters in an open primary can choose a ballot for any party, regardless of their party affiliation. Texas uses a combination of open and closed primaries.

direct primary
A nominating system that allows voters to participate directly in the selection of candidates for public office.

runoff primary
Held after the first primary to allow party members to choose a candidate from the first primary's top two vote-getters if no candidate received a majority vote.

closed primary
A primary in which voters must declare their support for a party before they are permitted to participate in the selection of its candidates.

open primary
A primary in which voters are not required to declare party affiliation.

Some states use a variation of the open primary, called the top-two primary (California and Washington) or **jungle primary** (Louisiana). Here voters receive the same ballot, on which are printed all candidate names. Candidates from all parties run in a single election. If a candidate receives more than 50 percent of the vote, he or she is declared the winner. If no candidate receives more than 50 percent, the top two vote-getters will participate in a runoff election. A criticism of the open primary is that it gives voters of one party an opportunity to sabotage the primary of another party. This can occur when voters who normally affiliate with one party try to nominate a "fringe" candidate from the other who has little chance of victory in the general election. Criticisms of top-two and jungle primaries include (1) they may produce two candidates from the same party competing for the same office in the general election, and (2) they limit the possibility of a third-party or independent candidate's ability to win the nomination.

Texas Primaries Before 1905, various practices had been used to select a party's nominees for public office. With the enactment of the Terrell Election Law in 1905, however, Texas political parties gained the opportunity to conduct primaries. The Texas Democratic Party has held primaries since that year. The Republican Party did not begin conducting primaries until 1926.

Beginning in the early 1950s, it became common practice for Texans to participate in the primaries of the Democratic Party and then legally cross over to vote for Republican candidates in the general election, a practice known as **crossover voting**. Historically, Texas Republicans were more likely to engage in crossover voting. As the number of Republican candidates increased, however, the number of crossover Republican voters correspondingly declined. Today, Democrats in Republican-dominated counties (such as Collin, Denton, Midland, Montgomery, and Williamson) are likely to participate in crossover voting.

The Texas Election Code requires voters to identify their party affiliation at the time of voting, making Texas a combination of a closed primary state and an open primary state. Voter registration certificates are stamped with the party name when voters participate in a primary. Qualified voters may vote in the primary of any party, as long as they have not already voted in another party's primary or participated in another party's convention in the same year.

Administering Primaries In most states, political parties sponsor and administer their own primaries. The Texas Election Code allocates this responsibility to each party's county executive committee. The primary normally occurs the first Tuesday of March. In 2018, the primary was held on March 6, and in 2020, it will be held on March 3.

Individuals who want to run in a direct primary for their party's nomination for a multicounty district office or a statewide office must file the necessary papers with their party's state chair. This party official certifies the names of these persons to each county chair in counties in which the election is administered. Prospective candidates who want their names placed on the primary ballot for a county or precinct office must file with their party's county chair. County executive committees for each political party supervise the printing of primary ballots. If the parties conduct a joint primary, the county elections administrator or the

jungle primary
A nominating process in which voters indicate their preferences by using a single ballot on which are printed the names and respective party labels of all persons seeking nomination. A candidate who receives more than 50 percent of the vote is elected; otherwise, a runoff between the top two candidates must be held.

crossover voting
A practice whereby a person participates in the primary of one party, then votes for one or more candidates of another party in the general election.

📊 HOW DO WE COMPARE...

In Types of Primaries?

Most Populous U.S. States	Primary Type	U.S. States Bordering Texas	Primary Type
California	Top-two primary	Arkansas	Open
Florida	Closed	Louisiana	Jungle (two-round system)
New York	Closed	New Mexico	Closed
Texas	**Combination (open/closed)**	Oklahoma	Closed

Source: FairVote, http://www.fairvote.org/primaries#congressional_primary_type_by_state.

Competency Connection
⚙ CRITICAL THINKING ⚙

Is the primary election for members of the party to choose their nominee, or should all registered voters have the opportunity to participate?

county clerk administers the election. If each party conducts its own primaries, county chairs arrange for voting equipment and polling places in the precincts or voting centers. Together with the state executive committee, the county executive committee determines the order of names of candidates on the ballot and **canvasses** (that is, confirms and certifies) the vote tally for each candidate.

Financing Primaries Major expenses for running party primaries include renting facilities for polls (the places where voting is conducted), printing ballots and other election materials, and paying election judges and clerks. In recent years, approximately 30 percent of the cost of holding Texas primaries has come from filing fees paid by candidates. The balance of these expenses is usually paid by the State of Texas. For example, candidates for the office of U.S. senator pay a $5,000 filing fee, and candidates for governor and all other statewide offices pay a $3,750 filing fee. Candidates for the Texas Senate and the Texas House of Representatives pay $1,250 and $750, respectively.[59]

In lieu of paying a fee, a candidate may file a nominating petition containing a specified number of signatures of people eligible to vote for the office for which that candidate is running. A candidate for statewide office must obtain 5,000 signatures. Candidates for district, county, or precinct office, and for offices of other political subdivisions, must obtain either 500 signatures or the equivalent of 2 percent of the area's votes for all candidates for governor in the last general election, whichever is less.

General and Special Elections

The date prescribed by Article I of the U.S. Constitution for congressional elections is the first Tuesday following the first Monday in November of even-numbered years (for example, November 6, 2018 and November 3, 2020). Presidential elections take place on the same day in November every four years (for example, November 3, 2020 and November 5, 2024).

canvass
To scrutinize the results of an election and then confirm and certify the vote tally for each candidate.

off-year or midterm election

A general election held in the even-numbered year following a presidential election.

special election

An election called by the governor to fill a vacancy (for example, U.S. congressional or state legislative office) or to vote on a proposed state constitutional amendment.

In Texas's general elections involving candidates for state, district, and county offices, the candidate who receives a plurality (the largest number of votes) in a contest is the winner. Even if no candidate wins a majority, because of votes received by third-party or independent candidates, the state does not hold a run-off election. Thus, Representative Will Hurd was reelected to Congress in 2018 after receiving 49.17 percent of the vote. Elections for governor and other state-wide officers serving terms of four years are scheduled in the off year. These **off-year or midterm elections** are held in November of the even-numbered years between presidential elections (for example, November 6, 2018 and November 8, 2022). Along with most other states, Texas follows this schedule to minimize the influence of presidential campaigns on the election of state and local officials. Elections to fill offices for two-year or six-year terms must be conducted in both off years and presidential years.

In addition, **special elections** are called to vote on constitutional amendments and local bond issues, as well as fill interim vacancies in legislative and

⊠ KEEPING CURRENT

Election 2020

How will Texas look in the 2020 elections and beyond? While Beto O'Rourke became a national political star and ran a close race against Senator Ted Cruz, he lost the election. Several statewide races were also close, though all were won by Republicans. Governor Abbott easily defeated Lupe Valdez, and Republicans retained control of the state legislature and won a majority of U.S. House seats. Why then would one expect anything different in 2020 and beyond?

There are indications that political change is coming to Texas: Beto O'Rourke's close race in 2018, Hillary Clinton's closer than expected loss in 2016, Democratic Party legislative gains in 2018 (12 Texas House seats, 2 Texas Senate seats, and 2 Congressional seats), and Democratic wins in urban counties suggest political change is coming to Texas.

The state's diversifying electorate and a leftward shift among young Texans appear to be weakening the Republican Party's control in Texas. The GOP's strongest supporters are older whites, yet each year there are fewer of them. Democrats have their strongest support among people of color and young whites, and that is the part of the electorate that is growing. Electoral

change may be coming to Texas because of a generational replacement, and this could make Texas competitive in the 2020 presidential and legislative elections. If Texas becomes competitive in presidential elections, or goes Democratic, it will have national political implications and transform the Electoral College Map.

As for election laws and administration, the 86th State Legislature failed to pass a law that would have made it a felony for an ineligible voter to vote. The Texas Senate did not confirm Secretary of State nominee David Whitley after a failed attempt to investigate the citizenship of 98,000 registered voters. Investigations found that the list was flawed and that many citizens were erroneously flagged as non-citizens. Defenders of both actions claimed these were both efforts at maintaining election security. Critics charged they were efforts to suppress the vote.

Sources: Juan Carlos Huerta and Beatriz Cuartas, "Is Texas Finally Turning Blue? We Looked at the Electorate to Find Out." December 18, 2018, *The Monkey Cage,* https://www .washingtonpost.com/news/monkey-cage/wp/2018/12/18/are-texass-demographics-finally-turning-the-state-blue-we-looked-at-the-electorate-to-find-out/?noredirect=on&utm_term= .c9d1d22f97a1; Mary Tuma, "Whitley Sinks, Voting Rights Don't." May 31, 2019, *The Austin Chronicle,* https://www.austinchronicle .com/news/2019-05-31/whitley-sinks-voting-rights-dont/.

congressional districts. If no candidate obtains a majority in a special election, a runoff contest between the top two contenders must be conducted to determine a winner. For example, on December 11, 2018, voters participated in a special election to fill a vacancy for Senate District 6. Four candidates filed to fill the Houston area Senate seat, with Democrat Carol Alvarado receiving 50.37 percent of the vote, followed by Democrat Ana Hernandez with 24.36 percent. Since Alvarado received a majority, no runoff election was needed. Vacancies in state judicial and executive offices are filled by gubernatorial appointment until the next general election and do not require special elections. Special elections for local governments (cities and counties) are discussed in Chapter 3, "Local Governments."

> ✓ **5.5 Learning Check**
>
> 1. True or False: Political parties are responsible for conducting general elections.
> 2. What is the difference between open and closed primaries?
>
> *Answers at the end of this chapter.*

CONCLUSION

Although most obstacles to voting have been abolished and Texas election laws have extended voting periods and simplified the elections process, many Texans do not exercise their right to vote. In national, state, and local elections, Texans vote at or below the national average. In addition, because education, income, and race and ethnicity are critical factors affecting voter turnout, concern is increasing that decisions are being made by an "elite" minority.

CHAPTER SUMMARY

LO 5.1 Analyze the components of a political campaign. Political campaigns have evolved from candidate speeches on a courthouse lawn or from the rear platform of a campaign train to sophisticated organizations that utilize media, targeted emails, and social networking resources to win voter support. As a result, political campaigns have become increasingly expensive. Texas laws are relatively weak, and federal regulations of campaign financing have been limited by judicial decisions and loopholes in disclosure laws.

LO 5.2 Describe the impact of Texas's changing demographics on politics. Racial and ethnic factors are strong influences on Texas politics and shape political campaigns. The increasing size of the Latino population makes Latinos an important factor in elections. However, lower levels of political activity than in the population at large limit an even greater impact of the Latino electorate. A majority of Latino voters and super majorities of African American voters participate in Democratic primaries and vote for Democratic candidates in general elections.

LO 5.3 Describe the evolving role of women in Texas politics. Texas women did not begin to vote and hold public office for three-quarters of a century after Texas joined the Union. Before 1990, only four women had won a statewide office in Texas. By the 1990s, the number of women elected to statewide office increased dramatically. Moreover, women served as mayors in about 150 of the state's towns and cities. In several elections early in the 21st century, women led all candidates on either ticket in votes received. Female candidates held the top two positions on the Democratic Party's ticket in 2014.

The number of women elected recently to state office has declined. Despite their electoral victories in Texas and elsewhere across the nation, fewer women than men seek elective public office. As customs, habits, and attitudes have changed, opportunities for women in public service have expanded.

LO 5.4 Explain how the voting process promotes and inhibits voter participation.
For most Texans, voting is their principal political activity. Registration is required before a person can vote and is intended to determine in advance whether prospective voters meet all the qualifications prescribed by law. Federal voting rights legislation has expanded the electorate, simplified voter registration, and encouraged voting. In addition, Texas law provides an early voting period to begin 17 days before an election or 10 days before a runoff. However, recent U.S. Supreme Court decisions and Texas's restrictive voter identification law have been criticized for inhibiting voter participation.

LO 5.5 Identify the differences among primary, general, and special elections. Primary elections are elections conducted within a political party to nominate candidates who will run for public office in a subsequent general election. General elections are conducted in November of even-numbered years to elect county, state, and federal officials from among candidates nominated in primary elections (or for small parties, in nominating conventions). Special elections are called by the governor to fill a vacancy (for example, U.S. congressional or state legislative office) or to vote on a proposed state constitutional amendment.

KEY TERMS

affirmative racial gerrymandering, p. 171
at-large district, p. 171
Campaign Reform Act, p. 161
canvass, p. 187
closed primary, p. 185
crossover voting, p. 186
dark money, p. 163
direct primary, p. 185
early voting, p. 171
election judge, p. 181
elections administrator, p. 181
general election, p. 184

gerrymandering, p. 170
grandfather clause, p. 170
hard money, p. 161
independent candidate, p. 157
independent expenditures, p. 162
jungle primary, p. 186
literacy tests, p. 170
motor-voter law, p. 172
off-year or midterm election, p. 188
open primary, p. 185
political action committee (PAC),
    p. 160
poll tax, p. 169

primary, p. 184
runoff primary, p. 185
soft money, p. 161
sound bite, p. 157
special election, p. 188
super PAC, p. 162
Texas Election Code, p. 178
Texas Ethics Commission, p. 161
universal suffrage, p. 169
voter turnout, p. 173
voting center, p. 180
voting precinct, p. 180
white primary, p. 170

LEARNING CHECK ANSWERS

 5.1   **1.** Texas is a large state and it is impractical for candidates to attempt to visit all of it. Statewide candidates must use advertisement on TV and radio, and also on social media.

2. False. Texas has no limits on donations to candidates for statewide office.

✓ 5.2   **1.** African Americans are more supportive of Democratic Party candidates than Latinos.

2. Latinos are an important group because the Latino population is growing and by 2040 is expected to be the majority population in the state.

✓ 5.3   **1.** False. There are more men serving in the legislature than there are women.

2. Women still shoulder more responsibilities for family and home than men do; some mothers feel obliged to care for children in the home until their children finish high school; and some voters hold prejudices against women.

✓ 5.4   **1.** Two former obstacles to voting in Texas included poll taxes and all-white primaries.

2. False. Texas law allows any qualified voter to vote from 17 to 4 days preceding a scheduled election or first primary and from 10 to 4 days preceding a runoff primary.

✓ 5.5   **1.** False. Political parties are responsible for primary elections. Government officials are responsible for conducting general elections.

2. Closed primaries are restricted to registered members of a political party. Any registered voter can participate in an open primary.

6 The Media and Politics

Learning Objectives

6.1 Compare the ways in which Texans get their information today with past patterns.

6.2 Describe the roles of the media in Texas politics.

6.3 Discuss the roles of the media in modern Texas election campaigns.

6.4 Analyze the issue of ideological bias in the Texas media.

6.5 Distinguish how print and electronic media are regulated by government.

6.6 Discuss representation of women and ethnic minorities in Texas media.

6.7 Discuss the positive and negative effects of changes the media are undergoing in Texas.

IMAGE 6.1 Students in a computer lab at the University of Texas Rio Grande Valley Brownsville Campus.

Robert Daemmrich Photography Inc/Corbis/Getty Images

Competency Connection
☼ CRITICAL THINKING ☼

Texans who want to stay informed are transitioning from reliance on newspapers and television to the Internet and social media. How well are you served by this change? Why? After reading the chapter, think about whether you would give the same answer.

The **media** have long had a major impact on politics in Texas and the nation. They play a major role in maintaining our democracy: informing citizens and leaders about what governments and politicians are doing and the debates about those actions, sometimes reporting information officials would rather we didn't know; affecting the issues that governments consider seriously; and, to some degree, shaping public opinion. In carrying out these roles, the media both affect and are affected by the other political actors—government and political leaders, interest groups, and the public. Because of the importance of the media and their diverse nature, serious debate surrounds whether and what kinds of bias exist and the rapidly changing nature of the media (such changes as the decline of newspapers, the growth of the Internet and social media, and the growing concentration of ownership of newspapers, television, and digital media). These topics are explored in this chapter.

In many ways, Texas is a unique state. However, as we will see, the media and their role in politics are similar to national patterns in most respects—with a few important exceptions. This chapter looks at national patterns and whether and how they play out in Texas.

This text distinguishes between three types of media: The term *print media* is generally accepted for newspapers and news magazines. Here, we refer to radio and television as *electronic media* and distinguish between broadcast and cable television. The Internet and social media are commonly referred to as *digital media*. Second, note that the word *media* is plural; for example, "The media *have* long had a major impact."

◩ Where Do We Get Our Information?

LO 6.1 Compare the ways in which Texans get their information today with past patterns.

The simple answer to the question of where we get our information is that it comes from newspapers and news magazines, television and radio, and the Internet and social media. However, the complete answer is more complex. Most people get news from more than one source, and whether they remember the information depends on the trust they have for the source and a number of other factors. Newspapers were once the dominant source of news. Today, however, newspapers are in decline in both numbers and readership, although they remain very important for national and state leaders. Television news is widely watched but is thin in content and is being outpaced by the Internet and social media.

Although often absent in discussions of sources of news, family and friends are an important source of news for many people. The most common way that people (almost three-quarters of all Americans) begin the process is, not surprisingly, from conversations—in person or over the phone. Almost two-thirds of adults follow up the information from family and friends by seeking the story in

Follow *Practicing Texas Politics* on Twitter @PracTexPol

media
Major means of mass communication.

the news media—traditional or new. Americans still count more on news organizations than family and friends for information, but they tend to be suspicious of both sources.[1]

In the past, newspapers and later television were the major sources of news. However, as Tables 6.1 and 6.2 show, the Internet is now challenging television news for more viewers. By 2016, which medium ranked first depended on how the question was asked. Also note that most people rely on more than one source of news. During 2016, only 9 percent of people relied on a single kind of source for information about the presidential campaign. Eighty percent consulted three or more types of sources (listed in Table 6.1). Another change is that a substantial majority of people (72 percent) get at least some news from mobile devices.

Table 6.2 shows that Texans and the nation have similar patterns of attention to sources of news. Among Texans, Internet and television are the most common sources of news, significantly leading radio and newspapers.

TABLE 6.1 Where People Learned about the 2016 Presidential Election

(Percentage of U.S. adults who learned about the presidential election in the past week from…)	%
Television	**78**
Local TV news	57
Cable TV news	54
National nightly network TV news	49
Late night comedy show	25
Digital	**65**
News websites or apps	48
Social networking site	44
Issue-based group websites, apps, or email	23
Candidate or campaign group websites, apps, or emails	20
Radio	**44**
Print newspaper	**36**
Local daily newspaper in print	29
National newspapers in print	23

Note: Numbers do not add to 100 percent because respondents could name more than one source of information.

Source: Jeffrey Gottfried, Michael Barthel, Elisa Shearer, and Amy Mitchell, "The 2016 Presidential Campaign - A News Event That's Hard to Miss," *Pew Research Center - Journalism & Media*, February 4, 2016, http://www.journalism.org/2016/02/04/the-2016-presidential-campaign-a-news-event-thats-hard-to-miss.

— Competency Connection —
☼ **CRITICAL THINKING** ☼

There are many sources of news. Can you rank them in terms of which are better sources? What factors did you consider in your ranking?

TABLE 6.2 Attention to News in the Types of Media in Texas and the Nation: How Many Times a Person Followed the 2016 Campaign (Percent)

Number of Times	TV		Internet		Newspaper		Radio	
	Texas	U.S.	Texas	U.S.	Texas	U.S.	Texas	U.S.
None	7	9	17	14	48	39	41	38
One or Two	28	23	15	16	22	22	19	22
Several	33	34	31	32	16	21	21	22
A Good Many	32	34	37	38	14	18	19	18
Total Percentage	100	100	100	100	100	100	100	100

Source: "2016 National Election Study Time Series," *Survey Documentation and Analysis,* University of California, Berkeley, http://sda.berkeley.edu, analyzed by author, January 15, 2019.

— Competency Connection —
☼ CRITICAL THINKING ☼

The table shows few major differences in paying attention to the news between the national and Texas samples. Why do you believe this similarity exists?

Print Media: Newspapers and News Magazines

Newspapers were long *the* news media for Americans. Nationally, newspapers began in the colonies in the early 1700s and had become important sources of political news by 1750. After 1800, they grew in number and news content, increasing from 92 newspapers in 1789 (the effective date of the U.S. Constitution) to 1,200 in 1835. The number of U.S. newspapers peaked at just over 2,600 at the beginning of the 20th century and declined to 1,286 dailies by 2016. Circulation peaked at 37 percent of the population in 1947 and then declined to 15 percent by 2009.[2] From the first newspaper in Texas, the *Gaceta de Tejas* (which may have published only one or two editions in 1813), to Texas's independence, few newspapers were actually published in the state. By 1860, there were 82. Most ceased publication during the Civil War, but the number of newspapers increased soon after the War and on into the 20th century.

By 1965, Texas ranked third in the nation in number of daily newspapers, and 80 percent of Texas households subscribed to at least one newspaper. However, competition from television slowed the growth of newspapers, and the advent of the Internet put them into decline. Newspapers have been particularly harmed by loss of advertising to Internet sites. Loss of classified ads to such sites as Craigslist has been especially damaging to revenue. By 2017, the state's 67 daily newspapers represented 57 percent of the number (118) that had been available in 1975.[3] Nevertheless, the five largest Texas cities had newspapers that ranked in the top 29 of the nation in circulation in 2015. (The *Dallas Morning News* was 4th and the *Houston Chronicle* 11th.) Like most newspapers, all have reduced staff and news pages.

Weekly newspapers have declined by about a third just since 2000; 397 were published in 2017.[4] Weeklies provide local social and political news but little state or national news. (Lots of pictures of kids, awards, and weddings greatly help circulation.) They tend to serve small towns and counties, suburban areas, college campuses, and communities with common interests, such as business, legal, military, and ethnic groups. One listing shows 50 ethnic newspapers in the state serving Latinos, African Americans, or major Asian groups.[5] Decline of the major dailies has given an opening to alternative newspapers in larger cities, notably the *Dallas Observer*, *Houston Press* (online-only beginning in 2017), and *Austin Chronicle*. Availability of print news has been boosted to some extent by the rise of several newspapers to national circulation, particularly the *Wall Street Journal*, *New York Times*, *Washington Post*, and *USA Today*. These dailies, of course, carry little Texas state and local news.

News magazines have always been fewer in number and read by fewer people. However, such periodicals are quite influential because they tend to be read by elites. Because news magazine reporters have more time to gather information and study it, their stories often provide more perspective than those published in newspapers. With its large population, Texas would seem a likely candidate for several competing news magazines. However, this competition has not emerged. Progressives and liberals have read the *Texas Observer* since 1954, but there is not a comparable conservative news magazine. *Texas Monthly*, an award-winning magazine, covers some politics but since its 2016 ownership change focuses more on social and cultural stories. Its article on the best and worst legislators after each biennial session of the Texas legislature is watched with trepidation by legislators up for reelection. As is detailed below, political websites on the Internet have taken up some of the slack from the shortage of state news magazines.

IMAGE 6.2 Delivering newspapers on a bike: A vanishing piece of Americana.

Vstock LK/Alamy Stock Photo

— Competency Connection —
✿ **CRITICAL THINKING** ✿

Will local newspapers survive the Internet challenge? Why or why not?

The print media have been particularly important sources of political information for at least four reasons. First, compared with television and radio, print media have the space to cover more stories and to develop these stories in greater detail. Although many in the general public are satisfied with only headlines and highlights, opinion leaders and those actually involved in government and politics need more detail and more complete coverage. Hence, the second reason for the importance of newspapers is that they are the major source of news for the elite (the better educated, more affluent population and political leaders).

Third, newspapers remain the largest gatherers of news. Print media have more reporters to find the news and are more often the ones who break stories (that is, initially report them). Major national newspapers and two wire services—New York City-based Associated Press (AP) and London-based Reuters—provide much of the national and international news that appears in other newspapers, on television and radio, and on Internet news sites and blogs. Newspapers, thus, tend to set the news agenda for broadcast news and the Internet.

Finally, major print media today require that stories be vetted for accuracy and attempt to follow standards of objectivity in reporting. Objectivity and vetting are only gradually developing on the Internet and are often problems on the two leading cable news channels, Fox on the right (the conservative side) and MSNBC on the left (the liberal side). (See the section later in this chapter, "Bias?")

The decline of local newspapers in Texas and elsewhere is important for at least two additional reasons. First, local newspaper reporters are often responsible for exposing corruption and graft in public life. (See the later section, "Investigative Journalism.") Second, when cities had competing newspapers, their presence facilitated public debate because editorial boards commonly took opposing stances on political issues. Through 1995, Houston had two dailies, the *Chronicle* (sometimes called the *Comical*) and the now defunct *Post* (sometimes called the *Pest*). Editorial positions changed somewhat with ownership, but editors' views for each paper often conflicted. In the mid-1980s, San Antonio's *Express* and *News* combined to form the *Express-News*, and in 1993, the *San Antonio Light* went out of business. The Dallas–Fort Worth Metroplex is currently served by two major newspapers. On their editorial pages, the *Dallas Morning News* often reflects center-right (moderate conservative) and conservative views and the *Fort Worth Star-Telegram* center-left (moderate liberal) and centrist perspectives.

Electronic Media: Radio and Television

Commercial radio in the United States began in the 1920s and by the 1930s entered its two-decade "Golden Age." Radio, however, did not penetrate Texas and the rest of the South in the 1930s to the degree that it did elsewhere. In Texas and other states, coverage of the war fronts during World War II enhanced the standing of radio, as did its value as a distraction from the horrors of war. Nationally and in Texas, radio remains pervasive. Ninety-nine percent of American homes have one or more radios receiving broadcasts from more than 11,000 radio stations. In Texas, there are 1,032 stations, compared to 464 newspapers.[6]

Radio is an important source of entertainment, particularly music, but it has limited value as a source of political news. Radio stations usually provide five minutes of news on the hour—headlines without much detail. For state and national news, most stations have at best a small news staff and depend on stories from the news services or feeds from such sources as the Texas State Network or, more recently, Fox News Radio. Local news tends to lack substance, and politics must compete with local social, cultural, and sports events for the short time available.

Two developments have increased the news impact of radio: the rise of talk radio and the development of radio focused on news. In the 1980s, politically oriented radio call-in talk shows became popular. Two decisions by the federal government had a major impact on this phenomenon in Texas and elsewhere. In 1987, the Federal Communications Commission (FCC) abolished the Fairness Doctrine that required stations to provide both sides of controversial topics they chose to air. Under the Fairness Doctrine, stations effectively had to provide both liberal and conservative commentators in the small world of talk radio. Without the Doctrine, conservatives, with a bigger audience, quickly outpaced the liberals.

In a second change, the federal Telecommunications Act of 1996 facilitated the development of large chains of radio stations, which in turn made easier the syndication of popular talk radio programs. This made talk radio available to more stations and their listeners. iHeartMedia, Inc. (formerly Clear Channel Communications), headquartered in San Antonio, for example, has become a major player in talk radio. It is a holding company involved in radio and television, outdoor advertising, and online programming. It is the largest owner of radio stations in the country (850), including 72 in Texas. iHeartMedia's seven news and talk radio stations in Texas cover all of the major metropolitan areas in the state except Austin.

Since 1991, conservative Rush Limbaugh has been the most listened to talk show host in the United States, followed more recently by other conservatives, such as Sean Hannity (whom some consider more influential because of his connection to President Trump), Glenn Beck, and Mark Levin. Conservative talk radio is heard almost entirely on commercial radio, whereas liberal commentators make more use of community radio. Political talk radio peaked in popularity in the 2000s, although it retains a large audience and is making increasing use of streaming, podcasts, Twitter, and Facebook.

In Texas, nationally syndicated talk show hosts have substantial followings, along with hosts who have Texas origins, such as Alex Jones, Michael Berry, Neal Boortz, Joe Pagliarulo, and Dan Patrick. Patrick's popularity led to a state senate seat and then his election as lieutenant governor in 2014 and 2018. Austin-based Alex Jones mixes conspiracy theories and conservatism. His denial of the Sandy Hook School shooting led to lawsuits, and in 2018, he was banned from four major online platforms, including YouTube and Facebook, for "promoting violence and hate speech."

Talk radio has provided an opportunity for its predominantly conservative audience to air their views and create a sense of community. Talk shows generally are a mix of opinion and entertainment with some news. Opinion and entertainment often taint the news, which is seldom fact-checked. More than half of listeners simply reinforce their preexisting views. Nevertheless, research also shows that regular listeners are influenced by the views they hear.[7]

The political role of radio has also been enhanced by the availability of all-news stations—some local, some part of large chains, and some from satellite radio, which provides a variety of news formats. In addition, public radio provides substantial coverage of local, state, and national news. Examples include Austin's KUT, KERA in Dallas, Houston's KUHF, and Texas Public Radio, which operates several stations in San Antonio and the Hill Country. In Austin, KUT's coverage is enriched by a partnership with the online newspaper *The Texas Tribune*. Over time, public radio stations in different Texas cities have combined resources for special reporting projects such as TXDecides and StateImpact.

Regularly scheduled television broadcasting in the United States began in 1928. However, Texas did not have commercial television until after World War II, when the industry began to flourish nationally. In 1948, WBAP-TV, the first television station in Texas and the South, was opened by Amon G. Carter, publisher of the *Fort Worth Star-Telegram* and a pioneer in Texas radio. In the 1950s, television flourished in the state. It appears that Texas paralleled the nation in the expansion of television. Nationally, the number of households with television expanded from 9 percent in 1950 to 97 percent in 1975, a percentage that has held steady to the present. Today, 80 percent of households have cable or satellite, although the proportion is declining among younger viewers. As of late 2017, there were 133 television stations in Texas, 11 of which are Public Broadcasting System (PBS) stations, covering 90 percent of the state's population.

Television news today comes in at least five different formats. From the most to the least used by the public, they are local news, cable news (particularly Fox, MSNBC, and CNN), network news (NBC, CBS, and ABC), political talk shows, and late night comedy shows.

IMAGE 6.3 Symbols of the new media: Facebook, Twitter, and the Tumblr site for Texas's online newspaper, *The Texas Tribune*.

Source: www.facebook.com; www.twitter.com; http://texastribune.tumblr.com.

Competency Connection
◉ SOCIAL RESPONSIBILITY ◉

How have the Internet and social media influenced the reliability of news?

Digital Media: The Internet and Social Media

In comparison to the other media, the Internet is a recent phenomenon with its roots in the 1960s. The blooming of what we think of as the Internet and **social media** came in the period 1994–2004. Since that time, there has been an explosive growth of websites, both in number and function. Not surprisingly, the Internet has become a vital part of politics and society. As Table 6.1 indicates, about two-thirds of Americans learned about the 2016 election campaign from the Internet. As we will see below, successful candidates and political movements now rely on the Internet.

Today, **news websites** and political **blogs** are increasingly important outlets for news. It is now quite rare for a Texas newspaper (including weeklies) or television station not to have a website providing a range of news and often blogs. Some of these sites are extensive; some are not. The connection with social media is also strong. Logos for such sites as Facebook, Twitter, YouTube, Tumblr, Pinterest, Instagram, and LinkedIn are commonly found on the state's newspapers, television stations, and magazines and their respective Internet sites. (See the three in Image 6.2.) Logos encourage readers to join conversations happening on these sites about current issues. Some users prefer to log in through social media to navigate news sites and to post comments.

In addition, since 2009, the *Texas Tribune* has been a high-quality nonprofit online newspaper that reaches a wide range of people, including most of the state's political elite. Texas has long had political newsletters that cover major issues and happenings—generally for a fee. The *Quorum Report*, for example, has been a self-described source of "information and gossip" since 1983 and went online in 1998. *Capitol Inside* has provided news and analysis since 2003.

Over the last decade, political blogs (regularly updated websites providing information and/or opinion) have become increasingly important in Texas politics. They tend to provide opinion (from diatribes to serious analysis) and news (commonly with the author's spin). They entertain, provide information, reinforce views, bring together like-minded citizens, and sometimes coordinate action. From 2006 to 2015, one of the more influential political blogs in the state was written by *Texas Monthly* senior executive editor Paul Burka. Since his retirement, *Texas Monthly Politics* has become more prominent.

The two major political parties, most statewide and some local candidates, and a multitude of interest groups maintain blogs, along with authors from both the left and right. Examples of ideological blogs on the left include *Off the Kuff* (self-described as Texas's longest running progressive political blog) and *Grits for Breakfast* (postings focused on criminal justice reform and available since 2004). Examples on the right include *Texas Conservative Review* (by a longtime Republican activist, published since 2002), *Big Jolly Politics* (with a range of conservative views sprinkled with humor, published since 2009), and *Texas Insider* (with coverage of national and state issues for 200,000 readers and posted daily since 2003). Part-time blogs often come and go, and recently because of problems with advertising revenue, some established Texas political blogs have effectively ceased or changed platforms (for example, Internet to podcast).

social media
Websites and computer applications that allow users to engage in social networking and create online communities. Social media provide platforms for sharing information and ideas through discussion forums, videos, photos, documents, audio clips, and the like.

news website
An Internet site that provides news. These sites are often affiliated with a newspaper or television station, but increasingly, many are independent.

blog
A website or web page on which a writer or group of writers record opinions, information, and links to other sites on a regular basis.

Over time, the use of social media has grown considerably among all demographic groups. Today, almost two-thirds of Americans over age 18 use social networking sites such as Facebook and Twitter, up from 7 percent in 2005. Social network usage is little affected by gender, race/ethnicity, or place of residence (urban, suburban, or rural). Education and income make some difference. Only age makes a substantial difference, and even then the oldest generation is not absent. Ninety percent of those ages 18 to 29 use social networking sites, compared to 35 percent of those age 65 and older.[8] Which site is preferred evolves over time. Facebook continues to be the most used site, but many younger users are focusing more on other sites, such as Snapchat.

As can be seen in Figure 6.1, age also has a strong impact on where people get news. Among younger adults (ages 18–29), social media is viewed as the most helpful source. For older generations, cable news is preferred, and appreciation of social media declines with age.

Many people get news from social networking sites. For example, in 2016, 70 percent of Texans reported learning campaign news from social media.[9] However, news exposure is often incidental to searching for other information. Thus, social media users have more exposure to news but may disregard or forget the message because it was not their primary focus. The range of news topics users find is broad. For example, entertainment news about celebrities is the most common kind of information accessed on Facebook. News about national government and politics is fourth, and local government is seventh (Figure 6.2).

Those who learn about a news story on Facebook may then access a news site. However, those who go directly to a news website spend three times as long there as those who arrive through Facebook.[10] Twitter is particularly important for following news as it happens and seeing comments on the event. Half of social network users have shared the news they gather on Twitter with others on the site, and almost half have discussed the information online. However, research shows that social media does not always facilitate discussion of important topics on-line or in person. Many users are reluctant to discuss topics when they perceive that their audience might disagree with them.[11]

Individuals also contribute to news reporting by posting photos (14 percent) or video (12 percent) they took at an event. Videos of policing incidents, for example, have a major impact on public discussion of police practice. Nationally, the racial conflict that followed a videoed police shooting in Ferguson, Missouri, focused public attention, but racially based incidents in Texas also produced debate in 2015–2016—for example, police response to African American teenagers at a McKinney pool party, the arrests and apparent beating of African American and Latino jaywalkers on Sixth Street in Austin, and the use of force against African American and Latino schoolchildren by school police in San Antonio and Round Rock. Body and dashboard cameras (sometimes eventually posted on line) have also helped to clear police in other incidents.

Groups also make use of online videos to further their cause. In 2015, a California anti-abortion group posted secretly taped videos of a conversation with a Planned Parenthood representative in Houston. In the discussion, group members asked about the possibility and cost of obtaining fetal tissue from aborted fetuses for research. There followed a firestorm of reactions in Texas and Washington, D.C. The effect of the incident carried into proposals made in the 2019 legislature. The videos proved a major blow to Planned Parenthood even though a Harris County grand jury cleared the organization of any violation of the law and indicted the videographers for tampering with a government document (a driver's license) and purchase or sale of human organs (the charge they attempted to make against Planned Parenthood). Both charges were later dropped.

A problem with the increasing role of blogs and ordinary citizens in generating and disseminating news is a lack of standards for honesty and vetting (checking for accuracy), something more likely to happen with the traditional media. Blogs and social media can quickly spread false or distorted information. Online fact-checking for both traditional and digital media is increasing. Politifact.com has a Texas-specific section, and other sites, such as Factcheck.org and Snopes.com cover Texas along with the rest of the nation. Like the facts they check, these fact-checkers should not be taken as definitive. The reader should examine how the site decided something was true or false.

✓ 6.1 Learning Check

1. From which media do most people get their news today?
2. From which medium did most people get their news in the early 20th century?

Answers at the end of this chapter.

FIGURE 6.1 Relation of Age to the Perception of the Most Helpful Source of Information about the Presidential Campaign

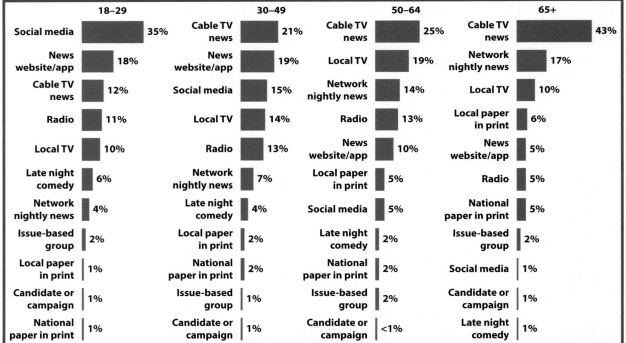

Source: Jeffrey Gottfried, Michael Barthel, Elisa Shearer, and Amy Mitchell, "The 2016 Presidential Campaign—a News Event That's Hard to Miss," Pew Research Center, February 4, 2016, http://www.journalism.org/2016/02/04/the-2016-presidential-campaign-a-news-event-thats-hard-to-miss.

18–29
Social media	35%
News website/app	18%
Cable TV news	12%
Radio	11%
Local TV	10%
Late night comedy	6%
Network nightly news	4%
Issue-based group	2%
Local paper in print	1%
Candidate or campaign	1%
National paper in print	1%

30–49
Cable TV news	21%
News website/app	19%
Social media	15%
Local TV	14%
Radio	13%
Network nightly news	7%
Late night comedy	4%
Local paper in print	2%
National paper in print	2%
Issue-based group	1%
Candidate or campaign	1%

50–64
Cable TV news	25%
Local TV	19%
Network nightly news	14%
Radio	13%
News website/app	10%
Local paper in print	5%
Social media	5%
Late night comedy	2%
National paper in print	2%
Issue-based group	2%
Candidate or campaign	<1%

65+
Cable TV news	43%
Network nightly news	17%
Local TV	10%
Local paper in print	6%
News website/app	5%
Radio	5%
National paper in print	5%
Issue-based group	2%
Social media	1%
Candidate or campaign	1%
Late night comedy	1%

— Competency Connection —
☼ CRITICAL THINKING ☼

People in different age groups turn to different media sources for information based on how helpful they perceive those sources to be. What factors might contribute to these different perceptions?

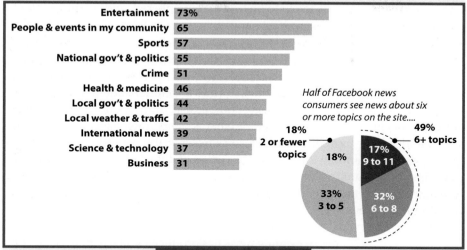

FIGURE 6.2 Percent of Facebook News Consumers Who Regularly See News on Facebook about...

Entertainment — 73%
People & events in my community — 65
Sports — 57
National gov't & politics — 55
Crime — 51
Health & medicine — 46
Local gov't & politics — 44
Local weather & traffic — 42
International news — 39
Science & technology — 37
Business — 31

Half of Facebook news consumers see news about six or more topics on the site....

18%
2 or fewer topics

49%
6+ topics

17%
9 to 11

18%

33%
3 to 5

32%
6 to 8

Source: Katerina Eva Matsa and Amy Mitchell, "8 Key Takeaways about Social Media and News," Pew Research Journalism Project, March 26, 2014, http://www.journalism.org/2014/03/26/8-keytakeaways-about-social-media-and-news.

— Competency Connection —
⚙ **CRITICAL THINKING** ⚙

What do you think of the quantity and quality of news provided through social media?

✪ The Media's Roles in Politics

LO 6.2 Describe the roles of the media in Texas politics.

The media are commonly said to fill four roles in U.S. and Texas politics: to provide information for the public and decision makers, to help citizens maintain democracy, to help shape the public agenda (what government does and doesn't do), and to influence citizens' views.

Providing Information

The first role, providing information, is basic and sounds simple. Over seven in ten adults report following news somewhat or very closely. However, transfer of information to the public is complex. Most people are not involved in politics and at best care only marginally about what is happening politically. They are more likely to hear and remember ideas and important but unexciting information if it comes from someone they trust. This source may be a trusted newscaster such as Walter Cronkite (1916–2009), the Texan who was anchor for CBS's nightly news program for 19 years, or local news anchors such as Houston's Bill Balleza, Dallas–Fort Worth's Brian Curtis, Austin's Amanda Salinas, or San Antonio's Randy Beamer. Bloggers and talk show hosts also may fill this role.

Trusted opinion leaders are most often friends or relatives who pay close attention to the news on traditional or new media and pass on the information to people they know. Because these leaders are known and trusted, the information they provide is more likely to be heard, remembered, and further explored. A majority of Americans who hear about a story from friends and family follow up by seeking a full news story.[12]

Knowing something about an issue increases the probability that related media stories will be heard and remembered. Thus, members of the political elite are more likely to pay attention to the news and to get more out of it than the general public. They know more initially, and because of their knowledge, they feel a greater incentive to become aware of what is happening. Research shows that a substantial, long-term difference exists between ordinary citizens and political leaders in understanding the news and in levels of knowledge (remembering and putting it into context). Many scholars see a growing knowledge divide between the informed and the less informed.

An impediment to gaining information for both an interested public and the elite is the softening of the news. Growth in the number and range of alternatives to newspapers and network evening news has produced a sharp increase in competition for advertising dollars, which are closely connected to audience size. To gain more readers/listeners, news providers have increased the amount of entertainment in news broadcasts (often referred to as **soft news**). Concomitantly, they have decreased the quantity of news focused on facts and affecting public policy (referred to as **hard news**). Local television news in Texas and elsewhere has long focused on accidents, crime, and the reaction of local residents to national events. As a result, although crime has declined in many cities such as Houston and Dallas, regular viewers of local news often believe that crime is increasing. Similarly, followers of talk radio, one of the ideological cable television networks (Fox or MSNBC), or ideological Internet blogs may develop more political knowledge but also come to accept inaccurate or incomplete versions of reality.

Digital media make important contributions to the flow of information to the public. They remove filters put in place by traditional media that limit direct access to information and allow the public to communicate directly.[13] Friends and family now have a major role in contributing and disseminating news. Not only do stories get posted on social networking sites, but users have the chance to include their own views and experiences.

The site Reddit, for example, allows users (rather than media professionals) to select the most important stories of the day. Unfortunately, the news role of social media has a fundamental conflict without an easy answer. On the one hand, few people use sites such as Reddit (7 percent in 2016), and for those users, entertainment value often trumps substantive value in the news chosen. On the other hand, considerable evidence supports the charge that news selection by professional journalists is elitist in nature and does not resonate with a large part of the public.

Government, interest groups, and the elite want to get the word out to the public. This goal long meant trying to get the print and electronic press to cover their concerns as news. Today, the Internet and social media provide an array of

soft news
News that is more entertaining, sensationalized, covers only the surface, and has little connection to public policy.

hard news
News that focuses on the facts, provides more depth, and commonly has implications for public policy.

direct outlets for users that avoid the filtering by professional journalists: their own Internet sites; advertisements on others' sites; blogs; and social media sites like Facebook, Twitter, and Instagram. If someone "likes" or "follows" a politician or interest group on a social media site, it is possible to contribute directly to the news feed and help spread the "news" by sharing a post.

Most Texas state officials make substantial use of the Internet to connect directly with citizens. The official website of the Office of the Governor urges viewers to "Connect with Gov. Abbott," listing Facebook, Twitter, Flickr, RSS Feed, Email, YouTube, LinkedIn, and Instagram. The Texas Comptroller's website, long referred to as "Window on State Government," has become a major source of information on the state that has enhanced the role of the comptroller.

Maintaining Democracy

A second task often assigned to the media is protecting democracy. Historically, the media have played a key protective role, but the quality of the protection has varied greatly. Media play a vital informational role for both ordinary citizens and leaders. Without the media reporting what is happening, citizens would be unable to make intelligent decisions in voting and other forms of political participation. We would be dependent on what the government and interest groups tell us. We also rely on the media to investigate and dig out information that government officials and special interests wish to hide. Over time, the ability of the press to fill these roles has fluctuated.

The Partisan Past Throughout the 19th century, newspapers in Texas and the nation were highly partisan, often scurrilous, and not addicted to the truth. For example, newspapers around the state were strongly divided on the personality of Sam Houston in both the editorial and news pages. When newspapers reemerged after the Civil War, they divided sharply over Reconstruction's Governor Edmund J. Davis. Nevertheless, the sensationalistic and exaggerated stories, known as "**yellow journalism**," published by the Hearst and Pulitzer newspapers at the close of the 19th century laid a foundation for investigative journalism, according to some historians. Others see yellow journalism as the ancestor of today's supermarket tabloids. In any event, the *Galveston News* in the second half of the 19th century began to move away from harsh partisanship, and by the end of the century most Texas newspapers were following suit.

Two factors seem to have contributed to this movement toward more even-handed reporting. One was the growth of news services such as the Associated Press, which meant that newspapers were sharing the same story. The other was the increasing reliance on advertising revenue. Technological changes made possible the publication of large runs of a newspaper, which increased circulation. Publishers had to become more moderate and professional because they could not afford to alienate either advertisers or subscribers. Advertisers then and now look at circulation numbers to determine whether to buy advertising space and how much to pay.

yellow journalism
Journalism that is based on sensationalism and exaggeration.

Professionalism and Democracy In the 20th century, **professionalism** gradually became the standard for American and Texas journalists. To be professional, reporting should be objective, neutral, and accurate, not based on partisanship, ideology, or the economic interest of reporters or owners of media outlets. Professional journalism has long been seen as important to democracy. Citizens and leaders gain a fuller and more accurate picture of events, and government and special interests get away with less. However, there are other perspectives.

Advocacy journalists strive for accuracy but reject objectivity (presenting both sides well). Ideological publications, such as the *Texas Observer*, practice advocacy. In 2018, it was rated "Left Biased" for story selection and "High" for factual reporting.[14] In newspapers, the distinction is easier to see. It is on the news pages that professionalism—objectivity and neutrality—should apply. Advocacy is practiced on the editorial pages. In television news, the news and opinion segments tend to be less clearly separated.

Professionalism requires honesty in reporting. In 2018, a *Houston Chronicle* reporter raised questions with the editor about the accuracy of a colleague's stories. The *Chronicle* hired an independent journalist to review the stories, which led to the retraction of eight stories, correction of 64 more, and the resignation of the accused reporter.

Professionalism is, of course, an ideal, and most suppliers of news are judged by how close they come to the ideal, not by whether they are perfect. Several trends have chipped away at the standards of professionalism. Critics have noted that professional journalists tend to see official sources (that is, government officials and other powerful people) as reliable, legitimate, and knowledgeable. Thus, professionals may overreport views of the government and the elite while neglecting the views of others.

Texas has two good recent examples. Reporters seem to have long taken at face value the bragging by legislative leaders about their balancing of the Texas state budget when the federal government has not been able to do so. The fuller picture is that the state constitution makes it virtually impossible for the legislature to appropriate more than the comptroller predicts the state will have available to spend. Also, the legislature has often used an array of accounting maneuvers or tricks. Similarly, reporters long appeared to readily accept state officials' claims of the "Texas Miracle"—Texas's adding jobs during the recent Great Recession. Low taxes and minimal regulations were said to be the basis of the state's success. However, the ups and downs of the Texas economy created by the fluctuations in the oil industry led many observers to argue that the "Texas Miracle" was produced by the oil shale boom, geography, and population growth, not governmental policy.

Similarly, being objective means presenting multiple perspectives on an issue. However, if there is no debate among the powerful, concerns by ordinary citizens may be neglected. For example, in 2004, the state effectively capped the number of special education students schools could serve. The public was unaware of this until a 2016 investigation by the *Houston Chronicle* reported the policy and that as many as 250,000 students may have been denied help. Public outcry and a 2018 federal report reversed the policy. Also, an issue may have two sides among political leaders and a third position held by the public that goes unreported in

professionalism
Reporting that is objective, neutral, and accurate.

the news. For example, in the recent debate over anti-abortion legislation passed by the legislature since 2013, most of the reporting focused on the two extremes—prolife and prochoice. However, for years the largest segment of the public has tended to reject the two extremes—no abortion at all or abortion for any reason. Americans are more likely to believe that abortion should be available, but only under certain circumstances.[15] The independent nature of Internet and social media interactions gives hope that citizen views not reflected in elite opinion will also be heard.

In recent years, the national media have become more **adversarial**. Aggressive use of investigations, publicity, and exposure of corruption has given them more independence and prominence. The sharp conflict between President Trump and the press has reinforced this trend at the national level. Whether the adversarial approach has happened in Texas remains an open question, at least in the case of the traditional media (print and broadcast). From the time of Democratic Party dominance to today's Republican dominance, critics have complained that the media are too friendly to state leaders and fail to challenge their policies.

Many observers believe that the national media are more partisan today than during most of the last century. Clearly, some forms of media in Texas are partisan: blogs, social media, and talk radio/television. But the traditional media (newspapers and local television news) tend not to be heavily partisan. In terms of newspapers, differences are more a matter of degree than absolute. The editorial policy of the *Fort Worth Star-Telegram*, for example, is commonly seen as center-left and its neighbor the *Dallas Morning News* as center-right. They and the major newspapers in San Antonio, Austin, and Houston all endorsed favorite son George W. Bush for president in 2004. In four presidential elections from 2004 to 2016, all five endorsed at least one Republican and one Democrat. In 2012, of Texas's 12 largest newspapers, eight endorsed Republican Mitt Romney and two Democrat Barack Obama. In 2016, newspapers in the state and nation overwhelmingly rejected Republican Donald Trump. In Texas, eight endorsed Democrat Hillary Clinton, one Trump, and one "not Trump." That year, the *Dallas Morning-News* endorsed a Democrat for president for the first time since before World War II, while recommending five Republicans, one Libertarian, and one Democrat for statewide office.

In the 2016 Democratic presidential primary, the major newspapers in Dallas, Houston, and San Antonio endorsed the moderate liberal Hillary Clinton over the more liberal Bernie Sanders. In the Republican primary, these three, along with the *Fort Worth Star-Telegram* and the *Waco Tribune-Herald*, split their endorsements among Jeb Bush, John Kasich, and Marco Rubio, who were generally considered more mainstream Republican candidates. The *Austin American-Statesman* did not endorse presidential candidates in 2012 or 2016 but summarized the message of the major Texas papers making endorsements as: "Please, please … don't pick Ted Cruz or Donald Trump, and let pragmatism prevail." (Trump, the eventual victor, was far from a conventional candidate and strongly anti-Republican establishment. Cruz, a U.S. Senator from Texas, was the most ideological conservative among the viable candidates.) In 2018, the major newspapers in Dallas, Fort Worth, Houston, and San Antonio each endorsed Republican Abbott for governor and Democrat O'Rourke for the U.S. Senate.

adversarial
Reporting featuring opposition and a combative style. Also called *attack journalism*.

Investigative Journalism We look to the media to keep our public officials honest by asking hard questions and investigating suspicious actions. Unfortunately, the ability of national and Texas media to conduct investigations has declined. The reduction in number of reporters is a major reason. An important tool for the watchdog role of the Texas media is use of open meetings and open records.

Many government officials in Texas are reluctant to share information about how public money is spent, how decisions affecting the public interest are made, or what information was used in making decisions. Failing to share information with the public may hide self-serving decisions or avoid opposition to policies preferred by decision makers. Government officials sometimes argue that they want to protect the public or that compiling information is difficult and costly. Some agencies, (notably, the Texas Commission on Environmental Quality and the Railroad Commission) are said to have a culture of hostility to the idea of public information.

In the past, meetings of school boards and other public boards were often closed to the public. However, during the 1973 session of the legislature, in the aftermath of the Sharpstown scandal (discussed below), the public interest group Common Cause received strong support from other public interest groups and the media to push through **open meetings** and **open records** legislation. (A weak open meetings law was passed in 1967. The open records act is now officially the Public Information Act.)

There is disagreement among informed observers as to how effective the laws have evolved to be today. Some see them as among the strongest in the country. However, the legislature has added a multitude of exceptions, and noncompliance and obstruction by state and local agencies are often problems. In its 2015 report, the Center for Public Integrity gave the state an F in public access to information and ranked it 48th among the states.[16]

Under open meetings law, government boards must discuss proposals and make their decisions in meetings open to the public. There are a few exceptions, such as personnel matters, contracts, and real property purchases or sales that can be discussed in executive (closed) session, but even then, actual decisions generally must be made in sessions open to the public. Ordinary citizens can, of course, attend, but it is reporting by the media that makes information widely available. Some cities and other government units now stream their meetings and make minutes and other documents available over the Internet.

Most reports, communications, and paperwork generated within executive agencies may be requested by citizens, and the agency must respond within 10 working days or ask the Attorney General whether they have to divulge the information. It must then provide the information "within a reasonable time, without delay." If the information is not provided, the requestor may sue, but lawsuits are expensive and thus more likely to be filed by organizations or affluent individuals. In 2013, the legislature updated requirements to clarify the inclusion of emails under open records laws. No reason need be given for an open records request, and there is no restriction on use of the information. Those most likely

open meetings
Meetings of public entities that are required by law to be open to the public.

open records
Government documents and records that are required by law to be available to the public.

to ask for records are the news media, advocacy groups, and activists within the community.

As with open meetings laws, open records laws include some restrictions as to what can be released, and this limitation can lead to difficulties obtaining information. For example, following the deadly 2013 fertilizer plant explosion in the town of West, the state fire marshal aggressively inspected all 104 ammonium nitrate facilities in the state. When a reporter requested copies of some of the reports, the documents were so heavily redacted (marked through) that they were useless to the reporter. After requesting a state attorney general's opinion, the reporter received more information, although the attorney general's office ordered the fire marshal to redact the names and addresses of facilities. During 2013–2014, the Texas Attorney General issued a series of opinions to state agencies ruling that the location of toxic chemicals should not be made public because of the danger of terrorism. The opinions highlight the conflict between keeping information from those who would do us harm and the public's needing to know where it is safe to live, to go to school, or to work.

The *Dallas Morning News* reported in January 2015 on their year-long study of open records compliance in North Texas. They sent five requests each to 113 local governments and found:

> Inconsistent treatment of the release of public information, giving rise to systemic violations of the law…
>
> - Widely varied costs for basic information, ranging from free to thousands of dollars.
> - Routine flouting of the law's response time deadlines.
> - An inability or refusal to provide some or all information about public expenditures in a searchable, electronic format.[17]

At the state level in early 2016, Agriculture Commissioner Sid Miller was criticized by the press for failing to comply with open records requests for emails about a state-funded trip to Oklahoma. Miller had received a so-called "Jesus Shot" to take away pain for life while on the trip. Critics argued the travel was personal and not government-related. Prior to the release of the emails, Miller reimbursed the state for his travel expenses.

The media not only report information they gather from open meetings and open records requests, but they also report information obtained by others using data the state requires to be reported. For example, candidates, lobbyists, and officeholders are required to report financial information, such as campaign contributions and expenditures, to the Texas Ethics Commission, which places the information online but not always in a readily usable form. Public interest groups, such as Texans for Public Justice, often compile the information to make patterns clearer. (In recent years, they reported on campaign contributions in Austin city elections and oil and gas industry contributions to legislators and regulators.) Because Texas lags behind other states in making information available online in understandable form, Texans must rely heavily on nongovernment entities to obtain and provide the information. The online *Texas Tribune* has developed several searchable databases, including salaries of public employees, the Texas Public Schools Explorer, higher education outcomes, and prisons.

Political Scandals and the Texas Media One of the roles often portrayed for the press is investigating wrongdoing by government and its leaders. Texas has a long history of political scandals and conflicts in which the media have played a significant but seldom leading role. The Texas press more commonly spreads the word and keeps the pot boiling, which allows time for concerned citizens and leaders to seek reforms. The classic case is the Sharpstown stock fraud scandal of the early 1970s in which federal prosecutors filed charges that resulted in criminal convictions. The media gave substantial coverage to the scandal and the subsequent actions of the "Dirty Thirty," a group of legislators who forced public discussion of the issues involved. As a result, Governor Preston Smith (named as an unindicted coconspirator), Lieutenant Governor Ben Barnes (who was not a participant in the conspiracy), and a large majority of the legislature were swept from office. A flurry of mild reforms followed.

In three other prominent cases, media investigations uncovered corruption. In the mid-1950s, the managing editor of the *Cuero Record* won a Pulitzer Prize for exposing the defrauding of veterans by the state land commissioner, Bascom Giles, who went to prison. Following up on Sharpstown, in the 1970s, the media and prosecutors found widespread corruption, such as illegal hiring of relatives and theft of legislative stamp allotments. In the late 1980s, media investigations produced changes in the membership on the Texas Supreme Court.

Scrutiny of the Texas Supreme Court began when two San Antonio newspapers questioned decisions by justices that favored their campaign contributors. That led to a fuller investigation by *Texas Monthly* and then a national story in 1987 by the investigative television program *60 Minutes*. In a rare move, the Texas Commission on Judicial Conduct publicly reprimanded two justices. Three justices took early retirement. Tenacious reporting changed personnel on the court and contributed to its moving from all Democrats to all Republicans. But this did not change the fundamental problem: judges and justices still have to raise money for their election campaigns—$1.5 to $2 million for a single campaign for the Texas Supreme Court. A decade later, in 1998, *60 Minutes* revisited the high court and found the same problem. Before, Democratic justices had favored their contributors: plaintiffs' attorneys. Now, Republican justices were favoring their contributors: business and insurance. (For further discussion of this issue, see Chapter 10, "The Judicial Branch.")

In both the Sharpstown and Texas Supreme Court cases, the changes were in personnel, not fundamental changes in the system. Because the system remains unchanged, so too does the likelihood of future abuses. Serious reform is a hard sell in Texas.

Setting the Public Agenda

A third major role of the media is its substantial contribution to setting the public agenda (called **agenda setting**)—that is, influencing which issues are dealt with by government. There are a multitude of problems affecting the public, but if public officials are not aware of them, nothing happens. In addition, officials may be aware of problems but not want to act. For example, low funding for mental health resources in Texas has created major problems for many Texans, but strong resistance to spending the money to increase social services has long left Texas among the lowest states in per capita mental health expenditures. Without the public's becoming aware and highly concerned, state leadership can ignore the problem. When a substantial segment of the public or major leaders become aware of issues, action is more likely.

An example of media influence on policy took place in early 2014. The plan of the Texas Department of Transportation (TxDOT) to build a bypass around the town of Snook would have required cutting down several trees and damaging others in a stand of 200- to 300-year-old live oaks. When residents protested in the nearby Bryan/College Station media, TxDOT promised an attempt to save some but not all of the trees. A Facebook page and an online petition were created. Then, within days of the story's appearing in a major daily, the *Houston Chronicle*, TxDOT devised a new plan that would move traffic safely, save the trees, and stay within budget.

The Texas media have a limited influence on agenda setting. Competing with the media in setting the public agenda are the governor, legislative leaders, and interest groups, who have more power and resources. Texas's leaders are also learning to use the Internet and social media to push their agendas. Chapter 9, "The Executive Branch," gives examples of how governors Perry and Abbott used the new media to affect the public agenda.

In addition, the decline in the number of reporters, the fragmented nature of the state's executive branch, the large number of local governments (particularly thousands of special districts and multiple county offices), and reliance on nonlocal and out-of-state collectors of information make it likely that many possible agenda items will be missed by the Texas media. Although the Texas press influences major state-level agenda items and many local issues, it has too few resources to cover, let alone influence, the majority of state agencies, county offices, and special districts.

Moreover, the elitist nature of the state political system and the power of special interest groups assure substantial competition for media attention. Grassroots movements, such as the Tea Party and the #MeToo Movement, have learned to use social media combined with traditional methods, such as rallies and demonstrations, to gain the attention of the public and leaders. However, the ability of ordinary citizens to come together over an issue of concern to them and use the new media sources to add their cause to the public agenda still appears to be in its infancy (but an infancy with possibilities of healthy growth).

agenda setting
Affecting the importance given issues by government and public leaders.

📋 STUDENTS IN ACTION

A Diverse Career and the Changing Media

Ademide Adedokun was born in London to Nigerian parents and moved to Katy, Texas, when she was nine. At Sam Houston State, she was a double major—history and political science—and active in the university and community. Among other awards, she was selected as the Outstanding Female Student at the university. With a career in public service in mind, she interned with the City of Huntsville and in the office of the local congressman, Kevin Brady.

It is common for congressional staff members to begin as interns, and this was Ademide's route. With the support of Congressman Brady and his chief of staff, she took a staff position with Congressman Pete Olson. In both positions, she worked with constituents. From there, she moved to the staff of the commandant of the Coast Guard in Washington, D.C., where she assisted the communications director in both internal and external messages. In 2012, she received a Master of Public Administration degree from American University in Washington, D.C., and was promoted to speechwriter for the commandant.

Ms. Adedokun was struck by the diversity of the media. "The media has changed," she said, "and that means that we use a variety of methods to transmit messages: internal websites, external

wavebreakmedia/Shutterstock.com

websites, speeches, video, and any other method we can think of."

Asked what she learned from being a political science major, she said, "Political science taught me how to write. You cannot enter the professional world without the knowledge of how to write using correct grammar and punctuation. During the course of a workday, no matter what profession you choose, you're going to write e-mails, reports, memos, and every other kind of document."

Source: Interview by Mike Yawn.

Competency Connection
💬 COMMUNICATION SKILLS 💬

What preparation is needed by journalists and others in the media? Would you prefer that journalists have more preparation in the techniques of the trade (such as research, investigation, writing, and speaking) or in the field on which they report (such as politics, business, or sports)?

Shaping Our Views?

A fourth role often attributed to the media is to shape our perceptions of events and issues. Many people believe that the media tell us what to believe—that is, they create opinion. Research finds little evidence for this view. Rather, it finds a much more complex process in which the media play important roles. We have seen that the media are a major source of information. However, this effect is reduced because we are more likely to perceive an issue and its importance if we already know something about the topic or if the information comes from a trusted source, such as a friend or favorite newscaster. Then, we are more likely to "hear" the news. Similarly, students in an introductory political science class are likely to find the news makes more sense (and therefore remember it) as they learn more background and context from the course.

Personal connection also affects our behavior. In the 2010 national elections, researchers found that putting a reminder that "Today is election day" at the top of Facebook news feeds and a button to click for polling place locations increased turnout by 60,000 voters. However, adding pictures of Facebook friends who voted increased the number by 280,000. That is, invoking people's social networks yielded an additional four voters for every one voter who was directly mobilized.[18]

Do the media change our minds? If we actually have a developed opinion, the answer is "not often." The reason is found in the concept of selective perception and retention. As a general rule, we tend to hear and remember those ideas that support what we already believe and to reject those views that conflict with our own. Consistently, when a group of Republicans and Democrats gather in the same room to listen to their parties' gubernatorial candidates debate issues, most of the group come away thinking that their candidate made the stronger arguments and won the debate. This tendency means that the media are unlikely to change the minds of those who strongly support candidates or issues, but they may have an effect on marginal supporters. Attack ads are a case in point.

Attack Ads Scurrilously attacking your opponent was a common practice in 18th- and 19th-century politics. Though generally less mean-spirited and less common today, **attack ads** (personal attacks) are still an important part of national and state politics. Advertisements that are negative toward the opponent are quite common and can rise to sharp attacks. A major reason that candidates run attack ads is that they work—on two levels. Negative ads tend to influence the tone and content of news coverage. Said another way, they often generate free media coverage. Second, votes may be won by negative ads. The public tends to accept accurate attacks on the issues, and negativity is often more interesting (and thus more memorable) than positive ads.

People regularly complain about negative campaign ads, but the importance of the political race and the repetition of the ads cause many to "hear" the charges. Convinced supporters will tend to reject the charges made in the ads, but marginal supporters may become less certain and abstain from voting for the candidate. This result seems to be the strongest electoral effect of attack ads. Research shows that as the number of negative ads increases, news coverage tends to become more negative, which lowers participation and trust in government. Although negativity and incivility have always had a role in American politics, research indicates that hearing and seeing negative or disrespectful behavior in the media increases the likely impact on our emotions and therefore on our view of politics.[19]

A classic example of successful attack ads is the 2002 race for governor between Democrat Tony Sanchez, Jr., and Republican Rick Perry. Sanchez, a wealthy oilman and banker from the border city of Laredo, was part of the

attack ad
An advertisement meant as a personal attack on an opposing candidate or organization.

Democrats' "Dream Team," composed of a Mexican American (Sanchez), an African American (Ron Kirk), and a moderately conservative Anglo (John Sharp) running for the top three offices on the ballot. The hope was to energize the Democratic Party's two ethnic bases and to compete with the Republicans for the large conservative Anglo vote. Republicans ran a series of attack ads trying to taint Sanchez with allegedly laundering drug money through his bank. Although the ads appear not to have reduced support from strong Democrats, they probably contributed to the failure of Sanchez's candidacy to mobilize Latino voters sufficiently to overcome the Republican advantage among Anglo voters.

The 2014 governor's race between Republican State Attorney General Greg Abbott and Democratic State Senator Wendy Davis included a great deal of mudslinging. One fight focused on the compelling life narratives each used. (Davis' biography was that of a divorced teenage mother living in a trailer who worked her way to Harvard and political success. Abbott's life story was one of perseverance—the victim of a freak accident that put him in a wheelchair, who persevered to serve on the state Supreme Court and as Attorney General.) Abbott's campaign accused Davis of exaggerating her hardships, while Davis' campaign accused Abbott of winning $10.7 million in a lawsuit over his injury but then as a public official blocking suits by others who were injured. In the 2018 U.S. Senate race, Republican incumbent Ted Cruz made substantial use of attack ads. Democratic challenger Beto O'Rourke avoided negative campaigning until the final month, when he released a series of attacks on Cruz's policy positions.

Priming and Framing Two related concepts are important in understanding the impact of the news on our views: priming and framing. Most issues can be seen in different ways. **Priming** may indicate how important an issue is or which part of a situation is most important. A classic example happened in the 1990 gubernatorial election between liberal Democrat Ann Richards and conservative Republican Clayton Williams. Through much of the campaign, the focus was primarily on the ideological differences between the two. As the conservative candidate in a conservative state, Williams maintained a comfortable lead. But then Williams told a joke to a group of reporters comparing rape to the weather and later refused to shake Richards's hand over charges she had made. As a result, his persona suddenly became the major focus for the press and many voters. (What kind of Southern man won't shake a woman's hand, and is he an insensitive sexist?) Poll results began to change, and Richards was narrowly elected. (Cable news, the Internet, and social media greatly speed the spread of news. The impact of these gaffes would be even larger today.)

priming
The news media indicating how important an issue is or which part of a situation is most important.

framing
Providing meaning or defining the central theme of an issue.

Framing provides meaning or defines a central theme. For example, lawsuits against doctors for malpractice, against employers for unsafe work conditions, and against manufacturers for selling harmful products were long viewed by much of the public as entertaining tidbits or as examples of the little guy/gal striking back at the powerful. However, in the early 1980s, groups of business people, doctors, and conservatives began a two-decades long public relations campaign to reframe the issue as important and costly to all Texans. Efforts focused on convincing the public that frivolous claims and expensive awards from these lawsuits were driving doctors out of the state, raising prices, and cutting into the economy. The campaigns changed the minds of enough people that the legislature passed legislation in 2003, and the public approved a constitutional amendment in that same year, to limit the damage awards for these claims.

The abortion controversy in Texas has created two related framing battles. In each legislative session since 2011, the Texas legislature has passed legislation affecting abortion, such as defunding Planned Parenthood, limiting and regulating abortion, and placing requirements on abortion clinics. Generally, prolife (antiabortion) legislators and groups have framed the debate in terms of abortion and human life, while prochoice (proabortion) supporters have framed the issue in terms of women's health and control of their own bodies. Even after a 2016 U.S. Supreme Court decision striking down Texas's restrictions on abortion clinics passed in 2013, supporters continued to frame the legislation as making the clinics safer, while opponents focused on access, arguing that the closing of clinics made abortion less available and more difficult (the argument accepted by the court).

What Research Finds Our understanding of the influence of the media has undergone substantial change over time. Pundits long suggested a hypodermic model in which the powerful media persuaded the unsophisticated citizenry. However, researchers found little evidence for this effect. It was followed by a minimal effects model that said the media could only reinforce and activate existing predispositions. Again, the evidence led in a different direction. Today, researchers find considerable evidence for a *subtle effects* model. The media are not all-powerful but are influential in important ways. In the words of Professors Rosalee Clawson and Zoe Oxley, "This tradition argues that the media influence citizens through agenda setting, priming, and framing; the media influence what citizens think about, which issues or traits citizens bring to bear when evaluating political leaders, and which considerations shape their thinking on political issues."[20]

Who is most likely to be influenced by the media? Research suggests the media have the most influence on those who lack background information or developed opinions, on people who rely on only one news source or news from one ideological viewpoint, and on issues that are far removed from daily life, such as false teeth or air conditioning for prison inmates (actual issues in 2018).

> **✔ 6.2 Learning Check**
>
> 1. Are the media today becoming more or less able to investigate government wrongdoing?
> 2. What does media framing mean?
>
> *Answers at the end of this chapter.*

✪ Campaigns and Citizen Participation

LO 6.3 Discuss the roles of the media in modern Texas election campaigns.

The media play a major role in campaigns for public office and citizen attempts to be heard. With the decline in the ability of political parties to mobilize voters, television and newspapers have long been the major mechanism for candidates to reach potential voters. In a state as large as Texas, this effort is an extremely expensive undertaking and one that is not always successful. The rise of the Internet and social media has given candidates more ability to reach out directly to voters. The new media have also provided new tools for citizen groups to organize and to try to sell their message.

Campaigns and the Traditional Media

What happens in campaigns illustrates the four major roles of the media just discussed. In the past, candidates relied on rallies and mobilization by local leaders and party organizations. With the advent of television and the decline of political parties, candidates for national, state, and many local offices now rely on the mass media to get their message out. They seek press coverage of their events, generate situations and issues they hope the media will cover, and buy ads. For years, the ads have made heavy use of television, although by 2008 the Internet was gaining ground.

The "How Do We Compare?" table shows 20 media markets in Texas, 8 more than California. As a result, the cost of a traditional media campaign is substantial. For example, the 2002 Texas gubernatorial campaign cost candidates (and their supporters) a record $95 million. In the hotly contested 2018 U.S. Senate race, Ted Cruz and Beto O'Rourke spent $126 million, while in that year's less contested governor's race, all candidates raised $78 million in contributions. Not surprisingly, candidates seek as much free media coverage as possible. Campaign events are designed more to gain news coverage than to involve those citizens attending, who are often more backdrop than participants.

The relationship between candidates and the press is often testy. Both need each other, but they have different goals. The candidate wants free and friendly coverage; the press wants entertaining news stories—controversy, scandals, and candidate mistakes. Candidates at both the state and national level want to control or at least influence the news. In Texas, the news environment makes it easier for the candidates to exercise control. There are fewer reporters; many of them know the candidate; and there is less of a press culture of asking challenging questions. This environment led to problems for Governors George W. Bush and Rick Perry, who went directly from working only in Texas state politics to running for president. They were not used to the rough-and-tumble aspects of national news, and as a result fared poorly in public debates and other encounters with reporters. Opportunities for direct contact with citizens through social media have enhanced the ability of candidates to bypass traditional media. Facebook and Twitter are now commonly used by candidates and office holders.

One of the complaints about news coverage of campaigns is that it tends to be **horserace journalism**; that is, it focuses more on who is winning than on the issues. Even after officials are elected, stories continue to focus on competition. For example, will Beto O'Rourke run for president in 2020? Once again, entertainment appears to triumph over content. A strong reason for horserace coverage is that news management wants a large audience and prefers stories that alienate neither side.

horserace journalism
News that focuses on who is ahead in the race (poll results and public perceptions) rather than policy differences.

🖿 HOW DO WE COMPARE...

In Media Access?

Most Populous States	Number of Media Markets (2018)	Newspaper Circulation Per Capita (2010)	Percentage of Households with a Computer (2016)	Percentage of Households with Internet Access (2016)
California	12	0.16	90	86
Florida	10	0.14	88	82
New York	9	0.31	87	82
Texas	**20**	**0.08**	**87**	**81**
States Bordering Texas				
Arkansas	4	0.15	81	71
Louisiana	7	0.12	81	75
New Mexico	2	0.12	81	75
Oklahoma	4	0.13	84	78

Sources: "US Map of Nielsen Media Markets," *Block,* October 22, 2018, http://bl.ocks.org/simzou/6459889; Statistical Abstract, 2012, Table 1136, *U.S. Census Bureau,* http://www.census.gov/library/publications/2011/compendia/statab/131ed/information-communications.html; and National Center for Education Statistics, *Digest of Education Statistics,* Table 702.60, March 2018, https://nces.ed.gov/programs/digest/d17/tables/dt17_702.60.asp?current=yes.

—— Competency Connection ——
⚙ CRITICAL THINKING ⚙

Texas has the lowest per capita newspaper circulation of all eight states but has higher Internet access than its smaller neighbors. What factors do you think contribute to this circumstance?

Digital Campaigning

The 2008 and 2012 presidential campaigns saw the Internet and social media come of age as a part of campaigning. Mainstream media provided blogs and online news coverage. YouTube, Facebook, and other social media provided outlets for candidates and citizens alike. Candidates began to use the Internet in a major way, putting up high-quality campaign sites and using social media to get out their message.

Barack Obama was particularly successful in using the new media in both of his presidential campaigns. For example, identifying and microtargeting potential younger voters through their email and social media accounts, his campaign was able to increase support and voter turnout among 18- to 24-year-olds. John F. Kennedy's 1960 presidential campaign is commonly seen as marking a revolution in how television would transform campaigns. Obama's campaign had the same effect on Internet and social media usage. In 2016, Donald Trump made the tweet a major campaign tool.

In Texas, statewide and local campaigns make heavy use of the Internet and social media. In his highly successful 2010 gubernatorial campaign, Governor

Perry adapted established campaign practices to modern-day reality, while his primary and general election opponents ran more traditional campaigns. Rather than use direct mail, phone banks, and knocking on the doors of strangers, the Perry campaign asked volunteers to identify 12 friends and turn them out to the polls. Facebook messages to friends were encouraged. Perry refused to meet with newspaper editorial boards (who decide on endorsements) and instead relied on friendly bloggers, social media, and personal appearances. He gave away no yard signs because, his campaign staff believed, they don't work. (Supporters could buy a sign if they wished.) Social media were used to get Perry's voters organized, connected, and to the polls.[21]

Ted Cruz's upset victory in the 2012 Republican primary for the U.S. Senate was fueled in significant part by skillful use of the Internet and social media. Among other efforts, the campaign advertised and raised funds on a multitude of platforms, targeted people who "liked" those who had endorsed Cruz, manipulated key words for Google searches, and used "promoted Tweets" (paid ads on Twitter that show up first in search results). Cruz continued heavy use of social media in his 2016 presidential bid and 2018 senate reelection campaign. His opponent in 2018, Beto O'Rourke, also made extensive use of the Internet, social media, and texting. O'Rourke appears to have spent more than any other candidate in the nation on social media advertising. The social media ads by both candidates were carefully targeted at different groups and were particularly important for O'Rourke's highly successful fundraising.

By the 2014 Texas elections, the Internet and social media were a standard part of Texas campaigns. However, many traditional national, state, and local candidates were caught unawares by the new media, suffering embarrassment and sometimes defeat. Cell phone pictures and videos of candidates' off-the-cuff remarks and mistakes are common on social media. Some go viral. Conservative lieutenant governor candidate Dan Patrick accidentally tweeted in February 2014:

> "MARRIAGE=ONE MAN & ONE MAN. Enough of these activist judges."
>
> —*Dan Patrick (@DanPatrick) February 26, 2014*

Even though he quickly changed the tweet, it remains on the Internet. (Readers should remember that comments and pictures posted on the Internet are likely to be there forever.)

The Internet sometimes encourages or facilitates harsh comments that might not be made face-to-face. In the 2014 and 2018 gubernatorial campaigns, candidates used Facebook and Twitter to promote discussion of their issues but often had a difficult time limiting negative and scurrilous comments posted about their opponents.

civic engagement
Actions by citizens to address issues of public concern.

Citizen Participation in the Digital Age

One of the charges against digital media is that use of the Internet and social media contributes to lower **civic engagement** (citizen actions to address issues of public concern). The idea is that because digital communication is not face-to-face, users are not well connected to other people and society. However, research by the Pew Research Internet Project does not support this view. Based on a 2012 survey of Internet users, researchers concluded that major growth occurred in political activity on social networking sites during the years 2008 to 2012. Politics, for most users, is not just a social network activity. Users are frequently active in other aspects of civic life. The study also found a common pattern: lower education and income tend to decrease civic participation. However, among Facebook and Twitter users, education and income had less effect. Finally, the young are as likely as older adults to be engaged in some political activities and are more likely to be politically active on social networking sites.

Studies have consistently shown that Texans are low in civic engagement compared to the rest of the nation. Texas is below the national average in such areas as the proportion of people voting, involved in groups, donating to charity, and volunteering. This lack of engagement is also true online. Both face-to-face and online, Texans are below the national average in discussing political or community issues with friends and family.[22]

Like candidates, citizens on both the left and right have learned to use digital media to increase their influence in the political arena. The Tea Party's success in organizing grassroots campaigns, for example, is commonly attributed to the aggressive use of social media. Similarly, skillful use of the digital media on the last day of the first special session of the 2013 legislature temporarily blocked antiabortion legislation and boosted State Senator Wendy Davis into the Democratic nomination for governor. Davis filibustered an antiabortion bill for almost 13 hours, forcing a second special session to be called to pass the bill. The filibuster was streamed live on YouTube to 180,000 viewers. Twitter was used to bring protestors to the state capitol to support Davis, and there were 570,000 tweets about the filibuster that day.[23]

> ✓ **6.3 Learning Check**
>
> 1. Why are statewide election campaigns so expensive in Texas?
> 2. Are political campaigns using the Internet and social media more effectively?
>
> *Answers at the end of this chapter.*

✪ Bias?

LO 6.4   Analyze the issue of ideological bias in the Texas media.

Given the important roles played by the media, it is not surprising that activists of all persuasions often believe the media are biased against them, today often calling stories they don't like "fake news." Certainly in the 19th century, bias was the norm. However, growth of journalistic professionalism in the 20th century increased public confidence. Through the mid-1980s, the majority of the American public believed the press was relatively unbiased. Since that time, however, substantial majorities have come to perceive bias in the media. Interestingly, social media are substantially less trusted than news organizations or family and friends. (This may be largely because of the tendency to trust those we know over those people and institutions we don't know.) Like most public institutions in the last half century, public trust in the media has declined. Yet, research indicates that while some types of media have become more partisan and ideological, most of the mainstream media still adhere to standards of objectivity and neutrality. To understand this conclusion requires explanation.

It is well established by research that over the last 30 years a larger proportion of reporters have been more liberal and aligned with the Democratic Party than is the general population,[24] while newspaper management has long tended to be more conservative and Republican. Many from both groups do not fit these tendencies, but the pattern is strong and persistent. Owners and publishers tend to be more conservative, possibly because of their greater affluence and business position. Newspapers have traditionally endorsed candidates for public office, and the choices (particularly for the top offices) generally reflect the position of owners and managers. Nationally, in the 22 presidential elections from 1932 to 2016, Republicans received more newspaper endorsements (17 elections) than Democrats (4 elections). (In 1996, some 70 percent of newspapers made no presidential endorsement!)

Texas's pattern is more complex. In the long period of Democratic Party dominance, both parties generally nominated conservative candidates; but in the Democratic primary, there was often a contest between a liberal and one or more conservatives. Texas newspapers, with some exceptions, generally supported conservatives.

Media Bias and the News

Do personal preferences of reporters and publishers affect coverage of the news? The answer is yes in countries with a partisan press, as was the case in the United States until the 20th century. Today, traditions of professionalism are the standard for journalists. These professional standards hold that the press should report the facts as they are, not the way journalists want them to be, and that opinion should be clearly separated and identified as such. This view has dominated Texas newspapers and television since the early 1900s with, of course, some exceptions. However, the pattern is changing or at least being challenged at both the national and local levels.

Since 2010, the two cable news networks with the largest audiences have been Fox, with a significant lead, and MSNBC, with a small lead over CNN. Importantly for the future, CNN and Fox substantially outdistance MSNBC in digital traffic—both desktop and mobile.[25] Fox has a conscious bias to the right (conservative), while MSNBC leans left (liberal). CNN (Cable News Network), the pioneer in cable news, has a tradition of objective reporting. Recently, however, many of its commentators have tended more liberal and less careful of facts than the straight news reporters. In 2012, about 54 percent of CNN's news time was factual reporting, while 46 percent was commentary or opinion. By comparison, Fox spent 55 percent of its news time on commentary and opinion and MSNBC 85 percent.[26]

There is considerable danger in relying on commentators for information. When Punditfact examined 171 statements made by Fox's news personalities and their guests, researchers found that 59 percent were mostly false, false, or "pants on fire" false. Only 22 percent of these statements were labeled true or mostly true. Of 28 assertions made by liberal MSNBC commentator Rachel Maddow, 45 percent were labeled in one of the false categories and 39 percent true or mostly true. By comparison, reporters and guests on CNN (considered a more traditional television news outlet) received a score of 53 percent true or mostly true and 27 percent partially or completely false.[27] (Note that percentages are for comments examined, not all comments.)

Talk radio has long been dominated by conservatives at both the local and national level. On the Internet, a wide range of blogs make it easy for users to get their information from congenial sources that entertain and reinforce the reader's views. Texas has popular blogs on both the right and left, with fewer in the center. A relatively new phenomenon is the growth in popularity of humorous political talk shows on television—for example, *Real Time with Bill Maher* and *Last Week Tonight with John Oliver*—and the significant number of people who get their political information from these entertainment sources. Unlike talk radio, these programs have tended to be more liberal.

The growth of social media increases the role of friends and opinion leaders in originating and framing issues. Availability of sites such as YouTube and Twitter increases self-selection of what news and views to receive. This practice leads to confirmation bias in which people become more fixed in their beliefs and attitudes because they seek out information that supports their beliefs.[28]

Objective reporting still remains an imperfectly followed standard for the three major television broadcasting networks (CBS, NBC, and ABC), the public networks (NPR, PRI, and PBS), and the major newspapers of Texas. At times, the media deviate from objectivity. When George W. Bush ran for governor and later for president, he was initially viewed negatively by a large number of the reporters covering him. When he ran for governor, he was seen as uninformed and trading on his father's name. When he ran for president, he was tainted with the negative paintbrush often applied by the national press to Texas politicians such as President Lyndon Johnson and presidential candidate Rick Perry (a rube from the country, unsophisticated, and poorly educated). However, in both campaigns, Bush was able to charm many reporters who warmed to him and gave him more favorable coverage.

From his arrival in the U.S. Senate, Texan Ted Cruz used blunt, combative rhetoric and showed an unwillingness to follow many of the informal rules of the Senate aimed at reducing open conflict. This attitude resonated with his supporters but created a variety of enemies among other senators (both Democrats and Republicans). The negativity was reflected in his coverage by the media. A similar phenomenon followed in his 2016 presidential bid. He tended to be viewed negatively by the press but received substantial coverage because extreme statements by the former Princeton debater provided entertaining sound bites.

What Research Finds

Is there partisan or ideological bias in the media? The findings are clear but nuanced. There is little objective evidence of systematic ideological or partisan bias in the mainstream media.[29] Major newspapers and network television news generally adhere to the standards of objectivity and journalistic professionalism. In the words of media scholar Timothy E. Cook, "Newsmaking is a collective process more influenced by the uncritically accepted routine workings of journalism as an institution than by attitudes of journalists."[30] With some notable exceptions, reporters and managers tend to act professionally and not let their ideological preferences dictate their choice of stories or direct the tone of their reporting. The ideological divide between reporters and managers probably also tends to reduce ideological or partisan bias, as each group moderates the views of the other.

Nevertheless, today more debate occurs between the "talking heads" representing differing interpretations on television, and more analysis stories are in newspapers and on the Internet. Many examples of biased coverage of issues and events can be found; however, they balance out over the long run. Where the media have become highly partisan and ideological is in areas in which consumers can choose their source of information and entertainment—Fox or MSNBC, which blog, which talk show?

Two other forms of bias are also noted in the media: a bias toward the entertaining over the important, and a commercial bias. Both are discussed later in the chapter in the section "Change in the Media."

✓ 6.4 Learning Check

1. Do studies find that there is a bias in the media to the left or right?
2. In which area of the media is partisanship increasing?

Answers at the end of this chapter.

✪ Regulation

LO 6.5 Discuss the nature and consequences of media regulation by government.

In many countries, the media are owned or heavily regulated by government. In the United States, the First Amendment to the U.S. Constitution protects freedom of the press, which has meant little regulation of newspapers. Broadcast media (radio and television) were long regulated under federal law to ensure they "serve the public interest, convenience, and necessity." In comparison to regulation in other Western nations, regulation in the United States has been minimal.

Regulation of Print and Broadcast Media

U.S. courts have been particularly suspicious of **prior restraint** or censorship before information can be made available to the public. The key idea is that government should not restrict the free flow of ideas beforehand, although certain kinds of statements may lead to punishment after publication or speech. For example, in *New York Times Co. v. United States*, 402 U.S. 713 (1971), the U.S. Supreme Court allowed publication of a highly classified government study of the Vietnam War popularly known as *The Pentagon Papers*, even though government officials argued that their publication might damage national security. Protection against prior restraint also applies to the Internet. In a 2014 case (*Kinney v. Barnes*, 443 SW3d 87), the Texas Supreme Court held that authors of existing defamatory online posts (statements that are untrue and damaging) may be required to take them down. However, courts cannot prohibit future such posts because that would be prior restraint. (Defamation is discussed below under "State and Local Regulation.")

One of the ironies in legal treatment of the media is the difference in governmental responses to criticism of government and obscenity. U.S. courts have protected the right of the media to criticize government more than is the case in most

prior restraint
Suppression of material before it is published, commonly called censorship.

other countries. The Federal Communications Commission (FCC), however, has regulated obscenity more tightly than have most other Western nations.

At the national level, the FCC is responsible for media regulation. The agency has a reputation for responding to special interests and being ineffective in protecting the public interest, although it has done better in protecting individuals from unfair publicity. In cable television's early days, broadcast television successfully lobbied for regulations that imposed major and costly restrictions on cable TV. The broadcast television industry sought to protect its turf through government rules restricting competitive programming and requiring cable to provide new services not required of the broadcasters. It took 20 years to overcome the opposition and see a reduction of these rules.

Today, the FCC still regulates broadcast television. Radio and cable television were deregulated in 1996. Media are subject to general laws, such as those regulating business practices and monopolies.[31] The Internet has not experienced the degree of regulation faced by the broadcast media and cable but has had to deal with a number of legal issues over time: copyright protection, pornography, cybersecurity, the harvesting of personal information from the Internet, and government spying.

Internet Regulation

Perhaps the most significant regulatory issue facing the Internet today is **net neutrality**, which means that Internet service providers must treat all data on the Internet equally, not providing faster connection speeds for a premium price and not curbing access or slowing transmission of lawful content. In 2015 under pressure from President Obama, a reluctant FCC approved new rules favoring net neutrality. In late 2017, under President Trump, the FCC repealed the rules. The 22 states with Democratic attorneys general then filed suit to keep net neutrality. The Texas Attorney General joined two other Republican states in a court brief against the Democrats' suit. Some states are moving to require net neutrality within their boundaries, but this appears unlikely in Texas. Opponents of net neutrality argue it stifles innovation, while supporters fear censorship, pay-to-play, and harm to small business.[32]

State and Local Regulation

State and local governments may regulate the media in areas not covered by FCC rules. In Texas, regulation has been minimal, although issues over franchises for cable outlets have been a source of considerable conflict. A long-standing free press issue was resolved in 2009 when Texas became the 37th state to pass a **shield law** protecting journalists from having to reveal certain confidential sources. The law, called the Free Flow of Information Act, allows reporters to protect their sources by not having to testify or produce notes in court. Journalists argued that they were not able to carry out their investigative role if they could not protect the identity of their sources. Prosecutors opposed such measures because they believed protection of sources impeded evidence gathering. Both sides finally agreed to a compromise that protects most sources but requires journalists to identify anyone the journalist witnessed committing a felony.

net neutrality
A legal principle that Internet service providers and government officials should treat all data on the Internet equally, not discriminating or charging differentially and not blocking content they do not like.

shield law
A law protecting journalists from having to reveal confidential sources to police or in court.

Under American common law, and now much statutory law, **defamation** of a person is a civil (not a criminal) wrong. That is, anyone who says or prints untrue information that damages a person's reputation may be subject to a civil lawsuit. If the comment is written, it is called **libel**; if spoken, it is **slander**. Because of the protection of freedom of the press and of speech in the First Amendment to the U.S. Constitution, libel and slander are much more difficult to prove than is the case in Europe and much of the rest of the world. What constitutes defamation varies from state to state and in federal law. In all cases, the

IMAGE 6.4 Public events such as protest marches and memorial services are mechanisms citizens have to spread their message widely. To be effective, they must capture the attention of the media, and even then, a major problem is the inability to control events and how the actions will be interpreted. In July 2016, out-of-state police-involved shootings of African Americans sparked demonstrations in Dallas, which received local, state, and national coverage on both traditional and new media. Then, at a peaceful march, a heavily armed sniper killed five police officers and wounded seven police and two civilians. This produced even greater coverage. In this picture, mourners hold a candlelight vigil as a memorial to the slain and wounded.

Anadolu Agency/Contributor/Getty Images

— Competency Connection —
◈ **SOCIAL RESPONSIBILITY** ◈

Is the growth of the Internet and social media making protests less necessary or more effective tools of citizen action?

defamation, libel, and slander
Communicating something untrue that damages a person's reputation (defamation) may be subject to a civil lawsuit. If the comment is written, it is called libel; if spoken, it is slander.

statement's being true is an absolute defense. Since a 1964 U.S. Supreme Court case (*New York Times Co. v. Sullivan*, 376. U.S. 254), public figures suing for defamation have a heavier burden than do ordinary citizens. In addition to proving that a statement is false and harmful, public figures must prove that it was made with "actual malice." (Public figures include political leaders, celebrities, and some others who may have received unwanted notoriety.)

A tactic used by companies, organizations, and wealthy individuals to deter negative comments in the media has been to sue for libel, thus saddling defendants with heavy costs to defend themselves. These "strategic lawsuits against public participation" or **SLAPP** have often had a chilling effect on public discussion of misdeeds. In 2011, Texas joined the majority of states in passing anti-SLAPP legislation. Together with amendments in 2013 and state court decisions through 2018, Texas's law prohibiting frivolous defamation lawsuits is one of the strongest in the country. Additionally, reporters are protected from lawsuits if a source provides false information.

Defamation suits arising from statements on the Internet are increasing. Information on the Internet, including social media, tends to be permanent and searchable. Whether anonymous or not, many find it easier to make negative comments on the Internet than in person. Although the right to post comments anonymously is protected by the First Amendment, libel is not. Providers may be forced to identify the "speakers." In 2012, a Texas jury awarded a Texas couple $13.8 million in a defamation suit against individuals who had posted "anonymous" posts on Topix.com (which provided discussion forums for local areas). The jury award was thrown out by the trial judge because of technicalities in the trial, and the appeals court upheld the judge's decision. However, Topix was required to provide information about those making the comments so that they no longer remained anonymous.[33]

> ✔ **6.5 Learning Check**
>
> 1. Which medium is most regulated today?
> 2. Which level of government has traditionally regulated media the most?
>
> *Answers at the end of this chapter.*

⬟ Latinos, African Americans, and Women in Texas Media

LO 6.6 Discuss the representation of women and ethnic minorities in Texas media.

Although African American and Latino Texans have a rising middle class, they are still underrepresented among decision makers and those who influence decisions, including the media. In 2018, for example, ethnic minorities were 39 percent of the U.S. population but only 23 percent of journalists and 19 percent of newsroom managers. These proportions have changed little over the last two decades. For the last decade, ethnic minorities graduated from journalism schools in similar proportions to Anglos but were less likely to be hired. Diversity tends to be lowest at small local newspapers and TV stations, the places where journalists traditionally seek their first job. Women, who are slightly more than half the population were 42 percent of both newsroom journalists and managers in 2018. As in much of the economy, women journalists tend to make less than their male colleagues.[34]

SLAPP
Strategic lawsuits against public participation are suits filed primarily to silence criticism and negative public discussion.

Data for Texas are less systematic but seem to follow the national pattern. Examinations in 2016 and 2018 of websites for a sample of Texas news outlets revealed that Texas racial and ethnic employment patterns mirrored national patterns. For example, of 32 members of the Capitol press corps (reporters assigned to cover state government in Austin), 15 were women (better than the national average), but there were no African Americans or Spanish surname individuals. Similarly, a study of the political pundits quoted or interviewed in the Texas media during the 2014 campaign found that seven political scientists were the dominant sources—quoted 1,331 times. All were Anglo males.[35]

Why do these numbers matter? In addition to issues of equity, traditional ethnic minorities are now a majority of Texas's population. Critics observe that to cover all Texans requires people who are familiar with the state's various communities and who speak the same language as the audience. Otherwise, reporting may be "incomplete, tone-deaf, or biased." Today, non-Anglo Texans are portrayed more often, with fewer stereotypes, and in a wider variety of contexts than was previously true. But critics see continuing, if subtle, stereotypes and stories focusing on family problems, crime, and traditional subordinate roles (such as maid, gardener, and unskilled labor). Media representation of successful minority group members is the exception.[36]

An example of the lack of attention to minority Texans is the cover page of the state's leading monthly magazine—*Texas Monthly*. (Editors commonly see the cover page as the most important page.) From its founding in 1973 through 2016, of 507 covers, African Americans appeared 18 times, 9 of those as a major focus. Included were two maids serving white women, a hustler, athletes, and a congresswoman. Latinos appeared 9 times (3 of those covers were of the singer Selena).

Shortages of minority group members in newsrooms may also affect how events are interpreted. Critics, for example, report a difference in the view of racial groups reflected in the news coverage of the 2015 biker shoot-out in Waco: "The biker shoot-out saw no extended conversation about gun control, mental illness, 'White thug life' nor family breakdown. The latter typically comes up specifically when news media covers Black-on-Black homicides."[37]

A small but significant number of ethnic news media outlets can be found in Texas and across the nation. One site's listing of media outlets in Texas included 26 Latino-, 9 African American-, 9 Asian-, and one Russian–oriented paper. The site also identified 15 Latino broadcast stations.[38] In the Pew Research Center's listing of Spanish language weeklies publishing in 2015, *La Voz de Houston* had the third largest circulation in the nation at 190,000. Four weeklies had circulation over 100,000 each, and the eight Texas weeklies listed had a total circulation over 720,000. *Univision*, the largest Spanish-language network in the United States, began in San Antonio in 1962. The second largest, *Telemundo*, started its Texas operations in Dallas in 2002.[39]

Nationally, African American-oriented media have a long history and are still the most prevalent, although the traditional African American media have lost audience in recent years. In Texas, with a smaller population, African American media are second to Latino media. Of 12 African American-owned television stations in the nation, there is one in Texas, KPEJ in Odessa. Nationally, in 2015, there were 13 African American websites with over one million unique visitors monthly, ranging from 1.2 to 9.7 million per site. None were based in Texas, but Texas content was carried. As is the case generally, websites received more visits from mobile devices than desktop computers.[40]

✓ 6.6 Learning Check

1. Today, are women and ethnic minorities found in the news media in similar proportions to their numbers in the state's population?

2. In the news, are minority Texans portrayed in a fashion similar to Anglos?

Answers at the end of this chapter.

⚡ Change in the Media: More Participation, More Sources, but Less News?

LO 6.7 Discuss the positive and negative effects of changes the media are undergoing in Texas.

The nature of the media is changing rapidly. From the 19th century through the first half of the 20th century, newspapers were the major source of news for Texans. But in the second half of the 20th century, television came to be the dominant source of information for Americans and Texans alike. Now, in the 21st century, the Internet and social media challenge television news for viewers, particularly among the young. Many see these changes as positive: people now have a wider range of choices for their news and can get it according to their own schedule and wishes. Through the Internet, people have more opportunity to participate in collection and distribution of news. Others see the changes as fraught with dangers for citizens' level of accurate information.

What do we know? First, newspapers remain the major gatherers of news. Television and Internet news depends heavily on major newspapers for originating stories. In the case of Internet news, an ongoing debate continues as to whether enough people will pay for news on the Internet and whether enough advertisers can be obtained to finance the level of news gathering now provided by newspapers. Second, the need to draw audiences by being more entertaining has decreased the amount of hard news across the media. Third, a proliferation of channels on television and blogs on the Internet has led to increased **niche journalism** (also called **narrowcasting**) that appeals to a narrow audience, which often leads to more extreme ideological and partisan views.

Concentration of Ownership

Another change profoundly affecting the media is a growing concentration of ownership. Today, around seven corporations (depending on the latest mergers) own most of the national newspapers, news magazines, broadcast television networks, and cable news networks, as well as publishing houses, movie studios, telephone companies, and Internet service providers.[41] At this writing, the corporations and some of their media are AT&T (telecommunications companies and Warner Media, which controls CNN and HBO); Disney (ABC, ESPN, and

niche journalism (narrowcasting)
A news medium focusing on a narrow audience defined by concern about a particular topic or area.

several movie studios); Viacom (170 networks in 160 countries and Paramount Pictures); CBS Corporation (Showtime and CBS); Rupert Murdoch companies (Fox television and *Wall Street Journal*); and the largest cable provider, Comcast (NBC, MSNBC, Telemundo, and Universal Pictures).

Corporations that own media outlets tend to be conglomerates; that is, they own companies that make or sell a variety of products, not just entertainment and information. A major concern is that they will pressure their own media to avoid negative reporting on the other companies in the conglomerate.

In Texas, local ownership of the media has declined sharply. Of the major Texas newspapers, only the *Dallas Morning News* is still owned by a Texas company, the A. H. Belo Corporation, which also owns the *Denton Record-Chronicle*. A spin-off, Belo Corporation, owned several Texas television stations but merged into the Gannett Co., headquartered in Virginia. Gannett in turn created a broadcast and digital media company, TEGNA, which owns 52 television stations, including 13 in Texas. They include stations in Austin (KVUE), Dallas–Fort Worth (WFAA), Houston (KHOU), and San Antonio (KENS). The *Houston Chronicle* and *San Antonio Express-News* are two of the six Texas newspapers published by the Hearst chain; the *Fort Worth Star-Telegram* is one of 29 dailies in 14 states published by the McClatchy Company; and the *Austin American-Statesman* was purchased in 2018 by GateHouse Media, which has been criticized for cutting costs to the point of harming news coverage. Of San Antonio's iHeartMedia's 850 radio stations, 72 are in Texas.

Homogenization Concentration of media ownership has four consequences that worry critics. The first is **homogenization of news**—the increased likelihood that the same stories will be presented in the same way, stories that in the past might have been affected by local and regional culture and concerns. Other critics refer to the *illusion* of choice—many ways to get the same news. Chains tend to provide the same feed to all the radio or television stations they own, for example. Ownership concentration has combined with tendencies of both newspapers and the electronic media to respond to their limited resources by reducing (or eliminating) reporters who gather news. Instead, media outlets rely on wire services, outside networks (such as Texas State Network News), or corporate feeds. A quarter of the 952 U.S. television stations that air newscasts do not produce their own news programs. Additional stations have sharing arrangements under which much of their content is produced outside their own newsrooms.[42]

In a state as large and diverse as Texas, homogenization represents a considerable change. Although the Internet provides more diversity in the presentation of news, so far the lack of revenue, reporters, and professional standards makes it more reactive and opinion oriented than traditional news reports. A study by the Pew Trust found that 99 percent of the stories covered by blogs originated in the traditional media and were then rebroadcast through bloggers.

Occasionally, however, the blogosphere does generate news and forces the traditional media to take notice. For example, in 2011, *TheAustinBulldog.org*, an essentially one-person operation, and the *Austin American-Statesman* newspaper used Texas's open records law to request personal emails by Austin city council

homogenization of news
Making news uniform regardless of differing locations and cultures.

members discussing city business. In 2016 in a lawsuit filed by the *Bulldog*, a Texas appeals court ruled that the city had to provide the emails. In El Paso, the website *Chucoleaks.org* has played a major role in a similar controversy over emails and city decision making.

Soft News A second consequence of growing concentration of ownership is the decline in the amount of news and its "softening." Prior to the 1980s, the news departments of the three major television networks (NBC, CBS, and ABC) were substantially shielded from profit expectations, and their evening news broadcasts were *the* national news, most of it hard news. However, in the mid-1980s, new ownership took over the three networks and demanded more advertising revenue from news. In this period, technological change allowed the emergence of competition from cable television. (CNN debuted in 1980, and a wide array of new and entertaining programs and networks soon followed.) Having to compete for audience share, network news executives sought more entertainment value by reducing the amount of hard news and increasing the emphasis on scandal, horserace coverage of political campaigns, and controversial sound bites. Eventually, softer coverage of news would come to CNN, NPR, and PBS. The ideological networks, Fox and MSNBC, have made their staple a minimum of hard news combined with entertaining spin and drawing in the ideological faithful as viewers.

Less State and Local News Part of the accepted wisdom in Texas and elsewhere is that "All politics is local." However, an examination of candidate speeches and partisan and ideological blogs shows traditional state and local issues being overwhelmed by national issues. Blogger Erica Grieder notes that "Transportation and water, two of the biggest issues facing the state, have been largely sidelined in favor of the same set of issues that animated voters in the Iowa [presidential] caucuses…: immigration and sanctuary cities [and] the correct way to refer to radical Islamist terrorism…"[43] Part of the reason for this nationalization of politics is the nationalization of the news.

In Texas, the national trends toward softer news and the concentration of ownership have added to a long-existing pattern of providing minimal attention to state and local news. Nonlocal owners of the state's newspapers have shown little interest in state and local news. In addition, publishers have cut staff, and, very importantly, reduced the size of the **Capitol press corps**. The number of reporters assigned to cover state news in Austin by Texas news outlets dropped from 66 in 1991 to about 50 in 2000 and then to 32 in 2016. For example, San Antonio's *Express-News* and the *Houston Chronicle*, both owned by the Hearst Corporation, now share an Austin bureau. Generally, the Capitol press corps is exclusively print journalists. The decline in full-time reporters covering state government means less investigative journalism to provide oversight of what our government does and doesn't do. Some observers are less concerned, believing that the Internet will fill the void.[44]

The decline of the traditional Capitol press corps should be seen in perspective. First, it is a phenomenon affecting most other large states. Second, some observers believe that it is mitigated to some degree in Texas by other factors.

Capitol press corps
Reporters assigned to cover state-level news, commonly working in Austin.

NPR reporter Elise Hu argues this case and notes that "Texans love reading about Texas—the notion of Texas exceptionalism, it seems, drives demand."[45]

Local television news in Texas and elsewhere is often cited as an example of soft news. Studies regularly identify much the same pattern as a 2012 Pew Research Center study. Almost two-thirds of local news coverage dealt with traffic, weather, crime, accidents, and human interest. Houston's KTRK was part of an earlier study and followed the pattern. Soft or not, local television news is watched regularly by about half of Americans, a greater number than watch network news. Perhaps the reason is captured by the Pew researchers' conclusion:

> Local TV news *is* more likely than other media we studied to try to portray regular people from the community and how they feel about things, rather than just officials. The reporting was straightforward and mostly strictly factual, with little of the journalist's opinion thrown in…. Viewers got straight news from their local TV stations, and it was certainly about the community.[46]

Commercial Bias A final concern arising from the growing concentration of media ownership is commercial bias and conflict of interest—that is, favoring the owners' company by presenting favorable stories or ignoring the bad the company does. Traditionally, advertising provides 80 percent of newspaper revenue and subscriptions provide 20 percent. Highly dependent on advertisers and needing to be responsive to corporate owners, reporters and editors face pressure to avoid angering either. Thus, "[i]n a survey of 118 local news directors, more than half report that advertisers try to tell them what to air and not to air—and they say the problem is growing."[47] One-third of newspaper editors report that they would not feel free to publish news that might harm their parent company.[48] According to reports, several employees of ABC who were critical of Disney practices were fired when the company acquired control of ABC. In Texas, Clear Channel (predecessor of iHeartMedia) was accused of censoring reporters' opinions.[49] As corporations invest more heavily in digital sites, some observers fear that commercial bias will intrude further into the Internet.

Beyond concerns about protecting parent companies, concentration of media ownership has raised issues about an elitist bias in news (a tendency to present topics and views congenial to the wealthy and powerful but not necessarily to the rest of the population). Additional potential biases sometimes argued include those favoring large corporations and their owners' views about the nature of capitalism and against organized labor. Examples often cited are corporate support for "right to work" laws that make it more difficult for unions to organize and for provisions that weaken access to workers' compensation (medical assistance for job-related injuries). On the latter issue, there was some media support for the state's weak workers' compensation system in the past. However, in 2015 and 2016, Texas newspapers, and particularly the *Dallas Morning News*, provided scathing reporting and commentary on the inadequacy of the system. (See Chapter 12, "Public Policy," for more information on workers' compensation.)

In authoritarian countries, publicly owned media commonly reflect government's views. However, in democratic societies, publicly owned media are more often independent and of high quality. National Public Radio (NPR), the Public Broadcasting System (PBS), and local public radio and TV stations receive a small amount of public financing. These entities raise most of their money from individual and corporate donors. Although public stations attract a more liberal audience, they have worked to avoid bias in their news reporting. The online *Texas Tribune* attempts to avoid partisan or ideological bias. Nevertheless, reliance on contributions from individuals and corporations has raised claims of conflict of interest.[50]

▣ POINT/COUNTERPOINT

Will the Internet and Social Media Be Able to Replace the Quantity and Quality of News Now Provided by Traditional Media?

THE ISSUE For more than a half century, the print media, radio, and television have provided a substantial amount of news in a relatively unbiased, professional manner. However, the Internet and social media are rapidly changing the pattern. Newspapers, the major gatherers of news, are in sharp decline, and television news has become softer and, in the case of cable news, more ideological. Internet news sites are increasing in number, and social media are becoming more diverse and more important sources of news.

The greater number of media options for both news and entertainment has increased competition between news and entertainment, in many ways melding the two together. At the same time, competition for advertising dollars has reduced revenue. As a result, less money has been available to hire reporters. Some claim this competitive environment and fewer professionals have had a negative effect on the quantity and quality of news.

FOR	AGAINST
1. Throughout its history, the media have been in constant change. This shift to digital media is simply another step in its evolution.	1. With so many choices, the present trend will continue. People will tend to choose entertaining news over hard and professional news. Soft news will be competing with partisan news.
2. Ultimately, advertising dollars will move to Internet news sites, and social media will continue to adapt to meet people's needs.	2. Audience size is key. Advertising dollars will go to entertainment over news and try to censor reporting when advertisers sponsor news.
3. Social media are producing a new approach to news by providing information while entertaining, eliminating traditional news media filters that limit direct access to information, and giving ordinary people tools to uncover and report the news.	3. Amateurs will not be able to produce the quantity and quality of news now provided by professionals even with new tools.

— Competency Connection —
☼ CRITICAL THINKING ☼

Over the next decade, what will be lost and what will be gained as we move to more dependence on the Internet and social media for our news?

For Good and for Bad: The Rise of the Internet and Social Media

Traditional media's coverage of government and politics is still dominant but is gradually being supplemented, modified, and replaced by the Internet and social media. Local television news, for example, has experienced some long-term decline in viewership but is still regularly watched by almost half the total population. Age, however, plays a major role. Close to three of five persons age 50 and over watch local news, compared to half that proportion for those ages 18–29.[51] A similar pattern exists for following the news in newspapers. However, traditional media are adapting, and the line between traditional and digital media is blurred.

Texas television stations and newspapers now commonly have an Internet site and provide varying proportions of their news via the Internet. In the words of one executive, "We are not a TV station anymore as much as a provider of news on multiple platforms."[52] A quarter of newspaper revenue now comes from the digital side. News sites for most major Texas newspapers do not yet match the quality of those of major national papers; however, most are improving.

One of the major new issues for newspapers, in particular, is whether to provide news on the Internet for free or by subscription. The *Dallas Morning News, Fort Worth Star-Telegram, Austin American-Statesman*, and *Houston Chronicle* provide some news free but reserve much news to paid subscribers. The online *Texas Tribune* is free.

The nature of the transition toward providing news digitally is illustrated in The Pew Research Center for Journalism and Media's listing of the 51 most used online news sites. Twenty-six of the sites are connected to traditional media, such as newspapers and television. For example, sites for the *Houston Chronicle* and *Dallas Morning News* newspapers are respectively 32 and 51 on the list. The 25 remaining sites originated essentially on the Internet.[53]

Two points should be noted about the transition to Internet news. One is that traditional media, particularly newspapers, continue to generate most news found on the Internet. Second, the development of digital newsrooms is still quite fragile. Most digital sites remain unprofitable.[54] The decline of newspapers and magazines has resulted in the elimination of far more editorial jobs than those created in digital newsrooms. Prospects that the digital revolution will provide the quantity of news now generated by traditional media are only a possibility, not a reality. Digital media are still a work in progress that will likely deliver less news in the short term.

The Future?

A great deal of debate exists about the future news role of the Internet and social media, including within the team that wrote this book. Objective observers generally reject the view that citizens and professionals will quickly replace traditional news media with something even better. They also reject the view that news will inevitably degenerate into ideological fiefdoms with no concern for the facts. Consumers of news will inevitably play a major role in the changes. The Pew Research Center, which does a great deal of polling about the media, concluded that "Overall our findings show a public that is cautious as it moves into today's more complex news environment and discerning in its evaluation of available news sources."[55]

The media will continue to change, as they have for almost three centuries. Newspaper reporters are still the most important gatherers of news. However, economic considerations mean that newspapers and news magazines will continue to lose readers and advertising dollars. As they decline, the amount of news collected is likely to decline as well. Television news departments are also under financial pressure and will not be able to take up the slack. Both the number of people using the Internet and social media and innovations in how these media are used will continue to grow.

Three critical questions face the digital media. First, can they take up the slack from the decline of traditional media and provide the quantity of hard news necessary to keep leaders and the public adequately informed? In the short term, objective observers believe social media will fail as a provider of sufficient trustworthy news. Over the longer term, success seems more likely. Blogs and Internet news sites already gather and disseminate news. However, they will need more advertising revenue to hire reporters. Social media already supplement news gathering, and their output is increasing. However, the way social media are structured means that news gathering tends not to be systematic. There are many sites, varied orientations, and fluctuation in the quality and number of individual contributions. News too often is secondary to entertainment.

Second, will the news provided by nonprofessional digital media users maintain journalistic standards of professionalism? One very possible outcome is the continuation of the competition between news and entertainment. The greater ability of people to choose their news sources and the need for advertising revenue to pay for technology favor continuation of the present emphasis on soft news and a wide range of partisan venues.

Advertisers are already pumping money into the Internet, including social media. Ideological and partisan groups are becoming more sophisticated in pursuing their goals through sites that proclaim lofty goals but simultaneously promote the interests of their sponsors. Standards of professionalism are still strong among reporters in both the traditional and new media, and the independent nature of social media may help keep news from tending to one extreme or the other.

Third, will the digital revolution increase the gap between the informed and the uninformed? For the news junkie (someone who follows news stories closely), an incredible amount of data and informed opinion are readily available. But for the average person, the entertainment value of soft news and the ability to select congenial views keep many ill-informed.

Government regulations will play a role. Most new communication technologies face demands for regulations that limit use, raise costs, and in general limit

⊠ KEEPING CURRENT
Election 2018 in Texas

As in the past, media coverage of Texas election campaigns was lighter than at the national level. However, both Texas and national media covered the state election more vigorously than in most midterms because of the possibility of an upset in the U.S. Senate race, the charisma of candidate Beto O'Rourke, and the possibility of the Senate and House races affecting the balance of power in the U.S. Congress. The most attention was paid to the Senate race, with horse race journalism topping issue differences. To the degree that Texas candidates and media focused on issues, much of the discussion was again on national issues, with major state problems getting short shrift. The one partial exception was border security, which was also a national issue.

Unlike past years, the race for governor received little attention, in large part because of both candidates' low-key campaigns and the near certainty of Governor Abbott's reelection. Except for some congressional and state legislative races, most down-ballot races received little attention. The ouster of the county judge in Harris County (Houston) by a political unknown came as a surprise because of the neglect of coverage of the demographic changes that led to the Democratic sweep. Texas newspapers continued to cut staff and the number of pages, while local television news provided local color but little depth. On the other hand, Internet and social media news was spurred by the campaign. Social media continued to increase in importance in campaigning, particularly in the U.S. Senate race.

✔ 6.7 Learning Check

1. Are the changes in the news media trending toward more or less news being gathered?
2. Are people using social media as a news source?

Answers at the end of this chapter.

competition with the established media. Legitimate concerns about defamation, free speech and press, government honesty and responsiveness, Internet neutrality, and public and private censorship will also keep government involved. Battles over the Internet are fought in courts, legislative bodies, and regulatory bodies.

Humans and the Internet have shown a remarkable ability to adapt and change. As this chapter shows, the news media have experienced centuries of change. The current transition to digital media is one more step down that path. Texas media will continue to be an integral part of that journey.

CONCLUSION

In many areas, Texas has patterns that differ significantly from those of the nation, but the media at both levels have remarkably similar histories and patterns. Newspapers were long the major outlet for news and remain important today, particularly as gatherers of news and as the source of the details of the news for the elite. Today, television is being overtaken by the Internet and social media as the major source of news for Texans, particularly among the young. Soft news and the decline in the number of reporters are major concerns. Growth in the number of ways to receive news provides the elite and news junkies a wealth of information. Potentially, social media provide more opportunity for ordinary Texans to participate in the reporting of news and to select how and what they receive. The concern is that the rise of social media is making news softer and more ideological.

The media continue to play a number of vital roles, albeit playing some better than others: informing citizens and leaders, maintaining democracy, setting the public agenda, and influencing our views. Diversity remains a major challenge. Changes in ownership of the media, availability of better campaign techniques for office seekers and citizen groups, and movement toward predominance of the Internet and social media portend both challenges and opportunities.

CHAPTER SUMMARY

LO 6.1 Compare the ways in which Texans get their information today with past patterns. The sources of news for Texans are changing. Newspapers were most important in the 1800s and the first half of the 20th century. Today, the interested public gets news from multiple sources. Newspapers are still important, but the Internet and social media are now overcoming television as Texans' most-used source. A major concern with the changes is the decline in the amount of actual news received by the public.

LO 6.2 Describe the roles of the media in Texas politics. There are many platforms from which to receive news, but the content of the news appears to be in decline. Absorbing the news requires some effort and certain conditions, which means that interested citizens and leaders are likely to gain much more from the news than the average citizen. Historically, the press was highly partisan and often an unreliable source of accurate information. In the 20th century, the press became a more professional provider of information in Texas and the nation, although in recent years the media have become more adversarial. The media have used the state's open meetings and open records laws to provide more information about public policymaking. In Texas and the nation, the ability to investigate is in decline because of corporate influence and lack of money, but the state's press has generally played a positive role in exposing political scandals. The media, together with political leaders and interest groups, participate in setting the agenda of what government will or will not consider. Texas media have worked at this role but face difficulties and are not always successful. The media seldom change people's minds, but they do affect public opinion through priming and framing. They help to shape what we think about and the evaluations we make.

LO 6.3 Discuss the roles of the media in modern Texas election campaigns. The media play a significant role in campaigns through the ads they run and the coverage they give candidates. Because the media and the candidates have different goals but need each other, the relationship is often conflictual. Each tries to manipulate the other. Use of the Internet and social media in campaigns has become very important and more sophisticated beginning in 2008.

LO 6.4 Analyze the issue of ideological bias in the Texas media. Research indicates that there is not a net bias in the media toward one party or ideology, although many parts of the media—talk shows, the two ideological cable networks, and blogs—have become more partisan. Researchers have found evidence of a commercial bias and a strong preference for news that is entertaining, rather than important but boring or difficult to understand.

LO 6.5 Discuss the nature and consequences of media regulation by government.
The national government has taken primary responsibility for regulation of the media. Newspapers have never faced substantial regulation, and today only broadcast television is still heavily regulated. The major legal issue facing the Internet is whether and how to apply the idea of net neutrality. In Texas, defamation, particularly through the Internet, remains an important topic.

LO 6.6 Discuss the representation of women and ethnic minorities in Texas media.
In Texas and the nation, women and ethnic minorities are underrepresented in journalism, and the proportions are even lower in management positions. One consequence is less representation in the news provided. Texas does have a tradition of ethnic news media, which will probably become more prevalent on the Internet.

LO 6.7 Discuss the positive and negative effects of changes the media are undergoing in Texas. Newspapers have long been the major gatherers of news. Their decline has meant fewer reporters actually gathering news for other forms of media to use. The growth of cable news and the increasing role of Internet blogs and social media are giving impetus to softer news and more opportunities for partisanship. Digital media provide more opportunity for citizen participation and innovation and will probably become the dominant media outlet for news. How that will affect news is the subject of a major debate.

KEY TERMS

adversarial, p. 207

agenda setting, p. 211

attack ad, p. 213

blog, p. 200

Capitol press corps, p. 229

civic engagement, p. 218

defamation, libel, and slander,
    p. 224

framing, p. 214

hard news, p. 204

homogenization of news, p. 228

horserace journalism, p. 216

media, p. 193

net neutrality, p. 223

news website, p. 200

niche journalism (narrowcasting),
    p. 227

open meetings, p. 208

open records, p. 208

priming, p. 214

prior restraint, p. 222

professionalism, p. 206

shield law, p. 223

SLAPP, p. 225

social media, p. 200

soft news, p. 204

yellow journalism, p. 205

LEARNING CHECK ANSWERS

 1. Television is now similar to digital forms as a source of news. For the young, the Internet and social media are most important.

2. In the early 20th century, most people got their news from newspapers.

 1. With fewer reporters, the media are less able to investigate government wrongdoing.

2. Media framing is the media giving a meaning or central theme to an issue.

6.3
1. The biggest factor in the high cost of Texas political campaigns is having to advertise in so many media markets.
2. Yes, political campaigns are using the Internet and social media more effectively.

6.4
1. No, examples of bias tend to balance out.
2. Partisanship tends to appear most consistently in areas in which consumers can choose their preferred ideological presentation, such as blogs, talk shows, and cable television.

6.5
1. Broadcast television is the most regulated medium.
2. The federal government has regulated media the most.

6.6
1. No, women and, more so, ethnic minorities are currently underrepresented in Texas newsrooms.
2. Reporting on minority Texans has improved but is still different in important ways, such as negative stereotyping.

6.7
1. With fewer reporters and the decline of newspapers, less news is being gathered.
2. Yes, many people rely on social media for their news, although other forms of media are more important over all.

The Politics of Interest Groups

7

Learning Objectives

7.1 Explain what are interest groups, why they form, and what are their essential characteristics.

7.2 Describe the types of interest groups and analyze the qualities of a powerful interest group.

7.3 Evaluate the kinds of activities that interest groups use to influence Texas government.

7.4 Analyze how interest groups are regulated and evaluate the effectiveness of these laws.

IMAGE 7.1 Students at a rally opposing a proposed Texas law that would allow concealed handguns on college campuses.

Bob Daemmrich/Alamy Stock photo

Competency Connection
COMMUNICATION SKILLS

What are your views on concealed handguns on college campuses? How would you convey your position to others?

The typical focus of politics is on nomination and election of citizens to public office. There is, however, much more to politics than that. Politics is perhaps best understood as the process of influencing public policy decisions to protect and preserve a group, to achieve the group's goals, and to distribute benefits to the group's members. Organized people demand policies that promote their financial security, education, health, welfare, and protection.

Because government makes and enforces public policy decisions, it is not surprising that people try to influence officials who make and apply society's rules or policies, nor is it surprising that one important approach is through group action. History shows that people who organize for political action tend to be more effective in achieving their goals than persons acting alone. This principle is particularly true if a group is well financed. Money plays a big role in state government and state elections, and groups that help politicians finance their campaigns often achieve their goals.

✪ Interest Groups in the Political Process

LO 7.1 Explain what are interest groups, why they form, and what are their essential characteristics.

When people attempt to influence political decisions or the selection of the men and women who make such decisions, they usually turn either to political parties (examined in Chapter 4), the media (examined in Chapter 6), or interest groups (the subject of this chapter). Interest groups participate in a variety of activities to obtain benefits and favorable laws and policies for their members.

What Is an Interest Group?

An **interest group** may be identified as a pressure group, a special interest group, or a lobby. It is an organization whose members share common views and objectives. To promote their interests, such groups participate in activities designed to influence government officials and policy decisions for the benefit of group members or their cause. When a group or individual communicates directly with a government official to influence the official's decision on a policy matter, this activity is called lobbying. For example, during every regular legislative session, the Independent Colleges and Universities of Texas (ICUT), an organization of more than 40 private colleges and universities, lobbies the legislature against cuts to the Texas Equalization Grants (TEG), a student aid program that provides financial assistance to students who attend these institutions of higher education.

Different types of businesses and industries also seek to influence government officials. For instance, oil and gas production is an important industry in Texas. During the 84th legislative session (2015), the Texas Independent Oil Producers and Royalty Owners, a 3,000-member organization that protects mineral exploration rights, aligned against environmental groups like the Sierra Club in

Follow *Practicing Texas Politics* on Twitter **@PracTexPol**

interest group
An organization that seeks to influence government officials and their policies on behalf of members sharing common views and objectives (for example, labor unions or trade associations).

support of a proposed bill that prohibited local governments' banning hydraulic fracturing in oil and gas production. Legislators passed the bill. (For a discussion of this bill, see Chapter 3, "Local Governments.")

Although political parties and interest groups both attempt to influence policy decisions by government officials, they differ in their methods. The principal purpose of party activity is to increase the number of its members who are elected or appointed to public offices, in order to gain control of government and achieve party goals. In contrast, an interest group seeks to influence government officials (regardless of their party affiliation) to the advantage of the group. In general, an interest group wants government to create and implement policies that benefit the group, without necessarily placing its own members in public office.

Part of the purpose of economic groups (for example, the Texas Association of Business) and professional groups (such as the Texas Trial Lawyers Association) is to make their policy preferences known to government officials. Interest groups act as intermediaries for people who share common interests but reside throughout the state. Essentially, interest groups add to the formal system of geographic representation used for electing many officeholders. Such organizations serve the interests of their members by providing functional representation within the political system. They offer a form of protection by voicing the interests of groups like businesspeople, laborers, farmers, religious groups, racial/ethnic groups, teachers, physicians, and college students across the state. These groups are composed of people who have similar interests but who may not constitute a majority in any city, county, legislative district, or state.

The Reasons for Interest Groups

Growth and diversity of interest groups in the United States continue unabated. An increasingly complex society has much to do with the rate of growth of interest groups in the country and within states. Political scientists Allan Cigler and Burdett A. Loomis contend that these growing numbers, plus high levels of activity, distinguish contemporary interest group politics from previous eras.[1] Interest groups proliferate in Texas and throughout the country for several reasons.

Legal and Cultural Reasons In *NAACP v. Alabama*, 357 U.S. 449 (1958), the U.S. Supreme Court recognized the **right of association** as part of the right of assembly guaranteed by the First Amendment to the U.S. Constitution. This decision greatly facilitated the development of interest groups, ensuring the right of citizens to organize for political, economic, religious, and social purposes.

The nation's political culture has traditionally encouraged citizens to organize themselves into a bewildering array of associations—religious, fraternal, professional, and recreational, among others. Americans have responded by creating literally thousands of such groups. In the 1960s and 1970s, for example, social movements sparked interest group activities on issues involving civil rights, women's rights, student rights, and opposition to the Vietnam War. In Texas, controversies over social issues (such as the ban on same-sex marriage), education policy issues (such as school finance), immigration reform, and gun rights have sparked new groups and revitalized existing interest groups. For instance,

right of association
The U.S. Supreme Court has ruled that this right is part of the right of assembly guaranteed by the First Amendment to the U.S. Constitution and that it protects the right of people to organize into groups for political purposes.

in 2012, Texans for Real Efficiency and Equity in Education, an education group, formed to intervene in the latest round of public school finance lawsuits. Their solution to problems in the school system was to form charter schools as an alternative. In 2013, the Reform Immigration for Texas Alliance (RITA) formed as a statewide network dedicated to building support for comprehensive immigration reform with fair, humane, and sensible policies, as well as to advocate for the preservation of allowing undocumented students to attend college at in-state tuition rates. Other interest groups, such as Texas Carry, formed to advocate for the right to keep and bear arms, especially the right to openly carry handguns. In 2015, the Texas legislature approved Texans' right to do so. The bill was signed into law by Governor Abbott at an indoor gun range.

Decentralized Government In a **decentralized government**, power is not concentrated at the highest level. Decentralization is achieved in two principal ways. First, the federal system divides power between the national government and the 50 state governments (as explained in Chapter 2, "Federalism and the Texas Constitution"). In turn, each state shares its power with local governments: counties, cities, and special districts. Second, within each level of government, power is separated into three branches, or departments: legislative, executive, and judicial. This separation of powers is especially apparent at the national and state levels.

A decentralized structure increases the opportunities for interest groups to form and influence government. This structure provides different access points for groups to fight their battles at different levels of government and within different branches at each level. For instance, Bike Texas has been unsuccessful in obtaining legislation at the state level to protect bicyclists on Texas roads. Nevertheless, the organization pressed successfully for protective city ordinances, such as in Austin, El Paso, Fort Worth, and San Antonio. In addition, before the statewide ban on texting while driving in 2017, more than 60 cities (including Arlington, Austin, Corpus Christi, El Paso, Galveston, and San Antonio) had already passed city ordinances banning texting while driving, especially in school zones.

The Strength of the Party System and Political Ideologies Two other factors have precipitated the influence of interest groups: strength (or weakness) of the party system and political ideologies. First, the absence of unified and responsible political parties magnifies opportunities for interest group action. A lack of strong, organized political parties can particularly affect policymakers (both state and local). In such cases, public officials are less likely to vote along party lines and therefore are more susceptible to pressure from well-organized interest groups, particularly if candidates rely on campaign contributions from these groups. In recent years, the Republican Party has dominated the Texas legislature and other statewide elective and appointive positions. Factions have developed within the Republican Party, however. At present, the Texas Tea Party has become a powerful faction within the Texas Republican Party, exercising considerable influence in the GOP's primaries and its state conventions (see Chapter 4, "Political Parties"). These factions tend to weaken party unity. Furthermore, liberal and conservative ideologies (developed and distinct orientations of political, social, and economic beliefs,

decentralized government
Decentralization is achieved by dividing power between national and state governments and separating legislative, executive, and judicial branches at both levels.

especially about the preferred role of government) have not been strong factors in Texas's two-party system. Public officials tend to rely more on their constituents or on the issues and less on ideology. In the end, public officials are susceptible to the pressures of interest groups.

Characteristics of Interest Groups

Citizens may join an interest group for different reasons, whether financial, professional, or social. Students who graduate from college often find themselves joining a professional or occupational group (Table 7.1).

In some cases, people join an interest group simply because they want to be part of a network of like-minded individuals working for a cause. The interest group often provides members with information and benefits and usually tries to involve them in the political process. Such a description suggests that any organization becomes an interest group when it influences or attempts to influence governmental decisions.

There are almost as many **organizational patterns** as there are interest groups. This variety arises from the fact that in addition to lobbying, most interest groups perform nonpolitical functions that are of paramount importance to their members. Texas Impact, for example, is a centralized statewide religious grassroots network representing several faith communities in Texas. It emphasizes charitable and spiritual activities, such as assisting low-income people in applying for social-welfare benefits, but also undertakes interfaith legislative advocacy.

Some interest groups are highly centralized organizations that take the form of a single controlling body. An example of such a centralized group currently operating in Texas is the National Rifle Association. Other groups are decentralized, consisting of loose alliances of local and regional subgroups. Their activities may be directed at either the local, state, or national level. Many trade associations (such as the Texas Mid-Continent Oil and Gas Association) and labor unions (such as those affiliated with the American Federation of Labor-Congress of Industrial Organizations [AFL-CIO]) are examples of decentralized organizations active in Texas politics. Other types of decentralized interest groups, including the National Women's Political Caucus (a women's rights organization) and Common Cause (a public interest group dedicated to government reform), have both state and local chapters in Texas.

Interest groups are composed chiefly of persons from professional and managerial occupations. Members of interest groups tend to have greater resources than most individuals possess. For instance, members are more likely to be homeowners with high levels of income and formal education who enjoy a high standard of living. Participation in interest groups, especially active participation, varies. Many citizens are not affiliated with any group, whereas others are members of several. Recent technology provides individuals easier access to interest group membership, unlike the registration paper forms of the past. For example, the Texas Community College Teachers Association (TCCTA) gives potential members an opportunity to join and register for conferences online. The site includes several resources, web links, and access to financial and

organizational pattern
The structure of a special interest group. Some interest groups have a decentralized pattern of organization. Others are centralized.

IMAGE 7.2 TCCTA's website shows one approach of how interest groups attract new members.

New to TCCTA?

Just a few reasons TCCTA is right for you!

>> High quality, high value professional development

>> Low cost professional liability insurance

>> Effective advocacy before the Texas Legislature and state agencies

>> A robust, statewide network of colleagues

Join Now!

Filemaker Central

— Competency Connection —
⚙ **CRITICAL THINKING** ⚙

Review the resources that TCCTA provides only for its members. If you were a college professor at a community college, which of these resources would convince you to join?

liability insurance benefits. In addition, TCCTA maintains Facebook and Twitter accounts, a blog, and information on the use of social media in classrooms. Some individuals, however, will not join an interest group—especially when they believe that they still benefit without actually having to join and pay the costs of membership.[2] People who receive benefits without paying the cost of membership, either in time or money, are called "free riders."

An organized group of any size usually comprises an active minority and a passive majority. As a result, decisions are regularly made by relatively few members. These decision makers may range from a few elected officers to a larger body of delegates representing the entire membership. Organizations generally leave decision making and other leadership activities to a few people. Two factors may explain limited participation in most group decisions: widespread apathy among rank-and-file members and the difficulty of removing entrenched leaders. Factors that influence **group leadership** include the group's financial resources (members who contribute most heavily usually have greater weight in making decisions), time-consuming leadership duties (only a few people can afford to devote much of their time without compensation), and the personality traits of leaders (some individuals have greater leadership ability and motivation than others).

group leadership
Individuals who guide the decisions of interest groups. Leaders of groups tend to have financial resources that permit them to contribute money and devote time to group affairs.

✔ **7.1 Learning Check**

1. Name at least two factors that motivate interest group formation.
2. True or False: Most interest groups have an active membership.

Answers at the end of this chapter.

TABLE 7.1 Texas Professional and Occupational Associations*

Health Related
Texas Dental Association
Texas Health Care Association
Texas Hospital Association
Texas Medical Association
Texas Ophthalmological Association
Texas Nurses Association
Texas Physical Therapy Association
Texas Counseling Association
Law Related
Texas Criminal Defense Lawyers Association
Texas Civil Justice League
Texas Trial Lawyers Association
Mexican American Bar Association of Texas
Texas Women Lawyers
Texas Young Lawyers Association
Texas Association of Consumer Lawyers
Education Related
Texas American Federation of Teachers
Texas Association of College Teachers
Texas Classroom Teachers Association
Texas PTA (Parent Teacher Association)
Texas Community College Teachers Association
Texas State Teachers Association
Texas Library Association
Texas Association of College and University Student Personnel
Texas Faculty Association
Texas School Counselor Association
Texas Association of School Administrators
Miscellaneous
Association of Environmental and Engineering Geologists (AEG) Texas
Texas Society of Architects
Texas Society of Certified Public Accountants
Intelligent Transportation Society (ITS) Texas

All organizations listed can be found on the Internet.

—— Competency Connection ——
⁂ **PERSONAL RESPONSIBILITY** ⁂

Review Table 7.1 on professional interest groups. Given your professional goals, which interest group might you join? What, do you suppose, would be the advantages of joining a professional interest group?

✪ Types of Interest Groups

LO 7.2 Describe the types of interest groups and analyze the qualities of a powerful interest group.

The increasing diversity of American interest groups at national, state, and local levels of government permits groups to be classified in several ways. Not only can interest groups be studied by organizational patterns (such as centralized versus decentralized, as discussed earlier), they can also be categorized according to the level or branch of government to which they direct their attention. Some groups exert influence at all levels of government and on legislative, executive (including administrative), and judicial officials. Others may try to spread their views among the general public and may best be classified according to the subject matter they represent. Some groups do not fit readily into any category, whereas others fit into more than one. In this section, we examine various types of interest groups: economic groups, professional and public employee groups, social groups, and public interest groups.

Economic Groups

Many interest groups exist primarily to promote their members' economic self-interest. These organizations are the most common in Texas and are known as **economic interest groups**. Traditionally, many people contribute significant amounts of money and time to obtain the financial benefits of group membership. Thus, some organizations exist to further the economic interests of a broad group, such as trade associations, whereas others seek to protect the interests of a single type of business, such as restaurant associations. The Texas Association of Business (generally known as TAB) is an example of a broader type of interest group, known as an umbrella organization because it represents a variety of smaller groups and coordinates their state and national government activities. More than 4,000 businesses from a variety of industries and the state's local chambers of commerce are all members of TAB. Individual corporations, such as communications giant AT&T, use the political process to promote a company's particular economic interests.

Business Groups Businesspeople understand they have common interests that may be promoted by collective action. They were among the first to organize and press national, state, and local governments to adopt favorable public policies. **Business organizations** typically advocate lower taxes, a lessening or elimination of price and quality controls by government, and minimal concessions to labor unions. At the state level, business organizations most often take the form of trade associations (groups that act on behalf of an industry). The Texas Gaming Association (a group that favors the creation of destination casino resorts in the state) is an interest group that has lobbied the state legislature in recent legislative sessions in support of gambling interests. Two of the many other Texas trade associations are the Texas Association of Builders, TAB, (a group that focuses on creating a positive environment for the housing industry) and the Texas Good

economic interest group
An interest group that exists primarily to promote their members' economic self-interest. Trade associations and labor unions are classified as economic interest groups because they are organized to promote policies that will maximize profits and wages.

business organization
An economic interest group, such as a trade association (for example, Texas Gaming Association), that lobbies for policies favoring business.

Roads and Transportation Association (a group made up of highway construction contractors, chambers of commerce members, professionals, and transportation experts, among others, dedicated to ensuring efficient transportation and increased funding for highways).

In past legislative sessions, Texas businesses and their representatives have succeeded in enacting many of their policy preferences into law. One notable case study is the impact of campaign contributions on the GOP-controlled 78th Legislature (2003). Some reports indicated that TAB, along with Texans for Lawsuit Reform, contributed more than $2.6 million to support Republican candidates in key legislative races in 2002. Subsequently, the newly GOP-controlled Legislature passed several "business friendly" bills. One of the more significant bills limited lawsuits against manufacturers, pharmaceutical companies, and retailers.[3] Furthermore, the tobacco industry successfully defeated a statewide ban on smoking in public places, hiring as many as 40 lobbyists in 2009.[4] Big business (such as oil and gas, banking and finance, and insurance) has also been successful in defending tax breaks and corporate subsidies in past legislative sessions. One tax that businesses pay is the franchise tax, a special tax charged for the privilege of doing business in the state. (For a discussion of the franchise tax, see Chapter 11, "Finance and Fiscal Policy.") In past legislative sessions, small businesses were effective in adding a permanent minimum $1 million deduction to the small business franchise tax exemption. The franchise tax rate was further reduced by 25 percent. This reduction resulted in estimated annual savings to Texas businesses of approximately $1.3 billion.

Labor Groups Unions representing Texas workers, though relatively active, are not as numerous or powerful as business-related groups. The state's **labor organizations** seek, among other goals, government intervention to increase wages, especially the state's minimum wage. In addition, labor groups work to obtain adequate health insurance coverage, provide unemployment insurance, and promote safe working conditions. Although Texans are traditionally sensitive to the potential political power of organized labor, certain industrial labor organizations are generally regarded as significant in Texas government. These groups are the Texas affiliates of the AFL-CIO (comprising 1,300 local unions and more than 230,000 members), the Communication Workers of America, and local affiliates of the International Brotherhood of Teamsters. For a highly industrialized state with a large population, union membership in Texas is small compared with that of most other states.

Texas is one the few states with union membership rates below 5 percent. As of 2017, only 4.7 percent of Texas's wage and salary workers belong to a union, according to the U.S. Bureau of Labor Statistics. With the pending cuts in education, health care, and state jobs in the 2011 legislature, several unions began relying on rallies as a means of expressing opposition. The Texas State Employees Union was a leading organizer of the "Save Our State Rally," one of the largest recorded rallies, with an estimated 6,000 to 7,000 people participating at the steps of the state Capitol. Although this rally brought considerable media attention, the unions were unsuccessful in preventing budgetary cuts made during the legislative session. The Texas State Employees Union continued to hold a "lobby day"

labor organization
A union that supports public policies designed to increase wages, obtain adequate health insurance coverage, provide unemployment insurance, promote safe working conditions, and otherwise protect the interests of workers.

IMAGE 7.3 Pro-Medicaid expansion rally at the Texas Capitol in Austin, Texas.

Marjorie Kamys Cotera/Bob Daemmrich Photography/Alamy Stock Photo

— Competency Connection —
⊚ **SOCIAL RESPONSIBILITY** ⊚

Rallies at the Texas Capitol are often a powerful strategy used by interest groups to mobilize their members. How important are rallies for conveying their message to policymakers?

rally of their members and supporters during subsequent legislative sessions, along with a series of mini-lobby days for different state employee groups, such as retirees, parole officers, and university workers. Although successful in obtaining a 2.5 percent pay raise for state workers in the 84th legislative session, the pay raise was allocated to mandatory employee contributions to the state retirement fund. Thus, the pay raise did not put more money in employees' pockets.

Professional/Public Employee Groups

Closely related to economic interest groups are groups dedicated to furthering the interests of a profession, such as physicians or attorneys. Public employees have also organized to advance their interests. Teachers have been especially active in their efforts to influence government decisions.

Professional Groups Standards of admission to a profession or an occupation, as well as the licensing of practitioners, concern **professional groups**. Examples of Texas professional and occupational associations are the State Bar of Texas (attorneys), the Texas Health Care Association, and the Texas Society of Certified Public Accountants. (See Table 7.1 for a list of some of the more

professional group
An organization of physicians, lawyers, accountants, or other professional people that lobbies for policies beneficial to members.

important Texas professional and occupational associations.) Professionals are more effective if they organize in groups that advocate for their interests. Physicians won a significant victory in the 76th Legislature in 1999, when Texas became the first state to allow doctors to bargain collectively with health maintenance organizations over fees and policies. The Texas Medical Association (TMA) successfully lobbied for passage of a constitutional amendment, Proposition 12, that authorized the state legislature to impose a $250,000 cap for non-economic damages in medical malpractice cases. TMA also won approval in the state legislature for a new medical school in the Rio Grande Valley and an increase in the state's cap on student loans for young physicians in order to increase the number of primary care doctors. In recent years, TMA has sought, albeit unsuccessfully, to improve the Medicaid system by ensuring physician payments, as well as improving access to quality health care and expanding Medicaid funding under the Patient Protection and Affordable Care Act so that compensated care is available to more Texas patients.

With regard to teacher groups, the last time teachers were successful in significantly increasing salaries and improving health packages was in 1999. At that time, they persuaded the state legislature to increase pay raises for every public school teacher, librarian, and registered school nurse in Texas. Legislators also fully or partially funded state-supported health insurance for public school teachers and other school employees, both active and retired. Teacher organizations, such as the Texas American Federation of Teachers, have continued to lobby to boost school funding, as well as to oppose school finance legislation that they believe provides inadequate funding and would intrude on local control of school matters. In recent legislative sessions, teacher associations have participated in rallies outside the state Capitol. (For more on school finance, see Chapter 11, "Finance and Fiscal Policy.") Teacher organizations have also been vocal with regard to changes in curriculum requirements by the State Board of Education and high-stakes standardized testing mandates set by the legislature and the Texas Education Agency. (For more on education policy affecting public schools, see Chapter 12, "Public Policy and Administration.")

Public officer and employee groups of state and local governments organize to obtain better working conditions, higher wages, more fringe benefits, and better retirement packages. The Texas State Employees Association, which represents government employees, for instance, lobbies for legislation that prevents job cuts and increases pay and health care benefits.

Among state government employees, the oldest and largest group is the Texas Public Employees Association with more than 15,000 active and retired state employees across the state. City government groups include the Texas City Management Association and the Texas City Attorneys Association. Through their organizational activities, these public officer and employee groups resist efforts to reduce the size of state and local governmental bureaucracies (though not always with success). The County Judges and Commissioners Association of Texas and the Justices of the Peace and Constables Association of Texas, for example, have been instrumental in assuring that measures designed to reform Texas's justice of the peace courts and county courts reflect their members' interests. Two of

public officer and employee group
An organization of city managers, county judges, law enforcement or other public employees or officials that lobbies for public policies that protect group interests.

the state's largest police unions, the Texas Municipal Police Association (TMPA), which represents more than 27,000 local, county, and state law enforcement officers, and the Combined Law Enforcement Associations of Texas (CLEAT), which represents more than 24,000 members, joined forces to lobby for police officer rights. When the 2015 legislature was in the final stages of the open-carry bill (a law that allows licensed gun owners to openly display their weapons), the TMPA took the position that the organization supported open carry but had concerns with an amendment that prevented police officers from asking to see a person's handgun license simply because he or she was openly carrying a gun. The amendment was not included in the final bill. Texas's open-carry law went into effect in January 2016. In addition, police organizations went on record in support of the statewide legislative proposal that banned texting while driving.

Social Groups

Texas also has a wide array of **social interest groups**. These include racial and ethnic organizations, civil rights organizations, gender-based organizations, religion-based organizations, and several public interest groups.

Racial and Ethnic Groups Leaders of Texas's **racial and ethnic groups** recognize that only through effective organizations can they hope to achieve their cherished goals. Examples of these goals include eliminating racial discrimination in employment; improving public schools; increasing educational opportunities; and obtaining greater representation in the state legislature, city councils, school boards, and other policymaking bodies of government.

One formidable group, the National Association for the Advancement of Colored People (NAACP), is an effective racial interest group. According to the Texas State Historical Association, chapters of the Texas NAACP were established during the World War I era, with the first chapter forming in El Paso in 1915. This organization has been successful in influencing public policies relating to school integration and local government redistricting. The NAACP also effectively fought for hate crimes legislation that enhances penalties for crimes on the basis of race, color, disability, religion, national origin, gender, or sexual preference.[5] In addition, the organization continues to advocate strict enforcement against racial profiling. Texas law defines racial profiling as an action by law enforcement personnel on the basis of an individual's race, ethnicity, or national origin as opposed to the individual's behavior or information identifying the individual as being engaged in criminal activity. Beginning in 2011, the Texas NAACP actively opposed making a Confederate battle flag image available on specialty Texas license plates. The organization successfully appealed to the Texas Department of Motor Vehicles to prevent legitimizing a symbol that, in their view, represents brutality and fear and that is used by hate groups to promote a racist ideology. The U.S. Supreme Court ultimately struck down these specialty license plates, concluding that the state did not create a "limited public forum" that allowed an individual's freedom of expression. Instead, the Court held in *Walker v. Sons of the Confederate Veterans* (2015) that license plates signified "government speech,"

social interest group
A group concerned primarily with social issues, including organizations devoted to civil rights, racial and ethnic matters, religion, and public interest protection.

racial and ethnic groups
Organizations that seek to influence government decisions that affect a particular racial or ethnic group, such as the National Association for the Advancement of Colored People (NAACP) and the League of United Latin American Citizens (LULAC), which seek to influence government decisions affecting African Americans and Latinos, respectively.

and the state had a right to reject these plates.[6] In addition, the NAACP, along with Latino groups, strongly advocated against the controversial voter ID law that went into effect (for more on this issue, see Chapter 5, "Campaigns and Elections"). Asian Americans in recent years have also formed organizations and political action committees or PACs (groups that raise and distribute money to political candidates), such as the Network of Asian American Organizations, which serves the interests of Asian American communities in Central Texas.

In Texas, Latino groups, especially Mexican American organizations, are more numerous than African American interest groups. The oldest Latino group, the League of United Latin American Citizens (LULAC), was founded in 1929 in Corpus Christi.[7] LULAC has worked for equal educational opportunities for Latinos, as well as for full citizenship rights. It continues to advocate for adequate public school funding, Mexican American Studies curriculum in public schools, and bilingual education, as well as higher education policies, like the "Top Ten Percent Rule" and affirmative action, both of which are designed to ensure diversity of college and university student populations. In addition, LULAC successfully pressed for state funds to open the school of pharmacy at Texas A&M–Kingsville, which was named after the late state legislator and strong advocate for higher education, Irma Rangel.[8] LULAC has brought attention to the importance of the U.S. Census, as well as to the State Board of Education's unwillingness to incorporate more Hispanic historical figures in public school textbooks.

Another organization, the Mexican American Legal Defense and Education Fund (MALDEF), formed in 1968 in San Antonio, uses court action in pursuit of political equality, equal education, immigration rights, representation for Latinos, and most recently, attempts of voter suppression for recently naturalized citizens. Both LULAC and MALDEF have been instrumental in addressing redistricting, especially when it comes to voting rights. On behalf of a statewide coalition of Texas Latino organizations called the Texas Latino Redistricting Task Force, among other plaintiffs, MALDEF in 2012 successfully challenged the redistricting plans created by the Texas legislature for the U.S. House of Representatives and the Texas House. The group's attorneys claimed that the plans did not provide fair representation for Latinos. A three-judge federal court allowed creation of two out of the four newly established congressional seats as Latino-majority districts. This court also created an additional Latino-majority district in the Texas House of Representatives, thus increasing the number of Latino-majority districts to 34. MALDEF continues to challenge, with some success, the drawing of some congressional and state legislative districts that dilute the voting strength of ethnic and racial minorities. MALDEF has successfully advocated against anti-immigrant legislative proposals. But, it was unsuccessful in challenging the ban on "sanctuary cities" (municipalities with policies that prohibit local law enforcement officers from inquiring into the immigration status of a person or report violations to federal immigration enforcement officials), which was passed by the state legislature in 2017.

women's organization
A women's group, such as the League of Women Voters, that engages in lobbying and educational activities to promote greater political participation by women and others.

Women's Groups The Texas Women's Political Caucus is an example of a **women's organization** that promotes equal rights and greater participation by women in the political arena. The League of Women Voters of Texas is a nonpartisan organization advocating greater political participation and public understanding of governmental issues. It also assists voters in becoming better informed by publishing *The Texas Voters Guide*, which provides information about elections, candidates, and candidates' positions on various issues.

The Texas Federation of Republican Women, a partisan interest group with more than 10,000 members and more than 164 local clubs, provides resources for women to influence government actions and policies. This organization actively encourages Republican women to run for public office. Another organization that formed in 2003, in response to the dwindling number of Democratic women in the state legislature, is Annie's List. This organization recruits, trains, and supports progressive female candidates, as well as raises money for these candidates. Among their endorsements in the 2014 statewide races were Democratic candidates Wendy Davis for governor and Leticia Van de Putte for lieutenant governor, but both were defeated. In recent elections, the group endorsed a number of Latina and African American candidates for positions in the Texas Senate and Texas House of Representatives. The organization provides supporters with an opportunity to "Join our Movement" on their website. Annie's List also used social media to follow Senator Wendy Davis's 11-hour filibuster against a bill to restrict access to abortions in 2013. Members and supporters live-tweeted from the Capitol during the debate. The hashtag (#standwithwendy) garnered over 500,000 tweets during the course of her delaying tactic. Other interest groups, such as the Hispanic Women's Network of Texas, focus on the concerns and needs of Hispanic women. This statewide organization is dedicated to advancing the interests of Latinas in the public, corporate, and civic arenas. The Texas Latina List, which had its origin in Fort Worth, is a political action committee that recruits and funds Latina candidates at all levels of appointive and elective office. In 2018, the organization endorsed the first Latina to the U.S. Congress, Veronica Escobar from El Paso.

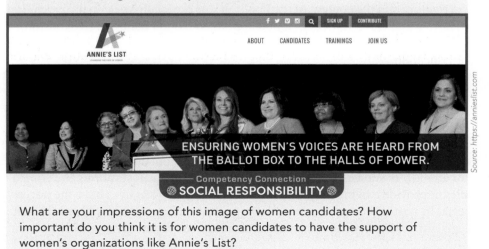

IMAGE 7.4 Annie's List is an example of a women's organization that focuses on electing women to public office.

Source: https://annieslist.com

ENSURING WOMEN'S VOICES ARE HEARD FROM THE BALLOT BOX TO THE HALLS OF POWER.

Competency Connection
◉ **SOCIAL RESPONSIBILITY** ◉

What are your impressions of this image of women candidates? How important do you think it is for women candidates to have the support of women's organizations like Annie's List?

Religion-Based Groups The Christian Coalition is an example of a **religion-based group**. With millions of Texans identifying themselves as conservative Christians, the organization continues to be one of the state's most influential political forces, though it had more momentum in the 1990s than it does now. This interest group engages in political action, primarily within the Republican Party. Issues that have precipitated the Christian Coalition's entrance on the political scene are abortion, homosexuality, limits on prayer in public schools, and decline of the traditional nuclear family.[9]

Other organizations have formed, such as Texas Values, which was founded in 2012, to educate the public about religious liberty and expression. In 2014, the group established Texas Values Action, a lobbying and advocacy organization, to openly support candidates and legislation that promote religious freedom without government interference or workplace retribution. This group raises money, endorses candidates, and sponsors activities to promote its agenda. In 2015, for instance, Texas Values Action claimed success in a citizen-initiated referendum that repealed Houston's antidiscrimination ordinance that prohibited discrimination based on a number of factors, including sexual orientation and gender identity. The organization was a strong proponent of the "bathroom bill," which sought to require public school students to use only bathrooms and lockers that matched the gender shown on their birth certificates.

The Texas Freedom Network was formed in the 1990s to oppose the increasing presence of the Christian Coalition. This organization monitors the activities of right-wing conservatives, musters liberal and mainstream voters, and provides an alternative voice on current political issues.[10] The Texas Faith Network, the official blog of the Texas Freedom Network, also created in the 1990s, monitors religious leaders statewide who represent the religious right and who attempt to influence political conservatives (usually Republicans). In recent decades, the Texas Freedom Network has worked on several issues, such as defending civil liberties, strengthening public schools, and especially maintaining the separation of church and state. The organization is also vocal in its opposition to social conservatives on the State Board of Education who influence the public school curriculum and the content of textbooks. It was especially vocal in its opposition in 2015 when Governor Greg Abbott appointed Donna Bahorich (R-Houston), a social conservative with ties to the Tea Party, to serve as Chair of the State Board of Education.

Another religion-based organization, the Texas Industrial Areas Foundation, operates in cities such as Dallas and in the Rio Grande Valley. It supports increased funding for parent training, easier access for children to qualify for Medicaid benefits, and extending Children's Health Insurance Program (CHIP) eligibility to more families.[11] Valley Interfaith, made up primarily of churches and schools, has successfully lobbied the Brownsville school district to increase wages for employees and has indirectly influenced other public institutions and companies to provide a living wage for their workers so they can live above the poverty level. In past legislative sessions, the organization has actively lobbied the state legislature, demanding restoration of funds cut from CHIP, expansion and

religion-based group
An interest group, such as the Texas Freedom Network, that lobbies for policies to promote its religious interests.

increases in Medicaid funding, and increases in state funding for public schools, as well as an equitable tax system that does not burden the poor.

Communities Organized for Public Service (COPS) in San Antonio, which has been active since the 1970s, and their affiliated organization, Metro Alliance, successfully lobbied the legislature to allow cities to use sales tax revenue to create job training and early childhood development programs.[12] In recent years, COPS/Metro leaders succeeded in raising wages for more than 5,000 low-paid employees of local governments and area hospitals. The city of San Antonio, for instance, voted in 2018 for a living wage of $15.00, benefiting its lowest paid workers.

Public Interest Groups

Unlike most other interest groups, **public interest groups** claim to promote the general interests of society, rather than narrower private or corporate interests. Environmental, political participation, education-related, and public morality (not directly associated with established religion) organizations are often identified as public interest groups.

Public interest organizations pursue diverse goals. Common Cause Texas, for example, focuses primarily on governmental and institutional reform. It advocates open meeting laws, public financing of political campaigns, and stricter financial disclosure laws. Texans for Public Justice supports efforts toward campaign finance reform, such as limitations on campaign contributions by political action committees and individuals. The Texas League of Conservation Voters uses a scorecard to monitor the voting records of state lawmakers who support environment-friendly "green" bills. These public interest organizations also use social media technology, such as Twitter and Facebook, to keep supporters connected. (See Table 7.2 for a partial list of Texas public interest groups.)

Texas Power Groups

Texas legislators readily identify the types of interest groups they consider most powerful: business-oriented trade associations (representing oil, gas, tobacco, chemical manufacturers, insurance, and railroads), professional associations (physicians, lawyers, and teachers), and labor unions. Other groups wielding considerable influence include brewers, truckers, automobile dealers, bankers, and realtors. Some of the most influential interest groups operating not only in Texas but also nationwide are general business organizations (for example, chambers of commerce), schoolteacher associations, utility companies, insurance companies and associations, hospital and nursing home associations, and bar associations for attorneys.[13]

Interest groups typified as **power groups** have several common traits. For one, these groups maintain strong links with both legislators (whose policy decisions affect group interests) and bureaucrats (whose regulatory authority controls activities of group members). Power groups often are repeat players in Texas politics, meaning they have been influencing politics in consecutive legislative

public interest group
An organization claiming to represent a broad public interest (such as environmental, consumer, political participation, or public morality) rather than a narrow private interest.

power group
An effective interest group strongly linked with legislators and bureaucrats for the purpose of influencing decision making and having a continuing presence in Austin as a repeat player from session to session.

TABLE 7.2 Texas Public Interest Groups*

Education Related
Texas Parent PAC
Texans for Education Reform
Environmental
Texas Campaign for the Environment
Texas Wildlife Association
Environment Texas
Sierra Club, Lone Star Chapter
Public Participation and Social Justice
Texas Association of Community Action Agencies
Communities Organized for Public Service
Public Citizen/Texas
Equality Texas
Public Morality
Mothers Against Drunk Driving
Texas Right to Life Committee
National Abortion and Reproductive Rights Action League Pro-Choice Texas

All organizations listed can be found on the Internet.

— Competency Connection —
⊗ **SOCIAL RESPONSIBILITY** ⊗

Review Table 7.2, which provides a sample of public interest groups. If given the opportunity, what central issue/concern would you create a public interest group around?

sessions for a long time. Another indication of power group influence is having headquarters in Austin. Many business-related associations, for example, own a headquarters building in the capital city. Others lease or rent buildings and office suites there. This proximity to the Texas Capitol and the main offices of state agencies provides regular contact with state officials and gives such associations a path to influence in state government.[14] In some cases, according to watchdog organizations, interest groups have received free use of meeting rooms in the Texas Capitol building for receptions.

One of the most influential power groups is the Texas Medical Association (TMA), formed in 1853. With a well-organized grassroots network, a skilled lobbying team, and more than 52,000 licensed physicians and medical students in Texas, TMA is one of the state's most powerful professional groups. According to TMA's figures, this group succeeded in passing as much as 90 percent of its agenda items back in the late 1990s.[15] Although TMA was not able to persuade the state legislature in 2013 to restore funding cuts in Medicaid from previous legislative sessions, the organization succeeded in preventing severe cuts to physicians' Medicaid payments so that doctors would continue seeing needy patients. In 2015, they successfully advocated for a significant expansion of funding for medical education, especially for medical residencies at hospitals. (For more on Medicaid funding, see Chapter 11, "Finance and Fiscal Policy.") Yet, the TMA, like other interest groups, is not always successful. In recent legislative sessions, TMA members and their lobbyists were unsuccessful in expanding Medicaid in Texas under the Affordable Care Act.

★ Interest Group Activities

LO 7.3 Evaluate the kinds of activities that interest groups use to influence Texas government.

When interest groups urge their members and others to become actively involved, they encourage people to participate in the political process. In some cases, interest groups even encourage members to consider running for public office. Groups benefit from having their supporters serve in decision-making positions, especially on influential boards and commissions. Local property taxpayers' associations, for example, frequently put forward candidates for public school boards and municipal offices in an effort to keep property taxes low. Likewise, when organizations of real estate agents or developers successfully lobby for placing their members in appointed positions on local planning and zoning commissions, they gain a distinct advantage. Because government officials need support for their policies, interest groups seek to mobilize and build that support, particularly for policies that form part of a group's goals and interests. Having the support or opposition of certain interest groups may determine the success or failure of bills, proposed budgets, appointments, and other policy matters.

Interest groups also are an outlet for discussions concerning policy issues. In doing so, they shape conflict and consensus in society. Conflict is the more usual outcome because each group is bent on pursuing its own limited ends. This commitment, in turn, leads to clashes with other groups seeking their own ends. Conflict is even more likely when addressing controversial issues, such as school finance, abortion, environmental protection, same-sex marriage, voter identification, redistricting, or immigration reform.

In some cases, however, certain issues may galvanize coalitions among various interest groups. For instance, groups representing teachers, parents, religious organizations, and civil rights organizations have rallied around the need for increased school funding. Even business organizations, such as the Texas Association of Business, joined forces. In 2011, for instance, many groups organized rallies called Save Texas Schools, which were centered on the issue of increased school funding and using the "rainy day" fund (the state's savings account) to cover any budgetary shortfalls. (For more on the rainy day fund, see Chapter 11, "Finance and Fiscal Policy.") In another unlikely coalition, during the 2015 legislative session, the Texas Association of Business joined forces with the pro-immigrant rights group, Reform Immigration for Texas Alliance (RITA). Their objective was to support legislation providing undocumented immigrants with

IMAGE 7.5 Along with tourists who visit the Capitol and government employees, lobbyists walk through the rotunda and halls as they seek to speak to state legislators.

Bernie Epstein/Alamy Stock Photo

— Competency Connection —
🔊 **COMMUNICATION SKILLS** 🔊

Lobbyists are an important component for the success of interest groups in the Texas Legislature. What do you think are some of the qualities of an effective lobbyist?

interest group technique
An action (such as lobbying, personal communication, giving favors and gifts, grassroots activities, electioneering, campaign financing by political action committees, and, in extreme instances, bribery and other unethical practices) intended to influence government decisions.

lobbying
Communicating with legislators or other government officials for the purpose of influencing decision makers.

an opportunity to obtain a state driver's license, or a state resident driver's permit, in order to make them eligible to buy car insurance. Political scientists know that interest groups use a wide range of techniques to influence policy decisions. These **interest group techniques** may be classified as lobbying; personal communication; giving favors and gifts; grassroots activities; electioneering; campaign financing by political action committees; and, in extreme instances, bribery and other illegal or unethical practices.

Lobbying

Lobbying is perhaps the oldest, and certainly the best-known, interest group tactic. According to Texans for Public Justice in 2014, "special interests spent up to $3 billion over the past decade on more than 72,000 Texas lobby contracts."[16] Identifying interest groups that hire lobbyists is one way to determine which interests are being represented before the state legislature and which are not. Lobbyists are individuals who are hired by an interest group. These full-time professional lobbyists attempt to influence government decision makers on behalf of special interests. Lobbying is most often directed at legislators and the lawmaking process, although it is also practiced within state agencies.

Not all lobbyists are full-time professionals. Most work for businesses and only occasionally go to Austin to speak to lawmakers about their concerns. Some lobbyists represent cities and counties. Among the most successful lobbyists are former state legislators, legislative aides, and gubernatorial aides. In recent years, Texas has ranked second in the country, after California, in money spent on lobbying the state government. At the same time, lobbyists generally outnumber the 181 Texas legislators by a ratio of roughly nine to one. Typically, the number of registered lobbyists increases during an election cycle. For the 2018 election cycle, there were 1,642 registered lobbyists. At the start of the 86th legislative session in 2019, the number stood at over 2,700 lobbyists.[17]

Some interest groups, such as the Texas Motorcycle Rights Association claiming to represent as many as 900,000 licensed motorcycle riders in Texas, will travel to Austin and hold a "lobby day" at the Capitol. On this occasion, association members meet with lawmakers about preserving bikers' rights. As this chapter's Students in Action feature suggests, even a "lobbyist for a day" requires a lot of planning and strategy in order to be an effective advocate. Another organization, Texas Interfaith Center, provides its members and supporters with information on its website on "faithful participation" and tips for meeting and interacting with legislators.

Personal Communication One of the main interest group techniques is personal communication by lobbyists. The immediate goal of lobbyists is to inform officials concerning their group's position on an issue. Because professional lobbyists are often experts in a specific field (and in some cases are former state officials), their tools of influence are the information and research they convey to public officials. The first task of the lobbyist is to gain access to legislators and other government decision makers. Once the lobbyist has made personal contact with a policymaker and captured the desired attention, he or she may use a variety of techniques to make that government official responsive to the group's demands, preferences, and expectations.

Because the process requires careful strategy, the lobbyist chooses the most appropriate time and place to speak with an official and determines how best to phrase arguments in order to have a positive impact. For maximum effectiveness in using this technique, a lobbyist must select the proper target (for example, a key legislative committee chair, regulatory agency administrator, county commissioner, or city zoning board member). Successful lobbyists rely heavily on a variety of technology, including smart phones, iPhones, iPads, Internet communications such as FaceTime, and other high-tech devices to store and communicate information. In fact, an important early study of interest group politics in Texas concluded that lobbying in the Lone Star State has shifted from an emphasis on personal argument to information-based communications.[18] A former Texas legislator compared lobbyists with pharmaceutical salespeople who explain new medicines to doctors who are too busy to keep up with the latest developments. In the same way, lobbyists provide data, information, and expertise about complex public policy issues to decision makers. For example, lobbyists representing the Texas Medical Society recruited Dr. Thomas Kim, a telehealth physician, to provide testimony to the House Public Health Committee on ways to regulate this new form of health care delivery in February 2016.[19] To perform their jobs effectively, successful lobbyists should clearly indicate the group they represent, define their interests, make clear what they want to do and why, answer questions readily, and provide enough accurate information for politicians and other officials to make judgments.

Successful lobbyists befriend as many legislators as possible, especially influential legislative leaders such as committee chairs, and they discover their interests and needs. These relationships are formed over time. Lobbyists also put pressure on sympathetic legislators to influence other legislators.

At present, no effective laws prohibit former Texas legislators (including former legislative presiding officers) from becoming lobbyists and immediately lobbying former colleagues. As of 2017, according to the National Conference of State Legislatures, at least 38 states required some kind of waiting period, ranging from the conclusion of the legislative session during which the legislator resigns to two years, before a legislator can become a lobbyist.[20] These lobbyists, and the interest groups that contract with them, are more likely to have connections in the state legislature than most other lobbyists. An ethics reform bill, SB 19, which addressed this "revolving door" problem was ultimately defeated in the 84th legislative session.[21] In 2017, Governor Perry, a strong advocate of ethics reform, signed into law the requirement that state elected officials who do business with cities, counties, and other governmental entities must disclose on personal financial statements their contracts with the Texas Ethics Commission. For many supporters, this law provides more government transparency and addresses potential conflicts of interests.[22]

Favors and Gifts Another lobbying technique used by interest groups, and especially by lobbyists, involves giving favors and gifts to legislators and other government decision makers. Common favors include arranging daily or weekly luncheon and dinner gatherings; providing free liquor, wine, or beer; furnishing tickets for entertainment events, air transportation, and athletic contests; and giving miscellaneous gifts. Gifts may include flower bouquets and spa treatments for female lawmakers or, for male lawmakers, guns, knives, and deer processing. Free tickets for Cowboys and Texans games, along with free access to some of the biggest collegiate football games across the state, are also commonplace and legal gifts for lawmakers from lobbyists, so long as the value of freebies for any one legislator from an individual lobbyist does not exceed $500 per calendar year. There are limits on the value of "travel gifts" for public officials and candidates, as well as for state agency employees.[23] In addition, public officials must report gifts valued at more than $250 to the Texas Ethics Commission.

Grassroots Activities Yet another influential technique used by interest groups is grassroots lobbying. Interest groups rely heavily on pressure from a grassroots network of organization members and sympathizers. Interest groups

📋 STUDENTS IN ACTION

Lobbyist for a Day

Since 2003, at the start of every spring semester in odd-numbered calendar years, a delegation of faculty, staff, and students from St. Mary's University in San Antonio* are recruited and trained on the principles of lobbying. The lobbying team goes to the Capitol for the day to lobby targeted state legislators and senators to try to increase, or at a minimum maintain, funding for Texas Equalization Grants (TEG) funding. This particular source of funding for college students was authorized first in the 1970s to provide an opportunity for low-income students to attend private colleges and universities in Texas.

In 2015, several students were selected to lobby the Texas legislature for this one-day event. One of the students was Karla Sotelo, a TEG recipient and political science major. What follows are her impressions of this experience.

Students mobilizing to take action.

Student lobbyist for the day

The Spring semester of 2015 yielded unexpected opportunities for me. It was only my second semester in college, and I was surprised to find out that I had been one of the few selected students to be part of the St. Mary's University Student Delegation to advocate for the Texas Equalization Grant (TEG) at the state's Capitol. As a political science major, I was thrilled that I had been presented with the opportunity to sit and meet with elected officials to address issues that impact the success of St. Mary's students and higher education in Texas. I had been given the chance to have my voice heard and eagerly accepted the offer. In preparation for the Biennial Texas Equalization Grant Student Advocacy Day, we were briefed on the TEG grant and asked to conduct more in-depth research about what would happen if TEG funding were reduced or cut completely. I realized that as a TEG recipient, not only did I rely on this grant, but so did many of the students here at St. Mary's.

Preparing to lobby

We arrived in the early morning in Austin on February 10th, dressed for success and ready to take on the task at hand. Before we could immerse ourselves into the hustle and bustle of the Capitol, we met with lobbyists who gave us a quick run-through of what to expect before meeting our legislators. They taught us how to properly convey the importance of TEG funding to our legislators by using facts and our personal stories. They explained how we would most likely meet with a legislator's staff member, reminding us that staff members play an important role within the legislative process and policymaking. After the meeting was adjourned, I was ready to make my mark at the state Capitol in Austin.

Lobbying for the first time

My first appointment was with one of my representatives from my hometown. I spoke to a staff member about why I chose to attend St. Mary's University and how the TEG made it possible for me to study at a private university. I spoke about my personal life, emphasizing my financial hardships and how the TEG had helped me become a first-generation college student in my family, allowing me to explore and pursue a career in politics.

I would have never thought that I would have had the opportunity to experience lobbying first-hand at the Capitol during my second semester in college. I was living the dream of any political science major. Not only was I advocating on behalf of myself, but also for future students in financial need. Speaking in favor of the TEG grant gave me a sense of civic duty to my community.* It is necessary to

(Continued)

Odilon Dimier/Alamy Stock Photo

articulate and address the issues that are important to us. Lobbying for the TEG grant strengthened my desire for advocacy and political participation.

*Part of St. Mary's University's mission is dedicated to civic engagement and servant leadership.

Source: Essay written by Karla Sotelo, March 4, 2016.

Competency Connection

◉ **SOCIAL RESPONSIBILITY** ◉

Although not professional lobbyists, "student lobbyists for the day" play an important role in conveying their concerns to policymakers. How important do you think it is to meet with state representatives and senators and talk to them about an an issue that directly affects you?

---

attempt to create an image of broad public support for a group's goals, mobilizing support when it is needed. The Internet has emerged as a significant forum for grassroots lobbying. Interest groups and lobbyists are increasingly using social media, such as Facebook, Twitter, Instagram, text alerts, and blogs. These communication methods are designed to generate information favorable to an interest group's cause and to spread that information widely among legislators, other policymakers, and the general public. Interest groups create Facebook pages to connect with supporters, gather signatures on petitions, or announce events. Another tactic, called "astrotweeting" uses fake social media accounts to provide a false impression of the number of supporters or opponents an issue actually has. Petition websites are also becoming more common for interest groups to demonstrate support for their positions, although some groups like the Texas Electric Cooperatives argue this approach is much less effective than letters and face-to-face contact with elected officials. The Texas State Teachers Association (TSTA) is very effective at communicating its agenda to its membership through Flickr and Facebook. Another education-related organization, Texans for Education Reform, formed in 2013 to promote charter schools and online virtual schools, also uses social media such as tweets to inform the public and its supporters about issues. The organization successfully lobbied the Legislature to increase the maximum number of charter schools in Texas. (For more on charter schools, see Chapter 12, "Public Policy and Administration.")

Electioneering

electioneering
Active campaigning by an interest group in support of, or in opposition to, a candidate; actions urging the public to act on an issue.

Participating in political campaign activities, or **electioneering**, is widespread among interest groups. These activities usually center on particular candidates but may also revolve around issue advocacy. If a candidate who favors a group's goals can be elected, the group has a realistic expectation that its interests will be recognized and protected once the candidate takes office. Interest group participation in the election process takes various forms. Publishing or otherwise publicizing the political records of incumbent candidates on a group's website is one of the simplest and most common forms of interest group participation.

Since the 2008 election, an explosion of YouTube videos has provided interest groups with opportunities to disseminate support for candidates or issues. Providing favored candidates with group membership information, mailing lists, and email lists is another valuable contribution that helps candidates solicit money and votes. In addition, groups may allow candidates to speak at their meetings, thus giving them opportunities for direct contact with voters and possible media coverage or Facebook coverage. Public endorsements can also benefit candidates, sending a cue to the group's membership and other interested voters with regard to which candidates they should support. Facebook pages are also created to generate "likes" for candidates and can facilitate garnering campaign contributions.

Another type of group participation in electioneering involves "Get Out the Vote" (GOTV) campaigns—that is, the favorable vote. Typically, increasing favorable voter turnout entails mailing campaign propaganda, making phone calls to members, registering voters, transporting voters to the polls, and door-to-door canvassing (soliciting votes). Social media, again, provide significant tools for rallying a candidate's base. For instance, Texas's controversial abortion bill, passed in the 2013 legislative session, generated a lot of activity on the Internet from groups on both sides of the issue. As mentioned earlier, Wendy Davis's filibuster on the Senate floor resulted in, what some observers called, a "tweetstorming" tactic. Proposed gun legislation during the 2015 legislative session created the most discourse on social media on both sides of the issue on Twitter.[24] The Official Hashtag of the Texas Legislature, #Txlege, also recorded over 29,000 mentions during the 84th legislative session.[25] Controversial issues, such as the "bathroom bill" in 2017, dominated social media.

Campaign Financing by Political Action Committees

Because political campaigns are becoming more expensive with each election, contributions from interest group members constitute an important form of participation in both federal and state elections. Although individuals continue to make personal financial contributions to candidates, some campaign funds also come from political action committees (PACs) (see Chapter 5, "Campaigns and Elections"). The Texas Ethics Commission defines a PAC as "a group of persons that has a principal purpose of accepting political contributions or making political contributions." Texas statutes prohibit direct political contributions by corporations and labor unions to individual candidates. These and other groups, however, may form PACs composed of their employees or members.

PACs have the task of raising funds and distributing financial contributions to candidates who are sympathetic to their cause. A PAC may also influence political campaigns involving issues that affect the group's vital interests. Currently, Texas imposes no limits on what PACs (or individual citizens for that matter) can raise or contribute to candidates running for statewide offices or a legislative seat, except in judicial races. Proposals to place limits on the amounts that citizens and PACs can contribute to candidates have not been given serious consideration by the legislature, although some limits and deadlines have been placed on campaign contributions to judicial candidates. In addition, legislators and statewide officeholders cannot accept campaign donations during a legislative session.

⊞ POINT/COUNTERPOINT

Should Campaign Contributions Be Limited?

THE ISSUE Most observers of Texas politics would agree that money plays a big role in political campaigns. Unlike the federal government, except for judicial elections, Texas law does not restrict the amount anyone can contribute to a state political campaign. That campaign donations are unregulated appears to enhance the role of money in elections. Yet the ability to donate money to election campaigns is also a form of political expression and free speech protected by both the Texas Constitution and the U.S. Constitution.

FOR	AGAINST
1. In states with no campaign contribution limits, it is difficult for anyone to successfully challenge an incumbent.	1. Campaign contributions to political candidates are a form of freedom of expression protected by the First Amendment of the U.S. Constitution.
2. Without a cap on campaign contributions, money controls politics, and wealthy individuals and PACs have tremendous influence in public policymaking.	2. Campaign contributions to candidates and public officials guarantee only access, not policy outcomes.
3. Disclosure of campaign contributions under current laws does not convey a complete picture of the role of money in elections.	3. Limits on campaign contributions have a chilling effect on the right to participate in the democratic process.

Source: Edwin Bender, "Evidencing a Republican Form of Government: The Influence of Campaign Money on State-Level Elections," *Montana Law Review*, 74, no. 1 (2013): 165–82.

─ Competency Connection ─
⊛ CRITICAL THINKING ⊛

Campaign contributions by PACS are a major way that interest groups participate in elections. Do you believe there should be reasonable limits, if any, on political campaign contributions?

PAC activities and their influence continue to increase. According to the Texas Ethics Commission, more than 2,000 active PACS registered at the start of 2019.[26] (See Table 7.3 for a list of some of the top Texas contributors during the 2016 election cycle.) Typically, PAC contributions have been dominated by interests representing the business sector, ideological groups (which have partisan affiliations), single-interest groups (which have only one interest, such as the Texas Right to Life PAC), and labor. During the 2018 election cycle, one PAC that supports Democratic candidates, ACTBlue Texas, was one of the top ten contributors.[27]

During one of the more contentious gubernatorial elections in 2014, the Republican nominee at the time, Greg Abbott, raised $11.5 million in the second half of 2013 and began 2014 with $27 million in his war chest (a common name for a candidate's campaign account). In contrast, the Democratic nominee, Wendy Davis, reported having raised $12.5 million. From the period of late

🔢 HOW DO WE COMPARE...

In Total Contributions in U.S. Congressional Races?

Most Populous U.S. States	Total Contributions*	Percent Given to Democrats	Percent Given to Republicans	Ranking** to Democrats	Ranking** to Republicans
California	$594,311,273	66.9	28.7	1	42
Florida	$207,945,216	41.2	55.3	31	20
New York	$472,126,312	71.8	24.5	5	44
Texas	**$289,163,859**	**39.2**	**57.1**	**34**	**18**
U.S. States Bordering Texas					
Arkansas	$ 25,581,604	28.0	69.8	46	3
Louisiana	$ 25,172,234	17.9	76.0	50	2
New Mexico	$ 14,889,819	66.9	29.1	7	42
Oklahoma	$ 23,382,191	26.0	68.4	48	4

*This figure includes PAC contributions to candidates, individual contributions to candidates and parties, and soft money contributions to parties in federal elections. (Soft money contributions are unlimited funds spent independently by supporters to benefit a candidate or by a party to educate voters.)

**Refers to how the state compares with all 50 states. For example, Texas's percentage of contributions to Republicans ranked 18th highest in the nation.

Source: "Open Secrets," *Center for Responsive Politics*, data reported as of January 8, 2019, http://www.opensecrets.org/states/.

Competency Connection
⚙ CRITICAL THINKING ⚙

Analyze this table. What are your initial impressions regarding the amount and percentage of PAC contributions by interest groups contributed to Texas congressional candidates for Democrats versus Republicans in comparison to the other states?

February until June of 2014, each candidate raised more than $11 million. Yet, Greg Abbott held a $36 million cash advantage over Wendy Davis' $13 million within less than four months of the election. In the end, Greg Abbott was elected governor. During the 2018 gubernatorial election, incumbent Greg Abbott raised a significant war chest of over $75 million compared to the war chest of Democrat nominee, Lupe Valdez, of close to $2 million. (For more on the gubernatorial election, see Chapter 9, "The Executive Branch.")

Perhaps the best indication of power among interest groups is the connection between the election campaign contributions of PACs and lobbying activities. It takes a coordinated effort by an interest group to influence one part of the political process (the campaign) while also affecting policy decisions in other areas (the legislative and executive branches). In this way, interest groups can exercise far greater control over the output of the Texas legislature and other officials than their numbers would indicate.

TABLE 7.3 Top Texas Contributors, (including PACs) in Spending by Category, 2016 Election

Donor	2015–2016 Spending	Category
1. Texas Association of Realtors	$9,132,640	Business group
2. National Association of Realtors	$4,145,366	Business group
3. Texans for Lawsuit Reform	$3,936,560	Focuses on lawsuit restrictions
4. Associated General Contractors of Texas	$2,116,675	Business group
5. Texas Medical Association	$2,007,834	Professional group
6. Empower Texans	$1,855,479	Supports Republicans
7. Border Health PAC	$1,550,000	Supports Health Access
8. Associated Republicans of Texans	$1,300,517	Supports Republicans
9. Texans for Education Reform	$1,155,524	Focuses on education reform
10. Texas Trial Lawyers Association	$1,139,931	Professional group

Note: List includes only interest groups. Period includes the two-year election cycle ending in December 2016.

Source: "Texas PACs: 2016 Election Cycle Spending," *Texans for Public Justice, 2016,* http://info.tpj.org/reports/Top%20Donors%20 2016.pdf.

— Competency Connection —
✿ **CRITICAL THINKING** ✿

Analyze this chart. What are your initial impressions regarding the types of interest groups that are among the top donors in Texas elections? In your opinion, do certain interest groups have undue influence in Texas politics?

Bribery and Unethical Practices

Bribery and blackmail, though not common in Texas, nevertheless have occurred in state and local government. One of the most notorious examples of corruption took place in the 1970s. It was called the Sharpstown Bank scandal, and it rocked the legislature. House Speaker Gus Mutscher (D-Brenham) and others were convicted of conspiring to accept bribes for passing deposit insurance bills as requested by Houston banker Frank Sharp. After the scandal, the state legislature passed a law prohibiting candidates for the office of Speaker of the House of Representatives from giving supportive legislators anything of value for their help or support in a campaign for the speakership. The law now requires separate campaign finance committees for election as a representative and for the Speaker's race. Contributions, loans, and expenditures received and made by a House Speaker candidate must be reported to the Texas Ethics Commission.

In 1980, an FBI investigation revealed that Texas House Speaker Billy Clayton (D-Springlake) accepted (but did not spend) $5,000 intended to influence the awarding of a state employee insurance contract. Because he had not cashed the checks, a federal district court found Clayton innocent of all bribery charges. In January 1981, he was elected to a fourth term as Speaker of the House. After eight years as Speaker, Clayton left the House to become an influential lobbyist.

In 1991, five-time Texas House Speaker Gib Lewis (D-Fort Worth) was indicted on two misdemeanor ethics charges by a Travis County grand jury. Rather than face the possibility of a trial, subjecting him to a stiffer penalty, Lewis agreed to a plea bargain, was fined $2,000, and announced his decision not to seek reelection to the House of Representatives in 1992. He became a successful lobbyist.

Similar to former House speakers, the behavior of candidates for House speaker has not been immune from public scrutiny. Although Texas law prohibits a speaker candidate from donating money to House candidates' election campaigns, in 2002 state Representative Tom Craddick (R-Midland) donated $20,000 from his reelection campaign to Campaign for Republican Leadership, a political action committee. In turn, the PAC gave all of its $176,500 to eight Republican candidates for the Texas House of Representatives. After Republicans won a majority of House seats for the first time since Reconstruction, Craddick was elected as the first Republican Speaker in January 2003.

Political action committees have also been orchestrated by influential policymakers in the U.S. Congress with ties to Texas. For example, Texans for a Republican Majority (TRMPAC), was organized under the patronage of former U.S. House member Tom DeLay (R-Sugar Land). In 2002, TRMPAC was involved in raising money for GOP candidates seeking seats in the Texas House. Later, in cooperation with DeLay, former Speaker Craddick played a major role in the success of a 2003 congressional redistricting effort that resulted in the 2004 election of more Republicans in the Texas delegation to the U.S. House of Representatives. (For more on redistricting, see Chapter 8, "The Legislative Branch.") Craddick was not charged with violation of any law, but DeLay and three associates involved with TRMPAC were indicted in 2005 by a Travis County grand jury for money laundering and conspiracy to launder $190,000 of campaign contributions from corporate contributors.[28] After indictment, DeLay was forced to step down as majority leader in the U.S. House of Representatives. In June 2006, while awaiting trial, DeLay resigned from his congressional seat. Convicted and given a three-year sentence in 2011, DeLay remained free on bond during his appeal. His conviction was ultimately overturned in 2014 by the Texas Court of Criminal Appeals. In the end, DeLay's political career was ruined, but Republicans were successful in gaining a majority of congressional seats in Texas's delegation for the first time since Reconstruction.

✓ 7.3 Learning Check

1. Name two techniques lobbyists use to influence legislators.
2. Does Texas place limits on PAC contributions to state candidates, as the federal government does on federal candidates?

Answers at the end of this chapter.

⬢ Power and Regulation in Interest Group Politics

LO 7.4 Analyze how interest groups are regulated and evaluate the effectiveness of these laws.

Clearly, interest groups play a significant role in Texas politics. They have access to a number of strategies and tactics to influence elections and policy decisions. So, how are interest groups regulated? Are these regulations effective? Do interest groups have too much political influence in shaping public policy?

Regulation of Interest Group Politics

Prompted by media reports of big spending by lobbyists and a grand jury investigation into influence peddling, in 1991 the 72nd Legislature proposed a constitutional amendment to create the eight-member **Texas Ethics Commission** to enforce legal standards for lobbyists and public officials. Voters approved the amendment in November of that year, thereby allowing the eight commission members to be appointed by the governor (four members), the lieutenant governor (two members), and the House Speaker (two members).[29] This legislation was initially designed to increase the power of public prosecutors to use evidence that some contributions to lawmakers by lobbyists and other individuals are more than mere campaign donations. This legislation also expanded disclosure requirements for lobbyists and legislators, and it put a $500 annual cap on lobbyist-provided food and drink for a lawmaker. Additionally, the law bans honoraria (gratuitous payments in recognition of professional services for which there is no legally enforceable obligation to pay) and lobby-paid pleasure trips (unless a legislator makes a speech or participates in a panel discussion). Furthermore, state law requires public officials to disclose and describe any gifts valued at greater than $250.

The ethics law defines as illegal any campaign contribution accepted with an agreement to act in the contributor's interest. The problem, however, is the difficulty in proving that a candidate or public official has intentionally accepted a campaign contribution from a particular interest group in exchange for policy benefits. The law also prohibits a candidate or official from receiving a contribution in the Capitol building itself.

Detailed records of political contributions and how this money is spent must be filed with the Texas Ethics Commission between two and seven times each year. These records are open to the public and are available on the commission's website. Candidates for legislative and statewide office are required to file electronic campaign disclosure reports, so that this information can be made instantly available. Current law requires that all candidates file semiannual reports. In contested elections, however, candidates must file itemized contribution and expenditure reports every six months, and 30 days and eight days before the election.

Generally, contributions and expenditures made by candidates in the last two days prior to an election campaign need not be disclosed until the next semiannual report is due. At present, there are no laws in Texas preventing these last-minute contributions by interest groups. Therefore, interest groups can potentially alter the outcome of key races in the few days before the election. It is also not uncommon for special interests to make campaign contributions after the election takes place. Current law prohibits lawmakers and other elected state officials from raising money during the regular legislative session. However, these postelection, or "late train," donations typically take place immediately following the November election until early December.

On its website, the Texas Ethics Commission lists the names of lobbyists and their clients, as well as payments received by each lobbyist. The commission's records, however, do not give a complete picture. Lobbyists do not have to

Texas Ethics Commission
A state agency that enforces state standards for lobbyists and public officials, including registration of lobbyists and reporting of political campaign contributions.

report exact dollar amounts for their contracts; they only need to indicate ranges. For example, compensation from each client is reported as less than $10,000, and then in $15,000 increments up to more than $500,000. For anything over $500,000, the exact amount is required. In addition, lobbyists are required to notify their clients if they represent two or more groups with competing interests, as well as notify the Texas Ethics Commission about any possible conflicts. This information, however, is not made available to the public or lawmakers.

The Texas Ethics Commission (TEC) is also authorized to hear ethics complaints against state officials, candidates for office, and state employees, although its budget and staff are typically very small and allow only a limited number of reviews each year. For the 2018 year, there were 68 sworn ethics complaints.[30] Most infractions center on penalties against campaign and PAC treasurers who failed to file reports; missed filing deadlines; or provided faulty reports on contributions, earnings, or expenditures. These types of infractions center on violations of the Texas Election Code. Fines are then assessed by the Ethics Commission on any infractions. On rare occasions, the TEC reviews complaints by state officials against organizations.

On occasion, the TEC may also issue subpoenas. Beginning in 2014, the Texas Ethics Commission, in response to an official complaint by two Republican lawmakers, issued a subpoena to a Tea Party-affiliated conservative group, Empower Texas. This action sought release of a donor list and communication records with lawmakers, after the group refused to register as a lobbyist and allegedly abide by ethics rules. Empower Texas continues to challenge the central authority of the TEC to enforce campaign finance laws in the courts.

When the names of donors are not disclosed by an interest group, donations are referred to as secret money—some observers also call this "dark money." This phenomenon has become increasingly present in campaign contributions by organizations. One of the more contentious legislative proposals during the 2013 legislative session would have required nonprofit organizations that spend money on political campaigns to disclose the names of their donors. Although the legislature passed the bill, former Governor Perry vetoed it.[31] Another failed attempt to regulate dark money was proposed during the 84th legislative session by Representative Byron Cook (R-Corsicana). This action was opposed by Lt. Governor Dan Patrick and Governor Abbott. Cook was unsuccessful in proposing a constitutional amendment to require nonprofit organizations to disclose the names of their contributors during the 85th legislative session in 2017.[32]

Reform advocates and others contend that staff members with the Ethics Commission are restricted from investigating complaints because of strict confidentiality rules. In addition, the complainant must be a Texas resident and demonstrate proof of residency. The complaint must be filed on a form provided by the commission and include information about the respondent and the complainant. Once the complaint has been filed, the TEC must immediately attempt to contact the respondent.[33] The Texas Ethics Commission is required to dismiss any Election Code complaint if the respondent claims that the violation was a clerical error and corrects the mistake within two weeks. This requirement also effectively weakens the ability of the agency to impose fines for most infractions.[34]

Some political reform groups, such as Common Cause Texas, claim that although some ethics laws are in place, they remain ineffective. Furthermore, questionable connections between lobbyists and legislators are largely unchecked. For instance, when former Governor Perry first took office, he issued a "strict" revolving-door lobbying policy for his staff, preventing staff members from leaving their employment to become lobbyists. He drew criticism shortly thereafter, however, when he hired senior staff personnel who had been registered as lobbyists during the preceding legislative session. For many observers, special interests had entered the governor's office through a revolving back door.

Although Texas law prohibits corporations and unions from providing campaign contributions directly to candidates, soft money can be directed to state Republican and Democratic party coffers for "administrative expenses." In light of the U.S. Supreme Court decision in *Citizens United v. Federal Election Commission* (2009), the Texas Ethics Commission issued an advisory opinion stating that corporations and unions are allowed to make expenditures independent of a political candidate, such as paying for political advertising that calls for the election or defeat of candidates, so long as they do not coordinate with the candidate's campaign. In February 2014, the TEC adopted another rule requiring PACs, *before* they receive donations from corporations or unions, to provide an affidavit that they intend to "act exclusively as a direct expenditure committee."[35]

As a result of *Citizens United*, a proliferation of super PACs was created, especially at the federal level. Super PACs raise unlimited sums of money from corporations, unions, associations, and individuals. Then PACs are allowed to spend unlimited amounts to directly target and advocate for or against specific political candidates. In 2014, Texas's prohibition of super PACs for state elections was overturned by the U.S. Fifth Circuit Court of Appeals. Now, similar to federal law, state super PACs raise unlimited sums for independent expenditures. Federal law requires a super PAC to report the names of its donors, unless a nonprofit organization is involved. State law requires the disclosure of the names of all donors regardless of the involvement of a nonprofit organization. During the 2012 presidential primary elections, Rick Perry benefited from these super PACs, especially from one called "Make Us Great Again."[36] After withdrawing from the Republican presidential nomination race, Perry received approval from the Federal Election Commission to form his own PAC or super PAC with funds remaining from his presidential campaign, or to transfer these funds to his gubernatorial campaign account.

A powerful relationship continues between campaign contributions and policy decisions. For some observers, little has changed since creation of the Texas Ethics Commission, as the system is still set up to favor incumbents.[37] All attempts to significantly reform campaign finance have been defeated. Proposed reforms have included contribution limits for individuals and PACs in legislative and statewide races, as well as full disclosure laws. As the late journalist Molly Ivins observed, "Texas is the Wild Frontier of campaign financing."[38] Campaign contributions are also connected to influential political appointments for state boards and commissions made by the governor. Although the regulatory authority of the Texas Ethics Commission was strengthened in 2003 as a part of a review by the Sunset Advisory Commission, many observers argue that the commission's powers are inadequate for the job it is intended to perform.[39] (For more information on the Sunset Advisory Commission, see Chapter 9 "The Executive Branch.")

Interest Group Power and Public Policy

The political influence of interest groups is determined by several factors. Some observers argue that a group with a sizable membership, above average financial resources, a knowledgeable and dedicated leadership, and a high degree of unity (agreement on and commitment to goals among the membership) will be able to exert virtually limitless pressure on governmental decision makers. Others point out that the more the aims of an interest group are consistent with broad-based public beliefs or stem from issue networks (coalitions that form around a particular policy issue), the more likely the group is to succeed and wield significant power. They also observe that if interest groups are well represented in the structure of the government itself, their power will be enhanced materially. Also, it is noted that a structure of weak governments will ordinarily produce strong interest groups.

From a different point of view, others insist that factors external to the group are also highly relevant. Research indicates that a strong relationship exists between the larger socioeconomic conditions in a state and the power of interest groups. These findings have led some observers to conclude that states with high population levels, advanced industrialization, significant per capita wealth, and high levels of formal education are likely to produce relatively weak interest groups and strong political parties. Interestingly, despite a large population, Texas is among the states with strong interest groups and relatively weak political parties. Compared with other states, scholars ranked Texas as one of 26 states where interest groups dominate or fluctuate in power over time.[40] The Center for Public Integrity (CPI), in its analysis of transparency and accountability of state governments in 2015, graded Texas below a D; only 3 states received better than a D+.[41] The Lone Star State received a grade of F in eight of the 13 categories, including lobbying disclosure, political campaign financing, and accountability for all three branches of government. According to the Center, the lower the grade the greater the likelihood of corruption in a state.

Three circumstances explain why states such as Texas may not fit the expected pattern. First, many Texas interest groups are readily accepted because they identify with free enterprise, self-reliance, and other elements of the state's individualistic political culture. The influence of the state's traditionalistic political culture suggests a reliance on a political elite to control governmental decisions and limited involvement by the general public. As a result, many Texans are predisposed to trust interest groups (especially business interest groups) and their lobbyists. Second, the century-long one-party Democratic tradition in Texas and the subsequent one-party Republican trend have rendered interparty competition negligible in many counties and districts. Furthermore, low levels of political participation, along with the absence of strong parties and meaningful competition between parties, has made Texas government vulnerable to the pressures of strong interest groups and their lobbyists. Finally, the Texas Constitution of 1876 and its many amendments have created state and local governments beset by weak, uncoordinated institutions. Faced with a government lacking sufficient strength to offer any real opposition, interest groups often obtain decisions favorable to their causes.

Pinpointing Political Power

Assessing the political power and influence that interest groups have in American government is difficult, and determining the extent of their power in Texas is especially complex. There is no simple top-down or bottom-up arrangement. Rather, political decisions (especially policy decisions) are made by a variety of individuals and groups. Some of these decision makers participate in local ad hoc (specific purpose) organizations; others wield influence through statewide groups. Ascertaining which individuals or groups have the greatest influence often depends on the issue or issues involved.

The political influence of any interest group cannot be fairly calculated by looking at only one political asset, whether it be money, status, knowledge, organization, sheer numbers, or in today's world, social media capabilities. Nevertheless, we may safely conclude that organized interest groups in Texas often put the unorganized citizenry at a great disadvantage when public issues are at stake.

✔ **7.4 Learning Check**

1. True or False: Texas's campaign finance laws often involve public disclosure by public officials and lobbyists.

2. True or False: The Texas Ethics Commission is the primary state agency regulating political contributions and expenditures by lobbyists and public officials.

Answers at the end of this chapter.

CONCLUSION

As we have learned, there are numerous interest groups in Texas. They exert tremendous influence over public decisions at all levels and in all branches of government. Some interest groups, however, have more influence than others. They participate in an assortment of activities and use a variety of techniques to influence government. What's more, few, if any, regulations effectively control the power of interest groups in Texas. These factors suggest that interest groups will continue to play a significant role in Texas politics for years to come.

CHAPTER SUMMARY

LO 7.1 Explain what are interest groups, why they form, and what are their essential characteristics. Interest groups act on behalf of their members to influence policy decisions made by government officials. Various factors foster interest group formation or effectiveness, such as legal and cultural reasons, a decentralized government, and the strength of the party system and political ideologies. Interest group participation influences public policy at all levels and within each branch (legislative, executive, and judicial) of Texas government. Involvement in an interest group provides members with information and opportunities to become active in the political process. Interest groups vary by organizational pattern, membership, and leadership.

LO 7.2 Describe the types of interest groups and analyze the qualities of a powerful interest group. In general, all interest groups at all levels of government can be classified according to their interests, membership, and the public policies they advocate. Among the types of interest groups that are trying to influence government policies and policymakers are those interested in economic issues, the professions, public employment matters, social issues, and the public good. Some interest groups are more powerful than others when one considers their financial resources and success rates within the legislature.

LO 7.3 Evaluate the kinds of activities that interest groups use to influence Texas government. Interest groups are involved in all types and areas of political activity. They serve various functions, which include recruiting candidates for public office, shaping consensus on issues, and providing an outlet for concerned citizens. To influence policy decisions, interest groups use several techniques, including lobbying, personal communication, giving favors and gifts, grassroots activities, electioneering, campaign financing by political action committees (PACs), and in extreme cases, resorting to bribery and other unethical or illegal practices.

LO 7.4 Analyze how interest groups are regulated and evaluate the effectiveness of these laws. An eight-member Texas Ethics Commission is charged with enforcing legal standards for lobbyists and public officials. Although money is a powerful influence over policy decisions, the state only limits campaign contribution amounts for judicial candidates and places few other restrictions on donations. Texas's campaign finance laws are best characterized as involving public disclosure by public officials, lobbyists, and PACs.

KEY TERMS

business organization, p. 246
decentralized government, p. 241
economic interest group, p. 245
electioneering, p. 260
group leadership, p. 243
interest group technique, p. 256
interest group, p. 239
labor organization, p. 246

lobbying, p. 256
organizational pattern, p. 242
power group, p. 253
professional group, p. 247
public interest group, p. 253
public officer and employee group, p. 248
racial and ethnic groups, p. 249

religion-based group, p. 252
right of association, p. 240
social interest group, p. 249
Texas Ethics Commission, p. 266
women's organization, p. 250

LEARNING CHECK ANSWERS

 7.1 **1.** Legal decisions, political culture, a decentralized government, the strength of the party system, and political ideologies are among the factors that contribute to the formation of interest groups.

2. False. Active membership will vary, depending on the organization and leadership of the organization.

7.2 **1.** False. Unlike most interest groups, public interest groups are interested in promoting the public interest.

2. In Texas, business groups are generally more powerful than labor groups.

7.3 **1.** Lobbyists use personal communication as well as favors and gifts to influence legislators.

2. Unlike federal law, Texas law does not limit campaign contributions by PACs to candidates for a state office (with the limited exception of judicial candidates).

7.4 **1.** True. Texas's campaign finance laws often involve disclosure by public officials and lobbyists, though critics would argue that current disclosure requirements are not sufficient to reform the system.

2. True. The Texas Ethics Commission is the primary state agency regulating the political contributions and expenditures by lobbyists and public officials.

The Legislative Branch

8

Learning Objectives

8.1 Describe the structure of the Texas legislature.

8.2 Describe the membership of the Texas legislature.

8.3 Compare the organization of the Texas House of Representatives and the Texas Senate.

8.4 Outline the responsibilities of the Texas legislature.

8.5 Explain the influences on legislators' voting decisions.

IMAGE 8.1 Ready for a quick draw?

AP Images/Eric Gay

Competency Connection
⊛ SOCIAL RESPONSIBILITY ⊛

Does openly carrying firearms make society safer or more dangerous?

In April 2007, a deranged student went on a shooting rampage at Virginia Tech University. In a systematic attack, the student chained and locked entry doors to a classroom building and then moved from room to room killing 32 faculty and students and wounding 17. Virginia Tech did not allow licensed handgun owners to bring their weapons on campus. During the interim of the 80th (2007) legislative session, the Texas House Committee on Law Enforcement studied the impact of laws that banned concealed gun license holders from carrying guns on college campuses. The committee recommended the elimination of this ban.

In each session of the Texas legislature from 2009 to 2013, campus carry laws designed for self-defense and to deter shootings were proposed but not enacted. (For a discussion of arguments for and against campus carry, see this chapter's Point/Counterpoint feature.) Finally, in 2015, in what one journalist believes should be remembered as the Gun Legislature,[1] the 84th Legislature enacted Senate Bill 11. This campus carry bill passed in the Senate by a party-line vote whereby all of the 20 Republicans voted for it and all of the 11 Democrats voted against it. Only seven Democrats voted for the bill when it passed by a vote of 94 to 47 in the House of Representatives. One House Republican and 46 House Democrats voted against it. In the same session, the Texas legislature enacted HB 910, which authorizes licensed handgun carriers to carry handguns openly in belt or shoulder holsters while in many public places (see photo above) but not, for example, in a court room or on a college or university campus. One unforeseen result of gun rights activism was action by the House to install panic buttons in the offices of representatives. This measure was taken at the beginning of the 84th regular session, after open carry activists confronted Rep. Poncho Nevárez (D-Eagle Pass) in his office.[2]

Effective on August 1, 2016, Texas's public universities (like Sam Houston State University or the University of Texas at Austin) had to decide how to develop policies that would comply with campus carry legislation. For public community colleges (like Austin Community College and Blinn College), the effective date was set a year later: August 1, 2017. With input from students, faculty, and staff, the president of each public institution of higher education decides (with board of regents review) which campus facilities and areas will be open for licensed carriers of concealed handguns. Many students cannot obtain a license because they are not 21 years of age, or at least 18 and an active or honorably discharged member of the U.S. armed forces, or cannot pass a criminal history background check.[3] Campus areas from which guns are banned must be marked with off-limits notices. Campus carry rules must be posted, and these rules must be available on the institution's website. Private colleges and universities (like Baylor University or St. Mary's University) are free to restrict or even prohibit the carrying of weapons on campus. Both SB 11 and HB 910 were backed strongly by Governor Greg Abbott. He attracted publicity by signing these bills at Red's Indoor Range (a firing range and gun store) in Pflugerville (near Austin) in June 2015.

Enacting gun laws and other legislation by any elected representative body is a slow, frustrating, and often disappointing process. Most citizens are impatient with political tactics and procedural delays, even if their policy objectives are eventually achieved. They often dislike the inevitable compromises involved in the legislative process.

Nevertheless, our legislators perform work of vital importance. They make laws that affect the life, liberty, and property of all persons in the state. After years of research, Professor Alan Rosenthal (1932–2013) of Rutgers University concluded: "[Legislatures] are far from perfect, yet they are the best we have, and preferable to any conceivable alternative. Not only that, they actually work, albeit in rather messy and somewhat mysterious ways—representing, lawmaking, and balancing the power of the executive."[4] After reading this chapter on the Texas legislature, you can decide whether Rosenthal's conclusions apply to the Lone Star State.

⊠ POINT/COUNTERPOINT

Should Concealed Carry of Handguns on Campuses Be Retained?

THE ISSUE In 2015, as reported at the beginning of this chapter, the Texas Legislature passed, and Governor Greg Abbott signed, Senate Bill 11 authorizing licensed persons to carry handguns on the campuses of institutions of higher education. This controversial legislation is an example of how state laws can have an impact on students and others.

FOR	AGAINST
1. Holders of handgun licenses are armed to defend themselves and others.	1. Concealed handguns distract students from learning and promote a culture of fear.
2. Private institutions can opt out of allowing handguns on campus.	2. Law enforcement officers will have difficulty distinguishing between criminal shooters and licensed handgun bearers.
3. Institutions can be flexible in creating rules to regulate campus carry.	3. Guns on campus could result in fatal accidents and more suicide.
4. The number of licensed carriers is relatively small, since a large majority of students are under age 21 or cannot qualify at ages 18 to 20 because they are not active or former military personnel.	4. Institutions of higher education could have difficulty recruiting faculty and staff as well as attracting students.

Source: Major Issues in the 84th Legislature, Focus Report 84-7 (Austin: House Research Organization, Texas House of Representatives, September 22, 2015), 112–113.

— Competency Connection —
✿ **CRITICAL THINKING** ✿

What are reasons for and against allowing private colleges and universities to opt out of campus carry?

Legislative Framework

LO 8.1   Describe the structure of the Texas legislature.

In Texas's Declaration of Independence, delegates complained that the Mexican government "had dissolved, by force of arms, the state Congress of Coahuila and Texas, and obliged our representatives to fly for their lives from the seat of government, thus depriving us of the fundamental right of representation." That fundamental right was subsequently established in the Constitution of the Republic of Texas and in all of Texas's five state constitutions, wherein Texans have entrusted the power to enact bills and adopt resolutions to popularly elected legislators. These powers are the essence of representative government. Other legislative functions include proposing constitutional amendments, adopting budgets for state government, levying taxes, redistricting, impeaching and removing executive and judicial officials if warranted, and investigating issues.

In Texas and 40 other states, the larger chamber of the **bicameral** (two-chamber, or two-house) legislature is called the House of Representatives. Some other states use the terms Assembly, House of Delegates, or General Assembly. Only Nebraska has a **unicameral** (one-chamber, or one-house) legislature with 49 senators. In the 49 states with bicameral legislatures, the larger chamber ranges in size from 40 members in Alaska to 400 members in New Hampshire. Texas has 150 members in its House of Representatives. The smaller legislative chamber is called the Senate. Alaska has the smallest Senate with 20 members; Minnesota has the largest with 67. The Texas Senate has 31 members.

Election and Terms of Office

Voters residing in representative and senatorial districts elect Texas legislators. Representatives are elected for two years. Senators are usually elected for four years. Terms of office for members of both houses begin in January of odd-numbered years.

Legislative redistricting for both the Texas House and the Senate occurs in the first odd-numbered year in a decade based on the results of the federal census. After the 2010 census, redistricting efforts began in 2011. In each even-numbered year, voters elect a new House of Representatives, as in 2012, 2014, 2016, and 2018. A new Senate was also elected in 2012. Because Senate terms are four years, however, in January of the next odd-numbered year (for example, 2013), senators draw lots by choosing from 31 numbered pieces of paper sealed in envelopes. The 16 who draw odd numbers get four-year terms, and the 15 who draw even numbers get only two-year terms. Thus, in 2014, elections were held for 15 positions in the Senate. Approximately one-half of the senators (that is, 15 or 16 as in 2016) are then elected in each even-numbered year through 2020.

A legislator may be expelled by a two-thirds majority vote of the membership of the legislator's chamber. If a legislator dies, resigns, or is expelled from office, the vacancy is filled by special election called by the governor. A legislator called to active military duty for more than 30 days retains the office if he or she appoints a qualified temporary replacement who is approved by the appropriate

bicameral
A legislature with two houses or chambers, such as Texas's House of Representatives and Senate.

unicameral
A one-house legislature, such as the Nebraska legislature.

chamber. As of 2019, three male representatives had been called to military duty. Each appointed his wife as a temporary replacement.[5]

Sessions

Texas law requires **regular sessions** to begin on the second Tuesday in January of each odd-numbered year (for example, January 8, 2019). In practice, these regular biennial sessions always run for the full 140 days, as authorized by the Texas Constitution (for example, through May 27, 2019). A beneficiary of these legislative sessions is the Austin economy because legislators and lobbyists spend millions for housing, food, beverages, and entertainment during each session.

The governor may also call **special sessions**, lasting no longer than 30 days each, at any time. From 2001 through 2014, Governor Rick Perry called 12 special sessions on a number of matters including congressional and legislative redistricting and imposing limitations on abortion. During special sessions, the legislature may consider only those matters placed before it by the governor. Special sessions are unpopular with legislators and costly to taxpayers. Per diem costs to cover legislators' travel and living expenses for all of the 181 legislators equal about $40,000 per day and total about $1,200,000 for a 30-day session. The three special sessions convened by Governor Perry in 2013 cost Texas taxpayers more than $2.5 million.[6] Governor Abbott did not call a special session until his second two years in office (January 2017 to January 2019).

regular session
A session of the Texas legislature that is constitutionally mandated and begins on the second Tuesday in January of odd-numbered years and lasts for a maximum of 140 days.

special session
A legislative session called by the governor and limited to no more than 30 days.

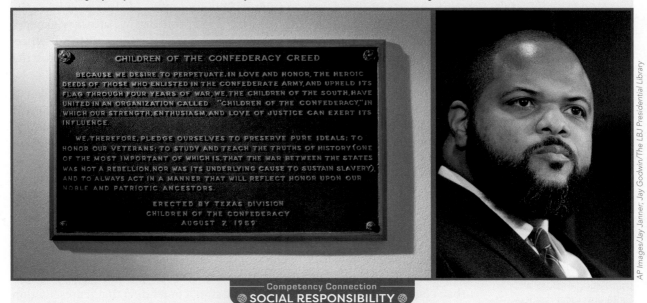

IMAGE 8.2 Representative Eric Johnson (D-Dallas) led the effort to remove the "Children of the Confederacy" plaque from the Texas Capitol. Johnson was elected as mayor of Dallas in June 2019.

AP Images/Jay Janner, Jay Godwin/The LBJ Presidential Library

— Competency Connection —
⊛ **SOCIAL RESPONSIBILITY** ⊛

Why do you believe the Children of the Confederacy plaque is controversial?

Districting

Providing equal representation in a legislative chamber involves dividing a state into districts with approximately equal numbers of residents. Population distribution changes constantly as the result of migration, births, and deaths. Therefore, legislative district boundaries must be redrawn periodically to ensure equitable representation. Such redistricting can be politically disadvantageous to a legislator. It may take away areas of constituents who have provided strong voter support; it may add an area of constituents who produce little support and much opposition; or it may produce a new district that includes the residences of two or more representatives or senators, only one of whom can be reelected to represent the district.[7]

In Texas, the first legislative and congressional elections in districts determined by the 2010 census were conducted in November 2012 for offices filled in January 2013. For the previous 10 years, the 2000 census was the basis for legislative and congressional representation.

State Legislative Districts The Texas Constitution requires reapportionment (allotment of seats according to population) and redistricting (drawing new district lines to reflect population change) in the first legislative session after the federal census. In the decades after 1876, however, the legislature sometimes failed to divide the state's population after each census and to map new districts for legislators. Thus, some districts for state representatives and senators became heavily populated and greatly underrepresented. Others experienced population decline or slow growth, resulting in overrepresentation.

In 1948, legislative districting inequities led to the adoption of a state constitutional amendment designed to pressure the legislature to remedy this situation. Now, the legislature's failure to **redistrict** during the first regular session after a decennial census brings the Legislative Redistricting Board into operation. This board consists of five *ex officio* (that is, "holding other office") members: the lieutenant governor, Speaker of the House of Representatives, attorney general, comptroller of public accounts, and commissioner of the General Land Office. The board must meet within 90 days after the legislative session and redistrict the state within another 60 days.

Although the legislature drew new legislative districts after the federal censuses of 1950 and 1960, the Texas Constitution's apportionment formulas for the Texas House and Senate discriminated against heavily populated urban counties. These formulas were not changed until the U.S. Supreme Court held in *Reynolds v. Sims*, 377 U.S. 533 (1964) that "the seats in both houses of a bicameral state legislature must be apportioned on a population basis." This "one person, one vote" principle was first applied in Texas by a federal district court in *Kilgarlin v. Martin*, 252 F. Supp. 404 (1965).

In December 2015, the U.S. Supreme Court heard a Texas case (*Evenwel v. Abbott*, 578 U.S. ___ [2016]) that could have upset the "one person, one vote" principle. This case involved Republicans Sue Evenwel of Titus County (a rural county near Texarkana) and Edward Pfenninger of Montgomery County (a suburban county near Houston). They sued the state, contending that representation in the Texas Senate should be based on voter-eligible population rather than total population. Considering only the voter-eligible population excludes children,

redistrict
Redrawing of boundaries after the federal decennial census to create single-member districts with approximately equal population (for example, legislative, congressional, and State Board of Education districts in Texas). Local governments must also redistrict for some positions. Congressional districts must be as close to equal population as possible. State and local districts may vary in population by 5 percent or so.

prisoners, and noncitizen adults. The U.S. Supreme Court rejected this argument, noting that all 50 U.S. states use total population as the basis for redistricting. The court left unclear whether total population is the only basis for determining district population for state legislative districts. Speaking for the Project on Fair Representation, which supported the lawsuit by Evenwel and Pfenninger, Edward Blum expressed disappointment with the decision but asserted "the issue of voter equality is not going to go away."[8]

Redistricting by the Texas legislature often sparks complaints about **gerrymandering**, a practice that involves drawing districts to include or exclude certain groups of voters in order to favor one group or political party. Usually, gerrymandered districts are oddly shaped rather than compact. The term "gerrymander" originated to describe irregularly shaped districts created under the guidance of Elbridge Gerry, governor of Massachusetts, in 1812. The political party holding the most positions in the legislature often benefits in elections conducted after redistricting. Many state and federal court battles have been fought over the constitutionality of Texas's legislative districting arrangements.

Members of the Texas Senate have always represented **single-member districts**—that is, the voters of each district elect one senator. Redistricting according to the 2010 federal census provided for an ideal population of 811,147 (the total state population of 25,145,561 divided by 31) in each senatorial district. Many of the 31 senatorial districts cover several counties, but a few big-city senatorial districts are formed from the territory of only part of a county (see Figure 8.1).

Until 1971, a Texas county with two or more seats in the House was a **multimember district** in which voters elected representatives at-large to represent the whole county. Voters in these counties voted in all House races in the county. In 1971, however, single-member districts were established in Harris, Dallas, and Bexar counties. Four years later, single-member districting was extended to all counties in which voters elected more than one representative. The change to single-member districts was largely a result of court actions. Election results demonstrate that single-member districts reduce campaign costs and increase the probability that more African American and Latino candidates will be elected. As a result of the 2010 federal census, redistricting provided each state representative district with an ideal population of 167,637 (total state population divided by 150). (See Figure 8.2.)

Because members of the state legislature attempt to gain political advantage for their political party through gerrymandering, redistricting is a complex process that is often resolved in the courts. Redistricting after the 2010 census was no exception. Beginning in 2011, the 82nd Legislature passed redistricting bills for Texas House, Senate, and congressional district boundaries. The plans favored the election of Republicans. Since members of historical minority groups, especially African Americans and Latinos, tend to vote for Democratic candidates, the redistricting plans also appeared to reduce the influence of these voters.

Under the provisions of the federal Voting Rights Act in force in 2011, Texas was required to obtain preclearance from the U.S. government for any changes in voting laws and voting boundaries. Texas's history of discrimination against minority voters forced this requirement on the state. Changes had to be approved

gerrymandering
Drawing the boundaries of a district, such as a state senatorial or representative district, to include or exclude certain groups of voters and thus affect election outcomes.

single-member district
An area that elects only one representative to a policymaking body, such as a state House, state Senate, or U.S. Congress.

multimember district
A district in which all voters participate in the election of two or more representatives to a policymaking body, such as a state House or state Senate.

FIGURE 8.1 Court-Ordered Texas State Senate Districts. The accompanying map shows districts wholly or partially within Harris County.

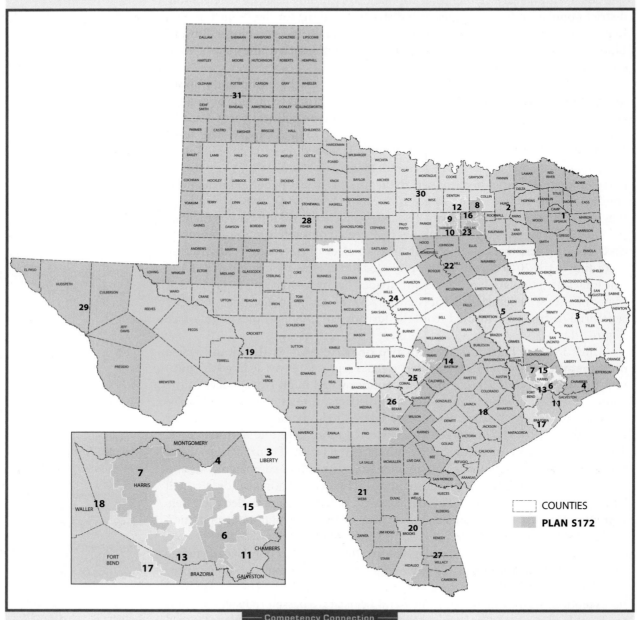

Competency Connection
☼ **CRITICAL THINKING** ☼

Should drawing maps that favor the election of members from a specific political party (partisan gerrymandering) be illegal?

FIGURE 8.2 Court-Ordered Texas State House Districts (for electing state representatives). The accompanying maps show districts wholly or partially within urban counties.

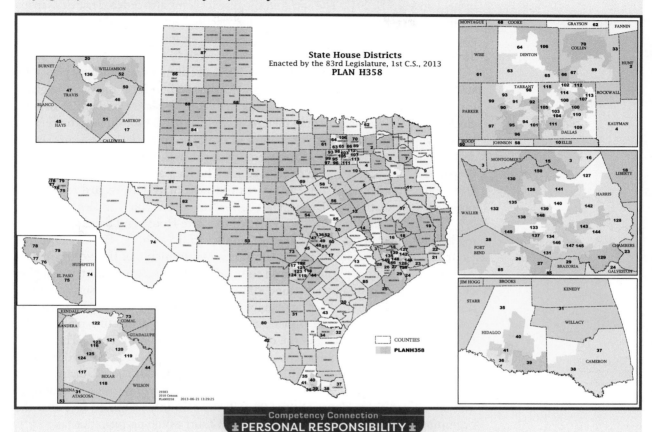

Competency Connection
‡ PERSONAL RESPONSIBILITY ‡

Should the courts be able to redraw boundary lines approved by the state legislature? Why or why not?

by either the U.S. Department of Justice or the U.S. District Court in Washington, D.C. Then-Attorney General Greg Abbott sent the redistricting plans to the U.S. District Court. All plans were found to discriminate against minority voters and were denied preclearance.

Private citizens can also challenge the fairness of redistricting plans. Several members of historical minority groups and organizations that represent these groups filed lawsuits in the U.S. District Court for the Western District of Texas in San Antonio. The lawsuits, consolidated into the case of *Perez v. Perry*, claimed that the redistricting plans discriminated against Latinos and African Americans. Because the 2012 party primaries could not be held until district boundary lines were established, a three-judge panel from the San Antonio district court drew interim maps for use in that year's primaries. The fairness of these maps was challenged by Republicans, and the case was appealed directly to the U.S. Supreme Court. That court ordered the maps redrawn in a way that was more consistent with the legislature's original Republican-friendly redistricting plans. The San Antonio district court followed this directive, redrew the maps, and ordered that party primaries be held on May 29, 2012. The San Antonio district court also ordered use of its maps for the November general elections. In that election, voters elected 95 Republicans and 55 Democrats to the Texas House, 19 Republicans and 12 Democrats to the Texas Senate, and 24 Republicans and 12 Democrats to the U.S. House.

The court-drawn maps used in the 2012 elections were temporary and the state-drawn maps had been denied preclearance; therefore, the 83rd Legislature (2013) had to produce redistricting plans for legislative and congressional elections. Although legislators failed to accomplish this task during the regular legislative session, they were successful in doing so in a special session. Senate and congressional boundary lines were identical to those of the redrawn maps prepared by the San Antonio district court. The map approved for use in Texas House elections varied from the court's redrawn map with regard to 14 state representative districts in Dallas, Harris, Tarrant, and Webb counties.

The day before Governor Perry signed the state House and Senate redistricting bills into law, in the case of *Shelby County v. Holder* (2013), the U.S. Supreme Court ruled that the automatic preclearance requirements of the Voting Rights Act were no longer applicable. Those complaining that a law or redistricting plan discriminates against racial or ethnic minorities must now file a lawsuit and prove discrimination. The redistricting plan for the Senate was not challenged, but a new lawsuit was filed against the House and congressional redistricting plans by the U.S. Department of Justice and the original plaintiffs in *Perez v. Perry*. The federal district court in San Antonio ordered interim use of the legislature's 2013 redistricting map for the House in the 2014, 2016, and 2018. In August 2018, a U.S. district court in San Antonio declared that the Texas Legislature must redraw unconstitutionally gerrymandered Texas House District 90 in Tarrant County within 45 days after the beginning of the 86th legislative session or that court would perform this task.

U.S. Congressional Districts In the year after a federal census, the Texas legislature must draw new boundaries for the state's U.S. congressional districts (from which representatives to the U.S. House of Representatives are elected). Population in the respective districts must be as close to equal as possible. Results of the 2010 federal census increased the number of Texas seats from 32 to 36, each with an ideal population of 698,488. Because the Texas legislature did not pass a congressional redistricting bill in its 2011 regular session, the task was performed in a special session. Then the redistricting plan was submitted for review by a three-judge panel of the U.S. District Court in Washington, D.C. That court denied preclearance in August 2012. Congressional redistricting followed a path similar to the House redistricting plan, including use of temporary maps in 2012, a new plan by the legislature in 2013, and a subsequent lawsuit. In the general election of 2012, Republicans elected 24 congressmen (23 Anglos and 1 Latino), while Democrats elected 12 (2 Anglos, 5 African Americans, and 5 Latinos). In the 2014 general election, 25 Republican congressmen were elected and 11 Democrats. Results in 2016 included the election of 25 Republicans and 11 Democrats.

New congressional districts were drawn in a special session of the Texas Legislature in 2013, but this districting plan essentially adopted the court-drawn

FIGURE 8.3 Court-Ordered Interim U.S. Congressional Districts (for electing U.S. representatives). Accompanying map shows districts wholly or partially within Harris County.

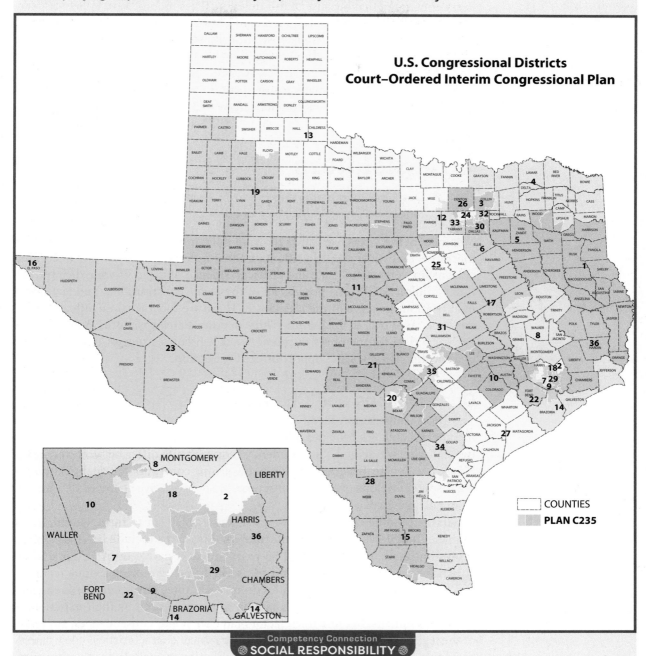

U.S. Congressional Districts
Court–Ordered Interim Congressional Plan

COUNTIES
PLAN C235

Competency Connection
◉ SOCIAL RESPONSIBILITY ◉

If a particular ethnic or racial group is primarily responsible for an increase in population in a state, should that group be entitled to the possibility of more representation in the U.S. Congress for members from their ethnic or racial group?

plan for the 2012 election. Governor Rick Perry signed the redistricting bill on the day following the U.S. Supreme Court's ruling in *Shelby County v. Holder*. Perry contended that because of this decision Texas did not have to get preclearance. Nevertheless, the U.S. Department of Justice and minority groups insisted that Texas had discriminated against minority voters and that preclearance was required under Section 3 of the Voting Rights Act. Without reaching a final decision, the federal district court in San Antonio ordered interim use of the 2013 congressional districting maps for the primaries and general election in 2014, 2016, and again in 2018 when Republicans won 23 seats and Democrats won 13.

Legislators

LO 8.2 Describe the membership of the Texas legislature, including legislators' formal and informal qualifications and compensation.

Members of the Texas legislature may not hold another government office. Furthermore, they must meet specific state constitutional qualifications concerning citizenship, voter status, state and district residence, and age. Despite such restrictions, millions of Texans possess all of the legal (constitutional and statutory) qualifications to serve in the legislature. These are the formal qualifications for an office. As is true of the memberships in other state legislatures, however, biographical data for members of recent Texas legislatures suggest many informal qualifications that restrict opportunities for election.

Qualifications and Characteristics

The Texas Constitution specifies the formal qualifications for House and Senate members. Table 8.1 provides a list of formal qualifications for positions in the two chambers. Age and state residency requirements differ between the Texas House and Senate. If a question arises concerning constitutional qualifications or if a dispute develops over election returns, each legislative chamber determines who will be seated.

In order to be elected, the typical Texas legislator also meets a number of informal qualifications. These informal qualifications include being an Anglo Protestant male between 35 and 50 years of age, a native-born Texan, and an attorney or a businessperson who has served one or more previous terms of office. Although such characteristics do not guarantee any predetermined reaction to issues and events, legislators tend to be influenced by their experiences and environments. Because these factors can have policy consequences, any study of the legislature must account for the biographical characteristics of legislators. See Table 8.2 for data on political party affiliation, racial/ethnic classification, gender of legislators, and turnover from selected legislatures from 1971 to 2019.

Gender and Ethnic Classifications Anglo men dominate the Texas legislature, and almost all Anglo men in the legislature are Republicans (only 10 of the 181 legislators in the 86th legislative session are Anglo male Democrats).

TABLE 8.1 Constitutional Qualifications for Membership in the Texas Legislature

Qualification	House	Senate
Citizenship	U.S. citizen	U.S. citizen
Voter status	Qualified Texas voter	Qualified Texas voter
Residence in district to be represented	One year immediately preceding election	One year immediately preceding election
Texas residence	**Two years immediately preceding election**	**Five years immediately preceding election**
Age	**21 years**	**26 years**

Source: Constitution of Texas, Art. 3, Secs. 6 and 7.

— Competency Connection —
☼ **CRITICAL THINKING** ☼

What do longer residency requirements and being older suggest about the role of senators compared to representatives?

As reflected by Table 8.2, over time the legislature has become more diverse and includes more women and members of historical minority groups in 2019 than it did in 1971. Although more than 50 percent of the state's population is female, approximately 22 percent of state legislators are women. Reports of male legislators meowing like cats when their female colleagues debate each other; making comments about female legislators' physical attributes; and, according to some, treating women with general disrespect caused one legislator to describe the Texas House and Senate as "the last of the good ol' boys' clubs."[9]

Representation of members of historical racial or ethnic minorities increased substantially from the late 1960s through the early 1990s. Both African Americans and Latinos have been underrepresented in the Texas legislature. Texans elected the first Asian American legislator in the 1960s. Voters did not elect another Asian American for almost 40 years. No Asian American has ever been elected to the Texas Senate.

Political Party Affiliation In 1961, no Republican held a seat in the Texas legislature. When the legislature convened in 1997, the GOP had a Senate majority. By January 2003, Republicans controlled both the Senate and the House. Since that year, each chamber has produced more "party line" votes.

Throughout the first decade of the 21st century, Republicans increased their strength in both the Texas House of Representatives and the Texas Senate. In 2011, Republicans achieved supermajority status (two-thirds of total membership) in the Texas House of Representatives, with 101 Republican representatives compared to 49 Democrats. Republican representation in the Texas Senate has fluctuated between 19 and 20 of the 31 senate seats since 2007. Although most of the increase in Republican strength resulted from elections, between 2009 and 2012, four Democratic representatives switched to the GOP. In the elections from

IMAGE 8.3 Governor Greg Abbott, Lieutenant Governor Dan Patrick, and Speaker Dennis Bonnen (R-Angleton).

Bob Daemmrich/Alamy Stock Photo

— Competency Connection —
COMMUNICATION SKILLS

What message, if any, do you believe our state leaders sought to convey by being photographed with Governor Abbott's dog?

2012 to 2019, Democrats increased their numbers in the House of Representatives, winning 55 seats in the Texas House in 2012, 52 in 2014, 56 in 2016, and 67 in regular and special elections in 2018 and 2019. The numbers remained fairly constant in the Senate, where Democrats won 12 seats in 2012, 11 in 2014, 11 in 2016, and 12 in 2018.

Central city residents usually elect African American and Latino Democrats, whereas Republican senators and representatives receive their strongest support from rural and suburban Anglo voters. Residents of Mexican border districts largely elect Latino Democrats.

Education and Occupation In government, as in business, most positions of leadership call for college credentials. Although not a formal constitutional requirement for election to the Texas legislature, in recent years nearly all members attended one or more institutions of higher education. Most of them could claim a bachelor's degree, and many had graduate or professional degrees (especially in law).

Traditionally, Texas legislators have included many attorneys and business owners or managers. Lesser numbers of real estate and insurance people, as well as some farmers, ranchers, and teachers, also have served. Health-care professionals, engineers, and accountants have held few legislative seats, although four of the members of the 86th Legislature were physicians (three senators and one representative). Laborers have held almost none.

TABLE 8.2 Texas Trends in Legislative Representation for Selected Legislatures (1971–2019)

Number of Regular Session	Year of Regular Session	Political Party		Racial/Ethnic Classification				Gender		
		Dem.	Rep.	Anglo	Latino	African American	Asian American	Men	Women	Turnover
HOUSE OF REPRESENTATIVES: 150 MEMBERS										
62nd	1971	140	10	137	11	2	0	149	1	20.0%
63rd	1973	133	17	131	11	8	0	145	5	46.7%
67th	1981	114	36	119	18	13	0	139	11	24.0%
68th	1983	115	35	117	21	12	0	137	13	27.3%
72nd	1991	92	58	117	20	13	0	131	19	20.1%
73rd	1993	91	59	110	26	14	0	125	25	22.8%
77th	2001	78	72	108	28	14	0	120	30	8.4%
78th	2003	62	88	105	30	14	1	118	32	24.0%
82nd	2011	49	101	101	30	17	2	118	32	23.3%
83rd	2013	55	95	96	33	18	3	119	31	28.7%
84th	2015	52	98	95	35	17	3	120	30	16.7%
85th	2017	56	95	94	37	16	3	121	29	13.3%
86th	2019	67	83	92	38	17	3	120	30	20.0%
SENATE: 31 MEMBERS										
62nd	1971	29	2	29	1	1	0	30	1	12.9%
63rd	1973	28	3	29	2	0	0	30	1	48.4%
67th	1981	24	7	27	4	0	0	30	1	26.7%
68th	1983	26	5	26	4	1	0	31	0	32.3%
72nd	1991	23	8	24	6	2	0	27	4	16.7%
73rd	1993	18	13	23	6	2	0	27	4	25.8%
77th	2001	15	16	22	7	2	0	27	4	6.5%
78th	2003	12	19	22	7	2	0	27	4	22.6%
82nd	2011	12	19	22	7	2	0	25	6	6.5%
83rd	2013	12	19	22	7	2	0	25	6	19.4%
84th	2015	11	20	22	7	2	0	24	7	12.9%
85th	2017	11	20	22	7	2	0	23	8	12.9%
86th	2019	12	19	23	6	2	0	22	9	19.6%

Source: Texas Legislative Reference Library, Texas Legislative Council, and the unofficial count of the Office of the Secretary of State, https://elections.sos.state.tx.us/index.htm.

Competency Connection
COMMUNICATION SKILLS

What do you believe are the most important trends in the membership of the Texas legislature since 1971?

Lawyer-legislators may receive retainers (payments) from corporations and special interest groups, with the understanding that legal services will be performed if needed. Some question whether lawyer-legislators are hired for their legal abilities, to delay a court proceeding with a continuance, or to influence legislation. An attorney who serves in the legislature can obtain a continuance (that is, a postponement) of any case set for trial during a period extending from 30 days before to 30 days after a legislative session. To avoid abuse of this privilege, judges can deny a continuance if a lawyer was hired to assist with a case within 10 days of trial or any related legal proceeding. Payments received for obtaining a continuance must be disclosed. A legislator may not represent paying clients before state agencies. (For a discussion of state agencies, see Chapter 9, "The Executive Branch.")

Religious Affiliation The Texas Constitution guarantees freedom of religion and prohibits use of public funds for the benefit of a sect or religious group. Even though Texans recognize separation of church and state, a legislator's religious beliefs may play a critical role in the formulation of public policy. These factors are especially important when considering legislation involving issues related to moral behavior (such as abortion or gambling) and some economic matters (such as state aid to church-related schools). Although the religious affiliation of each legislator is not a matter of record, a review of self-reported religious preferences indicates that Catholic senators and representatives are most numerous in Texas, followed by Baptists, Methodists, Presbyterians, and Episcopalians.

Legislative Experience In a legislative body, experience is measured in terms of turnover (that is, first-termers replacing experienced members who have retired or lost an election) and tenure (years served in a legislative chamber). For the five most recent Texas legislatures (82nd–86th), the average turnover in the House was about 20 percent of the membership every two years. In the Senate, it was about 14 percent. Turnover tends to be greater for the first legislature after redistricting or in the event of a scandal like the Sharpstown Bank scandal that occurred in 1971 after disclosure of corruption involving banker Frank Sharp and some legislators. Table 8.2 provides information on the turnover rate for elections immediately preceding and following redistricting since 1971.

The average length of service by legislators in the most recent legislatures was more than six years in both the House and the Senate. Many senators served first as representatives. In 2019, for example, 14 of the 31 senators in the 86th Legislature had served as representatives. After a term in office, an incumbent is more likely to win an election than is an inexperienced challenger.

As a general rule, lawmakers become most effective after they have spent two or more years learning procedural rules related to enacting legislation and working with constituents, bureaucrats, lobbyists, fellow legislators, and other elected officials. Several representatives and senators have held their current positions for decades. The most senior member of the House, Tom Craddick (R-Midland), was first elected in 1968; the most senior member of the Senate, John Whitmire (D-Houston), was first elected to that chamber in 1982. (Senator Whitmire was in the House of Representatives for 10 years prior to his service in the Senate.) Texas is one of 35 states that does not have term limits for legislators. Even though some Democrats and Tea Party Republicans have worked to achieve term limits for state-level officeholders (including legislators), these efforts have failed.

Compensation

The lowest-paid state legislators in the nation are from New Hampshire. These elected officials are paid $200 per year with no per diem (compensation to cover expenses). Although New Mexico does not pay members of its legislative bodies any annual salary, legislators receive up to $161 per diem for each day the legislature is in session. In contrast, California's annual salary of $107,241 is more than any other state pays its legislators. Texas's state senators and representatives receive low pay, reasonable allowances, and a relatively generous retirement pension after a minimum period of service.

Pay and Per Diem Allowance Originally, Texas legislators' salaries and per diem (daily) personal allowances during a regular or special session were specified by the state constitution and could be changed only by constitutional amendment. Now, as authorized by a constitutional amendment, the Texas Ethics Commission sets the per diem expense allowance. In addition, this commission may recommend salary increases for legislators and even higher salaries for the Speaker and the lieutenant governor; however, Texas voters must approve all such recommendations and therefore make the ultimate decision. The $600 monthly salary ($7,200 per year) has not increased since 1975.

For the 86th Legislature, which convened in January 2019, the per diem allowance to cover meals, lodging, and other personal expenses was $221 for senators, representatives, and the lieutenant governor. This per diem amounted to a total of $30,940 per official for the 140-day regular session. When the legislature was not in session, members could receive a maximum of 12 per diem payments of $206 during each month if they were working on state business.

Expense Allowances At the beginning of a session, each chamber authorizes contingent expense allowances. For example, during the 86th regular session, the House authorized every representative's operating account to be credited monthly with $15,250. The monthly allowance for the interim was $13,500. House members use money in this account to cover the cost of official work-related travel within Texas, postage, office operations, and staff salaries. Representatives can also use money from campaign contributions to supplement their assistants' salaries and their own travel allowances. Some legislators use political donations to pay rent for housing in Austin.

For the 86th regular session, each senator had a monthly allowance of $43,000 for intrastate travel and staff salaries, but beginning in June, it was reduced to $41,000. Other expenses for carrying out official duties (for example, subscriptions, postage, telecommunications, and stationery) were paid from the Senate's contingent expense fund. Like representatives, Senate members can supplement staff salaries with money from campaign contributions.

Staff members assist legislators with office management, research, constituent service, and communication. Although assistance in responding to postal mail and email is a staff function, communications via social media, especially Twitter, is of increasing importance for legislators. Many legislators have staff to manage these accounts, but some elected officials prefer to handle their social networking accounts directly. In the 86th legislative session, most of the state's representatives and senators had active Twitter accounts.

Retirement Pension Under the terms of the Texas State Employees Retirement Act of 1975, legislators contribute 8 percent of their state salaries to a retirement fund. Retirement pay for senators and representatives amounts to 2.3 percent of the state-funded portion of a district judge's annual base salary ($140,000 in fiscal years 2020 and 2021) for each year served and cannot exceed the annual salary of state district judges. For example, should Representative Tom Craddick or Senator John Whitmire retire, he would be eligible for the maximum $140,000 in annual retirement benefits.

Legislators with a minimum of 12 years of service may retire at age 50 with an annual pension of $38,640. Those with at least eight years of service may retire at age 60 with a pension of $25,760 per year. Many legislators do not serve long enough to qualify for a pension, but for those who are eligible, payments can begin while they are relatively young.

📊 HOW DO WE COMPARE...

In Salary of Legislators?

Annual Salary of Legislators for the Year of the Last Regular Session

Most Populous U.S. States	Annual Salary	U.S. States Bordering Texas	Annual Salary
California	$107,241	Arkansas	$40,188
Florida	$ 29,697	Louisiana	$22,800
New York	$ 79,500	New Mexico	$ 0*
Texas	**$ 7,200**	Oklahoma	$38,400

*Legislators in New Mexico receive mileage and a $161 per diem allowance but no annual salary.

Source: "Comparison of State Legislative Salaries," *Ballotpedia*, https//ballotpedia.org/Comparison_of_state_legislative_salaries.

Competency Connection
✦ CRITICAL THINKING ✦

How do you account for the wide range of salaries for state legislators? Is the salary of Texas legislators adequate or should they be paid more or less?

In 2017, the 85th Legislature enacted Senate Bill 500, which directs withholding retirement pensions for legislators and other elected officials convicted of crimes such as bribery, embezzlement, tampering with a government record, and perjury, while in office.[10]

🔀 Legislative Organization

LO 8.3 Compare the organization of the Texas House of Representatives and the Texas Senate.

Merely bringing legislators together in the Capitol does not ensure the making of laws or any other governmental activity. Gathering people to transact official business requires organized effort. The formal organization of the Texas legislature features a presiding officer and several committees for each chamber. The informal organization involves various caucuses that do not have legal status.

Presiding Officers

The Texas Constitution establishes the offices of president of the Senate and Speaker of the House of Representatives. It designates the lieutenant governor as president of the Senate and provides for the election of a Speaker to preside over the House of Representatives.

President of the Senate: The Lieutenant Governor The most important function of the lieutenant governor of Texas is to serve as **president of the Senate**.[11] Just as the vice president of the United States is empowered to preside over the U.S. Senate but is not a member of that national lawmaking body, so too the lieutenant governor of Texas is not a member of the state Senate. The big difference between them is that the lieutenant governor presides over most sessions and plays a leading role in legislative matters (see Table 8.3 for powers), whereas the vice president seldom presides or becomes involved in the daily business of the U.S. Senate.

Chosen by the people of Texas in a statewide election for a four-year term, the lieutenant governor is first in line of succession in the event of the death, resignation, or removal of the governor. When the governor is absent from the state, the lieutenant governor serves as acting governor and receives the gubernatorial salary, which amounted to more than $400 per day at the beginning of 2019. Ordinarily, however, the lieutenant governor's salary is $600 per month, which amounts to about $20 per day.

Because of the lieutenant governor's powers (most of which have been granted by Senate rules rather than by the Texas Constitution), this official is perhaps the most powerful elected officer in the state, especially when the legislature is in session. Shortly before taking office in January 2015, Lieutenant Governor Dan Patrick appointed 55 business leaders (mostly Republicans and campaign donors) to six citizen committees to advise him on economic development, economic

president of the Senate
Title of the lieutenant governor in his or her role as presiding officer for the Texas Senate.

forecasting, energy, tax policy, transportation, and water.[12] At the end of the 84th regular session, Patrick told reporters, "I will never be running against Greg Abbott for governor." Then he added, "I will be lieutenant governor. This will be my last job in Texas. I love this job. This is where the action is. It's a lot of fun."[13]

If the lieutenant governor dies, resigns, or assumes another office, the Senate elects one of its members to serve as acting lieutenant governor. At the beginning and end of each session, the Senate elects a president pro tempore, who presides when the lieutenant governor is absent or disabled.

Speaker of the House The presiding officer of the House of Representatives is the **Speaker of the House**, a representative elected to that office for a two-year term by the House in an open (that is, not secret) vote by the House membership.[14] Proceedings in the House are controlled by the Speaker (see Table 8.3). Many observers argue the Speaker is the second most powerful official in state government. House rules authorize the Speaker to name another representative to preside over the chamber temporarily. The Speaker may also name a member of the House, who is typically a strong supporter of the Speaker, to serve as permanent speaker pro tempore for as long as the Speaker desires. A speaker pro tempore performs all the duties of the Speaker when that officer is absent.[15] The Speaker occupies an apartment in the Capitol.

Speaker of the House
The state representative elected by House members to serve as the presiding officer for that chamber.

TABLE 8.3 Comparison of Powers of Presiding Officers

Lieutenant Governor (President of the Senate)	Speaker of the House
Issues interim charges to standing committees for subjects to be studied in the interim between regular sessions	Same as Lieutenant Governor
Creates and abolishes committees	Same as Lieutenant Governor
Appoints Senate committee and subcommittee chairs and vice chairs	Same as Lieutenant Governor
Appoints all members of Senate committees and subcommittees	Appoints most members of House committees and subcommittees (limited by seniority rules)
Determines the Senate committee to which a bill will be sent after introduction	Same as Lieutenant Governor
Recognizes senators who wish to speak on the Senate floor or make a motion	Same as Lieutenant Governor
Votes only to break a tie vote	Votes (rarely) on bills and resolutions
Serves as joint chair of the Legislative Council, the Legislative Budget Board, and the Legislative Audit Committee	Same as Lieutenant Governor

Competency Connection
☼ **CRITICAL THINKING** ☼

How important is it for representatives and senators to be political allies of the presiding officers? Are there consequences to being an opponent of the presiding officers?

Because of the Speaker's power, filling this House office involves intense political activity. Lobbyists make every effort to ensure the election of a Speaker sympathetic to their respective causes, and potential candidates for the position begin to line up support several months or even years before a Speaker's race begins. Long before this election, anyone aspiring to the office of Speaker will attempt to induce House members to sign cards pledging their support. House rules, however, prohibit soliciting written pledges during a regular session. Once elected, a Speaker usually finds it easier to obtain similar pledges of support for reelection to the speakership.

Speaker candidates must file with the Texas Ethics Commission. No limitations on donations exist. According to judicial decision, any attempts to limit spending are unconstitutional because such restrictions would "significantly chill political speech protected by the First Amendment" of the U.S. Constitution.[16]

With bipartisan support, Joe Straus (R-San Antonio) began serving as Speaker in 2009 when a coalition of Democrats and Republicans succeeded in ousting Speaker Tom Craddick (R-Midland). Tea Party activists within the Republican Party unsuccessfully challenged Straus, a moderate Republican, both for reelection to his representative's seat and the speakership.[17] When opposed by Tea Party–backed Rep. Scott Turner (R-Frisco) in a speakership contest at the beginning of the 84th regular session, Straus won by a vote of 127 to 19.[18] At the end of that session, Straus announced that he would seek the speakership again in 2017.[19] Straus won primary and general elections in 2016, and he was reelected speaker. In 2019, Dennis Bonnen (R-Angleton) was elected speaker at the beginning of the 86th regular session.[20]

Committee System

Presiding officers appoint committee members, designate committee chairs and vice chairs, and determine the standing committees to which bills will be referred. To consider legislation that crosses the jurisdictional lines of standing committees, they may appoint select committees. In addition, presiding officers may appoint members of joint interim study committees composed of senators and representatives (and in some cases, private citizens). Joint committees make recommendations for consideration by both the House and the Senate. (See Table 8.4 for the 86th Legislature's standing committees and the numbers of members in each.) Because House and Senate committees play important roles in the fate or fortune of all bills and resolutions, selection of committee members goes a long way toward determining the amount and type of legislative output during a session. Permanent staff members are available to assist legislators with standing committee work on a continuing basis. Usually, these staff members also work on interim study committees created to examine legislative issues between regular sessions.

House Standing Committees In the Texas House of Representatives, **substantive committees** consider bills and resolutions relating to the subject identified by a committee's name (for example, elections or transportation). Substantive committees sometimes have subcommittees in which a few of the committee's members focus more closely on specific issues under the committee's

substantive committee
With members appointed by the House Speaker, this permanent committee considers bills and resolutions related to the subject identified by its name (such as, the House Agriculture and Livestock Committee) and may recommend passage of proposed legislation to the appropriate calendars committee.

TABLE 8.4 Standing Committees (with Numbers of Members), 86th Texas Legislature, January 2019–January 2021

House Standing Committees (substantive committees in regular print, *procedural committees* in italics)

1. Agriculture & Livestock (9)
2. Appropriations (27)
3. Business & Industry (9)
4. *Calendars* (11)
5. Corrections (9)
6. County Affairs (9)
7. Criminal Jurisprudence (9)
8. Culture, Recreation & Tourism (9)
9. Defense & Veterans' Affairs (9)
10. Elections (9)
11. Energy Resources (11)
12. Environmental Regulation (9)
13. *General Investigating* (5)
14. Higher Education (11)
15. Homeland Security & Public Safety (9)
16. *House Administration* (11)
17. Human Services (9)
18. Insurance (9)
19. International Relations & Economic Development (9)
20. Judiciary & Civil Jurisprudence (9)
21. Juvenile Justice & Family Issues (9)
22. Land & Resource Management (9)
23. Licensing & Administrative Procedures (11)
24. *Local & Consent Calendar* (11)
25. Natural Resources (11)
26. Pensions, Investments, and Financial Services (11)
27. Public Education (13)
28. Public Health (11)
29. *Redistricting* (15)
30. *Resolutions Calendars* (11)
31. State Affairs (13)
32. Transportation (13)
33. Urban Affairs (9)
34. Ways & Means (11)

Senate Standing Committees

1. Administration (7)
2. Agriculture (5)
3. Business & Commerce (9)
4. Criminal Justice (7)
5. Education (11)
6. Finance (15)
7. Health and Human Services (9)
8. Higher Education (9)
9. Intergovernmental Relations (7)
10. Natural Resources & Economic Development (11)
11. Nominations (7)
12. Property Tax (5)
13. State Affairs (9)
14. Transportation (9)
15. Veterans Affairs and Border Security (7)
16. Water and Rural Affairs (7)

Source: Texas Legislature Online, including websites for the House (https://house.texas.gov/committees) and Senate (https://senate.texas.gov/committees.php).

— Competency Connection —
⚙ **CRITICAL THINKING** ⚙

How could serving on a specific committee benefit a legislator?

jurisdiction. Seniority, based on years of service in the House of Representatives, determines a maximum of one-half the membership for substantive committees, excluding the chair and the vice chair. When a regular session begins, each representative, in order of seniority, designates three committees in order of preference. A representative is entitled to become a member of the committee of highest preference that has a vacant seniority position. The Speaker appoints other committee members.

Seniority does not apply to membership on **procedural committees**, each of which considers bills and resolutions relating primarily to an internal legislative matter (for example, the Calendars Committee, which determines when a bill will be considered by the full House). The Speaker appoints all members of procedural committees.

Although substantive and procedural committees are established under House rules adopted in each regular session, the Speaker independently creates **select committees** and **interim committees** and appoints all members. A Speaker usually creates select committees during a session to consider legislation that crosses committee jurisdictional lines or during an interim (between regular sessions) to conduct special studies.

Senate Standing Committees Senate rules provide for **standing committees** (though the rules do not identify them as substantive or procedural committees), select committees, and interim committees. Standing committees sometimes have subcommittees. As president of the Senate, the lieutenant governor appoints all committee members and designates the chair and vice chair of each committee. At the beginning of the 86th Legislature in 2019, Lieutenant Governor Dan Patrick kept his campaign promise to decrease the influence of Senate Democrats by giving most committee chairs to Republicans. Of the 11 Democratic senators, only John Whitmire (D-Houston) and Eddie Lucio, Jr. (D-Brownsville) were appointed as chairs of standing committees. In the House, Speaker Dennis Bonnen appointed 12 of the 67 Democrats to chair committees.

Legislative Caucus System

Legislative caucuses are organized on the basis of partisan, philosophical, racial, ethnic, or other special interests. Until the 1990s, Democratic leadership in the Texas House of Representatives and the Senate absorbed potential opponents within their teams and discouraged caucuses. By February 2019, however, 35 caucuses were registered with the Texas Ethics Commission as required by law. Although increasingly important for legislators and interest groups, legislative caucuses are prohibited from receiving public money. These groups stay connected to voters through Facebook, Twitter, Pinterest, and RSS feeds. Some groups attempt to heighten the impact of their messages by subscribing to services such as ShareThis. Supporters become a distribution network sending press releases and other information through their social networks. Some caucuses do not have web pages. They rely solely on Facebook and other social media platforms to engage voters who share their interests.

---

procedural committee
These permanent House committees (such as the Calendars Committee and House Administration Committee) consider bills and resolutions relating primarily to procedural legislative matters.

select committee
This committee, created independently by the House Speaker or the lieutenant governor, may consider legislation that crosses committee jurisdictional lines or may conduct special studies.

interim committee
A House or Senate committee appointed by the Speaker or lieutenant governor to study an important policy issue between regular sessions.

standing committee
A permanent Senate committee whose members are appointed by the lieutenant governor for the purpose of considering proposed bills and resolutions before possible floor debate and voting by senators.

legislative caucus
An organization of legislators who seek to maximize their influence over issues in which they have a special interest.

Party Caucuses The strengthening of party caucuses in each chamber of the Texas legislature was one indication that Texas was becoming a two-party state. The House Democratic Caucus was organized in 1981. In recent years, all Democratic legislators have been reported as belonging to their party's House or Senate caucuses. Under the leadership of Representative Tom Craddick (R-Midland), the House Republican Caucus was organized in 1989. Although they have no formal organizational role in either chamber, party caucuses take policy positions on some issues and promote unity among their members.

Racial/Ethnic Caucuses Racial and ethnic groups also organize and form voting blocs to maximize their power. Because African Americans and Latinos constitute significant minorities in the Texas legislature, it is not surprising that they have formed caucuses for this purpose. The Legislative Black Caucus concentrates on issues affecting African American Texans, such as hate crimes laws, the criminal justice system, and construction of the Texas African American History Memorial Monument on the State Capitol grounds.

The House-based Mexican American Legislative Caucus focuses on such issues as voting rights and providing higher education opportunities in South Texas and along the Mexican border. Members of the caucus led efforts to establish the University of Texas–Rio Grande Valley, a merger of UT-Pan American and UT at Brownsville. The new institution includes a medical school and receives funding from the Permanent University Fund (PUF), a state endowment financed by oil and gas royalties from state-owned natural resources. This funding was denied under previous law. Both the Mexican American Legislative Caucus and the Senate Hispanic Caucus include some Anglo and African American members who have large numbers of Latino voters in their districts.

Ideological Caucuses House-based ideological caucuses have also emerged. The Texas Conservative Coalition attracts Republicans and conservative Democrats, whereas the liberal Legislative Study Group appeals to many Democrats (including several who are also members of the Legislative Black Caucus and the Mexican American Legislative Caucus). The conservative and liberal caucuses reflect opposing views on most issues. A few representatives, however, belong to both caucuses.

Bipartisan Caucuses Some caucuses are framed around specific issues. Because an issue may be important to both Republicans and Democrats, caucus membership is bipartisan. For example, the House Women's Health Caucus supports legislation on issues related to women's health care. In 2013, members of the caucus, including its sole Republican, unsuccessfully opposed setting additional restrictions on abortion clinics.[21] A more inclusive bipartisan caucus is the "Farm-to-Table" Caucus founded by former Representative (now Senator) Lois Kolkhorst (R-Brenham) and Representative Eddie Rodriguez (D-Austin). In the 83rd legislative session, caucus members succeeded in passing bills that eased restrictions on "cottage foods" (foods prepared in home kitchens for commercial sale) and food sampling at cooking demonstrations

IMAGE 8.4 Representative Jodie Laubenberg (R-Parker) holds baby shoes symbolizing her claim that an anti-abortion bill will save lives. Supporting her are three other House members of the 83rd Legislature: (left to right) Linda Harper-Brown (R-Irving), Marsha Farney (R-Georgetown), and Cindy Burkett (R-Sunnyvale).

REUTERS/Alamy Stock Photo

— Competency Connection —
COMMUNICATION SKILLS

Is it an effective communication tool to use the baby shoes when discussing abortion rights?

✓ **8.3 Learning Check**

1. True or False: The Speaker of the House of Representatives presides over that body but cannot vote on a bill or resolution.

2. In the Texas Senate, who determines the committee to which a bill will be sent after its introduction?

Answers at the end of this chapter.

and farmers' markets.[22] Organized in 2015, the Border Caucus is based on geography, not party identification; but its current members are House Democrats representing districts on the Mexican border. Their objectives are to promote economic development along the border and to counter negative publicity about the area.[23]

⬟ Legislative Operations

LO 8.4 Outline the responsibilities of the Texas legislature.

As the chief agent in making public policy in Texas state government, the legislature must have powers to function. Legislators also need immunity from interference while performing their official duties. Thus, lawmaking is governed by detailed rules of procedure for each legislative chamber.

Powers and Immunities

Although bound by restrictions found in few state constitutions, the legislature is the dominant branch of Texas government and the chief agent in making public policy. Legislators control government spending, which makes state agencies and personnel—and, to some extent, units of local government—dependent upon them. Composed of one or more appropriation bills, the biennial state budget authorizes state spending. The budget is the most important legislation for regular (and sometimes special) sessions. To become law, an appropriation bill must pass in both legislative chambers, but it is subject to the governor's line-item veto power (see Chapter 9, "The Executive Branch"). Although appropriation bills may originate in either the House or the Senate, all revenue-producing bills, such as a bill that imposes a state tax, must originate in the House. (For more on taxing and spending, see Chapter 11, "Finance and Fiscal Policy.") Along with their powers, lawmakers have immunities from prosecution designed to allow them to function freely.

Making Public Policy The most typical exercise of legislative power involves making public policy by passing bills and adopting resolutions. All proposed legislation must be introduced by an elected senator or representative in the appropriate chamber; however, private citizens often communicate their desire for new laws to elected officials. Commentators frequently criticize the legislative process, noting that campaign donors and their lobbyists are more likely to gain support for their proposals than the average citizen.

Each bill or resolution has a distinctive abbreviation that indicates the chamber of origin, and every legislative proposal is given a number indicating the order of introduction. For example, SB10 would be the tenth bill introduced in the Senate during a session. An official website, Texas Legislature Online, maintains the history, text, analysis, and any fiscal note for each proposed bill or resolution. If requested, it alerts a legislator or any other person to any bill filed on a topic.

A **simple resolution**, abbreviated HR (House Resolution) if introduced in the House and SR (Senate Resolution) if introduced in the Senate, involves action by one chamber only and is not sent to the governor. Adoption requires a simple majority vote (more than one-half) of members present. Matters dealt with by simple resolution affect only the chamber that is voting on the resolution and include rules of the House or Senate, procedures for House or Senate operations, and invitations extended to nonmembers to address a particular chamber.

After adoption by simple majority votes of members present in both the House and the Senate, a **concurrent resolution** (HCR or SCR) is sent to the governor, who has two options: sign it or veto it. Typical examples are resolutions that request action by the U.S. Congress; grant permission to sue the state; or name state icons, such as the state squash (pumpkin) and state musical instrument (guitar). In addition, the chambers adopt a concurrent resolution to adjourn at the end of any legislative session—a measure that does not require approval by the governor.

simple resolution
A resolution that requires action by one legislative chamber only and is not acted on by the governor.

concurrent resolution
A resolution adopted by House and Senate majorities and then approved by the governor (for example, a request for action by Congress or authorization for someone to sue the state).

Adoption of a **joint resolution** (HJR or SJR) requires approval by both houses but no action by the governor. The nature of a joint resolution determines whether a simple majority or a two-thirds vote is required. Proposed amendments to the Texas Constitution are examples of joint resolutions requiring a two-thirds majority vote of the membership of each house. Ratification of proposed U.S. constitutional amendments that require a vote of state legislatures are approved with a joint resolution adopted by simple majority votes of members present in both houses. Likewise, the same simple majority vote is required to adopt a joint resolution requesting creation of a constitutional convention for proposing amendments to the U.S. Constitution.

Before enactment, a proposed law is known as a **bill** (House bill [HB] or Senate bill [SB]). Each regular session brings forth an avalanche of bills, but only 18 percent became law in 2017. In that year's regular session of the 85th Legislature, 4,333 bills were introduced in the House and 2,298 in the Senate. Together, both chambers enacted 700 House bills and 511 Senate bills. The governor vetoed 36 House bills and 14 Senate bills.[24]

For purposes of classification, bills fall into three categories: special, general, and local. A special bill makes an exception to general laws for the benefit of a specific individual, class, or corporation. Of greater importance are general bills, which apply to all people or property in all parts of Texas. To become law, a bill must pass by a simple majority of votes of members present in both the House and the Senate, but a two-thirds majority vote of the membership in each chamber is required to pass an emergency measure that will take effect as soon as the governor signs it. A local bill creates or affects a single unit of local government (for example, a city, county, or special district). Such bills usually pass without opposition if sponsored by all legislators representing the affected area.

Administrative and Investigative Powers The legislature also defines the responsibilities of state agencies and imposes restrictions on them through appropriation of money for operations and through **oversight** of activities. One form of oversight involves requiring state agencies to make both periodic and special reports to the legislature.

Both the House and the Senate receive information from the state auditor concerning irregular or inefficient use of state funds by administrative agencies. The auditor is appointed by (and serves at the will of) the Legislative Audit Committee. This six-member committee is composed of the Speaker, the chair of the House Appropriations Committee, the chair of the House Ways and Means Committee, the lieutenant governor, the chair of the Senate Finance Committee, and a senator appointed by the lieutenant governor.

Another control over state agencies is the legislature's Sunset Advisory Commission, which makes recommendations to the House and Senate concerning the continuation, merger, division, or abolition of nearly every state agency. Affected agencies are reviewed every 12 years (see Chapter 9, "The Executive Branch").

Most of the governor's board and commission appointments to head state agencies must be submitted to the Senate and approved by at least two-thirds of the senators present. Thus, the Senate is in a position to influence the selection

joint resolution
A resolution that must pass by a majority vote in each house when used to ratify an amendment to the U.S. Constitution or to request a constitutional convention to propose amendments to the U.S. Constitution. As a proposal for an amendment to the Texas Constitution, a joint resolution requires a two-thirds majority vote in each house.

bill
A proposed law or statute.

oversight
A legislative function that requires reports from state agencies concerning their operations; the state auditor provides information on agencies' use of state funds.

of many important officials. The unwritten rule of **senatorial courtesy** requires that the Senate "bust" (reject) an appointment if the appointee is declared "personally objectionable" by the senator representing the district in which the appointee resides. Consequently, a governor will privately seek prior approval by that senator before announcing a selection.

To support its power to exercise oversight of administrative agencies and to investigate problems that may require legislation, the legislature has the authority to subpoena witnesses, administer oaths, and compel submission of records and documents. Such action may be taken jointly by the two houses as a body, by one house, or by a committee of either house. Refusal to obey a subpoena may result in prosecution for contempt of the legislature, which is punishable by a jail sentence of from 30 days to a year and a fine ranging from $100 to $1,000.[25]

Impeachment and Removal Powers The House of Representatives has the power to **impeach** all elected state judges and justices in Texas. The House may also impeach elected executive officers, such as the governor, and appointed state officials, such as members of boards of regents for public university systems. In 2013, Speaker Joe Straus directed the Select Committee on Transparency in State Agency Operations to investigate and consider impeachment of University of Texas System regent Wallace Hall for possible violations of his duties as a regent. A 2014 report alleged Hall had committed impeachable offenses, including releasing student information and pressuring university officials.[26] Although Hall avoided being the first unelected state official to be impeached, he was publicly reprimanded and censured by the investigatory committee.

Impeachment involves bringing charges by a simple majority vote of House members present. It resembles the indictment process of a grand jury (see Chapter 10, "The Judicial Branch"). Once impeached, an official is suspended from office until the Senate issues judgment. Following impeachment, the Senate conducts a proceeding with the Chief Justice of the Texas Supreme Court presiding, after which it renders judgment. Conviction requires a two-thirds majority vote of the Senate membership. The only punishment that the Senate may impose is removal from office and disqualification from holding any other public office under the Texas Constitution. If a crime has been committed, the deposed official may also be prosecuted before an appropriate court.

Immunities In addition to their constitutional powers, state senators and representatives enjoy legislative immunities conferred by the Texas Constitution. They may not be sued for slander or otherwise held accountable for any statements made in a speech or debate during a legislative proceeding. This protection does not extend to remarks made under other circumstances. They may not be arrested while attending a legislative session or while traveling to or from the legislature's meeting place for the purpose of attending, unless charged with "treason, felony, or breach of the peace."

Rules and Procedures

Enacting a law is not the only way to get things done in Austin. Passing bills and adopting resolutions, however, are the principal means whereby members of the

senatorial courtesy
Before making an appointment, the governor is expected to obtain approval from the state senator in whose district the prospective appointee resides; failure to obtain such approval will probably cause the Senate to "bust" the appointee.

impeach
Process in which the Texas House of Representatives, by a simple majority vote, initiates action (brings charges) leading to possible removal of certain judicial and executive officials (both elected and appointed) by the Senate.

Texas legislature participate in making public policy. The legislature conducts its work according to detailed rules of procedure.

To guide legislators in their work, each chamber adopts its own set of rules at the beginning of every regular session. Usually, few changes are made to the rules of the preceding session. Whether a bill is passed or defeated depends heavily on the skills of sponsors and opponents in using House rules and Senate rules. Experienced legislators are more likely to have bills approved because of their understanding of the rules and stronger relationships with the leadership.

The lieutenant governor and the Speaker decide questions concerning interpretation of rules in their respective chambers. Because procedural questions may be complex and decisions must be made quickly, each chamber uses a **parliamentarian** to assist its presiding officer. Positioned on the dais immediately to the left of the lieutenant governor or Speaker, this expert on Senate or House rules provides answers to procedural questions.

How a Bill Becomes a Law

The Texas Constitution calls for regular legislative sessions divided into three periods for distinct purposes. The first 30 days are reserved for the introduction of bills and resolutions, action on emergency appropriations, and the confirmation or rejection of recess appointments (appointments made by the governor between sessions). The second 30 days are generally devoted to committee consideration of bills and resolutions. The remainder of the session, which amounts to 80 days, is devoted to floor debate and voting on bills and resolutions. Throughout a session, action may be taken at any time on an emergency matter identified by the governor and incorporated into a bill that is introduced by a legislator. The full process of turning a bill into a law is complex; however, certain basic steps are clearly outlined.

Although most bills can originate in either chamber, the following paragraphs trace the path of a bill from introduction in the House to action by the governor.[27] Figure 8.4 illustrates this procedure.

1. Introduction in the House Any House member may introduce a bill by filing electronically with the chief clerk (or, as required by the Texas Constitution, filing 11 copies of a bill related to conservation and reclamation districts with that official). This staff person supervises legislative administration in the House. Prior to a regular session, members and members-elect (newly elected but not yet having taken the oath of office) may prefile bills as early as the first Monday after the November general election. Members may prefile bills 30 days before the start of a special session (so long as the bills relate to the topic for which the governor convened that session). It is common practice for an identical bill, known as a **companion bill**, to be introduced by a senator in the Senate at the same time the bill is introduced in the House. This action allows simultaneous committee action in the two chambers.

parliamentarian
An expert on rules of order who sits at the left of the presiding officer in the House or Senate and provides advice on procedural questions.

companion bill
Filed in one house but identical or similar to a bill filed in the other chamber; this simultaneous filing speeds passage of a bill because committee consideration may take place at the same time in both chambers.

2. First Reading (House) and Referral to Committee After receiving a bill, the chief clerk assigns it a number in order of submission, although the first few numbers are reserved for the most important bills, such as the budget. Then the bill is given to the reading clerk for the first reading. The reading clerk reads aloud the caption (a brief summary of the bill's contents) and announces the committee to which the bill has been assigned by the Speaker.

3. House Committee Consideration and Report Before any committee action, the committee staff must distribute a bill analysis that summarizes important provisions of the bill to committee members.[28] The committee chair decides whether the bill needs a fiscal note (provided by the Legislative Budget Board) projecting the costs of implementing the proposed legislation for five years. The committee chair also decides whether a bill requires the Legislative Budget Board to prepare an impact statement. Among the types of bills requiring an impact statement are those that would alter punishment for a felony offense or change the public school finance system.

As a courtesy to sponsoring representatives, most bills receive a committee hearing at which lobbyists and other interested persons have an opportunity to express their views. House rules require public notice of any formal meeting or public hearing. Witnesses may also submit online videos. Public hearings are livestreamed, and these hearings are archived on the Texas Legislature Online site. The committee chair decides whether a bill will go to a subcommittee for a hearing. A subcommittee includes only some members of the full committee. After a hearing, the subcommittee submits a written report to the committee. Recommended changes to proposed bills may be made by amendments, in which event the legislature must vote on each proposed amendment, or by substituting a new bill for the proposed bill.

Two committees determine the order in which bills are cleared for floor action. The Local and Consent Calendars Committee and the Calendars Committee conduct sessions that are open to the public, the press, and all representatives. The Local and Consent Calendars Committee assigns three types of legislative proposals to the Local, Consent, and Resolutions Calendar. The following are examples of these types of bills that were passed in the 85th regular session in 2017:

- *Local bills* affecting a limited number of localities, districts, counties, or municipalities: HB 2194 by Rep. Phil King (R-Weatherford), requiring certain counties to appoint members of the Weatherford Junior College board

- *Consent bills* that are uncontested and not likely to face opposition: HB 355 by Rep. John Raney (R-Bryan), prohibiting certain sex offenders from residing on the campus of an institution of higher education

- *Noncontroversial resolutions*, other than congratulatory and memorial resolutions: HCR 72 by Rep. Drew Darby (R-San Antonio), designating Big Spring as the Lighted Poinsettia Capital of Texas

FIGURE 8.4 Route Followed by a House Bill from Texas Legislature to Governor

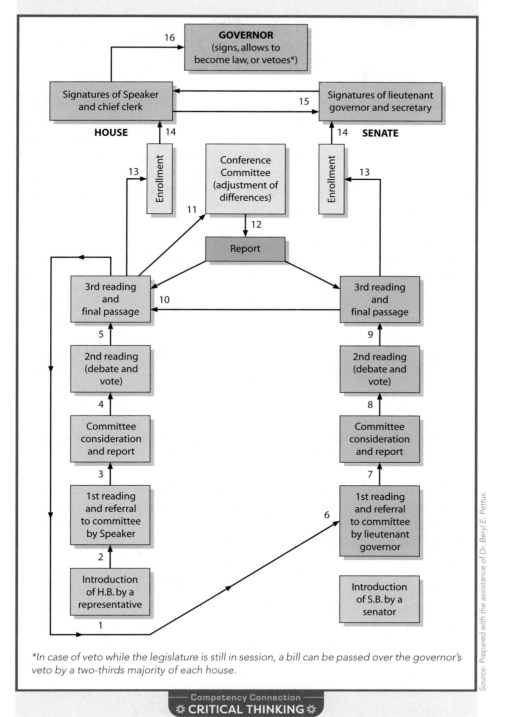

In case of veto while the legislature is still in session, a bill can be passed over the governor's veto by a two-thirds majority of each house.

Source: Prepared with the assistance of Dr. Beryl E. Pettus.

Competency Connection
✿ CRITICAL THINKING ✿

Should the process for a bill's becoming a law be simplified or made more complex?

The Calendars Committee places other bills on four daily calendars. The following are examples of these types of bills passed in the 85th regular session in 2017:

- The *Emergency Calendar*, for bills needing immediate action, as well as all taxing and spending bills: SB 4 by Sen. Charles Perry (R-Lubbock), banning "sanctuary cities" by prohibiting local policies that restrict enforcement of federal immigration law

- The *Major State Calendar*, for nonemergency bills that change policy in a major field of government activity and that have a major statewide impact: SB 2 by Sen. Paul Bettencourt (R-Houston), limiting local property tax increases

- The *General State Calendar*, for nonemergency bills having statewide application but limited legal effect and policy impact: HB 62 by Rep. Tom Craddick (R-Midland), imposing a statewide ban on reading, writing, or sending a text while driving

- *Constitutional Amendments Calendar*, for proposed constitutional amendments: HJR 37 by Rep. Eric Johnson (D-Dallas), authorizing the legislature to permit financial institutions to award prizes by lot (at random) to promote savings (subsequently adopted by Texas voters)

Within 30 days after receiving a bill, a calendars committee must decide by record vote whether to place the bill on a calendar for floor consideration. After this period expires, any representative may introduce a motion on the House floor to place the bill on an appropriate calendar. If the motion is seconded by five representatives and adopted by a simple majority vote, the House may schedule the bill for floor action without approval of a calendars committee. This procedure is seldom attempted. Because of the authority to decide if a bill will be placed on the calendar, the chair of the Calendars Committee is often identified as the fourth most powerful state government official, only less powerful than the lieutenant governor, the Speaker, and the governor.

4. Second Reading, Debate, and Vote (House) Usually, the second reading is limited to caption only. The author of a bill, the committee member reporting on behalf of the committee, or another designated member has the privilege of beginning and ending floor debate with a speech of not more than 20 minutes. Other speakers are limited to not more than 10 minutes each, unless extra time is granted. A computer on each representative's desk provides easy access to the text of amendments proposed during floor debate. After discussion ends and any amendments are added, a vote is taken on "passage to engrossment" (preparation of an officially inscribed copy). A quorum (the minimum number required to do business) is constituted when at least two-thirds of the House members (100 representatives) are present.

Approval of a bill on second reading requires a simple majority vote. A motion may be made to suspend the rules by a four-fifths majority vote of members present and to give the bill an immediate third reading. Thus, an exception can be made to the constitutional rule that all bills must be read on three separate days, though an exception for the third reading is seldom made in the House.

Provisions of the Texas Constitution, statutes, procedural rules, and practices within the respective chambers govern legislative voting. A record vote usually involves an electronic system. Votes are recorded and tallied as each representative presses the button on a desktop voting machine. This action turns on a light (green, yes; red, no; white, present but not voting) beside the representative's name on the two huge tote boards mounted on the wall behind the House Speaker's podium. House and Senate journals list the record votes of members of the respective chambers. Any House member may call for a record vote. House rules prohibit **ghost voting** (pressing the voting button for another representative) unless a member has given permission for the vote to be cast. When a representative asks for "strict enforcement," the voting machine of an absent member is locked.

Occasionally (especially at the end of a session), representatives engage in lengthy debates on bills they do not oppose (called buffer bills) or on the actual bill they are opposing. Such action is intended to prevent the House from voting on a bill that would probably be approved if brought up for a vote. This delaying action is called **chubbing**. In 2013, House Democrats engaged in chubbing to delay action on a bill that was designed to reduce the number of abortion providers in the state (SB 5). In the last two days of the first special session, Democratic representatives provided procedural challenges to the consideration of a bill on punishment for 17-year-old capital murderers. This tactic, coupled with extensive debate on SB 5 and the proposal of more than 25 amendments, kept the Senate from considering the bill until the final day of the special session. The delay was sufficient to allow for a successful filibuster by State Senator Wendy Davis (D-Ft. Worth) in the Texas Senate. In a second special session, a similar bill passed. Chubbing can be ended if 100 or more members vote to suspend House rules, as was done to pass the campus carry bill (SB 11) in 2015. In that same year, however, chubbing by House Democrats was successful in killing HB 4105 that would have prevented use of state or local government funds to issue same-sex marriage licenses.

To limit legislative logjams and discourage uninformed voting in the final days of a regular session, House rules contain prohibitions against second and third readings for the following bills:

- Nonlocal House bills during the last 17 days
- Local House bills during the last 10 days
- Senate bills during the last five days

Other detailed restrictions apply to House actions on the 126th to 139th days of a regular session. On the 140th, or final, day, House voting is limited to correcting bills that have passed. The Senate has similar end-of-session restrictions on considering legislation.

5. Third Reading and Final Passage (House)

On the third reading, passage of a bill requires a simple majority vote of members present. Amendments may still be added at this stage, but such action requires a two-thirds majority vote. After the addition of an amendment, a copy of the amended bill is made, checked over by the chief clerk, and stamped "Engrossed."

ghost voting
A prohibited practice whereby one representative presses the voting button of another House member who is absent.

chubbing
A practice whereby representatives engage in lengthy debate for the purpose of using time and thus preventing a vote on a bill that they oppose.

6. First Reading and Referral to Committee (Senate) After a bill passes on the third reading in the House, the chief clerk adds a statement certifying passage and transmits the bill to the Senate (where the original House number is retained). In the Senate, the secretary of the Senate reads aloud the House bill's caption and announces the committee to which the bill has been assigned by the lieutenant governor. All House bills sent to the Senate must have a Senate sponsor; likewise, all Senate bills sent to the House must have a House sponsor.

7. Senate Committee Consideration and Report Senate procedure differs somewhat from House procedure. A senator may "tag" any bill by filing a request with either the Senate secretary or the committee chair to notify the tagging senator 48 hours before a hearing will be held on the bill. A tag usually kills the bill if done during the last days of a session.

If a majority of the committee members wants a bill to pass, it receives a favorable report. Bills are listed on the Senate's Regular Order of Business in the order in which the secretary of the Senate receives them. Unlike the House, the Senate has no calendar committees to control the flow of bills from standing committees to the Senate floor. At the beginning of each session, however, the Senate Administration Committee parks a "blocker" at the head of the line. For the 86th regular session in 2019, there were two blocking measures by Sen. Bryan Hughes (R-Mineola): SB 409 establishing a county park beautification program and SJR 30 authorizing the state to receive gifts of historic value. Bills arriving later are designated "out of order," and a vote of three-fifths (19 senators) is required to suspend the regular order (that is, bypass the blocker bill) and bring the "out-of-order" bill to the Senate floor for debate. Before 2015, Senate rules required a two-thirds vote (21 senators) to bypass a blocker bill.[29] While serving as a senator, Dan Patrick (R-Houston) vigorously opposed that rule, arguing it gave the Democratic minority too much power. After his election as lieutenant governor, Patrick pushed successfully for the **three-fifths rule** requiring a smaller majority vote to bring a bill to the floor.

8. Second Reading, Debate, and Vote (Senate) As with second readings in the House, the Senate debates the bill and considers proposed amendments. A computer on the desk of each senator displays the texts of proposed amendments. During the debate, custom permits a senator to speak about a bill as long as physical endurance permits. This delaying tactic is known as **filibustering**. But a filibuster may be stopped if another senator is recognized for the privileged, nondebatable motion to "move the previous question," which means requiring an immediate vote. The motion must be seconded by at least five senators and requires a majority vote of senators present. Another privileged, nondebatable motion that can halt a filibuster is a motion to adjourn or recess. A filibuster is most effective if undertaken toward the end of a session when time is short.

In 2013, for example, Senator Wendy Davis killed an abortion bill (SB 5) during the 83rd Legislature's first special session. Through a series of procedural challenges from both Republicans and Democrats, Republican senators ended the filibuster with less than 15 minutes remaining. An outburst erupted from the crowd observing

three-fifths rule
A procedural device to control bringing bills to the Senate floor for debate.

filibustering
A delaying tactic whereby a senator may speak, and thus hold the Senate floor, for as long as physical endurance permits, unless action is taken to end the filibuster.

the Senate from the gallery located above the Senate chamber. The chaos continued so long that a timely vote did not occur. Several prochoice/proabortion organizations joined to create a "tweetstorm" of support for Davis's filibuster. Among the 547,000 tweets to #standwithwendy was one from then-President Barack Obama that was retweeted another 20,000 times. In addition, a livestream of the debate was available online and supporters live-blogged from the Capitol urging followers across the nation to contact local media outlets about the filibuster.[30]

When debate ends, a roll call vote is called by the secretary of the Senate. Unless a senator holds up two fingers to indicate an intention to vote no, the presiding officer usually announces that the chamber unanimously approves the bill after only a few names are called. The vote is recorded only if requested by three senators. A computer-controlled board at the front of the chamber shows how each senator has voted. Each vote requires a quorum of 21 senators present. A simple majority of "yea" votes of members present is sufficient to pass a bill.

9. Third Reading and Final Passage (Senate) If passed on the second reading, a bill can have its third reading immediately, assuming the rules have been suspended. This action is routinely taken in the Senate by the required four-fifths majority vote of members present. Amending a bill on the third reading requires a two-thirds majority vote of members present. A simple majority vote is required for passage.

10. Return to the House After passage by the Senate, a House bill returns to the chief clerk of the House, who supervises preparation of a perfect copy of the bill and delivers it to the Speaker. When an amendment has been added in the Senate (as usually happens), the change must be voted on in the House. If the House is not prepared to accept the amended bill, the ordinary procedure is to request a conference. Otherwise, the bill will die unless one of the chambers reverses its position.

11. Conference Committee When the two chambers agree to send the bill to conference, each presiding officer appoints five members to serve on the **conference committee**. Attempts are made to adjust differences and produce a compromise version acceptable to both the House and the Senate. At least three Senate members and three House members must agree before the committee can recommend a course of action in the two houses. The author of the bill usually serves as the conference committee chair.

12. Conference Committee Report The conference committee's recommended settlement of questions at issue must be fully accepted or rejected by a simple majority vote in each chamber. Most recommendations are accepted. Both chambers, however, may agree to return the report to the committee, or on request of the House, the Senate may accept a proposal for a new conference.

13. Enrollment After both chambers have accepted a conference report, the chief clerk of the House prepares a perfect copy of the bill and stamps it "Enrolled." The report is then presented to the House.

conference committee
A committee composed of representatives and senators appointed to reach agreement on a disputed bill and recommend changes acceptable to both chambers.

14. Signatures of the Chief Clerk and Speaker When the House receives the enrolled bill and the conference committee report, the bill is identified by chamber of origin and read by number only. Subsequently, it is signed by the chief clerk, who certifies the vote by which it passed. Then the House Speaker signs the bill.

15. Signatures of the Secretary of the Senate and the Lieutenant Governor Next, the chief clerk of the House takes the bill to the Senate, where it is read by number only. After certifying a passing vote, the secretary of the Senate signs the bill. Then the lieutenant governor does likewise.

16. Action by the Governor While the legislature remains in session, the governor has three options:

- Sign the bill
- Allow the bill to remain unsigned for 10 days, not including Sundays, after which time it becomes law without the chief executive's signature, or
- Within the 10-day period, veto the bill by returning it to the House, unsigned, with a message giving a reason for the veto (or to the Senate if a bill originated there).

The Texas Constitution requires a vote of "two-thirds of the membership present" in the first chamber that considers a vetoed bill (in this case, the House of Representatives) and a vote of "two-thirds of the members" in the second chamber (in this case, the Senate) to override the governor's veto.[31]

After a session ends, the governor has 20 days, counting Sundays, in which to veto pending legislation and file the rejected bills with the secretary of state. A bill not vetoed by the governor automatically becomes law at the end of the 20-day period. Because the legislature is no longer in session, the governor's postadjournment veto is of special importance because it cannot be overridden. Usually, the governor vetoes relatively few post-adjournment bills.

> **✓ 8.4 Learning Check**
>
> 1. What is the most typical way in which the legislature exercises its legislative power?
> 2. True or False: Members of the Texas House of Representatives have no way to delay a vote on a bill through debate.
>
> *Answers at the end of this chapter.*

⬟ Influences Within the Legislative Environment

LO 8.5 Explain the influences on legislators' voting decisions.

In theory, elected legislators are influenced primarily, if not exclusively, by their constituents (especially constituents who vote rather than those who make big campaign contributions). In practice, however, many legislators' actions bear little relation to the needs or interests of the "folks back home." Texas senators and representatives are not completely indifferent to voters, but many of them fall short of being genuinely representative.

Large numbers of citizens are uninterested in most governmental affairs and have no opinions about how the legislature should act in making public policy.

Others may have opinions but are inarticulate or unable to communicate with their legislators. Therefore, lawmakers are likely to yield not only to the influence of the presiding officers in the House and Senate but also to pressure from the governor. A threatened gubernatorial veto can kill a bill, as occurred with proposed legislation to ban texting while driving during the 83rd legislative session.

📋 STUDENTS IN ACTION

An Internship in Texas Government

"Senator [Rodney] Ellis' leadership and determination to help our youth prepared me to become the youngest African American City Council Member in the history of Georgetown, Texas."

—Shelley P. Davis, former Texas legislative intern

Student interns in the Texas Legislature are good examples of students in action.

If working in government appeals to you, whether as an elected official, political activist, or government employee, you could become a Student in Action through the Texas Legislative Internship Program (TLIP). Established by then-Senator Rodney Ellis (D-Houston) in 1990, the program is administered by the Office of Government Affairs at Texas Southern University. Internships are available in the spring semester of each academic year. Selected students intern with elected officials in government offices and for nonprofit advocacy organizations at the national, state, and local levels. In years in which the legislature is in session, interns who are in Austin have the opportunity to learn the legislative process through their work with more senior members of the legislature or in the offices of the governor and lieutenant governor.

College undergraduates with at least 60 hours of college credit and graduate and law students are eligible to apply for the program. Admission is competitive and requires exceptional writing skills and computer literacy. Through their work in the designated offices, students gain practical experience and assist with research and writing on work-related projects. Those accepted into the program must negotiate with their colleges to receive between 6 and 15 college credit hours. Interns receive a $7,500 stipend (as of 2019). Videoed testimonials from student participants are posted on the Texas Senate's TLIP website for each class of interns since 2001. The program also has its own Facebook page. More than 700 students have participated in the program. Many have remained active in politics, either running for office themselves or working in political campaigns. Three TLIP graduates served in the Texas legislature during the 86th legislative session: Representatives Ana Hernandez (D-Houston), Armando Walle (D-Houston), and Ron Reynolds (D-Missouri City).

— Competency Connection —
⚖ PERSONAL RESPONSIBILITY ⚖

Would you recommend that a college student apply for a legislative internship? Why or why not?

The chair of the Senate Transportation Committee allowed the bill to die in committee, remarking, "If it is not going to pass in the governor's mansion, why do we need to go through this?"[32] A similar bill was enacted in 2017. Other powerful political actors include the attorney general and judges who determine the constitutionality of laws; the state comptroller, who estimates state revenue for budgeting purposes; and lobbyists, who seek to win voluntary support or force cooperation for legislation that benefits the special interests they represent.

Events influence the introduction and passage of laws. See the Point/Counterpoint feature for the effect of "active shooter" incidents on college campuses and proposed laws. Additional sources of information and influence include research organizations and the media.

Research Organizations

Policymakers need reliable information. Most Texas legislators depend heavily on information provided by their staffs, by administrative agencies, and by lobbyists. In addition, legislators obtain information from official research bodies and independent providers of public policy research, sometimes called "think tanks."

The Texas Legislative Council Authorizing special research projects by its staff is one function of the Legislative Council. This council is overseen by the lieutenant governor (joint chair), the Speaker of the House (joint chair), six senators appointed by the lieutenant governor, the chair of the House Administration Committee, and five representatives appointed by the Speaker. The council's employees provide bill drafting, advice for legislators, legislative research and writing, publishing and document distribution, interim study committee research support, demographic and statistical data compilation and analysis, computer mapping and analysis, and other computer services.

The House Research Organization A bipartisan steering committee of 15 representatives—elected by the House membership for staggered four-year terms—governs the House Research Organization (HRO). Although the HRO is an administrative department of the House, it is independent of the House leadership. Its annual operating budget is set by the steering committee and the House Administration Committee.

In addition to producing reports on a variety of policy issues and House procedures, the HRO prepares the *Daily Floor Report* for each day the legislature is in session. In this publication, HRO personnel analyze important bills to be considered, providing a summary of bill content and presenting arguments for and against each bill. After a regular session, the HRO staff publishes a report on the session's important bills and resolutions, including some that were defeated.

The Senate Research Center Organized under the secretary of the Senate, the Senate Research Center analyzes bills under consideration by the Senate and conducts research on diverse issues. Primarily, it responds to requests from Senate members for research and information. The lieutenant governor, however, as president of the Senate, also calls on the center's information and expertise.

The center's periodic publications range from the semimonthly *Clearinghouse Update*, which presents brief accounts of issues facing Texas and the nation, to *Highlights of the [regular session number] … Legislature*, which summarizes hundreds of bills and joint resolutions for each regular session. Some other publications produced by the center include *The Senate Guide to Ethics and Financial Disclosure* and *Legislative Lexicon*, which defines words, terms, and phrases that form the "legislative lingo" used by legislators and staff.

The Center for Public Policy Priorities Founded in 1985 as an Austin office of the Benedictine Resource Center, the Center for Public Policy Priorities has been operating as an independent nonprofit organization since 1999. Its principal focus is on the problems of low- and moderate-income families in Texas. Legislators and other public officials have used its policy analyses on issues ranging from state taxation and appropriations to public education and health-care access. But some critics, like former House Appropriations Committee chair Rob Junell (D-San Angelo), insist that research by staff of "The Center for Too Many P's" is tainted with liberal bias.

The Texas Public Policy Foundation Established in 1989 in San Antonio, the Texas Public Policy Foundation (TPPF) is primarily funded by conservative activists. The foundation focuses its research on issues supporting limited government, free enterprise, private property rights, and individual responsibility. Using policy research and analysis, TPPF seeks to influence Texas government by recommending its findings to legislators and other policymakers, group leaders, media reporters, and the general public. An editorial in the liberal *Texas Observer* asserted in 2005 that "the Texas Public Policy Foundation has become the in-house think tank of the state's current Republican leadership."[33] In fact, the activities and influence of the foundation continue to increase as it operates from a new headquarters building near the Capitol. Of the top 25 Twitter accounts accessed by members of the 83rd Legislature (2013), for example, the only research organization on the list was the Texas Public Policy Foundation.[34]

The Media

Before the development of social media, measuring the influence of media on legislators' political decisions was difficult. Identifying the Twitter accounts most frequently followed by legislators now provides insight into the media sources on which officials rely for information. The most frequently followed is the online news site for the *Texas Tribune*. Other important media sites include *Quorum Report* (a daily online newsletter that focuses on Texas politics and state government), the *Austin American-Statesman*, *Texas Monthly*, and *Texas Insider* (a site that redistributes press releases and articles from multiple sources).[35] In addition, newsletters and other publications produced for subscribers or members of special interest groups highlight legislators' actions. On some policy issues, lawmakers may be impressed by newspaper editorials and articles, postings by bloggers, and editorial cartoons.[36]

✓ 8.5 Learning Check

1. True or False: The House Research Organization influences the House through the *Daily Floor Report*, which presents arguments for and against each bill.

2. How do social media provide insight on media sources that are important to legislators?

Answers at the end of this chapter.

★ KEEPING CURRENT
The 86th Legislature

Because Lieutenant Governor Dan Patrick chaired Donald Trump's presidential campaign in Texas, Trump's victory boosted Patrick's status among other Republicans and strengthened his leadership as president of the Texas Senate for the following 85th and 86th sessions. After Joe Straus (R-San Antonio) did not seek reelection in 2018, he was replaced as Speaker by Dennis Bonnen (R-Angleton) at the beginning of the 86th session. More than 7,300 bills were filed and more than 1,400 were passed during that session and sent to Governor Greg Abbott. Bills passed include authorization for state funding of economic development, restrictions on property taxes, increased funding for public education, legalization of cultivation and processing of hemp, taxation generally more favorable for business rather than consumers, and banning red-light cameras for traffic control. Among bills not passed was one that proposed expansion of Medicaid coverage for new mothers. Appointed as secretary of state by Governor Abbott in December 2018, David Whitley resigned shortly before the end of the 86th regular session, after he failed to obtain confirmation by the Senate. Whitley's handling of an investigation concerning the citizenship of registered voters caused all Senate Democrats to unite and block his appointment. In response, Governor Abbott vetoed some bills sponsored by Democratic senators and appointed Whitley to a job in the governor's office with an annual salary of $205,000 after the state agreed to pay $450,000 in court fees.

CONCLUSION

The framework of the Texas legislature reflects public demand for representative government. Legislators are chosen in popular, partisan elections. Much of the work of both the House and the Senate is done in committees, but floor debate and votes on bills and resolutions attract more public attention. Through their control of state taxing and spending, legislators have an immediate impact on the state's economy and the well-being of all Texans.

CHAPTER SUMMARY

LO 8.1 Describe the structure of the Texas legislature. The Texas legislature is a bicameral legislature composed of 31 senators elected for four-year terms and 150 representatives elected for two-year terms. Biennial regular sessions are limited to 140 days, and special sessions called by the governor are limited to 30 days. New legislative districts are drawn after each federal decennial census.

LO 8.2 Describe the membership of the Texas legislature. Legislators must be U.S. citizens, qualified Texas voters, and residents of their districts for one year. Minimum Texas residence is one year for representatives and two years for senators. Minimum age is 21 for representatives and 26 for senators. Legislators tend to be white, male, middle-aged Republicans. They are paid $7,200 per year in salary, but they also receive per diem payments and generous retirement benefits after several years of service.

LO 8.3 Compare the organization of the Texas House of Representatives and the Texas Senate. The lieutenant governor presides over the Senate, and the Speaker presides over the House. Both appoint committee members and name committee chairs and vice chairs for their respective chambers. Senators and representatives form legislative caucuses, which are groups with common interests. There are party caucuses for Democrats and Republicans, racial/ethnic caucuses for African Americans and Mexican Americans, ideological caucuses for conservatives and liberals, and some bipartisan caucuses organized around specific public policy issues.

LO 8.4 Outline the responsibilities of the Texas legislature. Legislators have primary responsibility for adopting public policy. In addition, they can check the power of the executive and judicial branches through the use of their investigative and impeachment powers. Constitutional provisions and rules of the House and Senate control the detailed process whereby a bill is passed in both chambers. The governor may sign a bill, allow it to become law without signing, or veto it. A veto kills a bill unless the veto is overridden by a two-thirds vote in each chamber.

LO 8.5 Explain the influences on legislators' voting decisions. In theory, voters have the most influence over legislators because voters elect them to office. In practice, legislators are influenced by a number of third parties. Among the individuals and entities that influence legislators' policy decisions are the governor and other state officials, lobbyists, research organizations, and the media.

KEY TERMS

bicameral, p. 276
bill, p. 299
chubbing, p. 305
companion bill, p. 301
concurrent resolution, p. 298
conference committee, p. 307
filibustering, p. 306
gerrymandering, p. 279
ghost voting, p. 305
impeach, p. 300

interim committee, p. 295
joint resolution, p. 299
legislative caucus, p. 295
multimember district, p. 279
oversight, p. 299
parliamentarian, p. 301
president of the Senate, p. 291
procedural committee, p. 295
redistrict, p. 278
regular session, p. 277

select committee, p. 295
senatorial courtesy, p. 300
simple resolution, p. 298
single-member district, p. 279
Speaker of the House, p. 292
special session, p. 277
standing committee, p. 295
substantive committee, p. 293
three-fifths rule, p. 306
unicameral, p. 276

LEARNING CHECK ANSWERS

 8.1   **1.** A governor has more authority in a special session because he sets the legislative agenda and the time for meeting.

2. False. Gerrymandered districts are legal so long as they do not dilute minority voting strength.

✓ 8.2 **1.** False. Although many legislators are practicing Christians, no religious requirements for elected office are included in state law.

2. The legislator's per diem allowance will be higher, at $221 per day during the 86th legislative session. Legislators receive only $600 per month (or $7,200 per year) in salary.

✓ 8.3 **1.** False. The Speaker of the House of Representatives can vote on bills or resolutions, although he often chooses not to do so.

2. The president of the Senate, who is the lieutenant governor, determines the Senate committee to which a bill will be sent after introduction.

✓ 8.4 **1.** The legislature most frequently exercises its legislative power by passing bills and resolutions.

2. False. Members of the Texas House of Representatives can use chubbing to delay a vote on a bill.

✓ 8.5 **1.** True. The House Research Organization influences the House through the *Daily Floor Report* that provides arguments for and against each bill.

2. Social media sites such as Twitter allow researchers to measure the number of times a legislator accesses a media outlet's account.

The Executive Branch

9

Learning Objectives

9.1 Analyze gubernatorial elections and the impact of campaign funds on the politics of the governorship.

9.2 Summarize how the constitution and laws of Texas provide resources, as well as succession and removal procedures, for the governor.

9.3 Discuss the informal powers of the governor.

9.4 Explain the effect of checks and balances on the executive powers of the governor.

9.5 Analyze the shared power of the executive and legislative branches.

9.6 Illustrate powers the governor exercises over the judicial branch of state government.

9.7 Describe the powers of the secretary of state and elected department heads.

9.8 Describe the role of the bureaucracy in governing the state of Texas.

IMAGE 9.1 Governor Greg Abbott visits state troops in Weslaco, near the border with Mexico, in April of 2018.

Bob Daemmrich/Alamy Stock Photo

Competency Connection
◎ SOCIAL RESPONSIBILITY ◎

How can Texas best balance human rights with security at the border?

On July 14, 2013, Texas Attorney General Greg Abbott announced that he would seek the Texas Republican Party's nomination for governor. He made the announcement on the 29th anniversary of the day that a falling oak tree changed his life forever, breaking his back, damaging his kidneys, and confining him permanently to a wheelchair. Abbott credits the accident with giving him a "spine of steel" and a focus not on the challenges life brings but on his response to challenges. When he met and overcame Democratic Texas Senator Wendy Davis's challenge in the 2014 gubernatorial election, Abbott's victory marked the end of an era in the Lone Star State. For most young Texans, Rick Perry was the only governor they had ever known, having served a record 14 years in the governor's office.

Perry's long tenure made him a nationally recognizable figure. He parlayed his name recognition into two campaigns for the U.S. presidency, an appearance on *Dancing with the Stars*, and eventually a position as U.S. Secretary of Energy in the Trump administration. Given the level of attention and media coverage the office receives, you might be surprised to learn that, unlike the president of the United States and the governors of most other states, the position of Texas governor is a relatively weak one with regard to formal powers.

Several of Texas's political traditions and institutions stem from the state's experiences after the Civil War (1861–1865). Even today, the state's executive structure shows the influence of anti-Reconstruction reactions against Governor E. J. Davis's administration (1870–1874). When Davis made aggressive use of state government power in an effort to enfranchise and protect freed slaves, a large majority of Anglo Texans complained that numerous abuses of power occurred, committed by state officials reporting directly to Governor Davis.[1] This piece of Texas history helps explain why, after more than 140 years, many Texans still distrust the "strong" executive model of state government. The U.S. president (with Senate approval) appoints and can independently remove members of a cabinet. In Texas, however, Article IV of the Texas Constitution establishes a multiheaded executive branch, or plural executive, over which the governor has only limited formal powers (see Figure 9.1).

As you learn about the workings of the executive branch of Texas government, consider an observation by Dr. Brian McCall, a former member of the Texas House of Representatives and subsequently chancellor of the Texas State University System. In his book *The Power of the Texas Governor: Connally to Bush*, McCall states: "It is widely reported that the governorship of Texas is by design a weak office. However, the strength of an individual governor's personality can overcome many of the limitations imposed on the office."[2] As you read this chapter, answer the following questions: Is the current head of Texas's executive branch a strong governor? How much power should other elected and appointed officials in this branch have?

Follow *Practicing Texas Politics* on Twitter **@PracTexPol**

FIGURE 9.1 The Structure of Texas Government: Important Agencies and Offices (with number of governing body members)

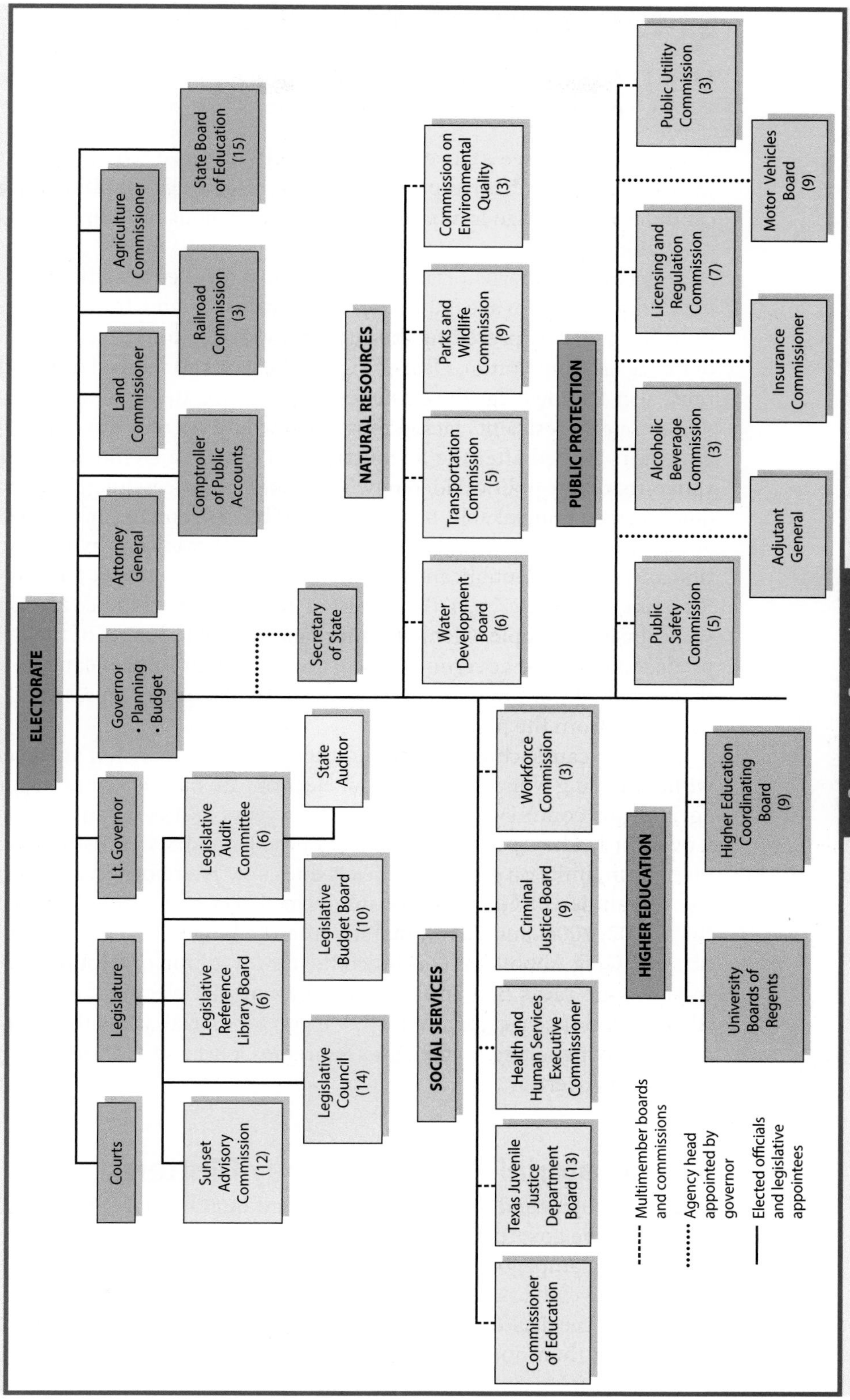

ELECTORATE

Courts

Legislature

Lt. Governor

Governor
• Planning
• Budget

Attorney General

Comptroller of Public Accounts

Land Commissioner

Agriculture Commissioner

Railroad Commission (3)

State Board of Education (15)

Sunset Advisory Commission (12)

Legislative Reference Library Board (6)

Legislative Audit Committee (6)

Legislative Council (14)

Legislative Budget Board (10)

State Auditor

Secretary of State

NATURAL RESOURCES

Water Development Board (6)

Transportation Commission (5)

Parks and Wildlife Commission (9)

Commission on Environmental Quality (3)

SOCIAL SERVICES

Texas Juvenile Justice Department Board (13)

Health and Human Services Executive Commissioner

Criminal Justice Board (9)

Workforce Commission (3)

Commissioner of Education

HIGHER EDUCATION

University Boards of Regents

Higher Education Coordinating Board (9)

PUBLIC PROTECTION

Public Safety Commission (5)

Alcoholic Beverage Commission (3)

Licensing and Regulation Commission (7)

Public Utility Commission (3)

Adjutant General

Insurance Commissioner

Motor Vehicles Board (9)

----- Multimember boards and commissions

.... Agency head appointed by governor

—— Elected officials and legislative appointees

✿ CRITICAL THINKING ✿

What are the advantages and disadvantages of having a plural executive?

❖ Gubernatorial Elections

LO 9.1 Analyze gubernatorial elections and the impact of campaign funds on the politics of the governorship.

Texas does not have a governor who merits the title "chief executive." Nevertheless, limited executive power does not discourage ambitious gubernatorial candidates who wage multimillion-dollar campaigns in their efforts to win this prestigious office.[3]

Successful gubernatorial candidates must meet constitutional prerequisites, including minimum age (30 years), U.S. citizenship, and Texas residency (for five years immediately preceding the gubernatorial election). According to Section 4 of the Texas Constitution's Bill of Rights, the governor and all other officeholders must also acknowledge the existence of a Supreme Being. There are also numerous extralegal restraints facing those who would become governor. Historically, governors elected after the Reconstruction Era were Democrats with a conservative-moderate political ideology. This mold for successful gubernatorial candidates seemed unbreakable, but William P. ("Bill") Clements, Jr. (in 1978 and 1986) and George W. Bush (in 1994 and 1998) broke tradition by becoming Texas's first and second Republican governors, respectively, since E. J. Davis. (See *Texas Almanac, 2016–2017*, p. 470, for a list of Texas governors since 1874.) As conservative businesspeople, Clements and Bush resembled most of their Democratic predecessors in the governor's office; however, their Republicanism, and the fact that they had not previously held elective public office, represented a dramatic departure from the past.[4]

Republican Rick Perry entered the governor's mansion at the end of 2000 without having won a gubernatorial election. He had served as a state legislator, agriculture commissioner, and for two years as lieutenant governor before Governor Bush was elected president of the United States. Although most states place term limits on governors, Texas does not. Therefore, in addition to serving the remainder of Governor Bush's term, Perry was elected three times after that (2002, 2006, and 2010), making him the longest serving governor in Texas history.[5] Greg Abbott has continued the new tradition of Republican dominance in statewide races by winning the gubernatorial elections of 2014 and 2018. Abbott combined a career in the private sector as a lawyer with a career in public service, having served on the Texas Supreme Court and as attorney general before becoming governor.

Gubernatorial Politics: Money Matters

Regardless of a candidate's background and qualifications, to be a serious contender for the governor's office, he or she must raise significant money to fund a campaign. Campaign funds allow candidates to buy advertising time, hire consultants, travel the state, and stage rallies. In politics, money talks. It is often, but not always, the deciding factor. In 2002, South Texas Democrat Tony Sanchez, Jr. spent more than double the amount raised by incumbent Rick Perry but lost by a wide margin. Since then, the winners of every gubernatorial election in Texas have raised and spent significantly more than their opponent. Governor Abbott continued raising funds through his first term, and by the beginning of 2017 (nearly two years before election day), he already had a war chest of $34.4 million. By election day, the governor and groups supporting him had amassed over $75 million to support his reelection. His opponent, Lupe Valdez, and her supporters raised less than $1.7 million for her campaign.[6]

The practice of buying influence with campaign contributions permeates American politics. After pumping millions of dollars into a winning gubernatorial election campaign, donors of large amounts of money are often appointed to key policymaking positions. Texas politics is no exception; the governor appoints members of important boards and commissions.

▧ POINT/COUNTERPOINT

Should the Texas Constitution Be Amended to Limit Terms Served by the State's Governor?

THE ISSUE Rick Perry became governor of Texas for two years after Governor George W. Bush won the presidential election of 2000. Subsequently, Perry was elected to three four-year terms, making his total tenure as governor a record-breaking 14 years. Thirty-six states impose term limits on governors, but Texas and 13 other states do not have such restrictions. In 2015, Senator Don Huffines (R-Dallas) made an unsuccessful attempt to amend SJR 88 to include term limits.

FOR	AGAINST
1. Limited terms produce new officeholders with fresh ideas.	1. Voters will not reelect someone who is incompetent or corrupt.
2. Election for a limited time causes an officeholder to place the interests of the public above that of a political party or special interests.	2. Representative democracies are based on the principle of popular election, which should not be restricted by reelection control.
3. Shorter tenure results in less corruption and fewer scandals.	3. Longer service provides more experience, which enhances governing skill.
4. Each term increases the age of an officeholder and the probability of death while in office.	4. A governor constrained by term limits will be disadvantaged when dealing with unelected lobbyists and bureaucrats, and with elected legislators and judges not subject to term limits.

Based on Einer Elhauge, "Are Term Limits Undemocratic?" *University of Chicago Law Review*, 64 (Winter, 1997), 83–201.

Competency Connection
⚜ COMMUNICATION SKILLS ⚜

Which elected leader might you contact to share your views on term limits, and how would you craft your message?

Candidates also use their fundraising efforts to symbolize the support they hold among the people of Texas. Thus, they work hard to publicize large totals at filing deadlines or to put a positive spin on smaller totals. After a July 2018 filing deadline, Abbott announced a campaign war chest of $28.9 million, nearly 130 times more than the $222,000 held by opponent Lupe Valdez. Still, Valdez remained positive, releasing the statement, "These are hard-earned funds coming from everyday Texans who know that our vision of the future is the way forward. We may not have tens of millions, but we've gained ground in the polls over the last two months and our message continues to resonate with everyday Texans."[7]

Gubernatorial Politics: Budgetary Influence

In addition to campaign donations, money can also serve as a tool to gain legislators' support for a governor's agenda. Lacking sufficient constitutional powers, a Texas governor must rely heavily on skills in personal relations, competent staff assistance from communications professionals, and talent for both gentle persuasion and forceful arm-twisting. Although arm-twisting is usually done without publicity, this secrecy is not always the case. For example, Governor Abbott asked conservative pastors to pressure Texas lawmakers for

IMAGE 9.2 Governor Greg Abbott on a trade mission to Cuba

DESMOND BOYLAN/AFP/Getty Images

Competency Connection
◈ **SOCIAL RESPONSIBILITY** ◈

Are the costs of gubernatorial travel abroad worth the benefits to the state of Texas?

support of SB6, a bill that would have blocked transgender people from using public restrooms that match their gender identities. He then announced that he would create and publish a list of those who did not support the bill and 19 of his other positions, saying, "No one gets to hide. No one gets to play neutral. Everyone has to be all in."[8]

Yet arm-twisting has its legal limits. In April 2014, after complaints were filed by Texans for Public Justice, Special District Judge Bert Richardson impaneled a grand jury in Travis County (Austin) to determine whether Perry abused his power in following through on a threat to veto $7.5 million in state funding for public corruption prosecutors. In August 2014, Perry became only the second Texas governor to be indicted. (The other was James E. "Pa" Ferguson in 1917.) The indictment charged Perry with "abuse of official capacity," a first-degree felony punishable by up to 99 years in prison. It also charged him with "coercion of a public servant," a third-degree felony that can result in up to 10 years in prison.[9] For a discussion of this indictment, see Chapter 3, "Local Governments." In February 2016, the Texas Court of Criminal Appeals ruled in Perry's favor on the abuse of power charge and upheld a lower court's ruling with regard to the unconstitutionality of the coercion law.[10]

⬧ Overview of the Governorship

LO 9.2 Summarize how the constitution and laws of Texas provide resources, as well as succession and removal procedures, for the governor.

The constitution and laws of Texas endow the governor with certain benefits and resources. They also provide procedures for removing a governor from office and providing a successor if the governor does not finish an elected term.

Compensation and Benefits

The biennial state budget for fiscal years 2020–2021 set the governor's salary at $153,750 per year, which is the same as salaries for the state's attorney general and comptroller of public accounts.[11] In 2011, Governor Perry stirred controversy when his federal campaign filings forced him to disclose that in addition to his salary, he also received retirement benefits from the state worth more than $92,000 per year. In a complex process that did not have to be disclosed under state law, Perry was able to retire as a state employee while continuing to receive pay as an elected official.[12] Shortly after Perry left office, such "double-dipping" was banned (except for district attorneys) by House Bill 408 enacted by the 84th Legislature.

State money pays the governor's expenses for official trips but not travel expenses for political campaigning or other nonofficial activities. Nevertheless, the Department of Public Safety provides personnel to protect the governor at all times at state expense. Travel expenses and overtime for Perry's security detail during the 160 days he campaigned for the Republican Party's 2012 presidential nomination cost the state more than $3.6 million. This information caused some Texans to insist that such expenses be covered by campaign funds.[13] The Texas Supreme Court ruled that separating expenses between the governor's campaign and official functions would require the Department of Public Safety to provide a detailed breakdown of how money for the governor's security is spent. To do so, according to the court, compromises a governor's safety and is therefore confidential.[14]

With Greg Abbott in the governor's office, the cost of his security detail is likewise paid by Texas taxpayers. Abbott has traveled extensively throughout the United States and abroad during his terms as governor. He made trips to promote Texas businesses, publicize his book, speak at political events, take vacations, and campaign for himself and other Republican candidates. By March of 2018, Abbott's travel and security detail had already cost taxpayers over $1 million. That was prior to extended trips to India and Japan and prior to the most of his reelection campaign travel.[15] Other fringe benefits of the governor's office include staff and housing in the Governor's Mansion, which is open for tours on a limited basis. Whether taxpayers are responsible for a governor's legal expenses resulting from a criminal investigation is unresolved. Although taxpayers paid more than $132,000 for Governor Perry's legal representation prior to indictment, post-indictment he used his campaign funds. Political supporters may also cover the costs of luncheons, dinners, receptions, and other social activities at the governor's residence and elsewhere.[16]

The Texas Constitution forbids the governor and other executive officers (except the lieutenant governor) from holding any other civil or corporate office, and the governor may receive neither compensation nor the promise of pay for other employment after taking office. Nevertheless, governors do own property and make investments while serving. To avoid the appearance of conflict between their personal economic interests and the public's interest, both Governors Bush and Perry placed their assets in blind trusts (a legal arrangement whereby holdings are administered by others and the elected official does not know which assets are in the trust). Governor Abbott did not do so.

Former governors also obtain benefits. For the year after leaving office and moving to a new home in Round Top (population 90, Fayette County), Rick Perry reported state retirement income of $133,215 resulting from his salary as governor. As a well-connected politician, however, he found opportunities for other income. Prior to being nominated by President Trump to the position of Energy Secretary, Perry made hundreds of thousands of dollars a year in 2015 and 2016 by taking advantage of a variety of opportunities. He worked as a consultant for a heavy equipment company owned by one of his former campaign donors and appointees. He served on the board of Energy Transfer Partners, a Dallas pipeline company owned by another longtime donor, and served on the board of Sunoco Logistics Partners. He worked as chief strategy officer for the Florida lobbying operations of dental insurance company MCNA Dental, which had contributed money to his presidential bid. He also received payment for speeches and media appearances, including a spot on *Dancing with the Stars*.

FIGURE 9.2 The Office of the Governor

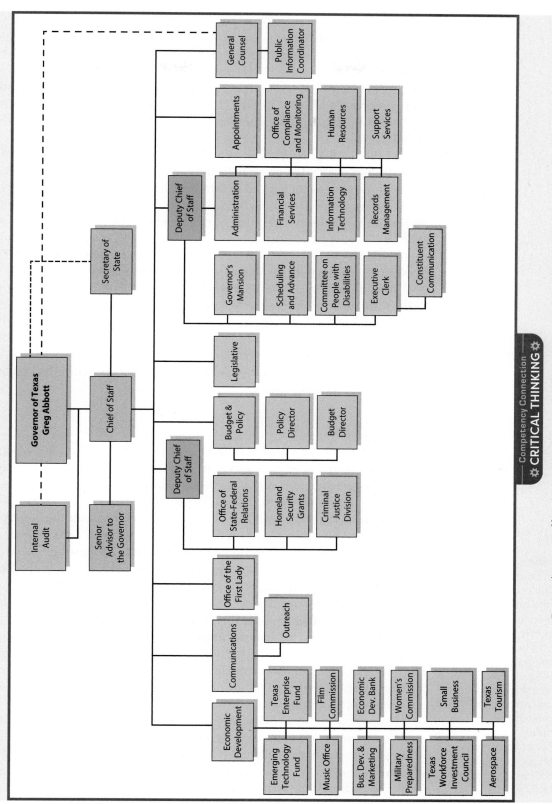

Does a larger staff make a governor more effective or less efficient?

Staff

The Texas governor's hands are often tied when dealing with the state bureaucracy, but the chief executive's personal staff continues to function under direct gubernatorial supervision. A governor's success in dealing with lobbyists, legislators, reporters, and the general public depends largely on staff input and support. The **governor's office** staff directs programs mandated by the legislature, such as statewide planning (see Figure 9.2). The governor can appoint and remove staff members.

As the state's population grew and governors embellished their roles in the 20th century, staff size burgeoned. Although fiscal belt-tightening has required recent governors to cut back, staff numbers are still substantially greater than in earlier years. From more than 300 on Governor Ann Richards's staff at the end of her term in January 1995, that number had dropped to 277 under Governor Abbott 22 years later. Even the size of Abbott's staff dwarfed the 68 full-time staff employees who served under Governor John Connally in the 1960s. The governor's office has also become more diverse over time.

The influence of a governor's appointed assistants and unofficial advisers on gubernatorial decisions is open to speculation. Protecting their chief is still a primary function of many staff assistants, particularly the press secretary (who tries to schedule interviews with friendly journalists) and the director of appointments (who evaluates potential appointees). All Texas governors have placed close friends and political associates in staff positions—persons who can be relied on for their loyalty to the chief executive.

Succession

Should a governor die, resign (as did George W. Bush after his 2000 election to the U.S. presidency), or be removed from office (as was James E. "Pa" Ferguson after his impeachment in 1917), or should a governor-elect refuse to take office or be permanently unable to fill the office, a successor serves for the remainder of the governor's four-year term. The lieutenant governor heads the constitutional order of succession. Next in line is the president pro tempore of the Senate. After these two officials, the legislature has designated the following line of succession: Speaker of the House, attorney general, and chief justices of the 14 courts of appeals in ascending numerical order, beginning with the chief justice of the First Court of Appeals and ending with the chief justice of the Fourteenth Court of Appeals, both of whom have their primary seats in Houston.

If the governor is temporarily unable to serve, is temporarily disqualified, or is impeached, the lieutenant governor exercises the powers of the governor until the governor becomes able or qualified to serve or is acquitted of impeachment charges. The lieutenant governor becomes acting governor while the governor is absent from the state. In the absence of both of these officials, the president pro tempore of the Texas Senate acts as governor. By custom, the Texas governor and lieutenant governor arrange their schedules so that, on at least one occasion during the tenure of a president pro tempore, both are conveniently out of state at the same time. In such circumstances, the president pro tempore of the Senate has the honor of becoming acting governor until the governor or lieutenant governor

governor's office
The administrative organization through which the governor of Texas makes appointments, prepares a biennial budget recommendation, administers federal and state grants for crime prevention and law enforcement, and confers full and conditional pardons on recommendation of the Board of Pardons and Paroles.

🏛 HOW DO WE COMPARE...

In Governor's Compensation and Staff Size?

Most Populous U.S. States	Governor's Annual Salary	Number of People Working in the Governor's Office	U.S. States Bordering Texas	Governor's Annual Salary	Number of People Working in the Governor's Office
California	$195,803	88	Arkansas	$143,820	60
Florida	$130,273	276	Louisiana	$130,000	93
New York	$179,000	180	New Mexico	$110,000	33
Texas	**$153,750**	**277**	Oklahoma	$147,000	34

Source: The Book of the States: 2018 (Lexington, KY: Council of State Governments, 2018), 110.

— Competency Connection —
⚙ CRITICAL THINKING ⚙

Is the Texas governor compensated too little, an appropriate amount, or excessively?

returns. If the president pro tempore is absent too, the Speaker of the House becomes acting governor.

Although the governor receives full pay when away from Texas, an acting governor receives an amount equal to the governor's daily pay (about $420) for each full day served. During Perry's run for the Republican Party's 2012 presidential nomination, the state paid Lieutenant Governor David Dewhurst a total of $29,589.[17] Even after Perry announced that he would not pursue another term as Texas governor in July 2013, Dewhurst was paid for more than 50 days as acting governor in less than a year. With an eye on another potential run for president, Perry used his final term as governor to travel around the country and to foreign destinations, such as Switzerland, Israel, London, and Palau. During his first term in office, Governor Abbott made trips to Mexico, Cuba, Europe, Israel, and Australia.

Removal from Office

Impeachment by the House of Representatives and conviction by the Senate form the only constitutionally prescribed method of forcing a Texas governor from office before the end of a term. Article XV, Section 1, of the Texas Constitution states, "The power of impeachment shall be vested in the House of Representatives." Each article of impeachment (similar to a grand jury's indictment) must be approved by a simple majority vote of the House. To remove the governor, one or more impeachment articles must be approved by a two-thirds majority vote of the senators present. Once impeached, a governor is suspended from office and may not exercise any authority unless the senators decide against conviction at the end of the Senate trial.

The penalty for conviction on an impeachment charge is removal from office and disqualification from holding any other appointive or elective office at state or local levels in Texas. But conviction does not bar the person from holding a federal office, such as U.S. senator or representative. After removal, a former governor who has been ousted for violating a criminal law may be tried and convicted in a regular trial. Violation of a civil law may subject the individual to a money judgment. Grounds for removing governors or other officials in the executive branch are not stipulated in the Texas Constitution. Impeachment proceedings are highly charged political affairs with legal overtones.

Although all of Texas's state constitutions have provided for impeachment and removal of the governor, only Governor James E. "Pa" Ferguson has been impeached and removed. His troubles stemmed from misuse of state funds and a feud with faculty and administrators of the University of Texas. On September 25, 1917, the Senate convicted Ferguson on 10 articles of impeachment, one of which charged him with official misconduct. The other nine articles involved violations of the state's banking laws and use of state funds for private gain. Although indicted and subsequently removed from office, Ferguson did not stand trial in a criminal proceeding. Reporting the outrage of University of Texas students and powerful alumni when Ferguson used his veto power on the university's state appropriation, one historian noted, "Soon after Ferguson's 'war' with the University, the Ex-Students' Association voted to remain an independent organization, outside the sphere of state control, where it would be free to defend the University again if needed."[18]

This same group united in 2013 to protect University of Texas President William Powers from efforts by the University of Texas System Board of Regents to force his resignation. Powers resigned in 2014, but his resignation did not become effective until June 2015.

✔ 9.2 Learning Check

1. True or False: The Texas governor's staff is smaller today than ever before.
2. What is the constitutional procedure for removing a governor from office?

Answers at the end of this chapter.

◪ Informal Powers of the Governor

LO 9.3 Discuss the informal powers of the governor.

A governor's ability to sway public opinion and to direct or influence the actions of other government officials depends on more than constitutional powers or powers conferred by the legislature. Informal powers are not based on law; rather, they stem from a governor's popularity with the public and are based on traditions, symbols, and ceremonies.

Many of the governor's speeches and public appearances reflect his role as chief of state, but others are political or even inspirational (for example, Governor Abbott visited a student assembly at Santa Fe High School in 2018 when students returned to school for the first time after the mass shooting there).[19] Although there was no opposition to his invitation to speak at the catholic St. Thomas University in Houston, more than 2,000 students at the University of North Texas signed an online petition requesting a different commencement speaker when Abbott was invited to address their graduation ceremony in May 2015. Reasons for opposing the invitation included Abbott's opposition to same-sex marriage and Denton's ban on "fracking," but UNT officials rejected the petition.[20]

Of course, a governor cannot accept all invitations to deliver speeches or participate in dedications, banquets, and other public events. Within the limits of time and priorities, however, every governor does attempt to play the role of chief of state. The breadth and depth of this role cannot be fully measured, but its significance should not be underestimated in determining a governor's success. Effective governors must be able to make impressive speeches, to remain at ease while communicating in interviews with newspaper and television reporters, and to communicate directly with Texans by writing (usually with staff assistance) newspaper articles of their own.[21]

In his 2010 campaign, Rick Perry recognized and made full use of the potential of social media as a campaign tool, and he continued to use it after the election to enhance his informal powers. He established direct links to his social media accounts through the official web page of the Office of the Governor, on which he also provided links to sign up for email updates, an RSS feed, and podcasts of his speeches. By the end of his time as governor, and with an eye on a potential run for the presidency in 2016, Perry's Facebook, Google, and Twitter pages were being updated several times a week. The posts highlighted his legislative victories; provided links to videos of his interviews and flattering news stories; and included pictures from his travels, holiday greetings to supporters, and more. He also regularly posted to Flickr, YouTube, Instagram, and LinkedIn. Direct communication with the public without the filter of the media allowed Perry to rally support for his causes and campaigns quickly and effectively.

Even without the national celebrity status that Perry gained through his 2012 presidential campaign, Greg Abbott began his term in 2015 with almost 400,000 likes on his Facebook page. By the beginning of his second term in office, Governor Abbott's Facebook politician page had almost 1.3 million likes, and his Office of the Governor Greg Abbott page had more than 90,000 likes. At the same time, Abbott's personal Twitter account had more than 239,000 followers and his official account more than 164,000. Although Abbott's YouTube channel had only 1,800 subscribers, he had posted 339 videos that reached over 1 million views. Abbott also used Flickr, where he had posted over 760 photos; LinkedIn, with over 500 followers; and Instagram, where he had almost 440 posts and over 9,100 followers. He has also attempted to build followings on Pinterest and Vimeo, with less success. As did Governor Perry, Governor Abbott uses his social media accounts to enhance his informal powers by engaging the public directly and managing his image in the media.[22]

Public involvement of family members may be a source of support for a governor. Laura Bush, for example, enhanced her husband's image as a governor committed to improving education. A former librarian, her First Lady's Family Literacy Initiative Program for Texas and Texas Book Festival promoted literacy and reading. Anita Perry, with bachelor's and master's degrees in nursing and 17 years of experience in various fields of nursing, often spoke on such topics as Alzheimer's disease, breast cancer awareness, and prevention of family violence. In addition, she worked with her husband to host the annual Texas Conference for Women, which addresses such issues as women's health care, personal growth, and professional development. She made history by working as a consultant for the Texas Association Against Sexual Assault. No wife of any earlier governor was employed while her husband was in office.[23]

Cecilia Abbott, the first Latina first lady in Texas history, is a former teacher and principal in Catholic schools. She left her job as managing director of community relations for a health-care provider to play a larger role in her husband's campaign but has maintained a lower profile than her predecessors. Though she prefers to avoid the media spotlight, in 2016 she launched an initiative called "Texanthropy" to promote voluntarism and service to others. She also partnered with the Texas Department of Family and Protective Services to increase support for children and families in the state's child welfare system. Texas's First Lady leads by example, volunteering for and visiting nonprofit organizations and charities, serving on the boards of several educational organizations, and maintaining memberships in numerous philanthropic groups.[24]

Like Rick Perry, Governor Abbott has gained national attention with statements concerning national affairs as well as state politics. On January 8, 2016, for example, he gave the keynote speech at the annual policy orientation event for the Texas Public Policy Foundation. In this address, Abbott unveiled a 92-page plan titled "Restoring the Rule of Law with States Leading the Way."[25]

Five months after gaining national attention with his Texas Plan, Abbott published a book that has been distributed throughout the country: *Broken but Unbowed: The Fight to Fix a Broken America.*[26] This volume is an autobiographical account of Abbott's struggle to survive the accident that put him in a wheelchair for the rest of his life, and it is linked to a description of the conservative policy battles that led to his Texas Plan. The book was released to the public at the time of the Texas Republican Party's state convention in May 2016, two years before the next gubernatorial election. Although Abbott has denied that he has interest in running for president in 2020, it remains to be seen whether he will seek the GOP nomination and election as U.S. president in future elections.

> **✓ 9.3 Learning Check**
>
> 1. True or False: The governor's informal powers are not based on law.
> 2. True or False: Public involvement of family members may be a source of support for the governor.
>
> *Answers at the end of this chapter.*

▣ Executive Powers of the Governor

LO 9.4 Explain the effect of checks and balances on the executive powers of the governor.

The governor of Texas is inaugurated on the third Tuesday in January of every fourth year, always in the odd-numbered year before a presidential election (for example, January 20, 2015). In the inauguration ceremony, the governor swears "to cause the laws to be faithfully executed."

Executive powers of the governor include nominating individuals to fill appointive offices (subject to approval of the Senate) and exercising limited control over state administration as authorized by the Texas Constitution and by statutes enacted by the Texas legislature. These powers are used to do the following:

- Nominate (and in some cases remove) state officials
- Deal with problems caused by civil disorder and natural disasters
- Participate in state budget making and budget management
- Announce policies by issuing executive orders

- Make public proclamations for ceremonial and other purposes
- Promote the economic development of Texas

In some respects, the governor exercises executive powers like those wielded by heads of other large organizations (for example, university presidents, business chief executive officers, union leaders, or the U.S. president), though with obvious differences. Of course, the executive powers of the governor of Texas resemble those of the country's other 49 state governors; however, different state laws and state constitutions give some governors more executive powers and other governors less.

Appointive Power

One of the most significant executive powers of the Texas governor is **appointive power**. The same laws that create administrative agencies allow a governor to nominate friends and political supporters. The governor's ability to nominate citizens for these positions, subject to approval by the Texas Senate, remains both an important political tool and a fundamental management power.

Department heads appointed by the governor include the secretary of state; the adjutant general, who heads the Texas Military Forces; the executive director of the Office of State-Federal Relations; the executive commissioner of health and human services; commissioners of education, insurance, and firefighters' pensions; and the chief administrative law judge of the State Office of Administrative Hearings (SOAH). The governor has the power, "notwithstanding other law," to designate and change the chairs of most state boards and commissions, either by designating a current member or appointing a new member to serve as chair. Not affected by this law are the presiding officers of governing bodies of higher education institutions and systems, along with those who advise or report to statewide elected officials other than the governor. Because he served for so long, Governor Perry managed to appoint allies and supporters to every appointed position available, making him more powerful than perhaps any governor in Texas history. As a result, Governor Abbott entered office with significantly less influence in the executive branch than his predecessor.[27]

Gubernatorial appointive power is not without certain legal and political limitations. The Texas Constitution requires that all appointees (except personal staff) be confirmed by the Senate with a two-thirds vote of senators present. This practice is known as "advice and consent," and it applies to the appointees of U.S. presidents and governors in most other states as well. To avoid rejection by the Senate, the governor respects the tradition of senatorial courtesy by obtaining approval of the state senator representing a prospective appointee's senatorial district before sending that person's name forward for Senate confirmation. Political prudence also demands that the appointments director in the governor's office conduct a background check on the appointee to avoid possible embarrassment—as occurred when, for example, Governor Dolph Briscoe appointed a dead man to a state board.

Texas governors may try to circumvent the Senate by making appointments while the Senate is not in session. The Texas Constitution, however, requires that these **recess appointments** be submitted to the Senate for confirmation within 10 days after it convenes for a regular or special session, though confirmation hearings do not have to occur immediately. Failure of the Senate to confirm

appointive power
The authority to name a person to a government office. Most gubernatorial appointments require Senate approval by two-thirds of the members present.

recess appointment
An appointment made by the governor when the Texas legislature is not in session.

a recess appointment prevents the governor from reappointing that person to the same position.

One limitation on the governor's appointive power is that the members of most state boards and commissions serve for six years, with overlapping terms of office. Thus, only one-third of the members finish a term every two years. A first-term governor must work with carryovers from previous administrations, even if such carryovers are not supportive of the new governor.

The appointive power of the governor extends to filling vacancies for elected heads of the executive departments, members of the Railroad Commission, members of the State Board of Education, district attorneys, and judges (except those for county, municipal, and justice of the peace courts). These appointees serve until they are elected or replaced at the next general election. In addition, when a U.S. senator from Texas dies, resigns, or is removed from office before his or her term expires, the governor fills the vacancy with an interim appointee. That appointee serves until a successor is elected in a special election called by the governor. A vacancy in either chamber of the Texas legislature or in the Texas delegation to the U.S. House of Representatives does not result in an interim appointment. Instead, the governor calls a special election to fill the position. The winner of the special election serves until after the next regularly scheduled general election.

Removal Power

In creating numerous boards and commissions, the legislature gives the governor extensive appointive power but no independent **removal power** over most state agencies. This limitation restricts gubernatorial control over the state bureaucracy. The legislature limits the governor's independent removal power to members of the governor's staff and three statutory officials whose offices were created by the legislature: the executive director of the Department of Housing and Community Affairs, the executive commissioner of health and human services, and the insurance commissioner.

Elected department heads and their subordinates are not subject to the governor's removal power. Moreover, the governor cannot directly remove most board and commission officials. The governor may informally pressure an appointee to resign or accept another appointment, but this pressure is not as effective as the power of direct removal. Except for the few positions described previously, governors may not remove someone appointed by a predecessor. They may remove their own appointees with the consent of two-thirds of the state senators present; however, this authority still falls short of independent removal power.

removal power
Authority to remove an official from office. In Texas, the governor's removal power is limited to staff members, some agency heads, and his or her appointees with the consent of the Senate.

Military Power

Article 4, Section 7, of the Texas Constitution states that the governor "shall be Commander-in-Chief of the military forces of the State, except when they are called into actual service of the United States." Appointed by the governor, the adjutant general commands the three branches of the Texas Military Forces (with approximate personnel numbers): Texas Army National Guard (19,000), the Texas Air National Guard (3,000), and the Texas State Guard (2,000).

IMAGE 9.3 Governor Abbott appointed Major General Tracy Norris to be Adjutant General of Texas effective January 1, 2019. The first female to hold the position, Norris now commands the Texas Military Department.

AB Forces News Collection/Alamy Stock Photo

— Competency Connection —
✦ CRITICAL THINKING ✦

Should the Governor's appointment and removal power be expanded, kept the same, or reduced?

The president of the United States can order units of the Army National Guard and Air National Guard to federal service in time of war or national emergency. Pay for National Guard personnel while on active duty and for training periods (usually one weekend each month) is the same as that for regular military personnel of the same rank. Texas State Guard units serve within Texas and support the other two branches of the Texas Military Forces. For the most part, State Guard soldiers are not paid for training activities, but when activated by the governor, they receive full pay.

In June 1943, an African American in Beaumont, Texas, was accused of raping a white woman, sparking a riot in which as many as 4,000 Anglo citizens attacked African American neighborhoods and businesses with guns, axes, and hammers. Since all Texas National Guard personnel were in federal service because of World War II, acting governor A. M. Aiken used Texas State Guard units to impose **martial law** (temporary rule by state military forces and suspension of civil authority) on Beaumont.[28] The action was taken according to the constitutional provision that the governor "shall have power to call forth the militia to execute the laws of the State, to suppress insurrections, and to repel invasions." Until the constitution was amended in 1999, this power extended to "protecting the frontier from hostile incursions by Indians or other predatory bands."

martial law
Temporary rule by military authorities when civil authorities are unable to handle a riot or other civil disorder.

As circumstances demand, the governor authorizes the mobilization of Army and Air National Guard personnel to perform relief and rescue service in counties hit by hurricanes, floods, fires, and other natural disasters. In August 2017, Governor Abbott mobilized the entire Texas National Guard in response to Hurricane Harvey. The personnel actively assisted in search and rescue missions and recovery efforts. Mobilization of the state military for disaster relief is expected and common, but other uses are more controversial. In April 2015, Governor Abbott received much criticism when he responded to demands by conspiracy theorists by ordering the Texas State Guard to monitor U.S. military forces participating in Operation Jade Helm 15. This training exercise involved about 1,200 federal personnel operating in Texas and other states in the Southwest, but some people claimed that they feared President Obama would send in some of the Islamic State's foreign fighters or Texans' firearms would be confiscated by the United Nations.[29]

The Texas Army and Air National Guard personnel also fight alongside the U.S. Army, Navy, Air Force, and Marines in foreign combat. Since the invasion of Afghanistan in 2001, more than 33,200 Texas Guard personnel have served in Afghanistan, Iraq, and other countries. Despite this service, cuts to federal government spending meant that the Texas Guard lost many of their attack helicopters to active duty branches in 2014.[30]

Law Enforcement Power

In Texas, law enforcement is primarily a responsibility of city police departments and county sheriffs' departments. Nevertheless, the Texas Department of Public Safety (DPS), headed by the Public Safety Commission, is an important law enforcement agency. The governor appoints the commission's five members, subject to Senate approval. The director of public safety is appointed by the commission and oversees more than 8,000 personnel in the DPS. Included among the department's responsibilities are highway traffic supervision, driver licensing, and criminal law enforcement in cooperation with local and federal agencies.

If circumstances demand swift but limited police action, the governor is empowered to assume command of the Texas Rangers, a division of DPS composed of a small number of highly trained law enforcement personnel operating statewide. As of February 2019, membership in this elite group totaled 178 men (124 Anglo, 44 Latino, and 10 African American) and 4 women (2 Anglo and 2 Latina).

budgetary power
The governor is supposed to submit a state budget to the legislature at the beginning of each regular session. When an appropriation bill is enacted by the legislature and certified by the comptroller of public accounts, the governor may veto the whole document or individual items.

Budgetary Power

Gubernatorial **budgetary power** is subordinated in part to the legislature's prerogative of controlling the state's purse strings. By statutory requirement, the governor (assisted by personnel in the Governor's Office of Budget and Policy and the Legislative Budget Board) should prepare separate budgets for consideration by the legislature in regular session. Texas law requires distribution of the governor's budget to each legislator before delivery of the governor's State of the State message. Traditionally, both the House and the Senate have been inclined to give greater respect to the Legislative Budget Board's spending proposals. (For further discussion of the state's budget process, see Chapter 11 "Finance and Fiscal Policy.")

The Texas governor's principal control over state spending comes from the constitutional power to veto an entire appropriations bill or to use the **line-item veto** to eliminate individual budget items. In June 2015, Governor Abbott claimed a 2016–2017 budget reduction of about $295 million from use of line-item vetoes, but $62 million were vetoes of **contingency riders** for bills that the legislature did not pass. Still, the Legislative Budget Board claimed that the governor had overstepped his authority in targeting riders. State Comptroller Glenn Hegar put the disputed funds on hold and requested an opinion from Attorney General Ken Paxton. Paxton declared the vetoes to be valid, expanding the governor's power in budget negotiations. In June 2017, this decision allowed Abbott to cut approximately $95 million from environmental protection programs using the line-item veto. The governor used his line-item veto power to cut about $120 million from the proposed budget that year.[31] In 2019, he signed a $250 billion budget without issuing a single line-item veto.

The line-item veto is an important power even when not used because legislators may avoid including items in the budget that the governor signals he will veto. Governor Perry's decision to oppose Medicaid expansion is an example. Under the Affordable Care Act, the federal government covered 100 percent of expanded access to the federal health-insurance program for low-income citizens until 2017, gradually declining to 90 percent by 2020. Texas has the largest uninsured population in the nation. In the first five years under the expanded program, the state would have received $76 billion to provide health-care coverage for poorer citizens. Expansion was strongly supported by the Texas Medical Association, Texas Hospital Association, and many other groups. Yet opposition by Governor Perry and then by Governor Abbott was a clear signal to legislators that authorizing the funding would result in a gubernatorial veto. Therefore, expansion and funding were never proposed.[32]

Executive Orders and Proclamations

Although the Texas Constitution identifies the governor as the "Chief Executive Officer of the State," it does not empower him or her to tell other state officials what they must do unless such action is authorized by the legislature. Nevertheless, governors use executive orders to set policy within the executive branch and to create or abolish task forces, boards, commissions, and councils. Each **executive order** is identified by the governor's initials and is numbered chronologically.

Executive Orders are not used frequently in Texas, with Governor Abbott issuing only one each year in 2016 and 2017 and three in 2018. Some are ceremonial, as when Abbott issued executive order GA-04 honoring the memory of George H. W. Bush after his passing. Others have a more substantive impact. In 2009, Perry's 73rd executive order (RP73) affected college students and faculty when it directed the Texas Higher Education Coordinating Board, in cooperation with public colleges and universities, to look at "opportunities for achieving cost efficiencies." Subjects under review were state funding for higher education based on courses completed, faculty workload, distance learning, alternatives to new campuses, energy use, and cost of instructional materials. Executive Order RP75, issued in August 2011, related to the establishment and support of WGU Texas

line-item veto
Action by the governor to eliminate an individual budget item while permitting enactment of other parts of an appropriation bill.

contingency rider
Authorization for spending state money to finance provisions of a bill if the bill becomes law.

executive order
The governor issues executive orders to set policy within the executive branch and to create task forces, councils, and other bodies.

(a partnership with the Western Governors University), a nonprofit independent university offering "online degrees based on demonstrated competence as opposed to degrees based on credit hours, clock hours or grades."[33]

Another instrument of executive authority is the **proclamation**, an official public announcement often used for ceremonial purposes (for example, naming January 2019 "Human Trafficking Prevention Month"). Some proclamations declare a state of emergency, as in 2014, when extreme winter weather caused a shortage of liquefied petroleum gas and Governor Perry joined several other states in issuing a proclamation waiving certain regulations and requirements in order to deliver gas throughout the region. Some proclamations identify a county or other region to be a disaster area. For example, in August 2017, Governor Abbott proclaimed a state of disaster due to Hurricane Harvey. The damage was so extensive that over the following year, the proclamation was amended to cover additional counties until 60 were included as part of the disaster area. The governor continued issuing additional proclamations renewing the state of disaster for Hurricane Harvey each month into 2019.[34] Additional uses of proclamations include calling special sessions of the legislature, calling special elections, declaring emergency items to be immediately considered by the legislature, and announcing the ratification of amendments to the U.S. Constitution.

Economic Development

The governor's office has direct control over efforts to attract investment and move businesses to Texas from other states and countries. Not only did Governor Abbott recruit specific corporations, such as moving the U.S. headquarters for Fortune 500 health-care giant McKesson Corp. to Las Colinas near Dallas, he also oversaw media and public relations campaigns in other states.[35] When the United Kingdom voted to exit the European Union in 2016, Governor Abbott launched a media campaign in England. He urged company executives who were uncertain about the stability of their country's economy to relocate to Texas.[36]

The Texas Enterprise Fund (TEF), originally funded in 2003 with $295 million from the state's "rainy day" fund (an account intended to pay for state operations in times of emergency), is used to attract or retain industries. Additional multimillion-dollar appropriations for TEF were made in subsequent state budgets until 2013, when state funding was not requested by the 83rd Legislature. Instead the Office of the Governor asked to "retain the rider that allows for the reappropriation of unexpended balances and appropriation of revenue received in order to continue the program that is already in place."[37] To complement TEF money, Perry established TexasOne, a nonprofit, tax-exempt corporation that operated with directors appointed by the governor. Its primary mission was to attract businesses from other states and countries. In launching TexasOne, Perry invited major companies and business-related groups to support the fund for three years with a range of annual tax-deductible contributions.[38] Prospective contributors were informed that visiting executives would be given "red carpet treatment throughout: flight into Texas, limousine transportation, four-star hotel accommodations, reception on arrival, evening with local and state leadership, … etc."[39]

The Emerging Technology Fund (ETF) was designed to help small to midsize companies develop new technology for a wide range of high-tech industries.

proclamation
A governor's official public announcement (such as calling a special election or declaring a disaster area).

In 2014, the fund generated controversy even among Texas Republicans. Though ETF-funded businesses showed an overall positive return in terms of job creation and tax revenue during the life of the program, 16 recipients declared bankruptcy. Gubernatorial candidate Greg Abbott repeatedly declared that Texas should not be in the in the business of "picking winners and losers."[40] In 2015, Governor Abbott replaced the Emerging Technology Fund with the Governor's University Research Initiative. With the transfer of the $40 million remaining in the ETF, the new program is designed to bring nationally recognized researchers to universities in Texas. In June 2016, Governor Abbott reintegrated TexasOne into the Texas Economic Development Corporation (TxEDC), which continued to rely on member organizations for funding. Abbott considers TxEDC and the Governor's Office of Economic Development and Tourism (EDT) to be the pillars of his economic development strategy. In 2017, the Governor's Office and TxEDC launched "GO BIG IN TEXAS®" to promote Texas as a premier destination for businesses.[41]

✓ 9.4 Learning Check

1. True or False: Most gubernatorial appointments must be approved by a two-thirds vote of the House of Representatives.
2. What constitutional power allows the governor to exercise control over state spending?

Answers at the end of this chapter.

✪ Legislative Powers of the Governor

LO 9.5 Analyze the shared power of the executive and legislative branches.

Perhaps the most stringent test of a Texas governor's capacity for leadership involves handling legislative matters. The governor has no direct lawmaking authority, but **legislative power** is exercised through four major functions authorized by the Texas Constitution:

- Delivering messages to the legislature
- Signing bills and concurrent resolutions
- Vetoing bills and concurrent resolutions
- Calling special sessions of the legislature

However, the success of a legislative program depends heavily on a governor's ability to bargain with influential lobbyists and legislative leaders (in particular, the Speaker of the House of Representatives and the lieutenant governor).[42]

Message Power

Article 4, Section 9, of the Texas Constitution requires the governor to deliver a State of the State address at the "commencement" (beginning) of each regular session of the legislature, but this directive is not interpreted to mean the first day of the session. On occasion, the governor may also present other messages, either in person or in writing, to the legislature. A governor's success in using **message power** to promote a harmonious relationship with the legislature depends on such variables as the timing of messages concerning volatile issues, the support of the governor's program by the chairs of legislative committees, and the governor's personal popularity with the public.

legislative power
A power of the governor exercised through messages delivered to the Texas legislature, vetoes of bills and concurrent resolutions, and calls for special legislative sessions.

message power
The governor's effectiveness in communicating with legislators via the State of the State address at the commencement of a legislative session and other gubernatorial messages delivered in person or in writing.

IMAGE 9.4 Governor Greg Abbott greets Malik Jefferson after the Longhorns beat the Sooners on October 10, 2015.

Competency Connection
☼ **CRITICAL THINKING** ☼

How does visiting events like the Texas-Oklahoma football game strengthen the governor's informal powers?

Bill Signing Power

While the legislature is in session, the governor indicates approval by signing bills and concurrent resolutions within 10 days (not counting Sundays) after receiving them. Bills and concurrent resolutions that are neither signed nor vetoed by the governor during that period become law anyway. After the legislature adjourns, however, the governor has 20 days (counting Sundays) to veto pending bills and concurrent resolutions.

Most media coverage of signings is the result of photo ops staged in Austin or elsewhere weeks or even months after official signings. Defenders of these ceremonial re-signings contend that the events help inform Texans about new laws. Critics insist that the principal objective of the signings is to give favorable publicity to the governor, bill sponsors, and others who wish to be identified with the legislation.[43]

Veto Power

The governor's most direct legislative tool is the power to block legislation with a veto. During a legislative session, the governor vetoes a bill by returning it unsigned (with written reasons for not signing) to the chamber in which the bill originated. If the legislature is no longer in session, a vetoed bill is filed with the secretary of state. **Veto power** takes different forms. In addition to general veto authority, the governor has the line-item veto (described earlier in this chapter), which can be used to eliminate one or more specific spending authorizations in an appropriation bill while permitting enactment of the remainder of the budget. Using the line-item veto power to refuse funding for a specific agency, the governor can effectively eliminate that agency. This line-item veto authority places the governor in a powerful bargaining position with individual legislators in the delicate game of **pork-barrel politics**. That is, the governor may strike a bargain with a senator or representative in which the chief executive promises not to deny funding for a lawmaker's pet project (the pork). In return, the legislator agrees to support a bill favored by the governor.

During a session, the governor's veto can be overridden by a two-thirds majority vote in both houses; but overriding a veto has occurred only once since the administration of Governor W. Lee O'Daniel (1939–1941). In 1979, the House and Senate overrode Governor Clements's veto of a bill giving Comal County commissioners power to establish hunting and fishing regulations for the county. The strong veto power that the Texas Constitution gives to the governor and the governor's informal power of threatening to veto a bill are formidable weapons for dealing with legislators.

The governor of Texas may also exercise a **postadjournment veto** by rejecting any pending legislation within 20 days after a session ends. Because most bills pass late in a legislative session, the postadjournment veto allows the governor to veto measures without threat of any challenge. In 2019, Governor Abbott issued 51 postadjournment vetoes.

Throughout most of the 77th Legislature's regular session in 2001, Governor Perry vetoed only a few bills. But in what some critics termed the "Father's Day Massacre," he exercised 78 postadjournment vetoes at 9 P.M. on the last possible day to do so (June 17). Surpassing Governor Clements's 59 vetoes in 1989, Perry's total of 82 vetoes in 2001 set a record. For the following six regular legislative sessions, his veto totals varied between a low of 19 (79th, 2005) and a high of 51 (80th, 2007).[44]

Governor Abbott vetoed 50 bills passed by the 85th Legislature in 2017. Among the bills vetoed was one (SB 667) aimed at establishing a guardianship compliance program to protect elderly and incapacitated Texans from neglect and financial exploitation. The bill had near unanimous support in the legislature, with all members of the committee handling it signing on as coauthors. The bill passed the Texas Senate with the support of all but one senator. Legislators were so confident about the clarity of the problem and the solution that Abbott's veto, and his explanation that the bill represented "unnecessary bureaucracy and unnecessary spending," came as a surprise. Senator Judith Zaffarini said, "I was truly shocked and dismayed, and that is an understatement. I was just flabbergasted. We didn't even worry about a veto. Not of this bill."[45] The governor vetoed 55 bills and 2 concurrent resolutions passed by the 86th Legislature in 2019.

Special Sessions Power

Included among the governor's powers is the authority to call special sessions of the legislature. The Texas Constitution places no restrictions on the number of special sessions a governor may call, but the length of a special session is limited to 30 days. During a special session, the legislature may consider only

veto power
Authority of the governor to reject a bill or concurrent resolution passed by the legislature.

pork-barrel politics
A legislator's tactic to obtain funding for a pet project, usually designed to be of special benefit for the legislator's district.

postadjournment veto
Rejection by the governor of a pending bill or concurrent resolution during the 20 days after a legislative session ends.

those matters the governor specifies in the call or subsequently presents to the legislature. The two exceptions to this requirement of gubernatorial approval are confirmation of appointments and impeachment proceedings. The threat of calling a special session is a tool the governor wields to influence the legislature to heed his wishes.

Rick Perry called 12 special sessions during his 15 years as governor, including three sessions in 2013. The first of the 2013 special sessions drew national and international attention when Senator Wendy Davis (D-Ft. Worth) delivered a marathon filibuster against a bill to restrict access to abortions. Satisfied with the legislature's support of his legislative agenda, Governor Abbott did not call a special session after the 85th Legislature in 2015. In July 2017, Abbott called a special session at the urging of Lieutenant Governor Dan Patrick. Patrick wanted to pressure legislators to pass the controversial "bathroom bill" to require transgender individuals to use bathrooms corresponding to their sex at birth (SB6). Abbott agreed and added 19 additional items to the special session agenda, including antiabortion, education, property tax, and other proposals. On the last day of the special session, not a single one of Abbott's 20 items had received an up or down vote. The governor threatened to call another special session. Lawmakers passed nine items on his agenda and adjourned.[46]

> ✓ **9.5 Learning Check**
>
> 1. True or False: During a session, the governor's veto can be overridden by a two-thirds majority vote in the House and in the Senate.
> 2. How can the legislature be convened for a special session?
>
> *Answers at the end of this chapter.*

★ Judicial Powers of the Governor

LO 9.6 Illustrate powers the governor exercises over the judicial branch of state government.

The governor exercises a few formal judicial powers, including the power to do the following:

- Fill vacancies on state (but not county or city) courts
- Play a limited but outdated role in removing judges and justices
- Perform acts of clemency to undo or reduce sentences given to some convicted criminals

Appointment and Removal of Judges and Justices

More than half of Texas's state judges and justices first serve on district courts and higher appellate courts through gubernatorial appointment to fill a vacancy caused by the creation of a new state court or a judge's death, resignation, or removal from office. The Texas judicial system has been heavily influenced by Governor Perry, whose long tenure allowed him to appoint almost 250 judges. The vast majority of them share Perry's pro-business stance. As a result, winning cases against large corporations in Texas is difficult.[47] Like other governors, Perry used this power to diversify the state's judicial system. For example, Governor Perry twice made history with his appointments of Wallace B. Jefferson, initially as the first African American to serve on the Texas Supreme Court and then, in 2004, as the first African American chief justice of that court. Chief Justice Jefferson returned to the private practice of law in 2013. In 2004, Perry appointed his former general counsel, David Medina, a Latino, to the Texas Supreme Court; and in 2009, he named Justice Eva Guzman as the first Latina to serve on that court. Nearly all his appointees to the Texas Supreme Court won subsequent election.[48]

Governor Abbott was elected as a state district court judge in 1992. Three years later, Governor George W. Bush appointed him to the Supreme Court of Texas, where he served for seven years before being elected as the state's attorney general. During his first term as governor, Abbott appointed one Texas Supreme Court justice (Jimmy Blacklock), five District Courts of Appeals justices, and 24 District Court judges.

According to Article XV, Section 8, of the Texas Constitution, the governor may remove any jurist "on address of two-thirds of each house of the Legislature for willful neglect of duty, incompetence, habitual drunkenness, oppression in office, or other reasonable cause which shall not be sufficient ground for impeachment." Governors and the legislature have not used this process for many years. Instead, they have left removal of state jurists to other proceedings and to voters. (See Chapter 10, "The Judicial Branch," for a discussion of the disciplining and removal of judges and justices.)

Acts of Executive Clemency

Until the mid-1930s, Texas governors had extensive powers to undo or lessen punishment for convicted criminals through acts of clemency that set aside or reduced court-imposed penalties. A constitutional amendment adopted in 1936 reduced the clemency powers of the governor and established the Board of Pardons and Paroles, which is now a division of the Texas Department of Criminal Justice.

Release of a prisoner before completion of a sentence on condition of good behavior is called **parole**. The seven-member Board of Pardons and Paroles, along with 14 commissioners appointed by the Chair, grants parole without action by the governor. The governor, however, may perform various acts of executive clemency that set aside or reduce a court-imposed penalty through pardon, reprieve, or commutation of sentence. Only if recommended by the Board of Pardons and Paroles can the governor grant a full pardon or a conditional pardon; however, pardons are rare in Texas. In fiscal year 2017, for example, the board considered 92 requests for full pardon and recommended clemency for 16 of these cases, and the governor granted full pardons to seven. Governor Abbott continued the tradition of announcing pardons around Christmas each year. He granted between four and seven pardons per year during his first term in office.[49]

A **full pardon** releases a person from all consequences of a criminal act and restores the same rights enjoyed by persons who have not been convicted of crimes. Pardons can be granted posthumously. In 2010, Governor Perry granted a full pardon to Timothy Cole after DNA evidence proved he had been wrongfully imprisoned for more than 13 years. Unfortunately, Cole died in prison nine

parole
Supervised release from prison before completion of a sentence, on condition of good behavior.

full pardon
An act of executive clemency, on recommendation of the Board of Pardons and Paroles, that releases a convicted person from all consequences of a criminal act and restores the same rights enjoyed by others who have not been convicted of a crime.

years before the pardon.[50] As attorney general, Greg Abbott subsequently issued an opinion stating that pardons could be granted posthumously.

Under a **conditional pardon**, the governor may withhold certain rights, such as being licensed to practice a selected occupation. The governor may unilaterally revoke a conditional pardon if the terms of that pardon are violated.

The governor may also independently grant one 30-day reprieve in a death sentence case. A **reprieve** temporarily suspends execution of a condemned prisoner, but governors seldom grant reprieves. Rick Perry's decision not to grant a reprieve to Cameron Todd Willingham, who was executed in 2004, subjected the governor to substantial criticism when subsequent evidence suggested that Willingham might have been innocent. In the midst of controversy over the Willingham case, former governor Mark White stated in an interview on National Public Radio that it was time for Texas to reconsider use of the death sentence. White had strongly supported capital punishment while he was governor (1983–1987).[51]

If recommended by the Board of Pardons and Paroles, the governor may reduce a penalty through **commutation of sentence** and may remit (return) forfeitures of money or property surrendered as punishment. In June 2005 Governor Perry commuted the sentences of 28 death row inmates convicted of crimes committed when they were younger than age 18. He took this action after the U.S. Supreme Court ruled in *Roper v. Simmons*, 543 U.S. 551 (2005), that the Eighth Amendment's ban on cruel and unusual punishment precludes the execution of those who were minors at the time they committed their crimes. More than a decade and 140 executions later, Governor Abbott commuted his first sentence. Abbott spared the life of Thomas Whitaker less than an hour before his scheduled execution in February 2018. Whitaker will remain in prison for life without possibility of parole.[52]

✪ The Plural Executive

LO 9.7 Describe the powers of the secretary of state and elected department heads.

Politically, the governor is Texas's highest-ranking officer; but the governor and the lieutenant governor share executive power with four department heads elected for four-year terms. These department heads (with annual salaries budgeted by the legislature for the biennial period covering fiscal years 2020–2021) are the attorney general ($153,750), comptroller of public accounts ($153,750), commissioner of the General Land Office ($140,938), and commissioner of agriculture ($140,938). The secretary of state, with a salary of $132,924 in fiscal years 2020–2021, is appointed by, and serves at the pleasure of, the governor. Positions of governor, lieutenant governor, comptroller of public accounts, and commissioner of the General Land Office are created in Article IV of the Texas Constitution. The commissioner of agriculture holds an office created by statute, now located in the Texas Agriculture Code. These executive officials are referred to collectively as the state's **plural executive**. Also performing executive functions are the three elected members of the Railroad Commission of Texas

---

✓ **9.6 Learning Check**

1. True or False: A vacancy on a Texas district court or higher appellate court is filled by gubernatorial appointment.
2. Which Texas official has power to independently grant one 30-day reprieve in a death sentence case?

Answers at the end of this chapter.

conditional pardon
An act of executive clemency, on recommendation of the Board of Pardons and Paroles, that releases a convicted person from the consequences of his or her crime but does not restore all rights, as in the case of a full pardon.

reprieve
An act of executive clemency that temporarily suspends execution of a sentence.

commutation of sentence
On the recommendation of the Board of Pardons and Paroles, the reduction of a sentence by the governor.

plural executive
The governor, elected department heads, and the secretary of state, as provided by the Texas Constitution and statutes.

(six-year term, $140,937 salary) and the 15 elected members of the State Board of Education (four-year term, nonpaying).

Elected department heads are largely independent of gubernatorial control. However, with the exception of the office of lieutenant governor, should one of these positions become vacant during an official's term of office, the governor, with Senate approval, appoints a successor until the next general election.

Rep. Lyle Larson (R–San Antonio) points out that several states have a cabinet system wherein the governor appoints most agency heads. To increase efficiency and transparency in Texas, he and others suggest a series of constitutional amendments that would change the way the Lone Star State's top administrative officials are selected. Larson warns, "Though the status quo is comfortable and change rarely is, we must resist the temptation to avoid major overhauls that will ultimately improve our state." He insists, "If we want to change government, we need to change its architecture. Shaking the pillars of government can and often does lead to great outcomes."[53] Are Texans ready for a cabinet government rather than a plural executive?

The Lieutenant Governor

Constitutional qualifications for the office of lieutenant governor are the same as for the governor. Some observers consider the lieutenant governor to be the most powerful Texas official, yet the **lieutenant governor** functions less in the executive branch than in the legislative branch, where he or she serves as president of the Senate. The Texas Constitution requires the Senate to convene within 30 days whenever a vacancy occurs in the lieutenant governor's office. Senators then elect one of their members to fill the office as acting lieutenant governor until the next general election. Thus, the Senate chose Senator Bill Ratliff (R–Mount Pleasant) to replace Lieutenant Governor Rick Perry when Perry succeeded Governor George W. Bush following the 2000 presidential election.

The annual state salary for the office of lieutenant governor is only $7,200, the same as that paid to members of the legislature. Like legislators, the lieutenant governor may also hold a paying job in private business or practice a profession. For example, from 1992 to 1998, Lieutenant Governor Bob Bullock was affiliated with the law firm of Scott, Douglass, & McConnico, LLP, in Austin, from which he received a six-figure annual salary.

With experience as a conservative talk-show host in Houston, Patrick is a colorful campaigner; and with strong Tea Party support, he easily defeated Sen. Leticia Van de Putte (D–San Antonio) in the 2014 general election. Patrick chaired Donald Trump's 2016 presidential campaign in Texas. As president of the Senate for the 85th Legislature, Patrick took strong stands in favor of limiting local property tax increases and requiring transgender Texans to use restrooms that correspond with the sex noted on their birth certificates. He pushed Governor Abbott aggressively for a special session to address the bathroom bill when it failed to pass during the regular session. At the same time, he supported a variety of restrictions on abortion and government subsidies for private schooling and homeschooling.

lieutenant governor
Popularly elected constitutional official who serves as president of the Senate and is first in the line of succession if the office of governor becomes vacant before the end of a term.

The Attorney General

One of Texas's most visible and powerful officeholders is the **attorney general**. Whether joining lawsuits to overturn federal health-care reform, arguing affirmative action questions in court, or trying to resolve redistricting disputes, the state's chief lawyer is a major player in making many important public policy decisions. This officer represents the state in civil litigation and issues advisory opinions on legal questions if requested by state and local authorities. To qualify for the office of attorney general, one must have been a practicing attorney in Texas for at least five years before taking office.

In 2014, Sen. Ken Paxton (R-McKinney) was elected Attorney General to replace Greg Abbott, who was elected Governor. Then Paxton won the general election in November against Democratic challenger Sam Houston by over 20 percentage points.

With more than 4,100 employees, the Office of the Attorney General gives advice concerning the constitutionality of many pending bills. The governor, heads of state agencies, and local government officials also request opinions from the attorney general on the scope of an agency's or official's jurisdiction and the interpretation of vaguely worded laws. Although neither judges nor other officials are bound by these opinions, the attorney general's rulings are considered authoritative unless overruled by court decisions or new laws. In an advisory opinion in 2015, the attorney general stated that government officials, including county clerks, their employees, justices of the peace, and judges could refuse to issue marriage licenses or perform marriage ceremonies for same-sex couples, so long as the official had a "sincerely held religious belief" against such unions.[54]

Another power of the attorney general is to initiate, in a district court, quo warranto proceedings, which challenge an official's right to hold public office. Such action may lead to removal of an officeholder who lacks a qualification set by law or who is judged guilty of official misconduct. Among its many functions, the Office of the Attorney General enforces child support orders issued by state courts and administers the Crime Victims' Compensation Fund.

As attorney general, Greg Abbott filed 34 lawsuits against the federal government between 2002 and 2014. Three of the cases were filed while George W. Bush was serving as president. The remaining 31 were filed during the Obama administration. Most frequently, the attorney general sued the Environmental Protection Agency. He also brought lawsuits challenging the Affordable Care Act and asking federal courts to approve Texas's redistricting maps and voter identification law.[55] Attorney General Paxton continued the practice, suing to strike down Obama administration policies an additional 27 times. With the advent of the Trump administration, Paxton's focus shifted to using lawsuits to defend Trump's policy agenda and other socially conservative causes. For example, Texas initiated or joined lawsuits to allow businesses to refuse service to same-sex couples, to restrict the use of restrooms by transgender Americans, to place religious symbols in government buildings, to attack gun regulations, and to end DACA (a program allowing those brought as children to the United States illegally by their parents to remain in the country).[56]

The attorney general also submits *amicus curiae* briefs on behalf of the state's efforts to influence the outcome of court cases. In 2016, Paxton maintained his attack on the Department of Education's transgender bathroom policy, when his

attorney general
The constitutional official elected to head the Office of the Attorney General, which represents the state government in lawsuits and provides legal advice to state and local officials.

office filed an amicus curiae brief in a case filed by the State of Virginia challenging the Department of Education's directive.[57]

Although the attorney general is the state's chief legal officer, Paxton has had personal legal problems that have affected his service. Even before he won the GOP nomination with strong Tea Party backing in 2014, Ken Paxton was fined $1,000 by the State Securities Board for soliciting clients for an investment company without being licensed as an investment adviser. After the November 2014 election, Texans for Public Justice brought this matter to the attention of the Travis County district attorney. Subsequently, it was referred to the district attorney for Collin County, where Paxton had solicited clients for Mowery Capital Management. An investigation was conducted by Texas Rangers, and as a part of that investigation, additional evidence was discovered that indicated Paxton had also solicited investors, including some of his fellow legislators, for another company, Servergy, Inc. Paxton received 100,000 shares of stock for doing so and failed to disclose this information to potential investors. He had also failed to register as a dealer for this series of transactions. On July 28, 2015, a grand jury indicted Paxton on three felony charges. After numerous delays in bringing the case to court, the Texas Court of Criminal Appeals blocked payments to the special prosecutors in November 2018. The attorneys are seeking a rehearing. If they remain unpaid, they may be unable to continue the case. While awaiting trial in state court, Paxton was hit with a civil complaint by the federal Securities and Exchange Commission in 2016 for misleading investors. The federal case against him was dismissed by jurors two years later. Paxton claims the cases are political witch hunts. Though he won reelection in 2018, it was by less than four percentage points.[58]

The Comptroller of Public Accounts

One of the most powerful elected officers in Texas government is the **comptroller of public accounts**, the state's chief accounting officer and tax collector; but there are no formal qualifications for this office. After a biennial appropriation bill passes by a simple majority vote in the House and Senate, the Texas Constitution requires the comptroller's certification that expected revenue will be collected to cover all of the budgeted expenditures. Otherwise, an appropriation must be approved by a four-fifths majority vote in both houses. As explained in a newspaper editorial,

> The comptroller's estimate, always a touchy subject, has been more so since 2011, when then Comptroller Susan Combs issued what turned out to be a vastly underestimated estimate that showed a $27 billion dollar deficit. The Legislature responded with a $5.4 billion cut in public education spending. To this day, some conspiracy theorists, including members of our editorial board, suspect that the extreme lowball was deliberate and that bringing the public education system to its knees was an endgame.[59]

In 2014, Republican Glenn Hegar of Katy won election to the office of Comptroller of Public Accounts. He defeated Democratic challenger Joi Chevalier in his 2018 reelection bid. As the state's comptroller, Hegar supervises almost

comptroller of public accounts
An elected constitutional officer responsible for collecting taxes, keeping accounts, estimating revenue, and serving as treasurer for the state.

2,800 employees. The comptroller's office promotes the cause of transparency in government by maintaining the new Comptroller. Texas.Gov website. This site allows anyone to see how state tax money is being spent. For example, you can find the amount of money Hegar's department and other state agencies have paid to individual vendors for goods or services or to its employees for official travel expenses. One of the comptroller's duties is to designate hundreds of Texas financial institutions (mostly banks, but also a few savings associations and credit unions) to serve as depositories for state-collected funds. The comptroller's office also administers college savings plans, scholarships, and other financial aid.

As directed by the legislature, Hegar promotes consistency in accounting methods and standards by all state agencies; he does the same for Texas's counties, cities, and special districts. In a statement to the general public, he describes his job as like that of a corporation's chief financial officer (CFO) and explains, "A CFO's duties usually include keeping the books, monitoring cash flows and maintaining a constant watch on the company's financial health. And that's my job—except I work for you."[60]

The Commissioner of the General Land Office

Although less visible than other elected executives, the **commissioner of the General Land Office** is an important figure in Texas politics; but there are no formal qualifications for this government position. Since the creation of the General Land Office under the Constitution of the Republic of Texas (1836), the commissioner's duties have expanded to include overseeing the state's public lands and thus awarding oil, gas, and sulfur leases for lands owned by the state (including wind rights especially in the Texas tidelands); serving as chair of the Veterans Land Board; and sitting as an ex officio member of other boards responsible for managing state-owned lands. In addition to these responsibilities, the General Land Office maintains an archive of more than 35 million documents and historic maps relating to land titles in Texas. With about 575 employees, the General Land Office also oversees growth of the Permanent School Fund, which is financed by oil and gas leases, rentals, and royalties and which each year provides hundreds of millions of dollars to benefit the state's public schools.

In 2018, Land Commissioner George P. Bush sparked a battle with the State Board of Education over disbursement of education funds. Elected in 2014 and reelected in 2018, the Republican is a member of the third generation of the Bush family to hold office for Texas. He is the grandson of former Texas congressman and president of the United States George H. W. Bush, and nephew of former Texas governor and president of the United States George W. Bush. Under Commissioner Bush's leadership, the School Land Board declined in 2018 for the first time ever to allocate money from its fund to the State Board of Education (SBOE). In the past eight funding cycles, the School Land Board allocated part of its funding directly to school funding and part to the SBOE, which used it largely for textbooks. This time, Bush directed that all of its $600 million go to the Available School Fund, arguing that the land office's investment fund is more profitable and more directly beneficial to schools. After contentious hearings before the

commissioner of the General Land Office
As head of Texas's General Land Office, this elected constitutional officer oversees the state's extensive landholdings and related mineral interests, especially oil and gas leasing, for the benefit of the Permanent School Fund.

Texas Legislature, Bush agreed to release $55 million to the SBOE. Still, this was far less than the $490 million allocated in FY 2018–2019.[61]

Because the General Land Office administers vast landholdings for the state, the commissioner is involved in many legal disputes. In 2018, Commissioner Bush filed a federal lawsuit to lift habitat protections for the golden cheeked warbler, an endangered species of bird. Taking the warbler off the endangered species list would have opened a large area in Central Texas to increased development and road building. Environmental groups supported continued protections. In 2019, a U.S. district court judge affirmed a decision by the U.S. Fish and Wildlife Service to keep the warbler on the endangered species list. The case was only the latest instance of the Texas government aligning with property rights advocates to target a species for delisting. The strategy was pioneered and used extensively by former comptroller Susan Combs, who assisted Bush in the warbler suit.[62]

The Commissioner of Agriculture

Under Section 5, Chapter 11 of the Texas Agriculture Code, for at least five of the 10 years before taking office as **commissioner of agriculture** a person must have had significant experience in the business of agriculture and owned or operated farm, ranch, or timber land. These criteria are important, but identification with the state's voters (most of whom live in suburbs or central cities) is the principal requirement for winning the office.

This state officer oversees the nearly 620 employees in the Texas Department of Agriculture and is responsible for enforcing agricultural laws and for providing service programs to Texas farmers, ranchers, and consumers. Control over the use of often controversial pesticides and herbicides is exercised through the department's Pesticide Programs Division. This division restricts the use of high-risk chemicals; it licenses dealers, professional applicators, and private applicators who apply dangerous pesticides and herbicides on their own farms and ranches. Other enforcement actions of the department include inspections to determine the accuracy of commercial scales, pumps, and meters. Such inspections protect Texas consumers at grocery store scales, gasoline pumps, and other venues.

An endorsement by Governor Rick Perry and ties to rocker Ted Nugent helped Republican Sid Miller win election to the office of Agriculture Commissioner in 2014. He has generated controversy ever since. During his first year as commissioner of agriculture, Miller received criticism for some of his appointments and for bonuses paid to department employees, for dropping the ban on deep-fried food and soft drinks in school lunchrooms, and for making two Facebook postings considered by many viewers to be anti-Muslim. When the legislature failed to appropriate money that he had requested for his agency, Miller alienated many farmers, business people, and legislators by increasing fees charged for its services. In 2016, Texas Rangers investigated Miller's use of state and campaign money for 2015 trips to Oklahoma for medical treatment and to Mississippi to rope calves in a rodeo. Though he reimbursed travel costs to the state and prosecutors decided against pressing criminal charges, the Texas Ethics Commission fined Miller $500 for the Oklahoma trip four years

commissioner of agriculture
The elected official, whose position is created by statute, who heads Texas's Department of Agriculture, which promotes the sale of agricultural commodities and regulates pesticides, aquaculture, egg quality, weights and measures, and grain warehouses.

later in December 2018. Miller was an avid supporter of Donald Trump's 2016 presidential campaign, and Miller's Twitter account garnered national attention by identifying Hillary Clinton with a vulgar expletive. The commissioner's Facebook page receives much criticism because he regularly posts inflammatory attacks on people and groups with whom he disagrees and at times spreads false, misleading, or unsupported news stories. In his 2018 reelection bid, numerous

📋 STUDENTS IN ACTION

The Mickey Leland Environmental Internship Program

What IT Is

The Mickey Leland Environmental Internship Program was founded in 1992 by the Texas Water Commission, which was a predecessor to the current Texas Commission on Environmental Quality. While representing Houston districts in the Texas House of Representatives (1973–1979) and the U.S. House of Representatives (1979–1989), Mickey Leland worked to promote a clean and healthy environment, proving to be an effective leader on environmental issues within Texas, as well as the entire nation. Congressman Leland was a member of the Subcommittee on Health and Environment and encouraged public awareness in the protection of public health, as well as environmental issues. In 1989, this African American Texan died in a plane crash while flying to visit a Sudanese refugee camp in Ethiopia. The internship in his honor is designed to continue his work of increasing awareness of environmental issues, encouraging students to consider careers in the environmental field, and promoting the participation of minorities and the disadvantaged in environmental policy development. Learn more at the internship's website, https://www.tceq.texas.gov/jobs/mickeyleland.

What You Can Do

Undergraduate students enrolled full-time are eligible to apply for the internship program. Depending on your area of study, the internship offers the opportunity to fit a broad range of interests while

Mickey Leland Environmental Internship Program students, summer 2015

Texas Commission on Environmental Quality

providing a hands-on experience within the Texas legislature. Students are involved in the decisions and actions of the legislature, including researching and drafting legislation, as well as attending committee hearings, working on special projects, and assisting in general office operations.

How It Helps

Any internship provides the ever-important real-world experience that businesses and professionals look for upon graduation. The Mickey Leland Internship is no exception and encourages careers in law, political science, communications, psychology, and education, among others.

— Competency Connection —
✦ PERSONAL RESPONSIBILITY ✦

How might an internship like this one empower you to develop your own skills and benefit your state?

powerful statewide interest groups, including the Texas Farm Bureau, declined to endorse Miller despite endorsing every other Republican statewide candidate. In spite of the controversy, Miller survived a primary election challenge from two fellow Republicans and defeated Democratic challenger Kim Olson to win reelection in 2018.[63]

The Secretary of State

The only constitutional executive officer appointed by the governor is the **secretary of state**. This appointment must be confirmed by a two-thirds vote of the Senate. The secretary of state has a four-year term concurrent with that of the governor but may be dismissed by the governor at any time. Most secretaries of state do not serve for a full term. The secretary of state oversees a staff of approximately 180 people and is the chief elections officer of Texas. Principal responsibilities of the office include the following:

- Administering state election laws in conjunction with county officials
- Tabulating election returns for state and district offices
- Granting charters (organizational documents) to Texas corporations
- Issuing permits to outside corporations to conduct business within Texas
- Processing requests for extradition of criminals to or from other states for trial and punishment

With these diverse duties, the secretary of state is obviously more than just a record keeper. How the office functions is determined largely by the occupant's relations with the governor. Governor Abbott appointed David Whitley, his former deputy chief of staff and appointments director, to be the 112th Texas Secretary of State in December 2018. However, Whitley sparked national controversy by releasing a list of 98,000 registered voters who were at some point noncitizens and referred the list to the Office of Attorney General for potential prosecution for voter fraud. Civil rights groups sued when an investigation uncovered that tens of thousands of those on the list had become citizens and were eligible to vote. A federal judge found no evidence of voter fraud and ended the state's investigation. In February 2019, 12 Senate Democrats announced their opposition to Whitley's confirmation, enough to deny him the two-thirds majority he would need to be confirmed. In May of that year, Whitley resigned shortly before the vote that would have denied his confirmation. Governor Abbott immediately rehired him to a position in the governor's office.[64]

> **✓ 9.7 Learning Check**
>
> 1. True or False: Heads of state agencies may not request opinions from the attorney general concerning the scope of their jurisdiction.
> 2. What is one important power of the secretary of state for persons desiring to establish a Texas corporation?
>
> *Answers at the end of this chapter.*

⬖ The State Bureaucracy

LO 9.8 Describe the role of the bureaucracy in governing the state of Texas.

Texans' most direct connection to their state government is through the state's bureaucracy. Whether obtaining a driver's license, driving on the state's roads, or attending a public college or university, the state bureaucracy touches the lives of the state's residents. In addition to the plural executive positions, Texas has two

secretary of state
The state's chief elections officer, with other administrative duties, who is appointed by the governor for a term concurrent with that of the governor.

popularly elected boards (the State Board of Education and the Railroad Commission) and more than 200 appointed boards, commissions, and departments that implement state laws and programs in Texas. Although the governor, with Senate approval, appoints nonelected officials, once they are in office the governor must rely on persuasion and personal or political loyalty to exercise influence. The almost 325,000 state employees who staff the agencies perform the day-to-day work of government and create what we frequently call the bureaucracy. In addition to delivering services to the people of Texas, state agencies also regulate people, occupations, and businesses. Regulation commonly shifts costs and benefits from one group to another. For example, contaminated air hurts the quality of life and increases medical costs for children with respiratory problems such as asthma, as well as for the elderly; but regulations requiring special equipment to reduce emissions from smokestacks cost businesses money. Not surprisingly, regulatory policy is fraught with controversy. This section provides highlights of some of the more active agencies in the state.

The Institutional Context

The way in which the Texas executive branch is organized has a major effect on public policy. A key reason is that the fragmentation of authority strongly affects who has access to policy decisions, as well as how visible the decision process is to the public. The large number of agencies means they are covered less by the media and, therefore, are less visible to the public. The power of the one state official to whom the public pays attention (the governor) is limited. Special interest groups, on the other hand, have strong incentives (profits) to develop cozy relationships with agency personnel; and most agencies do not have to defend their decisions before a higher authority (such as the governor), although agency regulatory decisions can be appealed to state courts.

Fragmentation of the state executive into so many largely independent agencies was an intentional move by the framers of the Texas Constitution and later legislatures to avoid centralized power. Administering state programs through boards was also thought to keep partisan politics out of public administration. Unfortunately, this fragmentation simply changes the nature of the politics, making it more difficult to coordinate efforts and hold the agencies responsible to the public.

Boards governing state agencies are not typically full-time; instead, they commonly meet quarterly. In most cases, a full-time board-appointed executive director oversees day-to-day agency operations. Boards usually make general policy decisions and leave the details to the executive director; however, some boards are much more active and involved (for example, the Texas Commission on Environmental Quality). In recent years, the governor's influence has increased through the ability to name a powerful executive commissioner to run two major agencies—the Health and Human Services Commission and the Texas Education Agency. Two important boards—the Railroad Commission of Texas (RRC) (which regulates the oil and gas industry) and the State Board of Education—are elected. Members of both tend to be quite active; however, the State Board of Education is limited by its lack of authority over the commissioner of education, who heads the Texas Education Agency and reports to the governor.

Some agencies were created in the Texas Constitution. Others were created by the legislature, either as directed by the state constitution or independent of it. As problems emerge that elected officials believe government must address, they look to existing state agencies or create new ones to provide solutions. Sometimes, citizen complaints force an agency's creation. For example, citizen outrage at rising utility rates resulted in the creation in 1975 of the Public Utilities Commission (PUC) to review and limit those rates. (Lobbying by special interest groups and the orientation of gubernatorial appointments over time, however, have changed the direction of the PUC's policies to again draw the ire of consumer advocates.) Lobbying by special interest groups to protect their own interests is also important in the creation of agencies. The most famous Texas case was lobbying by the oil and gas industry in the early 20th century to have the Railroad Commission create a system of regulation to reduce economic chaos in the fledgling industry.

The **sunset review process** is an attempt to keep state agencies efficient and responsive to current needs. Each biennium, a group of state agencies is examined by the Sunset Advisory Commission, which recommends to the legislature whether an agency should be abolished, merged, reorganized, or retained. It is the legislature that makes the final decision. At least once every 12 years, each of about 140 state agencies and other government entities must be evaluated. (Universities and courts are not subject to the process.) The Sunset Advisory Commission is composed of 10 legislators (five from each chamber) and two public members. The commission has a staff of 27 employees. In 2018–2019, it reviewed 32 agencies, including the Texas Military Department, which includes the Texas Army National Guard, Texas Air National Guard, and Texas State Guard.

A major problem with the sunset review process, according to critics, is that the legislature has little taste for the abolition or major restructuring of large agencies. For example, the Sunset Advisory Commission's staff found that the mission and byzantine regulations of the Alcoholic Beverage Commission were hopelessly outdated, yet the legislature continued the commission with only minor changes. From the Sunset Advisory Commission's authorization in 1977 through 2017, a total of 481 agencies were reviewed (some agencies were reviewed multiple times). Eighty-two percent were retained, 8 percent were abolished, and 10 percent were reorganized in major ways (such as combining two or more agencies). Of those agencies retained, some had changes, such as adding public members (people not from the regulated industry) on governing boards, improving procedures, or changing policies. According to the commission, from 1982 through 2017, the sunset process saved the state more than $981 million . In 2019, Governor Abbott signed SB68 into law. The new law requires a strategic fiscal review and zero-based budgeting for all state agencies on a schedule tied to their sunset reviews. Instead of assuming current funding levels are justified, each agency must start with a budget of zero dollars and analyze each of its functions for its needs and costs.[65]

State Employees

For most people, the face of state government is the governor, legislators, and other top officials. However, most of the work of Texas state government (called **public administration**) is done by people in agencies headed by elected officials and appointed boards. These **bureaucrats** (public employees), though often the subject

sunset review process
During a cycle of 12 years, each state agency is studied at least once to see if it is needed and efficient, and then the legislature decides whether to abolish, merge, reorganize, or retain that agency.

public administration
The implementation of public policy by government employees.

bureaucrats
Public employees.

of criticism or jokes about inefficiency and "red tape" (the rules and procedures that bureaucrats must follow), deliver governmental services to the state's residents. The public may see them in action as a clerk taking an application, a supervisor explaining why a request was turned down, or an inspector checking a nursing home.

The nature of bureaucracy is both its strength and its weakness. Large organizations, such as governments and corporations, need many employees doing specialized jobs with sufficient coordination to achieve the organization's goals. That means employees must follow set rules and procedures so they can provide relatively uniform results. When a bureaucracy works well, it harnesses individual efforts to achieve the organization's goals. Along the way, however, red tape slows the process and prevents employees from making decisions that go against the rules. State rules should mean the same in Dallas as in Muleshoe, but making decisions may seem slow, and "street level" bureaucrats may not have the authority to make adjustments for differences in local conditions. Thus, bureaucracies are necessary but sometimes frustrating.

Number of State Employees Governments are Texas's biggest employers. In 2018, the equivalent of 324,368 Texans drew full-time state paychecks (including employees of public colleges and universities). Although this number sounds like a lot, it represents only about 1 percent of the state population and places Texas among the bottom 10 states in number of state employees per capita. Texas is following a national pattern. More populated states tend to have fewer government employees relative to their population. As populations grow, most states, including Texas, hire proportionately fewer employees. From 1993 to 2018, the number of state employees declined relative to the population in both Texas and the nation because of economies of scale (meaning that as agencies grow, they may require more total employees but not as many relative to the population they serve; for example, as demand increases, many employees may be able to process more cases in the same amount of time). Another reason Texas ranks so low compared to other states is that Texas state government passes a great deal of responsibility to local governments. When local government workers are included in calculating the number of government employees, the total number of public employees increases from 105 per 10,000 residents to 500 per 10,000 residents.[66]

Competence, Pay, and Retention Although most public administrators do a good job, some are less effective than others. Many observers believe that bureaucratic competence improves with a civil service system along with good pay and benefits. In the first century of our nation, many thought that any fool could do a government job, and as a result, many fools worked in government. From local to national levels, government jobs were filled through the **patronage system**, also known as the spoils system. Government officials hired friends and supporters, with little regard for whether they were competent. The idea was that "to the victor belong the spoils." **Merit systems**, on the other hand, require officials to hire, promote, and fire government employees on the basis of objective criteria, such as tests, education, experience, and performance. If a merit system works well, it tends to produce a competent bureaucracy. A merit system that provides too much protection, however, makes it difficult to fire the incompetent and gives little incentive for the competent to excel.

patronage system
Hiring friends and supporters of elected officials as government employees without regard to their abilities.

merit system
Hiring, promoting, and firing on the basis of objective criteria, such as tests, degrees, experience, and performance.

Texas has never had a merit system covering all state employees, and the partial state merit system was abolished in 1985. What replaced it was a highly centralized compensation and classification system covering most of the executive branch but not the judicial and legislative branches or higher education. The legislature sets salaries, wage scales, and other benefits. Individual agencies are free to develop their own systems for hiring, promotion, and firing (so long as they comply with federal standards, where applicable). Critics worried that the result would be greater turnover and lower competence. A survey of state human resource directors, however, indicates that agencies have developed more flexible personnel policies that provide some protection for most employees. Moreover, patronage appointments have not become a major problem in state administration. In the words of one observer, "It's not uncommon for state agencies to become repositories for campaign staff or former officeholders.... But there are no wholesale purges" when new officials are elected.[67]

In Texas, most employees (public and private) are "at will"—that is, they can be fired or can quit for good, bad, or no reason unless they are under a contract or union agreement. The employment relationship is voluntary. Employers cannot fire workers for illegal reasons, such as race, retaliation for reporting illegal activity, or exercising civil liberties. For example, in a Virginia case, a federal appeals court held that a sheriff violated his employees' free speech rights by firing them for "liking" his opponent's campaign site on Facebook.

In recent years, Texas state government employee turnover has been consistently high: 17 to 19 percent in fiscal years 2012–2018. By comparison, in fiscal year 2014, turnover was just over 6 percent for the federal government. In 2015, turnover cost the state government $361 million, according to the State Auditor's Office's most recent estimate. In 2018, turnover reached 19.3 percent, its highest rate since auditors began tracking it in 1990. Turnover was highest for workers in social services, criminal justice, custodial positions, and medical and health occupations. The highest turnover rate (29.8 percent) was in the Juvenile Justice Department. Exit surveys (filled out by employees leaving state employment) reveal that the top three reasons for leaving are retirement, desire for higher pay or better benefits, and desire for more satisfactory working conditions.[68]

Other nonfinancial factors attract state employees. Studies consistently show that large numbers of government employees have a strong sense of service and thus find being a public servant rewarding. Three perks also increase the attractiveness of public employment: paid vacations, state holidays, and sick leave.

Another incentive for employment can be equitable treatment. For many years, Texas state government has advertised itself as an "equal opportunity employer;" however, a 2016 study conducted by the *Dallas Morning News* disclosed significant pay gaps between white men and all other gender, ethnic, and racial groups (except for Asian Americans). On average female state government employees earned 92 cents for every dollar earned by their male counterparts in 2015. Pay disparities were even more pronounced for members of historical minority groups: Latinas earned 82 cents for every dollar earned by white men, and African American women earned 84 cents for every dollar earned by white men. The highest-paying positions were most frequently held by white men, and all high-level positions were more likely to be held by whites than any other racial or ethnic group. White men outearned all other groups on a job-by-job comparison as well. For example, of the 14 Systems Analyst VI positions in the Office of the Attorney General (split equally between men and women), men's annual average earnings were $98,705, compared to women's average salaries of $84,831, a 16 percent pay gap. Earnings gaps are still smaller in government than in the private sector, but in Texas, that gap is widening in contrast to shrinking pay gaps in both the private sector and in other state governments.[69] Table 9.1 compares government employment patterns of women and historical minority groups to private sector employment patterns for the same groups.

Education

State Board of Education Oversight of Texas education is divided between the 15-member elected **State Board of Education (SBOE)** and the commissioner of education, who is appointed by the governor to run the Texas Education Agency. Over the years, the sometimes extreme ideological positions taken by many SBOE members prompted the legislature to whittle away the board's authority. For several years, the board was even made appointive rather than elective. Today, the greater power over state education is in the hands of the

State Board of Education (SBOE)
A popularly elected 15-member body with limited authority over Texas's K-12 education system.

TABLE 9.1 Texas Minorities and Women in State Government Compared with the Total Civilian State Workforce (in percentage)*

Job Category	African American Govt.	African American Total Workforce	Hispanic American Govt.	Hispanic American Total Workforce	Female Govt.	Female Total Workforce
Official, administrator	11	8	15	22	54	40
Professional	11	11	16	20	56	55
Technical	18	14	26	29	61	55
Administrative support	18	14	34	36	82	72
Skilled craft	9	10	28	52	8	12
Service and maintenance	25	13	36	52	45	52
TOTALS	**18**	**12**	**22**	**37**	**57**	**45**

*State agencies' workforces include executive agencies and higher education for fiscal year 2018; statewide civilian workforce includes both private and public workers and is for calendar year 2016.

Note on interpretation: The first cell indicates that 11 percent of Texas government officials and administrators are African American; the next cell to the right shows that 8 percent of the officials and administrators in the state's total economy are African American.

Source: Compiled from "Equal Employment Opportunity and Minority Hiring Practices Report, Fiscal Years 2017–2018," Texas Workforce Commission, Civil Rights Division, January 2019, https://twc.texas.gov/files/twc/equal-employment-opportunity-minority-hiring-practices-report-2017-2018-twc.pdf.

Competency Connection
COMMUNICATION SKILLS

How would you describe the differences between the government workforce and the total workforce? Why do you think those differences exist?

commissioner of education through control of the Texas Education Agency, but the SBOE remains important and highly controversial.

Among the board's most significant powers are curriculum approval for each subject and grade, textbook review for public schools, and management of investment of the Permanent School Fund.[70] See Chapter 11, "Finance and Fiscal Policy," for a discussion of the state revenue designated for public schools.

Representing districts with approximately equal population (1.8 million), the 15 elected SBOE members serve without salary for overlapping terms of four years. The governor appoints, with Senate confirmation, a sitting SBOE member as chair for a two-year term. Governor Greg Abbott drew media attention to his appointment of Donna Bahorich in June 2015, a second-term board member representing District 6, which comprises parts of Harris County. Bahorich, who has strong ties to the Tea Party and Lieutenant Governor Dan Patrick, homeschooled her three sons before sending them to private school. Abbott reappointed Bahorich in 2017 for a second two-year term.[71]

In the Lone Star State, the **Texas Education Agency (TEA)**, headquartered in Austin, has 805 employees. Created by the legislature in 1949, the TEA today is headed by the **commissioner of education**, appointed by the governor to a four-year term with Senate confirmation. Under former Governor Rick Perry, commissioners were closely connected and responsive to the governor. In December 2015, Governor Greg Abbott appointed Mike Morath, a Dallas Independent School District Board trustee and school choice proponent, to serve as commissioner.

The TEA has oversight authority over the state's public and charter schools and monitors statewide testing. Based on performance results, the TEA issues school and district ratings and approves school accreditation. Prior to 2018, schools were rated as "met standards," "met alternative standard," or "improvement required." The rating was based on four indices that combine test results, graduation rates, and other indicators.[72] In 2017 the Texas Legislature passed House Bill (HB) 22, which established three categories for measuring performance: student achievement, school progress, and "closing the gaps," which measures progress among economically disadvantaged students. In 2018, school districts and individual campuses began receiving grades of "A" through "F" in each category and overall. The agency has power to revoke accreditation of school districts that consistently fail to meet performance or financial standards. Revocation can result in a school district's closure.

Much of what the TEA does goes unnoticed by the general public, but some decisions receive considerable attention and have effects beyond education. Ratings of schools are advertised to draw home buyers into neighborhoods and subdivisions, and the decision to close a school or school district has profound effects on the community it serves. Thus, TEA has been cautious and often takes less drastic steps before closing schools or districts, including charter schools. In 2015, the Texas Legislature passed a law that TEA must take over a school board or close campuses in a district once a school receives "improvement required" ratings in five consecutive years. Marlin ISD reached its fifth year in 2016, and in 2017, Commissioner Morath replaced its school board with a "board of managers." In 2018, the TEA revoked Marlin's accreditation, meaning the state of Texas no longer recognized it as a public school, but granted a one-year abatement

Texas Education Agency (TEA)
Administers the state's public school system of more than 1,200 school districts and charter schools.

commissioner of education
The official who heads the TEA.

shortly thereafter. The TEA also revoked the accreditation of nearby Buckholts ISD, but granted a two-year abatement in hopes the school might improve.[73]

Boards of Regents Texas's public university systems, public universities outside the systems, and the Texas State Technical College System are governed by boards of regents. Regents are appointed by the governor for six-year terms with Senate approval. A board makes general policy, selects each university's president, and provides general supervision of its universities. In the case of systems, the board usually selects a chancellor to handle administration and to provide executive leadership. The president of one of the universities may simultaneously serve as chancellor. Day-to-day operation of the universities is in the hands of the individual school's top officials (commonly the president and the academic vice president, though terminology varies). Governance of community colleges is by local boards, as discussed in Chapter 3, "Local Governments."

Texas Higher Education Coordinating Board The **Texas Higher Education Coordinating Board (THECB)** is not a superboard of regents, but it does provide some semblance of statewide direction for all public (not private) community colleges and universities. In the 2013 sunset review process, the legislature significantly changed the agency's focus from regulation of public higher education to coordination. The sunset bill removed significant parts of the agency's authority, including the power to consolidate or eliminate low-producing academic programs and to approve capital projects.

The nine members of the board receive no pay and are appointed by the governor to six-year terms with Senate approval. The governor also appoints a student representative as a nonvoting member for a one-year term. In June 2018, Governor Abbott appointed Michelle Q. Tran, a senior at the University of Houston's Honors College working toward a Bachelor of Science degree in Economics and Mathematics, to the THECB.[74]

Gubernatorial power also extends to designating two board members as chair and vice chair, with neither appointment requiring Senate confirmation. Governors have substantial influence over higher education because they generally have a close relationship with the board. The commissioner of higher education, who runs the agency on a day-to-day basis and plays a significant role in higher education policy, is appointed (and can be removed) by the board. Commissioner Raymund Paredes, originally from El Paso, has served as commissioner since 2004.

Texas Higher Education Coordinating Board (THECB)
An agency that provides some coordination for the state's public community colleges and universities.

executive commissioner of the Health and Human Services Commission
Appointed by the governor with Senate approval, the executive commissioner administers the HHSC, develops policies, and makes rules.

Health and Human Services

The Texas Health and Human Services Commission (HHSC) coordinates social service policy. Sweeping changes were launched in 2003 when the 78th Legislature consolidated functions of 12 social service agencies under the **executive commissioner of the Health and Human Services Commission**. This legislation also began a process of privatizing service delivery, creating more administrative barriers to services, and slowing the growth of expenditures.

The executive commissioner of the HHSC is appointed by the governor for a two-year term and confirmed by the Senate. The commissioner controls the agency directly and is not under the supervision of a board; instead, executive commissioners tend to respond to the governor. As a result, governors maintain considerable influence over this area of policy. In 2018, Governor Abbott appointed Courtney Phillips, former head of Health and Human Services in Nebraska, to be executive commissioner. She is assisted by the nine-member Health and Human Services Council in the development of agency rules and policy. Members of the Council are nominated by the governor and approved by the Senate. See Figure 9.3 for the commission's organization chart and tasks of the departments. The HHSC itself handles centralized administrative support services, develops policies, and makes rules for its agencies. In addition, the commission determines eligibility for various programs, such as Temporary Assistance for Needy Families (TANF), the Supplemental Nutritional Assistance Program (SNAP), the Children's Health Insurance Program (CHIP), Medicaid, and long-term care services.

IMAGE 9.5 Governor Abbott appointed Courtney Phillips to be executive commissioner of the Texas Health and Human Services Commission. Phillips is the former chief executive officer of the Nebraska Department of Health and Human Services.

AP Images/Matt Ryerson

Competency Connection
★ **PERSONAL RESPONSIBILITY** ★

To what extent should state government work to protect and improve the health and well-being of its citizens?

FIGURE 9.3 The Consolidated Texas Health and Human Services System

Source: Based on Texas Health and Human Services Commission, https://hhs.texas.gov/sites/hhs/files//documents/about-hhs/leadership/hhsc-org-chart.pdf

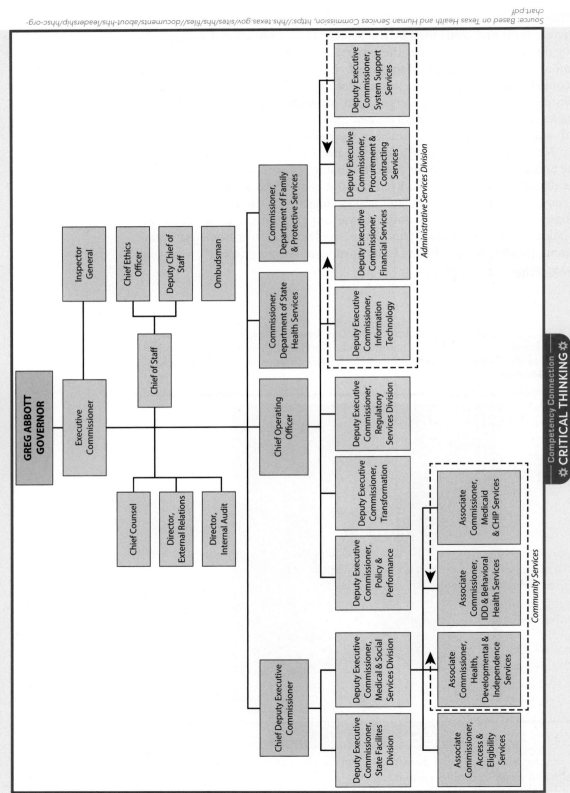

Competency Connection

✿ CRITICAL THINKING ✿

What is the most efficient and effective structure for the Texas Health and Human Services system?

Employment

Texas's state employment services cut across three areas of policy: human services, education, and economic development. The **Texas Workforce Commission (TWC)** receives appropriations from the legislature in the category of business and economic development, which probably works to its advantage because of the legislature's more friendly view of business and development. The agency serves both employers and workers. For employers, TWC offers recruiting, retention, training and retraining, outplacement services, and information on labor law and labor market statistics. For job seekers, TWC offers career development information, job search resources, training programs, and unemployment benefits. As part of this effort, the TWC matches unemployed workers with employers offering jobs. The TWC also collects an employee payroll tax paid by employers, which funds weekly benefit payments to unemployed workers covered by the Texas Unemployment Compensation Act. The unemployment benefits program provides temporary income to workers who have lost their jobs through no fault of their own. Typically, the amount paid to a qualified claimant depends on wages earned in an earlier quarter (three months).

The TWC is directed by three commissioners who receive a salary of $189,500 and are appointed by the governor, with consent of the Senate, for overlapping six-year terms. According to the statute that authorizes this commission, one member represents employers, one represents labor, and one is intended to represent the general public. In February 2016, Governor Abbott filled the labor seat on the commission by appointing Julian Alvarez, a former president of the Rio Grande Valley Partnership and Chamber of Commerce CEO. Concerning this appointment, Texas AFL-CIO President John Patrick complained, "I don't know too many workers who feel that the Chamber of Commerce really speaks for them. This makes it plain where working people stand in Gov. Abbott's agenda for Texas." Patrick described the governor's action as "a new dimension in appointing the fox to guard the henhouse."[75]

Economic and Environmental Agencies

State governmental agencies regulate business and industry, as well as provide services to make Texas an economically and environmentally inviting area in which to visit, live, and work. From regulating the oil and gas industry to building highways to balancing the needs of businesses and the environment, state agencies and their employees work to provide a quality of life acceptable to most Texans.

Railroad Commission of Texas The **Railroad Commission of Texas (RRC)** functions in several capacities, none of which has anything to do with railroads. Established in 1891 to regulate the railroads, it is the oldest regulatory agency in the state. However, in 2005, the RRC lost its last responsibilities for railroads. Today, the commission focuses primarily on the oil and gas industry. It grants permits for drilling oil and gas wells, regulates natural gas rates in rural areas, hears appeals of municipally set gas rates for residential and business customers, tries to prevent waste of petroleum resources, regulates pipeline safety, and oversees the plugging of depleted or abandoned oil

Texas Workforce Commission (TWC)
A state agency headed by three salaried commissioners that oversees job training and unemployment compensation programs.

Railroad Commission of Texas (RRC)
A popularly elected three-member commission primarily engaged in regulating natural gas and petroleum production.

and gas wells. The RRC also has jurisdiction over surface coal mining and uranium exploration.

Under law, the three commissioners are elected to six-year terms with one commissioner seeking election every two years. However, the RRC is often considered a way station in the career of rising politicians. Only a few stay six years, so many commissioners take office as a result of gubernatorial appointment. A high proportion come to office with much of their career in the oil and gas industry. The commissioners are full-time and earn $140,937 a year.

Public Utility Commission of Texas State regulation of Texas's utility companies did not begin until 1975 with the creation of the **Public Utility Commission of Texas (PUC)**. Its three members are appointed by the governor, with Senate approval, to overlapping six-year terms. They work full-time and earn $189,500 a year.

The PUC's regulatory authority is limited by both national and state policies. Its two major responsibilities are local phone service and electric utilities. PUC does not regulate long distance calling, wireless, or cable TV (regulated by the Federal Communications Commission [FCC]); natural gas utilities (Railroad Commission); water utilities (Texas Commission on Environmental Quality [TCEQ]); or municipal electric utilities (locally regulated).

Texas Department of Insurance The **commissioner of insurance** heads the Texas Department of Insurance (TDI), which regulates to some degree the $50 billion insurance industry in the Lone Star State. The commissioner is appointed by the governor for a two-year term and earns $202,383 a year. The Office of Public Insurance Counsel represents consumers in rate disputes. TDI deals with the wide range of insurance, including auto, health, home, life, wind, flood, and workers' compensation. It has a role in setting insurance rates, licenses agents and adjustors, and houses the state fire marshal.

Texas Department of Transportation The **Texas Department of Transportation (TxDOT)** deals with a wide range of transportation issues. Its major focus is the planning, design, construction, and maintenance of the state's highways and bridges (more than 80,000 miles). However, TxDOT is also involved, though to a much lesser degree, with aviation, intracoastal waterways, rail, public transportation, safety, and toll roads. The agency is headed by a five-member commission appointed by the governor, with Senate concurrence, to six-year overlapping terms. Drawing no state salary, each commissioner must be a "public" member without financial ties to any company contracting with the state for highway-related business. The commission selects an executive director who administers the department and maintains relations with the legislature and other agencies. The executive director earns $299,812 a year.

Texas Parks and Wildlife Department Responsibility for preserving Texas's natural habitats and managing public recreational areas lies with the **Texas Parks and Wildlife Department**. The nine unpaid members of its governing commission are appointed by the governor with Senate approval. The governor also designates the chair of the commission from among the members. Fees for fishing

Public Utility Commission of Texas (PUC)
A three-member appointed body with regulatory power over electric and telephone companies.

commissioner of insurance
Appointed by the governor, the commissioner heads the Texas Department of Insurance, which is responsible for ensuring the industry's financial soundness, protecting policyholders, and overseeing insurance rates.

Texas Department of Transportation (TxDOT)
Headed by a five-member appointed commission, the department maintains almost 80,000 miles of roads and highways and promotes highway safety.

Texas Parks and Wildlife Department
Texas agency that runs state parks and regulates hunting, fishing, and boating.

and hunting licenses and entrance to state parks are set by the commission. Game wardens, under the department, enforce state laws and departmental regulations that apply to hunting, fishing, trapping, and boating; the Texas Penal Code; and certain laws affecting clean air and water, hazardous materials, and human health.

Certification of Trades and Professions Citizens in more than 40 occupations—half of which are health related—are certified (licensed) to practice their profession by state boards. Each licensing board has at least one "public" member (not from the regulated occupation). All members are appointed to six-year terms by the governor with approval of the Senate. In addition to ensuring that practitioners qualify to enter a profession (giving them a license to practice), the boards are responsible for ensuring that licensees continue to meet professional standards.

Texas Commission on Environmental Quality (TCEQ) The **Texas Commission on Environmental Quality (TCEQ)**, commonly called "T-sec," coordinates the Lone Star State's environmental policies. Three full-time commission members earning $189,500 per year, an executive director earning $210,695 a year, and almost 2,700 employees oversee environmental regulation in Texas. The commissioners are named by the governor for six-year staggered terms. The governor designates one of the commissioners as chair, and the commissioners choose the executive director.

Texas Commission on Environmental Quality (TCEQ)
The state agency that coordinates Texas's environmental regulation efforts.

> ✓ **9.8 Learning Check**
>
> 1. True or False: The Sunset Advisory Commission has the authority to abolish state agencies.
> 2. Who has more control over public education in Texas: the commissioner of education or the State Board of Education?
>
> *Answers at the end of this chapter.*

CONCLUSION

Texas's constitutionally weak governor has grown stronger in recent years, but the term *chief executive* still does not accurately describe the head of the state's executive branch. The state constitution created a plural executive that diffuses power among a variety of independently elected officials. Governor Perry's power was enhanced by his long tenure and subsequent ability to appoint thousands of supporters to government posts. This advantage has begun to accrue to Governor Abbott because his ability to raise campaign money and to appeal to voters enabled him to win reelection. Use of executive, legislative, and judicial powers vested in the Texas governor by statutes and the state constitution—when combined with political leadership and informal powers not based on law—enhance the importance of the office. The executive branch also includes more than 200 appointed and elected boards, commissions, and departments that do the work of state government by implementing state laws and programs in the Lone Star State.

CHAPTER SUMMARY

LO 9.1 Analyze gubernatorial elections and the impact of campaign funds on the politics of the governorship. Successful gubernatorial candidates must meet the constitutional requirements for the office, including a minimum age of 30, U.S. citizenship, Texas residency, and acknowledgment of a Supreme Being. Historically, conservative-moderate Democrats dominated races for the office, though the trend in recent decades is for conservative Republicans to win decisive victories. Serious candidates must also procure substantial campaign funds. After election, governors often reward large campaign donors by appointing them to important government positions.

LO 9.2 Summarize how the constitution and laws of Texas provide resources, as well as succession and removal procedures, for the governor. The constitution and laws of Texas provide governors financial compensation of $153,750 per year, along with travel and security funds, fringe benefits, and a sizable staff. Succession procedures are in place for those who do not finish their terms because they resign, die, or are removed from office. Governors may be removed by House impeachment and Senate conviction, though this has only happened once.

LO 9.3 Discuss the informal powers of the governor. Since 1876, Texas governors have held a weak constitutional office. Governors rely heavily on their informal powers, which derive from their popularity with the public and are based on traditions, symbols, and ceremonies. Modern governors may enhance their informal powers by public appearances, use of traditional and electronic media, and support of family members.

LO 9.4 Explain the effect of checks and balances on the executive powers of the governor. The governor has power to appoint some department heads and members of the state's multiple boards and commissions, but only with approval of the Texas Senate. The legislature and the plural executive limit the governor's removal power. The governor checks the budgetary power of the legislature with strong veto powers, including a line-item veto. The governor may also use proclamations to call the legislature into special sessions.

LO 9.5 Analyze the shared power of the executive and legislative branches. To be successful in promoting their favored legislation, governors must bargain with lobbyists and legislators. To do so, they need to make skillful use of their formal legislative powers, which include delivering messages to the legislature, signing or vetoing bills and concurrent resolutions, and calling special sessions of the legislature.

LO 9.6 Illustrate powers the governor exercises over the judicial branch of state government. The governor fills vacancies on state courts caused by the creation of a new state court or a judge's death, resignation, or removal from office. Governors may remove judges, but only with direction by two-thirds of each house of the legislature, making it a rare occurrence. The governor may also grant clemency to undo or reduce sentences for some convicted criminals.

LO 9.7 Describe the powers of the secretary of state and elected department heads. All governors must share executive power with the lieutenant governor and four elected department heads: the attorney general (who acts as the state's chief lawyer), state comptroller (who acts as the state's chief accounting officer and tax collector), land commissioner (who manages the state's land and the revenue it produces), and agriculture commissioner (who both regulates and promotes Texas agriculture). The only appointed executive department head provided for in the Texas Constitution is the secretary of state, whose responsibilities include administering elections, granting charters and permits to corporations, and processing requests for extradition of criminals.

LO 9.8 Describe the role of the bureaucracy in governing the state of Texas. State boards, commissions, and departments are the agencies that implement laws and programs in Texas. Day-to-day work of governing the state is done by more than 325,000 state employees. Every 12 years (and sometimes more frequently) agencies are reviewed by the Sunset Advisory Commission. This small commission provides recommendations to the legislature on the continuation and any needed modifications for the reviewed agencies. Important state services like education, health, and human services are overseen by state agencies. In addition, insurance, business, and the environment are regulated by the state through boards, commissions, and departments.

KEY TERMS

appointive power, p. 329
attorney general, p. 342
budgetary power, p. 332
bureaucrats, p. 349
commissioner of agriculture, p. 345
commissioner of education, p. 353
commissioner of insurance, p. 358
commissioner of the General Land Office, p. 344
commutation of sentence, p. 340
comptroller of public accounts, p. 343
conditional pardon, p. 340
contingency rider, p. 333
executive commissioner of the Health and Human Services Commission, p. 354
executive order, p. 333
full pardon, p. 339

governor's office, p. 324
legislative power, p. 335
lieutenant governor, p. 341
line-item veto, p. 333
martial law, p. 331
merit system, p. 350
message power, p. 335
parole, p. 339
patronage system, p. 350
plural executive, p. 340
pork-barrel politics, p. 337
postadjournment veto, p. 337
proclamation, p. 334
public administration, p. 349
Public Utility Commission of Texas (PUC), p. 358
Railroad Commission of Texas (RRC), p. 357
recess appointment, p. 329

removal power, p. 330
reprieve, p. 340
secretary of state, p. 347
State Board of Education (SBOE), p. 352
sunset review process, p. 349
Texas Commission on Environmental Quality (TCEQ), p. 359
Texas Department of Transportation (TxDOT), p. 358
Texas Education Agency (TEA), p. 353
Texas Higher Education Coordinating Board (THECB), p. 354
Texas Parks and Wildlife Department, p. 358
Texas Workforce Commission (TWC), p. 357
veto power, p. 337

LEARNING CHECK ANSWERS

 9.1

1. Governors of Texas are constitutionally required to be U.S. citizens, to be Texas residents for five years immediately preceding the gubernatorial election, and to acknowledge the existence of a Supreme Being.
2. True. Major donors to gubernatorial campaigns are frequently appointed to government posts.

9.2

1. False. Although the size of the governor's staff has shrunk in recent years, it is much larger now than earlier in Texas history.

2. The Texas Constitution provides for impeachment by a simple majority vote of the House and conviction by a two-thirds majority vote of the Senate.

9.3 **1.** True. Informal powers of the governor are not based on law.

2. True. Public involvement of family members may be a source of support for the governor.

9.4 **1.** False. Most gubernatorial appointments must be approved by a two-thirds vote of the Senate.

2. The governor may veto an entire appropriation bill or use the line-item veto to eliminate individual budget items.

9.5 **1.** True. During a session, the governor's veto can be overridden by a two-thirds majority vote in the House and in the Senate.

2. The governor can call a special session.

9.6 **1.** True. A vacancy on a Texas district court or higher appellate court is filled by gubernatorial appointment.

2. The governor can independently grant one 30-day reprieve in a death sentence case.

9.7 **1.** False. The heads of state agencies, along with the governor and even local government officials, may request opinions from the attorney general on the scope of their jurisdiction.

2. The secretary of state grants charters to Texas corporations.

9.8 **1.** False. The Sunset Advisory Commission can recommend the abolition of an agency. Only the legislature can eliminate a state agency.

2. The commissioner of education has significantly more authority over state public and charter schools than the State Board of Education, because the commissioner heads the Texas Education Agency. Among its powers, this agency oversees statewide testing, determines if schools are meeting performance and financial standards, and has authority to close chronically noncompliant schools and school districts.

10 The Judicial Branch

Learning Objectives

10.1 Identify the sources of Texas law.

10.2 Compare the functions of all participants in the justice system.

10.3 Describe the judicial procedure for the adjudication of civil lawsuits.

10.4 Describe the judicial procedure for the adjudication of criminal cases.

IMAGE 10.1 Justice Don Willett, formerly of the Texas Supreme Court now on the U.S. Fifth Circuit Court of Appeals, and Texas's Tweeter Laureate, often tweeted 10 times or more per day. His tweeting was of concern to some U.S. senators.

Justice Don Willett ✓
@JusticeWillett

👤 Follow

#OpenCarry night at the judges' convention.
⚖️

RETWEETS 54   LIKES 138

7:35 PM - 30 Apr 2016

Source: Twitter

Competency Connection
⚖ PERSONAL RESPONSIBILITY ⚖

To assure people have confidence in the justice system, judges should be perceived as impartial. How could a judge's decision to tweet affect the public's impression of his or her impartiality?

For almost 20 years, in the small East Texas town of Appleby (Nacogdoches County), Preston Skelton and his wife lived next-door to Connie Moses and Helen Meeler, a retired teacher and nurse. The neighbors shared a common driveway. In 2009, a disagreement occurred about the location of the boundary line between their two properties. Over the next several months, law enforcement officials were called to the property numerous times as the disagreement intensified. On the morning of August 27, 2010, Moses and Meeler hired a worker to build a fence along the disputed property line. Skelton appeared with a rifle and ordered the worker and his neighbors to stop construction. He began shooting and killed both Moses and Meeler. The worker was able to escape. Skelton then ran into the nearby woods and fatally shot himself.[1]

Texas law provides peaceful ways to settle disagreements about property lines.[2] Disputants ask a neutral third party (a mediator or a judge) to review the evidence and determine the boundary line between properties. Although early societies permitted disputes to be settled by acts of personal revenge, modern societies depend on established rules and norms to resolve disagreements between parties. Therefore, one of the most important roles of the judicial system is the peaceful resolution of disputes. Some commentators suggest that without our judicial system, society would descend into anarchy,[3] as the opening example illustrates. Our courts have additional burdens, however. Texans, like all Americans, expect the decisions of their courts to be fair, just, and predictable.[4]

To render impartial verdicts that rely solely on facts and law, judges must be free from intimidation and violence. In 2015, a disgruntled criminal defendant critically injured Travis County District Judge Julie Kocurek. A subsequent survey, conducted by the Office of Court Administration, revealed that approximately 40 percent of participating trial court judges had concerns about their personal safety at work. In response, the 85th Legislature (2017) passed the Judge Julie Kocurek Judicial and Courthouse Security Act that requires special trainings and certifications for courthouse security personnel and prevents personal information about judges from being made public.

The United States is a nation of laws in which the national and state governments adopt laws that citizens are expected to obey. Citizens rely on courts to interpret and apply these laws to facts and resolve disputes accordingly. When a nation follows the rule of law, "respect for the law is paramount and disobedience of the law is punished."[5] The judicial system has a number of participants, including the disputing parties, lawyers, judges, and juries. When disagreements end up in the courts, procedural rules apply to assure a fair, just, and predictable result. As you learn about the judicial system, consider whether the Texas judicial system has met the ideal of being fair, just, and predictable.

⬟ State Law in Texas

LO 10.1 Identify the sources of Texas law.

Texans have given substantial power to their justice system. The Texas Constitution and state statutes grant government the authority, under appropriate circumstances, to take a person's life, liberty, or property. In addition to resolving disputes, the judicial branch interprets and applies state constitutional provisions, statutory laws, agency regulations, and the common law (traditions, customs, and practices that the court recognizes). Through their interpretations, judges are involved in the policymaking process. Yet judges attract less public attention than state legislative and executive officials, even though their decisions affect Texans every day. It is, therefore, important that the state's residents understand the purpose and workings of the judicial branch.

With more than 3,200 justices and judges, and almost that many courts, Texas has one of the largest judicial systems in the country. Including traffic violations, millions of cases are processed each year. Texas courts deal with cases involving **civil law** (for example, disputes concerning business contracts, divorces and other family issues, and personal injury claims). They also hear cases involving **criminal law** (proceedings against persons charged with committing a **misdemeanor**, such as using false identification to purchase liquor, which is punishable by a fine and jail sentence; or a **felony**, such as armed robbery, which is punishable by a prison sentence and a fine). A court's authority to hear and decide a particular case is its **jurisdiction**.

Sources of Law

Regardless of their jurisdiction, Texas courts interpret and apply state law.[6] These laws include the provisions of the Texas Constitution, statutes enacted by the legislature, regulations adopted by state agencies, and judge-made common law based on custom, tradition, and practice dating back to medieval England. A court may apply a constitutional provision, statute, regulation, or common law, or any combination of these laws, in the same case. Procedures for filing a case, conducting a trial, and appealing a judgment depend on whether the case is civil or criminal.

The Texas Constitution and statutes are available at Texas Legislature Online. Thomson Reuters Westlaw publishes the same information in *Vernon's Texas Statutes and Codes Annotated*. Newly enacted laws are compiled and made available through the Office of the Secretary of State's website. Agency regulations are codified in the *Texas Administrative Code*. Common law is found in individual court decisions. Although all levels of courts render decisions that affect the common law, only appellate court decisions are reported in the *South Western Reporter* series, published by Thomson Reuters Westlaw, and reported online through LexisNexis.

Code Revision

In 1963, the legislature charged the Texas Legislative Council with the responsibility of reorganizing Texas laws related to specific topics (such as education or taxes) into a systematic and comprehensive arrangement of legal codes. Almost 60 years later, the council continues to work on this project. In addition to piecemeal changes resulting from routine legislation, the legislature also sometimes undertakes extensive revision of an entire legal code. In 2003, the 78th Legislature authorized the council to compile all statutes related to local governments into the Special District Local Laws Code, a project that remained ongoing in 2019.

civil law
The body of law concerning disputes between individuals and other noncriminal matters, such as business contracts and personal injury.

criminal law
The body of law concerning felony and misdemeanor offenses by individuals against other persons and property, or in violation of laws or ordinances.

misdemeanor
Classified as A, B, or C, a misdemeanor may be punished by fine and/or jail sentence.

felony
A serious crime punished by fine and prison confinement.

jurisdiction
A court's authority to hear and decide a particular case.

✔ **10.1 Learning Check**

1. True or False: Civil law cases involve misdemeanors and felonies.
2. True or False: Texas state law includes judge-made common law based on custom and tradition.

Answers at the end of this chapter.

⬣ Courts, Judges, Lawyers, and Juries

LO 10.2   Compare the functions of all participants in the justice system.

Since the early 1700s, the structure of Texas's judicial system has been shaped by Western European influences. Under Spanish law three municipalities were established: Bexar (1716), Nacogdoches (1716), and Laredo (1787). Mexico continued the traditions of Spanish law, and Anglo settlers brought the influence of English judicial practices to the Republic of Texas. As the Lone Star State's population grew, its court system became more complex. Today's Texas judicial system has many participants, including more than 3,200 judges who preside over the state's courts, almost 100,000 attorneys who represent clients in legal proceedings, and thousands of jurors who decide the facts in both civil and criminal trials each year.

Article V of the Texas Constitution, "Judicial Department," vests all state judicial power "in one Supreme Court, in one Court of Criminal Appeals, in Courts of Appeals, in District Courts, in County Courts, in Commissioners Courts [which now have no judicial authority, as discussed in Chapter 3, 'Local Governments'], in Courts of Justice of the Peace and in such other courts as may be provided by law." In exercising its constitutional power to create other courts, the Texas legislature has established municipal (city) courts, county courts-at-law, and **probate** courts.[7] Probate matters relate specifically to decedents' estates, primarily establishing the validity of their wills; however, courts with probate jurisdiction also handle guardianship proceedings and mental competency determinations. Probate courts and county courts-at-law are referred to as statutory courts. The legislature has also authorized the creation of a number of specialty courts to meet specific needs of particular groups of the state's residents, such as veterans and children.

probate
Proceedings that involve the estates of decedents. Courts with probate jurisdiction (county courts, county courts-at-law, and probate courts) also handle guardianship and mental competency matters.

original jurisdiction
The power of a court to hear and decide a case first.

appellate jurisdiction
The power of a court to review and decide cases after they have been tried elsewhere.

exclusive jurisdiction
The authority of only one court to hear and decide a particular type of case.

concurrent jurisdiction
The authority of more than one court to try a case. For example, a civil dispute involving more than $200 but less than $10,000 may be heard in either a justice of the peace court, a county court (or county court-at-law), or a district court.

Trial and Appellate Courts

Texas's judicial system is complex. (See the structure of the current judicial system presented in Figure 10.1.) The law creating a particular court fixes the court's subject matter jurisdiction (civil, criminal, or both). Further, constitutional provisions or statutes determine whether a court has **original jurisdiction**, which is authority to try cases being heard for the first time; **appellate jurisdiction**, authority to rule on lower court decisions; or both. A court may have both exclusive and concurrent jurisdiction. A court that has **exclusive jurisdiction** is the only court with the authority to decide a particular type of case. **Concurrent jurisdiction** means that more than one court has authority to try a specific dispute. In that instance, a plaintiff selects the court in which to file the case. Qualifications and compensation for judges vary among the different courts, as shown in Table 10.1.

FIGURE 10.1 Court Structure of Texas

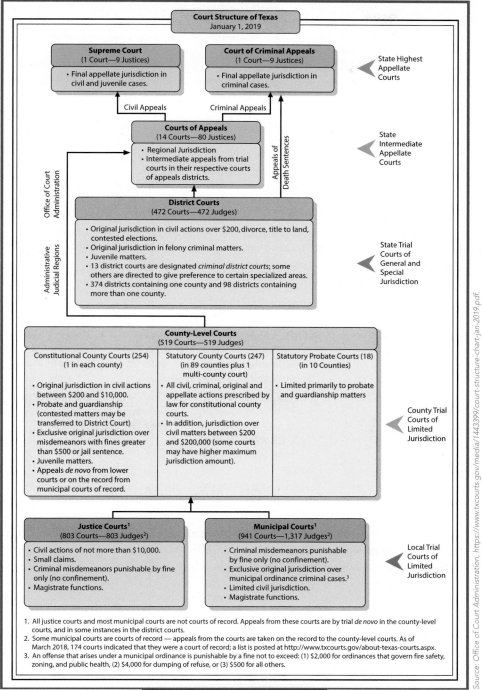

Court Structure of Texas
January 1, 2019

Supreme Court
(1 Court—9 Justices)
- Final appellate jurisdiction in civil and juvenile cases.

Court of Criminal Appeals
(1 Court—9 Justices)
- Final appellate jurisdiction in criminal cases.

State Highest Appellate Courts

Civil Appeals   Criminal Appeals

Courts of Appeals
(14 Courts—80 Justices)
- Regional Jurisdiction
- Intermediate appeals from trial courts in their respective courts of appeals districts.

Appeals of Death Sentences

State Intermediate Appellate Courts

Office of Court Administration

District Courts
(472 Courts—472 Judges)
- Original jurisdiction in civil actions over $200, divorce, title to land, contested elections.
- Original jurisdiction in felony criminal matters.
- Juvenile matters.
- 13 district courts are designated *criminal district courts*; some others are directed to give preference to certain specialized areas.
- 374 districts containing one county and 98 districts containing more than one county.

State Trial Courts of General and Special Jurisdiction

Administrative Judicial Regions

County-Level Courts
(519 Courts—519 Judges)

Constitutional County Courts (254) (1 in each county)	Statutory County Courts (247) (in 89 counties plus 1 multi-county court)	Statutory Probate Courts (18) (in 10 Counties)
• Original jurisdiction in civil actions between $200 and $10,000. • Probate and guardianship (contested matters may be transferred to District Court) • Exclusive original jurisdiction over misdemeanors with fines greater than $500 or jail sentence. • Juvenile matters. • Appeals *de novo* from lower courts or on the record from municipal courts of record.	• All civil, criminal, original and appellate actions prescribed by law for constitutional county courts. • In addition, jurisdiction over civil matters between $200 and $200,000 (some courts may have higher maximum jurisdiction amount).	• Limited primarily to probate and guardianship matters

County Trial Courts of Limited Jurisdiction

Justice Courts[1]
(803 Courts—803 Judges[2])
- Civil actions of not more than $10,000.
- Small claims.
- Criminal misdemeanors punishable by fine only (no confinement).
- Magistrate functions.

Municipal Courts[1]
(941 Courts—1,317 Judges[2])
- Criminal misdemeanors punishable by fine only (no confinement).
- Exclusive original jurisdiction over municipal ordinance criminal cases.[3]
- Limited civil jurisdiction.
- Magistrate functions.

Local Trial Courts of Limited Jurisdiction

1. All justice courts and most municipal courts are not courts of record. Appeals from these courts are by trial *de novo* in the county-level courts, and in some instances in the district courts.
2. Some municipal courts are courts of record — appeals from the courts are taken on the record to the county-level courts. As of March 2018, 174 courts indicated that they were a court of record; a list is posted at http://www.txcourts.gov/about-texas-courts.aspx.
3. An offense that arises under a municipal ordinance is punishable by a fine not to exceed: (1) $2,000 for ordinances that govern fire safety, zoning, and public health, (2) $4,000 for dumping of refuse, or (3) $500 for all others.

Source: Office of Court Administration, https://www.txcourts.gov/media/1443399/court-structure-chart-jan-2019.pdf.

Competency Connection
◉ **SOCIAL RESPONSIBILITY** ◉

How would simplifying the state's court system improve or harm the judicial system in Texas?

TABLE 10.1 Texas Judges and Justices

Court	Judicial Qualifications	Term of Office	Annual Salary	Method of Selection	Method of Replacement
Local Courts Municipal Courts	Varies; set by each city	Varies; set by each city	Paid by the city; highly variable	Appointment or election, as determined by city charter	Method determined by city charter
Justice of the Peace Courts	None	Four years	Paid by the county; highly variable, ranging from a few thousand dollars to more than $140,000	Partisan precinctwide elections	Commissioners Court
County Courts Constitutional County Courts	Must be "well informed" in Texas law; law degree not required	Four years	Paid by the county; highly variable, ranging from a few thousand dollars to more than $190,000	Partisan countywide elections	Commissioners Court
Statutory County Courts (courts-at-law and probate courts)	Age 25 or older; licensed attorney with at least four to five years' experience, depending on statutory requirements; two years' county residence	Four years	Paid by the state and county; somewhat variable ranging from $125,000 to more than $180,000; must be not less than $1,000 less than district judge in same county	Partisan countywide elections	Commissioners Court
State Courts District Courts	Ages 25–74; licensed attorney with at least four years' experience; two years' county residence	Four years	$140,000; county salary supplements; must be $5,000 less than court of appeals justices' salaries	Partisan districtwide elections	Governor, with advice and consent of Senate
Courts of Appeals	Ages 35–74; licensed attorney with at least 10 years' experience	Six years	$154,000 (justices); $156,500 (chief justices); county salary supplements; must be $5,000 less than Texas Supreme Court justices' salaries	Partisan districtwide elections	Governor, with advice and consent of Senate
Court of Criminal Appeals	Ages 35–74; licensed attorney with at least 10 years' experience	Six years	$168,000 (judges); $170,500 (presiding judge)	Partisan statewide elections	Governor, with advice and consent of Senate
Supreme Court	Ages 35–74; licensed attorney with at least 10 years' experience	Six years	$168,000 (justices); $170,500 (chief justice)	Partisan statewide elections	Governor, with advice and consent of Senate

Sources: Compiled from "Texas Association of Counties 2018 Salary Survey," https://www.county.org/TAC/media/TACMedia /Legislative/2018-Salary-Survey-Complete.pdf; Judicial Compensation Commission, "Report of the Judicial Compensation Commission," September 2018, http://www.txcourts.gov/media/1442408/jcc-2018-report-final.pdf.

— Competency Connection —
✿ **CRITICAL THINKING** ✿

Courts hear different types of cases. Should all judges have the same qualifications and receive the same compensation?

Local Trial Courts The courts with which Texans are most familiar are **municipal courts** and **justice of the peace** (JP) courts. These local trial courts handle, among other types of cases, charges involving Class C misdemeanors (including most traffic violations), the least serious category of criminal offenses. Municipal judges and justices of the peace, like other Texas justices and judges, may, but are not required to, perform marriages. After the U.S. Supreme Court declared same-sex marriage legal across the nation, several Texas JPs decided they would no longer perform weddings. Their right of refusal is permitted under state law. Local trial court judges also serve as magistrates of the state. In this latter capacity, these officials issue warrants for the arrest of suspects and conduct hearings to determine whether a person charged with a criminal act will be released on bail or jailed pending further court action.

More than 900 incorporated cities, towns, and villages in Texas have municipal courts. Although mayors of general law cities have authority to preside over municipal courts (unless the city council provides for the election or appointment of someone to perform this function), only 1 percent of municipal judges are mayors. Usually, municipal court judges of home rule cities are named by city councils for two-year terms. Under state law, only municipal judges who preside over municipal **courts of record** (courts with a court reporter or electronic device to record the testimony and proceedings) must be licensed attorneys under state law. City councils also set professional qualifications, as well as determine the number of judges and set judicial salaries for their municipalities.

Municipal courts have limited civil jurisdiction in cases involving owners of dangerous dogs. These courts have no appellate jurisdiction. Their original and exclusive criminal jurisdiction extends to all violations of city ordinances, and they have criminal jurisdiction concurrent with justice of the peace courts over Class C misdemeanors committed within city limits. Individuals dissatisfied with the result of a municipal court ruling can appeal the decision to the county court or a county court-at-law.

Approximately 20 percent of municipal courts are courts of record. Appeals from those courts are based on a transcript of trial proceedings. If a court is not a court of record, appeals receive a trial de novo (a completely new trial).

Justice of the peace courts have been a part of the Texas judicial system since ratification by popular vote of the Constitution of 1836 that provided the governmental structure for the Republic of Texas. A justice of the peace is elected by voters residing in a precinct with boundaries created by the county commissioners court. The Texas Constitution mandates the minimum number of precincts per county (one to four) according to population. County commissioners may exceed this minimum by creating up to eight precincts (also based on population) and establish the number of JPs (one or two) per precinct. In recent years, a few commissioners courts have abolished some justice courts to save money for their counties.

As in seven other states, the position of JP requires neither previous legal training nor experience.[8] Fewer than 10 percent of Texas's JPs (usually in large cities) are lawyers who may engage in private legal practice while serving as a

municipal court
City-run court with jurisdiction primarily over Class C misdemeanors committed within a city's boundaries.

justice of the peace
A judge elected from a justice of the peace precinct who handles minor civil and criminal cases, including small claims court.

court of record
A court that has a court reporter or electronic device to record testimony and proceedings.

justice of the peace. Within a year after election, a justice of the peace who is not a lawyer must complete an 80-hour course in performing the duties of that office. Thereafter, the JP is supposed to receive 20 hours of instruction annually, 10 hours of which must include topics related to civil trial procedure. Failure to complete annual training violates a JP's duties under the law. The State Commission on Judicial Conduct, a Texas agency that has the authority to discipline judges, can order justices who do not comply to complete mandatory education. Judges who demonstrate a misunderstanding of the law may also be required to take training. Forty judges and justices (including several justices of the peace) were ordered to complete additional education in 2017.

In urban areas, being a justice of the peace is a full-time job, whereas justices in many rural precincts hear few cases. In addition to presiding over the justice court, a justice of the peace serves as an ex officio notary public (someone who verifies signatures on legal documents). A JP also functions as a coroner, determining cause of death when the county commissioners court has not named a county medical examiner. Justice of the peace courts have both criminal and civil jurisdiction. In all cases, their jurisdiction is original. In criminal matters, these local courts try Class C misdemeanors; however, any conviction may be appealed to the county court or a county court-at-law for a new trial. Because these courts are not courts of record, all appeals are de novo (meaning a new trial is held).

Justices of the peace have jurisdiction over four types of civil cases: evictions, debt claims, repair and remedies, and small claims (civil disputes with less than $10,000 in controversy). Rules of evidence and procedure, though uniform for all justice courts, are not as formal for most cases as in other court proceedings. As a result, ordinary people can represent themselves more easily without hiring a lawyer, thus earning these courts the nickname "the people's court."[9] A justice may question witnesses directly to develop the facts in a case and limit the types and amount of potential evidence each party must provide the other party prior to trial (a process called discovery). In most debt collection cases, rules of evidence and procedure that are more formal still apply.

Exclusive civil jurisdiction of JP courts is limited to cases in which the amount in controversy is $200 or less, not including interest. Concurrent civil jurisdiction is shared with county courts (for amounts in controversy in excess of $200) and district courts (for amounts in controversy in excess of $500), so long as the disputed amount does not exceed $10,000. Appeals from JP courts, in which more than $250 is in controversy, are taken to the county level. The justice of the peace court is the court of last resort if the amount in controversy does not exceed $250, thus making its decisions final in these cases.

constitutional county court
Trial courts created in the Texas Constitution for each of Texas's 254 counties. If a county has one or more county courts-at-law, constitutional county courts do not usually hear and decide cases.

County Trial Courts Each of Texas's 254 counties has a **constitutional county court** and a county judge, as prescribed by the state constitution. In the more than 90 counties that have one or more county-level courts created by statute, county judges generally do not hear cases. Their time is devoted to administrative matters like budget preparation that does not involve court cases. Judges of constitutional county courts need not be attorneys. Statutory county court judges must be experienced attorneys. Like district court and appellate court judges, all county-level judges who preside over courts must take Texas Supreme Court–approved courses in court administration, procedure, and evidence.

Most constitutional county courts have original and appellate jurisdiction, as well as probate, civil, and criminal jurisdiction. Original civil jurisdiction is limited to cases involving between $200 and $10,000. Original criminal jurisdiction includes all Class A and Class B misdemeanors.

Appellate criminal jurisdiction extends to cases originating in JP courts and municipal courts. A constitutional county court's appellate jurisdiction is final with regard to criminal cases involving fines of $100 or less. For cases in which greater fines are imposed, the plaintiff may appeal to a court of appeals. Civil cases are heard on appeal from JP courts.

In counties with large populations, the legislature has authorized more than 250 statutory courts (most commonly called **county courts-at-law**) to relieve constitutional county court judges of some or all courtroom duties. With few exceptions, the criminal jurisdiction of county courts-at-law is limited to misdemeanors. Civil jurisdiction of most county courts-at-law is restricted to controversies involving amounts of $200 to $200,000. In 10 urban counties throughout the state, the legislature has created statutory county **probate courts** to handle the admission of wills to probate, a procedure to establish the validity of a will, as well as guardianship and mental competency proceedings. In guardianship proceedings, a court appoints someone to care for the person and/or the property of an individual who is unable to do so for him or herself because of age, physical disability, or mental incapacity.

State Trial Courts Texas's principal trial courts are district-level courts of general and special jurisdiction. Most state trial courts are designated simply as **district courts**. Some are criminal or civil district courts. Each district-level court has jurisdiction over one or more counties. Heavily populated counties may have several district courts with countywide jurisdiction.

Most district court judges are authorized to try both criminal and civil cases, though a statute creating a court may specify that the court give preference to one or the other. All felony criminal cases are matters of original jurisdiction. Misdemeanor jurisdiction is limited to cases transferred from constitutional county courts, cases specifically authorized by the state legislature, and offenses involving misconduct by government officials while acting in an official capacity. Appeal after a death penalty sentence is taken directly to the Court of Criminal Appeals. Other criminal convictions are appealed to an intermediate appellate court.

District courts have exclusive original jurisdiction over civil cases involving divorce, land titles, contested elections, contested wills, slander, and defamation of character, unless the legislature has granted concurrent jurisdiction to a county court-at-law. District courts have concurrent original jurisdiction with lower courts in controversies involving $200 or more; above the maximum dollar amount jurisdiction of those courts, district courts exercise exclusive civil jurisdiction. Appeals of civil cases go to courts of appeals.

county court-at-law
Trial courts created by statute to assume the responsibilities of constitutional county courts in counties with larger populations.

probate court
Statutory courts that only handle administration of decedent's estates, mental competency proceedings, and guardianship proceedings.

district court
State trial courts that hear and decide both civil and criminal cases.

Intermediate Appellate Courts The legislature has divided Texas into 14 state **courts of appeals** districts and has established a court of appeals in every district. Each of these courts has three or more judges or justices (a chief justice and from 2 to 12 justices). Their six-year terms are staggered so that one-third of the members are elected or reelected every two years. This arrangement helps ensure that at any given time—barring death, resignation, or removal from office—each appellate court will have two or more judges with experience on each court. Decisions are reached by majority vote of the assigned judges after they examine the written record of the case, review briefs (written arguments) prepared by the parties' attorneys, and hear oral arguments by the attorneys. At least three judges must hear and decide each case, unless the court's chief justice orders that the entire court hear and decide a case (an en banc proceeding). These courts hear appeals of civil and criminal cases from district courts and county courts (but not appeals involving the death penalty or DNA-forensic testing for individuals sentenced to death).

Final jurisdiction includes cases involving divorce, slander, boundary disputes, and elections held for purposes other than choosing government officials (for example, bond elections). Courts must hear appeals in panels of at least three justices. A decision requires a majority vote of a panel of justices.

Highest Appellate Courts Texas and Oklahoma are the only states in the Union that have **bifurcated** (divided) court systems for dealing with criminal and civil appeals. Texans continue to resist the creation of a unified judicial system, which would have a single appellate court of last resort for both criminal

courts of appeals
Intermediate-level appellate courts that hear and decide appeals from trial court decisions.

bifurcated
A divided court system in which different courts handle civil and criminal cases. In Texas, the highest-level appeals courts are bifurcated.

📊 HOW DO WE COMPARE...

In Salaries of Highest Court Justices and Judges?

Annual Salaries of Highest Court Justices and Judges (in dollars as of 2018)

Most Populous U.S. States	Amount*	U.S. States Bordering Texas	Amount*
California	$244,179	Arkansas	$174,925
Florida	$220,600	Louisiana	$169,125
New York	$230,200	New Mexico	$139,819
Texas	**$168,000**	Oklahoma	$145,914

*In most states (including Texas), the chief presiding judge or justice receives a supplement due to the additional workload. In Texas the amount is $2,500.

Source: National Center for State Courts, "Survey of Judicial Salaries," July 2018, https://www.ncsc.org/~/media/Microsites/Files/Judicial%20Salaries/Judicial-Salary-Tracker-Jul-2018.ashx.

Competency Connection
💬 **COMMUNICATION SKILLS** 💬

Share with a classmate, whether you believe Texas compensates its highest court justices and judges fairly?

felony cases and complex civil cases.[10] Both of Texas's highest courts have nine justices (Supreme Court) or judges (Court of Criminal Appeals) who serve six-year terms. One-third of the positions on each court are open for election or reelection in each general election. Members of the courts are elected on a state-wide basis. The Supreme Court of Texas and the Court of Criminal Appeals are authorized to answer questions about Texas law asked by federal appellate courts (for example, the U.S. Fifth Circuit Court of Appeals or the U.S. Supreme Court).

In Texas, the highest tribunal with criminal jurisdiction is the **Court of Criminal Appeals**. This court hears criminal appeals exclusively. Most appeals come to the court from courts of appeals. Death penalty defendants in capital felonies or DNA-forensic testing cases have an automatic right of appeal from a district court to the Court of Criminal Appeals. Of the almost 2,000 appeals received in 2017, only eight were direct appeals of death penalty or DNA verdicts.

Voters elect one member of the Court of Criminal Appeals as presiding judge. Sharon Keller, the first woman to head the Texas Court of Criminal Appeals, was elected in 2000. As of 2019, three of the other eight judges were women. Judge Elsa Alcala, the first Latina judge to serve on the court, decided not to seek reelection in 2018. She frequently challenged the constitutionality of

Court of Criminal Appeals
The state's highest court with criminal jurisdiction.

IMAGE 10.2 Courts of appeals and the Texas Supreme Court frequently convene on college and university campuses. Here the 10th Court of Appeals (Waco) conducts appellate hearings at Sam Houston State University (Huntsville).

The Center for Law, Engagement, and Politics

— Competency Connection —
⚙ **CRITICAL THINKING** ⚙

What are some advantages and disadvantages of having appellate courts travel to college campuses to conduct hearings?

Texas's death penalty. As of 2019, all judges on the court were Anglo. All members of the court since 1996 have been elected as Republicans; however, in December 2013, Justice Lawrence Meyers announced he would seek election to the Texas Supreme Court as a Democrat in the 2014 election.[11] This switch in party affiliation made Judge Meyers the first Democrat to hold statewide office since 1998. Meyers did not win election to the Supreme Court; but his term on the Texas Court of Criminal Appeals did not expire until January 2017—so he remained on that court. When Meyers did not win reelection in 2016, no Democrats remained in statewide office.

Officially titled the **Supreme Court of Texas**, the state's highest court with civil jurisdiction has nine members: one chief justice and eight justices. No Democrats have served on the Texas Supreme Court since 1998. When former Governor Rick Perry appointed Wallace Jefferson to the Texas Supreme Court in 2001, he became the first African American to serve on the court. Jefferson's elevation to chief justice in 2004 marked another first for African Americans on the court. In 2019, the court was less diverse than it had been throughout the 21st century. The nine-member court included no African Americans and only two women (one Latina and one Anglo). All of the justices were Republican.

This high court is supreme only in cases involving civil law. Because it has severely limited original jurisdiction (for example, cases involving denial of a place on an election ballot), nearly all of the court's docket involves appeals of cases that it determines must be heard. Much of the supreme court's work involves handling petitions for review, which can be requested by a party who argues that a court of appeals made a mistake on a question of law. If as many as four justices favor granting an initial review, the case is scheduled for argument in open court. In 2018, the Texas Supreme Court granted an initial review for approximately 13 percent of the more than 900 petitions that were filed, an increase over previous years. Justices do not make public their votes on petitions for review.

Other functions of the Texas Supreme Court include establishing rules of civil procedure for the state's lower courts and transferring cases to equalize workloads among the courts of appeals. Early in each regular session of the Texas legislature, the chief justice is required by law to deliver to the legislature a State of the Judiciary message, either orally or in written form.

The Texas Supreme Court has taken a leadership role in use of technology as a way to make courts with civil jurisdiction more efficient and to make court proceedings more accessible. In 2012, when the supreme court launched its mandatory e-filing program, former Chief Justice Wallace Jefferson declared, "The era of big paper is over."[12] All documents used in civil cases (except for juvenile cases) must now be submitted online through efiletexas.gov. For those interested, podcasts of oral arguments are available for downloading. The court's activities may also be followed through RSS feeds. Although Texas's official Tweeter Laureate, Justice Don Willett (formerly a member of the Texas Supreme Court), was silenced upon his appointment to the U.S. Fifth Circuit Court of Appeals, other justices maintain Twitter accounts. Justice Eva Guzman is among the more prolific tweeters.

#

Supreme Court of Texas
State's highest court with civil jurisdiction.

Specialty Courts Over the last decade, Texas has followed the national trend of developing **specialty courts** to deal with particular types of problems or specific populations. Among the approximate 250 specialized courts are "cluster courts," which are traveling courts that adjudicate only Children's Protective Services cases; drug courts, which focus on treatment options rather than incarceration for substance abusers; mental health courts; and veterans' courts, which deal with offenders who have suffered some type of mental disorder related to their military service experiences.[13]

Specialty courts are created by county commissioner's courts and, with regard to drug courts, municipalities as well. The courts have a dual rationale: efficiency and therapy. Courts with a nontherapeutic purpose, such as Children's Protective Services courts, are intended to increase the court system's efficiency by placing foster children into permanent homes more quickly. Others, such as drug courts, mental health courts, or veterans' courts, are designed with a therapeutic rationale. Their goal is to improve outcomes for participants through individualized treatment plans developed and monitored by attorneys, judges, and treatment personnel. If treatment is successful, the presiding judge can enter an order of nondisclosure for most offenders, thus keeping the public from learning about an offense. Some reviews of these courts suggest many are meeting their dual mission of efficiency and therapy; other studies offer less conclusive results.[14]

Alternative Dispute Resolution The state has adopted several methods to encourage litigants to resolve their disputes without going to trial. To reduce workloads, speed the handling of civil disputes, and cut legal costs, each county is authorized to set up a system for **alternative dispute resolution (ADR)**. This procedure allows an impartial third party who has training as a mediator or arbiter to negotiate disputes between and among litigants. ADR is frequently cited as a significant factor in the "vanishing jury trial."[15] Many lawsuits are now settled prior to trial. A settlement occurs when the parties resolve their disputes without going to trial.

Collaborative divorce is another nonadversarial method for resolving disputes outside the courtroom. If either spouse elects to litigate (go to court) after the process begins, attorneys for both spouses must resign. Under the Texas Family Code, families with children are encouraged to use collaborative procedures. If family violence is involved, however, the abuse victim must expressly request using a collaborative process, and the victim's lawyer must work with the client to devise procedures to limit the possibility of further violence.

Selecting Judges and Justices

Texas, along with Alabama and Louisiana, chooses all judges (except municipal judges) in partisan elections. Many commentators (including chief justices of the Texas Supreme Court) oppose this practice. Court of Criminal Appeals Judge Elsa Alcala cited the election of judges as her reason for not seeking reelection.

specialty courts
Courts designed to deal with particular types of problems, such as drug-related offenses or specific populations, such as veterans or foster children.

alternative dispute resolution (ADR)
Use of mediation, conciliation, or arbitration to resolve disputes among individuals without resorting to a regular court trial.

Harvard Law professor Jed Handelsman Shugerman noted that foreign countries that follow the American legal system seldom adopt "the peculiar [American] institution" of electing judges.[16] One complaint is the appearance that "justice is for sale" to the highest campaign donor.[17] Another is that elections unfairly favor Anglo judicial candidates.

▧ POINT/COUNTERPOINT

Should Texas Adopt the O'Connor Plan for the Selection of Judges?

THE ISSUE In 2014, former U.S. Supreme Court Justice Sandra Day O'Connor, in collaboration with the Institute for the Advancement of the American Legal System, developed the O'Connor Judicial Selection Plan (O'Connor Plan). Unlike the judicial selection plan followed by Louisiana, Alabama, and Texas in which judges at all levels of the courts are selected through popular, partisan elections, the O'Connor plan is a four-step process. Based on the Missouri plan, this judicial selection model attempts to overcome some of the criticisms of that plan. A broad-based nominating commission comprised mostly of nonlawyers nominates several qualified judicial candidates. The governor nominates someone from this list to the judgeship. If the governor fails to act, the commission appoints the judge. The judge serves at least two to three years in office and receives public performance evaluations from an evaluation commission, a predominantly nonlawyer panel. An uncontested, nonpartisan retention election is held so voters can decide whether to keep the judge. After that, the judge runs for reelection in uncontested, nonpartisan elections for each subsequent term in office.

FOR	AGAINST
1. Having an independent commission identify a list of potential judicial nominees based on merit assures a more qualified judiciary.	1. A system that relies on nominating commissions to identify judicial nominees is less democratic than popular, partisan elections because the nominee is not directly accountable to the voters.
2. Providing public evaluations of a judge's job performance gives the voters the necessary information to make informed voting decisions for retention elections.	2. Even if performance evaluations are made available, the likelihood that voters will review them is low.
3. Allowing for uncontested, nonpartisan elections holds judges accountable without forcing them to align with partisan or moneyed interests (a process that gives the perception that "justice is for sale").	3. Retention elections and uncontested reelections do not hold judges as accountable to the voters as popular elections do. Election results show that less than 1 percent of incumbent judges are removed by voters in uncontested elections. Almost 25 percent of incumbent judges are defeated each election cycle in states with popular elections.

Sources: Justice Sandra Day O'Connor (Ret.) and Institute for the Advancement of the American Legal System, "The O'Connor Judicial Selection Plan," *Institute for the Advancement of the American Legal System*, September 2014, http://iaals.du.edu/sites/default/files /documents/publications/oconnor_plan.pdf; Stephen J. Ware, "The Missouri Plan in National Perspective," *Missouri Law Review* 74 no. 3 (2009): 751–775.

— Competency Connection —
◉ SOCIAL RESPONSIBILITY ◉

What should voters know about judicial candidates prior to voting?

Judicial selection methods are far from uniform, with at least 15 different processes in use across the country.[18] Many opponents of the popular election of judges favor some version of the merit selection process initiated by the state of Missouri in 1940. The **Missouri Plan** features a nominating commission (frequently dominated by lawyers and judges) that recommends a panel of names to the governor whenever a judicial vacancy is to be filled. The governor must then decide whom to appoint from the list. If the governor fails to decide within a limited amount of time, the nominating commission appoints a judge from the list of recommendations. The appointee then serves for a year or so before the voters decide whether to give the new judge a full term. In subsequent elections, the judge runs unopposed for additional terms. If the voters do not approve a judge, then the nominating commission and governor must make another appointment on a similar trial basis. More than 99 percent of appointees are approved by the voters in their initial retention election and subsequent reelections.[19]

Others, especially some Texas legislators, favor an **appointment-retention system** for all courts of record. In this system, the governor appoints a judge and voters determine whether to retain the appointee. Reform proposals have consistently failed in the Texas legislature. At the very least, reformers argue, judicial elections should not be partisan. They agree with former Chief Justice Wallace Jefferson who observed, "a justice system built on some notion of Democratic judging or Republican judging is a system that cannot be trusted."[20] The 83rd Legislature (2013) approved the Joint Interim Judicial Selection Committee to study this issue and provide recommendations to the 84th Legislature. The committee issued no report. Despite the urgings of former Chief Justice Wallace Jefferson and current Chief Justice Nathan Hecht, neither the 84th nor the 85th Legislatures made changes to the judicial selection process. The 86th Legislature established the Texas Commission on Judicial Selection to evaluate alternative methods for selecting statutory county court judges and all state judges and justices.

Disciplining and Removing Judges and Justices

Each year, a few of Texas's judges and justices commit acts that warrant discipline or removal. These judges can be removed by the voters at the next election; by trial by jury; or if they are state court judges, by legislative address or impeachment. The State Commission on Judicial Conduct, however, plays the most important role in disciplining the state's judiciary. This 13-member commission is composed of six judges, each from a different level court; two attorneys; and five private citizens who are neither attorneys nor judges.

Commission staff sometimes undertake investigations on their own. After being stopped for driving while intoxicated, Justice Nora Longoria (13th Court of Appeals [Edinburg]) repeatedly identified herself as a judge and asked that she not be arrested. Although the charge was dismissed, the commission found that she appeared to be using her office to advance her own interest. A judge may also be accused of wrongdoing by written complaint. When Burnet County Judge James Oakley posted a Facebook comment that it was "time for a tree and a rope" in response to the arrest of an African American man accused of

Missouri Plan
A judicial selection process in which a commission recommends a panel of names to the governor, who appoints a judge for one year or so before voters determine whether the appointee will be retained for a full term.

appointment-retention system
A merit plan for judicial selection in which the governor makes an appointment to fill a court vacancy for an interim period, after which the judge must win a full term in an uncontested popular election.

murdering a police officer, the commission received multiple complaints. Claiming his comments referenced a Pace Picante ad, the judge maintained his post was not racially motivated. Nonetheless, the commission found his behavior compromised public perception of an impartial judiciary. Even though both judges were publicly reprimanded for discrediting the judiciary, voters reelected them to their respective positions in 2018.[21]

As Judge Oakley learned, social media can be problematic for judicial officials. In other states, judges have been reprimanded for posting comments about cases pending in their courts. Comments that appear to favor a particular litigant are a violation of judicial ethics.

Misuse of social media by judicial officials has presented other problems. Not only are judges responsible for their own behavior but also for their staff members' activities. Further complicating the issue is that using government-owned computers for postings could constitute misuse of government property. Court decisions have been challenged because a judge followed a party's attorneys on Twitter. When a Galveston County judge was publicly reprimanded by the commission for posting comments about a case in her court on her Facebook page, the Special Review Panel appointed by the Chief Justice of the Texas Supreme Court overturned the ruling. The panel agreed with the judge's assertion that she was attempting to keep voters informed about her court by reporting on upcoming cases.

Indeed, regular communication through social media can make the judicial process more transparent and judges more "human." A fine line marks the difference between transparency and inappropriate postings. Just as attorneys must do, judges must follow the same rules of communication for social media as for all other media. Tweeter Laureate and former Justice Don Willett observed, "Whether they're crafting a 140-page opinion or a 140-character tweet, judges must always be judicious."[22]

The State Commission on Judicial Conduct has often been criticized for being too lenient with judges.[23] In 2017, the commission resolved more than 1,300 complaints. Of the 62 cases that were not dismissed, the commission issued some form of sanction or suspension to 53 judges. Eight judges resigned to avoid disciplinary action. One judge had two cases against him. Table 10.2 provides an overview of complaints and sanctions by court type. Parties to lawsuits file the most complaints. Since the inception of electronic filing in 2016, complaints have increased.

The commission's jurisdiction extends to judges and justices at all levels of the court system. Both the presiding judge of the Court of Criminal Appeals, Sharon Keller, and the chief justice of the Texas Supreme Court, Nathan Hecht, have been disciplined by the commission. Both disciplinary actions were reversed in appellate proceedings.[24]

In addition to a public reprimand, any judge can receive a private reprimand or be ordered to take additional training. All punitive rulings can be appealed to the chief justice of the Texas Supreme Court, who appoints a Special Court of Review (a three-judge panel of appellate judges) to hear the appeal. The commission has the authority to recommend removal of a judge. Such a recommendation is considered by a seven-member tribunal appointed by the Texas Supreme Court.

TABLE 10.2 Disposition of Cases by Judge Type, 2017

Judge Type	Number of Judges	Number of Complaints	Portion of Total Complaints	Number of Sanctions	Portion of Total Actions
Municipal	1,326	85	5%	2	4%
Justice of the peace	802	319	21%	16	31%
Constitutional county court	254	90	6%	20	39%
Statutory county court	262	134	9%	0	0%
District court	469	623	40%	13	26%
Appellate	98	151	10%	0	0%
Senior or retired	386	73	5%	0	0%
Associate*	214	60	4%	0	0%
Total	3,811	1,535	100%	51	100%

*Full- or part-time judges appointed as masters, magistrates, or referees to assist with specific types of cases.

Source: "Fiscal Year 2017 Annual Report," State Commission on Judicial Conduct, http://www.scjc.texas.gov/media/46650/fy-17-scjc-annual-report.pdf.

Competency Connection
☼ **CRITICAL THINKING** ☼

The Commission on Judicial Conduct enforces judicial ethical standards. Does the commission appear too lenient? Why or why not?

If the tribunal votes to remove the judge, the decision may be appealed to the Texas Supreme Court.

The State Commission on Judicial Conduct also oversees an employee assistance program called Amicus Curiae. This program locates service providers for judges suffering from substance abuse or mental or emotional disorders. Judges receiving services through Amicus Curiae may do so through a self-referral or be referred by the commission. The commission has made no referrals since 2013. Participation is voluntary.

Lawyers

Both the Texas Supreme Court and the State Bar of Texas play roles in regulating the 100,000 practicing attorneys licensed by the state of Texas. The Supreme Court of Texas supervises the licensing of lawyers. Accreditation of law schools is largely a responsibility of the American Bar Association. Nine Texas law schools are fully accredited. The University of North Texas at Dallas College of Law, the state's newest law school, has received provisional accreditation and will be eligible to apply for full accreditation in 2020. Bills were proposed in the 86th Legislature to establish law schools in El Paso and the Rio Grande Valley, as well as allow distance learning through the UT Law School for students at UT-Rio Grande Valley. The State Bar of Texas oversees and disciplines the state's lawyers.

State Bar of Texas To practice, a licensed attorney must be a member of the State Bar of Texas and pay dues for its support. Because of lobbying activities, several lawyers sued the organization in 2019 arguing that mandatory dues violated the First Amendment. The state bar enforces ethical standards for Texas lawyers. An administrative agency of the state, the organization disciplines, suspends, and disbars attorneys. The advent of social media has presented special challenges for attorneys. Some have failed to recognize that maintaining a blog touting courtroom accomplishments is advertising. Others have not considered that communicating through a Facebook page with a judge presiding over a lawyer's case is prohibited.[25] Information about an attorney's professional disciplinary record is available from the Find-A-Lawyer link on the state bar's website. In addition, the entity oversees an extensive continuing legal education program.

Legal Services for the Poor Many attorneys and judges agree with former U.S. Supreme Court Justice Lewis Powell that "[e]qual justice under law is … one of the ends for which our entire legal system exists.… [I]t is fundamental that justice should be the same, in substance and availability, without regard to economic status."[26] Under the Bill of Rights in the Texas Constitution and the Sixth Amendment to the U.S. Constitution, indigent individuals accused of felonies are entitled to legal representation at the state's expense. A person whose claim arises from a physical injury may hire an attorney on a **contingency fee** basis, in which the lawyer is paid from any money recovered in a lawsuit or settlement. Representation in such legal matters as divorce, child custody, or contract disputes, however, requires the client to make direct payment to the attorney for legal services. Free legal help for civil cases is often provided by an attorney with the Legal Services Corporation, more commonly referred to as Legal Aid. Limited funding in recent years has reduced the assistance available through this program.

The Texas Access to Justice Foundation estimates that more than 90 percent of qualified applicants are denied services due to limited resources. Many middle-income individuals earn too much to qualify for legal aid but still cannot afford to hire an attorney. Lack of access to legal representation creates a "justice gap." To address this issue, in 2015, the Texas Supreme Court created the Commission to Expand Civil Legal Services. Chaired by former Texas Supreme Court Chief Justice Wallace Jefferson, the commission recommended study of self-representation issues and rules changes so attorneys could limit the scope of client representation to brief consultations. No subsequent action was taken after release of these recommendations.[27]

Another commission, the Texas Access to Justice Commission, was also created by the Texas Supreme Court to coordinate and increase delivery of legal services to the state's poor. This 15-member commission includes judges, lawyers, and private citizens. The State Bar of Texas and the Texas Access to Justice Foundation support and collaborate with these efforts. The foundation maintains a website that provides information, forms, and links to low- and no-cost legal services providers.

Attorney volunteers fill some of the legal representation gap. Special programs, such as Texas Lawyers for Texas Veterans, target particular populations for legal services provided by these private attorneys. State bar officials recommend that lawyers donate 50 hours per year assisting needy clients. In 2015, the state's

contingency fee
A lawyer's compensation paid from money recovered in a lawsuit or settlement.

🗒 STUDENTS IN ACTION

"[My client's] case makes me reflect on the various difficult choices people must make to risk everything and leave their home countries for an uncertain future."

— Norma Johnson,
University of Houston law student

Law schools offer a variety of legal clinics where law students, under the supervision of their professors, offer legal services to the poor. Frequently these clinics target a specific population and allow students to develop expertise in a particular specialty. The University of Houston Law Center (UHLC) sponsors five different clinics, including an immigration clinic.

Participation

To participate in the immigration clinic, students must enroll in a class that meets weekly in which they learn advocacy skills and immigration law. In addition, students are assigned immigration cases. Working under the supervision of professors, the law students represent clients from the initial client interview through the conclusion of the case, including representing clients before the Department of Homeland Security and in immigration courts.

Types of Cases

The clinic specializes in representing those seeking asylum because of political violence, immigrant victims of domestic violence, and children. Students also work with immigrants being held in detention centers across the state. Community outreach programs are provided for organizations that offer services to immigrants. The clinic sponsors continuing legal education programs for practitioners and partners with other organizations, such as the Tahirih Justice Center, a national organization that assists female immigrants. During Hurricane Harvey (2017), the groups helped immigrants with legal issues, including replacement of lost immigration documents. Both individual professors and the clinic have received local, regional, and national recognition for their work.

Dave and Les Jacobs/Blend Images/Getty Images

Law students often use their research skills to help others, such as undocumented immigrants.

Results

Students, in collaboration with their professors, have succeeded in obtaining permanent legal residency for clients and getting immigrants released from detention centers. In 2015, under the direction of UHLC Associate Clinical Professor Janet Beck, two students were able to obtain a credible fear interview for their five-year-old client. A credible fear interview is used to establish whether asylum should be granted because a significant possibility exists that an immigrant will be persecuted if he or she returns to the home country. The child's mother had previously been denied asylum. Based on the court's determination that the child had a credible fear of persecution and was therefore entitled to asylum, the mother's case was reconsidered. Obtaining the interview for the child after the initial determination to deny the mother's request for asylum was precedent setting and changed the Department of Homeland Security's procedures in such cases.

Source: "Immigration Clinic," *University of Houston Law Center*, https://www.law.uh.edu/clinic/immi.asp.

— Competency Connection —
⚙ SOCIAL RESPONSIBILITY ⚙

What value, if any, do you believe law clinics provide in preparing law students for the practice of law? What value, if any, do they provide to the community at large?

lawyers provided almost 2 million hours of free legal assistance and more than 1.25 million hours of reduced-fee legal work. In 2017, attorneys also contributed approximately $1.7 million to the Access to Justice Foundation.[28]

For-profit companies provide options for low-cost legal services through online self-help legal materials. Some of the sites include lawyer referrals for further assistance. The better-rated sites include FAQs, questionnaires that when answered can then be used to populate the form, and software to check the accuracy of the completed form. Interactive software and legal self-help books allow a person to write a will, obtain a divorce, or create a corporation. Legal documents that would cost hundreds, and sometimes thousands, of dollars if prepared by an attorney can be completed at little or no cost with self-help products. These sites, however, are not permitted to offer any advice on how to complete or adapt the forms to a specific transaction.

Juries

A jury system lets citizens participate directly in the administration of justice. Texas has two types of juries: grand juries and trial juries (also called petit juries). The state's Bill of Rights guarantees that individuals may be charged with a felony only by grand jury indictment. It also provides that anyone charged with either a felony or a misdemeanor has the right to trial by jury. If requested by either party, jury trials are required in civil cases. In recent years, the number of civil jury trials in Texas has steadily declined.

Grand Jury Composed of 12 citizens, a **grand jury** is chosen at random from a list of 20 to 125 prospective grand jurors selected and summoned in the same way that civil jury panels are identified. The grand jury process is then explained to the panel. Some judges attempt to elicit volunteers; others select the first 12 qualified jurors. In addition, four alternates are selected. Until 2015, Texas also allowed the use of a method called the "key man system" (nicknamed "pick-a-pal"), in which a panel of commissioners hand-selected potential grand jurors. Critics argued this method resulted in bias and a lack of diversity among grand jurors that undermined the community's confidence in the criminal justice system.[29] Following the model used by most states and the federal government, the 84th Legislature (2015) eliminated the key man system.

Members of a Texas grand jury must have the qualifications of trial jurors and not be a complainant (the accused) in a grand jury proceeding. County commissioners determine the pay for grand jurors, and thus pay varies across the state, although it is similar to pay for service on a trial jury. The district judge appoints one juror to serve as presiding juror or foreman of the jury panel. A grand jury's life is three months in length, though a district judge may extend a grand jury's term up to 90 days. During this period, grand juries have the authority to inquire into all criminal actions but devote most of their time to felony matters.

Although grand juries usually consider indictments for cases presented by the district attorney, they can act independently. Juries that refuse to follow the lead of the prosecutor are called "runaway grand juries." When the Collin County district attorney refused to investigate allegations of securities fraud against

grand jury
Composed of 12 persons (and four alternates) with the qualifications of trial jurors, a grand jury serves three months while it determines whether sufficient evidence exists to indict persons accused of committing crimes.

Attorney General Ken Paxton, the grand jury undertook its own investigation.[30] Ultimately, a special prosecutor was appointed and Paxton was indicted. Refusal to pay the special prosecutor delayed prosecution of the case through mid-2019.

If, after investigation and deliberation (often lasting only a few minutes), at least nine grand jurors decide there is sufficient evidence to warrant a trial, an indictment is prepared with the aid of the prosecuting attorney. The indictment is a written statement accusing some person or persons of a particular crime (for example, burglary of a home). An indictment is referred to as a true bill; failure to indict constitutes a no bill. In a misdemeanor case, a grand jury information (with the same effect as an indictment in a felony case) may be prepared, but is not constitutionally required, for prosecution. Jurors and witnesses are sworn to keep secret all they hear in grand jury sessions.

Petit Jury Although relatively few Texans ever serve on a grand jury, many can expect to be summoned for duty on a trial jury (**petit jury**). Official qualifications for jurors are not high. To ensure that jurors are properly informed concerning their work, the court gives them brief printed instructions (in English and Spanish) that describe their duties and explain basic legal terms and trial procedures. In urban counties, these instructions are often shown as a video in English and other languages common to segments of the county's population, such as Spanish or Vietnamese.

Qualifications, Selection, and Compensation of Jurors A qualified Texas juror must be

- A citizen of the United States and of the state of Texas
- Eighteen years of age or older
- Of sound mind
- Able to read and write (with no restriction on language), unless literate jurors are unavailable
- Neither convicted of a felony nor under indictment or other legal accusation of theft or any felony

Qualified persons have a legal responsibility to serve when called, unless exempted or excused. Exemptions include

- Being age 70 or older
- Having legal custody of a child or children younger than age 10
- Being enrolled in and attending a university, college, or secondary school
- Being the primary caregiver for an invalid
- Being employed by the legislative branch of state government
- Having served as a petit juror within the preceding two years in counties with populations of at least 200,000 or the preceding three years in counties with populations of more than 250,000
- Being on active military duty outside the county

Judges may excuse others from jury duty in special circumstances. A person who is legally exempt from jury duty may file a signed statement with the court

petit jury
A trial jury of 6 or 12 members.

clerk at any time before the scheduled date of appearance. In most counties, prospective jurors complete necessary exemption forms online. Anyone summoned for jury duty can reschedule the reporting date once (at least twice in urban counties), as long as the new date is within six months of the original. Subsequent rescheduling requires an emergency that could not have been previously anticipated, such as illness or a death in the family. Failure to report for jury duty or falsely claiming an exemption is punishable as contempt of court, and a guilty individual can be fined up to $1,000.

A **venire** (panel of prospective jurors) is chosen by random selection from a list provided by either the secretary of state, another governmental agency, or a private contractor selected by the county commissioners court. The list includes the county's registered voters, licensed drivers, and persons with identification cards issued by the Department of Public Safety. A trial jury is composed of six or twelve citizens, one of whom serves as foreman or presiding juror: six serve in a justice of the peace court, municipal court, or county court, whereas 12 serve in a district court. A jury panel generally includes more than the minimum number of jurors.

Attorneys question jurors through a procedure called **voir dire** (which means "to speak the truth") to identify any potential jurors who cannot be fair and impartial. Prospective jurors can expect to be asked about their social media habits, such as who they follow on Twitter. In some instances, attorneys will have reviewed veniremen's Facebook accounts and other social media sites. An attorney may challenge for cause any venire member suspected of bias. If the judge agrees with the attorney, the prospective juror is excused from serving. Some individuals try to avoid jury duty by answering voir dire questions in ways that make them appear biased.

An attorney challenges prospective jurors either by peremptory challenge (up to 15 per side, depending on the type of case, without having to give a reason for excluding the venire members) or by challenge for cause (an unlimited number). Jurors may not be eliminated on the basis of race or ethnicity. For a district court, a trial jury is made up of the first 12 venire members who are neither excused by the district judge nor challenged peremptorily by a party in the case. For lower courts, the first six venire members accepted form a jury. A judge may direct the selection of alternate jurors to replace any seated juror who can no longer serve. Once impaneled, jurors are sworn in and receive further instructions from the court. They will be instructed to avoid communication with others about the trial during the proceedings. Not only is direct communication disallowed, jurors are also prohibited from sending information about the trial through tweets, postings, or blogs. Attempts to communicate with parties to the trial, such as friending them on social media sites, is also prohibited.

Although daily pay for venire members and jurors varies from county to county, minimum pay for juror service is $6 for all or part of the first day of jury duty and may be as high as $50 for each subsequent day. Under state law, counties fund the first $6 per juror each day, and the state reimburses the counties up to $34 per juror for each subsequent day of service. Employers are not required to pay wages to an employee summoned or selected for jury duty; however, they cannot fire permanent employees for such service.

venire
A panel of prospective jurors drawn by random selection. These prospective jurors are called veniremen.

voir dire
Courtroom procedure in which attorneys question prospective jurors to identify any who cannot be fair and impartial.

✓ **10.2 Learning Check**

1. A court must have jurisdiction to hear a case. What does this mean?
2. True or False: It is the responsibility of the grand jury to determine whether a defendant is guilty.

Answers at the end of this chapter.

◰ Judicial Procedures in Civil Cases

LO 10.3 Describe the judicial procedure for the adjudication of civil lawsuits.

The term "civil law" generally refers to matters not covered by criminal law. The following are important subjects of civil law: **torts** (for example, unintended injury to another person in a traffic accident); contracts (for example, agreements to deliver property of a specified quality at a certain price); and domestic relations or family law (such as divorce). Civil law disputes usually involve individuals or corporations in lawsuits that seek money damages or injunctive relief (requiring someone to do or cease doing something). In criminal cases, a person is prosecuted by the state.

State legislatures frequently change both criminal and civil law. In recent years, the Texas legislature (through statutes and proposed constitutional amendments) and the people of Texas (by ratification of constitutional amendments) have greatly limited money damage recoveries in tort cases.[31]

In civil cases, plaintiffs may be eligible to recover for three different types of damages:

- Economic damages that include lost wages and actual expenses (for example, hospital bills)
- Noneconomic damages that include a loss in quality of life from causes, such as disfigurement, mental anguish, and emotional distress
- Exemplary or punitive damages that are intended to punish the defendant

Originally, juries determined the maximum amount of money judgments. Now, these recovery amounts, especially for noneconomic and exemplary damages, are restricted by law.

A major justification for limiting recoveries in tort cases is that individuals and businesses must pay high liability insurance premiums for protection against the risk of lawsuit judgments. After limitations were placed on recoveries in medical malpractice cases, many insurers reduced their malpractice insurance rates, and the number of physicians relocating to Texas increased. In 2017, the state issued twice as many new medical licenses as it did in 2003, the year the law was enacted. In that same period, the number of filed medical malpractice lawsuits dropped by 90 percent.[32] Physicians maintain they deliver better patient care because they no longer have to practice defensive medicine by over-prescribing medication or ordering unnecessary tests. As one doctor observed, "We understand that it's our job to practice good medicine. We don't need a lawyer to tell us that, or the threat or intimidation … of a lawsuit for that."[33]

Skeptics note that the cost of health care and health-insurance premiums for consumers has continued to rise.[34] Additionally, according to some observers, the most vulnerable patients, those in nursing homes and children, are denied access to the courts because their economic losses are small since they have no lost income, even though their noneconomic losses, such as pain and suffering, may be immense. Trial lawyers argue that the law has eroded "the rights and remedies" of injured parties.[35]

tort
An injury to a person or an individual's property resulting from the wrongful act of another.

Recoveries for other types of torts, such as those arising from product liability, have not been so restricted. In 2016, a Bexar County jury awarded almost $100 million to the parents and their young son for injuries the child sustained in an auto accident. The child was riding in the back seat of his father's Audi when the car was hit from behind. The car's front seat was designed to collapse backward in a rear-end collision. Plaintiffs alleged this design was defective, because when the seat collapsed, father's and son's heads collided. The child sustained permanent brain damage. Described as having been "at the top of his class" and a "born leader" prior to the accident, at the time of trial (four years after the accident), the 11-year-old had a vocabulary of five words, was in special education classes, and had uncontrollable seizures.[36] The case was settled for an undisclosed amount in March 2017.

Civil Trial Procedure

The Supreme Court of Texas makes rules of civil procedure for all courts with civil jurisdiction. These rules, however, cannot conflict with any general law of the state. Rules of civil procedure are enacted unless they are rejected by the legislature.

Civil cases normally begin when the **plaintiff** (injured party) files a petition, a document that includes the plaintiff's complaints against the **defendant** and the remedy sought—usually money damages. This petition is filed in the county in which the lawsuit is contemplated through efiletexas.gov and the court clerk issues a citation. The citation is delivered to the defendant, directing that person to answer the charges. To contest the suit, the defendant must file an answer to the plaintiff's charges. The answer explains why the plaintiff is not entitled to the remedy sought and asks that the plaintiff be required to prove every charge made in the petition.

Some individuals represent themselves pro se (without a lawyer) and file multiple frivolous lawsuits. If a defendant prevails in having the plaintiff declared a vexatious litigant by a court, the person's name is placed on a list maintained online by the Office of Court Administration. Vexatious litigants must either file a bond with the court or, in some instances, obtain prior permission before proceeding with a lawsuit. Through 2018, trial courts had declared approximately 250 individuals as being vexatious litigants, 15 percent of whom were inmates in Texas Department of Criminal Justice prisons.[37]

Before the judge sets a trial date (which may be many months or even years after the petition is filed), all interested parties should have had an opportunity to file their petitions, answers, or other pleas with the court. These instruments constitute the pleadings in the case and form the basis of the trial. Prior to the trial, the parties also have the opportunity to gather from each other information related to the pending case. This process, known as **discovery**, includes examining documents, obtaining written and oral answers to questions, inspecting property under the control of the other party, and similar activities. Information obtained during discovery may become evidence in the case. Among the items attorneys research are any electronic communications, such as email, a party might have created or received, as well as postings on social media sites. Some unethical practitioners attempt to friend a party to get into the more private areas of these sites.

plaintiff
The injured party who initiates a civil suit or the state in a criminal proceeding.

defendant
The person sued in a civil proceeding or prosecuted in a criminal proceeding.

discovery
Gathering information from the opposing party and witnesses in a lawsuit, including examination of relevant documents, obtaining written and oral answers to questions, inspecting property under the control of the other party, and similar activities.

Either party has the option to have a jury determine the facts. Over the past 25 years, the number of cases decided by a jury has decreased by more than 60 percent.[38] Less than 0.4 percent of civil lawsuits are tried to a jury. After the jury determines the facts, the judge applies the law to that version of the facts. If no one demands a jury, the trial judge decides all facts and applies the law. Fewer than one-third of all filed lawsuits are tried to the judge in a proceeding known as a bench trial. In recent years, the number of bench trials has also been in rapid decline while the number of cases settled by agreement between the plaintiff and defendant has increased (approximately 12 percent of civil law disputes and almost one-third of family law cases). The remaining cases are dismissed.

Trial and Appeal of a Civil Case

As a trial begins, lawyers for each party make brief opening statements. The plaintiff's case is presented first. The defendant has an opportunity to contest all evidence introduced and may cross-examine the plaintiff's witnesses. After the plaintiff's case has been presented, it is the defendant's turn to offer evidence and the testimony of witnesses. The plaintiff may challenge this evidence and testimony. The judge is the final authority as to what evidence and testimony may be introduced by all parties, though objections to the judge's rulings can be used as grounds for appeal.

In a jury trial, after all parties have concluded, the judge writes a charge to the jury, submits it to the parties for their approval, makes any necessary changes they suggest, and reads the charge to the jury. In the charge, the judge instructs the jury on the rules governing their deliberations and defines various terms. After the charge is read, attorneys make their closing arguments to the jurors; then the jury retires to elect one of its members to serve as the presiding juror (commonly referred to as foreman) and to deliberate.

The jury will not be asked directly whether the plaintiff or the defendant should win. Instead, the jury must answer a series of questions that will establish the facts of the case. These questions are called **special issues**. Judgment is based on jurors' answers. To decide a case in a district court, at least the same 10 of the 12 jurors must agree on answers to all of the special issues; in a county court or JP court, the same five of six must agree. If the required number of jurors cannot reach agreement, the foreman reports a hung jury. If the judge agrees, the jury is discharged. Any party may then request a new trial, which will be scheduled unless the case is dismissed. If the judge disagrees with the foreman's report, jurors continue to deliberate.

A jury's decision is a **verdict**. When there is no jury, the judge arrives at a verdict. In either case, the judge prepares a written decision, or the **judgment** or decree of the court. Any party may then file a motion for a new trial based on the reasons the party believes the trial was unfair. If the judge agrees, a new trial is ordered; if not, the case may be appealed to a higher court. A complete written record of the trial is sent to the appellate court. The usual route of appeals is from a county or district court to a court of appeals and then, in some instances, to the Texas Supreme Court.

special issues
Questions a judge gives a trial jury to answer to establish the facts in a civil case.

verdict
A judge's or jury's decision about a court case.

judgment
A judge's written opinion based on a verdict.

✓ **10.3 Learning Check**

1. What are the parties to a civil lawsuit called?

2. True or False: In a civil jury trial, jurors will be asked to decide which party should win.

Answers at the end of this chapter.

◨ Judicial Procedures in Criminal Cases

LO 10.4 Describe the judicial procedure for the adjudication of criminal cases.

Criminal cases occur when someone violates the rules of society by committing an offense for which the government can seek the offender's life, liberty, or property. Because a defendant risks losing his or her natural rights, the rules and procedures in criminal cases include many more checks on the system than in civil cases. From the moment a person is taken into custody until all appeals have been exhausted, the law is designed to assure the highest level of protection for the defendant's rights.

Criminal Justice System

Rules of criminal procedure are made by the legislature. The Texas Code of Criminal Procedure is written to comply with U.S. Supreme Court rulings regarding confessions, arrests, searches, and seizures. Additional rules of procedure have been adopted to promote fairness and efficiency in handling criminal cases.

Thousands of illegal acts (including traffic violations) are committed daily in Texas. After an arrest and before questioning, police must advise suspects of their constitutional rights to remain silent and to have an attorney present. When a prosecuting attorney (either the district attorney or the county attorney) files charges, a suspect must appear before a judicial officer (usually a justice of the peace), who names the offense or offenses charged and provides information concerning the suspect's legal rights. A person charged with a noncapital offense may be released on personal recognizance (promising to report for trial at a later date), released on bail by posting personal money or money provided for a charge by a bail bond service, or denied bail and jailed.

People who cannot afford to hire a lawyer must be provided with the services of an attorney in any felony or misdemeanor case in which conviction may result in a prison or jail sentence. In 2017, the state's taxpayers paid approximately $265 million to fund appointed counsel for indigent defendants. The 13-member Texas Indigent Defense Commission, comprised of judges, attorneys, and legislators, oversees the development of statewide policies and procedures for representation of the poorest defendants. In addition, the commission monitors county compliance and coordinates state monetary assistance for these programs. County taxpayers, however, bear more than 85 percent of the burden of indigent defense costs.[39]

Private attorneys, appointed by judges, provide most of the defense for indigent defendants; but an increasing number of counties maintain public defenders' offices to meet some of the representation needs of the poor. A study of the results achieved by the public defenders' office in Harris County found that although per case cost was higher for public defender representation ($946 versus $550), fewer defendants received guilty verdicts. Private criminal defense attorneys often oppose the creation of public defenders' offices, in part because they fear a loss of income; however, Harris County juvenile court judges continued to assign

85 percent of juvenile cases to private attorneys through 2018.[40] Public defenders in Harris County also attempt to be seen as a resource for all criminal defense attorneys, offering access to their law library and clothing appropriate for court appearances for criminal defendants. The Texas Fair Defense Act requires counties to devise standards for appointed counsel and establishes minimum attorney qualifications for the appointment of counsel for indigent defendants charged with capital crimes.

Under Texas law, the right to trial by jury is guaranteed in all criminal cases. Except in death penalty cases, defendants may waive jury trial (if the prosecuting attorney agrees), regardless of the plea—guilty, not guilty, or nolo contendere (no contest). To expedite procedures, prosecuting and defense attorneys may engage in plea bargaining, in which the accused pleads guilty in return for a promise that the prosecutor will seek a lighter sentence or will recommend community supervision. Usually, a judge will accept a plea bargain. If the defendant waives a trial by jury and is found guilty by a judge, that judge also determines punishment.

Criminal Trial and Appeal

After the trial jury has been selected, the prosecuting attorney reads an information (for a misdemeanor) or an indictment (for a felony) to inform the jury of the basic allegations of the state's case. The defendant then enters a plea.

As plaintiff, the state begins by calling its witnesses and introducing any evidence supporting the information or the indictment. The defense may then challenge evidence and cross-examine witnesses. Next, the defense presents its case, calling witnesses and submitting evidence that, in turn, the prosecution attacks. After all evidence and testimony have been presented, the judge charges the jury by instructing jurors on rules governing their deliberations and explaining the applicable law. Both prosecuting and defense attorneys then address final arguments to the jury before it retires to reach a verdict.

The jury must reach a unanimous decision to return a verdict of guilty or not guilty. If jurors are hopelessly split, the result is a hung jury. In that event, the judge declares a mistrial and discharges the jurors. When requested by the prosecuting attorney, the judge orders a new trial with another jury.

If a jury brings a verdict before a court, the judge may choose to disregard it and order a new trial on the grounds that the jury failed to arrive at a verdict that achieves substantial justice. In a jury trial, the jury may determine the sentence if the convicted person so requests; otherwise, the judge assesses the sentence. In a capital felony case in which the death penalty is being sought, the jury must determine punishment. A separate hearing on the penalty is held, at which time the person's prior criminal or juvenile record, general reputation, and other relevant factors may be introduced, such as facts concerning the convicted person's background and lifestyle as determined by a presentence investigation.

A convicted defendant has the right to appeal on grounds that an error in trial procedure occurred. All appeals (except for death penalty cases) are heard first by the court of appeals in the district in which the trial was held. A few of these appeals are ultimately reviewed by the Texas Court of Criminal Appeals. Death penalty appeals are made directly from a district court to the Texas Court of Criminal Appeals.

✓ **10.4 Learning Check**

1. True or False: A majority of jurors must return a verdict of guilty or not guilty.

2. A capital felony for which the defendant received the death penalty is appealed to which court?

Answers at the end of this chapter.

KEEPING CURRENT
The Impact on Texas

The popular, partisan election of judges affected judicial selection in both statewide and local elections in both 2016 and 2018. At the state level, voters elected only Republican candidates in both elections. The national split between urban and rural voters is also present in Texas. In urban areas like Dallas and Harris Counties, Democratic Party judicial candidates won all district court judgeships in 2016 and 2018. In 2018, Democrats also won all county and courts of appeals judgeships in these urban counties.

At the court of appeals level, Democrats now hold a majority on seven of the state's 14 courts of appeals. As with previous elections, the party affiliation, not the record or incumbency of a candidate, appeared to be the most important factor in the likelihood of a judicial candidate's winning election to office. One of the defeated Republican court of appeals justices, Brett Busby, was subsequently appointed to the Supreme Court of Texas.

Nationally, Donald J. Trump's election increased the possibility of at least one Texan being appointed to the U.S. Supreme Court. Despite a number of unflattering tweets from Tweeter Laureate Don Willett, Trump named him to the U.S. 5th Circuit Court of Appeals in 2017. Trump also considered Willett for the position on the U.S. Supreme Court now held by Justice Brett Kavanaugh.

Funding the Texas judicial system remains of primary concern to counties and judges. The 86th Legislature was asked to consider increasing financial support for attorneys for indigent defendants. Raising salaries and increasing longevity supplements for state judges were additional areas of concern. The State Commission on Judicial Compensation recommended a 15-percent increase in annual salary and payment of longevity supplements after four years of judicial service.

CONCLUSION

The Texas legal system is indeed confusing. From sorting out overlapping court jurisdictions to identifying elected judges and justices—the system appears to be shrouded in mystery and anonymity. Often understood only by those who use the system daily—Texas lawyers—decisions of criminal and civil court judges affect every Texan. For the justice system to work effectively, Texans must understand these complex proceedings. Technology has affected all aspects of the judicial branch. The ability of computers to process and organize large volumes of data has made the system more efficient. Ease of communication through social media has sometimes confused its users, whether judges, lawyers, or jurors. The move into the 21st century has included problems not contemplated by those who designed the judicial branch.

CHAPTER SUMMARY

LO 10.1 Identify the sources of Texas law. The role of courts is to settle disputes by interpreting and applying the law. Texas state law includes both civil law and criminal law. The sources of law include the state's constitution, its statutes, regulations, and the common law (judge-made law). In an attempt to organize its laws, the legislature has instructed the Texas Legislative Council to place laws that cover specific topics into codes.

LO 10.2 Compare the functions of all participants in the justice system. Both constitutional and statutory laws have been used to create the state's court system. Courts may have original or appellate jurisdiction, or both. Texas has local, county, trial, and appellate courts. Some trial courts are now specialty courts that provide more direct oversight of particular types of cases or involving specific populations. The state's emphasis on parties' resolving their disputes outside the courtroom has resulted in fewer trials. Almost all Texas judges are elected through popular, partisan elections, a system followed in only two other states. Once in office, a judge, as well as the lawyers who appear before him or her, are subject to regulation and discipline. There are two types of juries both of which are chosen from a panel of randomly selected veniremen: grand juries (which determine if adequate cause exists to bring a defendant to trial in a criminal case) and petit juries (which determine the facts in civil cases, whether a defendant is guilty or not guilty in a criminal case, and may determine punishment in criminal cases).

LO 10.3 Describe the judicial procedure for the adjudication of civil lawsuits. The civil justice system includes contract cases, tort cases, family law matters, and juvenile justice cases. The Texas legislature has limited the amount of punitive and noneconomic damages in some tort cases. In jury trials for civil cases, the jury determines the facts of the case by answering special issues, and the judge applies the law. In Texas's bifurcated court system, the highest appellate court for civil cases is the Texas Supreme Court.

LO 10.4 Describe the judicial procedure for the adjudication of criminal cases. Criminal law regulates many types of behavior. Protections that are built into the law, for accused felons in particular, include a defendant's being advised of his or her constitutional rights, the right to appointed counsel if someone is indigent, and the right to trial by jury. Felony defendants have the right to a grand jury indictment. Except in capital murder cases, a defendant can waive the right to a jury trial. Jury verdicts in criminal cases must be unanimous. In Texas's bifurcated court system, the highest appellate court for criminal cases is the Texas Court of Criminal Appeals.

KEY TERMS

alternative dispute resolution (ADR),
   p. 375
appellate jurisdiction, p. 366
appointment-retention system,
   p. 377
bifurcated, p. 372
civil law, p. 365
concurrent jurisdiction, p. 366
constitutional county court, p. 370
contingency fee, p. 380
county court-at-law, p. 371
courts of appeals, p. 372
Court of Criminal Appeals, p. 373

court of record, p. 369
criminal law, p. 365
defendant, p. 386
discovery, p. 386
district court, p. 371
exclusive jurisdiction, p. 366
felony, p. 365
grand jury, p. 382
judgment, p. 387
jurisdiction, p. 365
justice of the peace, p. 369
misdemeanor, p. 365
Missouri Plan, p. 377

municipal court, p. 369
original jurisdiction, p. 366
petit jury, p. 383
plaintiff, p. 386
probate, p. 366
probate court, p. 371
special issues, p. 387
specialty courts, p. 375
Supreme Court of Texas, p. 374
tort, p. 385
venire, p. 384
verdict, p. 387
voir dire, p. 384

LEARNING CHECK ANSWERS

 1. False. Misdemeanors and felonies are considered criminal law cases.

2. True. Texas courts interpret and apply judge-made common law based on custom and tradition dating back to medieval England, in addition to state laws that include the provisions of the Texas Constitution, statutes enacted by the legislature, and regulations adopted by state agencies.

 1. Jurisdiction means that the court has the authority to hear a particular kind of case. Jurisdiction may be granted in the Texas Constitution or in the statute creating a court.

2. False. A grand jury only determines if there is enough evidence to go to trial in a criminal case. A petit jury determines if a defendant is guilty.

 1. The parties to a civil lawsuit are the plaintiff, who is the injured party bringing the lawsuit, and the defendant, who is the person being sued.

2. False. In a civil jury trial, jurors answer special issues, or a series of questions about the facts in the case. The judge then applies the law to the answers to the special issues and renders a judgment establishing who won the case.

 1. False. A jury verdict in a criminal case, whether guilty or not guilty, requires a unanimous decision by the jury. If jurors are split, the result is a hung jury.

2. A capital felony for which the defendant received the death penalty is appealed directly to the Court of Criminal Appeals.

11

Finance and Fiscal Policy

Learning Objectives

11.1 Assess the fairness of Texas's budgeting and taxing policies.

11.2 Describe the sources of Texas's state revenue.

11.3 Describe the procedure for developing and approving a state budget.

11.4 Evaluate the effectiveness of the state's financing of public services.

IMAGE 11.1 The Texas Lottery Commission maintains a Twitter account

Texas Lottery ✓
@TexasLottery

👤+ Follow

RT to say "THANK YOU" to #TexasTeachers! #TeacherAppreciationDay

Thank You!

RETWEETS 3   LIKES 2

10:00 AM - 3 May 2016

Source: Twitter

— Competency Connection —
★ PERSONAL RESPONSIBILITY ★

Should ethical concerns about gambling influence whether a government-sponsored lottery is an appropriate revenue source for public education?

West Texas Intermediate Crude (WTI) is a stream of crude oil produced in Texas and southern Oklahoma. The per barrel price of WTI serves as the benchmark for the price of other crude oil produced in the United States. Through the first nine months of 2014, WTI sold for $90 or more per barrel. On June 16, 2014, it reached the highest price for the year when each barrel sold for $107.52. Beginning in October 2014, the price of WTI began a downward spiral. By the time the 84th Legislature convened on January 13, 2015, the per barrel price of WTI was $45.92.[1] What had been dubbed "The Texas Miracle," the ability of Texas to flourish in the midst of the Great Recession that began in 2008 and severely damaged the national economy, paused.

Oil, gas, and related industries comprised about 14 percent of the Texas economy in 2014. Shifts in profitability in these industries, therefore, had a significant impact on the state's economic well-being. Bolstered in part by the optimistic outlook of the Office of the Comptroller of Public Accounts, members of the Texas legislature went through the 84th legislative session reducing taxes and increasing spending. When the session ended on June 1, 2015, the price of oil had recovered to $62.87 per barrel suggesting that the comptroller's prediction of $65 per barrel was correct.[2] Then, in August 2015, oil prices tumbled. By January 20, 2016, WTI sold at $26.68 per barrel, its lowest price since 2003. Over the upcoming two years, the price rose to over $75 per barrel in October 2018 and then began to decline again to approximately $60 per barrel in May 2019.

Exploration and production slowed in the oil fields because of the low price of oil due to an oversupply. By the end of 2015, the Houston area reported an annual job loss of almost 18,000 employees from the oil and gas industry sector. Job losses in manufacturing and slowdowns in construction hiring were also linked to the troubled oil and gas industry.[3] From 2014 through April 2016, statewide job losses in oil and gas industries were estimated at 65,000 with an additional 185,000 people losing their jobs in industries that supported the oil and gas sector.[4] By June 2016, more than 40 Texas oil producers were in bankruptcy. Major energy companies like Chevron and Marathon Petroleum Corp. reported they were losing money. These companies not only produce oil and gas but they also refine it. Because of the low cost of crude oil, their refinery operations had continued to show a profit until 2016. Then, a backlog of petroleum products, like gasoline and heating oil, made these operations unprofitable. Cities and smaller towns in oil-producing areas of the state suddenly had a glut of apartments and housing. Fearful Texans spent less and further lowered tax revenue available to the state. In contemplation of a revenue shortfall, the Legislative Budget Board directed all state agencies to reduce their proposed 2018–2019 budget requests by 4 percent prior to submission. The 85th Legislature was forced to consider how to deliver services to the state's residents in a time of declining revenue. Prospects for the 86th Legislature were somewhat improved. By January 2019, both Chevron and Marathon reported profits; however, the number of Texas energy company failures had increased to 75, almost three-fourths of all industry bankruptcies.

This chapter examines the balance between costs and services; it provides an overview of the Lone Star State's fiscal policies, budgeting processes, and most costly public policy areas. Taxing, public spending, and governmental policy priorities will continue to have significant impacts on 21st-century Texans.

✪ Fiscal Policies

LO 11.1 Assess the fairness of Texas's budgeting and taxing policies.

During the 84th legislative session in 2015, legislators were able to extend Texas's traditional low-tax approach to **fiscal policy** (public policy that concerns taxes, government spending, public debt, and management of government money). The economic boost the Texas economy received from oil and gas prices of more than $90 per barrel, along with high levels of production, resulted in a budget surplus for the 2014 fiscal year. Ignoring the warning signs of $45 per barrel oil and relying on predictions that the worst was over, the legislature began eliminating and reducing taxes. When the predicted downturn occurred, the 85th legislative session (2017) struggled with less revenue. By 2019, the 86th Legislature once again had additional funds and was able to address public school finance and other more costly services.

Tax revenue includes state sales taxes, as well as taxes on specific items, such as cigarettes, motor vehicles, and gross receipts from businesses. Revenue sources other than taxes include oil and gas royalties, land sales, and federal grants-in-aid. When economic conditions are poor, the legislature achieves a balanced budget by using a number of accounting maneuvers, like deferring some mandatory payments beyond the end of the biennial budget period, encouraging early payment of taxes to speed up revenue collection, and intentionally underfunding high-cost items such as Medicaid.[5] In difficult economic times, the legislature also looks for ways to reduce spending, especially for high-cost items such as education and health care. When the economic outlook is more favorable, as it was in 2015, the legislature restores funding and reduces taxes. Once these taxes have been reduced, legislators are reluctant to increase them to raise revenue during subsequent economic downturns.

Texans remain committed to pay-as-you-go spending and low taxes, no matter the strength of the economy. The Lone Star State's fiscal policy has not deviated from its 19th-century origins. Today, the notion of a balanced budget, achieved by low tax rates and low-to-moderate government spending levels, continues to dominate state fiscal policy. Consequently, state government, its employees, and its taxpayers face the daily challenge of meeting higher demands for services with fewer resources.

The state's elected officials appear to adopt the view expressed by economist and Nobel Prize winner Milton Friedman (1912–2006) that "the preservation of freedom requires limiting narrowly the role of government and placing primary reliance on private property, free markets, and voluntary arrangements."[6] Texas legislators and other state leaders have repeatedly demonstrated a willingness to reduce services, outsource governmental work to decrease the number

fiscal policy
Public policy that concerns taxing, government spending, public debt, and management of government money.

of employees on the state's payroll, and maintain or lower tax rates as solutions to the state's fiscal problems.

Taxing Policy

Texans have traditionally opposed mandatory assessments for public purposes, or **taxes**. Residents have pressured their state government to maintain low taxes. When the state experiences budget surpluses as it did in 2014–2015, pressure increases to eliminate or lower taxes. The 84th Legislature repealed eight different taxes, including, among others, the fireworks tax, the oil regulation tax, and the controlled substances tax. A 25 percent reduction of the franchise tax, a tax paid by most businesses in Texas, saved taxpayers more than $2.5 billion in the 2016–2017 biennium. Because of weaker economic conditions in 2017, the 85th Legislature passed no major tax repeals or reductions.[7]

When additional revenues have been needed, Texans have indicated in poll after poll their preference for **regressive taxes**, which favor the rich and fall most heavily on the poor ("the less you make, the more government takes"). Under such taxes, the burden decreases as personal income increases. Figure 11.1 illustrates the impact of regressive taxes on different levels of income. An attempt to increase the sales tax rate in exchange for a reduction in property taxes failed in the 86th Legislature, however. The Legislative Budget Board's report that under

tax
A mandatory assessment exacted by a government for a public purpose.

regressive tax
A tax in which the effective tax rate decreases as the tax base (such as individual income or corporate profits) increases.

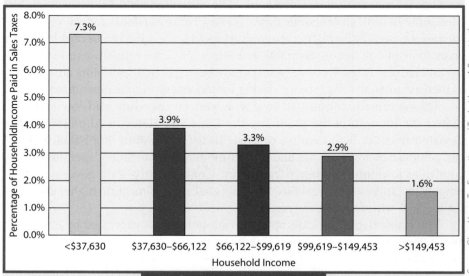

FIGURE 11.1 Percent of Average Annual Family Income Paid in Sales Tax in Texas (FY2018)

Source: Glenn Hegar, *Tax Exemptions and Tax Incidence: A Report to the Governor and the 85th Texas Legislature* (Austin: Texas Comptroller of Public Accounts, November 2018), https://comptroller.texas.gov/transparency/reports/tax-exemptions-and-incidence.

── Competency Connection ──
◉ SOCIAL RESPONSIBILITY ◉

What arguments support the fairness of poorer people paying a higher percentage of their income in taxes than the wealthy do?

this plan taxes would increase for anyone with an annual income of less than $100,000 was likely instrumental in the defeat.

Texas lawmakers have developed one of the most regressive tax structures in the nation. A general sales tax and selective sales taxes have been especially popular. **Progressive taxes** (taxes in which the impact increases as income rises—"the more you make, the more government takes") have been unpopular. Texas officials and citizens so oppose state income taxes that the state constitution requires a popular referendum before an income tax can be levied. The 86th Legislature determined even the possibility of a personal income tax was unacceptable. Legislators chose to ask voters to amend the Texas Constitution to prohibit any tax on personal income.

To finance services, Texas government depends heavily on sales taxes, which rank among the highest in the nation. In addition, the Lone Star State has a dizzying array of other taxes. The Texas state comptroller's office collects more than 60 separate taxes, fees, and assessments on behalf of the state and local governments.[8] Yet the sales tax remains the most important source of state revenue.

Many observers have criticized the regressive characteristics of Texas's tax system as being unfair. An additional concern is that the state primarily operates with a 19th-century land- and product-based tax system that is no longer appropriate to the knowledge- and service-based economy of the 21st century. Local governments rely heavily on real estate taxes for their revenue. More than half of the state's general revenue tax collections are sales and use taxes. Until 2006, business activities of **service sector** employers (including those in trade, finance, and the professions) remained tax-free. In that year, however, the state altered the franchise tax law to require most Texas businesses to pay taxes calculated on their profit margins. This extension of the franchise tax subjected many service sector entities to taxation.

Texas's tax structure ranks as the 21st most volatile in revenue fluctuation among the states.[9] Its reliance on severance taxes (those generated by oil, gas, and other minerals mined or pumped from the earth) contributes to this volatility. In addition, a comparison of sales and use tax collections ($31.9 billion) and franchise tax collections ($3.7 billion) for fiscal year (budget year) 2018 reflects the extent to which the Lone Star State persists in relying on sales tax revenue. Changes in Texas's economy, without corresponding changes in its tax system, are projected to continue to erode the tax base. Under the current structure, the part of the economy generating the greatest amount of revenue frequently pays the least amount in taxes.

The state also charges special fees and assessments that are not called taxes but involve payments to the government. Texas legislators, reluctant to raise taxes, have often assessed these fees and surcharges. Is a **fee**, defined as a charge "imposed by an agency upon those subject to its regulation,"[10] different from a tax? Some argue that such assessments represent an artful use of words, not a refusal to raise taxes, and that these charges meet the definition of a tax if the proceeds benefit the general public. For example, the state requires attorneys to pay an annual legal services fee to fund legal assistance for the poor. Attorneys who fail to pay this fee lose their right to practice law in the state. No matter the designation, this mandatory fee is money that an attorney must pay to finance government services for the general public.

progressive tax
A tax in which the effective tax rate increases as the tax base (such as individual income or corporate profits) increases.

service sector
Businesses that provide services, such as finance, health care, food service, data processing, or consulting.

fee
A charge imposed by an agency upon those subject to its regulation.

Budget Policy

Hostility to public debt is demonstrated in constitutional and statutory provisions that are designed to force the state to operate with a pay-as-you-go **balanced budget**. The Texas Constitution prohibits the state from spending more than its anticipated revenue "[e]xcept in the case of emergency and imperative public necessity and with a four-fifths vote of the total membership of each House."[11] In addition, the cost of debt service limits the state's borrowing power. This cost cannot exceed 5 percent of the average balance of general revenue funds for the preceding three years.

To ensure a balanced budget, the comptroller of public accounts must submit to the legislature in advance of each regular session a sworn statement of cash on hand and revenue anticipated for the succeeding two years. The amount certified includes revenue available in both the General Revenue Fund and the General Revenue-Dedicated Fund. Appropriation bills enacted at that particular session, and at any subsequent special session, are limited to not more than the amount certified, unless a four-fifths majority in both houses votes to ignore the comptroller's predictions or the legislature provides new revenue sources.

Texas accounts for the state's revenue and spending in several different budgets. The All Funds Budget includes all sources of revenue and all spending. In addition, reference is often made to the General Revenue Funds Budget. This budget includes the nondedicated portion of the **General Revenue Fund** (money that can be appropriated for any legal purpose by the legislature) plus some of the funds used to finance public education (the Available School Fund, the State Instructional Materials Fund, and the Foundation School Fund). Casual deficits (unplanned shortages) sometimes arise in the General Revenue Fund. Like a thermometer, this fund measures the state's fiscal health. If the fund shows a surplus (as happened in fiscal years 2014–2015), fiscal health is good; if a deficit occurs (as occurred in FY 2010–FY 2011), then fiscal health is poor. Less than one-half of the state's expenditures come from the General Revenue Fund; the remainder comes from other funds that state law designates for use for specific purposes.

The General Revenue–Dedicated Funds Budget includes more than 200 separate funds. Because of restrictions on use, these accounts are defined as **dedicated funds**. In most cases, the funds can only be used for their designated purposes, though in some instances money can be diverted to the state's general fund. Even amounts that can only be spent for a designated purpose may be manipulated to satisfy the mandate for a balanced budget. The legislature can incorporate any unspent balances into its budget calculations. In the 82nd legislative session, for example, the legislature refused to appropriate more than $5 billion in General Revenue–Dedicated Funds in order to give the appearance of a balanced budget. State lawmakers justify these actions by noting that the high costs of programs such as Medicaid force them to freeze these balances. Former State Representative Sylvester Turner (D-Houston, and then mayor of Houston) characterized this practice somewhat differently, calling it "dishonest governing,"[12] because it is an accounting trick that makes money appear available

balanced budget
A budget in which total revenues and expenditures are equal, producing no deficit.

General Revenue Fund
An unrestricted state fund that is available for general appropriations.

dedicated fund
A restricted state fund that has been identified to be spent for a designated purpose. If the fund is consolidated within the General Revenue Fund, it usually must be spent for its intended purpose. Some unappropriated amounts of dedicated funds, even those required to be used for a specific purpose, can be included in the calculations to balance the state budget.

on paper that in fact is not available. Subsequent legislative sessions varied in their reliance on unappropriated, dedicated funds to balance the budget. An attempt by the House of Representatives to restrict the number of dedicated funds that could be used to balance the budget failed in the 86th Legislature.

The Federal Funds Budget includes all funding from the federal government. These amounts must be spent for their designated purposes. Likewise, the Other Funds Budget includes an additional 200-plus dedicated funds, each of which must be spent for its stated purpose, such as the Property Tax Relief Fund that must be used to fund public education.

⊠ POINT/COUNTERPOINT

Should Texas Adopt a Constitutional Amendment to Eliminate the Use of Unspent Dedicated Revenue to Balance the Budget?

THE ISSUE In the 84th legislative session, State Representative Drew Darby (R-San Angelo) introduced HJR 111, a proposed constitutional amendment that would prohibit using unspent dedicated funds to balance the biennial budget. Although the Texas House unanimously approved the amendment, the Senate allowed the resolution to die in committee. He offered no similar proposal in the 85th or 86th legislative sessions.

Since 1991, the Texas legislature has used unspent money in General Revenue–Dedicated Funds to satisfy the constitutional mandate to balance the state's biennial budget. Texans have paid a variety of fees to provide government services to the state's residents and yet, often, the money is stockpiled and remains unspent. Although the money can only be used for its intended purpose, the comptroller can include funds in these accounts that have not been appropriated in order to certify that a state budget is balanced. Therefore, legislators forego or limit spending the money in these accounts so the comptroller can count it for certification. This practice gives the illusion that the budget is balanced on paper, even though the funds cannot be spent.

Failing to spend the money has consequences. For example, every licensed motorcyclist in the state pays an additional $5 for each license renewal. This fee is supposed to be used for motorcycle safety training and public awareness campaigns for all drivers. Yet, from 2005 until 2015, no money was distributed from the account and it accumulated more than $18 million. During that same period, motorcycle fatalities increased by 59 percent. Texas Department of Transportation officials argued that one reason for the increase in fatalities was the general public's lack of awareness on how to "share the road" safely with bikers. Spending biker license fees on safety awareness programs for motorists could have possibly saved lives.

FOR	AGAINST
1. Prohibiting the use of unspent dedicated funds to balance the state's budget would increase transparency in the budgeting process. Current practices are really "smoke-and-mirrors" accounting that makes legislators appear to be more fiscally responsible than they actually are.	1. In difficult economic times, the legislature needs the flexibility to use all available accounting maneuvers to achieve a balanced budget. 2. Without the ability to use unspent dedicated funds to balance budgets, critical programs, such as Medicaid, would be cut or taxes would be increased.

(Continued)

FOR	AGAINST
2. Because the legislature yields to the temptation not to spend dedicated funds, many important needs in the state are not being met. Dedicated funds should either be used for their intended purposes or returned to the taxpayers. To do otherwise is a broken promise.	3. The legislature reduced its reliance on unappropriated dedicated funds in the last two sessions on its own initiative. A constitutional amendment is, therefore, unnecessary and too restrictive.
3. Without the discipline of a constitutional amendment, legislators will continue to rely on unspent dedicated funds to give the appearance of a balanced budget.	

Sources: "Bill Analysis: HJR 111," *House Research Organization*, April 27, 2015, http://www.hro.house.state.tx.us/pdf/ba84r/hjr0111 .pdf#navpanes=0; Phil Prazan, "Millions of Dollars Sit in Accounts that Could Save Lives on the Road," *KXAN*, March 2, 2015, http:// kxan.com/2015/03/02/millions-of-dollars-sit-in-accounts-that-could-save-lives-on-the-road/; and Joe Straus, "The Texas House Puts a New Limit on Budget Growth," *Austin American-Statesman*, May 4, 2015.

— Competency Connection —
⊛ **SOCIAL RESPONSIBILITY** ⊛

How would you vote on this proposed amendment? Why?

✓ **11.1 Learning Check**

1. What are three characteristics of Texas's fiscal policy?

2. The state of Texas has one of the highest sales tax rates in the nation. It does not have a state income tax. Is Texas's tax structure an example of a regressive or a progressive tax system?

Answers at the end of this chapter.

Spending Policy

Historically, Texans have shown little enthusiasm for state spending. In addition to requiring a balanced budget, the Texas Constitution restricts increases in spending that exceed the rate of growth of the state's economy and limits welfare spending in any fiscal year to no more than 1 percent of total state expenditures. Consequently, public expenditures have remained low relative to those of other state governments. Texas has consistently ranked between 47th and 50th in state spending per capita. Although the state's voters have indicated moderate willingness to spend for highways, roads, and other public improvements, they have demonstrated much less support for welfare programs, recreational facilities, and similar social services.

🔳 Revenue Sources

LO 11.2 Describe the sources of Texas's state revenue.

Funding for government services primarily comes from those who pay taxes. In addition, the state derives revenue from fees for licenses, sales of assets, investment income, gambling, borrowing, and federal grants. When revenue to the state declines, elected officials have only two choices: (1) increase taxes or other sources of revenue or (2) decrease services. In times of projected budget shortfalls, as occurred prior to the 2012–2013 biennium, the legislature's favored responses have been to decrease services and manipulate accounts within the budget as described in the Point/Counterpoint feature in this chapter. When revenue is plentiful, as was the situation in 2014–2015, pressure builds to reduce taxes.

The Politics of Taxation

Taxes are but one source of state revenue.[13] According to generally accepted standards, each tax levied and the total tax structure should be just and equitable. Opinions vary widely about what kinds of taxes and what types of structures meet these standards. Conflicts are most apparent in the struggle to finance the state's public schools as elected officials strive to lower real estate taxes for the state's property owners and replace local funding with additional state-level taxes. Texas has a constitutional mandate to provide "an efficient system of public free schools," and the state's courts have defined adequate funding as a key element of this requirement. Determining who should pay taxes to finance public education is a challenge.

In 2006, despite resistance, the 79th Legislature modified and expanded the business franchise tax in an effort to lower property taxes. It also imposed a $1 tax on cigarettes, increased taxes on other tobacco products (except cigars), and required buyers to pay a tax on used cars at their presumptive value as determined by publications such as *Kelley Blue Book*. Since 2006, legislators have yielded to the demands of small business owners by reducing the number of businesses subject to the franchise tax and lowering the tax rate. Concomitantly, the legislature has increased taxes on tobacco products. These modifications reflect both the political strength of business owners and the ease of raising taxes on items that some people deem morally questionable.

Sales Taxes By far the most important single source of state tax revenue in Texas is sales taxation. (See Figure 11.2 for the sources of state revenue.) Altogether, sales taxes accounted for more than 60 percent of state tax revenue and 25 percent of all revenue in fiscal years 2016–2017. These sales taxes function as a regressive tax, and the burden imposed on individual taxpayers varies with spending patterns and income levels.

For almost 60 years, the state has levied and collected two kinds of sales taxes: a **general sales tax** and several selective sales taxes. First imposed in 1961, the limited sales, excise, and use tax (commonly referred to as the general sales tax) has become the foundation of the Texas tax system. The current (2019) statewide rate of 6.25 percent is one of the nation's highest (ranking as the 13th-highest rate among the 45 states that imposed a sales tax as of 2018). Local governments have the option of levying additional sales taxes for a combined total of state and local taxes at 8.25 percent (see Chapter 3, "Local Governments"). The base of the tax is the sale price of "all tangible personal property" and "the storage, use, or other consumption of tangible personal property purchased, leased, or rented." Among exempted tangible property are the following: receipts from water, telephone, and telegraph services; sales of goods otherwise taxed (for example, automobiles and motor fuels); food and food products (but not restaurant meals); medical supplies

general sales tax
Texas's largest source of tax revenue, applied at the rate of 6.25 percent to the sale price of tangible personal property and "the storage, use, or other consumption of tangible personal property purchased, leased, or rented."

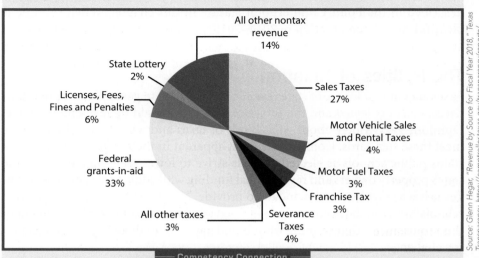

FIGURE 11.2 Sources of State Revenue, Fiscal Year 2018

All other nontax revenue 14%

Sales Taxes 27%

Motor Vehicle Sales and Rental Taxes 4%

Motor Fuel Taxes 3%

Franchise Tax 3%

Severance Taxes 4%

All other taxes 3%

Federal grants-in-aid 33%

Licenses, Fees, Fines and Penalties 6%

State Lottery 2%

Source: Glenn Hegar, "Revenue by Source for Fiscal Year 2018," Texas Transparency, https://comptroller.texas.gov/transparency/reports/revenue-by-source.

—— Competency Connection ——
✲ **CRITICAL THINKING** ✲

What other sources of revenue do you believe are available to the state of Texas?

sold by prescription; nonprescription drugs; animals and supplies used in agricultural production; sales by university and college clubs and organizations (as long as the group has no more than one fundraising activity per month); and equipment used in the manufacture, processing, or fabrication of tangible personal property.

Because the general sales tax primarily applies to tangible personal property, many services are untaxed. Sales taxes are charged for dry cleaning, football tickets, and parking; however, accountants, architects, and consultants provide their services tax-free. Because professional service providers and businesses represent some of the most powerful and well-organized interests in the Lone Star State, proposals that would require these groups to collect a sales tax have faced strong resistance. (See Chapter 7, "The Politics of Interest Groups.") Although the comptroller estimates that eliminating sales tax exclusions for professional and other service providers would generate more than $8 billion in additional annual revenue, even in difficult economic times, legislators have made no effort to change the law.[14]

Through mid-2018, as a result of decisions made as early as the 1960s by the U.S. Supreme Court, many goods sold via the Internet were exempt from a state's general sales tax. This prohibition was costly to state governments. Although such sales were subject to a use tax that was to be paid by the consumer, few purchasers made these payments and the cost of enforcement was prohibitive.

The U.S. Supreme Court had interpreted the Commerce Clause to prohibit states from forcing online retailers to charge sales tax on sales transactions, unless the seller had a facility or employee in the state. The physical presence of the facility or person created an affiliate nexus or connection to the state. Only Congress could authorize states to tax sales if the seller did not have an affiliate nexus. Then, in June 2018, the court reversed its previous decisions. In *South Dakota v. Wayfair*, 585 U.S. _____ (2018), the court held that merchants who have no affiliate nexus in a state but conduct considerable business in the state establish an economic nexus. That economic nexus is sufficient to allow states to tax the sales of remote online retailers. South Dakota's standard of applying the tax to online merchants whose annual sales exceeded $100,000 or 200 separate transactions met the court's definition of a business having conducted "considerable business" in the state. In Texas, any company that has $500,000 in sales must collect sales tax on purchases.

Noting the pervasiveness of Internet sales, the court determined that remote online retailers, who could avoid collecting sales taxes on their transactions, had an unfair advantage over in-state merchants who were required to charge these taxes. The court further recognized that requiring an affiliate nexus before a state legislature could levy taxes against a merchant created an artificial barrier to taxation in a world in which so many transactions occur virtually. In his opinion, Justice Anthony Kennedy observed: "A virtual showroom can show far more inventory, in far more detail, and with greater opportunities for consumer and seller interaction than might be possible for local stores." Without further changes to state laws, Texas's state comptroller did not believe Texas would experience a significant increase in sales tax collections as a result of this decision.[15]

Other sellers have argued that multiple rates and definitions of products subject to state sales taxes create a collection nightmare. Through the Streamlined Sales Tax Governing Board (SSTGB), 24 states, not including Texas, have signed Streamlined Sales and Use Tax Agreements that provide a uniform tax system to overcome these arguments. Approximately 2,000 online retailers voluntarily collect taxes for these states. South Dakota is a member of the SSTGB. The U.S. Supreme Court took note of this membership in upholding the constitutionality of South Dakota's sales tax on goods sold online.

The 86th Legislature sought to address some of the concerns regarding the collection of sales tax on Internet sales. Because local governments have authority to collect up to 2 per cent in sales taxes on items purchased within their jurisdictions and these rates vary, to limit confusion, the comptroller is now required to calculate a uniform local sales tax rate that online retailers collect. Additionally, companies such as Amazon often serve as a marketplace for sellers to promote their goods. The company operating the marketplace is now responsible for collecting and remitting sales taxes on goods sold through its site. As a result of this change, the Legislative Budget Board estimates an additional $700 million in taxes will be collected in the 2020–2021 biennium for state and local governments.

The Lone Star State has used its sales tax laws to negotiate jobs and an improved economy for Texans. In 2012, Amazon entered a settlement agreement for the payment of disputed sales taxes with then-Comptroller Susan Combs. Under terms of the agreement, Amazon began collecting sales taxes and agreed to invest more than $200 million in the state and create an additional 2,500 jobs. As of 2019, the company had approximately 15 fully operating fulfillment centers (several at least 1,000,000 square feet in size). Corporate officials stated that they had created thousands of well-paying jobs with health-care and retirement benefits for Texans.[16]

Since 1931, when the legislature first imposed a sales tax on cigarettes, many items have been singled out for **selective sales taxes**. These items may be grouped into three categories: highway user taxes, **sin taxes**, and miscellaneous sales taxes. Highway user taxes include taxes on fuels for motor vehicles that use public roads and registration fees for the privilege of operating those vehicles. Sin taxes have a dual purpose: to raise tax revenue and to curtail behaviors that are viewed as unhealthy or immoral. The principal sin taxes are those on cigarettes and other tobacco products, alcoholic beverages, and mixed drinks. One of the most contested taxes was a $5 fee added to admission fees to so-called gentlemen's clubs. The Texas Supreme Court rejected club owners' arguments that the law interfered with exotic dancers' free speech rights. In 2018, the state collected $15 million from this tax source, much less than the $103 million generated from the sale of beer. In that same year, the comptroller assessed "bikini bars" millions of dollars in unpaid taxes, arguing that partially clothed exotic dancers did not eliminate tax liability. Club owners sued.[17] Other selective sales taxes include hotel and motel room rentals ("bed tax") and retail sales of boats and boat motors.

Business Taxes As with sales taxes, Texas imposes both general and selective business taxes. A general business tax is assessed against a wide range of business operations. Selective business taxes are those levied on businesses engaged in specific or selected types of commercial activities.

Commercial enterprises operating in Texas have historically paid three general business taxes:

- Sales taxes, because businesses are consumers
- **Franchise taxes**, because many businesses operate in a form that attempts to limit personal liability of owners (that is, corporations, limited liability partnerships, and similar structures)
- Unemployment compensation payroll taxes, because most businesses are also employers

The franchise tax, which has existed for more than 100 years, is imposed on businesses for the privilege of doing business in Texas with limited liability protections provided by state law. As a part of the restructuring of the state's school finance system in 2006, the legislature expanded the franchise tax to include all businesses operating in a format that limited the personal liability of owners. Sole proprietorships; general partnerships wholly owned by natural persons; passive investment entities (such as real estate investment trusts or REITs); and small businesses, those that make $1 million or less in annual income or that owe less than $1,000 in franchise taxes, are exempt. The tax is levied on a business's taxable margin, which is the amount of money earned in Texas that is equal to the least of (1) total revenue minus the cost of goods sold, (2) total revenue minus compensation and benefits paid to employees, (3) 70 percent of total revenue, or (4) total revenue minus $1 million. For many businesses being able to deduct the cost of goods sold provides the most favorable tax treatment. In 2015, American

selective sales tax
A tax charged on specific products and services.

sin tax
A selective sales tax on items such as cigarettes, other forms of tobacco, alcoholic beverages, and admission to sex-oriented businesses.

franchise tax
A tax levied on the annual receipts of businesses that are organized to limit the personal liability of owners for the privilege of conducting business in the state.

Multi-Cinema (AMC), a movie theater company, sued the comptroller arguing that movies were the sale of a good. The Third Court of Appeals (Austin) ultimately determined that a special provision of the Texas Tax Code applied to movies, allowing them to be treated as a good. Because movies are goods, the appeals court held that AMC could deduct the entire cost of its theater and related equipment such as screens and sound systems. The comptroller has appealed this case to the Texas Supreme Court arguing that this decision could cost the state $1.5 billion per year in lost revenue. According to the House Ways and Means Committee, the court's holding challenged the stability of the state's margins tax revenue.

Although proponents estimated that the restructured franchise (margins) tax would produce about $6 billion in state revenue each fiscal year, actual collections have been far less. In the fiscal year of 2018, franchise tax collections were $3.7 billion. The 84th Legislature (2015) lowered the margins tax rate by 25 percent, thus lowering anticipated collections. For the two-year period covering the 2019–2020 biennium, the comptroller projected total collections of $8.2 billion (or approximately $4.1 billion per fiscal year). Collections remain well below the amounts predicted by the tax's original proponents. Several reasons have been cited for this shortfall, including a weak economy, the increase in the small business exemption to eliminate taxes on businesses earning less than $1 million a year, a definition of "cost of goods sold" that includes deductions not available under federal law, and decreases in the tax rate. The tax is highly unpopular among small business owners, who continue to seek its repeal, both in the legislature and in the courts.[18]

All states have unemployment insurance systems supported by **payroll taxes**. Paid by employers to insure employees against unemployment, these taxes are levied against a portion of the compensation paid to workers. Although collected by the state, the proceeds are deposited into the Unemployment Trust Fund in the U.S. Treasury. Benefits are distributed to qualified workers who lose their jobs.

The most significant of the state's selective business taxes are levied on the following:

- Oil and gas production
- Insurance company gross premiums
- Public utilities gross receipts

Selective business taxes accounted for approximately 15 percent of the state's tax revenue in the 2014–2015 biennium, when the economy was strong and oil and gas prices and production were high. By the 2016–2017 biennium, these taxes accounted for only 11 percent of the state's tax revenue. An upturn in oil and gas production and a moderate increase in prices for these commodities counterbalanced with the 84th Legislature's elimination of some selective business taxes increased the amount of projected revenue from selective business taxes in 2020–2021 by $4 billion from the 2014–2015 biennium collections.

One of the more important selective business taxes is the **severance tax**. Texas has depended on severance taxes, which are levied on a natural resource, such as oil or natural gas, when it is removed from the earth. Texas severance taxes are based on the quantity of minerals produced or on the value of the resource

payroll tax
An employer-paid tax levied against a portion of the wages and salaries of workers to provide funds for payment of unemployment insurance benefits in the event employees lose their jobs.

severance tax
An excise tax levied on a natural resource (such as oil or natural gas) when it is severed (removed) from the earth.

when removed. The Texas crude oil production tax and the gas-gathering tax were designed with two objectives in mind: to raise substantial revenue and to regulate the amount of natural resources mined or otherwise recovered. Each of these taxes is highly volatile, reflecting dramatic increases and decreases as the price and demand for natural resources fluctuate. The downturn in the oil and gas market that began in 2014 and continued through the 2016–2017 biennium had a devastating effect on this source of tax revenue. By the 2020–2021 biennium, oil and gas prices were expected to recover sufficiently to generate an estimated $10.7 billion in revenue, approximately $1 billion more than had been collected in the 2014–2015 biennium. Oil and gas production in Texas relies heavily on hydraulic fracture stimulation (fracking). Controversies about the environmental impact of this recovery method on groundwater and on underground stability and water supply could reduce production and, therefore, decrease severance tax revenue to the Lone Star State.[19]

Inheritance Tax Since 2005, federal law has not granted federal tax credits for payment of state inheritance taxes. As a result, Texas has collected no state inheritance or estate tax (frequently called a death tax) on the estates of individuals who died on or after January 1, 2005. The 84th Legislature (2015) repealed all of Texas's inheritance tax laws, noting that no significant taxes were collected under existing law ($12,000 in 2014) and that the comptroller did not need to invest resources in enforcing such an insignificant tax.[20]

Tax Burden The Tax Foundation places Texas well below the national average for the state tax burden imposed on its residents. In 2012, when state and local taxes were considered, the Lone Star State's tax burden ranked 46th among the 50 states. Texas also ranks as having one of the 15 most business-favorable tax systems in the nation. A candidate's "no new taxes" pledge remains an important consideration for many Texas voters and will likely result in state officials continuing to choose fewer services over higher taxes to balance the state budget.

Tax Collection As Texas's chief tax collector, the comptroller of public accounts collects more than 90 percent of state taxes, including those on motor fuel sales, oil and gas production, cigarette and tobacco sales, and businesses. Amounts assessed by the comptroller's office can be challenged through an administrative proceeding conducted by that office. Taxpayers dissatisfied with the results of their hearings can appeal the decision to a state district court.

Some taxpayers commit tax fraud by not paying their full tax liability. Electronic sales suppression devices and software, like zappers and phantom-ware, are used to report fewer sales than retailers actually have. These devices allow users to maintain an electronic set of books for tax purposes that erases some credit card and cash transactions from the register's memory. The devices and software are difficult to detect. Their use reduces the payment of any taxes based on a business's receipts, such as sales taxes, mixed drink taxes, and the gross margins or franchise tax. The possession, sale, purchase, or use of this type of device is a state jail felony, punishable by up to two years in a state jail.[21] (For a discussion of different categories of felonies and the related punishment, see Chapter 13, "The Criminal Justice System.")

Revenue from Gambling

The Lone Star State receives revenue from three types of gambling operations (called "gaming" by supporters): horse racing and dog racing (both live and simulcast), a state-managed lottery, and bingo. The state has an uncomfortable relationship with the concept of raising revenue through games of chance and other forms of wagering. Opposition from social conservatives and religious groups is strong. The state's most influential elected officials (Governor Greg Abbott and Lieutenant Governor Dan Patrick) disapprove any expansion of gambling activities in the state.[22] House Speaker Dennis Bonnen also does not prioritize expansion, yet proceeds from gambling activities provide revenue for needed services like public education.

In 2013, the Texas House of Representatives voted to abolish the Texas Lottery Commission. When proponents argued the legislature would have to replace $2.2 billion in biennial funding for public schools if the lottery were eliminated, some opponents changed their votes.[23] As a result, the Texas Lottery Commission will continue in existence through 2025, although the same bill created the Legislative Committee to Review the Texas Lottery and Texas Lottery Commission. When this committee investigated the viability of phasing out the lottery, it determined that funding provided to public education, veterans' benefits, and health-care facilities was valuable and that the lottery should be continued.[24]

Despite resistance from elected officials, owners and operators of gambling facilities, as well as the Texas Lottery Commission, continue to urge expansion of gambling opportunities. The state's three Native American tribes (the Kickapoo nation near Eagle Pass, the Alabama-Coushatta in East Texas, and the Tigua near El Paso) argue for the right to operate Las Vegas–style casinos. In 2016, the Alabama-Coushatta opened a casino-like facility south of Livingston that offered electronic bingo games. Within months, state officials sued the tribe seeking closure of the facility. A similar suit was filed against the Tigua. Both tribes obtained tribal recognition from the U.S. government under a 1987 treaty that prohibits them from engaging in any gaming activities not otherwise legal in Texas. Whether the Alabama-Coushatta and Tigua will be able to continue their gaming operations remains questionable. The lawsuits were ongoing as of 2019. The Kickapoo, who obtained tribal recognition from the United States prior to 1987, operate the Lucky Eagle Casino in Eagle Pass, without fear of closure. Gambling activities are restricted to games such as bingo and a slot-like machine based on bingo. Proposed legislation to allow casino-style gambling on tribal lands and in other areas of the state is regularly defeated, as occurred in the 86th Legislature.

Owners of horse racing operations have lobbied politicians for legalization of slot machines at their tracks. When the Texas Racing Commission voted to expand gambling at the state's dog and horse racing tracks to include historical racing terminals, in which players bet on unidentified, previously run races, the Legislative Budget Board froze funding to the agency. After a year-long battle, the commission rescinded its ruling and funding was restored.

The Texas Lottery has also tested the resolve of the state's leadership to contain gambling activities. When the Texas Lottery Commission's executive director explored creating games tied to the results of fantasy sports teams, Governor Abbott ordered agency employees to abandon these plans. In January 2016, Attorney General Ken Paxton issued an Attorney General Opinion that fantasy sports betting through online providers, such as DraftKings and FanDuel, is illegal in Texas.[25] Strong opposition to expanding gambling operations may yet yield to the state government's need for additional money in the years ahead.

Racing Pari-mutuel wagers on horse races and dog races are taxed. This levy has never brought Texas significant revenue, and betting has consistently declined since 2000. Proceeds from uncashed mutuel tickets, minus the cost of drug testing animals at the racing facility, revert to the state. In most years, the Racing Commission collects far less revenue than its operating expenses. Texas has four types of horse racing permits, ranging from Class 1 (with no limit on the number of race days per year) to Class 4 (limited to five race days annually). As of 2019, the Lone Star State had nine permitted horse racing tracks (four that were active, two that were training facilities, and three that were inactive) and three dog tracks providing live and simulcast racing events on which people could wager legal bets.

Lottery Texas operates one of 44 state-run lotteries, and participates in multistate lotteries: Mega Millions and Powerball. Through May 2019, Texans had won more than $60 billion in prizes since the first lottery tickets were sold in 1992. Chances of winning the state lottery jackpot, however, are 1 in 26 million. Texans have won 12 Mega Millions jackpots and only three Powerball jackpots since the state began participating in these lotteries in 2003. Chances of winning Mega Millions are 1 in 176 million. Powerball odds are even more daunting: 1 in 195 million.

The Texas Lottery Commission administers the state's lottery. Appointed by the governor, the five members of this commission serve six-year terms. Because the commission also oversees bingo operations (a power the 84th Legislature unsuccessfully attempted to take from the Lottery Commission), one member must have experience in the bingo industry. Among the commission's functions are determining the amounts of prizes, overseeing the printing of tickets, advertising ticket sales, and awarding prizes. The commission maintains a Twitter account through which the public receives regular updates on winning lottery numbers, upcoming jackpot amounts, and previous winners. Additionally, the account is used for public relations purposes to remind the general public of the lottery's benefits to the state. The image that opens this chapter represents such a reminder. Because lottery proceeds are used to support public education, urging Texans to thank public school teachers reinforces the connection between the lottery and the state's schools.

Most profits from the lottery are dedicated to public education spending. In 2018, almost $1.4 billion went to the Texas Foundation School Fund. This amount constituted only a small portion (6.5 percent) of the state's budgeted expenditure of approximately $21 billion on public education in that same year. Proceeds from a Veteran's Cash scratch-off game benefit the Veterans' Assistance Fund, which received $15.3 million from ticket sales in 2018. Unclaimed prizes from the Texas lottery revert to the state 180 days after a drawing. These funds are transferred to hospitals across the Lone Star State to provide partial reimbursement for unfunded indigent medical care. Five percent of ticket sale revenue is used to pay commissions to retailers who sell the tickets.

Bingo State law allows bingo operations to benefit charities (for example, churches, veterans' organizations, and service clubs). The 5 percent tax on bingo prizes over $5 in value is divided 50/50 between the state and local governments. State revenue from bingo taxes remains low. Local charities benefit somewhat from the portion of the proceeds that is distributed to them. In 2017, the last year for which information is available, these donations were approximately $31.2 million. In that same year, the Texas Lottery Commission reported gross receipts from charitable bingo games of almost $776 million, of which $590 million was used to pay winners' prizes. The Legislative Committee to Review the Texas Lottery and Texas Lottery Commission, created by the 83rd Legislature, evaluated the effect of mandatory charitable distributions on charitable bingo. As a result of their findings that 30 percent of the state's 1,095 licensed bingo charities received no donations from the operators who ran their games, the committee recommended minimum required distributions to the licensed charities.[26] No changes have been made to the law governing minimum required charitable distributions, however.

Other Nontax Revenues

Less than 50 percent of all Texas state revenue comes from taxes and gambling operations; therefore, other nontax revenues are important sources of funds. The largest portion of these revenues comes from federal grants. Figure 11.3 reflects the growth of this funding source over the last seven biennia. State business operations (such as sales of goods by one government agency to another government agency) and borrowing also are significant sources of revenue. In addition, the state has billions of dollars invested in interest-bearing accounts and securities.

Federal Grants-in-Aid Gifts of money, goods, or services from one government to another are defined as **grants-in-aid**. Federal grants-in-aid contribute more revenue to Texas than any single tax levied by the state. More than 95 percent of federal funds are directed to three programs: health and human services, business and economic development (especially highway construction), and education. In the 2020–2021 biennium, approximately one-third of state funding or $88 billion was anticipated from the federal government. This projection was

grant-in-aid
Money, goods, or services given by one government to another (for example, federal grants-in-aid to states for financing public assistance programs for poor Texans).

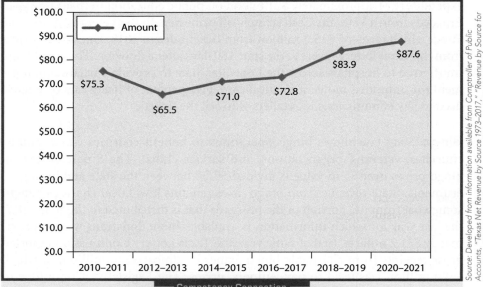

FIGURE 11.3 Federal Grants to Texas by Biennium (FY2010–FY2021) (in billions)

Amount

$100.0
$90.0
$80.0 — $75.3
$70.0
$60.0 — $65.5 $71.0 $72.8
$50.0
$40.0
$30.0
$20.0
$10.0
$0.0

$83.9
$87.6

2010–2011 2012–2013 2014–2015 2016–2017 2018–2019 2020–2021

— Competency Connection —

☼ **CRITICAL THINKING** ☼

Is Texas too reliant on federal grants to balance its budget?

consistent with the proportion of federal funding included in the state's budget over recent years.

State participation in federal grant programs is voluntary. Participating states must (1) contribute a portion of program costs (varying from as little as 10 percent to as much as 90 percent) and (2) meet performance specifications established by federal mandate. Funds are usually allocated to states on the basis of a formula. These formulae usually include (1) lump sums (made up of identical amounts to all states receiving funds) and (2) uniform sums (based on items that vary from state to state, such as population, area, highway mileage, need and fiscal ability, cost of service, administrative discretion, and special state needs).

Land Revenues Texas state government receives nontax revenue from public land sales, rentals, and royalties. Sales of land, sand, shell, and gravel, combined with rentals on grazing lands and prospecting permits, accounted for approximately 1 percent of the state's budget in the 2018–2019 biennium. A substantial portion of revenue from state lands is received from oil and natural gas leases and from royalties derived from mineral production. The instability of oil and natural gas prices causes wide fluctuations in the amount the state receives from these mineral leases. Collections for the budget year of 2018 represented a $300 million increase from the prior year's land revenues.

Oil and gas is not the only energy-related resource that provides revenue for the state. In addition, the General Land Office, the agency responsible for managing the more than 13 million acres of land surface and mineral rights that the state owns, leases onshore and offshore sites for energy production from wind, solar, and geothermal sources. Hard minerals, such as sand, gravel, caliche, and sulfur, are also mined from state-owned land, and the producers pay a royalty to the state. Because the General Land Office can take payment from oil and gas producers in cash or in kind, Texas also maintains an energy marketing program through which the state sells natural gas and electricity to local governments, public colleges and universities, and state agencies. The principal beneficiary of monies received from these programs is the Permanent School Fund. The General Land Office proclaims on its website that its business activities "turn oil into textbooks for Texas children."[27]

The Tobacco Suit Windfall Early in 1998, the American tobacco industry settled a lawsuit filed by the state of Texas. During a period of 25 years, cigarette makers will pay the Lone Star State $18 billion in damages for public health costs incurred by the state as a result of residents' tobacco-related illnesses. These funds support a variety of health-care programs, including the Children's Health Insurance Program (CHIP), Medicaid, tobacco education projects, and endowments for health-related institutions of higher education. Payments averaged approximately $500 million per year through 2015. Because of increases in taxes that have reduced consumption in Texas and other states, revenue from the sale of tobacco products has declined in recent years. As a result, the comptroller predicted that settlement payments from the tobacco lawsuit would continue to decline to approximately $400 million per year in the 2020–2021 biennium. An additional $2.3 billion is administered as a trust by the state comptroller to reimburse local governments (cities, counties, and hospital districts) for unreimbursed health-care costs.

Miscellaneous Sources Fees, permits, and income from investments are major miscellaneous nontax sources of revenue. Fee sources include those for motor vehicle inspections, college tuition, student services, state hospital care, and certificates of title for motor vehicles. The most significant sources of revenue from permits are those for trucks and automobiles; sale of liquor, wine, and beer; and cigarette tax stamps. These fees are collected by a variety of agencies at both the state and local levels of government. For example, the Department of Motor Vehicles collects motor vehicle registration and certificate-of-title fees through county tax collectors' offices; the State Board of Insurance collects insurance fees; and the Department of Public Safety collects driver's license, motor vehicle inspection, and similar fees. For the 2020–2021 biennium, the comptroller predicted an increase in income from these sources. This prediction is further evidence of Texas's strengthening economic condition.

At any given moment, Texas has billions of dollars on hand, invested in securities or on deposit in interest-bearing accounts. Trust funds constitute the bulk of money invested by the state (for example, the Texas Teacher Retirement Fund, the

State Employee Retirement Fund, the Permanent School Fund, and the Permanent University Fund). Investment returns closely track fluctuations in the stock market. Chaos in the financial markets that began in September 2008 had a direct effect on this revenue source. After a sharp decline in the 2008–2009 biennium, interest and investment income for the 2018–2019 biennium was almost twice that collected during the halcyon 2006–2007 biennium.

The Texas state comptroller is responsible for overseeing the investment of most of the state's surplus funds. Restrictive money management laws limit investments to interest-bearing negotiable order withdrawal (NOW) accounts, U.S. Treasury bills (promissory notes in denominations of $1,000 to $1 million), and repurchase agreements (arrangements that allow the state to buy back assets such as state bonds) from banks. Interest and investment income was expected to provide 1.1 percent of state revenue in the 2020–2021 biennium.

The University of Texas Investment Management Company (UTIMCO) invests the Permanent University Fund and other endowments for the University of Texas and Texas A&M University systems. Its investment authority extends to participating in venture capital partnerships that fund new businesses. Board members for UTIMCO include the chancellor and three regents from the University of Texas System, two individuals selected by the Board of Regents of the Texas A&M University System, and three outside investment professionals. This nonprofit corporation was the first such investment company in the nation affiliated with a public university.

The Public Debt

When expenditures exceed income, governments finance shortfalls through public borrowing. Such deficit financing is essential to meet short- and long-term crises and to pay for costly projects, such as prison construction. Most state constitutions, including the Texas Constitution, severely limit the authority of state governments to incur indebtedness.

Bonded Indebtedness For 75 years, Texans have sought, through constitutional provisions and public pressure, to force the state to operate on a pay-as-you-go basis. Despite those efforts, the state is allowed to borrow money by issuing **general obligation bonds** (borrowed amounts repaid from the General Revenue Fund) and **revenue bonds** (borrowed amounts repaid from a specific revenue source, such as college student loan bonds repaid by students who received the funds). Commercial paper (unsecured short-term business loans) and promissory notes also cover the state's cash flow shortages. Whereas general obligation bonds and commercial paper borrowings require voter approval, other forms of borrowing generally do not. Outstanding bonded debt, including bonds issued by the state's universities, was approximately $57 billion as of the end of fiscal year 2018, of which $30.5 billion was issued as revenue bonds; $7.8 billion was issued by state agencies but did not have to be repaid by the state; and the remainder consisted of general obligation bonds.[28]

general obligation bond
Amount borrowed by the state that is repaid from the General Revenue Fund.

revenue bond
Amount borrowed by the state that is repaid from a specific revenue source.

Bond Review Specific projects to be financed with bond money require legislative approval. Bond issues also must be approved by the Texas Bond Review Board. The four members of this board are the governor, lieutenant governor, speaker of the house, and comptroller of public accounts. This board approves all borrowings by the state or its public universities with a term in excess of five years or an amount in excess of $250,000.

Economic Stabilization Fund The state's Economic Stabilization Fund (popularly called the **Rainy Day Fund**) operates like a savings account. It is intended for use when the state faces an economic crisis and was originally created to prevent or eliminate temporary cash deficiencies in the General Revenue Fund. By legislative mandate, the balance cannot be reduced below $7 billion. The Rainy Day Fund is financed with one-half of any excess money remaining in the General Revenue Fund at the end of a biennium (an event that has only happened twice) and with one-half of 75 percent of oil and natural gas taxes that exceed 1987 collections (approximately $1.3 billion in that year). A constitutional amendment, approved by the voters in 2014, allocates the remaining one-half of excess oil and natural gas taxes to the State Highway Fund. If necessary, the legislature can direct the money intended for the State Highway Fund to the Rainy Day Fund. Withdrawals from the Rainy Day Fund require legislative approval by supermajorities. Three-fifths of members present must approve a withdrawal to cover deficits and two-thirds of members present must approve withdrawals for any other purpose. The 86th Legislature authorized the largest transfer in the Rainy Day Fund's history. Funds were used to cover costs of Hurricane Harvey damage and shortfalls in the teacher retirement system and Texas Tomorrow Fund (discussed later in this chapter).

Like a savings account, the Rainy Day Fund has provided temporary support for programs like public education, Medicaid, and the criminal justice system. Governor Rick Perry also used the account to finance business development funds, such as the Texas Enterprise Fund (TEF). Several scandals surrounding TEF and similar economic development programs resulted in substantial revisions to TEF by the 84th Legislature.

The weakness or strength of the Texas economy is revealed in collections by the Rainy Day Fund. Although a budget surplus transfer was made from the 2006–2007 budget, no transfers have been made since. When the 86th Legislature convened in January 2019, the Economic Stabilization Fund totaled $12.5 billion. The comptroller predicted no budget surplus would be available from the 2018–2019 biennium. The balance of the Rainy Day Fund remained below the maximum amount of $16.8 billion that could be held in the account. Deposits to the Rainy Day Fund are limited to an amount equal to 10 percent of revenue collections from the previous biennium. Should the maximum be reached, the state suspends transfers and deposits all earned interest in the General Revenue Fund. The comptroller has also sought authority to invest more of the Rainy Day Fund in higher-yield investments to protect against economic declines. This proposal was approved by the 86th Legislature in response to Comptroller Hegar's argument that Texas's previous investment strategy was like "burying the [state's] money in a hole on the Capitol lawn."[29]

Rainy Day Fund
A fund used like a savings account for stabilizing state finance and helping the state meet economic emergencies when revenue is insufficient to cover state-supported programs.

✔ 11.2 Learning Check

1. What is the largest source of tax revenue for the state of Texas?
2. What is the stated purpose of the Rainy Day Fund?

Answers at the end of this chapter.

⭐ Budgeting and Fiscal Management

LO 11.3 Describe the procedure for developing and approving a state budget.

The state's fiscal management process begins with a statewide vision for Texas government and ends with an audit.[30] Other phases of this four-year process include development of agency strategic plans, legislative approval of an appropriations bill, and implementation of the budget. Each activity is important if the state is to derive maximum benefit from the billions of dollars it handles each year.

Budgeting Procedure

A plan of financial operation is usually referred to as a **budget**. In modern state government, budgets serve a variety of functions, each important in its own right. A budget includes an estimate of anticipated revenue and outlines a plan for spending that shows a government's financial condition at the close of one budget period and the anticipated condition at the end of the next budget cycle. Based on estimated revenue, the budget also makes spending recommendations for the coming budget period. In Texas, the budget period covers two fiscal years. A **fiscal year** is a one-year budget period. Each fiscal year begins on September 1 and ends on August 31 of the following year. The fiscal year is identified by the initials FY (for "fiscal year") preceding the number for the ending year. For example, FY2019 began on September 1, 2018, and ended on August 31, 2019.

Texas is one of 19 states that have some form of a biennial (every two years) budget period. Many political observers argue that today's economy fluctuates too rapidly for this system to be efficient. The Lone Star State's voters, however, have consistently rejected proposed constitutional amendments requiring annual state appropriations.

Legislative Budget Board By statute, the **Legislative Budget Board (LBB)** is a 10-member joint body of the Texas House of Representatives and the Texas Senate. Its membership includes as joint chairs the lieutenant governor and the Speaker of the House of Representatives. Assisted by its director and staff, the LBB prepares a biennial (two fiscal years) current services–based budget. This type of budget projects the cost of meeting anticipated service needs of Texans over the next biennium.

Constitutional limits are in place to control how much the state can spend. The legislature has no discretion in how dedicated funds can be spent (although the funds are not required to be spent). The comptroller of public accounts furnishes the board with an estimate of the growth of the Texas economy covering the period from the current biennium to the next biennium. Legislative appropriations from undedicated tax revenue cannot exceed that rate of growth. Based on the comptroller's projections, the LBB capped the growth of appropriations from undedicated tax revenue at 9.9 percent for the 2020–2021 biennium.

budget
A plan of financial operation indicating how much revenue a government expects to collect during a period (usually one or two fiscal years) and how much spending is authorized for agencies and programs.

fiscal year
A one-year budget period. For Texas's state government, each fiscal year begins on September 1 and ends on August 31 of the following year.

Legislative Budget Board (LBB)
A 10-member body co-chaired by the lieutenant governor and the Speaker of the House. This board and its staff prepare a biennial current services budget. In addition, they assist with the preparation of a general appropriation bill at the beginning of a regular legislative session. If requested, staff members prepare fiscal notes that assess the economic impact of a proposed bill or resolution.

The board's staff also helps draft the general appropriations bill for introduction at each regular session of the legislature. If requested by a legislative committee chair, staff personnel prepare fiscal notes that estimate the potential economic impact of a bill or resolution. Employees of the LBB also assist agencies in developing performance evaluation measures and audits, and they conduct performance reviews to determine how effectively and efficiently state agencies are functioning.

Governor's Office of Budget and Policy Headed by an executive budget officer who works under the supervision of the governor, the Governor's Office of Budget and Policy (GOBP) is required by statute to prepare and present a biennial budget to the legislature. Traditionally, the governor's plan is policy based. It presents objectives to be attained and a plan for achieving them. As a result of this dual arrangement, two budgets, one legislative in origin and the other executive, should be prepared every two years. Governor Perry submitted separate budgets for each of the first four biennia of his administration (2001–2007). For the last three biennia (2009–2015) of his governorship, however, Perry proposed budgets that were the same or varied only minimally from those prepared by the LBB. Governor Abbott continued to follow the policy-based model in his proposed budgets. His 2020–2021 proposed budget included his priorities, such as public school finance reform and funding for research efforts at public universities. The governor did not include specific line item requests; rather he provided some general requests for "full funding" or increased funding in excess of prior years' budgets.[31]

Budget Preparation Compilation of each budget begins with development of a mission statement for Texas by the governor in cooperation with the LBB. That vision for the 2020–2021 biennium urged agency personnel to "maximize the efficient use of state resources in service to the agency's core mission."[32] Every even-numbered year, each operating agency requesting appropriated funds must submit a five-year strategic operating plan to the GOBP and to the LBB. These plans must incorporate the state's mission and philosophy of government, along with quantifiable and measurable performance goals. Texas uses performance-based budgeting; thus, strategic plans provide a way for legislators to determine how well an agency is meeting its objectives. For example, in 2018, the Commission on the Arts submitted a strategic plan in which the agency set a goal of providing and supporting arts and cultural grants. One performance measure was to assure that 6 percent of agency grants were awarded to rural counties. This goal met the agency purpose of advancing the state culturally in areas where others would likely not invest in arts and cultural programs.

Legislative Appropriation Request forms and instructions are prepared by the LBB. (See Figure 11.4 for a diagram of the budgeting process.) These materials are sent to each spending agency in late spring in every even-numbered year. For several months thereafter, representatives of the budgeting agencies work to complete their proposed departmental requests. An agency's appropriations request must be organized according to strategies that the agency intends to use

FIGURE 11.4 Texas Biennial Budget Cycle

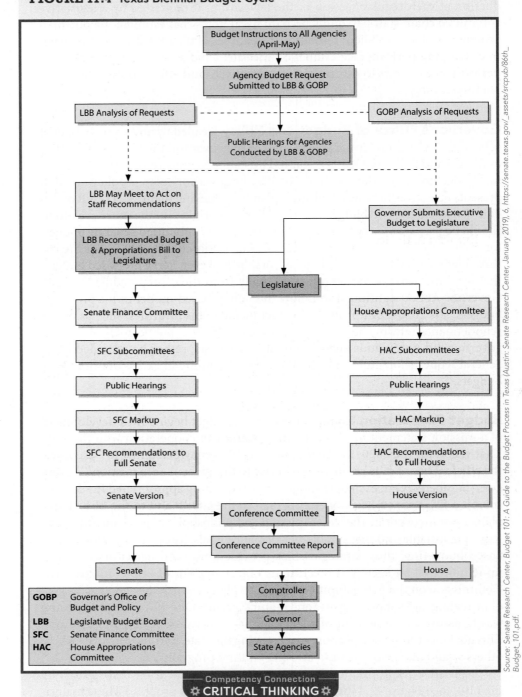

Budget Instructions to All Agencies (April–May)

Agency Budget Request Submitted to LBB & GOBP

LBB Analysis of Requests — GOBP Analysis of Requests

Public Hearings for Agencies Conducted by LBB & GOBP

LBB May Meet to Act on Staff Recommendations

Governor Submits Executive Budget to Legislature

LBB Recommended Budget & Appropriations Bill to Legislature

Legislature

Senate Finance Committee — House Appropriations Committee

SFC Subcommittees — HAC Subcommittees

Public Hearings — Public Hearings

SFC Markup — HAC Markup

SFC Recommendations to Full Senate — HAC Recommendations to Full House

Senate Version — House Version

Conference Committee

Conference Committee Report

Senate — House

Comptroller

Governor

State Agencies

GOBP	Governor's Office of Budget and Policy
LBB	Legislative Budget Board
SFC	Senate Finance Committee
HAC	House Appropriations Committee

— Competency Connection —
✿ **CRITICAL THINKING** ✿

How could Texas's budgeting process be made more efficient?

Source: Senate Research Center, Budget 101: A Guide to the Budget Process in Texas (Austin: Senate Research Center, January 2019), 6, https://senate.texas.gov/_assets/srcpub/86th_Budget_101.pdf.

in implementing its strategic plan over the next two years. Each strategy, in turn, must be listed in order of priority and tied to a single statewide functional goal.

By early fall in even-numbered years, state agencies submit their departmental estimates to the LBB and GOBP. These budgeting agencies then carefully analyze all requests and hold hearings with representatives of spending departments to clarify details and glean any additional information needed. At the close of the hearings, budget agencies traditionally compile their estimates of expenditures into two separately proposed budgets, which are then delivered to the legislature.

Thus, in each regular session, legislators normally face two sets of recommendations for all state expenditures to be made during the succeeding biennium. Since the inception of the **dual budgeting system**, the legislature has shown a marked preference for the recommendations of its own budget-making agency, the LBB, over those of the GOBP and the governor. Therefore, as noted earlier, the governor's proposed budget frequently varies little, if at all, from the LBB's proposed budget.

By custom, the legislative chambers rotate responsibility for introducing the state budget between the chair of the Senate Finance Committee and the chair of the House Appropriations Committee. At the beginning of each legislative session, the comptroller provides the legislature with a biennial revenue estimate. The legislature can only spend in excess of this amount upon the approval of four-fifths of each chamber. In subsequent months, the legislature debates issues surrounding the budget, and members of the Senate Finance Committee and the House Appropriations Committee conduct hearings with state agencies, including public universities and colleges, regarding their budget requests. During the hearings, agency officials are called upon to defend their budget requests and the previous performance of their agencies or departments. In the 86th Legislature, Senate Finance Chair Jane Nelson proposed, and the legislature approved, a form of zero-based budgeting. The procedure requires state agencies to justify every program and all agency spending during the sunset review process. The Sunset Review Board is authorized to make recommendations to the legislature on appropriate spending levels for each agency activity.

The committees then make changes to the appropriations bill (a practice known as "markup") and submit the bill to each chamber for a vote. (For a discussion of how a bill becomes a law, see Chapter 8, "The Legislative Branch.") After both chambers approve the appropriations bill, the comptroller must certify that the state of Texas will collect sufficient revenue to cover the budgetary appropriations. Only upon certification is the governor authorized to sign the budget. The governor has the power to veto any spending provision in the budget through the line-item veto (that is, rejecting only a particular expenditure in the budget). Disagreement arose between Governor Abbott and the LBB over the extent of the governor's line-item veto power after the end of the 84th legislative session. Legislators frequently add riders to the budget bill directing how some of the appropriations can be spent. For example, the legislature directed the Texas Education Agency to pay $193,000 in dues to the Southern Regional Education Board, an organization that supports the Common Core. This national education standard is opposed by many conservatives. Governor Abbott vetoed the rider. An unelected staff member of the LBB ruled that the rider was not an appropriation

dual budgeting system
The compilation of separate budgets by the legislative branch and the executive branch.

and, therefore, not subject to the governor's line-item veto. Attorney General Ken Paxton disagreed and issued an opinion that the governor's line-item veto authority extended to budget riders. The governor used this newfound power to veto budget riders in the budget passed by the 85th Legislature.

Budget Expenditures

Analysts of a government's fiscal policy classify expenditures in two ways: functional and objective. Services being provided by government represent the state's functional budget. When the money spent is categorized by the object of expenditures, such as employees' salaries, the budget report is described as objective. Figure 11.5 illustrates Texas's proposed functional expenditures for fiscal years 2018 and 2019. For more than five decades, functional expenditures have centered on three principal functions: public education, health and human services, and highway construction and maintenance (included under business and economic development). Subsequent biennial budgets reflected the same priorities.

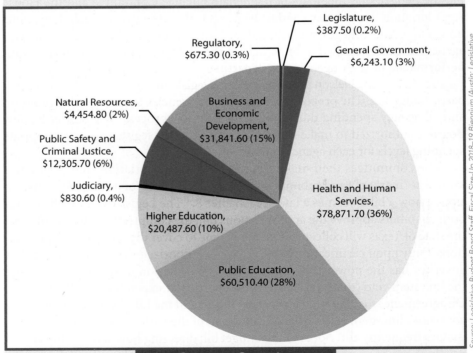

FIGURE 11.5 All Texas State Funds Appropriations ($216.6 billion) by Function for Fiscal Years 2018–2019 (in millions)

- Legislature, $387.50 (0.2%)
- General Government, $6,243.10 (3%)
- Regulatory, $675.30 (0.3%)
- Business and Economic Development, $31,841.60 (15%)
- Natural Resources, $4,454.80 (2%)
- Public Safety and Criminal Justice, $12,305.70 (6%)
- Judiciary, $830.60 (0.4%)
- Higher Education, $20,487.60 (10%)
- Health and Human Services, $78,871.70 (36%)
- Public Education, $60,510.40 (28%)

Source: Legislative Budget Board Staff, Fiscal Size-Up 2018–19 Biennium (Austin: Legislative Budget Board, September 2018), http://www.lbb.state.tx.us/Documents/Publications/Fiscal_SizeUp/Fiscal_SizeUp.pdf.

— Competency Connection —
★ PERSONAL RESPONSIBILITY ★

Based on how Texas spends its money, what services are most important to Texans? Do you agree with these decisions?

Budget Execution

In most state governments, the governor's office or an executive agency responsible to the governor supervises **budget execution** (the process by which a central authority in government oversees implementation of a spending plan approved by the legislative body). The governor of Texas and the Legislative Budget Board have limited power to prevent an agency from spending part of its appropriations, to transfer money from one agency to another, or to change the purpose for which an appropriation was made. Any modification the governor proposes must be made public, after which the LBB may ratify it, reject it, or recommend changes. If the board recommends changes in the governor's proposals, the chief executive may accept or reject the board's suggestions.

The proper functioning of Texas's budget execution system requires a coordinated effort among the state's political leadership. The board met twice in 2018, in July and November, to receive updates on the state's economic condition. The board met in January 2019 to set the budget growth rate for 2020–2021.

Purchasing

Agencies of state government must make purchases through or under the supervision of Texas Procurement and Support Services (TPASS), a division of the Office of the Comptroller of Public Accounts. Depending on the cost of an item, agency personnel may be required to obtain competitive bids. This division places greater emphasis on serving state agencies for which it purchases goods than on controlling what they purchase. It also provides agencies with administrative support services, such as mail distribution and management of vehicle fleets. In addition, the division negotiates contracts with airlines, rental car agencies, and hotels to obtain lower prices for personnel traveling on state business. These services are also available to participating local governments. The seven-member Council on Competitive Government, chaired by the governor, is required to determine exactly what kinds of services each agency currently provides that might be supplied at less cost by private industry or another state agency.

Facilities

A seven-member appointed board oversees the Texas Facilities Commission. This agency provides property management services for state facilities. In addition, agency personnel, in collaboration with the Longhorn Foundation, manage football tailgating on state property in Austin. The agency begins taking online reservations in June of each year.

Accounting

The comptroller of public accounts oversees management of the state's money. Texas law holds this elected official responsible for maintaining a double-entry system, in which a debit account and a credit account are maintained for each transaction. Major accounting tasks of the comptroller's office include processing

budget execution
The process whereby the governor and the Legislative Budget Board oversee (and, in some instances, modify) implementation of the spending plan authorized by the Texas legislature.

warrants (checks) used to pay state obligations, acknowledging receipts from various state revenue sources, and recording information concerning receipts and expenditures in ledgers. Contrary to usual business practice, state accounts are set up on a cash basis rather than an accrual basis. In cash accounting, expenditures are entered when the money is actually paid rather than when the obligation is incurred. In times of fiscal crisis, the practice of creating obligations in one fiscal year and paying them in the next allows a budget to appear balanced. Unfortunately, it complicates the task of fiscal planning by failing to reflect an accurate picture of current finances at any given moment. The comptroller issues monthly and annual reports that include general statements of revenues and expenditures. These reports allocate spending based on the object of expenditures that are the goods, supplies, and services used to provide government programs. Salaries, wages, and employment benefits for state employees consistently lead all objective expenditures.

Auditing

State accounts are audited (examined) under direct supervision of the state auditor. This official is appointed by and serves at the will of the Legislative Audit Committee, a six-member committee composed of the lieutenant governor; the Speaker of the House of Representatives; one appointed member from the Senate; and the chairs of the Senate Finance Committee, the House Appropriations Committee, and the House Ways and Means Committee. The auditor may be removed by the committee at any time without the privilege of a hearing.

With the assistance of approximately 200 staff members, the auditor provides random reviews of financial records and transactions after expenditures. Auditing involves reviewing the records and accounts of disbursing officers and custodians of all state funds to assure compliance with the law. Another important duty of the auditor is to examine the activities of each state agency to evaluate the quality of its services, determine whether duplication of effort exists, and recommend changes. The State Auditor's Office is also responsible for managing the state's compensation and job classification system and for reporting on employment and compensation needs to the legislature. The agency conducts audits in order of priority by reviewing activities most subject to potential or perceived abuse first. Its stated mission is to provide elected officials with information to improve accountability in state government.

> ✔ **11.3 Learning Check**
>
> 1. What is a fiscal year?
> 2. Texas has a dual budgeting system. How does this process work?
>
> *Answers at the end of this chapter.*

★ Future Demands

LO 11.4 Evaluate the effectiveness of the state's financing of public services.

Elected officials have worked to keep taxing levels low. As a result, Texas has also kept its per capita spending levels among the lowest in the nation. Some observers believe that this limited funding is merely deferring problems in the areas of education, social services, and the state's infrastructure to the coming years.

Problems that continue to compete for public money include increasing enrollment in our public schools, colleges, and universities; additional social service
needs; and an outdated infrastructure.

Public Education

The state, together with local school districts, is responsible for providing a
basic education for all Texas school-age children. Every week the local, state,
and national governments spend $1.2 billion to operate public schools in the
Lone Star State. Even so, state and local spending on public education remains
below the national average ($9,016 per student in Texas versus $11,762 nationally
for FY2016). Public education accounted for 28 percent of the state's projected
expenditures (approximately $30.3 billion per year) for the 2018–2019 biennium.
That amount of state funding accounted for less than 40 percent of the actual cost
of public education. All remaining costs for public education must be covered
with local taxes and federal grants.

This hybrid arrangement may explain some of the difficulties in operating and
financing Texas's schools. Is public education a national issue deserving of federal
funding, attention, and standards, similar to the interstate highway system, in
which the federal government pays for roads that connect all parts of the nation?
Or should education be a state function, similar to the state's role in building and
maintaining state highways so that all Texans are entitled to drive on the same
quality of paved roads? Or is public education a local responsibility, more akin
to city streets so that towns with more money have better-quality streets than
their poorer neighbors? Although education appears to integrate all three levels
of government—national, state, and local—into one system, confusion and conflict surround the fiscal responsibility and role of each in the state's educational
system. When the Texas legislature created the Property Tax Relief Fund in 2006,
state leaders predicted that by 2008 state funding would provide at least 50 percent
of public school funding. Through 2019, however, the state's share of funding for
public schools remained at less than 40 percent. The 25 percent reduction in the
gross receipts tax approved by the 84th Legislature reduced the proceeds of the
Property Tax Relief Fund further. The 86th Legislature reformed the public school
finance system, increased state support, and decreased local property taxes, all of
which were priorities for the Lone Star State's legislative and executive leadership.

Sources of Public School Funding Texas state government has struggled
with financing public education for almost half a century.[33] Table 11.1 provides a
history of relevant court decisions, state constitutional provisions, and legislative
responses that have established funding sources and shaped the ways in which
those sources are administered. In promoting public education, Texas state government has usually confined its activity to establishing minimum standards
and providing basic levels of financial support. School districts and state government share the cost of three elements—salaries, transportation, and operating
expenses. Local funding of school systems relies primarily on the market value
of taxable real estate within each school district, because local schools raise their

TABLE 11.1 History of Texas Public School Finance in the Courts

Case	Year	Question	Decision	Legislative Response
Rodriguez v. San Antonio (U.S. Supreme Court)	1971	Does Texas's school funding system violate the Equal Protection Clause?	No, because education is not a federally protected right.	None
Edgewood v. Kirby (Texas Supreme Court)	1989	Is Texas's school funding system "efficient" as required by the Texas Constitution?	No, a 9-to-1 difference in per-student funding is inefficient. An efficient system must produce "similar revenue for similar effort."	Decided to study the issue.
Edgewood v. Kirby (Texas Supreme Court)	1991	Is Texas's school funding system "efficient"?	No	Authorized county education districts.
Carrollton-Farmers Branch v. Edgewood (Texas Supreme Court)	1992	Do countywide education districts create a statewide property tax, a practice prohibited by the Texas Constitution?	Yes	Established a program to recapture wealth from property-rich districts to redistribute to property-poor districts (also known as the "Robin Hood" plan).
Edgewood v. Meno (Texas Supreme Court)	1995	Is a recapture program constitutional?	Yes, because it provides funding for a "general diffusion of knowledge."	None
West Orange-Cove v. Neeley (Texas Supreme Court)	2005	Does the need for most districts to tax at the maximum allowable tax rate create a statewide property tax?	Yes	Lowered the property tax by establishing the Property Tax Relief Fund at the state level.
Morath v. Texas Taxpayer and Student Fairness Coalition, et al. Multiple cases involving more than 600 school districts, parents, the Texas Association of Business, and the Texas Charter School Association (Texas Supreme Court)	2016	Is Texas's school funding system "efficient"?	Yes, the current school funding system meets "minimal constitutional requirements."	Legislature urged to revise the school funding system and "upend an ossified regime ill-suited for 21st century Texas," but not required to do so.

Sources: Compiled from Albert H. Kauffman, "The Texas School Finance Litigation Saga: Great Progress, Then Near Death by a Thousand Cuts," *St. Mary's Law Journal* 40, no. 2 (2008): 511–579; Morgan Smith, "A Guide to the Texas School Finance Lawsuits," *Texas Tribune*, February 29, 2012, http://www.texastribune.org/texas-education/public-education/how-navigate-texas-school-finance-lawsuits/; Morgan Smith, "Texas School Finance Trial Enters Phase Two," *Texas Tribune*, January 21, 2014, http://www.texastribune.org/tribpedia/school-finance/; and *Morath v. Texas Taxpayer and Student Fairness Coalition*, 490 S.W 3d 826 (2016).

— Competency Connection —
✿ CRITICAL THINKING ✿

What amount of financial support should the state provide for funding public schools?

share primarily through property taxes. Average daily attendance of pupils in the district, types of students (for example, elementary, secondary, or disabled), and local economic conditions determine the state's share.

In 1949, the Texas legislature passed the Gilmer-Aiken Law, intended to provide a minimum level of state support for every public school student in Texas. This law established the Minimum Foundation Program (now called the Foundation School Program). Local property taxes fund programs beyond the minimum level of services financed by the Foundation School Program. (For a discussion of school district taxing procedures, see Chapter 3, "Local Governments.")

Money to finance the Foundation School Program is allocated to each school system from the Foundation School Fund. This fund accounts for more than 70 percent of state funding for public schools. Other sources of state revenue are used to support public schools and include the following:

- The Available School Fund (revenue received from a variety of state taxes and income from the Permanent School Fund, primarily funded by public land proceeds)

- The School Taxing Ability Protection Fund (money appropriated by the legislature to offset revenue reduction incurred by rural school districts)

- The Texas Lottery

- The Property Tax Relief Fund (money appropriated to offset loss of revenue from local property taxes)

- The General Revenue Fund

Funding Equalization As Table 11.1 indicates, a continuing controversy surrounding public school finance in Texas has been court-mandated funding equalization. The legislatively enacted wealth equalization plan, labeled the **"Robin Hood" plan** by its critics, requires wealthier districts (those with a tax base equal to $319,500 or more per student) to choose among a series of options to reduce its wealth per student in a process called recapture. These funds are transferred to the state for redistribution to property-poor school districts. Despite court challenges, the "Robin Hood" plan has been found to be constitutional. One-third of the state-administered Property Tax Relief Fund may be used to equalize funding among districts. Despite continuing disparities in per student funding among school districts, the 86th Legislature restricted the amount of funding required of wealthier districts.

At the heart of the dispute regarding how to achieve equalized funding is whether all students in the state are entitled to receive the same quality of education. Although court decisions have granted Texas students the right to equal educational opportunities, these determinations do not address the reality that not all students enter school equally prepared to succeed. Frequently, parents of economically disadvantaged students are unable to offer their children the same learning opportunities as those provided by more affluent parents. To make up for this difference in preparation, both the state and federal governments provide additional funding to help school districts equalize learning outcomes for low-income students. The 84th Legislature approved approximately $120 million in

"Robin Hood" plan
A plan for equalizing financial support for school districts by transferring tax money from rich districts to poor districts.

additional funding for qualifying prekindergarten (pre-K) programs that serve low-income students. Although the 85th Legislature did not renew funding, the 86th Legislature provided funding and legal requirements for this initiative.

Many public officials and education experts have expressed concern that educating more economically disadvantaged students requires increases in the funding of public education, in addition to single grants for specific programs. Of the 5.3 million students enrolled in Texas's schools in 2016–2017, approximately 3.1 million were classified as economically disadvantaged. Yet, on a per-student basis, Texas ranks in the bottom third of states for expenditures and has only increased spending by approximately $350 per student since 2011. Unless funding levels increase, school districts will continue to struggle in their attempts to provide students with an adequate education to compete in the 21st-century workplace.

Public Higher Education

Like public schools, the public higher education system endures the dual pressures of increasing enrollment and declining state support. As a result of the Texas Higher Education Coordinating Board's Closing the Gaps initiative that extended from 2000 through 2015, college enrollment in the state's public colleges and universities increased by an additional 605,000 students through 2015 over 2000 enrollment levels. Closing the Gaps was replaced by the 60x30TX initiative in 2015. The primary goal of 60x30TX is to assure that at least 60 percent of 25- to 34-year-old Texans have a postsecondary credential (either a certificate or degree) by 2030. As of 2017, only 43.5 percent of 25- to 34-year-old Texans met this standard. To increase both completion rates and the number of students enrolling in colleges and universities, public institutions of higher education will have to increase faculty, staff, and facilities. Additional provisions of 60x30TX seek to make college more affordable and to lower student debt load. To achieve the cost-savings goals, colleges and universities will have to reduce costs. In addition, the Texas Higher Education Coordinating Board has called on the state legislature to increase funding for higher education.[34]

Furthermore, the success of this effort depends on more low-income, underprepared students enrolling in institutions of higher education. In 2018, fewer than 50 percent of students graduating from Texas high schools were career-ready or college-ready. This lack of preparation occurred in two-thirds of the state's top-ranked high schools. Results for lower-ranked schools were even worse.[35] To lower the cost of developmental education for these students, Texas now requires colleges to integrate developmental course work into credit-bearing courses.

State financial aid for college and university students is insufficient to meet demand. The 82nd Legislature reduced funding for higher education by more than 9 percent from 2010–2011 funding levels. Although the 83rd Legislature restored most funding for college operations and financial aid benefits to 2010–2011 levels, the 84th Legislature abolished the B-On-Time program that forgave loans for students who graduated within four or five years depending on their program. Because the number of eligible students who receive assistance is far lower than the number who qualify for aid, higher education institutions have reduced the amount of some awards.[36] At the same time, colleges and universities are increasing tuition to cover their operating costs. Low levels of state funding have forced students to bear more of the costs of their education by paying higher tuition and taking out more and larger loans.

At the core of this dilemma is a philosophical conflict about the nature of higher education and the role of government. Is higher education a public good that benefits society in which government should invest? Or, is higher education a commodity that benefits the individual who should, therefore, bear the cost of that personal benefit?

Public colleges and universities receive most of their state income through formula funding, a method that uses specific factors to calculate how much money each institution receives. In recent years, the governor, the legislature, and the Texas Higher Education Coordinating Board have argued for a change in the factors used to determine the state's portion of funding. Each favors an outcomes-based funding formula that links the amount of state funding for a college or university to the number of students who successfully complete courses and the number of students who graduate (and, if a community college, transfer to a university). Former Governor Rick Perry expressed his support for outcomes-based funding in 2011: "Texans deserve college graduation for their hard-earned tax dollars, not just college enrollment."[37] The 82nd Legislature then passed legislation requiring the Texas Higher Education Coordinating Board to develop an outcomes-based formula for funding public universities and colleges. The 83rd Legislature implemented outcomes-based funding for a portion of state money appropriated to community colleges. The Texas Higher Education Coordinating Board (THECB) requested that the 86th Legislature fund a supplement (or bonus) to universities equal to their number of graduates. The measure did not succeed. Proponents maintain that the emphasis on successful outcomes will improve higher education. Opponents argue that such a funding structure will reduce the amount of financial support institutions receive and will have a negative effect on students who need the most assistance.[38]

Community College Funding Public community colleges receive their funding from the following sources: student tuition and fees, the state of Texas, local taxpayers, the federal government, and private (individual, foundation, and corporate) donations. State financing of public community or junior colleges was restructured by the 83rd Legislature (2013) to include three components: core operations funding, contact hour funding, and success points funding (an outcomes-based measure). Each community college district in the state receives a minimum amount to cover core operations, $1.36 million per district for the 2018–2019 biennium. The legislature appropriates an additional amount ($1.52 billion in 2018–2019) based on a "contact hour of instruction" rate for vocational-technical and academic courses. This rate is determined by calculating the hours of contact between an instructor and students and, when combined with core operations funding, represents approximately 90 percent of state funding. Payment for achieving student success points provides the balance of state funding. These points are awarded based on student performance, including successful completion of courses, graduation, and transfer to a university.

After previous legislatures lowered the per point value of success points, the THECB requested an increase in 2019. No change was made. Funding for community colleges remains significantly below 1998 formula funding levels. Costs continue to increase, while state financial support declines. This gap in funding has been financed by students and local taxpayers.

Over the years, the legislature has reduced funding to community colleges by a greater percentage than university funding. One report by the *Texas Public Higher Education Almanac* suggests that 54 percent of undergraduates attend community colleges. The majority of these students are African American and Latino. For some observers, this reduction in funding constitutes inequality between universities and community colleges[39] and, arguably because of student population demographics, unequal treatment based on race.

University Funding Texas's state universities and the Texas State Technical College System obtain basic financing through tuition and legislated biennial appropriations from the General Revenue Fund. They also obtain money from fees other than tuition, such as student service and computer use fees (which are deposited in the General Revenue Fund), auxiliary services income (for example, rent for campus housing and food service fees), grants, gifts, and special building funds. The University of Texas and the Texas A&M University systems share revenue from the Permanent University Fund (PUF) investments and surface income from 2.1 million acres of public lands. Royalty income from oil and gas production from these public lands cannot be distributed. This revenue must be invested. An annual distribution is made through the Available University Fund (AUF). The University of Texas System receives two-thirds of this distribution and Texas A&M University and some of its system schools receive one-third. Total distributions from the AUF were approximately $900 million in 2018.

Controversy has surrounded limited state funding for universities in South Texas and border regions, most especially in the Rio Grande Valley. In 1987, unequal allocation of state funding for universities was challenged in the case of *Richards v. LULAC*, 868 SW2d 306 (1993). Although the plaintiffs failed to establish racial bias in the funding of higher education to the satisfaction of the Texas Supreme Court, in 1989 the legislature created the South Texas/Border Initiative with a focus on funding parity for higher education in these areas of the state.[40] The 83rd (2013) Legislature authorized the creation of a regional comprehensive university in the Rio Grande Valley that included a new medical school located in Harlingen. Combining the campuses of UT-Pan American (in Edinburg), UT-Brownsville (in Brownsville), and the Regional Academic Health Center (in Harlingen), the University of Texas Rio Grande Valley (UTRGV) was given direct access to PUF money. The university enrolled its first class in September 2015. Because UTRGV represented a combination of existing universities, the school also graduated its first class in December 2015. The medical school opened in 2016 and will graduate its first class in 2020.

Tuition Deregulation In late 2002, the University of Texas System led an effort to eliminate legislative caps on tuition and fees. According to university officials, funding limitations threatened the University of Texas at Austin's ability

📋 STUDENTS IN ACTION

Making a Difference in Education

Many professors require their students to complete group projects, but Professor Gilbert Schorlemmer at Blinn College goes beyond the traditional project. He requires students to "take something they're passionate about and make a difference," as former student Sarah Westerman described her group's project in Professor Schorlemmer's class.

What Sarah and fellow students Christopher Rieger, Michael Coleman, and Brooke Bayliss were passionate about was education and the high student dropout rates from Texas's public schools. Once the group began exploring the dropout issue, they wondered why students didn't stay in school. When they began to research student retention issues, they learned that many students have no incentive to finish high school. Because high schools focus on preparing students to pursue baccalaureate degrees, many schools neglect students who have little or no interest in obtaining a university diploma.

The group concluded that when students leave high school, they're treated like adults but they have no way to live like adults because high school graduates have no "real-world" skills. One limitation the group discovered was funding. The cost of equipment and instructors for trade programs is often greater than for academic courses. Many school officials seemed to lack an understanding of the role and importance of vocational programs in achieving student success. The concept of student success required a redefinition to remove the stigma attached to trade programs.

The group needed a way to deliver their message to school districts, the State Board of Education, the Texas Education Agency, and others interested in education reform. Professor Schorlemmer's project provided the answer. One requirement was to form a special interest group. The students formed the Texas Education Alternative Learning League (TEALL), a special interest group devoted to enhancing the reputation of vocational trade courses and increasing the number of offerings in the state's public high

Brooke Bayliss, Christopher Rieger, Michael Coleman, and Sarah Westerman

schools. If TEALL's mission interests you, you can find them on Facebook, Twitter, and YouTube. The group also made presentations to local school districts encouraging boards of trustees to devote resources to funding vocational programs.

What's the group's advice to students who share their desire to make a difference? In the words of group member Mike Coleman, "Find someone who knows the system. Find someone who believes in you." Brooke Bayliss suggests, "Pick something you care about. Work with your professors. You have to be able to look at your passion at four in the morning—and love it!"

Source: Interview with Brooke Bayliss, Christopher Rieger, Michael Coleman, and Sarah Westerman, May 2016.

Competency Connection
⊛ **SOCIAL RESPONSIBILITY** ⊛

What role should students have in making changes to Texas's public education system?

to remain a premier research institution. Despite fears that escalating tuition and fees would limit access to higher education for Texas's lower income students, the proposal became law in 2003.

Public universities, as well as public community colleges, quickly moved to raise tuition. Both the dollar increase in tuition and the rate of increase have been dramatic. Since 2003, universities have raised tuition rates and fees more than 170 percent above their 2002 levels. At the same time, state support of universities and community colleges has declined. Elected officials have expressed concern about the rapid increase in tuition and fees. Public universities are now required to establish programs that lock in tuition rates for four years for entering freshmen who choose to participate. The Texas Affordable Baccalaureate (TAB) Program, begun in 2014, is designed to lower the cost and shorten the time in which students can obtain baccalaureate degrees. Texas A&M-Commerce and South Texas College offer applied sciences baccalaureate degrees in organizational leadership at a cost of $750 per term. Other TAB participants accept competency-based credits for past work experience and offer their programs fully online in an effort to lower costs. Four community colleges (Brazosport, Midland, South Texas, and Tyler) now offer applied sciences and applied technology baccalaureate degrees at much lower tuition costs than their university counterparts. Many legislators believe that tuition rates will remain affordable only if the Texas legislature reclaims control of setting them.[41]

Texas Tomorrow Funds The Texas Guaranteed Tuition Plan and Tomorrow's College Investment Plan comprise the Texas Tomorrow Funds. The Tuition Plan provides a way for parents to save for their children's education and to lock in the cost of tuition and fees at the state's public colleges and universities. Tuition increases have also affected these programs. The Texas Tomorrow Fund is backed by the full faith and credit of the state of Texas. According to the fund's provisions, approximately 66,000 students must be educated at an anticipated expense to the state of $1.5 billion. As of 2019, the fund had an unfunded liability of approximately $615 million, an amount the state will be required to finance from general revenue. More than $210 million was allocated from the General Revenue Fund to pay these obligations for the 2020–2021 biennium. Because of rapid tuition increases, the state closed the fund to new participants in 2003. The fund reopened as the Texas Tuition Promise Fund in 2008, though at much higher rates. Most important, the Texas Tuition Promise Fund is not guaranteed by the full faith and credit of the state of Texas. College living costs can be covered by investment in Tomorrow's College Investment Plan.

State Grant and Loan Programs Rather than give money directly to colleges and universities, legislators across the country have preferred to give students the funding and allow them to select the institution at which the funds will be spent. The Texas Tuition Equalization Grants program, created in 1971, subsidizes tuition expenses for eligible students who demonstrate financial need and attend private, nonprofit colleges and universities in Texas. The student must maintain a 2.5 GPA to continue receiving aid. A second type of grant is the **TEXAS Grants Program** (Toward Excellence, Access, and Success), which is

TEXAS Grants Program
"Toward Excellence, Access, and Success" is a college financial assistance program that provides funding for qualifying students.

▦ HOW DO WE COMPARE...

In Tuition and Fees?

Average Tuition and Fees for Academic Year 2018–2019

Most Populous U.S. States	Public University	Public Community College	U.S. States Bordering Texas	Public University	Public Community College
California	$ 9,870	$1,430	Arkansas	$8,710	$3,700
Florida	$ 6,360	$3,250	Louisiana	$9,550	$4,190
New York	$ 8,190	$5,490	New Mexico	$7,130	$1,840
Texas	**$10,300**	**$2,620**	Oklahoma	$8,750	$4,380

Note: Tuition rates are for in-state students at public universities and community colleges.

Source: The College Board, "Tuition and Fees by Sector and State over Time," *Trends in College Pricing* (2018), https://trends .collegeboard.org/college-pricing/figures-tables/tuition-fees-sector-state-over-time.

Competency Connection
★ PERSONAL RESPONSIBILITY ★

Who should pay the costs of your college education: you or taxpayers?

the state's largest financial aid program. Qualified students receive grant funding to pay all tuition and fees at any public university in the state. They must be Texas residents, enroll in college within 16 months of high school graduation, show financial need, and have no convictions for a crime involving a controlled substance. Participating students must maintain a 2.5 GPA and complete at least 24 semester hours each academic year. The Texas Educational Opportunity Grant Program (TEOG) provides financial aid to financially needy community college students who maintain a 2.5 cumulative GPA and complete 75 percent of attempted hours. Students are only eligible for four years after initial enrollment, for the first 75 hours of attempted credit hours, or until receiving an associate degree.

Other programs are available to reward students who obtain their degrees quickly or to assist those who are aging out of the foster care system. Students who attempt no more than three credit hours beyond the hours required for their degree and graduate within four years of initial enrollment in college are eligible for a $1,000 rebate upon graduation from a public university. Youth between the ages of 16 and 23 who have aged out of the foster care system may be eligible for up to $5,000 annually for post-secondary education. Current information about all of these programs is available on the THECB's website. Utilizing social media, the THECB maintains Twitter, Pinterest, LinkedIn, and Facebook accounts and an interactive web tool, entitled Compare College TX, to help users learn about various aspects of higher education at Texas's public universities and colleges, including costs.

Public Assistance

Enrolling more students in high-quality public schools and institutions of higher education are ways in which Texas's political leaders hope to combat poverty. Income disparity between the wealthiest 20 percent of Texans and the poorest 20 percent widened throughout the first decades of the 21st century. Even after implementation of the federal Patient Protection and Affordable Care Act (Obamacare) a higher percentage and number of Texans continue to lack health insurance than residents of any other state. The number of children without coverage also ranks highest in the nation, in both percentage and sheer numbers. Poverty levels remain above the national average. Notable differences in levels of poverty also exist among racial and ethnic groups, and especially among children: African American children (33 percent), Latino children (35 percent), and Asian children (11 percent), compared to Anglo children (10 percent).

Increasing health-care costs for the poor present significant challenges to state government. The percentage of the total state budget dedicated to health and human services is second only to spending on all levels of education ($81.0 billion for education versus $78.9 billion for health and human services in the 2018–2019 biennium). The cost of Medicaid and the **Children's Health Insurance Program (CHIP)** (an insurance program with minimal premiums for children from low-income families) frequently exceeds budget allocations, even though many eligible individuals do not receive benefits from these programs.

Coverage for children remains an issue for lawmakers. In 2017, the state had the largest number of uninsured children in the nation: more than 835,000.[42] Some observers suggest that up to one-half of uninsured children qualify for Medicaid or CHIP and yet do not receive any health insurance benefits.

Limiting access to Medicaid lowers the state's obligation to pay for benefits, but at what cost? The federal government funds 60 cents of every dollar paid for Medicaid services. In addition, the federal portion of CHIP expenditures is approximately 84 cents of every dollar paid for medical services. The 83rd Legislature increased state funding for Medicaid to accommodate an additional 450,000 recipients by FY2015, because many children previously on CHIP are now eligible for Medicaid under the Affordable Care Act. Although the state refused to extend Medicaid benefits to adults who were not primary caregivers for a minor, it was not allowed to limit extending coverage to more children. According to some observers, state officials' refusal to expand Medicaid coverage to adults likely cost the state $100 billion in federal funding over the 10-year period from 2014 to 2024. Under the expanded program, the federal government is responsible for 90 percent of costs through 2024. Elected officials argued that the federal government provided no guarantee that such high levels of support would continue. Thus, any expansion could devastate the state's budget if these extraordinary levels of federal support were reduced. Ongoing court challenges to the Affordable Care Act could invalidate the law and eliminate federal support.

Much of the cost and care burden for uninsured residents, both children and adults, has shifted to local governments, hospitals, and the insured. Counties and hospitals must subsidize unreimbursed costs for treating the uninsured by charging higher rates to the insured, which translates into higher insurance premiums, as well as higher county property taxes. Analysts project a continuing increase

Children's Health Insurance Program (CHIP)
A program that provides medical insurance for minimal premiums to children from low-income families.

in indigent health-care costs in the years to come. The ability of local entities to meet the social service needs of the state's low-income residents is one of the key challenges of the 21st century.

Infrastructure Needs

In addition to demands for education, health, and human services, Texans look to state government to meet other needs. The state of Texas has a responsibility to provide an infrastructure for its residents, including both highway and water systems. Limited resources and growing demands are evident in the provision of these services as well.

Transportation Consistent with Texas's pay-as-you-go budget system is its pay-as-you-ride system of financing construction and maintenance of roads and highways. Texas roads have been financed through a combination of motor fuel taxes, motor vehicle registration fees, and the Federal Highway Trust Fund, to which certain federal highway user taxes are allocated. The Texas Department of Transportation's *Texas Transportation Plan 2040* reported that the state would require more than $545 billion to meet its roadway needs through 2040. Only about one-half of the needed funding is available under current funding strategies.[43]

Alternative sources of transportation funding increased in the 83rd and 84th Legislatures. In 2014, the 83rd Legislature proposed an amendment to the Texas Constitution to allow one-half of oil and gas taxes intended for the Rainy Day Fund to be diverted to the State Highway Fund (also identified as Fund 6). Proponents suggested this approval would provide an additional $1.5 billion annually for highway construction and maintenance. Voters agreed and approved the amendment by an overwhelming 80 percent majority. Through FY2018, the state transferred $5.4 billion in oil and gas taxes to the State Highway Fund. Voters approved a second amendment to the Texas Constitution in 2015 that dedicates a portion of sales tax revenue and motor vehicle sales, use, and rental taxes to the State Highway Fund. Although the Legislative Budget Board estimated these funds would total approximately $2.5 billion, in 2018 (the first year of implementation), the state transferred $2.25 billion. In addition, the 84th Legislature eliminated the diversion of monies intended for the Texas Highway Fund to other agencies (HB 20). This action resulted in an additional $1.3 billion in funding for road construction and maintenance. If fully funded, these amounts will exceed the $4 billion needed annually for a sufficient and safe infrastructure.[44]

Historically, as increases in roadway construction costs have exceeded funding, much of this expense has been transferred to users in the form of tolls. The reality of financing new highway construction with tolls was perhaps best expressed by former Texas Transportation Commission chair Ric Williamson, who described the policy as, "It's the no road, the toll road, or the slow road."[45] Increasing costs also required borrowing concessions, as authorized by Texas voters through constitutional amendment. Authorized in 2001, the Texas Mobility Fund allowed the state to issue bonds and use the proceeds for road construction. In 2015, the 84th Legislature prohibited any further borrowing by the fund. In 2018, an interim report by the House Transportation Committee recommended the creation of county Transportation Reinvestment Zones that could borrow money for transportation projects. The same report recommended reversal of the legislative prohibition on toll roads.

Water The ongoing Texas drought that began in 2007, abated briefly in 2008 and finally ended in 2015, has highlighted the state's water needs. In 2012, the Texas Water Development Board issued its state water plan. Six years in development, the plan had dire predictions for Texans if efforts were not made to increase the state's water supply in the coming years. Projected cost to provide adequate water supplies for anticipated population growth was $53 billion. If the state took no action, in the event of a significant drought, the report estimated annual losses of $12 billion in income and 115,000 jobs.[46] A constitutional amendment, ratified by voters in 2013, led to the creation of two special funds to finance, through low-interest loans, certain water projects under the State Water Plan to ensure the availability of adequate water resources in the future. In 2014, the comptroller of public accounts focused attention on the continuing need for additional state funding and more reliance on technology, noting that "conservation's not enough."[47]

The state's droughts are as dramatic as their endings. The Memorial Day Weekend Floods in 2015 left 23 Texans dead and caused millions of dollars in property damage. In 2017, Hurricane Harvey dumped as much as 60-plus inches of rain on large portions of Southeast Texas causing $125 billion in property damage and killing at least 68 people. Climatologists predict continued cycles of extreme droughts and floods. Texas's surging population will only worsen conditions as dwindling water supplies will be used to meet increased demand.[48] In March 2016, the U.S. Census Bureau reported that from July 2017 through June 2018, Texas had added 380,000 new residents, and three of the 10 fastest-growing metropolitan areas in the nation were in Texas (Dallas, Ft. Worth, and Austin metropolitan areas).[49] Concern continues over water supplies for the state.[50]

11.4 Learning Check

1. True or False: Tuition deregulation resulted in lower tuition at the state's public colleges and universities.

2. On which public service does Texas spend the most money?
   a. Education
   b. Welfare
   c. Highways
   d. Water

Answers at the end of this chapter.

CONCLUSION

Economists suggest that a full recovery from the global economic crisis that erupted in 2008 may take as long as 20 years. Although by 2013 Texas experienced a remarkable turnaround in its economy, signs of economic problems emerged in 2014 as oil prices plummeted. This uncertainty continued through 2018. Comptroller Glenn Hegar expressed concern in his 2018 Biennial Revenue Estimate about both the volatility of oil and gas prices and the unpredictability of national trade policies. He noted that Texas was the "nation's leading exporter, and any escalation in trade tensions would have an adverse effect on the state's economy." Although Texas's credit ratings remained high, Hegar also expressed concern about the state's long-term pension obligations and the potential negative effect on its credit ratings. The 86th Legislature focused on lowering property taxes and finding alternative revenue sources to finance the state's public school system. A well-educated and well-trained population remained a critical goal to assure a successful future.

CHAPTER SUMMARY

LO 11.1 Assess the fairness of Texas's budgeting and taxing policies. Texas remains a low-cost, low-services state. The Lone Star State has one of the most regressive tax systems in the United States because of its heavy reliance on the sales tax and its having no state income tax. Texans require that the state operate with a balanced budget, limit borrowing, and limit spending on social services.

LO 11.2 Describe the sources of Texas's state revenue. The state relies on taxes, fees, gambling revenue, sale of assets, oil and gas royalties, investments, and the federal government to fund state services. Rather than raise taxes, Texas's elected officials often increase fees, fines, and other assessments. Voters have restricted the amount of money the state can borrow. Additionally, the state has a Rainy Day Fund that operates like a savings account and is intended to provide one-time funding for emergencies.

LO 11.3 Describe the procedure for developing and approving a state budget. Each biennium, the Legislative Budget Board and the Governor's Office of Budget and Policy are required to prepare proposed budgets. Before a budget can be approved, the comptroller of public accounts must provide an estimate of available revenue for the upcoming biennium and certify that spending will not exceed revenue. Tax collection, investment of the state's surplus funds, and overseeing management of the state's money are responsibilities of the comptroller of public accounts. The governor and the Legislative Budget Board oversee implementation of the budget and have limited authority to redirect agency spending. The state auditor is responsible for examining all state accounts to ensure honesty and efficiency in agency spending of state funds.

LO 11.4 Evaluate the effectiveness of the state's financing of public services. State revenue pays for services to Texas's residents. Most state money pays for public education (including higher education) and public assistance, especially Medicaid. Higher numbers of low-income students enrolled in the state's public schools will likely increase the cost of public education. The burden for the cost of higher education is shifting to students, consistent with a philosophy that treats higher education as a commodity for which the individual is responsible. Providing access to medical care remains an important state issue, despite the Affordable Care Act. The state also has infrastructure needs. To repair the state's decaying roads and bridges, construct adequate roadways to meet the needs of a growing population, and overcome severe water shortages will be costly to the state's taxpayers in the years ahead.

KEY TERMS

balanced budget, p. 398
budget, p. 414
budget execution, p. 419
Children's Health Insurance Program (CHIP), p. 430

dedicated fund, p. 398
dual budgeting system, p. 417
fee, p. 397
fiscal policy, p. 395
fiscal year, p. 414

franchise tax, p. 404
general obligation bond, p. 412
General Revenue Fund, p. 398
general sales tax, p. 401
grant-in-aid, p. 409

LEARNING CHECK ANSWERS

 11.1

1. Texas requires a balanced budget, favors low taxes, and spends at low to moderate levels.

2. Texas has a regressive tax system, which means that poor people pay a higher percentage of their incomes in taxes than do wealthier residents.

 11.2

1. The general sales tax is the state's largest source of tax revenue.

2. The Rainy Day Fund is to be used when the state faces an economic crisis.

 11.3

1. A fiscal year is a budget year. The fiscal year for the State of Texas begins on September 1 and ends on August 31 of the following calendar year.

2. A state with a dual budgeting system requires both the executive branch and the legislative branch to prepare and submit proposed budgets to the legislature. In Texas, both the governor and the Legislative Budget Board submit proposed budgets.

 11.4

1. False. Since tuition deregulation, student tuition has risen 170 percent over 2002 levels at public colleges and universities.

2. The state spends more money on education than any other service.

12 Public Policy and Administration

Learning Objectives

12.1 Describe how public policy is made in Texas.

12.2 Analyze major challenges faced by the Texas education system.

12.3 Describe the major health and human services programs in Texas, and discuss how efforts to address the needs of its citizens have been approached.

12.4 Compare the roles of government in generating economic development while maintaining a safe, clean, and prosperous environment for the state's residents.

12.5 Describe the various aspects and complexities in Texas's immigration policy.

IMAGE 12.1 Texans, particularly students, have a long tradition of protesting government actions and demanding changes in policy. After the election of President Trump, women's marches were organized throughout the country. Here's a picture of the "Woman's March" in Austin.

Michael Silver Editorial/Alamy Stock Photo

Competency Connection
⚙ CRITICAL THINKING ⚙

Are marches an effective way for students to be heard? What are other ways for students to impact public policy?

One good way to see what is important in public policy is to follow the money. For many years in Texas, the state government has spent each year's budget on four areas. For example, in the 2018–2019 biennium (two-year budget cycle), the legislature appropriated $216.8 billion as follows:

- Education: 37 percent
- Health and human services: 36 percent
- Business and economic development: 15 percent
- Public safety and criminal justice: 6 percent
- Everything else: 6 percent[1]

In one other important policy area, the money trail leads to the private sector. Although regulation costs the state government little (0.3 percent of the total), it has profound cost effects on individuals, companies, and local governments. Regulation commonly shifts costs and benefits from one group to another. For example, contaminated air hurts the quality of life and increases medical costs for children with respiratory problems, such as asthma, as well as for the elderly, but regulations requiring special equipment to reduce emissions from smokestacks cost businesses money. Deciding who should pay the bill is controversial and is largely answered in the battles over government regulations.

State government policies profoundly affect the lives of all of us. Services, subsidies, taxes, and regulations affect students from kindergarten through graduate school, the impoverished, the middle class, the wealthy, and small and large businesses. State policies affect our safety and health as well as the profitability of businesses. The impact of a given policy varies by group. (Who gets a tax cut? Who doesn't?) Thus, public policy is a source of great conflict because groups compete to gain benefits and reduce costs to themselves. As we will see, some are better positioned than others to win this battle.

This chapter examines two aspects of public policy in Texas: (1) the circumstances of the situation and the behavior of the people and agencies who implement the policies and (2) the nature and impact of these policies. Covered are the major policy areas of education, health and human services, business and economic development, the environment, and immigration. The other big-ticket item in Texas state government—public safety and criminal justice—is covered in Chapter 13, "The Criminal Justice System," and details on state spending are provided in Chapter 11, "Finance and Fiscal Policy." The state's regulatory agencies are discussed in Chapter 9, "The Executive Branch."

★ Making Public Policy in Texas

Follow *Practicing Texas Politics* on Twitter @PracTexPol

LO 12.1   Describe how public policy is made in Texas.

public policy
What government does or does not do to and for its citizens.

Surprisingly, scholars who study public policy have not agreed on a single definition of the term "public policy." One simple and useful definition for **public policy** that is used in this chapter is: what government does or does not do to and for its citizens.[2] Policy is both action, such as state or local governments raising or lowering speed limits, and inaction, such as Texas state government not accepting federal funds for expansion of Medicaid under the Affordable Care Act (Obamacare).

Models of Policymaking

Scholars who study public policy have made use of several models, or conceptual maps, of how the process works. Models simplify and clarify our thinking and focus attention on important aspects of how systems work. No one model is sufficient by itself, but together, different models can give us a more complete picture. The following models are useful in explaining how public policy works:

- Institutional model, which focuses attention on the structure and processes of government in order to understand why some policies emerge and others do not.

- Group model, which focuses attention on the groups involved and their interests. It sees group interaction as the central element of politics and policy as the outcome of group struggles.

- Elite model, which holds that public policy reflects the preferences of social and economic elites. The public is seen as apathetic, and its opinions tend to be shaped by the elite.

- Rational model, which suggests that public policy should be determined by weighing costs and benefits and selecting the policies that produce the greatest benefits over costs. It is frequently invoked as the "way things should be" but seldom found to be the way policy development really works.

- Incremental model, which sees "new" public policy as only a slightly modified continuation of past policy. Policymakers do not review all policy regularly. They lack the time, resources, and incentive to do so. Rather, they take existing policies as a starting point, perhaps modify them slightly, and focus on new policies. (Clearly, the incremental model is a rejection of the rational model.)

All of these models are helpful in understanding policymaking in Texas. The organization of Texas government and its rules and practices, as we will see, give elites and some groups more access to policymakers than others. Chapter 7, "The Politics of Interest Groups," describes the large number and power of economic interest groups in our state, and throughout the book, the strong role of economic elites should be apparent.

Throughout the nation, the rational model is useful in seeing how policy could be improved, but it casts little light on actual processes. In Texas, legislators are part-time, and the legislature itself meets only part of every other year to consider literally thousands of proposals. Lawmakers have neither the time nor resources to gather all the information they would need to choose the best policy in each area. Similarly, the agencies that implement the laws passed by the legislature lack resources, and often incentives, to compile all the information they would need to weigh all costs and benefits.

With respect to the incremental model, some important breaks in Texas public policy have occurred, but once established, policies tend to change only incrementally. For example, testing was first mandated in Texas schools in 1980 and became a major policy tool in 1990. Through several changes in form, testing has remained a major tool of educational assessment ever since. Similarly, privatization of social services was first mandated by the legislature in 2003 and, through several ups and downs, has continued. (Privatization involves governments contracting with private companies to provide certain government services, in this case handling citizens' applications for social services such as Medicaid.) As we saw in Chapter 9, "The Executive Branch," the sunset process requires a substantial review of most state agencies every 12 years. Through the sunset process, the legislature has generally enacted only incremental changes for most agencies and abolished few smaller, weaker ones.

Not included in the previously listed models is the participatory democratic model in which the public shows high levels of interest, knowledge, and participation in civic life (levels of which tend to be low in Texas). In this model, citizens would understand their needs and through elections demand that their representatives enact policies reflecting the voters' wishes. In practice, clear messages from the electoral process that produce policy are quite rare. Most policy decisions made by the legislative or executive branches are unknown or poorly understood by the general public. Citizens who are part of the economic elite, belong to an interest group, or feel very strongly about an issue are more likely to be heard. For example, polling in 2018 conducted by the University of Texas in concert with the *Texas Tribune* indicated that 59 percent of registered voters approved of the continuation of the Deferred Action for Childhood Arrivals (DACA) policy, while 30 percent wanted to see it end. However, when looking at the issue of immigration, Texans seem split on whether to immediately deport undocumented immigrants or not—51 percent against and 44 percent in favor of immediate deportation.[3]

Individual citizens are not completely ignored in policymaking, but the process is complex, and citizen impact tends to be filtered through groups and the political process. While elections generally don't send clear, specific policy preferences to our elected representatives, campaigning, the interest groups that represent us, and the desire of elected representatives to avoid being defeated push policymakers to make policies the majority of the voting public support.

Studies comparing opinion and policy outcomes in the 50 states indicate that public policy is influenced by public opinion. There are similar findings at the national level. However, studies also indicate that public influence happens primarily for issues that are relevant and important to the public, and, therefore, issues to which the public pays attention.[4] Most Texas policy issues don't fit this description. One national study found that the strongest influence on public policy was the opinion of the affluent, followed in descending order by business interest groups, mass-based interest groups, and average citizens[5]—a pattern that may well fit Texas.

In addition to the models, the environment of Texas influences public policy. These include such factors as wealth and income level, political ideology, and political culture. Wealth and income affect the resources that different groups can use to influence the political process. It is also the case that wealthier states tend to spend more on government and poorer states less. Wealthier, urban, industrialized states such as California and New York tend to spend more money per capita on public services such as education. Poorer states such as Louisiana and Mississippi spend less. Texas has a large economy and is highly urban, which push it toward greater government spending. However, Texas is slightly below the national average for median household income, and Texans have a tradition of conservatism and an individualistic/traditionalistic political culture that values small government. The tension between the two forces has caused Texas to spend more per capita on government over time but to keep government much smaller than is the case in other large, urban states.

Another way of understanding how public policy is made is to look at the steps commonly involved. Generally, one or more interest groups begins the process by bringing problems to the attention of government officials and then lobbying for solutions that benefit members of the group. Second, political parties and chief executives (such as the Texas governor) often select and combine proposals of interest groups into a manageable number and include them as part of their program or agenda. In Texas, the weakness of the governor and the large number of agencies mean that agency heads play this role for most of the issues affecting their area of responsibility. (The agriculture commissioner, for example, tries to aggregate the demands made by the various agricultural interest groups and proposes his/her agenda to the legislature.)

Third, the legislature then accepts some of the proposals through the passage of laws, the creation or modification of agencies, and the appropriation of money to carry out the policies. Fourth, the executive branch implements the policies. At the national level, the president provides instructions for the agencies that actually carry out policies. In Texas, more than 200 agencies have substantial independence from the governor. Therefore, state agencies have more latitude and independence than federal agencies in determining legislative intent and in applying the law to unforeseen circumstances. Finally, when disputes arise about the interpretation of the law itself or its implementation by the executive branch, the Texas attorney general may be asked for an opinion, court suits may be filed, or the legislature may be lobbied for changes (or all of the above).

These steps are commonly followed in the order just discussed, but in many cases, steps are skipped or reversed. For example, in an emergency such as a major hurricane, the governor may take actions and issue directives (some with the force of law, others effectively suggestions) with little or no input from interest groups or the legislature. Making public policy is a dynamic and varied process.

Public policy is the product of a series of formal and, probably more important, informal interactions among a variety of groups and individuals. These participants include wealthy, powerful, and well-placed individuals; interest groups; the governor, agency heads, and other political leaders; legislative leaders and committees; judges and the Texas attorney general; and officials of the federal government. Which actors are more important at which stages varies. Interest groups try to influence every step of the process. They initiate proposals; lobby the parties, other interest groups, the governor and relevant agencies, and the legislature; and file court suits or amicus curiae (friend of the court) briefs. (Amicus curiae briefs are filed by someone interested in the outcome of a case but who is not a party to the lawsuit.)

The Institutional Context

The way in which the Texas executive branch is organized has a major effect on public policy. A key reason is that fragmentation of authority strongly affects who has access to policy decisions, as well as how visible the decision process is to the public. The large number of agencies means they are covered less by the media and, therefore, are less visible to the public. The power of the one state official to whom the public pays attention (the governor) is limited. Special interest groups and the economic elite, on the other hand, have strong incentives (profits) to develop cozy relationships with agency personnel, and most agencies do not have to defend their decisions before a higher authority (such as the governor). Thus, it is not surprising that comparative studies of the states find a strong role for interest groups and the elite in Texas policymaking.

Bureaucracy and Public Policy We often think of public administrators as simply implementing the laws passed by the legislature, but the truth is that they must make many decisions about situations not clearly foreseen in the law. Not surprisingly, their own views, their bosses' preferences, their agency's culture, and the lobbying they receive make a difference in how they apply laws passed by the legislature. Agencies also want to protect or expand their turf. Lobbyists understand the role of the bureaucracy in making public policy and they work just as hard to influence agency decisions as they work to influence legislation.

Public agencies also must build good relations with state leaders (such as the governor), key legislators, and executive and legislative staff members because these people determine how much money and authority an agency receives. Dealing with the legislature often involves close cooperation between state agencies and lobbyists for groups that the agencies serve or regulate. For example, the Texas Good Roads/Transportation Association (mostly trucking companies and road contractors) and the Texas Department of Transportation have long worked closely, and relatively successfully, to lobby the legislature for more highway construction money.

In Texas, three factors are particularly important in determining agencies' success in achieving their policy goals: the vigor and vision of their leadership, their resources, and the extent to which elites influence implementation (called **elite access**).

Many Texas agencies define their jobs narrowly and make decisions on limited, technical grounds without considering the broader consequences of their actions. Other leaders of agencies, however, take a proactive approach. The Texas Comptroller's Office, for example, became a major player in the Texas government, a more aggressive collector of state taxes, a problem solver for other agencies, and under Carole Keeton Rylander Strayhorn, a focus of controversy.

elite access
The ability of the business elite to deal directly with high-ranking government administrators to avoid full compliance with regulations.

In 2006, Strayhorn conducted a report on undocumented immigration in Texas. She reported that deporting undocumented immigrants in Texas would be too costly to the state at nearly $18 billion. Her report countered the tough immigration stance of her party.[6]

The second factor important in determining agencies' success is their resources. Historically, Texas government agencies have had minimal funds to implement policy. Consider the example of nursing homes, which are big business today and are primarily for-profit enterprises. Almost two-thirds of Texas nursing home residents depend on Medicaid to pay for their care. However, Medicaid rates, set by the state, have not increased as fast as costs. According to the Texas Health Care Association in 2014, "The state continues to reimburse providers nearly 20 dollars per day less than the cost of care."[7] As of 2016, Texas was ranked 47th among 50 states in nursing home care. Low rates depress nursing home profitability. Less scrupulous companies maintain profits by cutting staff and services.[8]

The third relevant factor is elite access. Nursing home company executives' access, for instance, to top-level agency administrators demonstrates this process. Nursing home residents are generally weak and unable to leave if service is bad or threatens their well-being. Therefore, residents depend heavily on government inspectors to ensure that they are treated well. Unfortunately, the number of nursing home inspectors in Texas has been like a roller coaster—sometimes up, sometimes down. When the number of inspectors relative to the number of residents decreases, the number of inspections decreases, and abuse tends to increase. Even when there are enough inspectors, nursing home company executives' connections to top-level agency administrators often ensure that infractions result in a slap on the wrist and a promise to do better.

One 2018 study ranked Texas fourth worst among the states in serious deficiencies per nursing home, but in the middle (21st) in the amount of average fines for violations.[9] A 2011 Texas State Auditor's report found that the Department of Aging and Disability Services (DADS) "rarely terminates its contracts with nursing facilities that have a pattern of serious deficiencies. In fiscal years 2014 and 2015, the department found that of more than 1,200 facilities, 328 had accounted for 94 percent of violations. Yet, of the 328 facilities, the state was able to collect fines from only 22. However, it reconsidered or rescinded all but one of those terminations."[10] Over the years, both the Health and Human Services Commission and the state attorney general have been criticized for their lack of fervor in pursuing nursing home violations.

As these reports indicate, weak leadership, lack of resources, as well as elite access make policy less effective and abuse more common in Texas nursing homes. Four other factors also contribute to lower quality care in Texas:

- The state's shortage of nurses, in part because of too few nursing programs
- The high proportion of lower income patients (who are less able to make effective demands)
- The number of larger nursing facilities (where patients are more anonymous and thus easier to neglect)
- The prevalence of for-profit facilities (which tend to reduce staff and services to lower expenses)

At least since the 1990s (when good data became available), Texas has had more severe and repeated violations of federal patient care standards than most other states. A study by a nursing home advocacy group ranked Texas the worst nursing home state, failing on six of eight statistical measures. A study by the Commonwealth Fund, the SCAN Foundation (Senior Care Action Network Foundation), and AARP (formerly the American Association of Retired Persons) as of 2017 ranked Texas's long-term care system 46th on quality of care, due largely to poor nursing home ratings. Harm to residents can include neglect, physical and verbal abuse, injury, and death. For-profit nursing homes tend to do more serious and repeated harm to residents than do government and nonprofit homes.[11] Clearly, government administrators greatly affect policy, and their decisions have an impact on people's lives.

⊞ Education

LO 12.2   Analyze major challenges faced by the Texas education system.

Texas's commitment to education began with its 1836 constitution, which required government-owned land to be set aside for establishing public schools and "a University of the first class." Later, framers of the 1876 constitution mandated an "efficient system of public free schools." This chapter examines the attempts of Texas public schools and universities to meet the needs of a changing student body and to improve the quality of education in a rapidly changing world. Chapter 11, "Finance and Fiscal Policy," discusses how and how much we pay to meet those challenges.

Public Schools

In the 21st century, public school students have increasingly come from families that are ethnic minorities or economically disadvantaged. According to Texas Education Agency data, in the 2017–2018 academic year, 52 percent of Texas students were Latino, 28 percent Anglo, 13 percent African American, 4 percent Asian, and 3 percent other (multiracial, Native American, and Pacific Islander). In addition, 59 percent of Texas students were economically disadvantaged (defined as those eligible for free or reduced-price lunches), and 19 percent had limited English language proficiency.

Historically, Texas has not served minority and less affluent students as well as it has Anglo and middle-class students. If this pattern continues, studies project that Texans' average income will decline, while the costs of welfare, prisons, and lost tax revenues will increase.[12] Table 12.1 provides data on how Texas's educational efforts and outcomes compare to those of other states.

One indication that the state can do better comes from *U.S. News and World Report*'s 2018 ranking of the nation's best high schools (based on criteria such as college readiness, math and reading scores, and graduation rates). About 6,000 high schools across the United States achieved a Best High School

TABLE 12.1 Effort and Outcomes in Texas Education (Rank Among the 50 States)

Texas Public Schools	
State and local expenditure per pupil	37th
Average teacher salary	28th
High school graduation rate	5th
Comparison of average scores in math on NAEP* for 8th graders	17 states higher than Texas, 16 similar, 16 lower
Comparison of average scores in reading on NAEP* for 8th graders	32 states higher than Texas, 14 similar, 3 lower
Percentage of high school students who play on a sports team	12th
Texas Public Higher Education	
Expenditure per full-time student	7th
Average university faculty salary	20th
Average community college faculty salary	25th
Average tuition and fees at public universities	21st**
Average tuition and fees at community colleges	3rd**
University graduation rate	32nd
Percent of population with a bachelor's degree or higher	28th

*National Assessment of Educational Progress, called the Nation's Report Card.

**21st and 3rd cheapest.

Source: "Texas Fact Book, 2014," *Legislative Budget Board, www.lbb.state.tx.us/Documents/Publications/Policy_Report/Fact_Book_2014.pdf;* "2016 Texas Public Higher Education Almanac," *Texas Higher Education Coordinating Board, http://www.thecb.state.tx.us; and* "National Assessment of Educational Progress, 2015," *National Center for Education Statistics, http://www.nationsreportcard.gov.*

— Competency Connection —
☼ **CRITICAL THINKING** ☼

Education is often said to be important to individuals, the state, and the nation. What do the numbers suggest about Texans' commitment to excellence in education?

Ranking. Of 1,500 Texas high schools, 601 made the list. Seventeen Texas high schools were ranked among the top 100 in the nation, including the nation's highest ranked school for the fifth year in a row, Dallas's School for the Talented and Gifted. Three schools making the top 100 were located in San Juan, Brownsville, and Mission, all in South Texas. Of the 20 highest-achieving high schools in Texas, 16 had a non-Anglo majority, and 12 had a majority of economically disadvantaged students.[13]

Today, more than 1,000 independent school districts and about 200 charter operators shoulder primary responsibility for the delivery of educational services to 5.3 million students. (Chapter 3, "Local Governments," discusses the organization and politics of local school districts.) Although local school districts have somewhat more independence than in the past, they are part of a relatively centralized system in which state authorities substantially affect local decisions, from what is taught to how it is financed. As was discussed in Chapter 9, "The Executive Branch," Texas public schools are heavily regulated by the Texas Education

Agency (TEA), headed by the state commissioner of education and, to a lesser extent, the State Board of Education (SBOE). Less regulated than the independent school districts and sometimes more controversial are charter schools.

Alternatives to Traditional Public Schools For many years, there has been controversy over where Texas schoolchildren should go to school. Today there are alternatives to traditional public schools for Texas children: private schools, homeschools, and charter schools. Other options include online learning programs and the High School Equivalency Program.

Over the years, some critics have called for vouchers as an option to public schools, labeling the issue as "school choice." Vouchers would use government funds to pay tuition for students attending private schools. In 2017, Governor Abbott and Lt. Governor Dan Patrick attended a rally on the steps of the Texas Capitol urging lawmakers to vote to give parents state money to attend private schools. However, in the 2019 legislative session, the support for school vouchers waned as the new speaker stated that the House would not pass legislation approving vouchers.

Supporters of vouchers argue that parents should have the choice to take their children out of low-performing public schools and place them in better-performing private schools. In addition, competition should encourage public schools to perform better. Opponents argue that vouchers would take better students, particularly middle-class children, out of the public schools. Loss of these students would likely lower their parents' political support to fund and improve public schools. They argue that the poor, who are the focal point of voucher arguments, would be unlikely to move their children in significant numbers.

Others have called for homeschooling, in which parents are responsible for their children's education. In 1994, the Texas Supreme Court ruled that homeschooling was a legal alternative to public schools. In Texas, the state has three requirements in order for homeschooling to be legal: the instruction must be real (not a sham), visual (such as a book or video screen), and cover at least five subjects (reading, spelling, grammar, mathematics, and good citizenship). There is no hard data on homeschooling in Texas. According to the National Household Education Survey, in the 2015–2016 school year, it was estimated that 166,403 students were homeschooled in Texas.

Supporters of homeschooling argue that parents will take more responsibility for their own children's education and teach them the family's values. Opponents argue that wide variation exists in educational outcomes. Many homeschooled students are well educated and go on to be successful in college and work; others get little education and are unable to compete effectively with their peers.

Charter schools are another option for Texas children. In 1995, the legislature authorized the issuance of charters to schools that would be less limited by TEA rules. Charter schools are open-enrollment, draw students from across district lines, use a variety of teaching strategies, and are exempt from many rules, such as state teacher certification requirements. State law requires fiscal and academic accountability for these schools, together with monitoring and accreditation by TEA. With greater flexibility legislators hoped charter schools could deal more effectively with at-risk students. Compared with students at traditional schools, charter school students are more economically disadvantaged, more are African American, slightly more are Latino, and fewer are Anglo.

Charter schools are public schools responsible to the state but not the local school district. Charters are granted to nonprofit corporations that, in turn, create a board to govern the school. The particular organizational structure varies from school to school. Charter schools commonly have multiple campuses. In 2017–2018, Texas had 774 charter schools serving 337,000 students (or more than 6 percent of all public school students).

In 2013, the Texas legislature passed a major revision of charter school regulations, including raising the cap on the number of charters granted from 215 in 2013 to 305 in 2019. The legislation also toughened standards and moved responsibility for initial charter approval from the SBOE to the commissioner of education. There has been some volatility in charter schools in the state. In 2016, TEA announced the closure of seven charter schools for failing to meet the higher accountability standards, an additional 11 charter schools closed voluntarily. As of October 2018, the total number of charters that had been granted was 329, of which 154 schools had closed (54 of those by TEA), leaving 175 active.[14]

Two major policy controversies have arisen over charter schools. Whether the state has adequately financed these schools has been the subject of lobbying efforts and court decisions. The effectiveness of their programs in improving student performance has also been disputed.

Charter schools receive most of their funding from the state based on attendance, with the rest coming from federal and private sources. They cannot impose taxes or charge tuition. They do not receive construction funding (a major cost for schools) from the state but can issue bonds (borrow) for new construction. Charter schools argue that under state funding formulas they have less revenue per pupil (by $1,000) than do traditional schools.[15] The calculations are complex, and opponents argue that the difference is actually small. After failing to convince the legislature to provide additional funding, the Texas Charter Schools Association filed suit over the issues of facilities funding and the state cap on the number of charters. In May 2016, the Texas Supreme Court ruled on this and other suits involving over half of the state's school districts. In its 100-page opinion, the court described Texas's school finance system as Byzantine but satisfying minimum constitutional requirements.[16] The opinion urged the legislature to fix the system but did not order it to do so. Thus, charter schools will have to convince the legislature that they need and deserve more money.

Charter school officials believe they have an ally in education commissioner, Michael Morath. He appointed three charter school experts to high-level positions in the TEA within months of taking office in 2016 and maintained cordial relations with the Texas Charter School Association.

The effectiveness of charter schools in meeting the needs of at-risk students is sharply debated. Some Texas charter schools have "compiled terrific records of propelling minority and low-income kids into college."[17] Some charter schools have given misinformation as they claim a 100 percent college acceptance rate. However, some charter schools require students be accepted to a four-year university in order to graduate, which is not known to the public. In the 2016 *U.S. News and World Report* listing of the nation's best high schools, 9 of the 20 best high schools in Texas were charter schools, located in Arlington, Houston (2), Westlake, Austin, Laredo, Brownsville, Edinburg, and San Juan. Some other charter schools have been marked by corruption and academic failure.

A six-year study (2007 to 2013) by Stanford University researchers found that charter school results varied by state. However, in 2017 another Stanford report found that students who attend Texas charter schools show more growth in reading compared to those attending Texas public schools. There was no significant difference found in math. Charter school students from low socio-economic backgrounds and English language learners gained more than their counterparts in traditional public schools.[18]

According to a study conducted from 2002 to 2011, greater variability in quality in the charter sector occurred in the earlier study years. Over time, as less competent schools closed, charter schools improved in average effectiveness to be comparable to traditional schools.[19] Other studies suggest a continuing variability in the quality of charter schools. These schools are still a work in progress, on average comparable to traditional schools in effectiveness, but widely variable in quality.

Two alternatives to public schools are online schools and the High School Equivalency Programs (HSEPs). Starting in 2009, the Texas Virtual School Network (TxVSN) began providing students and schools with online courses taught by state-certified and credentialed teachers. Third through twelfth grade students may be eligible through their schools. The HSEPs require students to be at least 16 years old. HSEP's focus on students at risk of not graduating or earning their high school diploma.

Testing One of the sharpest debates in Texas education is over the role of state-mandated standardized tests (sometime called accountability testing). The state's top policymakers agree that the educational system needs objective *assessment* of success or failure and *accountability* for that success or failure. Educators and political leaders are sharply divided, however, about how to assess student progress and whether student test scores should affect such matters as student graduation and teacher and administrator pay. Nevertheless, testing as a major assessment and accountability tool is now federal and state policy. Texas first mandated a standardized test in 1980 and began to rely heavily on testing in 1990. It has used five tests over the years, each more rigorous than its predecessors.

An essential component of the state testing program is the **Texas Essential Knowledge and Skills (TEKS)**, a core curriculum adopted in 1998 that sets out for every subject matter and grade level the knowledge students are expected to gain and use. This curriculum is required by the legislature and is approved by the State Board of Education.

The TEKS is similar to the Common Core, a curriculum used by 44 other states. Because Texas had invested time and money in developing TEKS and some experts found it marginally better in some areas than the Common Core, state authorities were inclined to keep their own system. When the federal government required states to switch to the Common Core to be eligible for a pool of funds

Texas Essential Knowledge and Skills (TEKS)

A core curriculum (a set of courses and knowledge) setting out what students should learn.

to encourage innovation, the issue became primarily ideological and about state versus federal authority. The 2013 legislature prohibited use of the Common Core by both state education agencies and local school districts. Because Texas is such a large textbook market, publishers adapted textbooks to reflect the TEKS. Some districts, however, use instructional materials in keeping with the Common Core.

The current testing program is the **State of Texas Assessment of Academic Readiness (STAAR)**. Mandated by the legislature in 2007 and 2009, STAAR went into effect in the spring of 2012. It included a number of key mandates:

- End-of-course examinations in the four high school core subject areas (math, science, English, and social studies).

- A requirement to pass both end-of-course tests and courses in order to graduate.

- For grades 3 through 8, new tests to assess reading and math for each level, as well as writing, science, and social studies for certain grade levels.

- The new tests and curriculum to be more closely tied to college readiness and preparation for the workplace.

- The new tests to be more rigorous and standards to be gradually raised through 2016.

In the first round of STAAR tests, statewide passing rates for freshmen varied from 55 percent for writing to 87 percent for biology. However, if the 2016 standards had been applied, a majority of students would have failed in each subject. Not surprisingly, the results were met with controversy.

Increasing the number of tests, how much they count, and their level of difficulty caused a strong backlash. In 2013, the legislature decreased the number of end-of-course tests from 15 to five and cut testing for high-performing students in grades 3 through 8. In 2015, the legislature allowed students to graduate if they passed three of five state end-of-course exams if a school committee approved; this was set to expire in 2017 but was extended to 2019. Overall, 92 percent of the Class of 2015 passed all five exams. Another 6 percent failed one or two tests, but most were able to graduate. Similarly, most grade school students failing an exam were promoted by a campus committee. In 2016, administration of the STAAR test was plagued with problems, and a group of parents filed suit to have its results for that year blocked.

One of the most controversial aspects of the testing programs is that test results are used to evaluate teachers, administrators, and schools. This practice, continued under STAAR, is intended to increase "accountability"—that is, to hold teachers and administrators responsible for increasing student learning. Many educators object to having their pay—and perhaps their jobs—depend on student performance as measured by a test, because student success is highly affected by students' backgrounds and home environments. The dilemma is that although research shows that quality teaching makes a major contribution to student learning, it is not clear whether tests adequately measure the teacher's contribution.

In January 2012, then-Texas education commissioner Robert Scott, who led much of the development of the use of tests as a policy tool in the state, said that

State of Texas Assessment of Academic Readiness (STAAR)
A state program of end-of-course and other examinations begun in 2012.

testing had become a "perversion." Over the previous decade, he argued, too much reliance had been placed on tests. He wanted test results to be "just one piece of the bottom line, and everything else that happens in a school year [to be] factored into that equation."[20]

Since the 1980s when standardized tests were first used, there have been cries of protest from parents, educators, schools districts, and the students themselves. Social conservatives argue that the program tramples on local control of schools, whereas African American and Latino critics charge that the tests are discriminatory. Educational critics complain that "teaching to the test" raises scores on the test but causes neglect of other subjects and skills. Questions were also raised when the federal No Child Left Behind program (now the Elementary and Secondary Education Act) produced substantially different evaluations of some schools than the Texas system (because the two assessment systems use different criteria). Supporters of testing argue that the policy holds schools responsible for increasing student learning. As proof, they point to improved test scores of most groups of students since the program began.

Because test results are so important to both students and their schools, there has been controversy over how high standards should be. Some parents and advocates for disadvantaged students argue that minimum passing scores are too high. STAAR's higher standards have created pushback. In August 2018, the Texas Education Agency replaced the pass/fail system for schools and now uses the A–F grading system to bolster accountability and transparency. However, in this new system, 40 percent of a school's rating will be based on STAAR test results. While school boards and others have argued against this new system, Lt. Governor Dan Patrick says the system is "here to stay."[21]

Some critics believe that national tests, such as the National Assessment of Educational Progress (NAEP), are better measures because they are not "taught to," and they provide a basis of comparison with changes in other states. In broad terms, Texas student performance (as measured on state and national tests) improved from at least 1980 to around 2011, and in varying degrees, gaps between Anglo, African American, and Latino students diminished. However, since that time, scores on the NAEP have tended to be flat or dropping. STAAR scores have shown little improvement. Table 12.1 compares NAEP scores in Texas to those of other states.

Both supporters and critics of testing tend to agree that STAAR is not working well but disagree as to why. Supporters of testing argue that the test needs to be more rigorous and that teachers and administrators need to stop fomenting fear and test anxiety. Opponents say students are over-tested, and the testing model has grown stale. Controversies over testing will continue.

Colleges and Universities

Texas has many colleges and universities—105 public and 42 private institutions of higher education serving more than 2.1 million students annually. A growing number of for-profit and nonprofit online institutions also offer degrees and certificates. Most potential Texas students live within commuting distance of a campus. Public institutions include 38 universities, 10 health-related institutions, 50 community college districts (many with multiple campuses), three two-year state colleges, and four colleges (with 10 campuses) of the Texas State Technical College System. All receive some state funding and, of course, state oversight and regulation.

The Struggle for Tier-One Status Texas has three universities widely recognized as being among the prestigious tier-one national research universities: Rice University (private), the University of Texas at Austin (public), and Texas A&M University in College Station (public). All three are ranked by *U.S. News and World Report* among the top 100 national universities, along with three private schools, Southern Methodist University, Baylor University, and Texas Christian University. Three other Texas universities made the second 100: University of Texas-Dallas (129th), University of Houston (171st), and Texas Tech University (187th).[22]

Among public universities, the University of Texas at Austin and Texas A&M University in College Station are commonly referred to as the state's "flagship" universities. They have traditionally been the most prestigious academically and the most powerful politically. Most observers believe that Texas needs more flagship universities to serve the increasing number of highly qualified students and to conduct the research necessary to attract new businesses and grow the economy. In 2009, a state constitutional amendment sought to increase the number of tier-one schools by giving access to funding to seven public universities through the Texas Research Incentive Program. These schools include the Universities of Texas at Arlington, Dallas, El Paso, and San Antonio; Texas Tech University; University of Houston; and University of North Texas (UNT). In 2016, these four institutions received the "Carnegie Tier One" status. In 2012, Texas State University, San Marcos, was added to the list of emerging research institutions by the Texas Higher Education Coordinating Board (THECB).

There are no universally accepted criteria for tier-one status. However, schools are expected to receive at least $100 million a year in research grants and belong to the prestigious, invitation-only Association of American Universities (AAU). In Texas, only the University of Texas at Austin, Texas A&M University in College Station, and Rice University are members. Another important step toward tier-one status is listing by the Carnegie Classification of Institutions of Higher Education as one of the 115 schools highest in research activity.

Access to Higher Education Two sets of issues have challenged Texas higher education in recent years: funding and providing access to Texas's highly diverse population. Low state funding and the sharp increase in tuition rates are discussed in Chapter 11, "Finance and Fiscal Policy."

Improving the educational opportunities of Texas's ethnic minorities and the economically disadvantaged is an important but controversial issue and one with a long history in the state. A 1946 denial of admission to the University of Texas law school on the grounds of race led to the "landmark [U.S. Supreme Court] case, *Sweatt* v. *Painter*, that helped break the back of racism in college

📋 STUDENTS IN ACTION

Booze and Ballots: A Tale of Two Different Times

"We involved a lot of students in the public sphere for the first time, and some continued to be involved. We saved some lives and had a lot of fun."

—Anonymous

Sam Houston State University Alumni Association

Texas law allows citizens of almost any political entity to vote their area wet (the sale of alcohol is allowed) or dry (the sale of alcohol is prohibited). Walker County, home of Huntsville and Sam Houston State University (Sam), voted dry in 1914 and remained so until 1971. That year, Citizens for a Progressive Huntsville, composed mainly of Sam students and led by two students, circulated a petition for an election to permit alcohol sales within the city. Most of the 916 who signed the petition were thought to be Sam students or faculty. Townspeople were reluctant to sign the petition because others could see their names on the list. When the vote was held by secret ballot, however, all four voting boxes favored a wet community, which won with 62 percent of the votes. An estimated 800 students voted (out of 3,118 total votes).

In 2008, a Sam student ran unsuccessfully for the Huntsville City Council. Although it was not part of his public message, he told fellow students that his major concern was to extend bar hours from 12 midnight to 2 A.M. Even so, he couldn't get his own fraternity brothers out to the polls.

In 1971, in the wet issue, campus activists found a concern that could pull together students of widely varying views. Nearly 40 years later, the presidential election of 2008 produced a larger-than-usual student vote, but there was no local student-led movement to capitalize on the bar hours issue.

What's the Advice to Students?

"Sometimes it takes an issue like booze to get people interested enough to act on other, more important matters."

Source: Interview with Kelsey Lea, Samantha Davis, William Niven, Connor Shields, and Gilbert Schorlemmer, May 7, 2014.

Competency Connection
⚙ CRITICAL THINKING ⚙

What issues mobilize students to action?

---

admissions" throughout the country.[23] Texas's long history of official and private discrimination still has consequences today. Although many Latinos and African Americans have become middle class since the civil rights of the 1960s and 1970s, both groups remain overrepresented in the working class and the ranks of the poor. Poverty rates for Hispanics and African Americans are twice the rate of Anglo-Americans in Texas. In 2018, Hispanics made up roughly 39 percent of the population, but over half, 51 percent, of those lived below the poverty level.

To deal with these inequalities, the Texas Higher Education Coordinating Board adopted an ambitious program in 2000, called Closing the Gaps, to increase college enrollment and graduation rates for all groups by 2015. The program was highly successful. By 2017, enrollment and graduation had increased markedly. African Americans receiving degrees or certificates went from 33,000 in 2015 to 41,027 in 2017; Latino graduates went from 88,000 to 111,344. As of 2017, 124,178 undergraduates categorized as "economically disadvantaged" had received their degree or certificate. This was more than halfway to the goal of 246,000 slated for 2030. The proportion of both men and women attending postsecondary programs has also increased. Building on the success of Closing the Gaps, the Coordinating Board developed a new plan, 60x30TX, to expand student achievement and build a "globally competitive Texas workforce by 2030." The goal is to assure that 60 percent of young Texans (ages 25–34) have a post-secondary credential (either a degree or certificate) by 2030. In 2016, 42 percent of young Texans had a degree or certificate. Based on the 2018 data and since the program was implemented, the annual number of certificates and bachelors and masters degrees awarded in Texas have increased 7.25 percent.[24] Texas public institutions of higher education are to serve all students well, regardless of ethnicity or economic background.

A study financed by the Bill and Melinda Gates Foundation concluded that if the goals of Closing the Gaps were achieved, "When all public [state and local] and private costs are considered, the annual economic returns per $1 of expenditures by 2030 are estimated to be $24.15 in total spending, $9.60 in gross state product, and $6.01 in personal income."[25]

Texas colleges and universities commonly describe themselves as equal opportunity/affirmative action institutions. **Equal opportunity** simply means that the school takes care that its policies and actions do not produce prohibited discrimination, such as denying admission on the basis of race or sex. **Affirmative action** means that the institution takes positive steps to attract women and members of historical minority groups. For most schools, affirmative action means taking such noncontroversial steps as making sure that the school catalog has pictures of all groups—Anglos and minorities, men and women—and recruits in predominantly minority high schools, not just schools with majority Anglo student populations. However, some selective universities have actively considered race along with other factors in admissions and aid, and other schools have offered scholarships for minority students. This side of affirmative action has created conflict.

Affirmative action issues have been largely addressed in the courts. Some Anglo applicants denied admission or scholarship benefits challenged the second form of affirmative action programs in the courts. In the case of *University of California v. Bakke* (1978), the U.S. Supreme Court ruled that race could be considered as one factor, along with other criteria, to achieve diversity in higher education enrollment; however, setting aside a specific number of slots for one race was not acceptable.[26] (Remember that U.S. Supreme Court decisions establish precedents that must be followed throughout the country.) Relying on the *Bakke* decision, the University of Texas Law School created separate admission

equal opportunity
Ensures that policies and actions do not discriminate on factors, such as race, gender, ethnicity, religion, or national origin.

affirmative action
Takes positive steps to attract women and members of racial and ethnic minority groups; may include using race in admission or hiring decisions.

pools based on race and ethnicity, a practice the U.S. Fifth Circuit Court of Appeals declared unconstitutional in *Hopwood v. Texas* (1996).[27] In 2003, the U.S. Supreme Court issued two rulings on affirmative action. In the Michigan case of *Grutter v. Bollinger*, the court ruled that race could constitute one factor in an admissions policy designed to achieve student body diversity.[28] On the same day in another Michigan case, *Gratz v. Bollinger*, the court condemned the practice of giving a portion of the points needed for admission to every underrepresented minority applicant.[29]

After the *Hopwood* ruling, Texas schools looked for ways to maintain minority enrollment. In 1997, Texas legislators mandated the **top 10 percent rule**, which provided that the top 10 percent of the graduating class of every accredited public or private Texas high school could be admitted to tax-supported colleges and universities of their choosing, regardless of admission test scores. Thus, the students with the best grades at Texas's high schools, including those that are heavily minority, economically disadvantaged, or in small towns, can gain automatic admission to a flagship institution or other public college or university of their choosing. The top 10 percent rule has helped all three groups. However, court challenges continued at the University of Texas at Austin.

For students not admitted on the basis of class standing, the University of Texas at Austin used a "holistic review" of all academic and personal achievements, which may take into consideration family income, race, and ethnicity (with no specific weight and no quotas). The use of race in the holistic review produced another court challenge (*Fisher v. University of Texas*), which was heard before the U.S. Supreme Court during the fall of 2012.[30] The Court held that a university's use of race must meet a test known as "strict scrutiny," meaning that affirmative action will be constitutional only if it is "narrowly tailored." Courts can no longer simply accept a university's determination that it needs to consider race to have a diverse student body. Instead, courts themselves will need to confirm that the use of race is "necessary." The Fifth Circuit Court found that the university met this standard, and the admissions program was upheld by the U.S. Supreme Court in 2016.[31]

Have student bodies at the two flagship schools changed in response to changes in the law? From fall 2010 to fall 2018, Anglos were a minority of incoming University of Texas at Austin freshmen—37 percent in 2017–2018—although they remained a majority of the total student body until 2012. In 2003–2004, Texas A&M University in College Station announced that it would not use race in admissions decisions but would increase minority recruiting and provide more scholarships for first-generation, low-income students. (First-generation students are the first in their immediate family to attend college.) The university also dropped preferences for "legacies" (relatives of alumni), who were predominantly Anglo. In Spring 2017, Anglos made up 62 percent of freshmen, while 70 percent of students were transfers.

The top 10 percent rule is controversial, especially among applicants from competitive high schools denied admission to the state's flagship institutions. In fall 2009, 86 percent of students offered admission to the University of Texas at Austin qualified by the top 10 percent rule, a situation that left little room for

top 10 percent rule
Texas law gives automatic admission into any Texas public college or university to those graduating in the top 10 percent of their Texas high school class, with limitations for the University of Texas at Austin.

POINT/COUNTERPOINT

Should Texas Continue to Use the "Top 10 Percent Rule"?

THE ISSUE To promote diversity in Texas colleges and universities without using race as an admission criterion, the state legislature in 1997 passed a law guaranteeing admission to any public college or university in the state to Texas students who graduate in the top 10 percent of their high school class. The law sought to promote greater geographic, socioeconomic, and racial/ethnic diversity. The law applies to all public colleges and universities in the state, but it has had its greatest effect on the two flagship universities—the University of Texas at Austin and Texas A&M University in College Station—prestigious schools with more qualified applicants than they can admit. The rule has increased minority representation at both schools but more so at the University of Texas. In 2009, the legislature capped automatic admission to the University of Texas at Austin at 75 percent.

FOR	AGAINST
1. The top 10 percent rule is doing what it was designed to do—increase diversity among highly qualified students.	1. The top 10 percent rule unfairly puts students who attend high schools with rigorous standards at a disadvantage. Thus, they are tempted to take lighter loads or attend less demanding high schools.
2. Virtually all top 20 percent students from competitive high schools who choose UT-Austin or TAMU-College Station gain admission there.	2. So many students are admitted under this one criterion that the universities have too little discretion, and students with other talents (such as music and the arts) are left out.
3. The problem is not that Texas has too many students entering schools under automatic admission. Rather, the issue is that Texas has too few flagship universities to accommodate the number of qualified students.	3. The rule is creating a brain drain. Many top students are leaving Texas to attend college in other states, where they often remain after graduation.

— Competency Connection —
✿ CRITICAL THINKING ✿

Underlying the argument about the top 10 percent rule is concern for opportunity and for diversity on campus. Should Texas look for an alternative to the top 10 percent rule? If so, what?

---

students to be admitted on the basis of high scores or other talents (such as music or leadership). According to the university's president, even football might have to be abolished. (No one believed him.) In response, the 2009 legislature modified the rule so that UT-Austin would not have to admit more than 75 percent of its students on the basis of class standing. The class standing that the university chose for admission varied by year: top 8 percent for fall 2016; 7 percent for 2015, 2017 and 2018; and 6 percent for 2019 and summer of 2020. Initially, the 75 percent cap was in effect only through the 2015–2016 school year; however, the 84th Legislature repealed the expiration date. In 2017, Texas Senator Kel Seliger (R-Amarillo) authored a bill to repeal the top 10 percent rule stating that doing so would lead to greater diversity in the long run. However, even with Governor Abbott's support for repeal or substantial modification, the bill did not make it to a vote.

✓ 12.2 Learning Check

1. Why is standardized testing so controversial in Texas?
2. What is the "top 10 percent rule" in Texas higher education?

Answers at the end of this chapter.

Health and Human Services

LO 12.3 Describe the major health and human services programs in Texas, and discuss how efforts to address the needs of its citizens have been approached.

Most people think of Texas as a wealthy state, and indeed, the Lone Star State has many wealthy residents and a substantial middle class. Texas, however, also has long been among the states with the largest proportion of its population in poverty. From 2000 to 2017, Texas's poverty rate varied between 15 to 18.5 percent of the population. It has declined in recent years, albeit irregularly. Poverty is particularly high for children and members of historical minority groups, as can be seen in Table 12.2. Poverty is highest in South Texas and about half of the metropolitan areas. It is lowest in suburban counties surrounding major metropolitan areas. Poverty is defined in terms of family size and income. In 2018 (the year for the latest poverty numbers), according to the federal poverty levels, for a family of three, poverty was an annual family income of less than $20,780; for a family of four, it was $25,100.

Even more Texans are low income, meaning they earn an income above the poverty line but insufficient for many "extras," such as health insurance. A common measure of low income is an income up to twice the poverty level. In 2018, 48 percent of Texas's children lived in low-income families.

Access to health care is a national issue that is even more acute in Texas. Although the state's major cities have outstanding medical centers, they are of little use to those who lack the resources to pay for care.[32] For at least the last decade, studies comparing health care in the various states consistently rank Texas near the bottom. For example, from 2007 to 2016, the Commonwealth Fund, a well-respected foundation, did five state-by-state comparisons of various aspects of health system performance. All ranked Texas in the bottom quarter of the states.[33]

A key factor in access to health care is health insurance. In Texas, the proportion of people without health insurance dropped from 26 percent in 2010, when the Affordable Care Act (Obamacare) became law, to 17 percent in 2017. With nearly 5 million uninsured, the state led the nation in proportion of uninsured, as it had since at least 1988. Uninsured rates are particularly high for Latino Texans, as the "How Do We Compare" table in this chapter shows. Texas also leads in the proportion of uninsured children.

The Patient Protection and Affordable Care Act (popularly known as ACA or Obamacare), passed by Congress in 2010, is aimed at improving this situation. Some provisions of the act are widely supported: for example, young adults up to age 26 can be on their parents' insurance, preexisting conditions are covered in many cases, and caps on lifetime benefits have been lifted.

The heart of the ACA is an attempt to provide health insurance to almost all Americans, requiring those who can afford it to purchase health insurance and expanding Medicaid to cover those who cannot afford to buy insurance on their own. Both provisions have met with controversy. Analysts attribute a significant part of the drop in the number of uninsured Texans to the ACA. For people who

TABLE 12.2 Families in Poverty in Texas and the United States (2017)

	Texas (Percent)	United States (Percent)
Families	12*	10
Anglos	7	8
Latinos	18	16
African Americans	17	20
Children 0–18	18	16
Adults 19–64	10	10
Age 65 and older	10	8

*Family income is used by many specialists in poverty as a better indicator. Among individual Texans, the percentage was 17.2.

Source: "State Health Facts," Kaiser Family Foundation, 2017, http://kff.org/statedata. Based on U.S. Census data.

— Competency Connection —
☼ **CRITICAL THINKING** ☼

How does poverty in Texas impact all Texans?

do not already have a health insurance plan that meets ACA requirements, states can provide insurance "exchanges" or "marketplaces" to assist them. For states such as Texas that opt not to have an exchange, the federal government's exchange provides assistance. Republicans in the U.S. Congress, along with President Donald Trump, have tauted calls to "repeal and replace" ACA, but as of May 2019, it remained. However, changes over the past few years have significantly impacted ACA. There have been estimates that half a million fewer people enrolled for ACA because of cuts to outreach and advertisement alone.

The second major effort of the ACA was to expand the coverage of **Medicaid**, the joint federal–state program to provide medical care to the poor. In June 2012, the U.S. Supreme Court upheld most of the Affordable Care Act in a suit brought by Texas and 25 other states (*National Federation of Independent Business v. Sebelius*, 132 S.Ct. 2566 [2012]). However, the court held that the national government could not use the threat to withhold existing Medicaid funds to coerce states into expanding Medicaid coverage. This holding allowed Texas and other states to opt out of Medicaid expansion.

Evolution of Social Services Since the Great Depression of the 1930s, state and national governments have gradually increased efforts to address the needs of the poor, the elderly, and those who cannot afford adequate medical care. In the 20th century, social welfare became an important part of the federal relationship (see Chapter 2, "Federalism and the Texas Constitution," and Chapter 3, "Local Governments"). Over time, the national government has taken responsibility for relatively popular social welfare programs, such as Social Security, Medicare, and

Medicaid
Funded in large part by federal grants and in part by state appropriations, Medicaid is administered by the state. It provides medical care for poor persons.

aid to the blind and disabled. The states, on the other hand, have responsibility for less popular welfare programs that have less effective lobbying behind them, such as Medicaid, Supplemental Nutrition Assistance Program (SNAP, formerly food stamps), and Temporary Assistance for Needy Families (TANF). The federal government pays a significant part of the cost of state social welfare programs, but within federal guidelines the states administer them, make eligibility rules, and pay part of the cost.

Health and human services programs are at a disadvantage in Texas for two reasons. First, the state's political culture values individualism, self-reliance, and business interests; thus, anything suggesting welfare is difficult to fund at more than a minimal level. In addition, the neediest Texans lack the organization and resources to compete with special interest groups representing the business elite and the middle class. Thus, the Lone Star State provides assistance for millions of needy Texans, but at relatively low benefit levels, and many people are left out.

Privatization When the legislature consolidated agencies under the Health and Human Services Commissioner in 2003, it also mandated a major change in the state's approach to social services—**privatization**. The belief is that private contractors can provide public services more cheaply and efficiently than can government. Under a legislative mandate, local social services offices and caseworkers were replaced with call centers operated by private contractors. Applicants for social services were encouraged to use the telephone and Internet to establish eligibility for most social services. A similar but much smaller privatized system had worked reasonably well in 2000. However, this new, larger system performed poorly. After 2003, the number of children covered by insurance dropped sharply, and eligible people faced long waits and lost paperwork. In response to these problems, the offshore private contractor was replaced, many state employees were rehired, and attempts were made to bring children back into the social welfare system. Still in 2010, a federal official complained about Texas's "five-year slide" to last place among states in the speed and accuracy of handling food stamp applications after privatization.[34] Promised savings and better service have yet to appear.

State officials say the problem is that privatization is still a work in progress and that there is no turning back. Critics argue that profit incentives for contractors and social services for the public are inherently in conflict. Officials have continued to promote privatization, but more gradually, with the result that some Texas social services are a mixture of public and private administration. Private contractors are both for-profit and nonprofit. An example is foster care, which has responsibility for about 28,000 children. With too little money, too few caseworkers, and inadequate accountability, foster care in Texas has performed poorly under both public and privatized management. Child welfare advocates view the current privatized plan as stretching limited resources even thinner and adding a layer of private bureaucracy.[35] In 2015, a federal judge in Corpus Christi ruled in a class-action lawsuit brought by a New York-based advocacy group that the Texas foster care system violated children's constitutional rights. The judge ordered reforms including more caseworkers and

privatization
Transfer of government services or assets to the private sector. Commonly, assets are sold and services contracted out.

appointed two special masters, both experts in the area of foster care to make recommendations to the state. In April 2016, Governor Abbott appointed the retired chief of the Texas Rangers, Hank Whitman, to lead the agency. Texas appealed the 56 recommendations from the experts appointed by the federal judge. In October 2018, the 5th Circuit Court of Appeals reviewed the case. The court agreed with the federal judge's assessment for major reform, but nevertheless scraped one key recommendation to limit the number of cases per caseworker. The court pulled other recommendations, and the dissent stated, "In place of the discipline imposed by the district court's order, the majority inexplicably affords what it terms a 'prudent' and 'creative' bureaucracy the flexibility to set its own course and to proceed at its own pace — ignoring that this is what DFPS has been doing for twenty years."[36]

Human Services

The Health and Human Services Commission (HHSC) administers a variety of programs, three of which have long received a great deal of attention and debate: TANF, SNAP, and Medicaid. All three are administered by the executive commissioner of HHSC within federal guidelines and are funded by the federal government and to a lesser extent by the state. In the words of budget analyst Eva DeLuna Castro, eligibility for these and other "public assistance programs in Texas is very restrictive compared to other states, the benefits are lower, and health benefits for poor adults are more limited. As a result, a smaller share of the poor in Texas receives any public assistance."[37] In addition, all three programs suffered financially from the budget cutbacks carried out by the 2011 legislature and only partially recovered in 2013 and 2015.

Most social welfare programs in Texas provide specific services or assistance for a specific need. SNAP, for example, provides a mechanism to buy food, and Medicaid provides access to medical care. **Temporary Assistance for Needy Families (TANF),** on the other hand, provides very limited cash assistance that can be spent for various needs. In Texas, the program is aimed at extremely poor families. For a family of three in 2018, the poverty level was $20,780 in annual income (or $1,731 per month). To receive TANF that year, a family of one parent and two children could earn no more than $2,256 a year (12 percent of the poverty level). The family would receive $295 a month, with a lifetime limit of 60 months if one of the recipients is an adult. Children who qualify for TANF benefits can receive benefits on their own until age 18. Along with other requirements, caretakers must be U.S. citizens or legal residents and agree to work or to enroll in a job training program.

According to HHSC, the "most common" TANF caretaker is a woman about 30 years old with one or two children younger than age 11. She is unemployed, has no other income, and receives a TANF grant of $295 or less per month for fewer than 12 months. In addition to the small amount of cash provided by TANF, recipients may receive benefits from other programs, such as SNAP and Medicaid. To reduce abuse, benefits for both TANF and SNAP are provided through a plastic Lone Star Card that functions like a debit card.

Temporary Assistance for Needy Families (TANF)
Provides financial assistance to the very poor in an attempt to help them move from welfare to the workforce.

A second federal–state program administered by the commission is the **Supplemental Nutritional Assistance Program (SNAP)**, formerly called food stamps. It makes food available to elderly or disabled people, families, and single adults who qualify because of low income, defined as no more than 130 percent of the poverty level. Approximately 80 percent of those who benefit from SNAP receive no TANF support. Benefits vary, depending on income and the number of people in a household. In 2018, for example, a qualified Texas household composed of three people could earn up to $2,858 a month and obtain groceries costing up to $505 each month. Adults between the ages of 16 and 59 must look for work or be in a work program. If they are employed, they cannot quit without a good reason.[38]

To assist in connecting eligible Texans to service providers, several private groups use social media sites, such as Twitter and Facebook, as well as blogs. A Fighting Chance for Texas Families provides information about resources and encourages users to share their stories of how they have survived in poverty in Texas.

Health and Mental Health Services

The third major federal–state program administered by HHS is Medicaid. Part of President Lyndon B. Johnson's Great Society initiatives in the 1960s, Medicaid is designed to provide medical care for the poor. Eligible are the aged, blind, and disabled; parents with dependent children with household incomes up to 15 percent of the poverty level; children with household incomes up to 201 percent of the poverty level (adults would not be eligible); and pregnant women with household incomes up to 198 percent of the poverty level. Resources not counted against the poverty level limit are a home, personal possessions, and a low-value motor vehicle. As of July 2018, Medicaid and the related children's program CHIP covered roughly 4.3 million Texans.

Not to be confused with Medicaid is **Medicare**, another Great Society initiative. A federal program providing medical assistance to qualifying applicants age 65 and older, Medicare is administered by the U.S. Department of Health and Human Services without use of state funds. Because Medicaid is considered welfare and serves the poor, it has much less political clout than Medicare, which serves a more middle-class clientele. Medicaid has much more difficulty gaining funding, and benefits for clients and reimbursements for service providers tend to be lower. Benefits are so low that the majority of Texas doctors now refuse new Medicaid patients, and nursing homes have trouble covering their costs. Medicare reimbursement amounts are set by the federal government, and while they are higher than those for Medicaid, they are also low, thus reducing physician access for some patients.

Under the 2010 national Affordable Care Act, states were required to expand Medicaid coverage to virtually all nonelderly adults and children earning up to 133 percent of the poverty level. States that did not provide expanded coverage risked losing their existing federal Medicaid funds. However, as mentioned earlier, the U.S. Supreme Court held that the federal government could

Supplemental Nutritional Assistance Program (SNAP)
Joint federal–state program administered by the state to provide food to low-income people.

Medicare
Funded entirely by the federal government and administered by the U.S. Department of Health and Human Services, Medicare primarily provides medical assistance to qualified applicants age 65 and older.

🖥 HOW DO WE COMPARE...

In (1) Proportion of Uninsured by Race/Ethnicity and (2) Expansion of Medicaid Under the Affordable Care Act (ACA)?

Most Populous States	(Percent)				(Yes/No)
	Anglo	Latino	African American	Total Population	Expanded Medicaid
California	5	12	6	8	Yes
Florida	13	22	17	8	No
New York	4	12	7	7	Yes
Texas	**12**	**29**	**17**	**20**	**No**
States Bordering Texas					
Arkansas	8	25	8	10	Yes*
Louisiana	8	28	10	10	Yes
New Mexico	7	NA	8	11	Yes
Oklahoma	12	26	17	16	No

*Expanded using an alternative method.
NA = Not available.
Source: "State Health Facts," *Kaiser Family Foundation*, 2017, http://kff.org/uninsured/state-indicator/rate-by-raceethnicity.

— Competency Connection —
☼ CRITICAL THINKING ☼

What patterns do you see in the data? Do the patterns appear to have any relation to whether states expanded Medicaid under the ACA?

not use threats of withholding funding to coerce expansion of Medicaid for adults. Thus, states have the option of participating in the expansion or keeping their existing adult programs. Coverage of children must be expanded. Editorials in most of Texas's major newspapers supported the expansion; however, in July 2012, then-Governor Rick Perry informed federal authorities that Texas would not participate in the expansion of Medicaid. As of May 2019, some 36 state (plus the District of Columbia) had expanded Medicaid coverage, and 14 (including Texas) had not done so (The "How Do We Compare" table shows the decision of other large states and Texas's neighbors.) As of 2019, public support for Medicaid expansion has remained strong, with 56 percent in support of expansion.

For those states participating, the federal government pays the entire cost of expansion for the first three years and at least 90 percent beyond that. Payments for primary care physicians are also raised to Medicare levels. Estimates are that opting out cost Texas over $100 billion.

Without the expansion of Medicaid, Texas remains a national leader in the number of uninsured. Nearly 1.7 million Texans (of the state's 5 million uninsured) are left uncovered by the decision. Several studies have examined the consequences of not expanding Medicaid and concluded that it will lead to preventable deaths. In Texas, one conservative projection is that 1,800 to 3,000 lives a year could be lost and large numbers of illnesses will not be detected early or will go untreated.[39] Nearly 640,000 Texans have no realistic access to insurance without the Medicaid expansion.

The Department of State Health Services (DSHS), a part of HHSC, performs a wide variety of functions, including public health planning and enforcement of state health laws. As with public assistance, state health policies are closely tied to several federal programs. One example is the Special Supplemental Nutrition Program for Women, Infants, and Children (WIC), a delivery system for healthy foods, nutritional counseling, and health-care screening.

A more visible role of the DSHS in Texas is providing information and resources on public health concerns. A few examples in the past decade have been Ebola, the Zika virus, and the HIV/AIDS epidemic. In September 2014, Texas's first Ebola case received substantial publicity and posed a challenge to the DSHS, which educates Texans on infectious diseases. In 2016, attention focused on the Zika virus, a serious mosquito-borne disease. A long-term problem in Texas is acquired immunodeficiency syndrome (AIDS) caused by the human immunodeficiency virus (HIV). It is commonly transmitted by sexual contact (both homosexual and heterosexual; three-fourths of Texas cases) and contaminated needles used by drug abusers (27 percent). AIDS is an international epidemic but has been more stable in Texas.

In 2017 among the 90,700 Texans living with HIV, 78 percent were male, 25 percent Anglo, 37 percent African American, and 32 percent Latino. HIV is the state's seventh leading cause of death among Texans ages 25–44. (For comparison, first are accidents, second suicides, and sixth homicides).[40]

A related problem is the continuing increase in the number of cases of sexually transmitted diseases (STDs) other than HIV/AIDS reported in Texas each year. This number reached nearly 192,300 in 2017. Persons between 15 and 24 years of age account for the majority of this total. The actual STD numbers are probably higher because not all STDs must be reported, and many cases are unreported. The Centers for Disease Control and Prevention saw an increase in the diagnosis of STDs across the country for the fourth straight year in 2017. In Texas, Houston leads the state with the highest rates of infections.[41]

The Texas departments of State Health Services and Aging and Disability Services provide public mental health programs for persons unable to afford private therapy. However, Texas's per capita funding for mental health programs has ranked 48th to 50th among the 50 states for years (in fiscal year 2013, $41 per capita, compared to the national average of $120).[42] The legislature did provide more funds in 2013 and 2015. Further, according to the *Texas Tribune*, in the 2017 legislative session, legislators launched "a community grant program for mental health services, addressed how health insurance companies offer mental health benefits, and funding to renovate state mental health hospitals." But

Texas still falls below most other states' efforts. As a result, the state serves only a fraction of those needing assistance. From at least 1995 to 2015, the number of psychiatric hospital beds per 100,000 population has declined, creating long waiting lists.[43]

State hospitals have a number of other problems:

- Large residential facilities are appropriate for a limited number of patients at best.
- State hospitals are deteriorating.
- Staffing problems, including inadequate training and rapid turnover, are rampant.

Reports of abuse in living centers brought an agreement in 2009 between the U.S. Department of Justice and Texas to increase the number of workers. Since then, the number of workers has increased, but the failure to increase wages for direct care workers has contributed to continuing high rates of neglect.

Like most states, Texas relies heavily on community outpatient services for mental health treatment, which is the cheaper and medically preferred option for most patients. Because of the shortage of programs, the number of patients receiving community mental health services has been relatively flat, fluctuating from 62,000 to 68,000 annually during the 2007 to 2013 period. Houston has roughly seven public mental health beds per 100,000 people, according to a study, whereas national standards state that the number of beds needs to be increased ten times. An unknown number of the mentally ill are detained in jails and prisons or living on the streets. Reportedly, there are roughly 18,000 inmates in the Harris County Jail, some 3,000 inmates receive psychiatric treatment at the jail every day, "more than any other mental health hospital in Texas."[44] For a discussion of mental health issues among inmates, see Chapter 13 "The Criminal Justice System."

Employment

The Texas Unemployment Compensation Act, funded by an employer-paid payroll tax and administered by the Texas Workforce Commission, is used to pay benefits to those who lose their jobs through no fault of their own (such as being laid off). The amount paid to the unemployed depends on wages earned in an earlier quarter (three months). In 2016, the maximum weekly compensation was $479, and the minimum was $65. In the same year, the average tax rate paid by employers was 1.46 percent of the first $9,000 of each employee's salary. The Great Recession which occurred from 2007–2009, increased unemployment and claims, although Texas unemployment remained below the national average. When the fall in the price of petroleum devastated the oil and gas sector, unemployment exceeded the national average.

Since 1913, Texas has had a **workers' compensation** program to help workers injured on the job receive medical care and recover some lost wages. Employers purchase insurance from private companies to cover expenses of those injured or made ill by work conditions. By the mid-1980s, the program had become

workers' compensation
A system of insurance that pays benefits to workers injured or made ill by their work.

highly controversial, with charges of low benefits for injured workers and high insurance premiums for employers. A two-year lobbying and legislative struggle produced a major modification of the program in 1989. A coalition of employers and insurance companies defeated a coalition of plaintiffs' lawyers and labor unions in the legislature. The process for injured workers became more administrative and less judicial. Workers were less likely to win and more likely to receive lower benefits. The major source of the problem, Texas's dangerous workplaces (particularly transportation, construction, and oil and gas) and lax safety standards, received scant improvement. Since 2000, Texas has generally led the nation in workplace deaths.

The workers' compensation system is governed by the Division of Workers' Compensation (DWC) of the Texas Department of Insurance. Since creation of the DWC in 2005, lawyers who represent injured workers have complained that the agency is too close to the insurance companies; and the commissioner testified in 2014 that workers are losing an increasing proportion of disputes in the agency's court-like system that resolves disputes. The number of claims by workers and insurance rates charged employers have declined.

Texas is the only state in the union that does not require employers to provide workers' compensation insurance. Failure to provide the insurance puts the employer at risk for expensive court suits, which are generally forbidden by law if the employer provides workers' compensation insurance. About two-thirds of Texas employers provide the insurance. A recent trend has been the development of opt-out plans in which the employer provides a private plan that generally covers fewer injuries, cuts off benefits sooner, and gives employers more control of the process.

> ### ✓ 12.3 Learning Check
>
> **1.** Why are health and human services programs at a disadvantage in Texas?
>
> **2.** Which program is better funded, Medicaid or Medicare?
>
> *Answers at the end of this chapter.*

◼ Economic and Environmental Policies

LO 12.4   Compare the roles of government in generating economic development while maintaining a safe, clean, and prosperous environment for the state's residents.

Education, health, and human services represent three-fourths of Texas state government expenditures. Business, economic development, and regulation together account for 13 percent of the budget, but they have a substantial and often direct effect on the lives of Texans. The state tries to generate economic development that, when successful, produces jobs and profits. Regulations affect the prices we pay for electricity and insurance, as well as the quality of the air we breathe.

Historically, regulation was supported as a means to protect the individual, the weak, and the general public against the economically powerful and special interests. In practice, this protection has been difficult to achieve because the benefits of regulation tend to be diffuse and the costs specific. For example, cleaner air benefits a broad range of the public, but few can put a dollar amount on their own personal benefit. On the other hand, companies that must pay to clean up their air emissions see a specific (and sometimes large) cost. Thus, they may perceive more incentive to spend money to fight regulation than do those who benefit from it.

Moreover, businesses are better organized, have more connections to policymakers, and employ more lobbyists than the public does. For most of Texas's history, including the long period of conservative Democratic domination, economic and regulatory policies have tilted toward business. The Republican ascendancy in recent years has enhanced this tendency, although consumer, environmental, and labor advocates are being heard.

Business, however, is not monolithic. Battles over taxes, subsidies, and regulation produce conflicts between different kinds of businesses. Established businesses, for example, often seek to limit competition by seeking regulation of newcomers. When cable television emerged, broadcast television successfully sought burdensome requirements and limitations that slowed the development of the new industry. Similarly, when the Texas legislature began to regulate smokestack emissions, established companies sought successfully to be "grandfathered" (that is, existing smokestacks were exempted from the new regulations, which gave old companies a cost advantage). In recent years, coal producers and users, natural gas companies, and wind energy farm operators and carriers have been at odds over issues such as environmental regulations, pipeline and powerline rights of way, and tax and subsidy policy. As a consequence of the divisions, some policy issues are fought by coalitions with business, labor, consumer, and environmental interests on both sides.

Business Promotion

Some cynical observers contend that the business of Texas government is business. Others argue that boosting business strengthens the economy and creates jobs that benefit the lives of all Texans. Certainly, the state's political culture and the strength of business lobbyists make government responsive to business. Free-market advocates who compare policies in the states have consistently identified Texas as a business-friendly state in the last decade. In 2018 the Small Business and Entrepreneurship Council ranked Texas second among the 50 states in "policy environment" for entrepreneurship, behind Nevada and far ahead of Texas's neighboring states. The same group ranked Texas second in its small business tax index in 2018, and another researcher found Texas to have the third least burdensome regulatory structure.[45]

There are costs to these rankings. In 2018, the Institute on Taxation and Economic Policy ranked Texas's tax system as the second most unfair state and local tax system in the country, which is putting more burden on those of lower income and less burden on those with more wealth. The Social Science Research Council's human development index is a composite of health, education, and income levels. It ranks Texas 34th.[46]

Economic Regulatory Policy

Have you ever complained about a high telephone bill, a big automobile insurance premium, or the cost of a license to practice a trade or profession for which you have been trained? Welcome to the Lone Star State's regulatory politics. For businesses seeking to boost profits or professional groups trying to strengthen their licensing requirements, obtaining or avoiding changes in regulations can be costly but rewarding. Less organized consumers and workers often believe they are left to pick up the tab for higher bills and fees and, on occasion, inferior service.

Traditionally, government regulation focused on prohibitions or requiring certain procedures to be followed. However, in the last decade, Texas regulators have increasingly sought to use economic competition to reduce costs to consumers and prevent harmful practices. This policy has produced great controversy. Although Texans tend to believe strongly in the merits of competition in much of the economy, there is not as much agreement that competition works for utilities and in protection of the environment. The reader will see this conflict played out across most of the areas of this section.

Business Regulation The Railroad Commission (RRC) and the Public Utility Commission (PUC) are among Texas's most publicized agencies. The former regulates the oil and gas industry, which experienced a spectacular resurgence in its influence during the recent oil boom, and the latter affects the telephone and electric power bills paid by millions of Texans.

Textbooks often cite the Railroad Commission as the classic case of "agency capture," a situation in which the regulated industry exerts excessive influence over the agency intended to regulate it. Despite legislation requiring protection of consumers and the environment, the RRC has long seen its major function as maintaining the profitability of the state's oil and gas industry. The industry's earlier decline and the state's greater economic diversity reduced industry dominance somewhat. However, the resurgence of the industry enhanced its political power and influence. The more recent decline that began in 2014 is once again reducing the industry's influence over state policies.

A controversy facing the RRC is hydraulic fracturing (generally called fracking). This process involves injecting large amounts of water, sand, and chemicals underground at high pressure to break up shale formations, allowing oil or gas to flow up the wellbore. Fracking and horizontal drilling have been key to the rebirth of the oil and gas industry in the state and nation. However, major questions have been raised about fracking's effect on the environment, including the safety of the underground water supply and the disposal of contaminated water that returns to the surface.

Given the state's growing water shortage, this additional use for water is causing concern. Another problem arising from exploration and production is the damage to roads in the area of the Eagle Ford Shale (in South Texas). Given the tendency of state agencies to define their role narrowly, neither problem may be readily addressed. The decline in oil and gas production may provide a more effective solution by reducing both water usage and road damage. Fracking has had an immediate consequence: an oversupply of oil and gas that has resulted in lower prices. Additionally, this new technology has had two longer term effects. First, it has extended the use of fossil fuels for decades. Second, the availability of relatively cheap and clean natural gas has reduced the carbon emissions created by much dirtier coal but also made it more difficult for clean, renewable sources of energy such as wind and solar to compete.[47]

Regulation of Public Utilities Through Competition The major responsibility of the Public Utility Commission of Texas (PUC) is regulation of local phone service (not long distance or wireless) and electric utilities. Since 2002, it has followed a national trend in state regulatory policy of relying on competition to protect consumer interests. Traditionally, the rates of utility companies, such as those providing electricity and telephone service, were set or approved by government regulators. (Prices were said to be *regulated*.) Texas regulators, responding to legislative direction, have embraced **deregulation**, under which business practices (such as setting rates) formerly strongly influenced by government rules are governed more by market conditions. The belief is that competition will produce fair prices and protect the public interest. Critics say they were half right.

Allowing consumers to choose their telephone service supplier was expected to result in reasonable telephone bills and reliable service from companies that must compete for customers. With the growth of competition from cell phones, this system seems to work. According to critics, however, deregulation of most Texas electricity suppliers has raised rates in comparison to those of other states—a reversal of two decades of lower-than-average rates under state regulation. A review of the average retail cost of a unit of power from 2011 to 2018 shows that the average price in the United States as of November 2018 was 12.95 cents per kilowatt hour (kWh). We fluctuate in our ranking, but as of January 2019, we were ranked 21st out of all 50 states in terms of the lowest average electric rate.[48] Over the last four years of regulation and the first 10 years of deregulation, electricity was relatively expensive but then saw an improvement. Both sides of the issue can claim support for their position.

Complicating the assessment is the significant drop in the wholesale cost of electricity (the price utilities pay power producers) from 2002 to 2016 brought about by natural gas replacing coal as the leading fuel for power plants, the decline in the price of natural gas, Texas's national lead in cheap wind power, adequate power supply, and slower than expected growth in demand for electricity. Also, consumers can shop among electricity providers and significantly reduce their rates, although most people do not do so.

Another comparison is between the 85 percent of Texans in the deregulated sector and the 15 percent served by regulated entities (such as municipal power companies in, for example, Austin and San Antonio). Regulated rates have been consistently lower.[49]

Insurance Regulation At the beginning of 2003, Texans who owned homes and automobiles paid the highest insurance rates in the country. Rates were

deregulation
The elimination of government restrictions to allow free market competition to determine or limit the actions of individuals and corporations.

unregulated and rising rapidly. In response to the public outcry, the 2003 legislature gave the commissioner of insurance authority to regulate all home insurers doing business in Texas. The following year, Texas began a largely deregulated "file and use" system for auto and homeowners insurance. Insurers set their own rates, but the commissioner of insurance is authorized to order reductions and refunds if rates are determined to be excessive. Advocates of this system expected it to produce reasonable rates by promoting competition among insurance companies. However, by 2018, Texas homeowner insurance rates were consistently high (seventh highest in the nation that year and $717 above the national average). In the more competitive car insurance industry, during the period 2010 to 2018, Texas fluctuated between the middle of the 50 states in average cost and being significantly higher. The cost of car insurance in Texas is nearly 27 percent more than the national average. In 2018, Texas had the 10th highest car insurance rates in the nation.[50]

Because of the frequent occurrence of natural disasters such as hurricanes, hail, and mold, insurance in Texas tends to be expensive. But are Texas rates more costly than necessary, as consumer groups argue? The "loss ratio," which is considered the best measure of insurance company profitability, is what a company pays in benefits as a percentage of the premium money it receives. The insurance industry prefers a loss ratio of 60 percent or less; consumer advocates prefer a higher percent. From 1995 to 2004, the average loss ratio for Texas insurance companies was 69 percent, and from 2005 to 2014, 59 percent[51]—a good decade for insurers, thanks to rate increases and only one year of losses. In the 84th Legislature, however, insurers supported legislation intended to limit homeowner lawsuits against them. Sponsored by Sen. Larry Taylor (R-Friendswood), an insurance agent, the bill passed the Senate but was not voted on by the House of Representatives. This limitation on insurer liability may well emerge in subsequent legislative sessions.

Regulating Highways Texans' love affair with their cars and pickups has led to traffic congestion and accidents. In recent years, Texans spent an average of 25 minutes commuting to work (one way), just at the national average. However, this number conceals huge differences—from a few minutes in small towns to much more than the average in densely populated areas and some suburbs. On the other hand, since 2000, the percentage of workers commuting by private vehicle has declined slightly in Texas's major cities.

With an increasing number of cars and trucks on the road, total accidents tend to increase. However, from 2010 to 2017, traffic deaths per 100 million miles driven remained relatively steady in the nation and Texas (for the state, from 1.27 deaths to 1.38). The reasons for the decline, according to research, are safer roads, vehicles, and behavior by drivers (such as use of seatbelts and designated drivers). In 2017, alcohol was involved in 51 percent of Texas traffic deaths compared to 62 percent for the nation. Speeding and, more recently, distracted driving are the other major causes of fatal accidents. In September 2017, a state law was passed that made it illegal to read, write, or send a text message while driving. In the same year, of more than 530,000 car accidents, 100,687 or 19 percent were caused by distracted drivers. One in every five car accidents in Texas was caused by a distracted driver.

While the state's record has improved over time, it does not compare well to that of other states. In 2017, Texas ranked the third worst for drunk driving, ninth for speeding, and ninth highest in deaths per 100 million miles driven. As of January 2017, not one day has passed in 16 years without a traffic related death in the state. Some states and cities have significantly lowered traffic accident rates, however.

The Texas Department of Transportation (TxDOT) is widely viewed as one of the most successful state agencies in lobbying the legislature for appropriations. However, it too follows the state pattern of scarce resources for government agencies. Highway mileage and public transportation have not kept up with population growth, and road and bridge maintenance has lagged seriously. Testimony in 2014 by Texas A&M Transportation Institute researchers indicated that Texas would need to spend $4 to $7.4 billion more each year to maintain 2010 mobility levels.[52]

In the face of strong legislative opposition to new taxes, how should improvements be financed? Texas has relied on government borrowing through bonds. This resource is approaching its limits. Historically, Texas officials showed a marked preference for toll roads built and run by private companies. However, strong public opposition to toll roads, particularly to privately run toll roads, resulted in their being limited by the 84th Legislature. For a discussion of toll roads and other issues related to infrastructure financing, see Chapter 11, "Finance and Fiscal Policy."

In keeping with state officials' encouragement of private transportation efforts, Texas Central Partners, a private developer, is planning a high-speed passenger rail for a 90-minute trip between Dallas and Houston. It will run through 11 counties with nearly 250 miles of track. As of 2018, it was hoped that the $20 billion plan will be complete by 2024, as the first bullet train in the nation. The biggest issues have been eminent domain concerns and public funding, but with nearly a third of the land acquired through sales, the plan is moving forward. The train is projected to bring in $2.5 billion in taxes and provide more than 1,000 permanent jobs.

Compared with highways, public transportation has less governmental and user support. Only a few Texas cities have light rail (such as Austin's Capital MetroRail) for public transportation. In Texas, 95 percent of public transportation is by bus. Statewide, the proportion of commuters using public transit has increased slightly since 2000, but cities have varied in usage (El Paso and Austin up but Dallas and Houston down).[53]

In 2016, Texas had eight urban transit agencies serving areas with 200,000 or more residents. These agencies provided approximately 90 percent of Texans' public transit trips. The most common organizational form (seven of eight) is a metropolitan transit authority (MTA), which is a local regional government that can impose taxes and service the central city and surrounding suburbs. The Texas Department of Transportation (TxDOT) has little role in the planning, finance, or operation of MTAs. In addition, 30 urban transit agencies and 39 rural transit systems served smaller communities. More than 135 operators provided transportation services to the elderly and to individuals with disabilities under varying arrangements with local governments.

Regulating Tourism, Parks, and Recreation Tourism is the third largest industry in the Lone Star State. The state park system attracts 7 to 10 million visitors a year (both Texans and out-of-state tourists) and usually generates over $1 billion a year for the economy. With Texas ranked 49th in state money spent on parks in the first years of this century, however, state parks were suffering deterioration in quality and services. Fewer parks and park amenities hurt business and were a loss to middle- and working-class Texans, many of whom depend on public parks for recreation. Since 2007, appropriations for Parks and Wildlife have fluctuated. The 2009 legislature kept the increased level of funding, but the revenue-strapped 2011 legislative session reduced the budget. The 2013 session increased appropriations but to less than the 2007 levels, which was reduced by the 2015 legislature. In 1993, the legislature passed a law that granted all money generated by taxes on sporting goods to be given to state parks and historic sites. However, only about 40 percent of the collected taxes have been given to state parks. A constitutional amendment was passed by the 86th legislative session which will require all taxes from sporting goods to go the parks and historic sites. In November 2019, the amendment would need a simple majority of votes for it to go into effect. A poll conducted by the Texas Parks and Wildlife Foundation found that 84 percent of Texans surveyed supported the protection of natural areas and found parks to be "necessary for a healthy and active lifestyle."[54]

Environmental Regulation

Among Texas's many public policy concerns, none draws sharper disagreements than how to maintain a clean and safe environment while advancing business development that will provide jobs and profits. Because of the nature of its industries and Texans' love for driving, the Lone Star State has been among the most polluted states for years. Our industries, for example, produce more toxic contaminants (chemical waste) than do those of any other state. This grim reality confronts local, state, and national policymakers, and the decisions of all three affect the quality of air and water.

Since the early 1970s, federal policies have driven state and local environmental efforts, with Texas state and local officials generally resisting or slowing the impact of federal policies. Mandates from the national level have been issued by the U.S. Environmental Protection Agency (EPA) and the U.S. Congress through the Clean Air and Clean Water Acts. Under the Obama administration, the EPA became more active, and the number of conflicts with Texas officials increased. Responses by Texas officials have included public complaints, legislation introduced by the state's representatives in Congress, requests for waivers, and state-filed lawsuits. Under former Attorney General Greg Abbott and his successor, Ken Paxton, suits against the federal government have become much more common, particularly in the environmental area. (From January 2009 when President Obama took office through May 2016, there have been 40 suits, including 21 against the EPA.) Concern about climate change and Texas's substantial greenhouse gas emissions have also increased federal–state conflict.

Texas businesspeople usually support state policies designed to forestall federal regulations. Tracking corporate Texas's every step, however, is a growing array of public watchdogs (such as the Sierra Club), who inform the public concerning environmental problems. Environmental groups have embraced technology to aid their cause. Cell phone cameras and GPS help documentation, and social media are major tools for organizing and informing the public.

Air and Water The Texas Commission on Environmental Quality (TCEQ) coordinates environmental policy in the state. Unfortunately, it has come under so much influence from the businesses it regulates that TCEQ is accused of being another instance of agency capture. For example, TCEQ's top leadership has often overruled recommendations from the agency's technical staff and specialists if they conflict with the business goals of those with political connections. The permitting of a West Texas nuclear waste site provides an example. In 2009, after several years of controversy and against the unanimous recommendation of staff specialists, TCEQ's executive director ordered a license issued to Waste Control Specialists, LLC for the construction of a low-level radioactive waste site. Within six months, the executive director left the agency and went to work for the operator. One observer has noted that from 1993 to 2010, "former TCEQ higher-ups—including commissioners, general counsels, and a deputy director … earned as much as $32 million lobbying for the industries they once policed."[55]

State policymakers must balance federal directives and state law with pressures from businesses and environmentalists, a major challenge. In recent years, TCEQ and the EPA have pushed the state's metropolitan areas to meet federal air standards, with moderate success. After changing its approach in 2005, Houston met federal smog standards in 2009 for the first time in 35 years. By 2014, it was meeting standards some days but missing them more often. By 2015, the city had reduced hazardous air pollution by 80 percent. Air quality has been a source of pride in San Antonio. Through 2018, it was the only major U.S. city never to have been in nonattainment status (though it had come close). Its success in gaining the Toyota plant came in part because of its clean air record. With a growing population and contaminants blowing in from

IMAGE 12.2 Cracks in the dry bed of Lake Lavon, northeast of Dallas. Texas's alternating periods of drought and flooding, together with the highly unequal distribution of rainfall from one region to another, make water policy a critical element of the state's development.

AP Images/Matt Slocum

— Competency Connection —
✿ **CRITICAL THINKING** ✿

We can't control the weather. What can we do to better deal with alternating drought and flooding?

the oil and gas production in the nearby Eagle Ford Shale, air quality has declined since 2008, and by 2015, local leaders were worried about receiving nonattainment status if the EPA toughened their standards.

Texas's growing population and economy have increased the demand for electrical power. Many of the recent environmental conflicts between the EPA and Texas have related to the pollution produced by coal-burning power plants. Significantly cleaner natural gas is becoming the preferred fuel for generating plants in Texas and elsewhere because of its lower cost. Wind and solar power are making small but growing inroads.

Water is another important issue in a state that is largely arid. Texas's growing population, industry, and irrigation-based agriculture face serious water shortages. In addition, drought and flooding are regular problems for many areas. TCEQ, working with local prosecutors, deals with contamination of waterways. Major sources of water pollution include industry (through both air emissions and improper disposal of toxic waste), agriculture (particularly from fertilizer, manure, and pesticide runoff), and poorly treated sewage. Three sets of interconnected issues frame the water supply debate:

- Conflicts over who controls the water: Under Texas law, surface water (in lakes and rivers) belongs to the state, but citizens and other entities may be granted rights to it. Water is overappropriated—that is, if every entity actually received the amount it has been allocated by the state, lakes and rivers would be dry. Underground water (called groundwater) has almost no regulation. Under the legal concept known as the **rule of capture**, landowners own the water below their property. Problems arise when upstream landowners pump so much water that downstream landowners' wells and springs dry up.

- The desire of metropolitan areas and drier Central and Western Texas to build lakes and pipelines to capture and move water from wetter areas, such as East Texas: Many communities want to keep their water. Others object to the loss of land to lakes and damage to rivers and wetlands. Closely related are conflicts among the users of water—agriculture, cities, and industry—and with environmentalists over who gets priority over water.

- Maintenance of the quality and quantity of underground water: Underground reservoirs of water, such as the Ogallala (a part of it is located in the Texas Panhandle) and Edwards (located in South Central Texas) aquifers, supply water for many cities, farms, and rivers. Depleting these underground water sources threatens the industries and people that rely on them.

rule of capture
A rule of law that a landowner can capture and own the natural resources extracted from the land. Thus, groundwater belongs to the landowner.

Most sides of the water disputes agree that Texas needs an effective water plan. The state has had a series of water plans, but they have had little impact. In 2013, the legislature agreed to a two-pronged approach. With the approval of the voters, $2 billion from the state's Rainy Day Fund would be used (1) to encourage conservation and (2) to build new water projects, such as reservoirs. No one believes that the plan will fully solve the water shortage problem, but people are encouraged that some action is being taken. The money is being used more for projects than conservation. With the continued growth of population and the needs of agriculture and industry, conflicts over water continue to grow in importance.

The issue of water supply is made worse by Texas's periodic droughts, which are often followed by flooding. From 1980 through 2018, Texas experienced more than 200 weather and climate disasters costing at least $1 billion each, including 26 droughts, 29 flood events, and 16 wildfire events.[56] A Senate bill passed during the 86th legislative session that would take $1.7 billion from the Rainy Day Fund to be used to pay for flood control projects and repairs from flooding throughout the state. (The 2010–2011 drought, for example, cost $8–13 billion. Associated fires destroyed more than 4 million acres of timber, pasture, and residences.) In the majority of years, there are lesser droughts or floods in one or more regions of the state. Water problems are also discussed in Chapter 1, "The Environment of Texas Politics," and financial implications are covered in Chapter 11, "Finance and Fiscal Policy."

Hazardous Waste Hazardous waste is a fact of modern life. From the use of low-level radioactive materials for disease diagnosis in hospitals to industrial production of plastics and chemicals on which we depend, we generate large quantities of dangerous waste. This waste ranges in danger from high-level radio-active material with potential toxicity for thousands of years to nonradioactive hazardous waste. Those who produce hazardous materials want to get rid of waste as cheaply as possible, and they have the money and incentive to succeed in keeping the costs of disposal low. Although environmental groups in Texas have increased in power and political skill, they generally can only delay and modify actions favored by pollution producers. For its part, much of the public simply says "Not in my backyard" (NIMBY).

In the case of low-level radioactive waste, there has been a series of political skirmishes stretching back to the 1970s, a lack of a coordinated plan, and a growing amount of waste. By 2009, a private radioactive waste dumpsite had been built in sparsely populated Andrews County near the border with New Mexico and a permit issued by TCEQ. By 2012, the first loads of waste had arrived. Initially, the waste was to be from Texas and Vermont, working through an interstate compact. However, from 2012 into 2016, 82 percent of the waste was from outside the two compact states.[57]

The substantial campaign contributions and lobbying by the site's developer, Waste Control Specialists, and its owner led to charges of crony capitalism (government officials favoring and subsidizing their friends in the private sector who have helped them). In 2018 the Texas site was the only one in the nation serving the estimated $30 billion a year demand for disposal,[58] and there were proposals to expand the dump's size and to allow storage of higher level radioactive waste.

Generated largely by Texas's petrochemical industry, nonradioactive hazardous waste stored in landfills presents another environmental dilemma. Poorly stored materials may leak into the water table or nearby waterways or contaminate the dirt above them. Some housing and commercial land developers covet landfill sites for their building projects because of costs and location. TCEQ has tended to approve less restrictive guidelines for these sites. As the state's population increases in the years ahead, even greater demands will be placed on the quality of its air, water, and land.

 **12.4 Learning Check**

1. True or False: Business regulation in Texas tends to be tough on businesses.

2. What are some demands that state environmental policymakers must balance?

Answers at the end of this chapter.

Immigration

LO 12.5   Describe various aspects and complexities in Texas's immigration policy.

Immigration policy is often thought of as a federal responsibility. In practice, however, states also are involved. A policy issue that has received attention from federal and state governments, including Texas, is how to treat immigrants without lawful immigration status (undocumented immigrants).

Chapter 1, "The Environment of Texas Politics," provides context regarding immigration for Texas and the federal government, and notes that several attempts at ending pro-immigration policies during the 84th Texas Legislature in 2015 failed. The attempts to eliminate a policy allowing noncitizens, including some immigrants without lawful immigration status, to pay in-state tuition at public universities and colleges failed. In 2017, the Texas legislature passed a bill banning "sanctuary cities," which allows the local law enforcement to question the citizenship of anyone they detain or arrest, including anyone stopped for a routine traffic stop.

The 84th Legislature did pass House Bill 11 (HB 11), a law that attempts to boost border security and fight crime linked to unlawful immigration.[59] Among

IMAGE 12.3 Texans react to President Trump's move to end DACA, they protest demanding a Dream Act to protect immigrants and their families.

EFE News Agency/Alamy Stock Photo

—— Competency Connection ——
✿ **CRITICAL THINKING** ✿

Whether DACA continues or ends, how will it impact Texas?

other provisions, HB 11 increased penalties for human smuggling, authorized hiring more state troopers, and created an intelligence center to analyze crime data.[60] For his part, Governor Abbott continued a policy begun by Governor Perry of using the Texas National Guard to patrol the Texas border with Mexico.[61]

Other states, such as Arizona and Alabama, have passed legislation that has been described as harsh toward immigrants.[62] Texas, on the other hand, continues to have a law, signed by Governor Perry in 2001, that grants in-state college tuition to some immigrants without lawful immigration status. A potential explanation for why Texas has different policies than those of other states is the role of business interest groups, in particular the influential Texas Association of Business. These business groups argued that repeal of the in-state tuition law would be bad for the economy because Texas businesses need a highly educated workforce.[63] Moreover, Mexican Americans are a major and growing part of the Texas electorate, and there has been a long and close, if sometimes testy, relationship with Mexico.

Business interest groups in Texas argue that the nation requires comprehensive immigration policy reform.[64] In 2012, President Barack Obama signed an executive order, the Deferred Action for Childhood Arrivals, known as DACA. The order allowed children brought to the United States illegally to apply for deferred action for deportation and to apply for a work permit with specific requirements. In 2018, in a U.S. district court, Texas Attorney General Ken Paxton requested an injunction against the federal government to end DACA. Paxton is requesting that the federal government stop issuing or renewing additional permits under DACA. The court agreed with the legal arguments made by Paxton in the case, but they declined to issue an injunction. On January 22, 2019, the U.S. Supreme Court declined to take up the case as requested by the president and others for the spring term. This means that the nearly 700,000 undocumented children (roughly 115,000 in Texas) who were brought to the United States illegally are protected, for now. The earliest the court could issue an opinion is in 2020. In December 2014, President Obama issued another executive order on immigration, known as Deferred Action for Parental Accountability (DAPA), which allowed as many as four million immigrants without lawful immigration status to remain in the United States. (See Chapter 1, "The Environment of Texas Politics," for more information on DAPA.) Texas, joined by 25 other states, sued the Obama administration on the legality of DAPA in the case of *United States v. Texas*. In February 2015, federal district court Judge Andrew Hanan, an appointee of George W. Bush, located in Brownsville, issued a stay prohibiting the implementation of DAPA, and the case was appealed to the U.S. Supreme Court. The Supreme Court reached a 4-4 tie in its decision, thus upholding the district court's decision.[65] The constitutionality of the president's executive order has not yet been determined.

Immigration policy is contradictory. The United States is a nation of immigrants, yet struggles to develop immigration policy. Some people say that they do not want immigrants, yet immigrants (whether with or without lawful immigration status) work (oftentimes in undesirable jobs), pay taxes, and are a reason why Texas continues to grow both economically and in population.[66]

✔ **12.5 Learning Check**

1. True or False: Texas business groups took an equally hard line on both border policy and treatment of undocumented immigrants.

2. Has Texas policy been harsher on border security or undocumented immigrants?

Answers at the end of this chapter.

CONCLUSION

A variety of actors beyond the legislature and governor shape Texas public policy, including the bureaucrats who implement the policy. The state's public policies affect many aspects of Texans' lives. The Texas education system faces challenges created by serving large numbers of disadvantaged students, coupled with a reluctance to devote sufficient state resources to education. The state has a large proportion of poor and working-class citizens in need of help in health and human services; this segment of the population has little political power to effectively satisfy their needs. In the areas of economic development and regulation, public policy has often tended to serve the interests of business over those of consumers. Immigration remains a controversial and unsettled issue for both the nation and the State of Texas.

CHAPTER SUMMARY

LO 12.1 Describe how public policy is made in Texas. Public policymaking is a dynamic process in which a variety of actors, including the bureaucracy, play a vital role in shaping the nature of policy. Models and the policymaking process are useful tools for understanding policy. Texas's political culture and political process produce public policies that are responsive to business and government elites but that provide a weaker social safety net than the majority of other states. The success of agencies in Texas is influenced by the vigor of their leaders, the lack of resources for most agencies, and elite access.

LO 12.2 Analyze major challenges faced by the Texas education system. Whether in public school districts, institutions of higher education, or the legislature, policymakers face the challenge of achieving educational excellence at a price that Texas taxpayers can afford and that voters will support. Texas schools face the challenge of a changing student body—more ethnically diverse and from less affluent families. Failure to respond to the challenge is likely to damage the state's economy. Testing remains a major tool for trying to improve education in the state. It is also a source of great controversy. Better serving the needs of Texas's rapidly diversifying population and the top 10 percent rule have been major issues in college admissions.

LO 12.3 Describe the major health and human services programs in Texas, and discuss how efforts to address the needs of its citizens have been approached. State responsibility for many public assistance programs and the state's high poverty rate continue to place demands on Texas's social service agencies to assist needy families and those physically or mentally ill, aged, or disabled. Health and human services programs in Texas are politically weak and poorly funded.

LO 12.4 Compare the roles of government in generating economic development while maintaining a safe, clean, and prosperous environment for the state's residents. Privatization of service delivery has a mixed record in Texas, with some major failures. Whether deregulation (the current direction of regulators) will be more effective than regulation in protecting the public interest remains unresolved; meanwhile, Texas consumers demand low-cost utilities, safe and plentiful drinking water, and cleaner air. State regulators tend to be protective of the industries they are charged to regulate. Deterioration of state parks because of funding shortages may cause Texas to lose tourist dollars. Texas has long had major pollution problems and public policies that have done little to improve the environment. Challenges to polluters are increasing, but change is slow. The ownership, protection, use, and availability of water have become major public policy issues.

LO 12.5 Describe the various aspects and complexities in Texas's immigration policy.
Texas immigration policy has contradictions that reflect the state's reality. The state's leaders express concern about the security of the border. Legislators passed a bill to assist in strengthening the border. On the other hand, Texas has not passed the kinds of strong anti-immigrant policies adopted in some other states. Business leaders have urged the adoption of legislation to encourage the education of young, undocumented immigrants. Texas business people also recognize that they need the workers and the purchasing power of immigrants, whatever their legal status.

KEY TERMS

affirmative action, p. 451

deregulation, p. 465

elite access, p. 440

equal opportunity, p. 451

Medicaid, p. 455

Medicare, p. 458

privatization, p. 456

public policy, p. 436

rule of capture, p. 470

State of Texas Assessment of
    Academic Readiness (STAAR),
    p. 447

Supplemental Nutritional Assistance
    Program (SNAP), p. 458

Temporary Assistance for Needy
    Families (TANF), p. 457

Texas Essential Knowledge and Skills
    (TEKS), p. 446

top 10 percent rule, p. 452

workers' compensation, p. 461

LEARNING CHECK ANSWERS

 12.1

1. False. Public administrators must make many decisions not clearly specified in the law. Their own views, their bosses' preferences, and their agency culture all make a difference in how they apply laws passed by the legislature.

2. The vigor of agency leaders, resources, and elite access are particularly important in determining how successful agencies are in achieving their policy goals.

 12.2

1. Major criticisms include whether the test used measures real learning, that tests overshadow or distort other learning (teaching to the test), whether tests should be used to evaluate teachers and administrators, that a particular test is too hard or too easy, that tests discriminate against some students, and that standardized testing weakens local control.

2. According to the top 10 percent rule, Texas students graduating in the top 10 percent of their high school class must be admitted to the public college or university of their choice.

12.3 **1.** Health and human services programs are at a disadvantage in Texas because of the state's political culture and the lack of resources and organization of those needing the services.

2. Medicare is better funded than Medicaid.

12.4 **1.** False. Regulation of business in Texas tends not to be tough on businesses (consider the Railroad Commission, for example).

2. State environmental policymakers must balance federal directives, business pressures, and demands from environmental groups.

12.5 **1.** False. Business groups played a major role in convincing political leaders to support education for potential workers, whatever their status.

2. Texas policy has been harshest toward border security.

13 The Criminal Justice System

Learning Objectives

13.1 Describe the different classifications of criminal offenses.

13.2 Analyze issues of the death penalty in Texas.

13.3 Explain the role of Texas's jail and prison system in handling corrections and rehabilitations.

13.4 Compare the juvenile justice system to the adult correctional system.

13.5 Evaluate the fairness of Texas's justice system.

IMAGE 13.1 Despite reform laws in Texas that have helped decrease recidivism, incarceration rates remain high.

Mayra Beltran/©Houston Chronicle

— Competency Connection —
✿ CRITICAL THINKING ✿

Texas has been rated one of the top states in terms of percentage of people incarcerated. What factors are contributing to high rates of incarceration in Texas?

On May 17, 2015, in Waco, Texas, bikers met at a Twin Peaks restaurant to discuss motorcycle rights and safety issues. Waco police and Department of Public Safety officers were assigned to monitor the meeting that day. Around noon a shooting broke out. Reports state that police shot at people who were firing shots at others. Police also returned fire to shots fired upon them. The shootout left 20 injured and nine dead—one member of the Bandidos Motorcycle Club, seven members of the Cossacks Motorcycle Club, and a biker who supported the Bandidos. There were so many suspects that police had to use the Waco Convention Center to process them. Police arrested 177 people at the scene and charged many of them with organized crime. Several people arrested said they were innocent bystanders and were not involved, including one retired San Antonio police detective. Arrested suspects were each ordered to be held on a $1 million bond by a Waco judge.

Stories conflict over what caused the shootout. Some bikers say it was a dispute over the design of the Cossacks "bottom rocker" vest patch. The bottom rocker is attached to the back of a member's vest and identifies the club's territory. Bandidos allegedly didn't want the Cossacks to wear a "Texas" bottom rocker. Other members say the brawl started when a member of the Bandidos ran over a Cossack member's foot. A police spokesman corroborated this version at the time of the incident. Court records state that "a war" between the Bandidos and the Cossacks had been going on since 2013.[1] According to the Texas Department of Public Safety's 2014 gang assessment, the Bandidos were a Tier 2 level threat, the second highest. (The Crips, Bloods, and Aryan Brotherhood of Texas were also at this level.) As of 2019, police still have no clear explanation of what started the shootout.

The federal Bureau of Alcohol, Tobacco, Firearms, and Explosives reported recovering 151 guns from the crime scene. According to the Associated Press and ballistics reports, a .223-caliber rifle caused the deaths of four people and injured one of the wounded. This rifle is the same caliber used by Waco police. Whether any of the bikers had the same type of rifle remains unclear.[2]

Defense attorneys for several bikers arrested after the shootout claimed that they were not given access to key evidence that might establish their clients' innocence, which would be a violation of the Michael Morton Law. (Morton was convicted of his wife's murder after the prosecutor failed to provide evidence that supported his innocence. He was subsequently exonerated.) Evidence that might exonerate an accused person is called **exculpatory evidence**. Further, attorneys noted that the McLennan County district attorney's office made the unusual demand that bikers sign a form stating they would not release any information about evidence to the media. Attorneys for the bikers filed a request with the court pursuant to the Morton Act. After the request was filed, the DA's office released the evidence without any condition.

In April 2016, charges were dropped against almost 40 bikers after the McLennan County grand jury failed to indict them. In May 2018, all but 37 of the original cases had been dismissed. Of the 37 cases, 24 of the individuals have been reindicted for different charges that include murder and first and second degree rioting. The trial of Jacob Carrizal, president of the Dallas chapter of

Follow *Practicing Texas Politics* on Twitter **@PracTexPol**

exculpatory evidence
Evidence that helps a defendant and may exonerate the defendant in a criminal trial.

Bandidos, was the only trial dealing with the original charges. In November 2017, Carrizal's case was declared a mistrial since the jury could not reach a unanimous decision. Abel Reyna, then–district attorney for McLennan County, came under heavy criticism for the handling of these cases. In 2018, Reyna was not reelected as district attorney. He faces several civil lawsuits based on his decisions in the Waco shootout and an FBI public corruption investigation. Barry Johnson, the new district attorney, will oversee the remaining cases in 2019.

In his opinion in *Brady v. Maryland*, 373 U.S. 83 (1963), U.S. Supreme Court Justice William O. Douglas observed, "Society wins not only when the guilty are convicted but when criminal trials are fair; our system of the administration of justice suffers when any accused is treated unfairly." The Waco shootout reminds us that we must continue to ask if anyone convicted of a felony might be innocent. In analyzing why prosecutors charged bikers with organized crime rather than murder, Sandra Guerra Thompson, a law professor at the University of Houston, stated, "It's less direct culpability that you have to prove. For the person who didn't use a weapon and who didn't commit a killing, all [prosecutors] have to prove is that [the defendant is] a member of a street gang." Some observers have speculated that because those involved were bikers, the police acted unfairly. As you learn about Texas's justice system, consider what the state does to make the system fair and what practices might interfere with that goal.

✪ Elements of the Criminal Justice System

LO 13.1 Describe the different classifications of criminal offenses.

The Texas **criminal justice system** classifies different types of crimes as either felonies or misdemeanors (discussed in Chapter 10, "The Judicial Branch"). The **Texas Penal Code** is a codified body of laws that covers crime and its punishment. After each legislative session, the State of Texas updates its penal code to include new laws while keeping the core chapters and titles the same. Punishment of crimes in Texas varies from a fine to imprisonment based on the severity and category of a crime. Arguments have been made for continuing to strengthen criminal justice laws and policies while at the same time examining concerns about how Texas carries out justice. Laws may be applied differently based on the resources of local law enforcement and the prevailing attitudes of one's community.

Criminal Justice Law

As of 2018, the State of Texas identified 2,971 crimes as felonies.[3] Less serious offenses are classified as misdemeanors. Features of the Texas Penal Code include **graded penalties** for noncapital offenses and harsher penalties for repeat offenders. First-, second-, and third-degree felonies may involve imprisonment and fines in cases involving the most serious noncapital crimes.

criminal justice system
The system involves prosecution, defense, sentencing, and punishment of those suspected or convicted of committing a crime.

Texas Penal Code
The body of Texas law covering crimes, penalties, and correctional measures.

graded penalties
Depending on the nature of the crime, noncapital felonies are graded as first degree, second degree, third degree, and state jail; misdemeanors are graded as A, B, and C.

enhanced punishment
Additional penalties or prison time for those who engage in organized crime or hate crimes, and for repeat offenders.

capital felony
A crime punishable by death or life imprisonment without parole.

Some lesser offenses (especially those involving alcohol and drug abuse) are defined as state-jail felonies (so-called fourth-degree felonies) and are punishable by fines and confinement in jails operated by the state. The three classes of misdemeanors (A, B, and C) may involve county jail sentences and/or fines. (See Table 13.1 for categories of noncapital offenses and ranges of penalties.) People who engage in organized criminal activity, repeat offenders, and those who commit hate crimes (crimes motivated by bias against a person's race, ethnicity, religion, age, gender, disability, or sexual preference) are punished as though the offender had committed the next higher degree of felony. This practice is called **enhanced punishment**.

Under the Texas Penal Code, a person commits murder if there is evidence of intent to kill or cause serious bodily harm to the victim. The presence of additional circumstances, such as the victim's age or role as a law enforcement official, can make the crime a **capital felony**, for which the death penalty may be applied.

TABLE 13.1 Selected Texas Noncapital Offenses, Penalties for First Offenders, and Courts Having Original Jurisdiction

Selected Offense	Offense Category	Punishment	Court
Murder Theft of property valued at $300,000 or more	First-degree felony	Confinement for 5–99 years or life Maximum fine of $10,000	District court
Theft of property valued at $150,000 or more but less than $300,000 Aggravated assault, including of a spouse	Second-degree felony	Confinement for 2–20 years Maximum fine of $10,000	District court
Theft of property valued at $30,000 or more but less than $150,000 Impersonating someone online	Third-degree felony	Confinement for 2–10 years Maximum fine of $10,000	District court
Theft of property valued at $2,500 or more but less than $30,000 Possession of four ounces to five pounds of marijuana	State-jail felony	Confinement for 180 days to 2 years Maximum fine of $10,000	District court
Theft of property valued at $750 or more but less than $2,500 Resisting arrest	Class A misdemeanor	Confinement for 1 year Maximum fine of $4,000	Constitutional county court and county court-at-law
Theft of property valued at $100 or more but less than $750 Terroristic threat	Class B misdemeanor	Confinement for 180 days Maximum fine of $2,000	Constitutional county court and county court-at-law
Theft of property valued at less than $100 Sexting (sending or possessing sexually explicit images of people 17 or younger by a minor)	Class C misdemeanor	No confinement Maximum fine of $500	Justice of the peace court and municipal court (if offense committed within city limits)

Competency Connection
❖ CRITICAL THINKING ❖

In analyzing Table 13.1, do the punishments fit the crimes?

Criminal Justice Policy

Policymaking in Texas takes into account public opinion, the state's budget, and federal court rulings. The Lone Star State's political culture requires elected officials to be seen as "tough on crime." Lengthy imprisonment is expensive, however, and Texas has one of the highest incarceration rates in the nation. Detention practices that do not result in cruel and unusual punishment (including provision of adequate facilities, health care, and prisoner safety) add to the cost of confinement. Increasing racial and ethnic diversity in Texas also creates tension among all its residents. These factors influence the state's policies with regard to criminal law.

Drug Crimes Since the 1980s, arrests for drug possession have ballooned in Texas. Most arrests are for possession of a controlled substance. Many people who are prosecuted for low-level drug crimes are dealing with a range of other issues, including mental illness, homelessness, and poverty. Prisons and jails are not equipped to treat these problems. Untreated inmates are more likely to continue using drugs and commit other crimes when released. Texas has relied heavily on incarceration as a primary response to drug offenses. However, state officials have slowly evolved in the methods used to handle drug crimes.

In the current century, state legislators have searched for less costly and more effective ways to address high incarceration rates for drug offenses. Solutions include easing parole criteria for nonviolent offenders, establishing in-prison treatment options, and creating specialty drug courts (see Chapter 10, "The Judicial Branch"). The 84th Legislature opted out of a 19-year-old federal policy that denied food stamps to felony drug offenders for life. Texas now allows those who are first-time felony drug offenders to receive food stamp benefits (although they are still ineligible for cash help through welfare). Offenders who commit second drug offenses lose these benefits. Forty-seven states have ended the food stamp ban based in part on a 2013 Yale University study that found denying food assistance made felons more likely to prostitute themselves to buy food.[4] Three states enforce a lifetime ban on food stamp benefits: West Virginia, South Carolina, and Mississippi. Texas and 23 other states have a modified ban. This means that there are stipulations on receiving aid, such as drug tests. In addition to denying social service benefits to drug offenders, criminal laws have included harsh penalties. As a result, state jail and prison populations have increased dramatically over the last 40 years. When Texas legislators shifted their focus to rehabilitation and reintegration of offenders into society, they achieved positive outcomes. After reforming its criminal justice policies, the Lone Star State experienced a nearly 20 percent reduction in crime.

Inefficiencies in the criminal justice system occur even before trial. A yearlong study in Harris County examined more than 6,500 felony and misdemeanor cases. Many defendants spent weeks or months in county jail awaiting punishment for minor offenses, including possession of small amounts of drugs.[5]

All Texas counties with populations over 550,000 must establish drug courts. These courts provide more extensive supervision than other programs. An example of a successful drug court is in Tarrant County, where a SWIFT

(Supervision With Intensive enForcemenT) Court was created in 2012. In a program described as "probation on steroids," offenders are closely monitored for strict compliance with probation conditions. These programs have been successful, but they are not available to all defendants.

Access to successful drug court programs by minorities and the poor can also be a problem. An *Austin American-Statesman* investigation found that the structure of the Travis County Drug Diversion Court's program limited access by disadvantaged groups. Although African Americans make up nearly 8 percent of the Travis County population, they represent 24 percent of all arrests for possession in 2017. The rate of conviction for African Americans is much higher than for whites. Yet, between 2010 and 2015, participation in the drug court program by African Americans and Latinos dropped by more than half. Judges observed that low minority participation rates were due in part to lawyers not referring their clients to the program. Defense attorneys argued that the program structure was time intensive and too inflexible. They complained that it required extensive therapy sessions, random drug tests, and additional community service for missed court appointments or failed drug tests. Lower recidivism rates and individual rehabilitation successes confirm that drug courts work. Travis County's drug court offers defendants the opportunity to keep their records clean if they complete the yearlong treatment plan.[6] When Texans who suffer from addiction are incarcerated, the county and state limit the addicted person's ability to become a healthy, productive member of the community. The cost is much lower for drug treatment programs than for incarceration: under $4,000 per inmate per year for treatment compared to almost $19,000 per inmate per year for incarceration.[7] Equal access to successful programs for all groups, regardless of race, ethnicity, or economic status, should have a positive effect in the criminal justice system; conversely, limited access may well have a negative effect.

Hate Crimes Since 1993, Texas law has provided enhanced punishment for hate crimes, which are criminal acts against another person motivated by bias or prejudice against a group of which the victim is a member. In 1998, one of Texas's most horrific hate crimes occurred in Jasper, located in East Texas. James Byrd, Jr., an African American man, was chained by his ankles to the back of a pickup truck and dragged for miles to his death by three white men. Authorities believe that he was conscious throughout the incident until his head hit the side of the road and he was decapitated. In response, the legislature passed the James Byrd, Jr. Hate Crimes Act in 2001. This act strengthened Texas law by identifying specific targeted groups who were the most likely victims of hate crimes.

Violent acts that are perpetrated on specific groups of Texans are a threat to all Texans. In 2017 (the most recent year for which data are available), the Federal Bureau of Investigation identified 190 criminal incidents as hate crimes in the state. Race was identified as the primary motivation for hate crimes, followed by hate crimes based on sexual orientation. Information provided by the FBI Hate Crimes Statistics reported that in 2017 Austin led the state in the number of hate crimes reported, with Dallas second.[8] Policymakers use the collected data to determine if laws and policies are effective.

While Texas's James Byrd, Jr. Hate Crimes Act protects against hate crimes based on race, religion, color, sex, disability, age, natural origin, or sexual orientation, it does not protect against offenses based on the victim's sexual identity or expression. According to State Representative Garnet Coleman (D-Houston), transgender people are 28 times more likely to experience physical violence than others.[9] Even so, the 84th Legislature failed to extend the Hate Crimes Act to include transgender people. Some Texas cities (including Austin, Dallas, Fort Worth, and El Paso) have ordinances to help protect transgender Texans.

It is noteworthy that district attorneys determine which cases are prosecuted as hate crimes. Their reluctance to use this law is reflected in the fact that there has been roughly one conviction per year in which the statute has been officially invoked. Often prosecutors have used the law as leverage for a **plea bargain**, in which defendants plead guilty to a lesser charge or receive a shorter sentence. In response, civil rights groups have called for a law that would require the Texas attorney general's office to conduct a study analyzing the effectiveness of the Hate Crimes Act. To date, no such law has been enacted.

✓ 13.1 Learning Check

1. What types of crimes may receive "enhanced punishment," and what does that mean?
2. True or False: Most low-level drug offenders have complicating issues such as homelessness and poverty.

Answers at the end of this chapter.

⬟ The Death Penalty

LO 13.2 Analyze issues of the death penalty in Texas.

Texas is one of 31 states, along with the federal government, that imposes the death penalty as punishment for the most serious crimes. The death penalty has taken many forms in Texas. Before 1923, counties carried out executions by hanging. After 1923, the legislature required the state to execute offenders by electrocution. Due to a series of court challenges, no executions occurred in Texas between 1964 and 1982. In 1972, in the case of *Furman v. Georgia*, 408 U.S. 238 (1972), the U.S. Supreme Court ruled that the state's use of the death penalty was unconstitutional because its use was arbitrary and racially biased.

Reinstitution of the Death Penalty

Following the *Furman* decision, Texas rewrote its death penalty laws in 1973 to meet the U.S. Supreme Court's demands for standardization and fairness. The first execution under the new law occurred in 1982, when Texas became the first state in the nation to use lethal injection. During the past three decades, no state has executed more capital felons than Texas (555 men and six women executed from January 1982 through May 2019). Texas has performed roughly 37 percent of the nation's executions even though only 8.1 percent of the nation's population lives in the Lone Star State.[10]

A capital murderer can receive the death penalty in a variety of circumstances. Murder becomes a capital felony if the victim was younger than 10 or if the victim was a police officer, firefighter, or prison employee acting in his or her official capacity. In addition, murders become capital felonies when they occur during the commission of another felony, such as robbery or rape. Murder for hire, serial murders (including killing an unborn child), and inmate-on-inmate murder are

plea bargain
An agreement between the prosecutor and the defendant in a criminal case in which the defendant agrees to plead guilty to a specific charge and in return gets certain concessions from the prosecutor, such as a reduction in charges, a shortened prison term, or probation.

also capital felonies. Although state law allows the death penalty after a second conviction for rape of a child under the age of 14 or in cases involving human trafficking in children for sexual purposes, legal commentators argue this law is unconstitutional. The U.S. Supreme Court has ruled that the death penalty can only be imposed for murder. Through April 2019, the Texas law had not been challenged.

After a jury has found a defendant guilty of a capital offense, jurors must unanimously determine whether the accused represents a continuing threat to society and whether circumstances in the defendant's life warrant life imprisonment rather than death. The minimum sentence for a capital felony is life imprisonment without parole. If the state seeks the death penalty, all jurors must agree to the sentence. The death certificate of someone who has been executed lists the cause of death as "judicially ordered execution." Capital punishment remains controversial.[11]

The issue of racial bias in the use of capital punishment has never been fully resolved. Trial courts have allowed testimony that a person's race may make the accused a continuing threat to society. In the case of Duane Buck, an African American who was sentenced to death for a 1995 murder in Houston, a psychologist testified, "race [was] a factor associated with future dangerousness." The psychologist provided similar testimony in five other cases involving black or Latino defendants. All were sentenced to death. In 2000, then–Texas Attorney General John Cornyn agreed to new trials for these five defendants because of possible racial bias in the psychologist's testimony. Buck, however, was not granted a new trial because his attorney, not the prosecutor, had hired the psychologist to testify about race. In 2011, Buck appealed to the U.S. Supreme Court, but his appeal was denied, even though the justices described the psychologist's testimony as "bizarre and objectionable." Buck filed a subsequent appeal claiming ineffective counsel because his lawyer had solicited the racially biased testimony that resulted in his conviction. On October 5, 2016, the U.S. Supreme Court heard oral arguments in Buck's case. His lawyers argued that the death sentence he was given was racially biased. On February 22, 2017, the U.S. Supreme Court ruled in favor of Buck. The Court stated, "law punishes people for what they do, not who they are."[12]

In Harris County, where Duane Buck was tried, prosecutors are three times more likely to seek the death penalty for black defendants than for whites. Research suggests that the victim's race and gender (white females) is significant in determining whether a defendant receives the death penalty, regardless of the defendant's race. African Americans are overrepresented on Texas's death row; they make up approximately 12 percent of the state's population but almost 44 percent of its death row inmates. The *Texas Tribune* has created an app called "Faces of Death Row" that shows photos of death row inmates, gives a summary of their crimes, identifies the age and race of each inmate and the location of each crime, and includes the amount of time each prisoner has spent on death row. Users can scan through over 200 inmate photos and use filters to find specific inmates based on age, gender, race, or time spent on death row.[13]

In addition to issues regarding racial bias, questions have arisen about the possible innocence of some of the people who have been executed, and concerns remain about the method used to execute capital felons and the callousness of some officials. For nearly 30 years (December 1982 through July 2012), Texas used a three-drug process that first rendered a prisoner unconscious, then induced paralysis, and finally stopped the heart. In 2011, prison administrators became concerned about a shortage of the execution drug used to render prisoners unconscious, sodium thiopental. Texas officials contacted Oklahoma officials for advice on dealing with the scarcity of the drug. Records show that the Oklahoma assistant attorney general wrote colleagues that the state might help Texas in exchange for football tickets to the Red River Rivalry, a football game between the University of Oklahoma and the University of Texas.[14] Although the lawyer was criticized for being so callous about the death penalty, no drugs were exchanged.

Because of the unavailability of some of the drugs in the three-drug mix, Texas prison officials now give a lethal injection of pentobarbital, the same drug used to euthanize animals. State officials stockpiled pentobarbital (sold under the trade name Nembutal) after European pharmaceutical manufacturers announced they would no longer produce the drug for use in human executions.[15] When Texas ran out of the drug in September 2013, the state turned to compounding pharmacies for custom-made pentobarbital. Compounding pharmacies are unregulated by the U.S. Food and Drug Administration (FDA). In October 2013, several death row inmates in Texas filed a federal civil complaint against the Texas Department of Criminal Justice (TDCJ). The complaint alleged that TDCJ had falsified a prescription for pentobarbital, purchased from a Houston compounding pharmacy, for an inmate and facility that did not exist. Attorneys for the inmates argued unsuccessfully that using untested drugs from unregulated pharmacies was against the Eighth Amendment's ban on cruel and unusual punishment. TDCJ did not have a physician's prescription for the compounded drugs, required by state law in most cases. When the pharmacy requested return of the pentobarbitol, TDCJ refused to do so.

In addition to altering the drug protocol for lethal injections and using compounding pharmacies to obtain the necessary drugs, states have responded to shortages in drug supplies in other ways. One approach is the sharing of drugs between states. When Texas officials needed an additional vial of pentobarbital for a 2013 execution, Virginia's Department of Corrections supplied the drug. In September 2015, Texas reciprocated by furnishing Virginia officials with three vials of pentobarbital for an upcoming execution.[16] In April 2016, the Virginia legislature authorized that state to contract with compounding pharmacies to supply drugs for executions. Further, the legislation allowed prison officials to keep confidential the names of the state's drug suppliers. Texas passed a similar law in 2015. The ability of the Lone Star State to maintain the confidentiality of its suppliers' names was under a court challenge. As of April 2019, the Texas Supreme Court ruled that TDCJ can withhold the name of the compounding pharmacy that provided execution drugs in 2014. As of May 2016, four states provided an alternative to lethal injections in the event that the needed drugs were unavailable. Texas had no such backup plan. Further complicating this issue is the lack of uniformity and oversight of death penalty practices.

Reviewing the Death Penalty

Imposition of the death penalty has declined across the United States and in Texas in recent years. Concerns about possible executions of innocent people have had some effect. (From 1973 through April 2016, Texas had released 13 wrongfully convicted death row inmates.) In addition, the option of life without parole has provided an alternative punishment for capital felons.

Some states have placed a moratorium on the death penalty.[17] A **moratorium** is a delay or suspension of an activity or law. In March 2019, California's Governor Gavin Newsom called a moratorium on executions in the state. Although the American Bar Association has encouraged all states with death penalty laws to do the same, Texas legislators have consistently rejected the idea. The Texas Moratorium Network (TMN) argues that if Texans were better educated on the death penalty, capital punishment would be temporarily, or perhaps even permanently, suspended.

One factor that supports continued use of the death penalty is deterrence. According to the Death Penalty Information Center, from 1990–2016, states with the death penalty had higher rates of homicide than states without the death penalty.[18] These findings have been challenged, however, as not establishing a causal relationship between executions and deterrence.[19] Some evidence supports this claim. According to the 2016 FBI Uniform Crime Report, southern states had the highest murder rates in the nation. Yet, these same states, particularly Texas, account for a majority (80 percent) of the nation's executions. A survey of the nation's top academic criminologists indicates that 88 percent of these experts do not believe the death penalty deters homicides.[20]

A problem in determining whether the death penalty deters crime is that the time between sentencing and execution is quite lengthy. According to the TDCJ, the average time spent on death row prior to execution is nearly 11 years.[21] Some argue the punishment loses its deterrent effect because people do not see the immediate impact of the death penalty. Former Texas attorney general Jim Mattox interviewed several condemned inmates who were ultimately executed. Based on the inmates' responses, Mattox concluded, "It is my own experience that those executed in Texas were not deterred by the existence of the death penalty. I think in most cases you'll find that the murder was committed under severe drug and alcohol abuse."[22]

Some capital defendants are exempt from the death penalty. As the result of U.S. Supreme Court decisions and state law, for example, the death penalty cannot be used as punishment for anyone who was younger than 18 when committing a capital crime (*Roper v. Simmons*, 543 U.S. 551 [2005]) or anyone who is "mentally retarded" (now classified as intellectually disabled) (*Atkins v. Virginia*, 536 U.S. 304 [2002]). This penalty cannot be imposed if a defendant is found to have been mentally incompetent at the time of committing a capital crime.

The death penalty cannot be carried out on a convicted person who is mentally ill. The defendant must understand the connection between the execution and the acts that led to the original conviction.[23] Establishing mental illness in Texas, however, requires significant evidence. As of 2019, the state has continued to seek the execution of a number of mentally ill inmates, including Bobby Moore, a case in which the U.S. Supreme Court tossed out a lower court's ruling that he wasn't intellectually disabled based on nonmedical standards; Andre Thomas, who was described by Texas Court of Criminal Appeals Judge Cathy Cochran as "clearly 'crazy,' but … also 'sane' under Texas law,"[24]; and John Battaglia, who, according to several forensic psychiatrists, suffered from bipolar disorder.

moratorium
The delay or suspension of an activity or law. A moratorium may be imposed when something is seen as needing improvement.

The U.S. Supreme Court under *Atkins v. Virginia,* allows each state to determine a procedure for determining intellectual disability. In April 2019, the Texas House passed a bill that would have created a pretrial hearing to determine intellectual disability that may have exempted one from the death penalty. However, the Texas Senate's Criminal Justice Committee removed the pretrial requirement from the bill. Ultimately, the bill went to a conference committee to reconcile the two versions of the bill, but a compromise could not be reached and it died. Currently, the state allows courts to determine how to decide a defendant's intellectual ability. In 1990, Bobby Moore fatally shot a store clerk during a robbery in Houston. He was sentenced to death. In 2017, the U.S. Supreme Court tossed out the Texas Court of Criminal Appeals decision that Bobby Moore was not intellectually disabled and thereby not exempt from the death penalty, even though Moore's history showed he was not able to understand the days of the week or do basic math at the age of 13.

In 2018, the prosecutor handling Moore's case requested life without parole, but again the Texas Court of Criminal Appeals rejected that he was intellectually disabled. The appeals court used a test to determine intellectual disability that includes questioning a neighbor or family member to see if the person believes someone is disabled. In 2018, the case was appealed back to the U.S. Supreme Court; and in February 2019, for the second time, the high court reversed Moore's death sentence stating that he is intellectually disabled making him exempt from the death penalty. Many had hoped this case would provide a path toward sound medical-based procedures to determine intellectual disability set by the Texas legislature, but substantial changes were not made during the 2019 legislative session.

▣ POINT/COUNTERPOINT

Should Administrative Segregation Be Used as an In-Prison Punishment?

THE ISSUE Death row inmates are placed in administrative segregation, also known as solitary confinement, throughout their entire time on death row. Other inmates in state and federal prisons across the United States receive the same punishment. As of 2016, as many as 100,000 inmates were in solitary confinement or administrative segregation in the United States. Texas leads the nation in the use of administrative segregation as an in-prison punishment.

Administrative segregation occurs when an inmate is separated and isolated from other inmates. The incarcerated person is placed in a room without any human contact except with prison guards. On weekdays prisoners may be in their cells up to 23 hours a day, emerging only to shower and spend time outdoors ("in the yard") under strict supervision. Weekend conditions are even more restrictive, with some prisoners remaining in isolation for up to 48 continuous hours. Inmates are placed in administrative segregation for a variety of reasons in addition to having received the death penalty, including: committing violent acts against correctional officers or other inmates, membership in a gang, or for their own safety.

Many proponents of administrative segregation believe it is an effective form of punishment. No court has ruled the practice to be a violation of the U.S. Constitution's ban on "cruel and unusual punishment." Yet others criticize the practice as being cruel, inhumane, and a violation of human rights. President Barack Obama became the first U.S. president to denounce the use of solitary confinement in prisons. As of 2016, at least one state (Colorado) has limited its use by no longer placing mentally ill inmates in administrative segregation. Other states (not Texas) are discussing reforms.

(Continued)

FOR	AGAINST

FOR

1. Administrative segregation can protect inmates from the general population. Inmates who are pedophiles, murderers, or ex–gang members may face threats from other prisoners. Administrative segregation provides security and protection, making it difficult for high-risk inmates to be harmed.

2. Administrative segregation provides correctional officers with the ability to maintain order. Guards may use administrative segregation as a form of punishment and also as a means of deterrence. Inmates do not want to face weeks or longer in isolation. Further, administrative segregation can be used when prisoners are a threat to staff or other inmates.

3. In some cases, administrative segregation can be used to keep prisoners safe from themselves. Inmates in solitary confinement are less likely to commit suicide because they are carefully monitored. In addition, suicidal prisoners often use objects in their cells, such as bedsheets, towels, phone cords, or personal items like socks to harm themselves. However, in administrative segregation they do not have access to these items. Therefore, solitary confinement can be used to keep inmates safe.

AGAINST

1. Administrative segregation may cause mental illness in inmates or exacerbate existing mental health conditions. Many inmates suffer from mental illness. Isolating an inmate may intensify a mental illness, causing hallucinations, delusions, paranoia, and disorientation. Inmates in isolation lose a sense of control of their environment, which leads to anxiety, claustrophobia, and violence toward prison officials or themselves. Prisoners such as death row inmates, with no hope of release and limited human contact, present a significant risk to themselves and correctional officers.

2. A primary goal of prisons should be to offer inmates a chance at rehabilitation. Solitary confinement is used as a punishment, in some cases for minor infractions. Rehabilitation of inmates requires human interaction and access to services and programs. Inmates in administrative segregation have no human contact other than with correctional personnel and no access to services or programs. Yet each year, about 1,200 Texas inmates are released directly from administrative segregation into society. Prisoners who go directly back into society may have difficulty reintegrating because of their previous lack of social interaction or emotional or mental problems.

3. Some deem administrative segregation a form of torture. The United Nations Convention against Torture states that "torture is an act through which severe pain and suffering, whether physical or mental, is inflicted intentionally on someone for punishment, intimidation, information, or other reasons, such as discrimination." Opponents say this description is applicable to administrative segregation.

Competency Connection
☼ **CRITICAL THINKING** ☼

What punishments do you believe are appropriate to lessen violence in prisons?

In May 2001, Battaglia called his ex-wife on the phone so she could hear him murder their nine-year-old daughter, Faith, and their six-year-old daughter, Liberty. After the shooting, Battaglia went with his girlfriend to a bar and a tattoo parlor, where he had two roses with the girls' names tattooed on his arm. He then left a voice message to his daughters, "I love you and wish you had nothing to do with your mother. She was evil and vicious and stupid."[25] Battaglia's attorney argued that his client was delusional and incapable of communicating effectively with his lawyers. In arguments before the U.S. Fifth Circuit Court of Appeals, the attorney noted that Battaglia believed that others were to blame for the murder of his daughters, including the Ku Klux Klan, his ex-wife, and even the Dallas County district attorney. In 2016, the Fifth Circuit Court of Appeals granted a stay of execution to allow lower courts to determine Battaglia's mental competency. However, Battaglia was found to be maligning, and his execution was reinstated. On February 1, 2018, he taunted his ex-wife, saying hello to her before he was injected with the lethal dose of phenobarbital.

> **✓ 13.2 Learning Check**
>
> 1. Which Supreme Court case deemed the death penalty unconstitutional in 1972 and why?
> 2. According to the Texas Department of Criminal Justice, what is the average time spent on death row before an execution?
>
> *Answers at the end of this chapter.*

★ Correction and Rehabilitation

LO 13.3 Explain the role of Texas's jail and prison system in handling corrections and rehabilitations.

Confinement in a prison (either a penitentiary or a state jail) or in a county or municipal jail is designed to punish lawbreakers, deter others from committing similar crimes, and isolate offenders from society, thus protecting the lives and property of citizens who might otherwise become victims of criminals. Ideally, while serving a sentence behind bars, a lawbreaker will be rehabilitated and, after release, will obey all laws, find employment, and make positive contributions to society. According to a *Houston Chronicle* article in 2018, the recidivism rate exceeds 60 percent in Texas. The article reviewed inmates in state prisons or jails who violate the conditions of their release or who commit other crimes after being released and are therefore resentenced to prison.[26] Juvenile justice systems, which actually conduct their proceedings as civil cases and are, therefore, outside the criminal justice system, have a similar design but with a greater emphasis on rehabilitation than punishment. Descriptions of the criminal justice system in this section relate to adults; references to the juvenile justice system include individuals between the ages of 10 and 16.

Texas's rate of incarceration has declined in recent years, although it remains high. As of 2018, Texas ranked seventh in the nation with the highest rate of incarceration. In response to high crime rates at the end of the 20th century, the Texas legislature and the Texas Board of Pardons and Paroles concentrated resources on incarceration and punishment. A few years later, the legislature shifted its emphasis to rehabilitation. This shift in policy reduced the rate of incarceration, as evidenced by a modest decrease in the inmate population between 2013 and 2014. In that period the prison population decreased by about 1 percent or approximately 2,200 inmates.[27] After 2014, changes in criminal justice policies and resulting practices continued to improve the integration and rehabilitation of inmates. This new focus has been instrumental in reducing both the number of people incarcerated and the crime rate.

The Texas Department of Criminal Justice

The principal criminal justice agencies of the state are organized within the Texas Department of Criminal Justice. This department has a four-part mission:

- To provide public safety
- To promote positive behavioral changes
- To reintegrate offenders into the general society
- To assist crime victims

The organizational structure of TDCJ includes governance by the nine-member nonsalaried Texas Board of Criminal Justice; a full-time executive director hired by the board; and directors of the department's divisions, who are selected by the executive director. Each division director is responsible for hiring division personnel. Nearly 37,000 Texans worked for TDCJ in 2018. These employees were responsible for a prison population in 2018 of approximately 140,000 inmates and in 2017 almost 100,000 parolees. The Community Justice Assistance Division monitors local community supervision programs that oversee an additional half a million offenders on probation.

Providing Public Safety For many years, the primary focus of the Texas legislature, and therefore the TDCJ, was on providing public safety. Legislators classified an increasing number of actions as felonies, lengthened sentences for all types of crimes, funded the construction of additional prison units, and balanced the state's budget by reducing drug treatment programs and other interventions intended to change behavior. Because a large prison population and high recidivism rates proved costly, a bipartisan legislative effort redirected funding efforts to expand treatment and counseling services.

The current focus on rehabilitation and reentry has reduced the escalating imprisonment rates Texas experienced in the 20th century. Reversing a decades-long trend, Texas's adult and juvenile prison populations began to decline in 2010. Officials predicted that the number of inmates in the state's prisons would remain steady and is expected to fall 1.6 percent below the TDCJ's operating capacity for fiscal years 2019 and 2024.[28] In a longer period (2012–2020), Texas's general population is expected to increase by 5 percent;[29] therefore, the incarceration rate remains in decline, even though the actual number of inmates may increase. Since 2011, Texas has closed eight state prisons, suggesting that increasing the use of probation and job training is a smart fiscal choice. Between 2005 and 2015, lower numbers of prisoners and fewer prison facilities saved taxpayers more than $3 billion.[30]

The TDCJ sector responsible for ensuring public safety is the Correctional Institutions Division. Staff members in this division supervise the operation and management of state prisons, state jails, and other specialized facilities. Private

📊 HOW DO WE COMPARE...

In Prison Incarceration Rates?

Number of Prisoners per 100,000 Adult State Residents (as of December 2016)
(includes both federal and state prisoners)

Most Populous U.S. States	Number of Prisoners per 100,000 Residents	U.S. States Bordering Texas	Number of Prisoners per 100,000 Residents
California	430	Arkansas	763
Florida	601	Louisiana	997
New York	325	New Mexico	438
Texas	761	Oklahoma	937

Source: E. Ann Carson, *Bureau of Justice Statistics Bulletin: Prisoners in 2016*, (Washington, D.C.: U.S. Department of Justice, January 2018), https://www.bjs.gov/content/pub/pdf/p16.pdf.

— Competency Connection —
☼ CRITICAL THINKING ☼

Analyze the chart. Does the rate of incarceration in neighboring states have an impact on Texas? If so, how?

---

contractors operate seven prisons, four state jails, and various prerelease, work, substance abuse, and intermediate sanctions facilities. Figure 13.1 shows the location of prison and state jail units in Texas.

Maintaining a trained workforce to provide security has been an ongoing problem for the Correctional Institutions Division. Historically, difficult working conditions, including low pay and a lack of air conditioning in prison facilities produced annual turnover rates for correctional officers is nearly 30 percent. High turnover rates create a number of problems. Demand for corrections officers sometimes results in the state's hiring candidates who have not been properly screened, who fail to meet physical requirements for the job, or who have not been adequately trained to deal with the challenging inmate population.[31] Salary increases, signing bonuses, and job cuts in the oil and gas industry may improve staff retention. As of April 2019, the average salary of full-time corrections officers was slightly more than $42,000 a year.

An additional problem faced by TDCJ is the lack of air conditioning in its facilities. A 2014 study conducted by the University of Texas Law School's Human Rights Clinic described prison conditions as "violating both international human rights standards and the Constitution." Since 2007, fourteen inmates have died because of extreme heat exposure inside Texas prisons. In 2013, more than 90 correctional officers reported heat-related illnesses. Inmates who suffer heat exhaustion or a heat stroke often avoid getting medical treatment because the

FIGURE 13.1 Facilities of the Texas Department of Criminal Justice

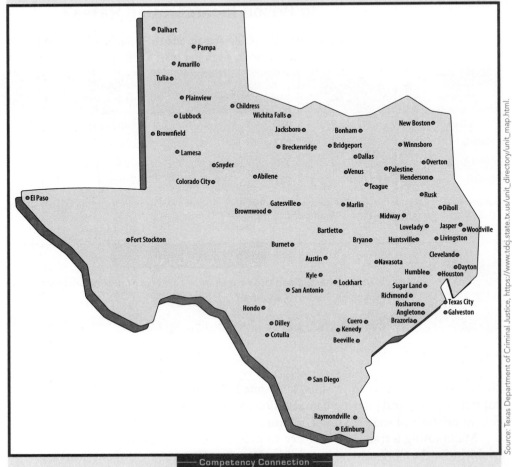

Source: Texas Department of Criminal Justice, https://www.tdcj.state.tx.us/unit_directory/unit_map.html.

— Competency Connection —
☼ **CRITICAL THINKING** ☼

How does having a state jail or prison facility in or near a community affect the community?

cost for doctor's visits has risen from a $3 copay to a $100 annual fee that is collected on the inmate's first physician's visit.[32]

In 2014, prisoners in the Wallace Pack Unit (Navasota) filed a lawsuit alleging lack of air conditioning was cruel and unusual punishment. The lawsuit was in response to 11 Texas inmates who died in the heatwave of 2011. The heat index outside the Pack Unit was over 100 degrees for 74 days in 2011. TDCJ has no maximum temperature standards for its facilities. In some Texas prisons, the heat index on a unit has been measured at nearly 150 degrees. TDCJ has claimed the primary reason for not installing air conditioning in Texas state prisons was the cost; yet in 2013, TDCJ spent $750,000 to install climate control units for

IMAGE 13.2 Texas state prisons do not have air conditioning, some units have large fans to circulate hot air during warm months.

Marjorie Kamys Cotera/Bob Daemmrich Photography/Alamy Stock Photo

— Competency Connection —
☼ **CRITICAL THINKING** ☼

Why should the state help inmates combat the severe heat in Texas prisons?

hogs living in the large barns on prison grounds. Although inmates can purchase personal fans in the commissary, the $20 cost is prohibitive for the state's many indigent prisoners. Clothing, such as shorts, that could keep inmates cooler is not provided, but is available for purchase in the commissary. Cost again is an issue for the indigent. Seventeen wrongful death lawsuits have been filed against TDCJ for heat-related inmate deaths. The union that represents correctional officers has expressed support for the plaintiffs' complaints. Since 2006, the TDCJ has paid over half a million dollars in workers' compensation claims for heat-related illnesses. In June 2014, some state prisons had large fans installed to reduce the heat. Even so, the Centers for Disease Control (CDC) stated that fans sold to inmates and the fans installed by TDCJ were ineffective in Texas's extreme heat conditions.[33] In February 2018, TDCJ settled the Pack Unit class action lawsuit and has agreed to install air conditioning in housing areas. Temporary units were used in the summer of 2018, but permanent air conditioning units should be installed by May 2020 for the Pack Unit only. TDCJ has since implemented revised heat protocols and has discussed other ways to combat hot conditions. However, the TDCJ has ignored this problem and the recommendations made by many organizations for many years, so it remains to be seen if or when all state prisons in Texas will have air conditioning.

The Lone Star State's prisons face other problems. Some staff members supplement low wages by smuggling in contraband for prisoners.[34] Smuggled cell phones are a major problem in Texas prisons, where inmates use them to maintain contact with gangs or to call family and friends. As of 2013, Texas set up two prisons with "managed access systems" that intercept calls and prevent inmates from using cell phones, as well as pinpointing a phone's location. The equipment acted as a cell tower that restricted access to authorized ID numbers. Legislators have not approved the program for systemwide implementation, which would cost $100 million per prison unit to install.[35] One of the program's strongest advocates is Senator John Whitmire (D-Houston), who, in 2008, received threatening calls from a death row inmate using a contraband cell phone. Senator Whitmire has also been the long-time chair of the Senate Criminal Justice Committee.

The state operates an offender telephone service, which until recently was too costly for inmates and their families. However, starting September 1, 2018, the cost went from 26 cents per minute down to 6 cents per minute. A typical 15-minute phone call was $4, but will now cost 90 cents. Phone call limits have been increased from 20 minutes to 30 minutes. TDCJ's director, Bryan Collier, said the agency wants to facilitate reentry and reintegration efforts for inmates with the new contract allowances. According to TDCJ, the state made $15 million from the inmate phone calls. Prison reformers argue that talking regularly with friends and family outside of prison is important to inmate rehabilitation. Prison experts observe that inmates tend to rehabilitate themselves once released if they have strong ties to those on the outside.[36]

In addition, several gangs exist within the prison system. In 2018, roughly 4,200 violent inmates and gang members (identified by prison officials as "security threat groups") were held in **administrative segregation**, sometimes referred to as solitary confinement. (See the Point/Counterpoint feature in this chapter.) Commentators argue that prisoners with no hope of release and limited human contact present a significant risk to correctional officers. In September 2017, Texas started moving away from using solitary confinement as a punishment, which ultimately only impacted 75 prisoners out of 4,000. A study conducted by the Association of State Correctional Administrators (ASCA) and the Liman Center for Public Interest Law at Yale University found that one-third of Texas prisoners had been in solitary confinement for six years or longer. The study looked at 42 state correctional systems and the Federal Bureau of Prisons. Texas was "in a league of its own when it comes to long-term solitary." In August 2013, 215 inmates were in solitary confinement, but by July 2017, the number had decreased to 76. During the same time frame, the number of inmates given administrative segregation decreased from 7,200 to roughly 3,940. TDCJ has focused on treatment and rehabilitation programs rather than administrative segregation. One such program, Gang Renouncement and Disassociation Process (GRAD), allows gang members to break ties with their gangs and go through a nine-month intensive program. The rehabilitation effort includes behavioral therapy, anger management courses, and substance abuse programs. Inmates who

administrative segregation
Commonly referred to as solitary confinement, this practice isolates an inmate in a separate cell as punishment, typically for violent or disruptive behavior.

successfully complete the GRAD program can be released from administrative segregation and returned to the general population.

The inmate population's general characteristics highlight some common issues, including poor education levels and substance abuse. Approximately 45 percent of Texas prisoners have less than a high school education, and one-third are functionally illiterate. Nationally and in Texas, the number of inmates with a serious mental illness is also high. Studies of jail and prison populations report that 23 percent of prisoners in the United States have been diagnosed with mental illness as of 2018. The profile of Texas prisoners in Table 13.2 identifies some characteristics of the state's incarcerated population.

Promoting Positive Behavioral Changes Several departments and divisions of TDCJ are responsible for programs to correct or modify the behavior of incarcerated felons. Training and instructional programs are used to rehabilitate inmates and equip them with a means of self-support after release. Self-discipline and education are the primary means of combating **recidivism** (criminal behavior resulting in reimprisonment after release). Every prisoner must be given a job

TABLE 13.2 Some Characteristics of Texas's Prison Population (2017)

Characteristic	Measurement (Percent)
Gender	
Male	92
Female	8
Race	
African American	33
Anglo	33
Hispanic	34
Type of Offense Leading to Incarceration	
Violent	56
Property	13
Drugs	16
Other	14
IQ	
Average	90.5 points

Source: "Fiscal Year 2017 Statistical Report," *Texas Department of Criminal Justice,* https://www.tdcj.texas.gov/documents/Statistical_Report_FY2017.pdf.

— Competency Connection —
☼ **CRITICAL THINKING** ☼

How might studying the characteristics of the prison population influence lawmakers' criminal justice policies?

recidivism
Criminal behavior that results in reincarceration after a person has been released from confinement for a prior offense.

but may elect not to work. Prisoners' labor saves money for Texas and for local governments and, in some instances, generates revenue for the state. Prisoners repair engines; manufacture furniture, including dorm room furnishings for several state universities; and even make the wooden gavels used by the presiding officers of the Texas legislature.

Southwestern Baptist Theological Seminary operates an extension program at the Darrington Unit, a maximum-security prison near Houston. Inmates can complete a four-year program for a bachelor of science in biblical studies that prepares them to assist chaplains and help counsel inmates. In 2018, the Heart of Texas Foundation provided a newly renovated $2.1 million building at the Darrington Unit. From May 2015 to May 2018, each year 33 to 35 inmates were awarded degrees. Program graduates are among the most violent criminals; but after graduation, they have traveled to prisons throughout the state to convince other inmates to change their ways. Prison officials report a reduction in prison violence since the program began. Unlike most inmate education programs that are designed to prepare prisoners for parole, Darrington Unit Seminary targets inmates who will likely never be released.

More than one-half of Texas prisoners are enrolled in vocational and academic classes offered through the prison system's Windham School District. In addition, some prisoners take community college and university courses. In 2014, almost 1,000 prisoners completed vocational training. Another 334 inmates graduated with college degrees ranging from associate's to master's. The state pays tuition costs for vocational training, but once released, the former inmate must reimburse the state. Tuition for college academic courses must be paid by the prisoner.

Reintegrating Offenders A major goal of treatment and education programs is to equip prisoners with the skills needed to succeed upon release. The Reentry and Integration Division provides extensive support to released offenders. This division has more than 60 reentry counselors located throughout the state to assist released inmates.

Two agencies are responsible for convicted criminals who serve all or a part of their sentences in the community: the Community Justice Assistance Division and the Parole Division. The Community Justice Assistance Division establishes minimum standards for county programs involving community supervision and community corrections facilities (such as a boot camp or a restitution center). In cases involving adult first-time offenders convicted of misdemeanors and lesser felonies, jail and prison sentences are commonly commuted to community supervision (formally called adult probation). These convicted persons are not confined if they fulfill certain court-imposed conditions. Through specialty courts, judges have also become directly involved in community supervision (see Chapter 10, "The Judicial Branch").

The Parole Division manages Texas's statewide parole and mandatory supervision system for convicted felons. The seven-member Board of Pardons and Paroles recommends acts of clemency (such as pardons) to the governor and grants or revokes paroles. The board's presiding officer employs and supervises 12 commissioners, who assist the board with parole and revocation decisions.

A three-member panel, comprised of at least one parole board member along with one or more commissioners, reviews inmate applications and decides whether to grant or deny parole. The board may impose restrictions deemed necessary to protect the community. If a parolee violates any conditions of release, a board panel determines whether to revoke parole.

Prisoners who have served some portion of their sentences may be eligible for parole. Felons who commit serious, violent crimes, such as rape or murder, must serve 30 to 40 years of "flat time" (without the possibility of having prison time reduced for "good-time" credit for good behavior). Other offenders may apply for parole after serving one-fourth of a sentence or 15 years, whichever is less (minus good-time credit).

Successful reintegration of offenders is complicated by a number of barriers to reentry. Not only do those convicted of felonies lose many civil rights, such as the right to serve on juries and administer estates, they, along with those convicted of misdemeanors, also encounter lifetime impediments to employment, housing, and student loans. According to the Equal Employment Opportunity Commission (EEOC), use of blanket exclusions against applicants with arrest or conviction records could violate civil rights laws. An employer can protect itself from a discrimination claim if they can show "its selection criteria is job-related and consistent with business necessity." It has been found that disqualification from employment and housing makes an offender's reintegration difficult. Many are calling for a new approach to support offenders' reintegration. Community programs, such as that offered by Goodwill of Central Texas, focus on offender assessment and case management while providing training and job placement assistance.[37] Goodwill officials realized that former prisoners need services and guidance as they transition out of the criminal justice system. Staff establish close relationships with ex-offenders and their families; and they provide support through different services, such as education and career help. Goodwill invites others to share their experiences and opinions through its Twitter site, #WorkIsTheAnswer. Programs such as Goodwill's help both the former inmate and the greater community because successful reentry lowers the likelihood of recidivism.

At the end of 2007, TDCJ prison units housed almost 154,000 adult inmates. By December 2018, that number was reduced to approximately 140,000 prisoners. In that period Texas's incarceration rate fell by 12 percent. The state's elected and appointed officials have adopted the view that the better solution is to have inmates on probation working toward integration into society rather than remaining behind bars. Further, this approach is helpful to taxpayers because of lowered costs—probation costs less than $2 a day per probationer compared to incarceration at a cost of more than $50 a day per inmate.[38]

The Texas legislature has passed several pieces of legislation aimed at reintegrating offenders back into society. The 84th Legislature sought to assist first-time offenders who receive deferred adjudication. Many who agreed to deferred adjudication assumed they had no criminal record, which was not true. Although charges were dismissed upon the successful completion of deferred adjudication, the offender still had a criminal record. Now, first-time offenders who successfully complete deferred adjudication after committing low-level, nonsexual, nonviolent crimes can petition a court to have their criminal records sealed to the general public. If the request is granted, the offender can check "no" on college, job, housing, and loan applications in response to questions about whether he or she has ever been convicted of a felony or misdemeanor.

The City of Austin has also taken steps to aid those who have served their jail or prison sentences. In 2015, Austin became the first city in the state to "ban the box," a movement that refers to eliminating the criminal-record box on employment applications. Only after a conditional offer of employment has been given can the employer initiate a background check. Austin, along with 11 states and 17 cities and counties, including Washington, D.C., applies these fair chance hiring policies to private employers.[39] These types of laws lessen the lifetime effect of a criminal conviction. Roughly three-fourths of people live in an area where "ban the box" or another fair-chance policy has been implemented.

Assisting Victims The fourth prong of TDCJ's mission directs attention to crime victims and their close relatives. The Victim Services Division provides information to crime victims about any change in an offender's status within the TDCJ system, as well as notification of pending parole hearings. Upon a finding of guilt, and before sentencing, victims may deliver victim impact statements in open court. They may also complete written statements that remain available to prison and parole officials. When an inmate is executed, up to five family members and close friends of the victim may witness the execution.

The State of Texas maintains a Crime Victims' Compensation Fund through the Office of the Attorney General. This program provides up to $50,000 to victims and their families for expenses related to a crime ($125,000 in the event of total disability). Covered costs include medical treatment, counseling, and burial expenses that are not covered by insurance or another government program, such as Medicaid. In June 2016, the attorney general's office opened an updated online system to allow advocacy agencies, law enforcement, prosecutors, and victim service providers access to the application form and other information for crime victims. The general public can only view historical information. Those seeking assistance can still contact the attorney general's office by phone. The program is funded by court costs, fees, and fines collected from convicted offenders, as well as juror donations of their compensation for serving as jurors.

Local Government Jails

In addition to prisons and state jails operated by the Texas Department of Criminal Justice, counties and cities across the state operate jails. These facilities are financed largely by county and municipal governments, respectively. Like penal institutions of the TDCJ, local government jails are used to control lawbreakers by placing them behind bars.

All but 19 Texas counties maintain a jail. Some counties have contracted with commercial firms to provide "privatized" jails, but most counties maintain public jails operated under the direction of the county sheriff. Originally established to detain persons awaiting trial and to hold those serving sentences for misdemeanor offenses, county jail facilities vary in quality and, except in some urban areas, do not offer rehabilitation programs. The Texas Commission on Jail Standards has oversight responsibility for county jails. These facilities have not been without problems.

Harris County has one of the largest detention facilities in the nation, housing on average 9,000 inmates at any point in time. The county also has the highest pretrial lock-up rate in the state and is less likely to release those arrested on personal recognizance bonds than other Texas counties. A personal recognizance bond authorizes a defendant's release based solely on his or her promise to appear at trial. Approximately 70 percent of Harris County jail inmates have not been convicted of any crime, but instead are awaiting trial because they cannot afford to post bond. In May 2016, Equal Justice Under Law, a non-profit civil rights group, filed a federal lawsuit against the county. The group claimed unfair practices because in setting bail, county officials failed to consider the financial ability of the defendant to post bail. Being held in county jail prior to trial is not only disruptive to people's lives, but jail conditions place them at risk of serious harm or even death. Fifty-five inmates died while in pretrial custody in Harris County from 2009 through 2015. Some died from untreated medical conditions; others from suicide; and still others as the result of beatings from fellow inmates. In 2017, U. S. District Judge Lee H. Rosenthal agreed that the bail system of Harris County was unfair to the indigent. The county, misdemeanor judges, the plaintiffs, and sheriff have all agreed on a new bail system that would allow roughly 85 percent of defendants to be release on personal recognizance.[40]

A disproportionate percentage of persons being detained are poor or members of historical minority groups. For example, African Americans make up 8 percent of Harris County's population, yet the jail inmate population is 48 percent African American. In April 2016, the district attorney for Harris County unveiled a criminal justice reform plan to reduce overcrowding in the county's jails and to address the disparate treatment of minorities and the poor. The overall three-year goal is to reduce the number of prisoners by approximately 1,800 inmates or 21 percent of the jail population. In 2017, District Attorney Kim Ogg helped begin a diversion program that would allow those caught with four ounces or less of marijuana to take a four-hour drug education program and thus avoid charges.[41] This program is estimated to help 10,000 people a year avoid spending time at the Harris County jail. In January 2019, District Attorney Ogg requested $21 million to hire additional prosecutors. The commissioner's court rejected the request. In a statement the district attorney said her office needs more resources and staff to ensure cases are processed quickly and fairly. However, the Texas ACLU and other civil rights organizations criticized her request because it could increase incarceration rates in Harris County.

Texas also has approximately 350 municipal jails, most of which are not regulated by the state. In large cities, these facilities often house hundreds of inmates who have been arrested for a variety of offenses ranging from Class C misdemeanors to capital murder. Those charged with more serious crimes are usually held temporarily until they can be transferred to a more secure county jail.

Private Prisons and Jails

In the 1980s, Texas had some of the nation's worst overcrowding due to the state's tough sentencing guidelines and a rise in illegal immigration apprehensions. Both state and local governments contracted with private companies to construct and operate prisons and direct prerelease programs. Texas has more privately operated incarceration facilities than any other state. Approximately 10 percent of Texas's inmates are housed in private prisons. These facilities are under the supervision of the Private Facility Contract Monitoring/Oversight Division of the TDCJ. The Texas Juvenile Justice Department oversees community-based private contract juvenile facilities. In addition to prisons and jails, private contractors also provide substance abuse treatment programs and halfway houses, where state and county prisoners are incarcerated in privately operated units.

In the past two decades, the state's elected officials realized that incarceration was too costly; thus, they began a move to reduce the length of prison sentences and to limit the number of inmates incarcerated for minor offenses. While good for taxpayers, the smaller prison population had a devastating effect on private prisons. In 2013, two private prisons were closed, one in Mineral Wells and the other in downtown Dallas, because they were no longer needed. In February 2015, prisoners rioted over alleged poor conditions that included lack of medical care and contaminated food at the Willacy County Correctional Center, a privately operated facility in Raymondville in South Texas. The facility was closed because of the extensive damage caused by the riot. From 2011 to 2017, the state closed eight prisons due to tight budgets and a shrinking prison population. The Legislative Budget Board estimated the state saved nearly $50 million because of the closures.[42]

Critics have expressed growing concern over a system that makes money on crime. High recidivism rates produce return "customers" and benefit private prisons. These "for profit" facilities provide little to no job training, and they make inmate–family interactions more difficult. For example, one private prison required prisoners to pay $1 per minute for video conference calls with family instead of allowing face-to-face visits. Both job training and family interaction are known to reduce recidivism, but private prisons have no incentive to provide either.[43]

✓ **13.3 Learning Check**

1. What are the two primary means of combating recidivism?
2. How has the change in the state's prison population affected private prisons?

Answers at the end of this chapter.

⊡ Juvenile Justice

LO 13.4 Compare the juvenile justice system to the adult correctional system.

Texas's juvenile justice system clearly distinguishes between youthful pranks and violent, predatory behavior. In general, young Texans at least 10 years of age but younger than 17 are treated as "delinquent children" when they commit acts that would be classified as felonies or misdemeanors if committed by adults. Children are designated as "status offenders" if they commit noncriminal acts, such as running away from home, failing to attend school, or violating a curfew established by a city or county. From 1957 to 2011, the Texas Youth Commission (TYC) was responsible for the rehabilitation and training of delinquent youth. After several years of scandal highlighting deficiencies in the agency, the 82nd Legislature (2011) abolished the TYC. The Texas Juvenile Probation Commission, the agency that oversaw county juvenile probation departments, was abolished at the same time. As a part of the sunset review process (see Chapter 9, "The Executive Branch"), the legislature created the Texas Juvenile Justice Department (TJJD) to assume the responsibilities of the abolished agencies. The 11-member board of TJJD, appointed by the governor with the consent of the Senate, is charged with unifying juvenile justice services from an offender's entry into the system through departure.

State and Local Agencies

Each county has a juvenile probation board that designates one or more juvenile judges, appoints a chief juvenile probation officer, and makes policies carried out by a juvenile probation department. When youth must be incarcerated, the responsibility rests with the TJJD. In fiscal year 2018, approximately 53,000 cases were referred to juvenile probation departments for disposition. The juvenile probation department has the discretion to impose a variety of punishments ranging from nonjudicial dispositions (such as referral to social service providers), to probation, to commitment to a TJJD secure facility. In 2015, only 1.4 percent of cases resulted in confinement of juveniles in TJJD facilities.[44] The primary goal of TJJD has shifted from sending juveniles to facilities far from their families to keeping them within their local area. If children must be removed from family settings, the law reflects a preference for group homes over correctional facilities.

For over a decade, the Texas Juvenile Justice Department has been rocked by physical and sexual abuse allegations involving staff and other offenders. In 2018, after a massive shakeup over the TJJD leadership, the director, Camille Cain, and others proposed short-term and long-term plans to Governor Abbott. Cain's ideas include some measures that will need legislative action.[45]

In 2017, one of the recent sex abuse scandals involved the Gainesville State School, located in North Texas. The scandal involved the conviction and 10-year sentence of a guard and the arrest of three other staff members in November 2017 for engaging in sex with youth in custody. Then, in January 2018, another four individuals were arrested on misdemeanor charges. In total, including the above, at least 10 staff and guards have been arrested and/or charged with abuse, plus one individual who was at large.[46] In the wake of the scandal given above, the new director of the TJJD has begun implementing a strategy to address problems. Director Cain noted in 2018 that the state-run youth lockups have been processing more reviews in order to release qualified youth. This led to an all-time low of 879 state youth lockups in June 2018, compared to roughly 5,000 in 2005. Recommendations have called for more community-based programs for youth offenders. Studies show that juvenile offenders closer to home in community-based supervised programs are less likely to reoffend then those in state facilities.[47] According to a study by the nonprofit Council of State Governments Justice Center, juveniles who were in state facilities are 21 percent more likely to be rearrested and three times more likely to commit a felony when they reoffend, when compared to those in community-based programs close to home.[48]

Research shows that it costs taxpayers $10,000 a year per person for community supervision versus $130,000 per juvenile a year in state-run facilities.[49] There has been a call by many to close state-run youth lockups and replace them with community-based rehabilitation and treatment centers.

Procedures

Although juvenile offenders are arrested by the same law enforcement officers who deal with adult criminals, they are detained in separate facilities. Counseling and probation are the most widely used options for dealing with juvenile offenders, but residential treatment and TJJD facilities remain as alternatives. An arresting officer has the discretion to release a child or refer the case to a local juvenile probation department. Other referrals come from public school officials, victims, and parents. Approximately 130,000 Texas youths enter the state's juvenile justice system annually.

Trials in juvenile courts are termed **adjudication hearings**. Juvenile courts are civil rather than criminal courts; therefore, any appeal of a court's ruling will be made to a higher court with civil jurisdiction. A few cases are ultimately appealed to the Texas Supreme Court. Juvenile court proceedings may be closed to the public by the presiding judge.

A juvenile determinate sentencing law covers more than 20 serious offenses. Under this sentencing provision, juveniles who commit offenses such as capital murder or aggravated sexual assault can be transferred to adult prisons when they reach the age of 19 and can be held there for as long as 40 years. In addition, approximately 1 percent of juveniles charged with serious crimes stand trial and are punished as adults. Prior to a determination of guilt, these young offenders remain in juvenile facilities "separated by sight and sound" from adult offenders; but once found guilty, convicted youth are transferred to the adult prison system.

An issue Texas legislators are trying to resolve is whether to raise the age of adulthood to 18 for criminal matters. Researchers and lawmakers find that steering 17-year-olds to juvenile courts and lockups instead of adult jails would save money, reduce arrest rates, and eliminate the inconsistent treatment of youth—they can be considered adults in the criminal justice system but still be regarded as children with regard to voting or buying lottery tickets and cigarettes. Federal law requires that 17-year-olds be separated from others when housed in adult prisons or jails, which may be costly to the state and counties. Most studies find that trying youths as adults results in these young people being more likely to reoffend than those held in the juvenile system under similar circumstances.[50] As of 2018, Texas was one of four states that excluded 17-year-olds from the juvenile system. These youthful offenders are handled entirely in the adult criminal justice system.[51] Advocates of reform, such as the Campaign for Youth Justice, argue that adulthood should start at age 18 for criminal justice purposes.[52] In June 2018, Missouri passed a bill that will move the age for juvenile jurisdiction from 17 to 18 by 2021, wherein they will no longer be placed in the adult system. Vermont will raise its juvenile status for those up to 19 years old by 2022, with some exceptions for violent offenses.

adjudication hearing
A trial in a juvenile court.

✓ 13.4 Learning Check

1. What agency oversees Texas's juvenile justice system?
2. True or False: Young Texans at least 6 years of age but younger than 19 are treated as "delinquent children" when they commit offenses that would be classified as felonies or misdemeanors if committed by adults.

Answers at the end of this chapter.

◘ Problems and Reforms: Implications for Public Policy

LO 13.5 Evaluate the fairness of Texas's justice system.

Legislators must deal with the 21st-century issues of overcrowding and mental illness in prisons, electronic and scientific technology, changing demographics, and misconduct by district attorneys. It is important for our policymakers to respond to issues within the criminal justice system that will assure fairness for all.

Overcrowding and Mental Illness in Prison

Decades of increasing problems with overcrowding in Texas prisons have begun to ease, with the state's overall prison population dropping from a high of 156,500 in 2011 to 140,000 in 2018. The decline comes as a result of aggressive work by the state government to create alternative sentencing options through special courts for drugs, veterans, prostitution, and drunk driving. In addition, expanded rehabilitation, probation, and parole options, together with a general drop in the crime rate, have resulted in a decrease in the state's prison population.[53] Still, many problems exist in the system, especially in municipal and county jails.

Overcrowded facilities and chronic understaffing have caused an increase in inmate-on-inmate violence resulting in serious injury or death. Telford Unit, a maximum security prison that holds more than 2,500 men, is located in Northeast Texas near Texarkana. The problems at this prison have a lot to do with the shortage of guards. In 2018, the prison was short 200 guards and operated with only 65 percent of full-time guards. The prison has the highest rate of vacancies in the state. It also has the highest rate of serious assaults on staff than any other prison in the state.[54] Furthermore, many inmates have complicating conditions such as mental illness. In Texas, based on the availability of psychiatric facilities, a person with a serious mental illness is 10 times as likely to be incarcerated as to receive treatment.[55] Results can be fatal. The high-profile 2015 death of Sandra Bland in the Waller County jail brought attention to the increasing problem of suicide among the incarcerated. In 2017, the Texas prison system had 34 suicides, the second highest number in the past decade. The Commission on Jail Standards has regulations on how to deal with inmates at risk of committing suicide, including face-to-face monitoring of the inmates while in custody. All 27 of the county jails in which one or more suicides occurred during the 2010–2015 period had been cited for violations of state regulations.[56]

Inmates at risk of suicide are often dealing with mental health issues. Harris County Judge Ed Emmett estimates that approximately one-third of inmates housed in county facilities are mentally ill. Harris County spends about $54 million a year to incarcerate those with mental illness. Many offenders have undiagnosed or untreated mental illnesses that may lead them to commit crimes.

The State Commission on Jail Standards has established screening procedures to determine whether someone taken into custody has mental health issues. In a 2015 study conducted by the Texas Public Policy Foundation, of the 98 counties responding to a survey on intake procedures, approximately 75 percent used screening forms to identify mental illness upon intake, slightly more than 40 percent used other medical records to check inmates' mental health history, and less than 35 percent notified magistrates when prescreening raised red flags.[57] Although many inmates receive treatment during their incarceration, once they are out of the system, they are left with little assistance. In the 86th (2019) legislative session, the TDCJ requested $281 million for the two-year budget for medical services for inmates, which will help with dental and other health-care costs, an aging population, and mental health issues. The legislature allocated close to $160 million to TDCJ for 2018–2019.[58]

Technology

Technology now touches many areas of the criminal justice system. Websites and social media provide different avenues for inmates to communicate with each other and the outside world. Forensic science, especially DNA testing, has been a resource that aids both defendants and prosecutors.

Since March 1980, Houston's KPFT has aired *The Prison Show* on Friday nights. This show can be heard live online and downloaded as a podcast. Additionally, the hosts maintain a Facebook page. Families and inmates have an opportunity to communicate through an on-air format. Friends and family members call in to the show while inmates listen. Sometimes the messages are words of encouragement and support; at other times, callers use the time to update an inmate about family matters such as a child's doctor visit.

Communication technology has raised new issues regarding prisoner contact with the outside world. Cell phones are now the most common contraband item, and their possession the least-prosecuted offense.[59] Although prisoners do not have direct access to the Internet, until 2016 many inmates had social media accounts, like Facebook pages, that were created and maintained by their families or friends. Some prison officials even advocated for Internet-enabled tablets to provide a distraction and deter inmates from inappropriate activities. In 2016, concerns over prisoners using the Internet to profit from their crimes or to continue criminal activity, along with social media policies that bar running an account in another person's name, led the TDCJ to take a harder line. The department announced a rule that bars inmates from having social media accounts, even if maintained by friends or family outside prison walls. Civil liberties advocates question whether the rule violates first amendment free speech rights.[60]

DNA testing, developed by geneticist Alec Jeffreys, transformed the criminal justice system. Biological evidence is used to identify suspects, as well as to exonerate the innocent. The state maintains a DNA database. Both TDCJ and TJJD collect DNA samples from all inmates convicted of felony-level offenses. Convicted felons who receive community supervision must provide DNA samples.

IMAGE 13.3 Administrative segregation's overuse has had a devastating impact on the mental health of inmates. Mental health issues need to be addressed by the criminal justice system of Texas in order to reduce recidivism, particularly, among the mentally ill inmates.

Andrew Lichtenstein/Corbis/Getty Images

— Competency Connection —
✿ **CRITICAL THINKING** ✿

What type of assistance should mentally ill inmates receive upon release?

Juveniles released on probation who have committed the most serious offenses (for example, murder, rape, or aggravated robbery) or who used a weapon to commit their offenses must also furnish DNA samples. Crime scene evidence can then be tested against the state's database samples. DNA evidence not only aids in identifying the guilty, it may also establish innocence, which is what occurred in the Michael Morton case. Morton was found guilty of murdering his wife in 1986 and spent 25 years in prison for a crime he did not commit. After meeting resistance from the Williamson County district attorney's office for seven years, Morton's attorneys were able to have a bloody bandana found at the crime scene tested for DNA evidence. The results set him free.[61] Delays that Morton experienced in having evidence submitted for testing are no longer possible due to laws passed by the 82nd Legislature (2011).

Laws, agencies, and commissions have been established by the state to prevent the miscarriage of justice. For example, state law requires all public crime labs to be accredited and DNA evidence to be held for retesting. An 11-member Texas Forensic Science Commission, appointed by the governor, investigates charges of negligence and misconduct.

Exoneration Issues

The Fourteenth Amendment to the U.S. Constitution guarantees that no state may "deprive any person of life, liberty, or property without due process of law." Rules and procedures that must be followed in criminal cases are specifically designed to protect people from losing life, liberty, or property as a result of arbitrary acts by the government. Even so, people are sometimes wrongfully convicted and incarcerated. A few of these inmates may subsequently be found innocent and released. When the state admits the person is innocent of the crime for which he or she was incarcerated, the prisoner is **exonerated**. According to the National Registry of Exonerations, a project of the University of Michigan Law School, 2,420 inmates across the nation were exonerated between 1989 and March 2019. Of this total, Texas had 360 exonerations, the most of any state in the nation.[62] Twenty-four percent of exonerations were at least partly based on DNA evidence.

Although DNA test results have contributed to the release of innocent prisoners, this evidence is not the panacea that will eliminate all wrongful imprisonment. In fact, only 23 out of 148 people who were released from prison in 2018 (nationally) had DNA evidence to exonerate them.[63] One of the least reliable forms of evidence, and perversely one of the most trusted forms, is eyewitness testimony. Although scientists have long suspected the accuracy of eyewitnesses, law enforcement officials and jurors have presumed its validity. In the 1930s, Yale University law professor Edwin M. Borchard reported on 65 cases in which innocent people were imprisoned because of faulty eyewitness evidence. As incarceration rates have risen, so too have wrongful incarcerations. According to the Innocence Project, a group that uses DNA evidence to obtain the exoneration and release of those wrongly convicted, inaccurate eyewitness identification was a factor in more than 70 percent of the 364-plus exonerees they had represented through 2018.[64] Research indicates several flaws in this type of evidence, including overlooking facial features of people of different races, transference to an individual encountered in a different setting, and poor recall due to the stress of being a crime victim or witness.[65] In response to these concerns, the 82nd Legislature revised state law in 2011 to require police departments and other agencies to develop written procedures for conducting photo and live lineups.

Although most people convicted of a crime are guilty, the probability of exoneration is remote, even for the innocent. The political reality is that to obtain a pardon and be fully exonerated requires the agreement of district attorneys, judges, the Board of Pardons and Paroles, and the governor. Posthumous pardons can be granted, should someone be exonerated after his or her death. The State of Texas compensates individuals wrongfully incarcerated. Someone found innocent after being imprisoned is entitled to $80,000 for each year he or she was wrongly incarcerated, $25,000 for each year on parole or required registration on a sex offender registry, tuition for training or college, a lifetime annuity, and assistance in accessing social service providers. Over the past 25 years, the state has paid over $93 million to more than 100 men and women who were wrongfully sent to prison. In 2017, Texas exonerated 23 people, which was the highest rate of exonerations in the country.[66] Lump sum payments can be made to the heirs of those exonerated after death. The 84th Legislature established the Timothy Cole Exoneration Review Commission to identify patterns in wrongful convictions and

exoneration
The state's officially declaring the innocence of someone who has been convicted of a crime.

make recommendations on how to limit the number of wrongful convictions in the state. (Timothy Cole was wrongfully convicted of sexual assault and died in prison in 1999. He was exonerated and fully pardoned in 2010.) The commission submitted its report in December 2016. In the report, the commission made broad recommendations to the legislature in such areas as recording interrogations, eyewitness identification, new practices for forensic science, false accusations and jail house informants.

Racial Bias in the Criminal Justice System

Changes in the state's demography have affected its justice system. The underrepresentation of African Americans and Latinos in elected and appointed leadership positions is matched by their overrepresentation in the criminal justice system.[67] If the race or ethnicity of those enforcing the law is consistently different from those against whom the law is enforced, the system has less credibility and may be viewed as unfair. Events in Texas and other states illustrate this point.

A Department of Justice report of policing and court practices in Ferguson, Missouri, following a police officer's shooting and killing of Michael Brown, an African American, found repeated examples of law enforcement bias against African Americans. Among examples of bias, the report cited racist emails sent by police and court officials and an arrest warrant system designed to generate revenue instead of promoting public safety, among other examples of bias.[68]

The arrest and subsequent death of Sandra Bland, a Prairie View A&M University employee, drew attention to the relationship between law enforcement and the African American community in Texas. Bland was pulled over for failing to use a turn signal. The situation escalated and she was arrested. As noted previously, Bland committed suicide while in jail. The incident drew attention to law enforcement tactics and whether the arresting officer took appropriate action or escalated the situation.[69]

The Texas Commission on Law Enforcement Standards and Education requires law enforcement agencies to provide annual racial profiling reports. Racial profiling is the practice of targeting members of historical minority groups for stops and searches. These racial profiling reports make public the number of traffic stops by race, gender, and age of the person stopped, as well as subsequent action, such as searches and arrests, that resulted from the stops. Instances of racial and ethnic bias are the subject of growing concern as Texas has evolved into a state in which two historical minority groups, African Americans and Latinos, make up the majority population.

The perception of racial bias in the criminal justice system can have deadly results for law enforcement personnel, as well. On the evening of July 7, 2016, in downtown Dallas, an African American sniper opened fire on police officers who were monitoring a peaceful demonstration against police shootings of African American men in Louisiana and Minnesota. Specifically targeting white officers, the shooter murdered five policemen and injured two civilians and seven other officers, before being killed by a bomb-rigged police robot. In reacting to the shootings, Dallas Police Chief Mike Brown, an African American, noted,

"All I know is that this must stop, this divisiveness between our police and our citizens."[70]

Questions remain about the targeting of members of historical minority groups by the police in the use of lethal force. In reviewing data that included information from three Texas police departments (Austin, Dallas, and Houston), Harvard economist Roland Fryer concluded that police were more likely to use nonlethal force with African Americans and Latinos than with whites. However, relying on information furnished by the Houston Police Department, Fryer found that officers were more likely to use lethal force against whites.[71] The findings were immediately controversial. Some pundits argued the study proved no racial bias in policing. Others noted the limited number of departments studied and reliance on self-reports by police of violent interactions made the findings meaningless. A few observed that the Houston Police Department was unique. Houston uses a community-based policing model in which officers are more familiar with the neighborhoods they patrol and work in partnership with community members to prevent and solve crimes. The department's racial and ethnic diversity mirrors that of the City of Houston and officers receive extensive training on community dynamics and problem-solving strategies.[72] According to the *Austin American-Statesman*, 20 percent of people shot by police in Texas were unarmed. Further, in 2015, 28 percent of those shot were black and another 28 percent were Hispanic. Effective September 1, 2015, all law enforcement agencies in Texas are required to submit reports to the Texas Attorney General's office on officer-involved shootings. Since the law passed, Houston has led the state in the number of shootings by police.

Misconduct by District Attorneys and Prosecutors

The main responsibility of a district attorney (DA) is to represent the State of Texas in criminal cases. The DA works with law enforcement officials to put together a criminal case that may be brought before criminal courts. Although most district attorneys are fair and effective, some unfortunately misuse their power. According to the *Texas Tribune*, there were at least 91 criminal cases between 2004 and 2012 in which "prosecutors committed misconduct, ranging from hiding evidence to making improper arguments to the jury."[73] In June 2018, Stacey Soule, a state prosecutor sat before the House Criminal Jurisprudence Committee and stated that the Court of Criminal Appeals had granted relief of only four cases of prosecutorial misconduct over the past year. The rate of official misconduct by law enforcement officials or prosecutors is highest in murder cases and child sexual assault cases. When misconduct occurs, prosecutors are rarely disciplined.[74]

The Code of Criminal Procedure requires that DAs not focus on convictions, but instead see that justice is done. At times, prosecutors are guilty of prosecutorial aggressiveness. In these instances, either law enforcement officials, including the DA, are blind to the possibility that the accused is innocent or use tactics that increase the likelihood of conviction. Ignoring the primary focus of achieving justice can have serious consequences for both the accused and the prosecutor.

In 1994, Anthony Graves was convicted of capital murder. Charles Sebesta, the DA, withheld exculpatory evidence and obtained false statements from witnesses in his efforts to send Graves to death row according to the U.S. Fifth

📋 STUDENTS IN ACTION

Correctional System Intern, Travis County Jail

Arisbeth Garcia, in her senior year at an Austin high school, wanted to intern for the Travis County jail. This internship was Arisbeth's opportunity to get a closer look at the criminal justice system and help decide her career path. As a correctional system intern, she shadowed a correctional officer. With 40 inmates in a "cube" area, Arisbeth was responsible for helping the officer with roll call, distributing lunches to prisoners, and generally helping monitor inmates.

Arisbeth learned a lot about the criminal justice system during that year as an intern. She noticed that many of the inmates were young. She's hoping to work with people, particularly youth, as a social worker to prevent them from becoming inmates.

Arisbeth's advice to students is to look for an internship in a field you are interested in; it's the best way to figure out what path you may want to pursue. She had a great experience interning with the Travis County jail and would recommend the internship program to any student planning a career in criminal justice. Arisbeth believes it's important to know different aspects of the system, whether one plans on becoming a social worker, correctional officer, or youth services provider. She wasn't sure what she wanted to do until she worked for the Travis County jail. While she learned a great deal from her internship, it also helped her know that she did not want to work in corrections directly. She believes internships are also good for helping students decide if a field of study is right for them. Students often spend years pursing a degree and later find they do not like the work in their field of study.

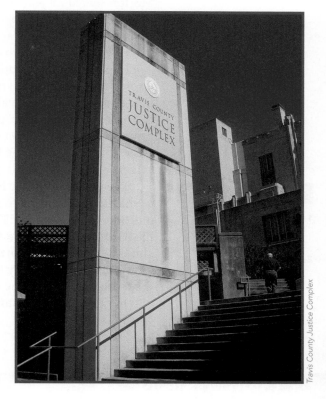

Travis County Justice Complex

Arisbeth's internship helped her when it was time to select a major in social work. It further helped her decide to use her education to find what would help youth stay out of prison.

Source: Interview conducted with Arisbeth Garcia on April 25, 2014.

— Competency Connection —
⚙ CRITICAL THINKING ⚙

What experiences have you had that have influenced your career decision?

Circuit Court of Appeals. Sebesta was disbarred for his conduct in February 2016.[75] Graves spent 12 years on death row for a crime he did not commit.

Another example of injustice by a DA can be observed in the case of Michael Morton. As a result of his failure to disclose exculpatory evidence to both the trial judge and Morton's attorneys, former Williamson County DA Ken Anderson was found in contempt of court. Further, the State of Texas brought a civil lawsuit accusing Anderson of official misconduct in the case. In November 2013, Anderson agreed to spend 10 days in jail, serve 500 community service hours, and pay a $500 fine to resolve the contempt case. In addition, his law license was revoked. Morton served 25 years for a crime he did not commit.

One case pending is that of Paul Storey. In 2006 during a robbery of a miniature golf course near Ft. Worth, Storey murdered the assistant manager. In 2008, he was sentenced to death. However, in 2017, the Texas Court of Criminal Appeals halted the execution because of a claim that the prosecutor had lied to jurors during the original trial. The prosecutor told the jury that the victim's family was for the death penalty, but the parents vigorously denied this statement; they strongly opposed the death penalty. As of May 2019, Storey remains on death row awaiting the decision of his sentence—will it be reduced to life without the possibility of parole? The Court of Criminal Appeals will review the claim and evidence to decide on the case.

The district attorney is a powerful figure in the criminal justice system. He or she has the authority to ask the courts, on behalf of the state, to take someone's life, liberty, or property. The opportunity to misuse that power was limited by the 83rd Legislature. The Michael Morton Law requires prosecutors to disclose almost all relevant information they have on a case to the defendant upon request. Any exculpatory information they have that might establish the defendant's innocence must be shared with the defendant as soon as the prosecutor obtains it, even if the information becomes available after the defendant is convicted.[76]

> ✔ **13.5 Learning Check**
>
> 1. True or False: DNA evidence is a panacea for exonerations.
> 2. What does the Code of Criminal Procedure require district attorneys to focus on?
>
> *Answers at the end of this chapter.*

CONCLUSION

The Texas criminal justice system is complex. Issues of fairness and efficiency remain paramount in ensuring that residents accept the legitimacy, or authority, of the criminal justice system. In recent years, the shift in Texas from punishment to rehabilitation has made the state a leader in reducing the number of prisoners and lowering the cost of the criminal justice system. The legal system, however, is not error-free. Issues of concern with criminal justice policies, the death penalty, rehabilitation, and fairness of the process need to be addressed. Only by understanding the system can citizens and lawmakers develop effective solutions.

CHAPTER SUMMARY

LO 13.1 Describe the different classifications of criminal offenses. Criminal law regulates many types of behavior. Less severe crimes are classified as Class A, B, or C misdemeanors and result in fines or detention in a county jail. More severe crimes include state-jail felonies; first-, second-, and third-degree felonies; and capital felonies. Policies have been adopted to deal with different criminal justice issues, such as substance abuse and hate crimes.

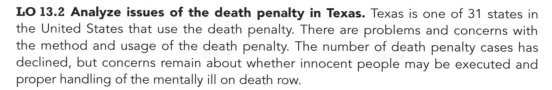

LO 13.2 Analyze issues of the death penalty in Texas. Texas is one of 31 states in the United States that use the death penalty. There are problems and concerns with the method and usage of the death penalty. The number of death penalty cases has declined, but concerns remain about whether innocent people may be executed and proper handling of the mentally ill on death row.

LO 13.3 Explain the role of Texas's jail and prison system in handling corrections and rehabilitations. Approximately 650,000 Texans were under the supervision of state and local judicial or correctional officers in 2014. Recent changes in state laws have emphasized the rehabilitative role of incarceration. The Texas Department of Criminal Justice has a four-pronged mission to handle issues of correction and rehabilitation: providing public safety, promoting positive behavioral changes, reintegrating offenders, and assisting crime victims.

LO 13.4 Compare the juvenile justice system to the adult correctional system. The juvenile justice system deals with correction and rehabilitation for juveniles (those between ages 10 and 16) and is administered through the Texas Family Code. Years of scandal at Texas Youth Commission (TYC) facilities resulted in abolition of the TYC and the Texas Juvenile Probation Commission. The Texas Juvenile Justice Department replaced those agencies in 2011.

LO 13.5 Evaluate the fairness of Texas's justice system. A number of issues remain problematic for the Texas justice system. These problems include overcrowding in county jails and mental illness in jails and prisons, effects of technological and scientific advances, the probable innocence of some inmates, possible racial and ethnic bias in the justice system, and misconduct among district attorneys.

KEY TERMS

adjudication hearing, p. 502
administrative segregation, p. 494
capital felony, p. 480
criminal justice system, p. 479

enhanced punishment, p. 480
exculpatory evidence, p. 478
exoneration, p. 506
graded penalties, p. 479

moratorium, p. 486
plea bargain, p. 483
recidivism, p. 495
Texas Penal Code, p. 479

LEARNING CHECK ANSWERS

 13.1 **1.** People who engage in organized criminal activity, repeat offenders, and those who commit hate crimes may receive enhanced punishment. This means the offender will be punished as though he or she had committed the next higher degree of felony.

2. True. Most low-level drug offenders are dealing with other issues like homelessness and poverty.

13.2   **1.** The Supreme Court ruled in *Furman v. Georgia* that the death penalty was unconstitutional because there was racial bias in its application.

2. According to the TDCJ, the average time spent on death row is nearly 11 years.

13.3   **1.** Self-discipline and education are the primary means of combating recidivism.

2. Private prisons are closing as the prison population decreases.

13.4   **1.** The legislature created the Texas Juvenile Justice Department (TJJD) to oversee Texas's juvenile system. TJJD replaced the abolished Texas Youth Commission (TYC) and the Texas Juvenile Probation Commission.

2. False. In general, young Texans at least 10 years of age but younger than 17 are treated as "delinquent children" when they commit crimes labeled felonies or misdemeanors if committed by adults.

13.5   **1.** False. Although DNA evidence has been used to obtain exonerations, fewer than 20 percent of the wrongfully imprisoned were released because of DNA evidence in 2015.

2. According to the Code of Criminal Procedure, a district attorney's primary responsibility is to seek justice, not convictions.

Glossary

Numbers in parentheses indicate the chapter in which the term is found.

adjudication hearing A trial in a juvenile court. (13)

administrative segregation Commonly referred to as solitary confinement, this practice isolates an inmate in a separate cell as punishment, typically for violent or disruptive behavior. (13)

adversarial Reporting featuring opposition and a combative style. Also called *attack journalism*. (6)

affirmative action Takes positive steps to attract women and members of racial and ethnic minority groups; may include using race in admission or hiring decisions. (12)

affirmative racial gerrymandering Drawing the boundaries of a district designed to favor representation by a member of a historical minority group (for example, African Americans) in a legislative chamber, city council, commissioners court, or other representative body. (5)

African American A racial classification applied to Americans of African ancestry. The term is commonly applied on the basis of skin color, omitting white Americans whose ancestors immigrated from Africa and including black Americans whose ancestors immigrated from the Caribbean, Latin America, and Europe. (1)

agenda setting Affecting the importance given issues by government and public leaders. (6)

alternative dispute resolution (ADR) Use of mediation, conciliation, or arbitration to resolve disputes among individuals without resorting to a regular court trial. (10)

Anglo As commonly used in Texas, the term is not restricted to persons of Anglo-Saxon lineage but includes those of European ancestry more generally. Traditionally, the term applies to all whites except Latinos. (1)

annex To make an outlying area part of a city. Now, this must be done by vote or petition of those to be annexed. (3)

appellate jurisdiction The power of a court to review and decide cases after they have been tried elsewhere. (10)

appointive power The authority to name a person to a government office. Most gubernatorial appointments require Senate approval by two-thirds of the members present. (9)

appointment-retention system A merit plan for judicial selection in which the governor makes an appointment to fill a court vacancy for an interim period, after which the judge must win a full term in an uncontested popular election. (10)

Asian American An ethnic classification for persons whose ancestry originates in the Far East, Southeast Asia, or the Indian subcontinent. (1)

at-large district Elected representatives who are elected from an entire entity, and not a single-member district. (5)

at-large election Members of a policymaking body, such as a city council, are elected on a citywide basis rather than from single-member districts. (3)

attack ad An advertisement meant as a personal attack on an opposing candidate or organization. (6)

attorney general The constitutional official elected to head the Office of the Attorney General, which represents the state government in lawsuits and provides legal advice to state and local officials. (9)

balanced budget A budget in which total revenues and expenditures are equal, producing no deficit. (11)

bicameral A legislature with two houses or chambers, such as Texas's House of Representatives and Senate. (8)

bifurcated A divided court system in which different courts handle civil and criminal cases. In Texas, the highest-level appeals courts are bifurcated. (10)

bill A proposed law or statute. (8)

biotechnology Also known as biotech, this is the use and/or manipulation of biological processes and microorganisms to perform industrial or manufacturing processes or create consumer goods. (1)

block grant Congressional grant of money that allows the state considerable flexibility in spending for a program, such as providing welfare services. (2)

blog A website or web page on which a writer or group of writers record opinions, information, and links to other sites on a regular basis. (6)

bond A mechanism by which governments borrow money. (3)

budget A plan of financial operation indicating how much revenue a government expects to collect during a period (usually one or two fiscal years) and how much spending is authorized for agencies and programs. (11)

budget execution The process whereby the governor and the Legislative Budget Board oversee (and, in some instances, modify) implementation of the spending plan authorized by the Texas legislature. (11)

budgetary power The governor is supposed to submit a state budget to the legislature at the beginning of each regular session. When an appropriation bill is enacted by the legislature and certified by the comptroller of public accounts, the governor may veto the whole document or individual items. (9)

bureaucrats Public employees. (9)

business organization An economic interest group, such as a trade association (for example, Texas Gaming Association), that lobbies for policies favoring business. (7)

Campaign Reform Act Enacted by the U.S. Congress and signed by President George W. Bush in 2002, this law restricts donations of soft money and hard money for election campaigns, but its effect has been limited by federal court decisions. (5)

canvass To scrutinize the results of an election and then confirm and certify the vote tally for each candidate. (5)

capital felony A crime punishable by death or life imprisonment without parole. (13)

Capitol press corps Reporters assigned to cover state-level news, commonly working in Austin. (6)

caucus A meeting at which members of a political party assemble to select delegates and make other policy recommendations at the precinct, county or state senatorial district, and state levels. (4)

Children's Health Insurance Program (CHIP) A program that provides medical insurance for minimal premiums to children from low-income families. (11)

chubbing A practice whereby representatives engage in lengthy debate for the purpose of using time and thus preventing a vote on a bill that they oppose. (8)

civic engagement Actions by citizens to address issues of public concern. (6)

civil law The body of law concerning disputes between individuals and other noncriminal matters, such as business contracts and personal injury. (10)

closed primary A primary in which voters must declare their support for a party before they are permitted to participate in the selection of its candidates. (5)

colonia A low-income community, typically located in South Texas and especially in counties bordering Mexico, that lacks running water, sewer lines, and other essential services. (3)

commission form A type of municipal government in which each elected commissioner is a member of the city's policymaking body and heads an administrative department (e.g., public safety with police and fire divisions). (3)

commissioner of agriculture The elected official, whose position is created by statute, who heads Texas's Department of Agriculture, which promotes the sale of agricultural commodities and regulates pesticides, aquaculture, egg quality, weights and measures, and grain warehouses. (9)

commissioner of education The official who heads the TEA. (9)

commissioner of insurance Appointed by the governor, the commissioner heads the Texas Department of Insurance, which is responsible for ensuring the industry's financial soundness, protecting policyholders, and overseeing insurance rates. (9)

commissioner of the General Land Office As head of Texas's General Land Office, this elected constitutional officer oversees the state's extensive landholdings and related mineral interests, especially oil and gas leasing, for the benefit of the Permanent School Fund. (9)

commissioners court A Texas county's policymaking body, with five members: the county judge, who presides, and four commissioners representing single-member precincts. (3)

commutation of sentence On the recommendation of the Board of Pardons and Paroles, the reduction of a sentence by the governor. (9)

companion bill Filed in one house but identical or similar to a bill filed in the other chamber; this simultaneous filing speeds passage of a bill because committee consideration may take place at the same time in both chambers. (8)

comptroller of public accounts An elected constitutional officer responsible for collecting taxes, keeping accounts, estimating revenue, and serving as treasurer for the state. (9)

concurrent jurisdiction The authority of more than one court to try a case. For example, a civil dispute involving more than $200 but less than $10,000 may be heard in either a justice of the peace court, a county court (or county-court-at-law), or a district court. (10)

concurrent resolution A resolution adopted by House and Senate majorities and then approved by the governor (for example, a request for action by Congress or authorization for someone to sue the state). (8)

conditional pardon An act of executive clemency, on recommendation of the Board of Pardons and Paroles, that releases a convicted person from the consequences of his or her crime but does not restore all rights, as in the case of a full pardon. (9)

conference committee A committee composed of representatives and senators appointed to reach agreement on a disputed bill and recommend changes acceptable to both chambers. (8)

conservative A person who advocates minimal intervention by government in economic matters and who gives a high priority to reducing taxes and curbing public spending, while supporting a more active role for government in traditional social issues. (4)

constable An official elected to assist the justice of the peace by serving papers and in some cases carrying out security and investigative responsibilities. (3)

constitutional amendment election Election, typically in November of an odd-numbered year, in which voters are asked to approve one or more proposed constitutional amendments. An amendment must receive a majority of the popular vote to be approved. (2)

constitutional amendment process Process for changing the Texas Constitution in which an amendment is proposed by a two-thirds vote of each chamber of the legislature and approved by a simple majority of voters in a general or special election. (2)

constitutional county court Trial courts created in the Texas Constitution for each of Texas's 254 counties. If a county has one or more county courts-at-law, constitutional county courts usually do not hear and decide cases. (10)

constitutional guarantees Rights and protections assured under the U.S. Constitution. For example, among the guarantees to members of the Union are protection against invasion and domestic uprisings, territorial integrity, a republican form of government, and representation by two senators and at least one representative for each state. (2)

constitutional revision Extensive or complete rewriting of a constitution. (2)

constitutional revision convention A body of delegates who meet to make extensive changes in a constitution or to draft a new constitution. (2)

contingency fee A lawyer's compensation paid from money recovered in a lawsuit or settlement. (10)

contingency rider Authorization for spending state money to finance provisions of a bill if the bill becomes law. (9)

council of governments (COGs) A regional planning body composed of governmental units (for example, cities, counties, special districts); functions include review and comment on proposals by local governments for obtaining state and federal grants. (3)

council-manager form A system of municipal government in which an elected city council hires a manager to coordinate budgetary matters and supervise administrative departments. (3)

county Texas is divided into 254 counties that serve as an administrative arm of the state and provide important services at the local level, especially in rural areas. (3)

county attorney An official elected to represent the county in civil and criminal cases, unless a resident district attorney performs some of these functions. (3)

county auditor A person appointed by the district judge or judges to check the financial books and records of other officials who handle county money. (3)

county chair Elected by county party members in the primaries, this key party official heads the county executive committee. (4)

county clerk An official elected to perform clerical chores for the county courts and commissioners court, keep public records, maintain vital statistics, and administer public elections, if the county does not have an administrator of elections. (3)

county convention A party meeting of delegates held in even-numbered years on a date and at a time and place prescribed by the party's state executive committee to adopt resolutions and to select delegates and alternates to the party's state convention. (4)

county court-at-law Trial courts created by statute to assume the responsibilities of constitutional county courts in counties with larger populations. (10)

county executive committee Composed of a party's precinct chairs and the elected county chair, the county executive committee conducts primaries and makes arrangements for holding county conventions. (4)

county judge An official popularly elected to preside over the county commissioners court, perform some administrative duties, and in smaller counties, hear civil and criminal cases. (3)

county sheriff A citizen popularly elected as the county's chief law enforcement officer; the sheriff is also responsible for maintaining the county jail. (3)

county tax assessor-collector This elected official no longer assesses property for taxation but does collect taxes and fees and commonly handles voter registration. (3)

county treasurer An elected official who receives and pays out county money as directed by the commissioners court. (3)

countywide tax appraisal district The district appraises all real estate and commercial property for taxation by units of local government within a county. (3)

courts of appeals Intermediate-level appellate courts that hear and decide appeals from trial court decisions. (10)

Court of Criminal Appeals The state's highest court with criminal jurisdiction. (10)

court of record A court that has a court reporter or electronic device to record testimony and proceedings. (10)

criminal justice system The system involves prosecution, defense, sentencing, and punishment of those suspected or convicted of committing a crime. (13)

criminal law The body of law concerning felony and misdemeanor offenses by individuals against other persons and property, or in violation of laws or ordinances. (10)

crossover voting A practice whereby a person participates in the primary of one party, then votes for one or more candidates of another party in the general election. (5)

cumulative voting When multiple seats are contested in an at-large election, voters cast one or more of the specified number of votes for one or more candidates in any combination. It is designed to increase representation of historically underrepresented ethnic minority groups. (3)

dealignment Occurs when citizens have no allegiance to a political party and become independent voters. (4)

decentralized government Decentralization is achieved by dividing power between national and state governments and separating legislative, executive, and judicial branches at both levels. (7)

dedicated fund A restricted state fund that has been identified to be spent for a designated purpose. If the fund is consolidated within the General Revenue Fund, it usually must be spent for its intended purpose. Some unappropriated amounts of dedicated funds, even those required to be used for a specific purpose, can be included in the calculations to balance the state budget. (11)

defamation, libel, and slander Communicating something untrue that damages a person's reputation (defamation) may be subject to a civil lawsuit. If the comment is written, it is called libel; if spoken, it is slander. (6)

defendant The person sued in a civil proceeding or prosecuted in a criminal proceeding. (10)

delegated powers Specific powers entrusted to the national government by Article I, Section 8 of the U.S. Constitution (for example, regulate interstate commerce, borrow money, and declare war). (2)

deregulation The elimination of government restrictions to allow free market competition to determine or limit the actions of individuals and corporations. (12)

Dillon's Rule A legal principle, still followed in the majority of states including Texas, that local governments have only those powers granted by their state government. (3)

direct primary A nominating system that allows voters to participate directly in the selection of candidates for public office. (5)

discovery Gathering information from the opposing party and witnesses in a lawsuit, including examination of relevant documents, obtaining written and oral answers to questions, inspecting property under the control of the other party, and similar activities. (10)

district attorney An official elected to serve one or more counties who prosecutes criminal cases, gives advisory opinions, and represents the county in civil cases. (3)

district clerk A citizen elected to maintain records for the district courts. (3)

district court State trial courts that hear and decide both civil and criminal cases. (10)

dual budgeting system The compilation of separate budgets by the legislative branch and the executive branch. (11)

early voting Conducted at the county courthouse and selected polling places before the designated primary, special, or general election day. (5)

economic interest group An interest group that exists primarily to promote its members' economic self-interest. Trade associations and labor unions are classified as economic interest groups because they are organized to promote policies that will maximize profits and wages. (7)

election judge Official appointed by the county commissioners court to administer an election in a voting precinct. (5)

electioneering Active campaigning by an interest group in support of, or in opposition to, a candidate; actions urging the public to act on an issue. (7)

elections administrator Person appointed to supervise voter registration and voting for a county. (5)

elite access The ability of the business elite to deal directly with high-ranking government administrators to avoid full compliance with regulations. (12)

eminent domain The power of the government to take private property for public uses, so long as just compensation is paid. (1)

enhanced punishment Additional penalties or prison time for those who engage in organized crime or hate crimes, and for repeat offenders. (13)

equal opportunity Ensures that policies and actions do not discriminate on factors, such as race, gender, ethnicity, religion, or national origin. (12)

exclusionary zoning The use of local government zoning ordinances to exclude certain groups of people from a given community. (1)

exclusive jurisdiction The authority of only one court to hear and decide a particular type of case. (10)

exculpatory evidence Evidence that helps a defendant and may exonerate the defendant in a criminal trial. (13)

executive commissioner of the Health and Human Services Commission Appointed by the governor with Senate approval, the executive commissioner administers the HHSC, develops policies, and makes rules. (9)

executive order The governor issues executive orders to set policy within the executive branch and to create task forces, councils, and other bodies. (9)

exoneration The state's officially declaring the innocence of someone who has been convicted of a crime. (13)

extraterritorial jurisdiction (ETJ) The limited authority a city has outside its boundaries. The larger the city's population size, the larger the reach of its ETJ. (3)

federal grants-in-aid Money appropriated by the U.S. Congress to help states and local governments provide needed facilities and services. (2)

fee A charge imposed by an agency upon those subject to its regulation. (11)

felony A serious crime punished by fine and prison confinement. (10)

filibustering A delaying tactic whereby a senator may speak, and thus hold the Senate floor, for as long as physical endurance permits, unless action is taken to end the filibuster. (8)

fiscal policy Public policy that concerns taxing, government spending, public debt, and management of government money. (11)

fiscal year A one-year budget period. For Texas's state government, each fiscal year begins on September 1 and ends on August 31 of the following year. (11)

framing Providing meaning or defining the central theme of an issue. (6)

franchise tax A tax levied on the annual receipts of businesses that are organized to limit the personal liability of owners for the privilege of conducting business in the state. (11)

full faith and credit clause Most government actions of another state must be officially recognized by public officials in Texas. (2)

full pardon An act of executive clemency, on recommendation of the Board of Pardons and Paroles, that releases a convicted person from all consequences of a criminal act and restores the same rights enjoyed by others who have not been convicted of a crime. (9)

general election Held in November of even-numbered years to elect county, state, and federal officials from among candidates nominated in primaries or (for minor parties) in nominating conventions. (5)

general obligation bond Amount borrowed by the state that is repaid from the General Revenue Fund. (11)

General Revenue Fund An unrestricted state fund that is available for general appropriations. (11)

general sales tax Texas's largest source of tax revenue, applied at the rate of 6.25 percent to the sale price of tangible personal property and "the storage, use, or other consumption of tangible personal property purchased, leased, or rented." (11)

general-law city A municipality with a charter prescribed by the legislature. (3)

gentrification A relocation of middle-class or affluent people into deteriorating urban areas, often displacing low-income residents. (1)

gerrymandering Drawing the boundaries of a district, such as a state senatorial or representative district, to include or exclude certain groups of voters and thus affect election outcomes. (5, 8)

ghost voting A prohibited practice whereby one representative presses the voting button of another House member who is absent. (8)

government A public institution with authority to formulate, adopt, implement, and enforce public policies for a society. (1)

governor's office The administrative organization through which the governor of Texas makes appointments, prepares a biennial budget recommendation, administers federal and state grants for crime prevention and law enforcement, and confers full and conditional pardons on recommendation of the Board of Pardons and Paroles. (9)

graded penalties Depending on the nature of the crime, noncapital felonies are graded as first degree, second degree, third degree, and state jail; misdemeanors are graded as A, B, and C. (13)

grand jury Composed of 12 persons (and four alternates) with the qualifications of trial jurors, a grand jury serves three months while it determines whether sufficient evidence exists to indict persons accused of committing crimes. (10)

grandfather clause Although not used in Texas, the law exempted people from educational, property, or tax requirements for voting if they were qualified to vote before 1867 or were descendants of such persons. (5)

grant-in-aid Money, goods, or services given by one government to another (for example, federal grants-in-aid to states for financing public assistance programs for poor Texans). (11)

grassroots Local (as in grassroots government or grassroots politics). (3)

group leadership Individuals who guide the decisions of interest groups. Leaders of groups tend to have financial resources that permit them to contribute money and devote time to group affairs. (7)

hard money Campaign money donated directly to candidates or political parties and restricted in amount by federal law. (5)

hard news News that focuses on the facts, provides more depth, and commonly has implications for public policy. (6)

home-rule city A municipality with a locally drafted charter. (3)

homogenization of news Making news uniform regardless of differing locations and cultures. (6)

horserace journalism News that focuses on who is ahead in the race (poll results and public perceptions) rather than policy differences. (6)

hydraulic fracturing Also known as "fracking," this method of extracting oil and natural gas involves forcing open fissures in subterranean rocks by introducing liquid at high pressure. (1)

impeach Process in which the Texas House of Representatives, by a simple majority vote, initiates action (brings charges) leading to possible removal of certain judicial and executive officials (both elected and appointed) by the Senate. (8)

implied powers Powers inferred by the constitutional authority of the U.S. Congress "to make all laws which shall be necessary and proper for carrying into execution the foregoing [delegated] powers, and all other powers vested by this Constitution in the government of the United States, or in any department or officer thereof." (2)

independent (candidate) A candidate who runs in a general election without party endorsement or selection. (4, 5)

independent expenditures Expenditures that pay for political campaign communications and expressly advocate the nomination, election, or defeat of a clearly identified candidate but are not given to, or made at the request of, the candidate's campaign. (5)

independent school district (ISD) Created by the legislature, an independent school district raises tax revenue to support its public schools. Voters within the district elect a board that hires a superintendent, determines salary schedules, selects textbooks, and sets the district's property tax rate. (3)

initiative A citizen-drafted measure proposed by a specific number or percentage of qualified voters that becomes law if approved by popular vote. In Texas, this process occurs only at the local level in home rule cities, not at the state level. (2, 3)

interest group An organization that seeks to influence government officials and their policies on behalf of members sharing common views and objectives (for example, labor unions or trade associations). (7)

interest group technique An action (such as lobbying, personal communication, giving favors and gifts, grassroots activities, electioneering, campaign financing by political action committees, and, in extreme instances, bribery and other unethical practices) intended to influence government decisions. (7)

intergovernmental relations Relationships between and among different governments that are on the same or different levels. (3)

interim committee A House or Senate committee appointed by the Speaker or lieutenant governor to study an important policy issue between regular sessions. (8)

Jim Crow laws Discriminatory laws that segregated African Americans and denied them access to public services for many decades after the Civil War. (1)

joint resolution A resolution that must pass by a majority vote in each house when used to ratify an amendment to the U.S. Constitution or to request a constitutional convention to propose amendments to the U.S. Constitution. As a proposal for an amendment to the Texas Constitution, a joint resolution requires a two-thirds majority vote in each house. (8)

judgment A judge's written opinion based on a verdict. (10)

jungle primary A nominating process in which voters indicate their preferences by using a single ballot on which are printed the names and respective party labels of all persons seeking nomination. A candidate who receives more than 50 percent of the vote is elected; otherwise, a runoff between the top two candidates must be held. (5)

junior college or community college district Establishes one or more two-year colleges that offer both academic and vocational programs. (3)

jurisdiction A court's authority to hear and decide a particular case. (10)

justice of the peace A judge elected from a justice of the peace precinct who handles minor civil and criminal cases, including small claims court. (3, 10)

labor organization A union that supports public policies designed to increase wages, obtain adequate health insurance coverage, provide unemployment insurance, promote safe working conditions, and otherwise protect the interests of workers. (7)

Latino An ethnic classification of Americans of Latin American origin. When applied to females, the term is Latina. We will use this term throughout the book in addition to the term "Hispanic," which refers to people who trace their ancestry to Spain and other Spanish-speaking countries. (1)

Legislative Budget Board (LBB) A 10-member body co-chaired by the lieutenant governor and the Speaker of the House. This board and its staff prepare a biennial current services budget. In addition, they assist with the preparation of a general appropriation bill at the beginning of a regular legislative session. If requested, staff members prepare fiscal notes that assess the economic impact of a proposed bill or resolution. (11)

legislative caucus An organization of legislators who seek to maximize their influence over issues in which they have a special interest. (8)

legislative power A power of the governor exercised through messages delivered to the Texas legislature, vetoes of bills and concurrent resolutions, and calls for special legislative sessions. (9)

liberal A person who advocates government support in social and economic matters and who favors political reforms that extend democracy, achieve a more equitable distribution of wealth, and protect individual freedoms and rights. Liberals tend to favor less government regulation in the private lives of individuals. (4)

libertarian A person who advocates minimal government intervention in both economic and social issues. (4)

lieutenant governor Popularly elected constitutional official who serves as president of the Senate and is first in the line of succession if the office of governor becomes vacant before the end of a term. (9)

line-item veto Action by the governor to eliminate an individual budget item while permitting enactment of other parts of an appropriation bill. (9)

literacy tests Although not used in Texas as a prerequisite for voter registration, the test was designed and administered in ways intended to prevent African Americans and Latinos from voting. (5)

lobbying Communicating with legislators or other government officials for the purpose of influencing decision makers. (7)

local government Counties, municipalities, school districts, and other special districts that provide a range of services, including rural roads, city streets, public education, and protection of persons and property. (2)

maquiladoras Industrial plants on the Mexican side of the border which are partnered with American companies. Such plants typically use low-cost labor to assemble imported parts for a wide range of consumer goods and then export these goods back to the United States or to other countries. (1)

martial law Temporary rule by military authorities when civil authorities are unable to handle a riot or other civil disorder. (9)

media Major means of mass communication. (6)

Medicaid Funded in large part by federal grants and in part by state appropriations, Medicaid is administered by the state. It provides medical care for poor persons. (12)

Medicare Funded entirely by the federal government and administered by the U.S. Department of Health and Human Services, Medicare primarily provides medical assistance to qualified applicants age 65 and older. (12)

merit system Hiring, promoting, and firing on the basis of objective criteria, such as tests, degrees, experience, and performance. (9)

message power The governor's effectiveness in communicating with legislators via the State of the State address at the commencement of a legislative session and other gubernatorial messages delivered in person or in writing. (9)

metro government Consolidation of units of local government within an urban area under a single authority. (3)

middle class Social scientists identify the middle class as those people with white-collar occupations (such as professionals and small business owners). (3)

misdemeanor Classified as A, B, or C, a misdemeanor may be punished by fine and/or jail sentence. (10)

Missouri Plan A judicial selection process in which a commission recommends a panel of names to the governor, who appoints a judge for one year or so before voters determine whether the appointee will be retained for a full term. (10)

moratorium The delay or suspension of an activity or law. A moratorium may be imposed when something is seen as needing improvement. (13)

motor-voter law Legislation requiring certain government offices (for example, motor vehicle licensing agencies) to offer voter registration applications to clients. (5)

multimember district A district in which all voters participate in the election of two or more representatives to a policymaking body, such as a state House or state Senate. (8)

municipal (city) government A local government for an incorporated community established by law as a city. (3)

municipal court City-run court with jurisdiction primarily over Class C misdemeanors committed within a city's boundaries. (10)

national supremacy clause Article VI of the U.S. Constitution states, "This Constitution, and the laws of the United States which shall be made in pursuance thereof; and all treaties made, or which shall be made, under the authority of the United States, shall be the supreme law of the land." (2)

Native American A term commonly used for those whose ancestors were living in the Americas before the arrival of Europeans and Africans. Another commonly used term in the United States is "American Indian." (1)

neoliberal A political ideology that advocates less government regulation of business and supports governmental involvement in social programs. (4)

net neutrality A legal principle that Internet service providers and government officials should treat all data on the Internet equally, not discriminating or charging differentially and not blocking content they do not like. (6)

news website An Internet site that provides news. These sites are often affiliated with a newspaper or television station, but increasingly, many are independent. (6)

niche journalism (narrowcasting) A news medium focusing on a narrow audience defined by concern about a particular topic or area. (6)

noneducation special districts Special districts, other than school districts or community college districts, such as fire prevention or municipal utility districts, that are units of local government and may cover part of a county, a whole county, or areas in two or more counties. (3)

nonpartisan election An election in which candidates are not identified on the ballot by party label. (3)

North American Free Trade Agreement (NAFTA) An agreement among Mexico, the United States, and Canada designed to expand trade by eliminating tariffs among the three nations. (1)

off-year or midterm election A general election held in the even-numbered year following a presidential election. (5)

open meetings Meetings of public entities that are required by law to be open to the public. (6)

open primary A primary in which voters are not required to declare party affiliation. (5)

open records Government documents and records that are required by law to be available to the public. (6)

ordinance A local law enacted by a city council or approved by popular vote in a referendum or initiative election. (3)

organizational pattern The structure of a special interest group. Some interest groups have a decentralized pattern of organization. Others are centralized. (7)

original jurisdiction The power of a court to hear and decide a case first. (10)

oversight A legislative function that requires reports from state agencies concerning their operations; the state auditor provides information on agencies' use of state funds. (8)

parliamentarian An expert on rules of order who sits at the left of the presiding officer in the House or Senate and provides advice on procedural questions. (8)

parole Supervised release from prison before completion of a sentence, on condition of good behavior. (9)

patron system A type of boss rule that has dominated areas of South Texas and Mexico. (1)

patronage system Hiring friends and supporters of elected officials as government employees without regard to their abilities. (9)

payroll tax An employer-paid tax levied against a portion of the wages and salaries of workers to provide funds for payment of unemployment insurance benefits in the event employees lose their jobs. (11)

permanent party organization In Texas, the precinct chairs, county and senatorial district executive committees, and the state executive committee form the permanent organization of a political party. (4)

Permian Basin Also known as the West Texas Basin, this sedimentary basin in western Texas and southeastern New Mexico is known for its rich deposits of petroleum and natural gas. (1)

petit jury A trial jury of 6 or 12 members. (10)

plaintiff The injured party who initiates a civil suit or the state in a criminal proceeding. (10)

platform A document that sets forth a political party's position on public policy issues, such as income tax, school vouchers, or the environment. (4)

plea bargain An agreement between the prosecutor and the defendant in a criminal case in which the defendant agrees to plead guilty to a specific charge and in return gets certain concessions from the prosecutor, such as a reduction in charges, a shortened prison term, or probation. (13)

plural executive The governor, elected department heads, and the secretary of state, as provided by the Texas Constitution and statutes. (9)

political action committee (PAC) An organization created to collect and distribute contributions to political campaigns. (5)

political culture Widely shared attitudes, habits, and general behavior patterns that develop over time and affect the political life of a state or region. (1)

political party An organization with the purpose of controlling government by recruiting, nominating, and electing candidates to public office. People have different beliefs and values about the role of government and the nature of society. Those who share the same beliefs and values often identify with a specific political party. (4)

politics The process of policymaking that involves conflict and cooperation between political parties and other groups that seek to elect government officials or to influence those officials when they make public policy. (1)

poll tax A tax levied in Texas from 1902 until voters amended the Texas Constitution in 1966 to eliminate it; failure to pay the annual tax (usually $1.75) made a citizen ineligible to vote in party primaries or in special and general elections. (5)

pork-barrel politics A legislator's tactic to obtain funding for a pet project, usually designed to be of special benefit for the legislator's district. (9)

postadjournment veto Rejection by the governor of a pending bill or concurrent resolution during the 20 days after a legislative session ends. (9)

power group An effective interest group strongly linked with legislators and bureaucrats for the purpose of influencing decision making and having a continuing presence in Austin as a repeat player from session to session. (7)

precinct chair The party official responsible for the interests and activities of a political party in a voting district; typical duties include encouraging voter registration, distributing campaign literature, operating phone banks, and getting out the vote on Election Day. (4)

precinct convention A convention, held at the voting precinct level, to adopt resolutions and to select delegates and alternates to the party's county or senatorial district convention. (4)

president of the Senate Title of the lieutenant governor in his or her role as presiding officer for the Texas Senate. (8)

presidential preference primary A primary in which the voters indicate their preference for a person seeking nomination as the party's presidential candidate. (4)

primary An election conducted within the party to nominate candidates who will run for public office in a subsequent general election. (5)

priming The news media's indicating how important an issue is or which part of a situation is most important. (6)

prior restraint Suppression of material before it is published, commonly called censorship. (6)

privatization Transfer of government services or assets to the private sector. Commonly, assets are sold and services contracted out. (12)

privileges and immunities Article IV of the U.S. Constitution guarantees that "citizens of each state shall be entitled to the privileges and immunities of citizens of the several states." According to the U.S. Supreme Court, this provision means that citizens are guaranteed protection by government, enjoyment of life and liberty, the right to acquire and possess property, the right to leave and enter any state, and the right to use state courts. (2)

probate Proceedings that involve the estates of decedents. Courts with probate jurisdiction (county courts, county courts-at-law, and probate courts) also handle guardianship and mental competency matters. (10)

probate court Statutory courts that only handle administration of decedent's estates, mental competency proceedings, and guardianship proceedings. (10)

procedural committee These permanent House committees (such as the Calendars Committee and House Administration Committee) consider bills and resolutions relating primarily to procedural legislative matters. (8)

proclamation A governor's official public announcement (such as calling a special election or declaring a disaster area). (9)

professional group An organization of physicians, lawyers, accountants, or other professional people that lobbies for policies beneficial to members. (7)

professionalism Reporting that is objective, neutral, and accurate. (6)

progressive Favoring and working for progress in conditions facing the majority of society or in government. (1)

progressive tax A tax in which the effective tax rate increases as the tax base (such as individual income or corporate profits) increases. (11)

property tax A tax that property owners pay according to the value of real estate and other tangible property. At the local level, property owners pay this tax to the city, the county, the school district, and often other special districts. (3)

public administration The implementation of public policy by government employees. (9)

public interest group An organization claiming to represent a broad public interest (such as environmental, consumer, political participation, or public morality) rather than a narrow private interest. (7)

public officer and employee group An organization of city managers, county judges, law enforcement or other public employees or officials that lobbies for public policies that protect group interests. (7)

public policy What government does to or for its citizens to meet a public need or goal as determined by a legislative body or other authorized officials. (1, 12)

Public Utility Commission of Texas (PUC) A three-member appointed body with regulatory power over electric and telephone companies. (9)

racial and ethnic groups Organizations that seek to influence government decisions that affect a particular racial or ethnic group, such as the National Association for the Advancement of Colored People (NAACP) and the League of United Latin American Citizens (LULAC), which seek to influence government decisions affecting African Americans and Latinos, respectively. (7)

racial covenants Agreements written into real estate documents by property owners, subdivision developers, or real estate operators in a given neighborhood, binding property owners not to sell, lease, or rent property to specified groups because of race, creed, or color. (1)

Railroad Commission of Texas (RRC) A popularly elected three-member commission primarily engaged in regulating natural gas and petroleum production. (9)

Rainy Day Fund A fund used like a savings account for stabilizing state finance and helping the state meet economic emergencies when revenue is insufficient to cover state-supported programs. (11)

realignment Occurs when there is a major change in the support of political parties. (4)

recall A process for removing elected officials through a popular vote. In Texas, this power is available only for home-rule cities. (3)

recess appointment An appointment made by the governor when the Texas legislature is not in session. (9)

recidivism Criminal behavior that results in reincarceration after a person has been released from confinement for a prior offense. (13)

redistricting Redrawing of boundaries after the federal decennial census to create single-member districts with approximately equal population (for example, legislative, congressional, and State Board of Education districts in Texas). Local governments must also redistrict for some positions. Congressional districts must be as close to equal population as possible. State and local districts may vary in population by 5 percent or so. (3, 8)

redlining A discriminatory rating system used by federal agencies to evaluate the risks associated with loans made to borrowers in specific urban neighborhoods. Today, the term also refers to the same practice among private businesses like banks and real estate companies. (1)

referendum A process by which issues are referred to the voters to accept or reject. Voters may also petition for a vote to repeal an existing ordinance. In Texas, this process occurs at the local level in home-rule cities. At the state level, state constitutional amendments and bonds secured by taxes must be approved by the voters. (3)

regressive tax A tax in which the effective tax rate decreases as the tax base (such as individual income or corporate profits) increases. (11)

regular session A session of the Texas legislature that is constitutionally mandated and begins on the second Tuesday in January of odd-numbered years and lasts for a maximum of 140 days. (8)

religion-based group An interest group, such as the Texas Freedom Network, that lobbies for policies to promote its religious interests. (7)

removal power Authority to remove an official from office. In Texas, the governor's removal power is limited to staff members, some agency heads, and his or her appointees with the consent of the Senate. (9)

reprieve An act of executive clemency that temporarily suspends execution of a sentence. (9)

reserved powers Reserved powers are derived from the Tenth Amendment of the U.S. Constitution. Although not spelled out in the U.S. Constitution, these reserved powers to the states include police power, taxing power, proprietary power, and power of eminent domain. (2)

revenue bond Amount borrowed by the state that is repaid from a specific revenue source. (11)

right of association The U.S. Supreme Court has ruled that this right is part of the right of assembly guaranteed by the First Amendment to the U.S. Constitution and that it protects the right of people to organize into groups for political purposes. (7)

right-to-work laws Laws that limit the power of workers to bargain collectively and form and operate labor unions, increasing the power of employers relative to their employees. (1)

"Robin Hood" plan A plan for equalizing financial support for school districts by transferring tax money from rich districts to poor districts. (11)

rule of capture A rule of law that a landowner can capture and own the natural resources extracted from the land. Thus, groundwater belongs to the landowner. (12)

runoff primary Held after the first primary to allow party members to choose a candidate from the first primary's top two vote-getters if no candidate received a majority vote. (5)

secretary of state The state's chief elections officer, with other administrative duties, who is appointed by the governor for a term concurrent with that of the governor. (9)

select committee This committee, created independently by the House Speaker or the lieutenant governor, may consider legislation that crosses committee jurisdictional lines or may conduct special studies. (8)

selective sales tax A tax charged on specific products and services. (11)

senatorial courtesy Before making an appointment, the governor is expected to obtain approval from the state senator in whose district the prospective appointee resides; failure to obtain such approval will probably cause the Senate to "bust" the appointee. (8)

senatorial district convention Held in even-numbered years on a date and at a time and place prescribed by the party's state executive committee in counties that have more than one state senatorial district. Participants select delegates and alternates to the party's state convention. (4)

senatorial district executive committee Composed of a party's precinct chairs who reside within a senatorial district, the senatorial district executive committee fills districtwide vacancies in nominations for office and performs other statutory and party duties. (4)

separation of powers The assignment of lawmaking, law-enforcing, and law-interpreting functions to separate branches of government. (2)

service sector Businesses that provide services, such as finance, health care, food service, data processing, or consulting. (11)

severance tax An excise tax levied on a natural resource (such as oil or natural gas) when it is severed (removed) from the earth. (11)

shield law A law protecting journalists from having to reveal confidential sources to police or in court. (6)

simple resolution A resolution that requires action by one legislative chamber only and is not acted on by the governor. (8)

sin tax A selective sales tax on items such as cigarettes, other forms of tobacco, alcoholic beverages, and admission to sex-oriented businesses. (11)

single-member district An area that elects only one representative to a policymaking body, such as a state House, state Senate, or U.S. Congress. (8)

single-member district election Voters in an area (commonly called a district, ward, or precinct) elect one representative to serve on a policymaking body (e.g., city council, county commissioners court, state House and Senate). (3)

SLAPP Strategic lawsuits against public participation are suits filed primarily to silence criticism and negative public discussion. (6)

social interest group A group concerned primarily with social issues, including organizations devoted to civil rights, racial and ethnic matters, religion, and public interest protection. (7)

social media Websites and computer applications that allow users to engage in social networking and create online communities. Social media provide platforms for sharing information and ideas through discussion forums, videos, photos, documents, audio clips, and the like. (1, 6)

soft money Unregulated political donations made to national political parties or independent expenditures on behalf of a candidate that is used to fund election activities but are not directly donated to a political campaign. (5)

soft news News that is more entertaining, sensationalized, covers only the surface, and has little connection to public policy. (6)

sound bite A brief statement intended to be easily quotable by the news media that is designed to convey a specific message that a campaign wishes to make. (5)

Speaker of the House The state representative elected by House members to serve as the presiding officer for that chamber. (8)

special district A unit of local government that performs a particular service, such as providing schools, hospitals, or housing, for a particular geographic area. (3)

special election An election called by the governor to fill a vacancy (for example, U.S. congressional or state legislative office) or to vote on a proposed state constitutional amendment. (5)

special issues Questions a judge gives a trial jury to answer to establish the facts in a civil case. (10)

special session A legislative session called by the governor and limited to no more than 30 days. (8)

specialty courts Courts designed to deal with particular types of problems, such as drug-related offenses or specific populations, such as veterans or foster children. (10)

standing committee A permanent Senate committee whose members are appointed by the lieutenant governor for the purpose of considering proposed bills and resolutions before possible floor debate and voting by senators. (8)

State Board of Education (SBOE) A popularly elected 15-member body with limited authority over Texas's K-12 education system. (9)

state convention Convenes every even-numbered year to make rules for a political party, adopt a party platform and resolutions, and select members of the state executive committee; in a presidential election year, it elects delegates to the national convention, names members to serve on the national committee, and elects potential electors to vote if the party's presidential candidate receives a plurality of the popular vote in the general election. (4)

state executive committee Composed of a chair, vice chair, and two members from each senatorial district, this body is part of a party's permanent organization. (4)

State of Texas Assessment of Academic Readiness (STAAR) A state program of end-of-course and other examinations begun in 2012. (12)

statutory county court Court created by the legislature at the request of a county; may have civil or criminal jurisdiction or both, depending on the legislation creating it. (3)

straight-ticket voting Voting for all the candidates of one party. (4)

stratarchy A political system in which power is diffused among and within levels of party organization. (4)

strong mayor-council form A type of municipal government with a separately elected legislative body (council) and an executive head (mayor) elected in a citywide election with veto, appointment, and removal powers. (3)

substantive committee With members appointed by the House Speaker, this permanent committee considers bills and resolutions related to the subject identified by its name (such as, the House Agriculture and Livestock Committee) and may recommend passage of proposed legislation to the appropriate calendars committee. (8)

suffrage The right to vote. (2)

sunset review process During a cycle of 12 years, each state agency is studied at least once to see if it is needed and efficient, and then the legislature decides whether to abolish, merge, reorganize, or retain that agency. (9)

super PAC Independent expenditure-only committees that may raise unlimited sums of money from corporations, unions, nonprofit organizations, and individuals. (5)

superdelegate An unpledged party official or elected official who serves as a delegate to a party's national convention. (4)

Supplemental Nutritional Assistance Program (SNAP) Joint federal-state program administered by the state to provide food to low-income people. (12)

Supreme Court of Texas State's highest court with civil jurisdiction. (10)

tax A mandatory assessment exacted by a government for a public purpose. (11)

tax increment reinvestment zone (TIRZ) Also called a Tax Increment Finance District (TIF). An area in which municipal tax incentives are offered to encourage businesses to locate in and contribute to the development of a blighted urban area. Commercial and residential property taxes may be frozen. (3)

Temporary Assistance for Needy Families (TANF) Provides financial assistance to the very poor in an attempt to help them move from welfare to the workforce. (12)

temporary party organization Primaries and conventions that function briefly to nominate candidates, pass resolutions, adopt a party platform, and select delegates to party conventions at higher levels. (4)

Tenth Amendment The Tenth Amendment to the U.S. Constitution declares that "the powers not delegated by the Constitution, nor prohibited by it to the States, are reserved to the States, respectively, or to the people." (2)

term limit A restriction on the number of terms officials can serve in a public office. (3)

Texas Bill of Rights Article I of the Texas Constitution guarantees protections for people and their property against arbitrary actions by state and local governments. Protected rights include freedom of speech, press, religion, assembly, and petition. (2)

Texas Commission on Environmental Quality (TCEQ) The state agency that coordinates Texas's environmental regulation efforts. (9)

Texas Constitution of 1876 The lengthy, much-amended state constitution, a product of the post-Reconstruction era that remains in effect today. (2)

Texas Department of Transportation (TxDOT) Headed by a five-member appointed commission, the department maintains almost 80,000 miles of roads and highways and promotes highway safety. (9)

Texas Education Agency (TEA) Administers the state's public school system of more than 1,200 school districts and charter schools. (9)

Texas Election Code The body of state law concerning parties, primaries, and elections. (5)

Texas Equal Legal Rights Amendment (ELRA) Added to Article I, Section 3, of the Texas Constitution, it guarantees that "equality under the law shall not be denied or abridged because of sex, race, color, creed, or national origin." (2)

Texas Essential Knowledge and Skills (TEKS) A core curriculum (a set of courses and knowledge) setting out what students should learn. (12)

Texas Ethics Commission A state agency that enforces state standards for lobbyists and public officials, including registration of lobbyists and reporting of political campaign contributions. (5, 7)

Texas Grange A farmers' organization, also known as the Patrons of Husbandry, committed to low levels of government spending and limited governmental powers; a major influence on the Constitution of 1876. (2)

TEXAS Grants Program "Toward Excellence, Access, and Success" is a college financial assistance program that provides funding for qualifying students. (11)

Texas Higher Education Coordinating Board (THECB) An agency that provides some coordination for the state's public community colleges and universities. (9)

Texas Parks and Wildlife Department Texas agency that runs state parks and regulates hunting, fishing, and boating. (9)

Texas Penal Code The body of Texas law covering crimes, penalties, and correctional measures. (13)

Texas Workforce Commission (TWC) A state agency headed by three salaried commissioners that oversees job training and unemployment compensation programs. (9)

third party A party other than the Democratic Party or the Republican Party. Sometimes called a "minor party" because of limited membership and voter support. (4)

three-fifths rule A procedural device to control bringing bills to the Senate floor for debate. (8)

top 10 percent rule Texas law gives automatic admission into any Texas public college or university to those graduating in the top 10 percent of their Texas high school class, with limitations for the University of Texas at Austin. (12)

tort An injury to a person or an individual's property resulting from the wrongful act of another. (10)

undocumented immigrant A person who enters the United States in violation of federal immigration law and thus lacks proper documentation and identification. (1)

unicameral A one-house legislature, such as the Nebraska legislature. (8)

universal suffrage Voting is open for virtually all persons 18 years of age or older. (5)

urban renewal The relocation of businesses and people, the demolition of structures, and the use of eminent domain to take private property for development projects. (1)

venire A panel of prospective jurors drawn by random selection. These prospective jurors are called veniremen. (10)

verdict A jury's or judge's decision about a court case. (10)

veto power Authority of the governor to reject a bill or concurrent resolution passed by the legislature. (9)

voir dire Courtroom procedure in which attorneys question prospective jurors to identify any who cannot be fair and impartial. (10)

voter turnout The percentage of voters (either voting age population, voting eligible population, or registered voters) casting a ballot in an election. (5)

voting center A countywide voting system that allows voters to vote, after being electronically verified, at any voting center in a county. (5)

voting precinct The basic geographic area for conducting primaries and elections; Texas is divided into more than 8,500 voting precincts. (5)

weak mayor-council form A type of municipal government with a separately elected mayor and council, but the mayor shares appointive and removal powers with the council, which can override the mayor's veto. (3)

white primary A nominating system designed to prevent African Americans and some Latinos from participating in Democratic primaries from 1923 to 1944. (5)

women's organization A women's group, such as the League of Women Voters, that engages in lobbying and educational activities to promote greater political participation by women and others. (7)

workers' compensation A system of insurance that pays benefits to workers injured or made ill by their work. (12)

working class Social scientists identify the working class as those people with blue-collar (manual) occupations. (3)

yellow journalism Journalism that is based on sensationalism and exaggeration. (6)

Endnotes

Chapter 1

1. For a critical view of Texas's influence nationwide, see Gail Collins, *As Texas Goes ... How the Lone Star State Hijacked the American Agenda* (New York: Liveright, 2012).

2. For census information, see "State and County QuickFacts," *U.S. Department of Commerce, Census Bureau,* July 1, 2018, https://www.census.gov/quickfacts/tx.

3. Daniel Elazar, *American Federalism: A View from the States,* 3rd ed. (New York: Harper & Row, 1984), 109–149. For a different view of political culture, see Dante Chinni and James Gimpel, *Our Patchwork Nation: The Surprising Truth about the "Real" America* (New York: Penguin Group, 2010) and its website at http://www.patchworknation.org. This view identifies 12 political cultures nationally, of which nine are present in Texas.

4. David Cullen and Kyle G. Wilkison, *The Texas Left: The Radical Roots of Lone Star Liberalism* (College Station: Texas A&M University Press, 2010).

5. See Mike Kingston, "A Brief Sketch of Texas History," in *Texas Almanac 2018–2019,* ed. Robert Plocheck (Austin, TX: Texas State Historical Association, 2016), 28–41. For a description of events that led to Texas's war for independence from Mexico, see James Donovan, *The Blood of Heroes: The 13-Day Struggle for the Alamo—and the Sacrifice that Forged a Nation* (New York: Little Brown, 2012).

6. For survey data on the views of Texans regarding the media and society, see "Texas Media & Society Survey: Topline Results 2018," *Annette Strauss Institute for Civic Life Moody College of Communication, University of Texas at Austin,* https://moody.utexas.edu/sites/default/files/2018%20Topline%20Results.pdf.

7. Kingston, "A Brief Sketch of Texas History," 43; and Rupert N. Richardson, Adrian Anderson, Cary D. Wintz, and Ernest Wallace, *Texas: The Lone Star State,* 10th ed. (Upper Saddle River, NJ: Prentice Hall, 2010), 151–154.

8. For an interactive map of Confederate symbols around the nation, see "Whose Heritage: A Report on Public Symbols of the Confederacy," *Southern Poverty Law Center,* https://www.splcenter.org/data-projects/whose-heritage.

9. Cal Jillson, *Lone Star Tarnished: A Critical Look at Texas Politics and Public Policy* (New York: Routledge, 2012), 154.

10. For an in-depth look at the Comanches and their role in Texas history, see S. C. Gwynne, *Empire of the Summer Moon: Quanah Parker and the Rise and Fall of the Comanches, the Most Powerful Indian Tribe in American History* (New York: Scribner, 2010).

11. James L. Haley, *Passionate Nation: The Epic History of Texas* (New York: Free Press, 2006), 6, 19, 230–231.

12. Frederick Law Olmsted, *A Journey Through Texas* (New York: Dix, Edwards, 1857; New York: Burt Franklin, 1969), 296. For more information on Texas Indian tribes, see David LaVere, *The Texas Indians* (College Station: Texas A&M University Press, 2004).

13. Jillson, *Lone Star Tarnished,* 60.

14. For links to important documents from Texas history, including the Ordinances of Secession, see *Lone Star Junction,* http://www.lsjunction.com/docs/secesson.htm.

15. John R. Ross, "Lynching," in *The Handbook of Texas Online,* http://www.tshaonline.org/handbook/online/articles/jgl01.

16. Jillson, *Lone Star Tarnished,* 61.

17. For information on Texas Latinos, a history of the civil rights movement in Texas, and more, see *The Handbook of Texas Online,* https://tshaonline.org/handbook/online.

18. Richard Fry and Kim Parker, "Early Benchmarks Show 'Post-Millennials' on Track to Be Most Diverse, Best-Educated Generation Yet," *Pew Research Center Social and Demographic Trends,* January 15, 2018, http://www.pewsocialtrends.org/2018/11/15/early-benchmarks-show-post-millennials-on-track-to-be-most-diverse-best-educated-generation-yet.

19. For more on the conflict over tribal gambling facilities in Texas, see Emily Foxhall, "Alabama-Coushatta Tribe Fights for Right to a Gaming Center—Again," *Houston Chronicle*, February 27, 2018, https://www.houstonchronicle.com/news/houston-texas/houston/article/Alabama-Coushatta-fight-for-the-right-to-a-gaming-12707848.php.

20. For more about recent trends in immigration to the United States, see Gustavo Lopez, Kristen Bialik, and Jynnah Radford, "Key Findings about U.S. Immigrants," *Pew Research Center Fact Tank*, November 30, 2018, http://www.pewresearch.org/fact-tank/2018/11/30/key-findings-about-u-s-immigrants.

21. Alexa Ura and Naema Ahmed, "Hispanic Texans on Pace to Become Largest Population Group in State by 2022," *Texas Tribune*, June 21, 2018, https://www.texastribune.org/2018/06/21/hispanic-texans-pace-become-biggest-population-group-state-2022.

22. For a comprehensive national list, see the NALEO Educational Fund's National Directory of Latino Elected Officials at http://www.naleo.org/pra_dir_2017.

23. For the most recent statistics, see "Poverty Rate by Race/Ethnicity," *Henry J. Kaiser Family Foundation*, http://kff.org/other/state-indicator/poverty-rate-by-raceethnicity; and Kids Count Data Center, *Annie E. Casey Foundation*, http://datacenter.kidscount.org/data/tables/8782-median-family-income-among-households-with-children-by-race-and-ethnicity?loc=45&loct=2#detailed/2/45/false/36/4038,4040,4039,2638,2597,4758,1353/17618.

24. Juan Carlos Huerta and Beatriz Cuartas, "Is Texas Finally Turning Blue? We Looked at the Electorate to Find Out," *Washington Post*, December 18, 2018, https://www.washingtonpost.com/news/monkey-cage/wp/2018/12/18/are-texass-demographics-finally-turning-the-state-blue-we-looked-at-the-electorate-to-find-out/?utm_term=.4888eb182b1a.

25. For extensive studies of religion in Texas and America, see "America's Changing Religious Landscape," *Pew Research Center*, May 12, 2015, http://www.pewforum.org/2015/05/12/americas-changing-religious-landscape; and Niraj Chokshi, "The Religious States of America, in 22 Maps," *Washington Post*, February 26, 2015, https://www.washingtonpost.com/blogs/govbeat/wp/2015/02/26/the-religious-states-of-america-in-22-maps.

26. Chokshi, "The Religious States of America, in 22 Maps."

27. For an interactive map of nationwide anti-mosque activity, see "Nationwide Anti-Mosque Activity," *ACLU*, May 2018, https://www.aclu.org/issues/national-security/discriminatory-profiling/nationwide-anti-mosque-activity.

28. "Muslim Immigration Ban," *The Texas Politics Project at the University of Texas at Austin*, February 2017, https://texaspolitics.utexas.edu/set/muslim-immigration-ban-february-2017.

29. For more information on the Texas transportation system, see "Pocket Facts," *Texas Department of Transportation*, http://ftp.dot.state.tx.us/pub/txdot-info/gpa/pocket_facts.pdf; and Kevin McPherson, Jessica Donald, and Bruce Wright, "Transportation Infrastructure," *Texas Comptroller of Public Accounts: Fiscal Notes*, https://comptroller.texas.gov/economy/fiscal-notes/2018/may/transportation.php.

30. "Census Bureau Reveals Fastest-Growing Large Cities," *U.S. Department of Commerce, Census Bureau*, May 24, 2018, https://www.census.gov/newsroom/press-releases/2018/estimates-cities.html.

31. Steve White, Lloyd B. Potter, Helen You, Lila Valencia, Jeffrey A. Jordan, Beverly Pecotte, and Sara Robinson, "Urban Texas," *Texas Demographic Center*, August 2017, http://demographics.texas.gov/Resources/publications/2017/2017_08_21_UrbanTexas.pdf.

32. Marc Seitles, "The Perpetuation of Residential Racial Segregation in America: Historical Discrimination, Modern Forms of Exclusion, and Inclusionary Remedies," *Journal of Land Use & Environmental Law* 14 (Fall 1998): 89–124, http://www.law.fsu.edu/journals/landuse/Vol141/seit.htm.

33. For examples in Austin, see "Austin Gentrification Maps and Data," *Governing the States and Localities*, http://www.governing.com/gov-data/austin-gentrification-maps-demographic-data.html.

34. Kiah Collier, "As Oil and Gas Exports Surge, West Texas Becomes the World's 'Extraction Colony,'" *Texas Tribune*, October 11, 2018, https://www.texastribune.org/2018/10/11/west-texas-becomes-worlds-extraction-colony-oil-gas-exports-surge.

35. Ryan Murphy and Jay Root, "Texas Republicans Getting Almost 90 Percent of Money Flowing into State Elections," *Texas Tribune*, February 19, 2018, https://www.texastribune.org/2018/02/19/texas-republicans-getting-almost-90-percent-money-flowing-state-electi.

36. Robert W. Gilmer, PhD, "The Economic Outlook for Houston in 2019: Oil Prices Are Up Again, but Oil Risk Continues," *Bauer College of Business, University of Houston: Institute for Regional Forecasting*, December 11, 2018, https://www.bauer.uh.edu/centers/irf/houston-updates.php.

37. James Cozine, *Saving the Big Thicket: From Exploration to Preservation, 1685–2003* (Denton: University of North Texas Press, 2004). See also Robert S. Maxwell, "Lumber Industry," and Ronald H. Hufford, "Tree Farming," *Handbook of Texas Online*, https://www.tshaonline.org/handbook/online/articles.

38. For updates on Texas drought conditions, see "Texas Drought Information," *Texas Commission on Environmental Quality*, https://www.tceq.texas.gov/response/drought.

39. Ryan Dezember, "Behind Lumber's Collapse: A Perfect Storm of Housing and Trade," *The Wall Street Journal*, January 2, 2019, https://www.wsj.com/articles/behind-lumbers-collapse-a-perfect-storm-of-housing-and-trade-11546437601.

40. For an account of the history of the early years of the oil industry in Texas, see Roger M. Olien and Diana Davids Olien, *Oil in Texas: The Gusher Age, 1895–1945* (Austin: University of Texas Press, 2002).

41. To track the price of oil over time, see "Crude Oil Price History Chart," *Macrotrends*, http://www.macrotrends.net/1369/crude-oil-price-history-chart; and for more detail on those prices, see "Petroleum and Other Liquids," *U.S. Energy Information Administration*, https://www.eia.gov/dnav/pet/pet_pri_spt_s1_m.htm.

42. "Oil Patch Bankruptcy Monitor," *Haynes and Boone, LLP*, August 1, 2016, http://www.haynesboone.com/~/media/files/attorney%20publications/2016/energy_bankruptcy_monitor/oil_patch_bankruptcy_20160106.ashx.

43. For the most recent revenue statistics, see the Texas Comptroller of Public Accounts' Texas Transparency website at http://www.texastransparency.org/State_Finance/Revenue/Revenue_Watch/all-funds.

44. Collin Eaton, "Texas Oil and Gas Workforce at 7-Year Low," *Houston Chronicle*, January 29, 2018, https://www.chron.com/business/energy/article/Even-with-oil-record-in-sight-Texas-energy-12533523.php.

45. Mitchell Schnurman, "Energy Saver: Dallas, San Antonio and Austin Keep Texas Growing," *Dallas Morning News*, January 25, 2016, http://www.dallasnews.com/business/columnists/mitchell-schnurman/20160125-enerenergy-saver-dallas-austin-and-san-antonio-keep-texas-growing.ece.

46. For a broad review of the many studies linking air pollution from the burning of fossil fuels to respiratory and cardiovascular disease, premature birth, infant and adult mortality, and more, see Bert Brunekreef and Stephen Holgate, "Air Pollution and Health," *The Lancet* 360 (2002): 1233–1242. For the American Academy of Pediatrics official statement about the impact on children, see "Ambient Air Pollution: Health Hazards to Children," *Pediatrics* 114, no. 6 (2004), http://intl-pediatrics.aappublications.org/content/114/6/1699.full.

47. To explore the Fortune 500 list, see http://beta.fortune.com/fortune500.

48. For an interactive map that illustrates renewable energy by state, see "Renewable Energy by State," *Energy.gov*, http://energy.gov/maps/renewable-energy-production-state.

49. For an overview of energy in Texas, see "Texas State Profile and Energy Estimates," *U.S. Energy Information Administration*, http://www.eia.gov/state/?sid=TX#tabs-1.

50. Patrick Graves and Bruce Wright, "Solar Power in Texas: The Next Big Renewable?," *Texas Comptroller of Public Accounts: Fiscal Notes*, https://comptroller.texas.gov/economy/fiscal-notes/2018/april/solar.php.

51. Joanna H. Slusarewicz and Daniel S. Cohan, "Assessing Solar and Wind Complementarity in Texas," *Renewables: Wind, Water, and Solar*, 5 (2018): 7, https://jrenewables.springeropen.com/articles/10.1186/s40807-018-0054-3.

52. For a brief history of the venture that served as a driving force to bring high tech to Texas, see "Sematech," in *The Handbook of Texas Online*, https://tshaonline.org/handbook/online/articles/dns03.

53. "Apple to Build New Campus in Austin and Add Jobs across the US," *Apple Newsroom press release*, December 13, 2018, https://www.apple.com/newsroom/2018/12/apple-to-build-new-campus-in-austin-and-add-jobs-across-the-us.

54. For key findings and an interactive map about the high-tech sector, see "Cyberstates," *CompTIA*, https://www.cyberstates.org/#interactiveMap?geoid=48.

55. "Annual Report on Growth Occupations and Growth Industries." *Texas Workforce Commission*, November 18, 2018, https://lmci.state.tx.us/shared/PDFs/Report_on_Texas_Growth_Occupations_2018.pdf.

56. "Biotechnology and Life Sciences," *Texas Economic Development Corporation*, https://businessintexas.com/industries/biotechnology-life-sciences.

57. Molly Ivins, "Top to Bottom Reform of Financial Structures Essential," *Dallas Times Herald*, June 3, 1990.

58. For more detail on Texas agricultural production, see "Texas Ag Stats," *Texas Department of Agriculture*, https://texasagriculture.gov/About/TexasAgStats.aspx.

59. M. Angeles Villarreal and Ian F. Ferguson, *The North American Free Trade Agreement (NAFTA)*, (Washington, DC: Congressional Research Service, April 16, 2015), https://www.fas.org/sgp/crs/row/R42965.pdf.

60. For an in-depth look at the difficulties facing *maquiladora* workers, see Stephanie Navarro, "Inside Mexico's Maquiladoras: Manufacturing Health Disparities," *Stanford Medicine,* http://med.stanford.edu/schoolhealtheval/files/StephanieNavarro_HumBio122MFinal.pdf.

61. Damien Cave, "Mexico Updates Death Toll in Drug War to 47,515, but Critics Dispute the Data," *New York Times,* January 11, 2012. For additional information about the drug war in Mexico and violence along the border, see George W. Grayson, *Mexico: Narco-Violence in a Failed State* (Piscataway, NJ: Transaction Publishers, 2009); Charles Bowden, *Murder City: Ciudad Juarez and the Global Economy, New Killing Fields* (New York: Nation Books, 2011); and Ricardo C. Ainslie, *The Fight to Save Juarez: Life in the Heart of Mexico's Drug War* (Austin: University of Texas Press, 2013).

62. Anna Yukhananov, "Murder Rate Climbs in Mexico, while Other Crimes Fall," *Reuters,* January 21, 2016, http://www.reuters.com/article/us-mexico-crime-idUSKCN0V005C; and Brianna Lee, "Mexico's Drug War," *Council on Foreign Relations Backgrounders,* March 5, 2014, http://www.cfr.org/mexico/mexicos-drug-war/p13689.

63. For sortable statistics on crime in the United States, see "Crime in the U.S.: 2017," *U.S. Department of Justice, Federal Bureau of Investigations,* https://ucr.fbi.gov/crime-in-the-u.s/2017.

64. Mary Beth Sheridan, "The Weirdly Great Relationship between Trump and Mexico's New Leftist President," *Washington Post,* December 14, 2018, https://www.washingtonpost.com/world/the_americas/the-weirdly-great-relationship-between-trump-and-mexicos-new-leftist-president/2018/12/13/c849fe64-fd75-11e8-a17e-162b712e8fc2_story.html?utm_term=.9a1127723b18.

65. Tracy Wilkinson, "A Year after Trump Reversed Obama's Opening to Cuba, the U.S. Is Sitting Out Havana's Political Revamp," *Los Angeles Times,* June 22, 2018, https://www.latimes.com/nation/la-na-pol-us-cuba-20180622-story.html.

66. Ana Gonzalez-Berrera and Jens Manuel Krogstad, "What We Know about Illegal Immigration from Mexico," *Pew Research Center FactTank,* December 3, 2018, http://www.pewresearch.org/fact-tank/2018/12/03/what-we-know-about-illegal-immigration-from-mexico.

67. Angelos Angelou, William Mellor, and Anthony Michael, "Texans for All: Economic Impact of Senate Bill 4," *AngelouEconomics,* November 2017, https://assets.documentcloud.org/documents/4177307/TexansForAll.pdf.

68. Mark Wiggins, "Republican Opposition Mounting to Texas 'DREAM Act' Repeal," *KHOU Online,* April 14, 2015, http://www.khou.com/news/local/texas/republican-opposition-mounting-to-texas-dream-act-repeal/148639890.

69. Maggie Astor, "Texas' Ban on 'Sanctuary Cities' Can Begin, Appeals Court Rules," *The New York Times,* March 13, 2018, https://www.nytimes.com/2018/03/13/us/texas-immigration-law-sb4.html.

70. *Regents of the University of California; Janet Napolitano v. U.S. Department of Homeland Security; Kirstjen Nielsen,* No. 18-15068 D.C. No. 3:17-cv-05211-WHA, http://cdn.ca9.uscourts.gov/datastore/opinions/2018/11/08/18-15068.pdf.

71. For a collection of reports on the border issue, see https://www.businessinsider.com/us-mexico-border-wall-photos-maps-2018-5#texas-is-the-state-with-by-far-the-longest-stretch-of-land-bordering-mexico-yet-91-of-its-border-has-no-man-made-barrier-at-all-27.

72. Carl Hulse, "After Veto, Some Lawmakers See a New Emergency: Fixing the Act Trump Invoked," The New York Times, March 16, 2019, https://www.nytimes.com/2019/03/16/us/politics/trump-veto-emergency-act.html.

73. Marice Richter and Lisa Maria Garza, "Texas Governor Extends National Guard to Monitor Border," *Reuters,* December 15, 2015, http://www.reuters.com/article/us-texas-immigration-idUSKBN0TZ01B20151216.

74. R. G. Ratcliffe, "Menéndez: Does Texas Still Need to Spend $800 Million on Border Security?," *Texas Monthly,* April 10, 2018, https://www.texasmonthly.com/politics/menendez-texas-senate-hispanic-caucus.

75. For articles covering the issue of family separation starting with the announcement of the zero-tolerance policy, see "Families Divided," *Texas Tribune,* https://www.texastribune.org/series/separated-immigrant-families-zero-tolerance/?page=1.

76. Andrew J. Kondash, Nancy E. Lauer, and Avner Vengosh, "The Intensification of the Water Footprint of Hydraulic Fracturing," *Science Advances* 4, no. 8 (August 15, 2018), http://advances.sciencemag.org/content/4/8/eaar5982.

77. For information about loan and grant programs, see "Financial Assistance," *Texas Water Development Board,* accessed January 9, 2019, http://www.twdb.texas.gov/financial/index.asp.

78. For more details, see "Top Ten Most—and Least—Green U.S. States," *Daily Finance,* April 22, 2011, http://www.dailyfinance.com/2011/04/22/top-earth-day-10-most-and-least-green-u-s-states.

79. Ann E. Smith, Will Gans, and Mei Yuan, *Estimating Employment Impacts of Regulations: A Review of EPA's Methods for Its Air Rules* (Washington, DC: U.S. Chamber of Commerce, February 2013), 9–12, https://www.uschamber.com/sites/default/files/documents/files/020360_ETRA_Briefing_NERA_Study_final.pdf.

80. For a variety of statistics regarding Texas students, see "Student Data," *Texas Education Agency,* https://tea.texas.gov/Reports_and_Data/Student_Data.

81. "Quality Counts 2018: State Report Cards Map," *Education Week*, October 10, 2018, https://www.edweek.org/ew/collections/quality-counts-2018-state-grades/report-card-map-rankings.html.

82. "Rankings of the States 2017 and Estimates of School Statistics 2018," *National Education Association*, http://www.nea.org/assets/docs/180413-Rankings_And_Estimates_Report_2018.pdf; and Ross Ramsey, "Analysis: Texas' school finance problem in one pesky chart," *Texas Tribune*, October 10, 2018, https://www.texastribune.org/2018/10/10/analysis-texas-school-finance-budget-lbb.

83. Patrick Svitek, "Governor Greg Abbott signs $11.6 billion school finance measure into law," *Texas Tribune*, June 11, 2019, https://www.texastribune.org/2019/06/11/texas-gov-greg-abbott-signs-116-billion-school-finance-measure-law/. For a sortable table of beginning and average teacher salaries by state, see "Teacher Salary Data by State," *Teaching Portal*, http://www.teacherportal.com/teacher-salaries-by-state.

84. For a variety of reports and data regarding teachers and administrators, see "Educator Reports and Data," *Texas Education Agency*, https://tea.texas.gov/Reports_and_Data/Educator_Data/Educator_Reports_and_Data/.

85. For a variety of indicators of economic well-being, see "Kids Count National Indicators," KIDS COUNT Data Center, Annie E. Casey Foundation, https://datacenter.kidscount.org/data#USA/2/16/17,18,19,20,22,21,2720/char/0; and "The 2018 Annual Homeless Assessment Report (AHAR) to Congress," *U.S. Department of Housing and Urban Development, Office of Community Planning and Development*, https://www.hudexchange.info/resources/documents/2018-AHAR-Part-1.pdf.

86. Matthew Buettgens, Linda J. Blumberg, and Clare Pan, "The Uninsured in Texas: Statewide and Local Area Views," *Urban Institute Health Policy Center*, December 2018, https://www.episcopalhealth.org/files/2715/4447/0560/201812.10_Uninsured_in_Texas_FINAL.pdf.

Chapter 2

1. David B. Walker, *The Rebirth of Federalism: Slouching toward Washington*, 2nd ed. (New York: Chatham House, 2000), 260.

2. Rick Perry, *Fed Up! Our Fight to Save America from Washington* (New York: Little, Brown and Co., 2010), 32.

3. For a discussion of the history and meaning of this clause, see Gary Lawson, Geoffrey P. Miller, Robert G. Natelson, and Guy I. Seidman, *The Origins of the Necessary and Proper Clause* (New York: Cambridge University Press, 2013).

4. *Garcia v. San Antonio Metropolitan Transit Authority*, 469 U.S. 528 (1985).

5. For a description of the procedure, see "The Solution," *Convention of States*, http://www.conventionofstates.com/solution. See also, Greg Abbott, *Broken Not Unbowed: The Fight to Fix a Broken America* (New York: Threshold Editions, 2016).

6. *U.S. Term Limits v. Thornton*, 514 U.S. 115 (1995).

7. *Sweatt v. Painter*, 339 U.S. 629 (1950).

8. Paul Burka, "The M Word," *Texas Monthly*, January 2006, 14–16.

9. *U.S. v. Windsor*, 570 U.S. 12 (2013).

10. *Obergefell v. Hodges*, 576 U.S. ___ (2015). See also Lauren McGaughy, "High Court Calls Same-Sex Marriage a Fundamental Right," *Houston Chronicle*, June 27, 2015.

11. *Kimel v. Florida Board of Regents*, 528 U.S. 62 (2000); *Alden v. Maine*, 527 U.S. 706 (1999); and *Seminole Tribe v. Florida*, 517 U.S. 44 (1996).

12. *Frew v. Hawkins*, 540 U.S. 431 (2004). See also Carlos Guerra, "High Court Orders Texas to Honor Its Word and Pay Up," *San Antonio Express-News*, January 15, 2004.

13. *Kelo v. New London*, 545 U.S. 469 (2005).

14. For a description of a common carrier, see "How Eminent Domain Works in Texas," *State Impact*, https://stateimpact.npr.org/texas/tag/eminent-domain. See also Morgan Smith and Jim Malewitz, "In Big Bend, Trans-Pecos Pipeline Clears Last Hurdle," *Texas Tribune*, May 6, 2016, https://www.texastribune.org/2016/05/06/big-bend-trans-pecos-pipeline-clears-last-hurdle.

15. *United States v. Lopez*, 514 U.S. 549 (1995).

16. *Gonzales v. Raich*, 545 U.S. 1 (2005).

17. "State Marijuana Laws in 2018 Map," Governing: The States and Localities, www.governing.com under Data/Safety/Justice.

18. Neena Satija, "Interactive: Texas vs. the Federal Government," *Texas Tribune*, January 17, 2017, https://www.texastribune.org/2017/01/17/texas-federal-government-lawsuits. See also Lauren McGaughy, "Texas vs. the Feds—A Look at the Lawsuits," *Houston Chronicle*, November 20, 2015, http://www.houstonchronicle.com/news/politics/texas/article/Texas-taxpayer-tab-for-suing-feds-tops-5-million-6647726.php.

19. *National Federation of Independent Business v. Sebelius*, 567 U.S. ___ (2012).

20. *King v. Burwell*, 575 U.S. ___ (2015). See also Tim Eaton, "U.S. Supreme Court Rules in Favor of Obama, Affordable Care Act," *Austin American Statesman*, June 26, 2015.

21. See Jess Bravin and Byron Tau, "Supreme Court to Rule on Obama's Bid to Block Deportations," *Wall Street Journal*, January 20, 2016. Also see *United States v. Texas*, 579 U.S. ___ (2016).

22. Sanford F. Schram, "Welfare Reform: A Race to the Bottom?" *Publius: The Journal of Federalism* 28 (Summer 1998): 1–8. (Special issue: "Welfare Reform in the United States: A Race to the Bottom?" edited by Sanford F. Schram and Samuel H. Beer.)

23. See Melissa B. Taboada, "Texas Applauds New Bill That Will Take Place of No Child Left Behind," *Austin American Statesman*, December 10, 2015.

24. For a legislative history of the resolution, refer to Texas Legislature Online, http://www.legis.state.tx.us/BillLookup/History.aspx?LegSess=84R&Bill=SCR1.

25. Perry, *Fed Up!* 187–188.

26. To review his proposal, see Greg Abbott, "Restoring the Rule of Law with States Leading the Way," *Office of the Governor*, http://www.gov.texas.gov/initiatives.

27. For a more detailed account of early Texas constitutions, see John Cornyn, "The Roots of the Texas Constitution: Settlement to Statehood," *Texas Tech Law Review* 26, 4 (1995): 1089–1218. (Note: The author served as a member of the Texas Supreme Court and as the state's attorney general before being elected to the U.S. Senate in 2002.)

28. Leobardo F. Estrada, F. Chris Garcia, Reynaldo Flores Macias, and Lionel Maldonado, "Chicanos in the United States: A History of Exploitation and Resistance," in *Latinos and the Political System*, ed. F. Chris Garcia (Notre Dame, IN: University of Notre Dame Press, 1988), 28–64. See also, Roberto Juarez, "The American Tradition of Language Rights: The Forgotten Right to Government in a 'Known Tongue,'" *Law & Inequality: A Journal of Theory and Practice* 13, 2 (1995): 495–518.

29. Charles William Ramsdell, *Reconstruction in Texas* (New York: Columbia University Press, 1910); and T. R. Fehrenbach, *Lone Star: A History of Texas and the Texans* (New York: Macmillan, 1968), especially chap. 22, "The Carpetbaggers."

30. Patrick G. Williams, *Beyond Redemption: Texas Democrats after Reconstruction* (Austin: University of Texas Press, 2007); Carl H. Moneyhon, *Edmund J. Davis of Texas: Civil War General, Republican Leader, Reconstruction Governor* (Fort Worth: TCU Press, 2010); and Barry A. Crouch, *The Dance of Freedom: Texas African Americans during Reconstruction*, ed. Larry Madaras (Austin: University of Texas Press, 2007).

31. An alternative view on writing Texas's seventh constitution is presented in Patrick G. Williams, "Of Rutabagas and Redeemers: Rethinking the Texas Constitution of 1876," *Southwestern Historical Quarterly* 106, 2 (2002): 230–253.

32. Roy Walthall, "Celebrate Texas's Anniversary with a Reorganized Constitution," *Waco Tribune-Herald*, March 5, 2011.

33. Jane Elliott, "Gay Marriage Ban Put in Texas Constitution," *Houston Chronicle*, November 9, 2005. See also "Summary Report of the 2005 Constitutional Election Results," *Secretary of State*, http://www.sos.texas.gov/elections/forms/enrrpts/2005con.pdf.

34. Ralph Haurwitz, "From College to Beach, All Amendments Pass," *Austin American-Statesman*, November 4, 2009; Holly Hacker, "Prop. 4 Would Let Colleges Tap Fund," *Dallas Morning News*, October 4, 2009; and "Constitutional Amendments Proposed for November 2009 Ballot," Focus Report No. 81-8 (Austin: House Research Organization, Texas House of Representatives, August 20, 2009), http://www.hro.house.state.tx.us/pdf/focus/amend81.pdf.

35. See "Analyses of Proposed Constitutional Amendments for November 5, 2013, Election," *Texas Legislative Council*, http://www.tlc.state.tx.us/docs/amendments/analyses13.pdf.

36. See H204Texas.org, http://www.h204texas.org/library/documents-library, and search for Prop6.

37. See Greg Abbott, "Governor Urges Vote for Prop. 6," *McAllen Monitor*, October 20, 2015.

38. See "Amendments Proposed for November 2015 Ballot: Focus Report," *House Research Organization*, http://www.hro.house.state.tx.us/pdf/focus/amend84.pdf.

39. See "Amendments Proposed for November 2017 Ballot: Focus Report," *House Research Organization*, http://www.hro.house.state.tx.us/pdf/focus/amend85.pdf.

40. *Book of the States*, 2017, "Constitutional Amendment Procedure: By Initiative," http://knowledgecenter.csg.org/kc/system/files/1.3%202016.pdf.

41. Texas's right-to-work law was enacted in 1947 by the 50th Legislature. The law bans the union shop arrangement whereby newly hired workers must join a union after employment.

42. Jim Lewis, "Getting Around to a New Constitution," *County* (January/February 1999): 11–13. For a profile of Representative Rob Junell and his collaboration with Senator Bill Ratliff, see Janet Elliott, "Maverick in the Middle," *Texas Lawyer* (January 1999): 19–20.

43. For the text of the Ratliff-Junell draft constitution, refer to Texas Legislature Online, http://www.capitol.state.tx.us/BillLookup/Text.aspx?LegSess=76R&Bill=HJR1.

44. See Roy Walthall, "Waco Group Reorganizes Texas Constitution," *Waco Tribune-Herald*, November 15, 2010; Roy Walthall, "Texas Constitution Needs Makeover," *Amarillo Globe-News*, October 23, 2011; and "Waco Group Hoping to Reorganize Texas Constitution," accessed October 31, 2013, www.WacoTrib.com.

45. For a legislative history of the concurrent resolution, refer to the Texas Legislature Online, http://www.capitol.state.tx.us/BillLookup/History.aspx?LegSess=84R&Bill=HCR37.

46. For an analysis of amendments proposed between 1976 and 1989, see James G. Dickson, "Erratic Continuity: Some Patterns of Constitutional Change in Texas Since 1975," *Texas Journal of Political Studies* 14 (Fall–Winter 1991–1992): 41–56.

47. For the text of Junell's constitutional proposal, refer to Texas Legislature Online, http://www.capitol.state.tx.us/BillLookup/Text.aspx?LegSess=77R&Bill=HJR69.

48. For detailed analyses of the contents of the Texas Constitution, see Janice C. May, *The Texas State Constitution: A Reference Guide* (Westport, CT: Greenwood Press, 1996); The Texas Constitution can be found at the Texas Legislature's website, http://www.constitution.legis.state.tx.us.

49. *Santa Fe v. Doe*, 530 U.S. 290 (2000).

50. *Van Orden v. Perry*, 545 U.S. 677 (2005).

51. For details concerning the struggle for equal legal rights, see Rob Fink, "Hermine Tobolowsky, the Texas ELRA, and the Political Struggle for Women's Equal Rights," *Journal of the West* 42 (Summer 2003): 52–57; and Tai Kreidler, "Hermine Tobolowsky: Mother of Texas Equal Rights Amendment," in *The Human Tradition in Texas*, ed. Ty Cashion and Jesus de la Teja (Wilmington, DE: SR Books, 2001), 209–220.

52. Jason Embry, "School Tax System Unconstitutional: State Supreme Court Wants a Fix by June 1," *Austin American-Statesman*, November 23, 2005. See also Gary Scharrer, "Justices Warn that Changes Will Have to Be Significant," *San Antonio Express-News*, November 23, 2005.

53. See Kiahh Collier, "Experts: Expect Early 2016 School Finance Ruling," *Texas Tribune*, September 17, 2015, https://www.texastribune.org/2015/09/17/experts-expect-early-2016-school-finance-ruling. See also, Kiahh Collier, "Texas Supreme Court Upholds School Funding System," *Texas Tribune*, May 13, 2016, http://www.texastribune.org/2016/05/13/texas-supreme-court-issues-school-finance-ruling.

54. *Shelby County v. Holder*, 570 U.S. ___ (2013).

55. See Manny Fernandez, "Texas' Voter ID Law Does Not Discriminate and Can Stand, Appeals Panel Rules, April 27, 2018, https://www.nytimes.com/2018/04/27/us/texas-voter-id.html.

Chapter 3

1. *Clinton v. Cedar Rapids and the Missouri River Railroad*, 24 Iowa 455 (1868).

2. *People v. Hurlbut*, 24 Mich. 44, 95 (1871).

3. Jesse J. Richardson Jr., Meghan Zimmerman Gough, and Robert Puentes, "Is Home Rule the Answer? Clarifying the Influence of Dillon's Rule on Growth Management," *Brookings Institution*, January 2013, http://www.brookings.edu/research/reports/2003/01/01metropolitanpolicy-richardson.

4. Bruce R. Lindsay and Francis X. McCarthy, *Stafford Act Declarations 1953-2014: Trends, Analyses, and Implications for Congress* (Washington, D.C.: Congressional Research Service, July 15, 2014), https://www.fas.org/sgp/crs/homesec/R42702.pdf.

5. Claudia Rivas, "Boundary Dispute Ends in San Patricio County's Favor," *The News of San Patricio*, October 21, 2018, https://www.mysoutex.com/san_patricio_county/news/features/boundary-dispute-ends-in-san-patricio-county-s-favor/article_0e25f9ce-d30f-11e8-8ca6-3b6e9468eca0.html.

6. "New Law Requires Local Government Meetings to Be Put Online," *McAllen Monitor*, January 10, 2016, http://www.themonitor.com/news/local/new-law-requires-local-government-meetings-to-be-put-online/article_8c3ff2d4-b809-11e5-ad07-cf2d076ff8ad.html.

7. See *Texas Local Govt. Code Ann. Chapter* 5 (1987). A good description of local governments is "Local Government in Texas" by the Texas Municipal League, https://www.tml.org/Handbook-M&C/Chapter1.pdf. The less common but real issue of ending a city government is discussed in Michelle Wilde Anderson, "Dissolving Cities," *Yale Law Journal*, 121 (April 2012): 1346–1447.

8. Russell Gold, "Texas Prohibits Local Fracking Bans," *Wall Street Journal*, May 15, 2015.

9. Matt Zapotosky, "This Might Be the Most Corrupt Little Town in America," *Washington Post*, March 5, 2016, https://www.washingtonpost.com/world/national-security/this-might-be-the-most-corrupt-little-town-in-america/2016/03/05/341c21d2-dcac-11e5-81ae-7491b9b9e7df_story.html; and Garrett Brnger, "Crystal City Will Hold Recall Election," *KSAT*, March 8, 2016, http://www.ksat.com/news/crystal-city-will-hold-recall-election.

10. Enrique Rangel, "Voters in Many Texas Towns Consider Recalls of Elected Officials," *Amarillo Globe-News*, November 30, 2013.

11. Alexa Ura, "Bathroom Fears Flush Houston Discrimination Ordinance," *Texas Tribune*, November 3, 2015, https://www.texastribune.org/2015/11/03/houston-anti-discrimination-ordinance-early-voting.

12. Adrienne Lafrance and Rose Eveleth, "Are Taxis Safer Than Uber?" *Atlantic*, March 3, 2015, http://www.theatlantic.com/technology/archive/2015/03/are-taxis-safer-than-uber/386207.

13. The seminal work is Robert Lineberry and Edmund Fowler, "Reformism and Public Policies in American Cities," *American Political Science Review* 61 (September 1967): 701–717.

14. Tex. Elec. Code Ann. §143.003 (2010).

15. Alan I. Abramowitz, "Why Section 5 Is Still Needed: Racial Polarization and the Voting Rights Act in the 21st Century," *Sabato's Crystal Ball* (Charlottesville, VA: University of Virginia Center for Politics), March 7, 2013, http://www.centerforpolitics.org/crystalball/articles/why-section-5-is-still-needed-racial-polarization-and-the-voting-rights-act-in-the-21st-century.

16. The definition of a minority opportunity district varies by source and situation. It is particularly affected by the degree of ethnic polarization in voting. Commonly, it would require that a group be 50 percent of the citizens of voting age; but for Latinos, the percentage may be as high as 65 percent. Rudolph Bush, "Justice Department Approves Dallas Redistricting Plan," *Dallas Morning News*, December 21, 2011.

17. See Robert Bezdek, David Billeaux, and Juan Carlos Huerta, "Latinos, At-Large Elections, and Political Change: Evidence from the Transition Zone," *Social Science Quarterly* 81 (March 2000): 207–225. Data collected from city websites by author, March 2012.

18. Florian Martin, "City of Houston Sued over Ballot Language for Term Limit Change," *Houston Public Media*, November 19, 2015, http://www.houstonpublicmedia.org/articles/news/2015/11/19/128113/city-of-houston-sued-over-ballot-language-for-term-limit-change.

19. *National Directory of Latino Elected Officials* (Los Angeles: NALEO Educational Fund, 2017). Sonia R. García, Valerie Martinez-Ebers, Irasema Coronado, Sharon Navarro, and Patricia Jaramillo, *Politicas: Latina Trailblazers in the Texas Political Arena* (Austin: University of Texas Press, 2008) provides biographical essays on the first Latina elected public officials in Texas; and Kinder Houston Area Survey, http://has.rice.edu, details changes in the attitudes of Houstonians each year from 1982 to 2018.

20. Loren Steffy, "Fire Fight," *Texas Monthly*, April 2014, http://www.texasmonthly.com/politics/fire-fight.

21. Mike Morris, "Pension Board Agrees to 3-year Deal with Parker," *Houston Chronicle*, March 7, 2015.

22. Josh McGee and Michelle Welch, *Swamped: How Pension Debt Is Sinking the Bayou City* (Houston: Laura and John Arnold Foundation, August 2015), http://www.arnoldfoundation.org/wp-content/uploads/Swamped_FINAL-5.pdf.

23. Mimi Swartz, "Towering Debts," *Texas Monthly*, February 2017, https://www.texasmonthly.com/politics/towering-debts.

24. Erica Grieder, "Pension Reform Deal May Not be Perfect, But It's Good for the City," *Houston Chronicle*, October 28, 2017, https://www.houstonchronicle.com/news/columnists/grieder/article/Grieder-Pension-reform-deal-may-not-be-perfect-12314611.php.

25. "Comparison of State and Local Government Spending in the United States," *US Government Spending*, https://www.usgovernmentspending.com/compare_state_spending_2018dH0D.

26. Dave Fehling, "Drop in Oil Tax Revenue 'Not Going to Be Pretty' for Texas," *Houston Public Media*, January 26, 2016, http://www.houstonpublicmedia.org/articles/news/2016/01/26/135115/drop-in-oil-tax-revenue-not-going-to-be-pretty-for-texas.

27. "WTI Crude Oil Prices," *Macrotrends*, March 4, 2019, https://www.macrotrends.net/2516/wti-crude-oil-prices-10-year-daily-chart.

28. Eduardo Porter, "When Public Outperforms Private in Services," *New York Times*, January 15, 2013, https://www.nytimes.com/2013/01/16/business/when-privatization-works-and-why-it-doesnt-always.html; Allegra Hill, "Competitive Contracting—Dull but Effective," *Austin American-Statesman*, December 8, 2015.

29. Texas Comptroller of Public Accounts, *Tax Rates and Levies by County*, http://www.window.state.tx.us/taxinfo/proptax/taxrates.

30. John Kiernan, "2015's States with the Highest and Lowest Property Taxes," *Wallet Hub*, https://wallethub.com/edu/states-with-the-highest-and-lowest-property-taxes/11585.

31. An interesting account of the problems facing a rural county undergoing population change is Dave Mann, "The Battle for San Jacinto," *Texas Observer*, February 10, 2006, 12–13 and 18–19.

32. Tony Plohetski, "Grand Jury Investigating Gov. Rick Perry Convenes," *Austin American-Statesman*, May 16, 2014.

33. Eric Nicholson, "Big Changes Are Coming to Dallas County's Godawful Truancy Courts," *Dallas Observer*, August 17, 2015, http://www.dallasobserver.com/news/big-changes-are-coming-to-dallas-countys-godawful-truancy-courts-7490001.

34. Jim Webre, "Treasurer Will Stay until Successor Appointed," *Sealy News*, December 17, 2004.

35. Tom Bower, "Toyota Incentives Gets County's OK," *San Antonio Express-News*, May 21, 2003; Vicki Vaughan, "Toyota Factories Back in High Gear," *MySanAntonio.Com*, September 14, 2011, http://www.mysanantonio.com/business/article/Toyotafactoriesback-in-high-gear-2170706.php; and David Hendricks and Richard Webner, "Toyota Expanding to Six-Day Production and Adding 200," *San Antonio Express-News*, September 3, 2015, http://www.expressnews.com/business/local/article/Toyota-expanding-to-six-day-production-hiring-200-6483358.php.

36. Sean Collins Walsh, "Travis County Oks $951 Million Budget, In-person Jail Visits," *Austin American-Statesman*, September 29, 2015.

37. Gyusuck Geon and Geoffrey K. Turnbull, "The Effect of Home Rule on Local Government Behavior: Is There No Rule Like Home Rule?" Georgia State University, September 2004, https://www.researchgate.net/publication/228426796_The_Effect_of_Home_Rule_on_Local_Government_Behavior_Is_There_No_Rule_Like_Home_Rule.

38. Gaby Galvin, "On the Border, Out of the Shadows," *US News*, May 16, 2018, https://www.usnews.com/news/healthiest-communities/articles/2018-05-16/americas-third-world-border-colonias-in-texas-struggle-to-attain-services.

39. Dennis Foley, "Are Texas Border Cities Actually Safer Than Other Cities?" *KTSA News*, January 9, 2019, https://www.ktsa.com/are-texas-border-cities-actually-safer-than-other-cities/.

40. Texas Education Agency, *Snapshot 2017*, 2018, https://rptsvr1.tea.texas.gov/perfreport/snapshot/2017/state.html.

41. Texas Comptroller of Public Accounts, *Tax Exemptions and Tax Incidence*, November 2018, comptroller.texas.gov/taxes/property-tax/docs/96-1740.pdf - 182k - 2018-02-07.

42. Joe Smith, TexasISD.com, September 13, 2018.

43. Reeve Hamilton, "Study: Texas Economy Benefits from Community Colleges," *Texas Tribune*, November 26, 2010, https://www.texastribune.org/2010/11/12/study-tx-economy-benefits-from-community-colleges; and "The Economic Impact of Community Colleges," *Window on State Government*, http://comptroller.texas.gov/specialrpt/workforce/2008/PDF/07_Economic_Impact.pdf.

44. Enrique Rangel, "Lawmakers, Landowners Keep Eye on Water Rights," *Amarillo Globe-News*, May 31, 2014.

45. Taylor Goldenstein, "Abbott Signs Bill Limiting Annexation," *Austin American Statesman*, updated September 22, 2018, https://www.statesman.com/NEWS/20170816/Abbott-signs-bill-limiting-annexation-powers-of-cities.

Chapter 4

1. Scott Clement and John C. Green, "The Tea Party and Religion," *Pew Research Center*, February 23, 2011, http://www.pewforum.org/2011/02/23/tea-party-and-religion.

2. For discussions of contemporary Texas conservatism, see Karl Rove, *Courage and Consequence: My Life as a Conservative in the Fight* (New York: Threshold, 2010); Tom Pauken, *Bringing America Home* (Rockford, IL: Chronicles Press, 2010); Gail Collins, *As Texas Goes . . . How the Lone Star State Hijacked the American Agenda* (New York: Liveright, 2012); and Wayne J. Thorburn, *Red State: An Insider's Story of How the GOP Came to Dominate Texas Politics* (Austin: University of Texas Press, 2014).

3. Jim Henson, "GOP Candidates, Voters and Creationism," *The Texas Politics Project*, December 17, 2013, https://texaspolitics.utexas.edu/blog/gop-candidates-voters-and-creationism.

4. David Kirby and Emily Ekins, "Libertarian Roots of the Tea Party," *Policy Analysis*, August 6, 2012, http://object.cato.org/sites/cato.org/files/pubs/pdf/PA705.pdf.

5. For a discussion of contemporary Texas liberalism, see Mary Beth Rogers, *Turning Texas Blue: What It Will Take to Break the GOP Grip on America's Reddest State* (New York: St. Martin's Press, 2016).

6. Charles S. Bullock, Donna R. Hoffman, and Ronald Keith Gaddie, "Regional Variations in the Realignment of American Politics, 1944–2004," *Social Science Quarterly*, 87 (September 2006): 494–518; and Robert S. Erikson and Kent L. Tedin, *American Public Opinion*, 9th ed. (Boston: Pearson, 2015).

7. For more information on the Populist Party in Texas, see Alwyn Barr, *Reconstruction to Reform Texas Politics, 1876–1906* (Dallas: Southern Methodist University Press, 2000).

8. Teresa Palomo Acosta, "Raza Unida Party," *The Handbook of Texas Online*, http://www.tshaonline.org/handbook/online/articles/war01.

9. Tex. Elec. Code Ann. §142.007 (2010).

10. For an alternate view, see Carl Moneyhon, *Edmund J. Davis of Texas: Civil War General, Republican Leader, Reconstruction Governor* (Fort Worth: TCU Press, 2010).

11. Dick Smith, "Department of Banking," *The Handbook of Texas Online*, http://www.tshaonline.org/handbook/online/articles/mcdcg.

12. See Gregg Cantrell, "A Host of Sturdy Patriots: The Texas Populists," in *The Texas Left: The Radical Roots of Lone Star Liberalism*, ed. David O'Donald Cullen and Kyle G. Wilkison (College Station: Texas A&M University Press, 2010), 53–73.

13. Nancy Beck Young, "Democratic Party," *The Handbook of Texas Online*, http://www.tshaonline.org/handbook/online/articles/wad01.

14. Jessica Montoya Coggins, "Fifty Years after 'Viva Kennedy' and Its Political Impact on Latinos," *NBC Latino*, November 15, 2013, http://nbclatino.com/2013/11/15/fifty-years-after-viva-kennedy-and-its-impact-on-latinos.

15. Acosta, "Raza Unida Party."

16. Nancy Beck Young, "Democratic Party," *The Handbook of Texas Online*, http://www.tshaonline.org/handbook/online/articles/wad01.

17. Eleanor Dearman and John Reynolds, "The Brief: Tea Party Remains Strong within GOP Ranks." *Texas Tribune*, November 13, 2015, http://www.texastribune.org/2015/11/13/brief.

18. "Texas Report," *Latino Decisions*, February 2014, http://www.latinodecisions.com/files/5413/9488/2480/Texas_AV_Report.pdf.

19. Zachary Roth, "Battleground Texas: Inside the Fight to Turn the State Blue," *MSNBC*, June 5, 2014, http://www.msnbc.com/melissa-harris-perry/the-fight-turn-texas-blue. For a postmortem on Battleground Texas, see Jamie Lovegrove, "Democrats' Alliance with Battleground Texas Shows Strains," *Texas Tribune*, February 8, 2016, https://www.texastribune.org/2016/02/18/battleground-texas-regroups-game-plan-unchanged.

20. Rogers, *Turning Texas Blue*, 31–36.

21. Mary Beth Rogers, "How to Turn Texas Blue," *Texas Observer*, January 19, 2016, http://www.texasobserver.org/how-to-turn-texas-blue; "2018 voter poll results: Texas," *Washington Post*, November 30, 2018, https://www.washingtonpost.com/graphics/2018/politics/voter-polls/texas.html?noredirect=on&utm_term=.ff71037d0226.

22. Samuel J. Eldersveld and Hanes Walton Jr., *Political Parties in American Society*, 2nd ed. (New York: Palgrave Macmillan, 2000), 125–126.

23. "General Rules for All Conventions and Meetings," *Republican Party of Texas*, http://3npv5lo075n4f1mrxbxvz8hv.wpengine.netdna-cdn.com/wp-content/uploads/2016/06/2016-Rules-06.09.16.pdf.

24. "Texas Delegate Selection Plan for the 2016 Democratic National Convention," *Texas Democratic Party*, http://www.txdemocrats.org/pdf/2016-Delegate-Selection-Plan-9.23.2015.pdf.

25. For example, in April 2016, delegates to the Green Party of Texas State Convention met to nominate statewide candidates and select delegates for the Green Party National Convention. Green Party presidential candidate Jill Stein was awarded 15 of the 23 delegates. "Stein Wins Majority of Texas Convention Delegates," *Green Party Watch*, April 10, 2016, http://www.greenpartywatch.org/2016/04/10/stein-wins-majority-of-texas-convention-delegates.

26. Rebecca Elliott, "Democrats Drop Texas Two-Step for 2016," *Houston Chronicle*, July 1, 2015.

27. Wilson Andrews, Kitty Bennett, and Alicia Parlapiano, "2016 Primary Results and Calendar," *New York Times*, http://www.nytimes.com/interactive/2016/us/elections/primary-calendar-and-results.html.

28. Harry Enten, "Super Guide to Super Tuesday—Republican Edition," *FiveThirtyEight*, February 29, 2016, http://fivethirtyeight.com/features/super-tuesday-preview-republican-presidential-election-2016.

29. Andrews, Bennett, and Parlapiano, "2016 Primary Results and Calendar."

30. "Travis County Democratic Party List of Candidates," *Travis County Clerk's Office*, http://traviscountyclerk.org/eclerk/content/images/sample_ballots/2016.03.01/2016_Dem_Joint_Primary.pdf.

31. "Travis County Republican Party List of Candidates," *Travis County Clerk's Office*, http://traviscountyclerk.org/eclerk/content/images/sample_ballots/2016.03.01/2016_Rep_Joint_Primary.pdf.

Chapter 5

1. "Turnout and Voter Registration Figures (1970–current)," *Texas Secretary of State*, http://www.sos.state.tx.us/elections/historical/70-92.shtml.

2. George N. Green, "O'Daniel, Wilbert Lee [Pappy]," *Handbook of Texas Online*, February 22, 2016, http://www.tshaonline.org/handbook/online/articles/fod11.

3. Issie Lapowsky, "The Dot-Vote Crusade to Defend Politicians from Cybersquatters," *Wired*, January 24, 2016, http://www.wired.com/2016/01/the-dotvote-crusade-to-defend-politicians-from-cybersquatters.

4. Andrea Zelinksi, "'She Can't Even Keep Track of Her Gun,' Gov. Abbott Attacks Rival Lupe Valdez over Missing Weapon." *Houston Chronicle*, August 17, 2018; Allie Morris, "Lupe Valdez's Pistol Found, Dallas County Sheriff's Office apologizes," *Houston Chronicle*, August 22, 2018.

5. Kim L. Fridkin and Patrick J. Kenney, "Variability in Citizens' Reactions to Different Types of Negative Campaigns," *American Journal of Political Science* 55, no. 2 (2011): 307–325.

6. "Most Expensive Races," *OpenSecrets.org*, https://www.opensecrets.org/overview/topraces.php?cycle=2018&display=currcandsout; "Texas Senate Race," *OpenSecrets.org*, https://www.opensecrets.org/races/summary?id=TXS2&cycle=2018.

7. "Payday Loans," *Federal Trade Commission*, https://www.consumer.ftc.gov/articles/0097-payday-loans.

8. Mitchell Schnurman, "Payday-Loan Industry Spreads the Money in Texas," *Dallas Morning News*, April 7, 2015.

9. "TRIBPEDIA: Texas Ethics Commission," *Texas Tribune*, http://www.texastribune.org/tribpedia/texas-ethics-commission/about.

10. Bipartisan Campaign Reform Act of 2002, 2 U.S.C. § 431 (2002).

11. "Super PACs," *OpenSecrets.org*, https://www.opensecrets.org/pacs/superpacs.php.

12. "Campaign Finance Guide for Judicial Candidates and Officeholders," *Texas Ethics Commission*, September 1, 2013, https://www.ethics.state.tx.us/guides/JCOH_guide.htm#CAMP_CONTR.

13. "Personal Financial Statement Form PFS - Instruction Guide," *Texas Ethics Commission*, June 19, 2014, https://www.ethics.state.tx.us/forms/PFS_ins.pdf.

14. "What Is 'Dark Money,' and How Are States Responding to It," *San Antonio Express-News*, December 20, 2015.

15. David Saleh Rauf, "Texas Set to Require Disclosure of Some 'Dark Money' Ads," *San Antonio Express-News*, October 6, 2015.

16. David Saleh Rauf, "Texas 'Dark Money' Rule Set for Court Fight Ahead of Primaries," *San Antonio Express-News*, November 23, 2015; and "Federal Judge Tosses Lawsuit Against Texas Dark Money Regulation," *San Antonio Express-News*, March 15, 2016, http://www.expressnews.com/news/politics/texas_legislature/article/Federal-judge-tosses-lawsuit-against-Texas-dark-6891323.php.

17. Francisco Pedraza and Bryan Wilcox-Archuleta, "Donald Trump Did Not Win 34% of Latino Vote in Texas. He Won Much Less," The Washington Post, December 2, 2016, https://www.washingtonpost.com/news/monkey-cage/wp/2016/12/02/donald-trump-did-not-win-34-of-latino-vote-in-texas-he-won-much-less/?noredirect=on&utm_term=.87354c83dccf.

18. "American Election Eve Poll 2018 - Texas - Latino, African American, and AAPI Voters," *Latino Decisions*, http://www.latinodecisions.com/files/3515/4155/5782/TX_2018_groups.pdf.

19. Olivia P. Tallet, "Parties Misjudge Latino Vote Power," *Houston Chronicle*, October 14, 2018.

20. Juan Carlos Huerta and Beatriz Cuartas, "Is Texas Finally Turning Blue? We Looked at the Electorate to Find Out," December 18, 2018, *The Monkey Cage*, https://www.washingtonpost.com/news/monkey-cage/wp/2018/12/18/are-texass-demographics-finally-turning-the-state-blue-we-looked-at-the-electorate-to-find-out/?noredirect=on&utm_term=.c9d1d22f97a1.

21. Catherine Rampell, "Trump Has Done the Opposite of Everything the GOP Said It Needs to Do to Survive," *Washington Post*, March 31, 2016, https://www.washingtonpost.com/opinions/opposite-day-at-the-trump-campaign/2016/03/31/92032d00-f77c-11e5-8b23-538270a1ca31_story.html.

22. Laura Meckler, "Republican Party Wrestles with Immigration Stance as It Courts Hispanics," *Wall Street Journal*, April 18, 2014.

23. "Latino Republican Voters in Texas," *NPR*, November 4, 2018, https://www.npr.org/2018/11/04/664103241/latino-republican-voters-in-texas.

24. "Texas Report," *Latino Decisions*.

25. "American Election Eve Poll 2018 - Texas - Latino, African American, and AAPI Voters." *Latino Decisions*, http://www.latinodecisions.com/files/3515/4155/5782/TX_2018_groups.pdf.

26. Ross Ramsey, Matt Stiles, Julián Aguilar, and Ryan Murphy, "Minorities Drove Texas Growth, Census Figures Show," *Texas Tribune*, February 18, 2011, http://www.texastribune.org/2011/02/18/minorities-drove-texas-growth-census-figures-show.

27. Michael Li, "A Look at Texas Voter Turnout by Ethnicity," *Burnt Orange Report*, May 9, 2013, http://www.burntorangereport.com/diary/13488/a-look-at-texas-voter-turnout-by-ethnicity.

28. William H. Frey, "Minority Turnout Determined the 2012 Election," *Brookings*, May 10, 2013, http://www.brookings.edu/research/papers/2013/05/10-election-2012-minority-voter-turnout-frey.

29. Alexa Ura, "Obama, Davis Ask Supreme Court to Reject Texas Abortion Law," *Texas Tribune*, January 5, 2016, https://www.texastribune.org/2016/01/05/obama-advocates-ask-high-court-reject-abortion-law.

30. Jay Root, "Davis' Daughters Fire Back at Critics of Their Mother," *Texas Tribune*, January 28, 2014, http://www.texastribune.org/2014/01/28/davis-daughters-fire-back-critics.

31. Marissa Evans, "2018 Was the Year of the Woman in Texas. Candidates Say It's 'Not a One-Time Deal,'" *Texas Tribune*, November 8, 2018, https://www.texastribune.org/about/staff/marissa-evans.

32. *Yick Wo v. Hopkins*, 118 U.S. 356, 370 (1886).

33. Christopher Long, "Ku Klux Klan," *Handbook of Texas Online*, August 20, 2013, https://www.tshaonline.org/handbook/online/articles/vek02.

34. Chandler Davidson, "African Americans and Politics," *Handbook of Texas Online*, March 5, 2016, http://www.tshaonline.org/handbook/online/articles/wmafr.

35. David Montejano, *Anglos and Mexicans in the Making of Texas, 1836–1886* (Austin: University of Texas Press, 1987), 143.

36. Sanford N. Greenberg, "White Primary," *Handbook of Texas Online*, March 5, 2016, http://www.tshaonline.org/handbook/online/articles/wdw01; and Charles L. Zelden, *The Battle for the Black Ballot: Smith v. Allwright and the Defeat of the All-White Primary* (Lawrence, KS: University of Kansas Press, 2004).

37. Janie Boschma, "What It's Like to Be a Nonwhite Lawmaker Representing a White-Majority District (and Vice Versa)," *Atlantic*, January 30, 2015, http://www.theatlantic.com/politics/archive/2015/01/what-its-like-to-be-a-nonwhite-lawmaker-representing-a-white-majority-district-and-vice-versa/431829.

38. For more information on racial gerrymandering and the use of at-large districts to disenfranchise minorities, see Christopher M. Burke, *The Appearance of Equality: Racial Gerrymandering, Redistricting, and the Supreme Court* (Westport, CT: Greenwood Press, 1999).

39. Todd J. Gillman, "Gov. Rick Perry Sees 'Victory for Federalism and the States' in Voting Rights Ruling," *Dallas Morning News*, June 25, 2013.

40. Sahil Kapur, "Justice Ginsburg Slams Supreme Court's 'Hubris' in Fiery Dissent on Voting Rights Act," *Talking Points Memo*, June 25, 2013, http://talkingpointsmemo.com/dc/justice-ginsburg-slams-supreme-court-s-hubris-in-fiery-dissent-on-voting-rights-act.

41. 42 U.S.C. Sec. 1973 (1982).

42. "2018 November General Election Turnout Rates," *United States Election Project*, December 14, 2018, http://www.electproject.org/2018g.

43. *Canvassing Report: City of San Antonio General and Bond Election, Saturday, May 6, 2017*, https://www.sanantonio.gov/LinkClick.aspx?fileticket=nAOt9SnAh5I%3D&portalid=0.

44. "Turnout and Voter Registration Figures (1970–current)," *Texas Secretary of State*, https://www.sos.state.tx.us/elections/historical/70-92.shtml.

45. Paul R. Abramson, John Aldrich, Brad T. Gomez, and David Rohde, *Change and Continuity in the 2012 and 2014 Elections* (Thousand Oaks, CA: CQ Press, 2016).

46. "2018 General Election U.S. Senator," *Texas Secretary of State*, https://elections.sos.state.tx.us/elchist331_race832.htm.

47. *United States Election Project*, http://www.electproject.org/home/voter-turnout/demographics; *Exit Polls*, https://www.cnn.com/election/2018/exit-polls/texas/senate.

48. Bryon Allen and Chris Wilson, "Just how big was turnout in Texas, and what does it mean?" *TribTalk*, January 7, 2019, https://www.tribtalk.org/2019/01/07/just-how-big-was-turnout-in-texas-and-what-does-it-mean/.

49. Gary Bledsoe and Jennifer L. Clark, "Texas Lawmakers Are Busy Making It Harder to Vote," *Dallas Morning News*, May 19, 2015.

50. Tim Eaton, "Federal Appeals Court: Texas' Voter ID Law Violates Voting Rights Act," *Austin American Statesman*, August 6, 2015; Jim Malewitz, "After Appeals Court Ruling Against Texas Voter ID Law, Now What?" *Austin American Statesman*, July 23, 2016; and Krista M. Torralva, "Texas Voters without Photo ID Can Cast Ballots, Judge Rules," *Corpus Christi Caller-Times*, August 10, 2016, http://www.caller.com/news/local/-texas-voters-without-photo-id-can-cast-ballots-judge-rules-39ba448d-10ec-2d5b-e053-0100007fea06-389778781.html; Jeremy Wallace, "Revised Texas Voter ID Law Upheld by Appeals Court," *San Antonio Express-News*, April 28, 2018.

51. Christian Belanger, "PolitiFact: Texas Voter ID Fraud Cases about as Rare as Lightning Hits," *Austin American Statesman*, August 24, 2015.

52. The *Texas Election Code* is a compilation of state laws that govern voter qualifications, procedures for nominating and electing party and government officials, and other matters related to suffrage and elections.

53. Tex. Elec. Code Ann. §11.001 (2010) and §11.002 (2013).

54. Tex. Elec. Code Ann. Sec. 82.001-Sec. 82.007 (2010).

55. Analeslie Muncy, "Texas Municipal Election Law Manual," 4th ed. (Denton: Texas Municipal Clerks Association, 2015).

56. "Electoral Systems," *ACE Electoral Knowledge Network*, http://aceproject.org/ace-en/topics/es/default.

57. Tex. Elec. Code Sec. 61.014 (2007).

58. "Starting a Party and Nominating Candidates." *Texas Secretary of State*, http://www.sos.state.tx.us /elections/candidates/guide/minor.shtml.

59. Tex. Elec. Code Ann. §172.024 (2013).

Chapter 6

1. "The State of the News Media 2013," *The Pew Research Center's Project for Excellence in Journalism*, http://www.stateofthemedia.org/overview-2013; and Amy Mitchell, "Key Findings on the Traits and Habits of the Modern News Consumer," *Pew Research Center*, July 7, 2016, http://www.pewresearch .org/fact-tank/2016/07/07/modern-news-consumer.

2. Harold W. Stanley and Richard G. Niemi, *Vital Statistics on American Politics, 2011–2012* (Washington, D.C.: CQ Press, 2012), Table 4.2.

3. *Texas Almanac 2018–2019* (Austin: Texas State Historical Association, 2018), 662–674; and Louise C. Allen, Ernest A. Sharpe, and John R. Whitaker, "Newspapers," *Handbook of Texas Online* (Austin: Texas State Historical Association), https://www.tshaonline.org/handbook/online/articles/een08.

4. *Texas Almanac 2018–2019*, 666–674.

5. "Texas Newspapers and News Media Guide," *ABYZ News Links*, http://www.abyznewslinks.com /unitetx.htm.

6. *Texas Almanac 2018–2019*, 666–674.

7. Robert S. Erikson and Kent L. Tedin, *American Public Opinion*, 8th ed. (Boston: Pearson Longman, 2011), 248–249.

8. Andrew Perrin, "Social Media Usage: 2005–2015," *Pew Research Center*, October 8, 2015, http://www .pewinternet.org/2015/10/08/social-networking-usage-2005-2015.

9. "2016 National Election Study Time Series," *Survey Documentation and Analysis*, University of California, Berkeley, http://sda.berkeley.edu, analyzed by author, January 15, 2019.

10. Monica Anderson and Andrea Caumont, "How Social Media Is Reshaping News," *Pew Research Center*, September 24, 2014, http://www.pewresearch.org/fact-tank/2014/09/24/how-social-media-is-reshaping-news.

11. Ibid., and Katerina Eva Matsa and Amy Mitchell, "8 Key Takeaways about Social Media and News," *Pew Research Journalism Project*, March 26, 2014, http://www.journalism.org/2014/03/26/8-key-takeaways-about-social-media-and-news.

12. "State of the News Media 2013," *Pew*.

13. Thomas Standage, *Writing on the Wall: Social Media—The First 2,000 Years* (New York: Bloomsbury, 2013). Standage argues that social media in different forms have existed and served this function for 2,000 years.

14. "Texas Observer," *Media Bias/Fact Check*, November 2, 2018, https://mediabiasfactcheck.com /the-texas-observer.

15. Erikson and Tedin, *American Public Opinion*, 111–112; Carroll J. Glynn et al., *Public Opinion*, 3rd ed. (Boulder: Westview, 2016), 278–279; and "Public Opinion on Abortion: Views on Abortion, 1995–2016, *Pew Research Center: Religion and Public Life*, http://www.pewforum.org /2016/04/08/public-opinion-on-abortion-2.

16. Ross Ramsey, "Analysis: A Cloudy Day for Sunshine Laws in Texas," *Texas Tribune*, February 7, 2018, https://www.texastribune.org/2018/02/07/analysis-cloudy-day-sunshine-laws-texas; "Texas Public Information Act," *Freedom of Information Foundation of Texas*, 2016, http://foift.org/resources /texas-public-information-act; and David Montgomery, "Texas Gets D- Grade in 2015 State Integrity Investigation," *Center for Public Integrity*, November 9, 2015, https://www.publicintegrity.org /2015/11/09/18532/texas-gets-d-grade-2015-state-integrity-investigation.

17. Forrest Wilder, "Ignoring the Lessons from West," *Texas Observer*, March 2014, 44; Mose Buchele, "Curious about Explosive Chemicals Near You? Texas Attorney General Says It's Secret," *StateImpact*, June 16, 2014, no longer online; and "Public Information in North Texas," *Dallas Morning News*, January 23, 2015, http://res.dallasnews.com/interactives/records.

18. Inga Kiderra, "Facebook Boosts Voter Turnout," *UC San Diego News Center*, September 12, 2012, http://ucsdnews.ucsd.edu/pressrelease/facebook_fuels_the_friend_vote.

19. Doris A. Graber and Johanna Dunaway, *Mass Media and American Politics*, 9th ed. (Los Angeles: CQ Press, 2015), 349.

20. Rosalee A. Clawson and Zoe M. Oxley, *Public Opinion: Democratic Ideals, Democratic Practice*, 3rd ed. (Washington, D.C.: CQ Press, 2017), 105.

21. Kasey S. Pipes, "Inside Rick Perry's Campaign Strategy," *FoxNews.com*, August 11, 2011, http://www.foxnews.com/opinion/2011/08/11/inside-rick-perrys-campaign-strategy-how-it-worked-in-his-race-for-governor-and.html; and Sasha Issenberg, *The Victory Lab: The Secret Science of Winning Campaigns* (New York: Broadway Books, 2013).

22. Aaron Smith, "Civic Engagement in the Digital Age," *Pew Research Internet Project*, April 25, 2013, http://www.pewinternet.org/2013/04/25/civic-engagement-in-the-digital-age-2.

23. Heather Kelly, "Texas Filibuster on Abortion Bill Rivets Online," *CNN.com*, June 26, 2013, http://www.cnn.com/2013/06/26/tech/social-media/texas-filibuster-twitter.

24. David H. Weaver, Randal A. Beam, Bonnie J. Brownlee, Paul S. Voakes, and G. Cleveland Wilhout, *The American Journalist in the 21st Century* (Mahwah, NJ: Lawrence Erlbaum Associates, 2007).

25. Jesse Holcomb, "Cable News: Fact Sheet," *Pew Journalism and Media*, April 30, 2015, http://www.journalism.org/2015/04/29/cable-news-fact-sheet.

26. "State of the News Media 2013," *Pew*.

27. "Statements Made on FOX," Punditfact, January 31, 2019, https://www.politifact.com/punditfact/tv/fox/; "Statements Made on CNN," https://www.politifact.com/punditfact/tv/cnn/; "Rachel Maddow's File," https://www.politifact.com/personalities/rachel-maddow.

28. Charles S. Taber and Milton Lodge, "Motivated Skepticism in the Evaluation of Political Beliefs," *American Journal of Political Science*, 50 (July 2006): 755–769.

29. Graber and Dunaway, *Mass Media and American Politics*, 344; Dave D'Alessio and Mike Allen, "Media Bias in Presidential Elections: A Meta-Analysis," *Journal of Communication*, 50 (Autumn 2000): 133–156; and W. Lance Bennett, *News: The Politics of Illusion*, 9th ed. (New York: Longman, 2012). The problems of objective reporting are discussed by long-time Texas reporter Bill Minutaglio in two of his columns on the "State of the Media" published in the *Texas Observer*: "Jim Moore Calls for *The Texas Tribune* to Distance Itself from Funders," May 10, 2014, and "To Each According to Greed: Rick Perry, Toyota and the Texas Enterprise Fund," June 12, 2014, http://www.texasobserver.org/blog/stateofmedia.

30. Timothy E. Cook, *Governing with the News: The News Media as a Political Institution*, 2nd ed. (Chicago: University of Chicago Press, 2005), 71.

31. Graber and Dunaway, *Mass Media and American Politics*, 44–46.

32. Debbie Lord, "What is Net Neutrality and What Does the Repeal of It Mean for You?" *Atlanta Journal Constitution*, June 13, 2018, https://www.ajc.com/news/national/what-net-neutrality-and-what-does-the-repeal-mean-for-you/dKzgY07FSMolRARKPHtw5N/.

33. *Lesher v. Coyel*, June 16, 2014 No. 05-12-01357-CV.

34. "American Society of News Editors, *The 2018 ASNE Newsroom Diversity Survey*, November 15, 2018, https://www.asne.org/diversity-survey-2018; and Michael Barthel, "In the News Industry, Diversity Is Lowest at Smaller Outlets," *Pew Research Center*, August 4, 2015, http://www.pewresearch.org/fact-tank/2015/08/04/in-the-news-industry-diversity-is-lowest-at-smaller-outlets.

35. Staff, "Seven Men Dominate Political Analysis in Texas," *Texas Research Institute*, March 26, 2015, http://texasresearch.org/blog/seven-men-dominate-political-analysis-texas.

36. Andrea Grimes, "State of the Media: Building a Better Punditocracy," *Texas Observer*, May 4, 2015, https://www.texasobserver.org/state-of-the-media-texas-political-media.

37. Merdies Hayes, "Mass Murders Expose Bias, Stereotypes in Media Coverage," *Our Weekly*, October 8, 2015, http://ourweekly.com/news/2015/oct/08/mass-murders-expose-bias-stereotypes-media-coverag.

38. *ABYZ News Links*, January 2019.

39. Elisa Shearer, "Hispanic Media: Fact Sheet," *Pew Journalism*, June 2016, http://www.journalism.org/files/2016/06/State-of-the-News-Media-Report-2016-FINAL.pdf.

40. Nancy Vogt, "African-American Media: Fact Sheet," *Pew Journalism*, April 29, 2015, http://www.journalism.org/2015/04/29/african-american-media-fact-sheet; and Nancy Vogt, "African-American Media: Fact Sheet," *Pew Journalism*, June 2016, http://www.journalism.org/files/2016/06/State-of-the-News-Media-Report-2016-FINAL.pdf.

41. Christine Barbour and Gerald C. Wright, *Keeping the Republic*, 6th ed. (Los Angeles: CQ Press, 2014), 562.

42. "State of the News Media, 2014," *Pew Research Journalism Project*, March 26, 2014, http://www.journalism.org/packages/state-of-the-news-media-2014.

43. Erica Grieder, "National State of Mind," *Texas Monthly*, March 2016, 16.

44. Paul Burka, "The Capitol Press Corpse," *Texas Monthly*, January 2008, http://www.texasmonthly.com
/story/capitol-press-corpse. An oft-cited pessimistic assessment is Mark Lisheron, "Reloading at the
Statehouse," *American Journalism Review*, September 2010, no longer online.

45. Elise Hu, "A Lively Political Press in a State Where Everything's Bigger," *NPR*, July 5, 2013, http://www
.npr.org/blogs/itsallpolitics/2013/07/05/197987945/a-lively-political-press-in-a-state-where-
everything-s-bigger.

46. "The State of the News Media, 2006," *Pew Project for Excellence in Journalism*, http://stateofthemedia
.org/2006/a-day-in-the-life-of-the-media-intro/local-tv.

47. "Local TV News Project 2001," *Pew Research Journalism Project*, November 1, 2001, http://www
.journalism.org/2001/11/01/local-tv-news-project-2001.

48. Ben H. Bagdikian, *The Media Monopoly*, 6th ed. (Boston: Beacon Press, 1997), 30.

49. Bagdakian, *The Media Monopoly*, p. xxii; Carol Guensburg, "When the Story Is about the Owner,"
American Journalism Review, 20 (December 1998), no longer online; and Gabriel Rossman, "Elites,
Masses, and Media Blacklists: The Dixie Chicks Controversy," *Social Forces*, 83 (2004): 61–78.

50. Bill Minutaglio, "Jim Moore Calls for *The Texas Tribune* to Distance Itself from Funders," *Texas
Observer*, May 10, 2014, https://www.texasobserver.org/close-comfort; and Andrea Grimes, "The
Trouble with Trib Talk," *Texas Observer*, July 14, 2014, https://www.texasobserver.org/trouble-tribtalk.

51. "State of the News Media 2013," *Pew*.

52. Mark Jurkowitz, "The Growth in Digital Reporting: What It Means for Journalism and News
Consumers," *Pew Research Center: Journalism and Media*, March 26, 2014, http://www.journalism
.org/2014/03/26/the-growth-in-digital-reporting.

53. "Digital: Top 50 Online News Entities (2015)," *Pew Research Center*, no longer online.

54. Jurkowitz, "The Growth in Digital Reporting."

55. Mitchell, "Key Findings."

Chapter 7

1. Burdett A. Loomis and Allan J. Cigler, "Introduction: The Changing Nature of Interest Group Politics,"
in *Interest Group Politics* 9th ed., ed. Allan J. Cigler and Burdett A. Loomis (Washington, D.C.: CQ
Press, 2015), 2.

2. Joseph M. Bessette, John J. Pitney Jr., Lyle C. Brown, Joyce A. Langenegger, Sonia R. García, Ted
A. Lewis, and Robert E. Biles, *American Government and Politics: Deliberation, Democracy and
Citizenship* (Boston: Wadsworth, 2012), 273.

3. Christy Hoppe, "Business Lobby Flexes Muscle in Legislature," *Dallas Morning News*, April 12, 2003.

4. Robert T. Garrett and Christy Hoppe, "Two Bills Down to Embers," *Dallas Morning News*, May 11, 2009.

5. Peggy Fikac, "Perry Signs Hate Crimes Legislation," *San Antonio Express-News*, May 12, 2001.

6. Gary Scharrer, "Board Rejects Rebel Plate," *San Antonio Express-News*, November 11, 2011. See
Walker v. Sons of the Confederate Veterans, 576 U.S. ___ (2015). See also, Aman Batheja, "Supreme
Court: Texas Can Ban Confederate License Plates," *Texas Tribune, June* 18, 2015, http://www
.texastribune.org/2015/06/18/supreme-court-rules-texas-confederate-license-plat.

7. For an examination of the origins of LULAC and its founders, Alonso S. Perales and Adela
Sloss-Vento, see Cynthia Orozco, *No Mexicans, Women, or Dogs Allowed: The Rise of the Mexican
American Civil Rights Movement* (Austin: University of Texas Press, 2009).

8. See Sonia R. García, Valerie Martinez-Ebers, Irasema Coronado, Sharon A. Navarro, and Patricia A.
Jaramillo, *Politicas: Latina Public Officials in Texas* (Austin: University of Texas Press, 2008).
Chapter 3 concerns Representative Irma Rangel.

9. For information on the role of the Christian Coalition, see James Lamare, Jerry L. Polinard, and
Robert D. Wrinkle, "Texas: Religion and Politics in God's Country," in *The Christian Right in
American Politics: Marching Toward the Millennium*, ed. John C. Green, Mark J. Rozell, and
Clyde Wilcox (Washington, D.C.: Georgetown University Press, 2003), 59–78.

10. Peggy Fikac, "Alliance Formed to Monitor Radical Right," *Houston Chronicle*, October 1, 1995.

11. See Dennis Shirley, *Valley Interfaith and School Reform: Organizing for Power in South Texas*
(Austin: University of Texas Press, 2002).

12. For a history of COPS, see Mark R. Warren, *Dry Bones Rattling: Community Building to Revitalize an
American Democracy* (Princeton, NJ: Princeton University Press, 2001).

13. Richard Kearney, "Political Parties, Interest Groups and Campaigns," in Ann O'M. Bowman and
Richard Kearney, *State and Local Government*, 9th ed. (Boston: Wadsworth Cengage Learning, 2014),
117–127.

14. H. C. Pittman, *Inside the Third House: A Veteran Lobbyist Takes a 50-Year Frolic Through Texas Politics* (Austin: Eakin Press, 1992), 219. See also John Spong, "State Bar," *Texas Monthly*, July 2003, 110–113, 148–149.

15. "Doctors' Orders: Medical Lobby Becomes a Powerhouse in Austin," *Wall Street Journal*, May 19, 1999.

16. "Austin's Oldest Profession: Texas' Top Lobby Clients & Those Who Service Them," *Texans for Public Justice*, 2013/2014, http://info.tpj.org/reports/pdf/Oldest2013WithCover.pdf.

17. Lobby Reports Search & Lists, "Static Lobby Registration Lists," *Texas Ethics Commission*, https://www.ethics.state.tx.us/tedd/2018LobbyGroupByLobbyist.pdf. See also https://www.ethics.state.tx.us/tedd/2019LobbyGroupByClient.pdf.

18. Keith E. Hamm and Charles W. Wiggins, "Texas: The Transformation from Personal to Informational Lobbying," in *Interest Group Politics in the Southern States*, ed. Ronald J. Hrebenar and Olive S. Thomas (Tuscaloosa: University of Alabama Press, 1992), 80.

19. "Testimony by Thomas J. Kim, MD, MPH, Committee on Public Health on Telemedicine in Texas," *Texas Medical Society*, February 10, 2016, https://www.texmed.org/Template.aspx?id=35277.

20. Revolving Door Prohibition, "National Conference of State Legislatures," December 15, 2017, http://www.ncsl.org/research/ethics/50-state-table-revolving-door-prohibitions.aspx.

21. "Major Issues of the 84th Legislature," *House Research Organization*, September 22, 2015, http://www.hro.house.state.tx.us/pdf/focus/major84.pdf, 66. See also, Jay Root, "Ethics Reform Not Swept Under Rug, But Not Sweeping Either," *Texas Tribune*, June 1, 2017, https://www.texastribune.org/2017/06/01/ethics-reform-not-swept-under-rug-not-sweeping-either.

22. Jay Root, "Legislature Approves Bill Requiring Disclosure of Government Contracts," *Texas Tribune*, May 28, 2017, https://www.texastribune.org/2017/05/28/bill-requiring-disclosure-government-contracts-approved.

23. Matt Stiles, "Are Gifts Used as Calling Cards or as Keys to Legislators' Offices?" *San Antonio Express-News*, February 5, 2009. See also David Saleh Rauf, "Free Tickets Just Part of Game for Legislators," *San Antonio Express-News*, September 8, 2013.

24. Tom Benning, "Gun Bills Dominated Social Media Chatter on the Legislature," *Dallas Morning News*, July 6, 2015, http://trailblazersblog.dallasnews.com/2015/07/gun-bills-dominated-social-media-chatter-on-the-legislature.html.

25. "#TXLEGE: The Official Hashtag of Texas," *Influence Opinions*, July 2015, http://influenceopinions.com/txlege-the-official-hashtag-of-texas.

26. Campaign Finance Reports Search & Lists. "Political Committee Lists," *Texas Ethics Commission*, http://www.ethics.state.tx.us/dfs/paclists.htm.

27. For an examination of the total expenditures by PACS during the 2018 election cycle, see Campaign Finance Reports Search & Lists, "Political Committee Lists, Total Contributions and Expenditures Each Year by PAC by Year, 2018," https://www.ethics.state.tx.us/dfs/paclists.htm. See also "Top 10 PACS of the 2018 Texas Election Cycle," at https://www.transparencytexas.org/top-ten-pacs-of-the-2018-texas-election-cycle.

28. Ralph Blumenthal and Carl Hulse, "Judge Lets Stand 2 of 3 Charges Faced by Delay," *New York Times*, December 6, 2005; and Gary Martin, "Texas Jury Indicts Delay," *San Antonio Express-News*, September 29, 2005.

29. "A Brief Overview of the Texas Ethics Commission and Its Duties," *Texas Ethics Commission*, September 22, 2009, https://www.ethics.state.tx.us/pamphlet/B09ethic.pdf. See also on the same website, "Campaign Finance Guide for Political Committees," *Texas Ethics Commission*, June 16, 2016, https://www.ethics.state.tx.us/guides/pac_guide.pdf.

30. "Sworn Complaint Open Orders," *Texas Ethics Commission*, https://www.ethics.state.tx.us/sworncomp/orders. See also a list of the most common complaints at https://www.ethics.state.tx.us/whatsnew/Most_Common_Sworn_Complaint_Violations.pdf.

31. "Vetoes of Legislation, 83rd Legislature," *House Research Organization*, August 21, 2013, http://www.hro.house.state.tx.us/pdf/focus/veto83.pdf.

32. David Saleh Rauf, "Dark Money Disclosure Fight Heading Back to the Texas Legislature," *San Antonio Express-News*, March 18, 2016.

33. Dave Lieber, "Texas Ethics Laws Are Tightened, but Not as Much as They Could Have Been," *Fort Worth Star-Telegram*, June 26, 2009. See also "2011 Legislation," *Texas Ethics Commission*, http://www.ethics.state.tx.us/whatsnew/leg2011.html.

34. "Lobby Watch: Ethics Commission's Teeth in Perry's Hands," *Texans for Public Justice*, June 16, 2011, http://info.tpj.org/Lobby_Watch/pdf/EthicsCommissionFines.pdf.

35. "U.S. Supreme Court Ruling in Citizens United v. Federal Election Commission," *Texas Ethics Commission*, http://www.ethics.state.tx.us/whatsnew/US_Supreme_Court_Ruling.html. See also, "Adopted Rules," *Texas Ethics Commission*, http://www.ethics.state.tx.us/tec/rules.htm.

36. Laylan Copelin, "State Law Holds Back Corporate Donations," *Austin American-Statesman*, January 2, 2011. See also Tom Benning, "Super PACs Pointed to Help Rick Perry's Presidential Run," *Dallas Morning News*, September 16, 2011.

37. Sam Kinch Jr. with Anne Marie Kilday, *Too Much Money Is Not Enough: Big Money and Political Power in Texas* (Austin: Campaigns for People, 2000).

38. Molly Ivins, "Who Let the PACs Out? Woof, Woof!" *Fort Worth Star-Telegram*, February 18, 2001.

39. "With Perry's Signature, Texas Campaign Laws Will Get Boost They Need," *Austin American-Statesman*, June 9, 2003; Ginger Richardson, "Stronger Ethics Rules Hang on House Vote," *Fort Worth Star-Telegram*, June 2, 2003.

40. Clive S. Thomas and Ronald J. Hrebenar, "Political Parties, Interest Groups and Campaigns," in *State and Local Government*, 8th ed., ed. Ann O'M. Bowman and Richard Kearney (Boston: Wadsworth, 2010), 157.

41. Nicholas Kusnetz, "Only Three States Score Higher than D+ in State Integrity Investigation; 11 Flunk," *Center for Public Integrity*, updated November 23, 2015, https://www.publicintegrity .org/2015/11/09/188693/only-three-states-score-higher-d-state-inntegrity-investigation-11-flunk.

Chapter 8

1. Nick Jimenez, "This Session Should Be Known as Gun Legislature," *Corpus Christi Caller-Times*, June 3, 2015.

2. Tim Eaton, "Texas House Members Approve Panic Buttons in Offices," *Austin American-Statesman*, January 15, 2015.

3. Kirk Evans, Edwin Walker, Michele Byington, and Randy Macchi, *Texas Gun Law: Armed and Educated*, 2016–2017 ed. (n.p.: Texas Law Shield, 2015), 220–222. Written from a pro-gun perspective by four attorney authors, this book is subtitled *A Complete Guide to Gun Law in Texas*. For 12 articles on guns in Texas, see *Texas Monthly*'s "The Guns Issue," April 2016.

4. Alan Rosenthal, *Heavy Lifting: The Job of the American Legislature* (Washington, DC: CQ Press, 2004), 246–247. See also Alan Rosenthal, *Engines of Democracy: Politics and Policymaking in State Legislatures* (Washington, DC: CQ Press, 2009), 8–11.

5. For the experiences of Melissa and Rick Noriega (D-Houston), see Paul Burka, "Duty Calls," *Texas Monthly*, March 2006, 12, 14, 16.

6. Ross Ramsey, "Texas Legislature's Special Session: An Emergency Easily Avoided," *New York Times*, June 14, 2013.

7. For chapters by Gary Keith and six other authorities on redistricting in the Lone Star State, see Gary Keith, ed., *Rotten Boroughs, Political Thickets, and Legislative Donnybrooks: Redistricting in Texas* (Austin: University of Texas Press, 2013).

8. Quoted by AP journalist Mike Sherman in "High Court Upholds '1 person, 1 vote,'" *Waco Tribune-Herald*, April 5, 2016. See also Michael S. Kang, "Gerrymandering and the Constitutional Norm Against Government Partisanship," *Michigan Law Review* 116 (December 2017): 351–420, michiganlawreview.org/wp-content/uploads/2017/12/116/MichLRev351_Kang.pdf and Lyle Denniston's opinion analysis, "Leaving a Constitutional Ideal Still Undefined," *SCOTUS blog* (April 4, 2016), http://www.scotusblog.com/2016/04/opinion-analysis-leaving-a-constitutional-ideal-still-undefined.

9. Olivia Messer, "The Texas Legislature's Sexist Little Secret," *Texas Observer*, July 31, 2013, http://www .texasobserver.org/the-texas-legislatures-sexist-little-secret.

10. Jay Root, "Bill Stripping Pensions from Felon Politicians Advances," *Texas Tribune*, May 8, 2017, http://www.texastribune.org/2017/05/08/bill-stripping-pensions-from-corrupt-politicians-advances.

11. Some former lieutenant governors have been the subjects of books that give insight into this role. Ben Barnes served as Speaker of the House from 1965 to 1969 and as lieutenant governor from 1969 to 1973. For information on his service as presiding officer in each chamber, see Ben Barnes with Lisa Dickey, *Barn Burning, Barn Building: Tales of a Political Life, From LBJ to George W. Bush and Beyond* (Albany, TX: Bright Sky Press, 2006). Bob Bullock's years as lieutenant governor (1991–1999) are covered in Dave McNeely and Jim Henderson, *Bob Bullock: God Bless Texas* (Austin: University of Texas Press, 2008). Bill Hobby's experiences and observations from 18 years as lieutenant governor (1973–1991) are related in Bill Hobby with Saralee Tiede, *How Things Really Work: Lessons from a Life in Politics* (Austin: Center for American History, University of Texas at Austin, 2010). For information on Lieutenant Governor David Dewhurst's 12 years in office (2003–2015), see his interview with Erica Grieder, "The David Dewhurst Exit Interview," *Texas Monthly*, December 2014, 126–127, 178, 180, 182, and 184. Erica Grieder provides a profile of Dan Patrick shortly after his 2014 election as lieutenant governor in her "Master of the Senate," *Texas Monthly*, December 2014, 122–125, 186, 188, 190, 192, 194, 200, and 205–206.

12. Chuck Lindell, "Dan Patrick Taps Republicans, Donors for Advisory Boards," *Austin American-Statesman*, January 16, 2015. For commentary on Patrick's leadership in the 84th regular session, see Chuck Lindell, "Dan Patrick: Glory Hog or Inspired Leader?" *Austin American-Statesman*, March 16, 2015; Jonathan Tilove. "As Lieutenant Governor, Dan Patrick Remains a 'Christian First,'" April 5, 2015; and Mike Ward, "Patrick Wins High Marks for Senate Leadership," *Houston Chronicle*, June 8, 2015.

13. Quoted by Tim Eaton and Chuck Lindell, "Sine Die: The Gavel Falls, the Session Ends," *Austin American-Statesman*, June 2, 2015.

14. The changing role of the Speaker since 1876 is described by authors Patrick L. Cox and Michael Phillips in *The House Will Come to Order: How the Texas Speaker Became a Power in State and National Politics* (Austin: University of Texas Press, 2010).

15. For one speaker pro tempore's responses to questions about his role in the 78th and 79th Texas legislatures, see Monica Gutierrez, "Turner on a Tightrope: A Few Questions with Speaker Pro Tempore Sylvester Turner," *Texas Observer*, June 24, 2005, 10–11, 18.

16. Laylan Copelin, "Judge Tosses Out Spending Restrictions for Speaker Elections," *Austin American-Statesman*, August 26, 2008. See also *Free Market Foundation v. Reisman*, 573 F Supp 2nd 997 (W.D. Tex. 2008).

17. Ross Ramsey, "That Old Speaker-Ousting G.O.P. Gang of 11, Down to 4," *New York Times*, September 8, 2013. Concerning opposition to Straus and his key lieutenants in the 2016 Republican primaries, see Erica Grieder, "Round the Bend," *Texas Monthly*, May 2016, 22 and 24.

18. Tim Eaton and Chuck Lindell, "Joe Straus Fends Off First Challenge to House Speaker Post in 40 Years," *Austin American-Statesman*, January 14, 2015.

19. Tim Eaton, "Joe Straus to Run for Another Term as Speaker, *Austin American-Statesman*, June 4, 2015; and Gilbert Garcia, "Tangling with Straus Is Tougher Than It Looks," *San Antonio Express-News*, July 31, 2015.

20. See John Gonzalez, "Speaker Straus Foils Conservative Challenge," *San Antonio Express-News*, March 2, 2016; and "Giving Up the Gavel: After Five Terms as House Speaker, Joe Straus Calls It Quits," an interview with R. G. Ratcliffe, *Texas Monthly*, December 2017, 54 and 56, https://www.texasmonthly .com/politics/joe-straus-giving-up-the-gavel.

21. Lisa Falkenberg, "Houston's Davis Is Sole GOP No Vote on Abortion Bill," *Houston Chronicle*, July 3, 2013.

22. Becca Aronson, "Bipartisan Caucus Lays Groundwork for Food Movement," *San Antonio Express-News*, May 31, 2013.

23. Steve Taylor, "New Caucus Set Up to Ensure Region Gets Its Message Across," *Rio Grande Guardian*, July 21, 2015.

24. See *Major Issues of the 85th Legislature*, Focus Report No. 85-8 (Austin: House Research Organization, Texas House of Representatives), December 18, 2017, 5, http://hro.house.texas.gov/pdf/focus/major85.pdf.

25. House and Senate Rules based on Acts 1985, 69th Leg., Chap. 478, Sec. 1.

26. Rusty Hardin & Associates, LLP, "Investigative Report to the House Select Committee on Transparency in State Agency Operations Regarding Conduct by University of Texas Regent Wallace Hall and Impeachment under the June 25, 2013 Proclamation," March 2014, http://www.house.state .tx.us/media/pdf/Investigative-Report-Committee-on-Transparency-in-State-Agency-Operations.pdf.

27. For a more detailed description of the lawmaking process, see *How a Bill Becomes a Law: 86th Legislature*, Focus Report No. 86-2 (Austin: House Research Organization, Texas House of Representatives), February 28, 2019, https//hro.house.texas.gov/pdf/focus/hwbill86.pdf.

28. For more information on how committees work, see *House Committee Procedures: 84th Legislature*, Focus Report No. 84-3 (Austin: House Research Organization, Texas House of Representatives, March 4, 2015), http://www.hro.house.state.tx.us/pdf/focus/compro84.pdf.

29. For a defense of the two-thirds rule, see Paul Burka, "First, Dew No Harm," *Texas Monthly*, February 2006, 16, 18.

30. Caitlin Dewey, "Wendy Davis 'Tweetstorm' Was Planned in Advance," *Washington Post*, June 26, 2013. During the filibuster, Senator Davis wore her famous pink Mizuno running shoes. By contrast, Davis's Republican successor, former Tea Party leader and abortion opponent Konni Burton, made her first Senate appearance wearing black cowboy boots marked "Stand for Life." See Dave Montgomery, "New Tarrant Senator Makes a Statement with Her Footwear," *Fort Worth Star-Telegram*, January 14, 2015.

31. As one authority explains, this difference in the two-thirds majorities required by Article IV, Section 14, represents "a mysterious error in the present constitution." See George D. Braden, *Citizens' Guide to the Proposed New Texas Constitution* (Austin: Sterling Swift, 1975), 15.

32. Terrence Stutz, "Senator Ripped for Killing Statewide Ban on Texting While Driving," *Dallas News*, May 28, 2013.

33. Dave Mann and Jake Bernstein, "UndemoCraddick," *Texas Observer*, February 18, 2005, 3.

34. "An Online Look at the Texas 83rd Legislative Session," *Influence Opinions*, June 2013, influenceopinions.com/white-paper-an-online-look-at-the-83rd-texas-legislative-session.

35. Ibid.

36. For a veteran Texas journalist's account of four decades of reporting on the Texas legislature, see Dave McNeely, "A Press Corps on the Lege," *Texas Observer*, May 27, 2005, 8–11. See also the biography of the late Molly Ivins (1944–2007), a liberal journalist who covered the Texas legislature for many years: Bill Minutaglio and W. Michael Smith, *Molly Ivins: A Rebel Life* (New York: Public Affairs, 2009).

Chapter 9

1. For a revisionist view of Davis and his administration, see Carl H. Moneyhon, *Edmund J. Davis of Texas: Civil War General, Republican Leader, Reconstruction Governor* (Fort Worth: Texas Christian University Press, 2010).

2. Brian McCall, *The Power of the Texas Governor: Connally to Bush* (Austin: University of Texas Press, 2009). For a broad view of governors across the country, see Alan Rosenthal, *The Best Job in Politics: Exploring How Governors Succeed as Policy Leaders*, rev. ed. (Washington, DC: CQ Press, 2012).

3. For former Governor Dolph Briscoe's account of his election campaigns and six years (1973–1979) as governor, see his *Dolph Briscoe: My Life in Ranching and Politics*, as told to Don Carleton (Austin: Center for American History, University of Texas at Austin, 2008), 151–261. A biography that tells Governor Ann Richards's story is Jan Reid, *Let the People In: The Life and Times of Ann Richards* (Austin: University of Texas Press, 2012). For an insider's view of George W. Bush's years as governor, see Karl Rove, "A New Kind of Governor," in Rove's *Courage and Consequences: My Life as a Conservative in the Fight* (New York: Threshold Editions, 2010), chap. 6.

4. See Carolyn Barta, *Bill Clements: Texian to His Toenails* (Austin: Eakin Press, 1996); Bill Minutaglio, *First Son: George W. Bush and the Bush Family Dynasty* (New York: Times Books, 1999); and Clarke Rountree, *George W. Bush: A Biography* (Santa Barbara, CA: Greenwood, 2011).

5. For grades on Perry's leadership in eight public policy areas, see Nate Blakeslee, Pamela Colloff, Erica Grieder, Mimi Swartz, and Brian D. Sweany, "The Rick Perry Report Card," *Texas Monthly*, July 2014, 80–95. This same issue of *Texas Monthly* includes Paul Burka's assessment of Perry's administration (pp. 24, 26, and 28) and Brian D. Sweany's lengthy interview, "Face to Face with Rick Perry," (pp. 74–78, 150–155, 157–158). For *The Texas Tribune's* analysis of Governor Perry's time in office, see "The Perry Legacy," https://apps.texastribune.org/perry-legacy.

6. For campaign finance information about Governor Abbott and many other politicians, see *Project Vote Smart*, https://votesmart.org/candidate/campaign-finance/50168/gregory-abbott#.XHBn3S2ZPVp.

7. Patrick Svitek, "Valdez Has $222,000 for General Election, a Fraction of Abbott's Millions," *Texas Tribune*, July 17, 2018, https://www.texastribune.org/2018/07/17/lupe-valdez-greg-abbott-millions-november-election.

8. Morgan Smith, "Gov. Abbott: I'm Keeping a List of Lawmakers Who Oppose Me during the Special Session," *Texas Tribune*, July 17, 2017, https://www.texastribune.org/2017/07/17/abbott-property-taxes-are-top-issue-special-session.

9. Brian Rosenthal and Patrick Svitek, "Grand Jurors Deny Politics Played Role in Perry Indictment," *Houston Chronicle*, August 19, 2014.

10. Sean Collins Walsh, "Rick Perry Criminal Case Officially Dismissed." *Austin American-Statesman*, April 7, 2016.

11. For an interactive list of government salaries, see "Government Salaries Explorer," *Texas Tribune*, https://salaries.texastribune.org.

12. Gary Scharrer and Richard Dunam, "Perry's Retirement, Pay Boost Spark Charges of Hypocrisy," *Houston Chronicle*, December 17, 2011.

13. For example, see Bob Ray Sanders, "Gov. Perry's Campaign Should Reimburse Texas," *Fort Worth Star-Telegram*, April 4, 2012.

14. "The Texas Supreme Court and Legislature Help Perry Cloak Travel Security Expenses," *Houston Chronicle*, July 10, 2011.

15. Peggy Fikac, "Out-of-State Travel Tab for Abbott's Security Tops $1 Million," *San Antonio Express-News*, April 29, 2018.

16. R. G. Ratcliff, "Perry's a Long Way from the Cotton Farm," *Houston Chronicle*, July 26, 2009; Jay Root, "Spending on Perry's Austin Mansion Hits $800,000," *Texas Tribune*, November 23, 2011, https://www.texastribune.org/2011/11/23/governors-mansion-spending-hits-800000/

17. Wayne Slater, "Rick Perry Won't Rule Out Another Presidential Bid," *Dallas Morning News*, February 7, 2012; and Peggy Fikac, "Our Travelin' Governor Perry Will Spend Even More Time on the Road," *Houston Chronicle*, September 12, 2011.

18. Jim Nicar, "A Summer of Discontent," *Texas Alcalde*, September/October 1997, 83. For detailed accounts of Jim Ferguson's downfall, which opened the way for Miriam "Ma" Ferguson to be elected governor for two terms, see Bruce Rutherford, *The Impeachment of Jim Ferguson* (Austin: Eakin Press, 1983); and Cortez A. M. Ewing, "The Impeachment of James E. Ferguson," *Southwestern Social Science Quarterly* 48 (June 1933): 184–210.

19. Laurel Wamsley, "UPDATE: Greg Abbott Visits Santa Fe High School Reopening After Shooting," *Houston Public Media*, May 29, 2018, https://www.houstonpublicmedia.org/articles/news/2018 /05/29/287932/classes-resume-at-texas-school-for-1st-time-since-shooting.

20. Anna M. Tinsley, "UNT Students Petition for a Speaker Other Than Texas Gov. Abbott," *Fort Worth Star-Telegram*, April 8, 2015; and Anna M Tinsley, "Protesters Escorted Out with Little Disruption as Abbott Speaks at UNT," *Fort Worth Star-Telegram*, May 17, 2015. Cecilia Abbott earned three degrees from St. Thomas University (bachelor's degree with a major in psychology, master's degree in education, and master's degree in theology), and she has served as a member of the board of directors for that university.

21. For example, see Gov. Greg Abbott, "Franchise Tax Relief Is Essential to Texas Economy," *Austin American-Statesman*, April 15, 2015.

22. See Abbott's social media accounts at https://www.gregabbott.com/stay-connected/. Note that LinkedIn does not reveal a person's total number of connections, listing anything over 500 connections as "500+."

23. Ken Herman, "First Lady of Texas Takes a New Job," *Austin American-Statesman*, November 7, 2003. Concerning her salary, see "Anita Perry's Salary Comes Indirectly from Governor's Backers," *Austin American-Statesman*, September 14, 2011. For Anita Perry's responses to questions about her life in politics, see her interview by Evan Smith, "Anita Perry," *Texas Monthly*, September 2005, 178–180, 182, 184.

24. For more on Texanthropy and Cecilia Abbott's other philanthropic endeavors, see "Texanthropy" at https://gov.texas.gov/first-lady/texanthropy.

25. For the text of Abbott's plan, see http://gov.texas.gov/files/press-office/Restoring_The_Rule_Of_ Law_01082016.pdf.

26. See Governor Greg Abbott, *Broken but Unbowed: The Fight to Fix a Broken America* (New York: Threshold Editions of Simon and Schuster, 2016).

27. Rick Casey, "Shift in Power Lies Ahead for Government in Texas," *Houston Chronicle*, April 4, 2014.

28. See James S. Olson and Sharon Phair, "Anatomy of a Race Riot: Beaumont, Texas, 1943," *Texana* 11, 1 (1973): 64–72; James A. Burran, "Violence in an 'Arsenal of Democracy,'" *East Texas Historical Journal* 14 (Spring 1976): 39–51; and Valentine Belfiglio, *Honor, Pride, Duty: A History of the Texas State Guard* (Austin: Eakin Press, 1995), 64.

29. Christy Hoppe, "Amid Conspiracy Talk, Abbott Orders Texas Guard to Keep an Eye on Federal Military Training," *Dallas Morning News*, April 29, 2015; and Lisa Falkenberg, "Abbott Fans the Flames of Radical Paranoids," *Houston Chronicle*, May 3, 2015.

30. Sig Christenson, "Texas Guard May See Its Copters Fly Away," *San Antonio Express-News*, January 19, 2014.

31. Edgar Walters, "Texas Governor Signs $217 Billion Budget, Vetoes $120 Million," *Texas Tribune*, June 12, 2017, https://www.texastribune.org/2017/06/12/texas-governor-signs-217-billion-budget-vetoes-120-million.

32. Steve Clark, "Perry Rejects Medicaid Expansion for Texas Residents," *Valley Morning Star*, July 10, 2012; and Edgar Walters, "With Hospital Funds in Question, Abbott Holds Firm On Medicaid Expansion," *Texas Tribune*, April 20, 2015, https://www.texastribune.org/2015/04/20/hospital-funds-question-abbott-holds-firm-against-.

33. RP75-Relating to the Establishment and Support of Western Governors University Texas," *Legislative Reference Library*, August 3, 2011, http://www.lrl.state.tx.us/scanned/govdocs/Rick%20Perry/2011 /RP75.pdf.

34. For all proclamations issued by Governor Abbott, see "Proclamations by Governor Greg Abbott," *Legislative Reference Library*, https://lrl.texas.gov/legeleaders/governors/displayProcs.cfm?governorID =45&legSession=&govdoctypeID=2.

35. Bill Hethcock, "Fortune 500 Company to Move Headquarters from California to DFW," *Dallas Business Journal*, November 30, 2018, https://www.bizjournals.com/dallas/news/2018/11/30/mckesson-relocates-headquarters-to-north-texas.html.

36. Lydia DePillis, "Texas v. the UK's Not as Easy a Sell as Gov. Abbott Thinks," *Houston Chronicle*, July 7, 2016.

37. Office of the Governor, *Legislative Appropriations Request for Fiscal Years 2014 and 2015*, August 30, 2012, p. 1, available online at http://governor.state.tx.us/files/financial-services/LAR_AY_2014-15.pdf.

38. See Ken Herman, "Lunch and Hunt with Perry for $150,000," *Austin American-Statesman*, November 5, 2003; Clay Robison, "Perry's Perks Go to Big Spenders," *Houston Chronicle*, November 5, 2003; and W. Gardner Selby, "Critic Pans Perry's Bid for Funds as 'Greedy and Seedy,'" *San Antonio Express-News*, November 5, 2003.

39. Quoted by Wayne Slater, "Perry Criticized for Soliciting Funds," *Dallas Morning News*, November 5, 2003.

40. Paul Weber, "Perry's Tech Fund Showing Gains," *Dallas Morning News*, February 5, 2014.

41. For the website of the Texas government's efforts to attract business to the state, see *GO BIG IN TEXAS*, https://businessintexas.com.

42. Details of legislative-executive relations are found in Patrick Cox and Michael Phillips, *This House Will Come to Order: How the Texas Speaker Became a Power in State and National Politics* (Austin: University of Texas Press, 2010); Bill Hobby and Saralee Tiede, *How Things Really Work: Lessons from a Life in Politics* (Austin: Center for American History, University of Texas at Austin, 2010); and Dave McNeely and Jim Henderson, *Bob Bullock: God Bless Texas* (Austin: University of Texas Press, 2008).

43. See Dave Montgomery, "Perry Defends Ceremonial Bill Signings that Hutchison Blasts as 'Phony,'" *Fort Worth Star-Telegram*, August 21, 2009.

44. See *Vetoes of Legislation*, 77th, 78th, 79th, 80th, 81st, 82nd, and 83rd Legislatures, Focus Reports No. 77-10, No. 78-11, No. 79-9, No. 80-6, No. 81-7, No. 82-5, and No. 83-6 (Austin: House Research Organization, Texas House of Representatives, 2001, 2003, 2005, 2007, 2009, 2011, and 2013).

45. Patrick Michels, "Abbott Veto Is a Major Setback for Oversight of Troubled Adult Guardianship System," *Texas Observer*, June 24, 2017, https://www.texasobserver.org/guardianship-veto.

46. Ryan Murphy and Annie Daniel, "Here's What Happened to Texas Gov. Greg Abbott's Agenda during the Special Session," *Texas Tribune*, August 16, 2017, https://apps.texastribune.org/special-session-issues.

47. Sommer Ingram, "Perry's Texas Supreme Court Picks Criticized as Too Business-Friendly," *Dallas Morning News*, October 31, 2011.

48. Beth Brown, "Supreme Court Is Elected, but Bears Perry's Stamp," *New York Times*, August 12, 2011.

49. Lauren McGaughy, "Christmas Clemency: Gov. Greg Abbott Pardons Six Texans, Two for Marijuana Possession," *Dallas Morning News*, December 21, 2018.

50. Angela K. Brown, "Texas Governor Gives Copy of Pardon to Man's Family," *Fort Worth Star-Telegram*, March 20, 2010.

51. Bob Ray Sanders, "Ex-Governor's Death Penalty Skepticism a Welcome Step," *Fort Worth Star-Telegram*, October 25, 2009.

52. Jolie McCullough, "Minutes Before Execution, Texas Gov. Greg Abbott Commutes the Sentence of Thomas Whitaker," *Texas Tribune*, February 22, 2018, https://www.texastribune.org/2018/02/22/texas-gov-greg-abbott-thomas-whitaker-death-sentence.

53. Lyle Larson, "The Shape of Texas Government Needs an Extreme Makeover," *Star-Telegram*, May 13, 2016, https://www.star-telegram.com/opinion/opn-columns-blogs/other-voices/article77536762.html.

54. "Rights of Government Officials Involved with Same-Sex Wedding Ceremonies," Opinion No. KP-0025, *Attorney General of Texas*, June 28, 2015, https://www.texasattorneygeneral.gov/opinions/opinions/51paxton/op/2015/kp0025.pdf.

55. WFAA Staff, "Greg Abbott: 'I Go Into the Office, I Sue the Federal Government,'" *WFAA.com*, October 30, 2013, http://www.politifact.com/texas/statements/2013/may/10/greg-abbott/greg-abbott-.

56. Chuck Lindell, "Ken Paxton Pivots from Suing Obama to Defending Trump Policies," *Statesman*, September 25, 2018, https://www.statesman.com/NEWS/20180127/Ken-Paxton-pivots-from-suing-Obama-to-defending-Trump-policies.

57. "Attorney General Paxton Files Amicus in Virginia School Bathroom Lawsuit," *Office of the Attorney General*, May 11, 2016, https://texasattorneygeneral.gov/news/releases/attorney-general-paxton-files-amicus-in-virginia-school-bathroom-lawsuit.

58. Michael Barajas, "With Texas Court Ruling, Ken Paxton's Felony Case May Fizzle," *Texas Observer*, November 21, 2018, https://www.texasobserver.org/with-texas-court-ruling-ken-paxtons-felony-case-may-fizzle.

59. "Comptroller's Calm Is What State Needs Now," *Corpus Christi Caller-Times*, January 28, 2016.

60. Glenn Hegar, "New Budget Protects Texas Interests," *Austin American-Statesman*, June 14, 2015.

61. Julie Chang, "Amid GOP Flap over Education Funding, George P. Bush Backs Down a Little," *Statesman*, November 20, 2018, https://www.statesman.com/news/20181119/amid-gop-zflap-over-education-funding-george-p-bush-backs-down-little.

62. Asher Price, "U.S. Judge Rebuffs George P. Bush Endangered Species De-Listing Effort," *Statesman*, February 8, 2019, https://www.statesman.com/news/20190207/us-judge-rebuffs-george-p-bush-endangered-species-de-listing-effort. See also Asher Price and Eric Dexheimer, "How Texas Fights Endangered Species Protections, Critter by Critter," *Statesman*, September 25, 2018, https://www.statesman.com/news/20180409/how-texas-fights-endangered-species-protections-critter-by-critter.

63. Emma Platoff, "Texas Ethics Commission Fines Agriculture Commissioner Sid Miller $500 over 2015 Rodeo Trip," *Texas Tribune*, December 21, 2018, https://www.texastribune.org/2018/12/21/sid-miller-texas-agriculture-commissioner-fine-rodeo. See also Alex Samuels, "Some Texas Interest Groups Are Endorsing in Every Statewide Race — but Not in Sid Miller's," *Texas Tribune*, October 4, 2018, https://www.texastribune.org/2018/10/04/sid-miller-agriculture-commissioner-2018-midterms.

64. Paul J. Weber, "Judge Orders Texas Not to Purge Voters After Botching List," *AP News*, February 27, 2019. See also Alexa Ura, "Former Secretary of State David Whitley back at Gov. Greg Abbott's office," *Texas Tribune*, May 31, 2019, https://www.texastribune.org/2019/05/31/former-secretary-state-david-whitley-back-greg-abbotts-office/.

65. "Final Results of Sunset Review: 2016–2017," *Sunset Advisory Commission*, August 2017, https://www.sunset.texas.gov/public/uploads/files/reports/Final%20Results%20of%20Sunset%20Reviews_8-31-17.pdf.

66. W. Gardner Selby, "Greg Abbott Says Texas Shockingly Has More State Workers Per Capita than California, Illinois," *Politifact Texas*, February 20, 2015, http://www.politifact.com/texas/statements/2015/feb/20/greg-abbott/greg-abbott-says-texas-shockingly-has-more-state-w. *Politifact Texas* gave this claim a half-truth rating because Governor Abbott "cherry-picked" states that made his claim seem valid and failed to note Texas's overall low ranking in the number of state employees.

67. Harvey Kronberg, quoted in Jonathan Walters, "Life after Civil Service Reform," *Human Capital Series, IBM Endowment for the Business of Government*, October 2002, 20, http://www.businessofgovernment.org/sites/default/files/LifeAfterCivilServiceRefo.

68. "An Annual Report on Classified Employee Turnover for Fiscal Year 2018," *The State of Texas State Auditor*, December 2018, http://www.sao.texas.gov/reports/main/19-703.pdf.

69. J. David McSwane, "Losing Ground," *Dallas Morning News*, March 31, 2016, http://interactives.dallasnews.com/2016/pay-gap.

70. For background and details, see Dana Jepson, *Fact or Fiction: The SBOE's Role in Textbook Adoption*, Focus Report No. 77-17 (Austin: House Research Organization, Texas House of Representatives, February 22, 2002). For a careful analysis of Texas education, including the SBOE, see Cal Jillson, *Lone Star Tarnished: A Critical Look at Texas Politics and Public Policy* (New York: Routledge, 2012), 103–127.

71. Valerie Strauss, "Texas Governor Picks Home-Schooler to Lead State Board of Education," *Washington Post*, June 26, 2015, https://www.washingtonpost.com/news/answer-sheet/wp/2015/06/26/texas-picks-home-schooler-to-lead-state-board-of-education.

72. "2015 Accountability Manual," *Texas Education Agency*, August 7, 2015, https://rptsvr1.tea.texas.gov/perfreport/account/2015/manual/index.html.

73. Shelly Conlon, "Marlin ISD Gets Formal Reprieve from State Closure," *Waco Tribune-Herald*, March 20, 2018, https://www.wacotrib.com/news/education/marlin-isd-gets-formal-reprieve-from-state-closure/article_fc36aad9-f28a-59dc-b68c-18e448418e45.html.

74. "Governor Abbott Appoints University Student Regents and Student Representative to the Texas Higher Education Coordinating Board," *Office of the Governor*, June 5, 2018, https://gov.texas.gov/news/post/governor-abbott-appoints-university-student-regents-and-student-representative-to-the-texas-higher-education-coordinating-board.

75. Quoted in "Valley Senators, AFL-CIO Differ on Alvarez Appointment to TWC," *Rio Grande Guardian*, February 22, 2016, http://riograndeguardian.com/valley-senators-afl-cio-differ-on-alvarez-appointment-to-twc.

Chapter 10

1. Michele Marcote, "3 Die in Shooting," *Daily Sentinel*, August 28, 2010, http://dailysentinel.com/news/local/article_3d7e23c8-b256-11df-a136-001cc4c002e0.html.

2. Tex. Civ. Prac. & Rem. Code Ann. § 37.004 (West 2008); Tex. Prop. Code Ann. § 22.001 (West 2014). For a discussion of judicial remedies for settling boundary disputes in Texas, see Philip Thomas Segura, "Disputing the Boundary of the Declaratory Judgment Act," *Baylor Law Review* 67, no. 1 (2015): 323–338.

3. Robert A. Carp, Ronald Stidham, Kenneth L. Manning, and Lisa M. Holmes, *Judicial Process in America*, 10th ed. (Thousand Oaks, CA: CQ Press, 2017), 8–9.

4. Leo E. Strine, Jr., "The Harold E. Kohn Lecture: Regular (Judicial) Order as Equity: The Enduring Value of the Distinct Judicial Role," *Temple Law Review* 87 (2014): 91–100.

5. Carp, et al., 11.

6. An easy-to-understand book about Texas law is Richard Alderman's *Know Your Rights: Answers to Texans' Everyday Legal Questions*, 9th ed. (Dallas: Lone Star Books, 2018). Also see, the People's Law School at http://www.law.uh.edu/peopleslaw.

7. Annual statistics and other information on the Texas judicial system are available from the Texas Judicial Council and the Office of Court Administration, http://www.txcourts.gov/about-texas-courts.aspx.

8. Matt Ford, "When Your Judge Isn't a Lawyer," *Atlantic*, February 5, 2017, https://www.theatlantic.com/politics/archive/2017/02/when-your-judge-isnt-a-lawyer/515568.

9. The State Bar of Texas's website includes a how-to manual for prosecuting a claim in justice courts, titled *How to Sue in Justice Court*, which is available at https://www.texasbar.com/AM/Template.cfm?Section=Consumer_and_Tenant_Rights1&Template=/CM/ContentDisplay.cfm&ContentID=24859.

10. See former Chief Justice Joe R. Greenhill, "The Constitutional Amendment Giving Criminal Jurisdiction to the Texas Courts of Civil Appeals and Recognizing the Inherent Power of the Texas Supreme Court," *Texas Tech Law Review* 33, no. 2 (2002): 377–404; Ben L. Mesches, "Bifurcated Appellate Review: The Texas Story of Two High Courts," *American Bar Association*, June 29, 2017, https://www.americanbar.org/groups/judicial/publications/judges_journal/2014/fall/bifurcated_appellate_review_the_texas_story_of_two_high_courts.

11. Jay Root, "Texas Democrats See Judge's Party Switch as Sign of Momentum," *Texas Tribune*, December 20, 2013, https://www.texastribune.org/2013/12/20/party-switch-gives-democrats-something-build/.

12. David Slayton and Megan LaVoie, "Paperless Courts," *Texas Bar Journal* 77 (January 2014): 24–26.

13. For a list of Texas's child protection courts and child support courts, see "Judicial Directory," *Office of Court Administration*, http://www.txcourts.gov/judicial-directory.aspx. For specialty courts that deal with criminal matters, see "Specialty Courts" *Office of the Governor*, https://gov.texas.gov/uploads/files/organization/criminal-justice/Specialty_Courts_By_County_December_2016.pdf.

14. Frank A. Sloan et al., "Do Specialty Courts Achieve Better Outcomes for Children in Foster Care than General Courts?" *Evaluation Review* 37 (October 2013): 3–34; and Robert D. Morgan et al., "Specialty Courts: Who's In and Are They Working?" *Psychological Services* 13 (2016): 246–253.

15. David Beck, "A Civil Justice System with No Trials: Are We Sure We Want to Go There?" *Texas Bar Journal* 76 (December 2013): 1073–1076; David W. Elrod and Worthy Walker, "Fact or Fiction: Are There Less Jury Trials and Lawyers? If So, What Do We Do About It?" *Litigation Commentary & Review* 53 (June/July 2010), http://www.elrodtrial.com/docs/publications/tadc%20jury%20trial%20speech.pdf.

16. Jeb Handelsman Shugerman, *The People's Courts: Pursuing Judicial Independence in America* (Cambridge, MA: Harvard University Press, 2012).

17. For a discussion of the way one attorney has supported opponents of judges who made unfavorable rulings against his clients, see Lisa Falkenberg, "System Appears to Let Lawyer Buy a Judge," *Houston Chronicle*, February 19, 2014.

18. Roy A. Schotland, "New Challenges to States' Judicial Selection," *Georgetown Law Journal* 95 (2007): 1077–1105.

19. Brian T. Fitzpatrick, "The Politics of Merit Selection," *Missouri Law Review* 74 (2009): 675–709.

20. Wallace Jefferson, "The State of the Judiciary," *Texas Bar Journal* 74 (April 2011): 282–284.

21. "Public Admonition, Honorable Nora Longoria, Justice 13th Court of Appeals; CJC NO. 14-1037-AP," *Texas Commission on Judicial Conduct* (March 13, 2015); CJC 17-0320-CO et al., *State Commission on Judicial Conduct* (April 5, 2018), http://www.scjc.texas.gov/disciplinary-actions/public-sanctions/fy-2018/judge-oakley.

22. John G. Browning and Don Willett, "Rules of Engagement: Exploring Judicial Use of Social Media," *Texas Bar Journal* 79 (February 2016): 100-102 at 102.

23. "Judicial Pratfalls," *Houston Chronicle*, May 7, 2014.

24. A discussion of the proceeding against Keller is available in Dave Montgomery, "Judge Who Refused to Keep Office Open in Death Row Case Shouldn't Be Removed, Ruling Says," *Fort Worth Star-Telegram*, January 21, 2010. The Special Court of Review's findings in this case can be accessed at http://caselaw.findlaw.com/tx-special-court-of-review-sct/1546619.html. For a discussion of the case against Chief Justice Nathan Hecht, see Paul Burka, "He's Doing a Hecht of a Job," *Texas Monthly*, July 31, 2007, http://www.texasmonthly.com/burka-blog/hes-doing-a-hecht-of-a-job. For a discussion of Justice Hecht's related case with the Texas Ethics Commission for soliciting funds to pay his lawyer's fees, see Chuck Lindell, "Nathan Hecht Pays $29,000 to End $1,000 Ethics Fine," *Austin American-Statesman*, October 28, 2015, http://www.statesman.com/news/news/nathan-hecht-pays-1000-to-end-29000-ethics-fine/npBNW. All cases against Hecht were resolved in 2015.

25. Christina Vassiliou Harvey, Mac R. McCoy, and Brook Sneath, "10 Tips for Avoiding Ethical Lapses When Using Social Media," *Business Law Today*, January 2014, http://www.americanbar.org/publications/blt/2014/01/03_harvey.html.

26. Lewis Powell, Address to the ABA Legal Services Program, American Bar Association Annual Meeting, August 10, 1976.

27. "Report of the Texas Commission to Expand Civil Legal Services," December 2016, http://www.txcourts.gov/media/1436563/complete-cecls-report.pdf.

28. Information on attorneys' pro bono work can be found in Nils Greger Olsson, "2015 Texas Attorney Survey: Pro Bono Report," August 2016, https://www.texasbar.com/AM/Template.cfm?Section=Archives&Template=/CM/ContentDisplay.cfm&ContentID=34184; and data on 2017 contributions to access-for-justice initiatives can be found at Texas Access for Justice Foundation, Justice for All Campaign, https://texasatj.org/justice-all-campaign.

29. *Major Issues of the 84th Legislature* (Austin: House Research Organization, September 22, 2015), 40–41.

30. R. G. Ratcliffe, "Grand Jury Goes Rogue on Attorney General Ken Paxton," *Texas Monthly,* April 9, 2015, http://www.texasmonthly.com/burka-blog/grand-jury-goes-rogue-on-attorney-general-ken-paxton.

31. For a discussion of the history of tort reform in Texas, see Mimi Swartz, "Hurt? Injured? Need a Lawyer? Too Bad!" *Texas Monthly*, November 2005, 164–169, 218–234, 254–258.

32. Joey Berlin, "Coming of Age: Celebrating 15 Years of Texas Tort Reform," *Texas Medicine*, September 2018, pp. 14–21, https://www.texmed.org/Template.aspx?id=48427.

33. Ibid.

34. David Arkush, Peter Gosselar, Christine Hines, and Taylor Lincoln, "Liability Limits in Texas Fail to Curb Medical Costs," December 2009, http://www.citizen.org/documents/Texas_Liability_Limits.pdf.

35. Lana Shadwick, "Texas Court Filings Are Down 17 Percent: Tort Reform Is Blamed," *Breitbart*, http://www.breitbart.com/texas/2015/03/08/texas-court-filings-are-down-17-percent-tort-reform-is-blamed.

36. Patrick Danner, "San Antonio Family Wins $124.5 Million Jury Verdict," *San Antonio Express News*, March 7, 2016, http://www.expressnews.com/business/local/article/San-Antonio-family-wins-124-5-million-jury-6875917.php.

37. "Vexatious Litigants," *Office of Court Administration,* http://www.txcourts.gov/judicial-data/vexatious-litigants.aspx.

38. Beck, "A Civil Justice System"; Elrod and Walker, "Fact or Fiction."

39. Texas Association of Counties, "Legislative Update: Indigent Defense," August 2018, https://www.county.org/TAC/media/TACMedia/Legislative/Indigent-Defense-Brief-Aug2018.pdf.

40. Tony Fabelo, Carl Reynolds, and Jessica Tyler, *Improving Indigent Defense: Evaluation of the Harris County Public Defender* (Austin: Council of Governments Justice Center), September 30, 2013; Neena Satija, "Harris County Judges and Private Attorneys Accused of Cronyism: 'Everybody Wins but the Kids,'" *Texas Tribune*, November 1, 2018, https://www.texastribune.org/2018/11/01/harris-county-texas-juvenile-judges-private-attorneys.

Chapter 11

1. "Spot Prices for Crude Oil and Other Petroleum Products," *U.S. Energy Information Administration*, http://www.eia.gov/dnav/pet/pet_pri_spt_s1_d.htm.

2. Glenn Hegar, *Biennial Revenue Estimate: 2016–2017 Biennium, 84th Texas Legislature* (Austin: Texas Comptroller of Public Accounts, January 2015), 5–6, https://www.comptroller.texas.gov/transparency/reports/biennial-revenue-estimate/2016-17/pdf/96-402.pdf.

3. Robert W. Gilmer, "Houston Economy in 2016: No Recovery in Oil Markets Brings Another Slow Year," *Institute for Regional Forecasting*, March 10, 2016, http://www.bauer.uh.edu/centers/irf/houston-updates-march16.php.

4. Chris Tomlinson, "What Really Happened with the Texas Miracle May Surprise You," *Houston Chronicle,* April 17, 2016.

5. "Texas Budget Challenges Are Not Over," *Texas Taxpayers and Research Association,* August 3, 2017, https://ttara.org/wp-content/uploads/2018/09/August2017TTARABudgetResearchReport_Final.pdf.

6. Milton Friedman, *Dollars and Deficits: Inflation, Monetary Policy, and Balance of Payments* (Saddle Brook, NJ: Prentice-Hall, 1968), 7.

7. Glenn Hegar, *A Field Guide to the Taxes of Texas* (Austin: Texas Comptroller of Public Accounts, December 2017) https://www.comptroller.texas.gov/transparency/revenue/docs/96-1744.pdf.

8. For a complete list of taxes and descriptions of each, see "Texas Taxes and Fees," *Texas Comptroller of Public Accounts*, https://www.comptroller.texas.gov/taxes/a-to-z.php.

9. "Fiscal 50: State Trends and Analysis," *The Pew Charitable Trusts*, January 29, 2019, https://www
.pewtrusts.org/en/research-and-analysis/articles/2014/05/19/fiscal-50-state-trends-and-analysis.

10. *San Juan Cellular Telephone Company v. Public Service Corporation of Puerto Rico* (First Cir.), 967 F
2nd 683 (1992).

11. Art. III, Sec. 49a, Texas Constitution (1942, amended 1999).

12. Rodney Ellis and Sylvester Turner, "Short-Sighted Cuts Costly to Poor," *Houston Chronicle*, August 29,
2011.

13. For an excellent resource that includes descriptions of the state's major tax sources and amounts collected in 2017, see Hegar, *A Field Guide to the Taxes of Texas*.

14. Glenn Hegar, *Tax Exemptions and Tax Incidence* (Austin: Texas Comptroller of Public Accounts,
November 2018), https://www.comptroller.texas.gov/transparency/reports/tax-exemptions-
and-incidence.

15. Glenn Hegar, *Biennial Revenue Estimate 2020–2021,* (Austin: Texas Comptroller of Public Accounts,
January 2019), https://comptroller.texas.gov/transparency/reports/biennial-revenue-estimate/2020-21.

16. Andrea Ahles, "Amazon to Open Second Fulfillment Center in North Fort Worth, Add 1,000 Jobs,"
Ft. Worth Star-Telegram, April 20, 2016, http://www.star-telegram.com/news/business/article72953667
.html.

17. *Texas Entertainment Association, Inc. v. Glenn Hegar, Comptroller,* Civil Action 1:17-CV-594.

18. Chris Tomlinson, "Texas Needs to Drop Its Franchise Tax and Come Up with Something Better,"
Houston Chronicle, April 5, 2016, http://www.houstonchronicle.com/business/columnists/tomlinson
/article/Franchise-tax-needs-to-go-better-business-tax-7230109.php. For an excellent discussion of the
history of the franchise tax, see Josh Haney and Chris Wright, "A History of the Texas Franchise Tax:
The Complex Evolution of Our Main Business Tax," *Fiscal Notes,* May 2015, https://www.comptroller
.texas.gov/economy/fiscal-notes/2015/may/franchisetax.php.

19. For articles on local protests to fracking and other concerns, see "Fracturing," *StateImpact:
Texas—Reporting on Power, Policy, and the Planet,* http://stateimpact.npr.org/texas/tag/fracking.

20. "Bill Analysis: Repealing the Inheritance Tax," *House Research Organization,* May 21, 2015, http://
www.hro.house.state.tx.us/pdf/ba84r/sb0752.pdf#navpanes=0.

21. Tex. Business and Commerce Code Ann. Sec. 326.001-326.002 (2013).

22. Brandi Grissom, "Texas Lottery Was in Hot Pursuit of DraftKings Daily Fantasy Game, Records
Show," *Dallas Morning News,* January 15, 2016, http://www.dallasnews.com/news/state
/headlines/20160115-records-texas-lottery-was-in-hot-pursuit-of-fantasy-sports-game.ece.

23. Dave Montgomery, "On Second Thought Texas House Opts Not to Kill Lottery Commission," *Fort
Worth Star-Telegram*, April 24, 2013.

24. Gromer Jeffers, "Gambling Bills Coming Up Losers in Legislature," *Dallas Morning News,* April 20,
2016, http://www.dallasnews.com/news/state/headlines/20150419-gambling-bills-coming-up-losers-
in-legislature.ece.

25. Ken Paxton, "Opinion No. KP0057: The Legality of Fantasy Sports Leagues under Texas Law," *Office of
the Attorney General,* January 19, 2016, http://media.oag.state.tx.us/mediaroom/2016/pdf/kp0057.pdf.

26. For a complete discussion of all the findings and recommendations, see "Legislative Committee
to Review the Texas Lottery and Charitable Bingo in Texas: Report to the 84th Legislature," *Texas
Senate,* November 2014, http://www.senate.state.tx.us/75r/Senate/commit/c895/downloads/c895.
InterimReport84th.pdf.

27. "Energy," *General Land Office of Texas*, http://www.glo.texas.gov/energy/index.html.

28. Texas Bond Review Board, *Annual Report 2018* (Austin: Texas Bond Review Board, December 2018),
http://www.brb.state.tx.us/publications_state.aspx#AR.

29. Jim Malewitz, "Plan to Overhaul Texas Rainy Day Fund and Boost Returns Losing Steam," *Texas
Tribune,* May 19, 2017, https://www.texastribune.org/2017/05/19/rainy-day-fund-overhaul-loses-
steam-senate; Glenn Hegar, "Long-Term Obligations and the Texas Legacy Fund," *Fiscal Notes,*
September/October 2018, https://comptroller.texas.gov/economy/fiscal-notes/2018/sep-oct/index
.php#article.

30. For an excellent description of the Texas budgeting process, see *Budget 101: A Guide to the Budget
Process in Texas* (Austin: Senate Research Center, January 2019), https://senate.texas.gov/_assets
/srcpub/86th_Budget_101.pdf.

31. Governor Greg Abbott, *2020–2021 Governor's Budget,* February 2019, https://gov.texas.gov/uploads
/files/press/Governors-Budget-FY-2020-2021.pdf.

32. Governor's Office Budget Division and Legislative Budget Board, "Instructions for Preparing and
Submitting Agency Strategic Plans: Fiscal Years 2019–2023," *Office of the Governor,* February 2018,
https://gov.texas.gov/uploads/files/organization/budget-policy/5110_Strategic_Plan_Instructions_
FINAL_posted_to_web_March_9.pdf.

33. Reynaldo Valencia, Sonia García, Henry Flores, and José Roberto Juárez, *Mexican Americans and the Law* (Tucson: University of Arizona Press, 2004), 29–37.

34. "Texas Higher Education Strategic Plan: 2015–2030, 60x30TX," July 2015, *Texas Higher Education Coordinating Board,* http://www.thecb.state.tx.us/reports/PDF/6862.PDF.

35. Alejandra Matos, "Texas Top-Ranked High Schools Don't Prepare Most Kids for College Data Shows," *Houston Chronicle,* September 28, 2018, https://www.houstonchronicle.com/news/local/article/Texas-top-ranked-high-schools-don-t-prepare-13266783.php.

36. Leslie Helmcamp, *Sizing Up the 2014–2015 Texas Budget: Student Financial Aid* (Austin: Center for Public Policy Priorities, August 30, 2013), http://forabettertexas.org/images/EO_2013_08_PP_BudgetSeries_FinAid.pdf.

37. Rick Perry, "State of the State Address, 2011," February 8, 2011, http://www.lrl.state.tx.us/scanned/govdocs/Rick%20Perry/2011/SOS_Perry_2011.pdf.

38. Thomas L. Harnisch, *Performance-Based Funding: A Re-emerging Strategy in Public Higher Education Financing* (Washington, DC: American Association of State Colleges and Universities, June 2011), http://www.aascu.org/policy.

39. Ronald Trowbridge, "Community Colleges Get Short Shrift in Funding," *Houston Chronicle*, July 12, 2013.

40. John Sharp, *Bordering the Future: Higher Education, Setting the Framework* (Austin: Office of the Comptroller of Public Accounts, July 1998); Richard R. Valencia, *Chicano Students and the Courts: The Mexican American Legal Struggle for Educational Equality* (New York: New York University Press, 2008), 255–267.

41. Julie Chang, "Dan Patrick: Lawmakers Should Regulate Tuition Again," *Austin American-Statesman*, April 26, 2016, http://www.statesman.com/news/news/dan-patrick-lawmakers-should-regulate-tuition-agai/nrB7j.

42. Joan Alker and Olivia Pham, "Nation's Progress on Children's Health Coverage Reverses Course," Georgetown University Health Policy Institute Center for Children and Families, November 21, 2018, https://ccf.georgetown.edu/2018/11/21/nations-progress-on-childrens-health-coverage-reverses-course.

43. Kevin McPherson, Jessica Donald, and Bruce Wright, "Transportation Infrastructure: Keeping Texas Moving," *Fiscal Notes,* May 2018, https://comptroller.texas.gov/economy/fiscal-notes/2018/may/transportation.php#article.

44. "Rainy Day Fund Turning into Revenue Flood," *Transportation Advocates of Texas,* January 5, 2014, http://transportationadvocatesoftexas.org/News%20Updates/1.5.14%20Revenue%20Flood.html.

45. Patrick Driscoll, "Gas Taxes Can't Fuel All Road Projects," *San Antonio Express-News*, December 4, 2005.

46. Texas Water Development Board, *Water for Texas: 2012 State Water Plan* (Austin: Texas Water Development Board, January 2012), http://www.twdb.texas.gov/waterplanning/swp/2012/index.asp, as amended by *Water for Texas: 2017 State Water Plan* (Austin: Texas Water Development Board, May 2016), http://www.twdb.texas.gov/waterplanning/swp/2017/doc/2017_SWP_Adopted.pdf.

47. Susan Combs, *Texas Water Report: Going Deeper for the Solution* (Austin: Office of the Comptroller of Public Accounts, January 2014).

48. Ari Phillips, "What Happens When the First Texas Town to Run Out of Water Gets Rainfall," *ClimateProgress,* June 4, 2015, http://thinkprogress.org/climate/2015/06/04/3664959/texas-town-drought-flood.

49. Claire Osborn, "U.S. Census: Texas Again Leads in Population Growth," *Austin Statesman*, December 24, 2018, https://www.statesman.com/news/20181224/us-census-texas-again-leads-in-population-growth.

50. Spencer Grubbs, Shannon Halbrook, Jessica Donald and Bruce Wright, "Texas Water: Planning for More," *Fiscal Notes*, April 2019, https://comptroller.texas.gov/economy/fiscal-notes/2019/apr/tx-water-planning.php.

Chapter 12

1. "Summary of Appropriations for the 2018–2019 Biennium," *Legislative Budget Board,* May 2017, https://comptroller.texas.gov/about/media-center/infographics/2017/budget-certification/http://www.lbb.state.tx.us/Documents/Appropriations_Bills/85/Conference_Bills/4083_Summary_CCR_SB1_2018-19.pdf.

2. The classic Robert L. Lineberry, *American Public Policy* (New York: Harper & Row, 1977), 2; and Thomas R. Dye, *Understanding Public Policy*, 15th ed. (Boston: Pearson, 2017), 1.

3. Ross Ramsey, "UT/TT Poll: A Hard Line on Immigration, But Not on Deporting "Dreamers","" *Texas Tribune*, October 23, 2017, https://www.texastribune.org/2017/10/23/uttt-poll-hard-line-immigration-not-deporting-dreamers.

4. For summaries of the research, see Rosalee A. Clawson and Zoe M. Oxley, *Public Opinion: Democratic Ideals, Democratic Practice*, 3rd ed. (Washington, DC: CQ Press, 2017), 352–356; and Carroll J. Glynn et al., *Public Opinion*, 3rd ed. (Boulder: Westview Press, 2016), 295–319.

5. Martin Gilens and Benjamin I. Page, "Testing Theories of American Politics: Elites, Interest Groups, and Average Citizens," *Perspectives on Politics* 12 (2014): 575.

6. Darryl Fears, "Texas Official's Report Ignites a New Border Conflict," *Washington Post*, December 15, 2006, http://www.washingtonpost.com/wp-dyn/content/article/2006/12/14/AR2006121401552.html?noredirect=on%20https://lawprofessors.typepad.com/immigration/files/TX.comptroller.report.pdf

7. "State Not Meeting Texas Nursing Home Costs for Taking Care of Medicaid Residents," THCA, August 2016, txhca.org/state-not-meeting-texas-nursing-home-costs-for-taking-care-of-medicaid-residents.

8. Amanda Fredriksen, "Improving the Quality of Texas Nursing Home Care," *AARP*, March 22, 2012, 9, http://www.senate.state.tx.us/75r/Senate/commit/c802/handouts12/0322-Fredriksen-AARP.pdf; and Dave Mann, "A Death in McAllen," *Texas Observer*, September 23, 2005, 6.

9. "Nursing Home Inspect," *ProPublica*, November 2018, http://projects.propublica.org/nursing-homes/state/TX.

10. "Intolerable Care," AARP of Texas, January 24, 2017, https://states.aarp.org/wp-content/uploads/2017/01/INTOLERABLE-CARE.pdf.

11. Jenny Deam, "Texas Ranks Last in U.S. in Nursing Home Care," *Houston Chronicle*, May 14, 2015, http://www.houstonchronicle.com/business/medical/article/Texas-ranks-last-in-U-S-in-nursing-home-care-6264584.php; Eric Nicholson, "Texas Leads the League in Bad Nursing Homes, Partly because It Won't Regulate the Offenders," *Dallas Observer*, December 18, 2012, http://www.dallasobserver.com/news/texas-leads-the-league-in-bad-nursing-homes-partly-because-it-wont-regulate-the-offenders-7139830; "Nursing Home Report Cards: Texas," *Families for Better Care*, 2014, https://nursinghomereportcards.com/state/tx/; Manuel Bojorquez, "Eleven States Get Failing Grades for Nursing Home Care," *CBS Evening News*, August 9, 2013, http://www.cbsnews.com/news/eleven-states-get-failing-grades-for-nursing-home-care; and "Long-Term Services & Supports State Scorecard," AARP, The Commonwealth Fund, and The SCAN Foundation, 2018, http://www.longtermscorecard.org/databystate/state?state=TX.

12. The seminal work on demographic change in Texas in the 21st century and the consequences of not meeting the needs of Texas minorities is Steve H. Murdock et al., *The New Texas Challenge: Population Change and the Future of Texas* (College Station: Texas A&M University Press, 2003); updated in Steve H. Murdock et al., *Changing Texas: Implications of Addressing or Ignoring the Texas Challenge* (College Station: Texas A&M University Press, 2014).

13. "Best High Schools in Texas," *U.S. News and World Report*, 2018, http://www.usnews.com/education/best-high-schools/search?state-urlname=texas.

14. "Summary of Charter Awards and Closures," *Texas Education Agency*, October 25, 2018, file:///Users/veronica.reyna/Downloads/Summary_of_Awards_and_Closures%20(1).pdf.

15. "Charter FAQ," *Texas Charter Schools Association*, http://www.txcharterschools.org/news-events/charter-faq. Although this is an advocacy group, earlier studies show similar results. Debra S. Haas examines 2005–2007 data in "An Analysis of Gaps in Funding for Charter Schools and Traditional Districts," *Institute for Public School Initiative, The University of Texas System*, http://utsystem.edu/ipsi. An analysis paid for by the Texas Charter School Association had similar conclusions for 2005–2009. See R. C. Wood & Associates, "Comparative Analyses of Revenues Generated from the Texas Foundation School Program for Independent School Districts and Charter School Districts," *ERIC* February 2011, http://eric.ed.gov/?id=EJ990974.

16. Kiah Collier, "Texas Supreme Court Upholds School Funding System," *Texas Tribune*, May 13, 2016, https://www.texastribune.org/2016/05/13/texas-supreme-court-issues-school-finance-ruling.

17. "Charter Schools No Cure-All for Black Students, Says Study," *UT News*, April 11, 2012, http://www.utexas.edu/news/2012/04/11/charter_vasquez_heilig; "Failure Is an Option," *Houston Chronicle*, January 31, 2010; and Jennifer Radcliffe, "Study Supports KIPP Success," *Houston Chronicle*, June 22, 2010.

18. "Charter School Performance in Texas," *Center for Research on Education Outcomes*, July 22, 2015, http://Credo.stanford.edu.

19. Patrick L. Baude, Marcus Casey, Eric A. Hanushek, and Steven G. Rivkin, "The Evolution of Charter School Quality," *The University of Chicago Harris School of Public Policy*, October 2014, http://harris.uchicago.edu/sites/default/files/Rivkin.paper_.pdf.

20. Morgan Smith, "Texas Schools Chief: Testing Has Gone Too Far," *Texas Tribune*, January 31, 2012, https://www.texastribune.org/2012/01/31/texas-school-chief-testing-has-gone-too-far.

21. Holly K. Hacker, "Love or Hate Them, New A-F Letter Grades for Texas Schools Are Here to Stay, Lt. Gov. Dan Patrick Says," *The Dallas Morning News*, January 2017, https://www.dallasnews.com/news/education/2017/01/11/love-hate-new-f-letter-grades-texas-schools-stay-lt-govdan-patrick-says.

22. "2019 Best Colleges: Colleges in Texas," *U. S. News and World Report*, http://colleges.usnews.rankingsandreviews.com/best-colleges/tx.

23. Paul Burka, "General Admission," *Texas Monthly*, April 2012, http://www.texasmonthly.com/story/general-admission; see also *Sweatt v. Painter*, 339 U.S. 629 (1950).

24. "2018 Texas Public Higher Education Almanac," *Texas Higher Education Coordinating Board*, Spring 2018, http://www.thecb.state.tx.us/reports/PDF/10900.pdf.

25. The Perryman Group, "A Tale of Two States—And One Million Jobs," *Texas Higher Education Coordinating Board*, March 2007, http://www.thecb.state.tx.us/reports/PDF/1345.PDF?CFID¼7562420&CFTOKEN¼51730738.

26. *University of California Regents v. Bakke*, 438 U.S. 265 (1978).

27. *Hopwood v. Texas*, 78 F.3d 932 (1996).

28. *Grutter v. Bollinger*, 539 U.S. 306 (2003).

29. *Gratz v. Bollinger*, 539 U.S. 244 (2003).

30. *Fisher v. University of Texas at Austin*, 133 S.Ct. 2411 (2013).

31. *Fisher v. University of Texas* (2016), 579 U.S. _____ (2016).

32. "A Red Flag," *Fort Worth Star-Telegram*, June 15, 2007. A similar argument is made by two health policy specialists from the University of Virginia, Arthur Garson Jr. and Carolyn Long Engelhard, "Texas Has Top Medical Centers but Provides Poor Health Care," *Houston Chronicle*, September 17, 2011, http://www.chron.com/opinion/outlook/article/Texas-has-top-medicalcentersbutprovides-poor-2174885.php.

33. David C. Radley, Doug McCarthy, and Susan L. Hayes, "Rising to the Challenge: The Commonwealth Fund Scorecard on Local Health System Performance," *Commonwealth Fund*, 2016, http://www.commonwealthfund.org/interactives/2016/jul/local-scorecard/; and "Featured Scorecards," *Commonwealth Fund, Health System Data Center*, http://www.commonwealthfund.org/Publications/Health-System-Scorecards.aspx. Another study, "Code Red," financed by Rice University, reached similar conclusions: Ruth Campbell, "Texas Health Care in Critical Condition," *Midland Reporter-Telegram*, April 1, 2007.

34. Robert T. Garrett, "Texas Faulted on Food Stamps," *Dallas Morning News*, January 13, 2010; and Editorial Board, "Privatization Failure Is Taxpayers' Burden," *Austin American-Statesman*, March 26, 2008.

35. Emily DePrang and Beth Cortez-Neavel, "Fostering Neglect," *Texas Observer*, June 2014, 19–25.

36. Emma Platoff and Edgar Walters, "Federal Appeals Court Finds Texas Foster Kids Were Endangered - But Strikes Down Some Attempts At Reform," *Texas Tribune*, October 18, 2018, https://www.texastribune.org/2018/10/18/foster-care-5th-circuit-order-reform.

37. Eva DeLuna Castro, "Poverty 101," *Center for Public Policy Priorities*, November 2011, http://www.cppp.org/files/8/2011_11_Poverty101.pdf.

38. For more information on these and other benefits, log on to *Your Texas Benefits* at http://www.yourtexasbenefits.com.

39. Dr. Howard Brody, "Expand Medicaid, Save Lives," *HoustonChronicle.com*, October 12, 2012, http://www.chron.com/opinion/outlook/article/Expand-Medicaid-save-lives-3950778.php. For other consequences, see Rachel Garfield, Anthony Damico, and Kendal Orgera, "The Coverage Gap: Uninsured Poor Adults in States That Do Not Expand Medicaid," *Kaiser Family Foundation*, June, 12, 2018, https://www.kff.org/medicaid/issue-brief/the-coverage-gap-uninsured-poor-adults-in-states-that-do-not-expand-medicaid.

40. "Texas HIV Surveillance Report 2017, Annual Report," *Texas Department of State Health Services*, July 27, 2018, https://www.dshs.texas.gov/hivstd/reports.

41. Jan Ross Piedad, "Bexar County Ranks Third for Most STD Cases in Texas as Nation Sees Record High," Texas Public Radio, September 19, 2018, https://www.tpr.org/post/bexar-county-ranks-third-most-std-cases-texas-nation-sees-record-high-rates.

42. "State Health Facts," *Kaiser Family Foundation*, accessed 2019, http://kff.org/other/state-indicator/smha-expenditures-per-capita/; and "Fiscal Size-Up, 2018–2019 Biennium," *Legislative Budget Board*, September 2018, http://www.lbb.state.tx.us/Documents/Publications/Fiscal_SizeUp/Fiscal_SizeUp.pdf.

43. Edgar Walters, "State Spending More on Mental Health Care, but Waitlist for Beds Grows," *Texas Tribune*, May 1, 2016, https://www.texastribune.org/2016/05/01/despite-state-spending-dearth-pysch-hospital-beds.

44. *Community Health Needs Assessment 2016* conducted by the Menninger Clinic, a psychiatric health system in Houston, https://www.menningerclinic.com/Assets/menninger-chna-final-report-6-30-16.pdf; Elizabeth Trovall, "Harris County Steps towards Mental Health Treatment Instead of Incarceration," *Houston Public Media*, October 10, 2018, https://www.houstonpublicmedia

.org/articles/news/in-depth/2018/10/10/307457/harris-county-steps-towards-mental-health-treatment-instead-of-incarceration.

45. "Small Business Policy Index 2018," *Small Business and Entrepreneurship Council*, February 2018, https://sbecouncil.org/wp-content/uploads/2018/02/SBPI2018-SBECouncil.pdf "The 50-State Small Business Regulation Index," *Pacific Research Institute*, July 2015, www.pacificresearch.org.

46. "Who Pays? A Distributional Analysis of the Tax Systems in All 50 States," 5th edition, *Institute on Taxation and Economic Policy*, January 2015, www.itepnet.org/whopays.htm; and "Measure of America: Human Development Index," Social Science Research Council, accessed July 5, 2016, www.measureofamerica.org/maps.

47. Russell Gold, *The Boom: How Fracking Ignited the American Energy Revolution and Changed the World* (New York: Simon and Shuster, 2014); reviewed by Michael Ennis, "The Rough Guide to Frackistan," *Texas Monthly*, May 2014, 56–64.

48. "Annual Average Electricity Price Comparison by State," *Official Nebraska Government Website, 2016*, http://www.neo.ne.gov/statshtml/204.htm; "Electricity Rates in Your State," Choose Energy, February 28, 2019, https://www.chooseenergy.com/electricity-rates-by-state.

49. Jim Malewitz, "Deregulated Electricity a Mixed Bag for Consumers," *Texas Tribune*, August 12, 2015, https://www.texastribune.org/2015/08/12/report-deregulated-electric-utilities-narrowing-pr.

50. "Average Cost of Insurance: Car, Home, Renters, Health, and Pet (2019)," *ValuePenguin*, http://www.valuepenguin.com/average-cost-of-insurance; "Homeowners Insurance Quote Review," *HomeownersInsurance.com*, 2016, htpp://homeownersinsurance.com/rates/; and "Car Insurance Rates by State, 2018 Edition," October 11, 2018, *Insure.com*, http://www.insure.com/car-insurance/car-insurance-rates.html.

51. Terrence Stutz, "Texas Home Insurers See Another Strong Year But Still Seek Limits on Lawsuits," *Dallas Morning News*, April 20, 2015, http://www.dallasnews.com/news/state/headlines/20150420-texas-home-insurers-see-another-strong-year-but-still-seek-limits-on-lawsuits.ece; and "Homeowners Insurance Loss Data in Texas," *Texas Department of Insurance*, http://www.helpinsure.com/home/documents/ex3lossdata.pdf.

52. "Testimony of Dr. David Ellis before the Senate Select Committee on Transportation Funding, Expenditures and Finance," *Texas A&M Transportation Institute*, June 24, 2014, http://tti.tamu.edu/policy/wp-content/uploads/2014/06/Senate-Select-Committee-Testimony-TTIb1.pdf; "TTI Helps Texas Legislators See into the Future," *Texas A&M Transportation Institute*, 2011, http://tti.tamu.edu/2011/06/01/tti-helps-texas-legislators-see-into-the-future/; and "Group Looks at Texas Road Repair, Safety & Traffic Issues," *CBSDFW*, January 17, 2013, http://dfw.cbslocal.com/2013/01/17/group-identifies-texas-transportation-problems.

53. "2018 Texas Transit Statistics," *Texas Department of Transportation*, December 2018, https://ftp.dot.state.tx.us/pub/txdot-info/ptn/transit_stats/2018.pdf.

54. Carlos Anchondo, "State Lawmakers Aim to Lock in Funding for Texas Parks, Historic Sites," *The Texas Tribune*, January 30, 2019, https://www.texastribune.org/2019/01/30/state-push-to-fully-fund-Texas-state-parks-and-historic-sites.

55. Forrest Wilder, "Agency of Destruction," *Texas Observer*, May 26, 2010, http://www.texasobserver.org/agency-of-destruction; and see Eliot Shapleigh, "Cronies at the Capitol: Connecting the Dots for TCEQ," in *Owner's Box* (El Paso: Shapleigh, 2010), 30–33.

56. "Billion Dollar Weather and Climate Disasters," *National Centers for Environmental Information*, accessed March 8, 2019, http://www.ncdc.noaa.gov/billions/mapping.

57. "Disposal Volume and Activity Table," *Texas Low Level Radioactive Waste Disposal Compact Commission*, 2017, http://www.tllrwdcc.org/reports-more/. Maine initially joined and then left the interstate compact before the disposal site was opened.

58. Christopher Helman, "Texas Billionaire Builds Giant Nuclear Waste Dump," *Forbes*, April 1, 2011, http://www.forbes.com/sites/christopherhelman/2011/04/01/texas-billionaire-builds-giant-nuclear-waste-dump; Julie Bykowicz, "Republican Donor Simmons Seeks Rule to Fill Texas Dump," *Bloomberg News*, April 5, 2012, http://www.bloomberg.com/news/articles/2012-04-05/republican-donor-simmons-seeks-rule-to-fill-texas-dump; and Kate Galbraith and Jay Root, "Texas Billionaire Nears Radioactive Waste Dump Victory," *Texas Tribune*, May 17, 2011, https://www.texastribune.org/2011/05/17/texas-billionaire-nears-radioactive-waste-dump-vic.

59. "Editorial: Out of Austin, Mixed Messages on Illegal Immigration," *Dallas Morning News*, June 6, 2015, http://www.dallasnews.com/opinion/editorials/2015/06/06/editorial-out-of-austin-mixed-messages-on-illegal-immigration.

60. Julián Aguilar, "Abbott Signs Sweeping Border Security Bill," *Texas Tribune*, June 9, 2015, https://www.texastribune.org/2015/06/09/abbott-signs-sweeping-border-security-bill.

61. Ibid.

62. Benjy Sarlin, "How America's Harshest Immigration Law Failed," *MSNBC*, May 9, 2014, http://www.msnbc.com/msnbc/undocumented-workers-immigration-alabama.

63. "Editorial: Out of Austin."

64. Ibid.

65. Adam Liptak and Michael D. Shear, "Obama Immigration Plan Seems to Divide Supreme Court," *New York Times*, April 18, 2016, http://www.nytimes.com/2016/04/19/us/politics/supreme-court-immigration.html?_r=0.

66. Nick Jimenez, "No Easy Answers in Resolving Immigration Problems," *Corpus Christi Caller-Times*, April 23, 2016, http://www.caller.com/columnists/nick-jimenez/no-easy-answers-in-resolving-immigration-problems-27aa034b-face-51df-e053-0100007f44e8-376786911.html.

Chapter 13

1. Skip Hollandsworth, "Gang Land," *Texas Monthly*, July 2015, http://www.texasmonthly.com/the-culture/gang-land.

2. Dana Schiller, "Waco Police Likely Struck 4 People Killed in Brawl," *Houston Chronicle*, December 11, 2015, http://www.houstonchronicle.com/news/houston-texas/houston/article/Report-Waco-police-likely-struck-4-bikers-killed-6692745.php.

3. The Texas Board of Pardons and Paroles (BPP) provides a list and severity ranking for every felony offense. This listing is available at http://www.tdcj.state.tx.us/bpp.

4. Brian M. Rosenthal, "First-Time Texas Drug Felons to Be Eligible for Food Stamps Again," *Houston Chronicle*, August 20, 2015. To review the Yale Medical School study, see Emily A. Wang, et al., "A Pilot Study Examining Food Insecurity and HIV Risk Behaviors Among Individuals Recently Released from Prison," *AIDS Education and Prevention* 25, no. 2 (2013): 112–123.

5. Nick Wing, "Our Bail System Is Leaving Innocent People to Die In Jail Because They're Poor," *Huffington Post*, February 23, 2017, https://www.huffingtonpost.com/entry/cash-bail-jail-deaths_us_57851f50e4b0e05f052381cb.

6. Jazmine Ulloa, "Drug Court Failing Black Offenders," *Austin American-Statesman*, December 26, 2015, http://www.mystatesman.com/news/news/local-govt-politics/drug-court-failing-black-offenders/nprby.

7. Caitlin Dunklee, Travis Leete, and Jorge Antonio Renaud, "Effective Approaches to Drug Crimes in Texas: Strategies to Reduce Crime, Save Money, and Treat Addiction," *Texas Criminal Justice Coalition*, January 2013, https://www.texascjc.org/system/files/publications/TCJC%20Addiction%20Primer%20%28Jan%202013%29.pdf.

8. Megan Menchaca, "Austin Leads Texas in Reported Hate Crimes in 2017," *The Daily Texan*, November 28, 2018, http://www.dailytexanonline.com/2018/11/28/austin-leads-texas-in-reported-hate-crimes-in-2017.

9. Ryan McCrimmon, "Hate Crimes, Sodomy Law Before House Panel," *Texas Tribune*, May 6, 2015, https://www.texastribune.org/2015/05/06/house-committee-takes-hate-crimes-anti-sodomy-law/; Maggie Astor, "Violence Against Transgender People Is on the Rise, Advocates Say," *The New York Times*, November 9, 2017, https://www.nytimes.com/2017/11/09/us/transgender-women-killed.html.

10. "Quick Facts: The Death Penalty System in Texas," *Texas Moratorium Network*, http://www.texasmoratorium.org/quick-facts.

11. For insight into possible racial bias in the use of the death penalty and one lawyer's experiences in defending death row inmates, see Bryan Stevenson, *Just Mercy: A Story of Justice and Redemption* (New York: Spiegel and Grau, 2015); see also Bruce Jackson and Diane Christian, *In This Timeless Time: Living and Dying on Death Row in America* (Chapel Hill: University of North Carolina Press, 2012). This book includes images of and interviews with Texas death row inmates. For a full discussion of the possible execution of an innocent man, see James Liebman, Shawn Crowley, Andrew Markquart, Lauren Rosenberg, Lauren Gallo White, and Daniel Zharkovsky, "Los Tocayos Carlos," *Columbia Human Rights Law Review* 43, no. 3 (2012): 711–1152.

12. "Race and the Death Penalty in Texas," *New York Times*, April 2, 2016, http://www.nytimes.com/2016/04/03/opinion/sunday/race-and-the-death-penalty-in-texas.html; Lawrence Hurley, "U.S. Top Court Backs Texas Death Row Inmate In Race Case," *Reuters*, February 22, 2017, https://www.reuters.com/article/usa-court-deathpenalty-idUSL1N1G70VT.

13. Jolie McCullough and Ben Hasson, "Faces of Death Row," *Texas Tribune*, May 12, 2016, https://apps.texastribune.org/death-row.

14. Ken Herman, "Drugs, Death, and the OU Game," *Austin American-Statesman*, April 1, 2014.

15. For a discussion of the Danish manufacturer's response to the use of Nembutal as part of the execution process, see Ed Pilkington, "Florida Execution: Drug Firm Protests to Governor over Lethal Injection," *Guardian*, September 27, 2011, https://www.theguardian.com/world/2011/sep/27/death-penalty-florida-pentobarbital-lethal-injection. For details about Texas's purchase of the drug, see Mike Ward, "Records: Texas Bought Execution Drugs Before Supply Dwindled," *Austin-American Statesman*, June 20, 2012.

16. Tom Dart, "Virgina to Execute Convicted Murderer after Texas Supplies Lethal Injection Drug," *Guardian,* September 25, 2015.

17. For a list of those states in which a moratorium is in force, see "Death Penalty in Flux," *Death Penalty Information Center,* http://www.deathpenaltyinfo.org/death-penalty-flux.

18. To see a comparison between states with the death penalty and states without death penalty, see "Deterrence: States without the Death Penalty Have Had Consistently Lower Murder Rates," *Death Penalty Information Center,* https://deathpenaltyinfo.org/deterrence-states-without-death-penalty-have-had-consistently-lower-murder-rates.

19. Kerwin Kofi Charles and Steven N. Durlauf, "Pitfalls in the Use of Time Series Methods to Study Deterrence and Capital Punishment," *Journal of Quantitative Criminology* 28 (February 2012): 45–66.

20. Traci L. Lacock and Michael L. Radelet, "Do Executions Lower Homicide Rates: The Views of Leading Criminologists," *Journal of Criminal Law and Crimonology,* 99, no. 2 (2009): 489–508.

21. Texas Department of Criminal Justice, "Death Row Facts," *Death Row Information, Texas Department of Criminal Justice,* http://www.tdcj.state.tx.us/death_row/dr_facts.html.

22. Richard C. Dieter, "On the Front Line: Law Enforcement Views on the Death Penalty," *Death Penalty Information Center,* February 1995, http://www.deathpenaltyinfo.org/front-line-law-enforcement-views-death-penalty#fn15.

23. *Panetti v. Quarterman,* 551 U.S. 930 (2007).

24. Brandi Grissom, "Trouble in Mind: How Should Criminals Who Are Mentally Ill Be Punished?" *Texas Monthly,* March 2013, http://www.texasmonthly.com/story/trouble-mind.

25. Jolie McCullough, "Execution Stayed for Dallas Accountant Who Killed Daughter," *Texas Tribune,* March 30, 2016; https://www.texastribune.org/2016/03/30/dallas-accountant-faces-execution-daughters-deaths; Tassneem Nashrulla and Chris Geidner, "Appeal Court Halts Texas Execution Amid Claims of Mental Illness," *Buzzfeednews.com,* March 30, 2016, https://www.buzzfeed.com/tasneemnashrulla/appeals-court-halts-texas-execution-amid-claims-of-mental-il?utm_term=.yilWZgzorm#.fixr07EWwk.

26. For a discussion of the history of the Texas prison system, see Robert Perkinson, *Texas Tough: The Rise of America's Prison Empire* (New York: Metropolitan, 2010). Some reviewers have faulted this book for not reflecting improvements in the Texas prison system in recent years; Marc Levin, "More Criminal Justice Reform for Texas in 2018," *Houston Chronicle,* January 16, 2018, https://www.houstonchronicle.com/opinion/outlook/article/Levin-More-criminal-justice-reform-for-Texas-in-12499603.php.

27. Nicole D. Porter, "The State of Sentencing 2015: Developments of Policy and Practice," *The Sentencing Project,* February 10, 2016, http://www.sentencingproject.org/publications/the-state-of-sentencing-2015-developments-in-policy-and-practice.

28. *Adult and Juvenile Correctional Population Projections: Fiscal Years 2019–2024* (Austin: Texas Legislative Budget Board, January 2019), https://www.lbb.state.tx.us/Documents/Publications/Policy_Report/4910_Correctional_Population_Projections_Jan_2019.pdf.

29. "Texas Population 2013," *World Population Statistics,* http://www.worldpopulationstatistics.com/texas-population-2013.

30. Mark Holden and Brooke Rollins, "Commentary: Texas Saved $3B Closing Prisons. Why Rehabilitation Works," *Austin American-Statesman,* September 25, 2018, https://www.statesman.com/news/20180209/commentary-texas-saved-3b-closing-prisons-why-rehabilitation-works.

31. Gaby Galvin, "Underfunded, Overcrowded State Prisons Struggle with Reform," *U.S. News & World Report,* July 26, 2017, https://www.usnews.com/news/best-states/articles/2017-07-26/understaffed-and-overcrowded-state-prisons-crippled-by-budget-constraints-bad-leadership.

32. Human Rights Clinic, University of Texas School of Law, *Reckless Indifference: Deadly Heat in Texas Prisons,* March 2015, https://law.utexas.edu/wp-content/uploads/sites/11/2015/04/2015-HRC-USA-Reckless-Indifference-Report.pdf; Lance Lowry, "Heat in Texas Prisons Is a Boiling Liability," *Austin American-Statesman,* January 2, 2014.

33. Ibid.

34. An investigation at one prison unit disclosed drug and money-laundering activities that allegedly involved both prisoners and prison staff members. In a recorded phone call between a prisoner and his father, the inmate observed that prison guards would continue to smuggle contraband "as long as there was money to be made." Mike Ward, "Prison Smuggling Detailed," *Austin American-Statesman,* May 6, 2010; and Mark Ward, "K2 Problem Invades Texas Prisons," *Texas Chron,* July 3, 2017, https://www.chron.com/news/politics/texas/article/K2-problem-invades-Texas-prisons-11262602.php.

35. Matthew Clarke, "Texas Begins Intercepting and Blocking Cell Phone Calls from Prisons," *Prison Phone Justice,* January 7, 2016, https://www.prisonphonejustice.org/news/2016/jan/7/texas-begins-intercepting-and-blocking-cell-phone-calls-prisons.

36. "Inmate Phone Costs Should Be Reasonable," *Beaumont Enterprise,* April 5, 2016.

37. Terrance Allen and Reginald Smith, "Different Approach Needed after Inmates Are Released," *Austin American-Statesman*, April 14, 2016.

38. Marc Levin and Ann Yanez Correa, "Correcting the Texas Justice System," *Fort Worth Star-Telegram*, September 1, 2015.

39. Beth Avery and Phil Hernandez, "Ban the Box: U.S. Cities, Counties, and States Adopt Fair Hiring Policies," *National Employment Law Project*, September 25, 2018, https://www.nelp.org/publication /ban-the-box-fair-chance-hiring-state-and-local-guide; "Austin Becomes First Fair Chance Hiring City in the South," *City of Austin's Mayor Adler*, March 25, 2016, http://www.mayoradler.com/austin-becomes-first-fair-chance-hiring-city-in-the-south/.

40. Gabrielle Banks, "Harris County Bail System Unconstitutional, Federal Judge Rules," *Chron*, February 14, 2018, https://www.chron.com/news/houston-texas/houston/article/Harris-County-bail-system-unconstitutional-11108210.php.

41. Brian Rogers, "In Harris County, Punishment for Marijuana Depends on Where You're Caught," *Houston Chronicle*, January 24, 2018, https://www.houstonchronicle.com/news/houston-texas/article /Bay-area-law-enforcement-others-ignore-Harris-12511261.php.

42. Brandi Grissom, "With Crime, Incarceration Rates Falling, Texas Closes Record Number of Prisons," *The Dallas Morning News*, July 2017, https://www.dallasnews.com/news/texas-legislature/2017/07/05 /crime-incarceration-rates-falling-texas-closes-record-number-lock-ups.

43. John MacCormack, "Private Prison Boom Goes Bust," *San Antonio-Express News*, August 23, 2015.

44. "Overview of the Texas Juvenile Justice System," *Legislative Budget Board*, March 2016, http://www .lbb.state.tx.us/Documents/Publications/Issue_Briefs/3081_TX_JJS.pdf.

45. Jolie McCullough, "Following Sexual Abuse Scandals, Texas Juvenile Justice Department Submits Plan to Revamp Agency," *The Texas Tribune*, June 1, 2018, https://www.texastribune.org/2018/06/01 /Texas-Juvenile-Justice-Department-greg-abbott.

46. Mike Ward, "Sexual Misconduct Investigations Target North Texas Youth Lockup," *Chron*, November 7, 2017, https://www.chron.com/news/politics/texas/article/Sexual-misconduct-investigation-targets-North-12337875.php.

47. "Study Shows Community-Based Supervision, Not State-Run Incarceration, Leads to More Success for Texas Youth in Juvenile Justice System," *Justice Center Council of State Governments*, January 29, 2015, https://csgjusticecenter.org/youth/press-releases/study-shows-community-based-supervision-not-state-run-incarceration-leads-to-more-success-for-texas-youth-in-juvenile-justice-system.

48. Ryan McCrimmon, "Study Touts Community Programs for Juvenile Offenders," *Texas Tribune*, January 29, 2015, https://www.texastribune.org/2015/01/29/study-keep-youth-offenders-in-their-community.

49. Ibid.

50. Nicole Scialabba, "Should Juveniles Be Charged as Adults in the Criminal Justice System," *American Bar Association*, October 3, 2016, https://www.americanbar.org/groups/litigation/committees /childrens-rights/articles/2016/should-juveniles-be-charged-as-adults.

51. Office of Juvenile Justice and Delinquency Programs, "Statistical Briefing Book: Juvenile Justice System Structures and Process," *U.S. Department of Justice*, October 1, 2015, http://www.ojjdp.gov /ojstatbb/structure_process/qa04101.asp.

52. Franco, Nils, "Raise the Age Bills Flourish in 2016," *Campaign for Youth Justice: Research and Policy*, March 15, 2016, http://cfyj.org/news/blog/item/raise-the-age-bills-flourish-in-2016. See also, Patrick Michels, "Bringing 17-Year-Olds into Juvenile Justice System," *Texas Observer*, April 2, 2015, https:// www.texasobserver.org/juvenile-justice-house-support-for-bringing-17-year-olds.

53. Matt Clarke, "Texas Prison Population Drops as Guard Shortage Persists," *Prison Legal News*, January 10, 2015, https://www.prisonlegalnews.org/news/2015/jan/10/texas-prison-population-drops-guard-shortage-persists.

54. Jolie McCullough, "'You're Not as Safe as You Should Be.' How understaffing is affecting one Texas prison," *The Texas Tribune*, May 9, 2018, https://www.texastribune.org/2018/05/09/understaffing-texas-prisons-telford-maximum-security-prison-timothy-da.

55. Brandi Grissom, "Suicides and Attempts on the Rise in Texas Prisons," *Dallas Morning News*, November 28, 2015, http://www.dallasnews.com/news/state/headlines/20151128-suicides-and-attempts-on-the-rise-in-texas-prisons.ece; and Matthew Clarke, "Prisoner Suicides and Attempts Increasing in Texas," *Prisoner Legal News*, March 9, 2017, https://www.prisonlegalnews.org/news /2017/mar/9/prisoner-suicides-and-attempts-increasing-texas.

56. Erica Hellerstein, "The Death Of Victoria Gray: How Texas Jails Are Failing Their Most Vulnerable Captives," *ThinkProgress*, September 15, 2015.

57. Kate Murphy and Christi Barr, "Overincarceration of People with Mental Illness: Pretrial Diversion Across the Country and the Next Steps for Texas to Improve Its Efforts and Increase Utilization," *Texas Public Policy Foundation: Center for Effective Justice*, June 2015, 11–12, http://www.texaspolicy .com/library/doclib/Overincarceration-of-People-with-Mental-Illness.pdf.

58. Jolie McCullough, "Texas House, Senate Budget Plans Tens of Millions Apart on Prisoner Health Care," *Texas Tribune*, January 18, 2019, https://www.texastribune.org/2019/01/18/texas-prisons-health-care-texas-legislature-budget-proposals.

59. Edgar Walters, "In Cellphone Contraband Cases, Few Face Charges," *Texas Tribune,* May 4, 2014, https://www.texastribune.org/2014/05/04/cellphone-contraband-cases-few-face-charges.

60. Madlin Mekelburg, "New Prison Rule Means Texas Jailbirds Can't Tweet," *Texas Tribune,* April 14, 2016, https://www.texastribune.org/2016/04/14/criminal-justice-department-banning-inmates-social.

61. Michael Morton, *Getting Life: An Innocent Man's 25-Year Journey from Prison to Peace* (New York: Simon and Schuster, 2014).

62. "Exoneration Map," *The National Registry of Exonerations*, http://www.law.umich.edu/special /exoneration/Pages/Exonerations-in-the-United-States-Map.aspx.

63. "Exonerations by Year: DNA and Non-DNA," *The National Registry of Exonerations,* March 10, 2019, https://www.law.umich.edu/special/exoneration/Pages/Exoneration-by-Year.aspx.

64. "DNA Exonerations in the United States," The Innocence Project, 2019, https://www .innocenceproject.org/dna-exonerations-in-the-united-states.

65. Colin G. Tredoux, Christian A. Meisner, Roy S. Malpass, and Laura A. Zimmerman, "Eyewitness Identification," *Encyclopedia of Applied Psychology*, vol. 1, ed. C. D. Spielberg (New York: Elsevier Academic Press, 2004), 875–887.

66. Sydney Greene, "Fewer Exonerations in Texas' Harris County Drove National Rate Lower Too, Study Finds," *Texas Tribune*, March 14, 2018, https://www.texastribune.org/2018/03/14/study-finds-harris-county-decreased-exonerations-last-year.

67. For a discussion of the criminal justice system's disparate impact on African Americans, see Michelle Alexander, *The New Jim Crow: Mass Incarceration in the Age of Colorblindness* (New York: New Press, 2010).

68. Mark Berman and Wesley Lowery, "The 12 Key Highlights from the DOJ's Scathing Ferguson Report," *Washington Post*, March 4, 2015, https://www.washingtonpost.com/news/post-nation/wp/2015/03/04 /the-12-key-highlights-from-the-dojs-scathing-ferguson-report.

69. K. K. Rebecca Lai, Haeyoun Park, Larry Buchanan, and Wilson Andrews "Assessing the Legality of Sandra Bland's Arrest," *New York Times*, July 20, 2015, http://www.nytimes.com/interactive/2015 /07/20/us/sandra-bland-arrest-death-videos-maps.html.

70. Manny Fernandez, Richard Pèrez-Peña, and Jonah Engel Bromwich, "Five Dallas Officers Were Killed as Payback, Police Chief Says," *New York Times,* July 8, 2016, http://www.nytimes.com/2016/07/09/us /dallas-police-shooting.html?_r=0.

71. Roland G. Fryer, Jr., "An Empirical Analysis of Racial Differences in Police Use of Force," Working Paper, *Harvard University*, July 2016, http://scholar.harvard.edu/fryer/publications/empirical-analysis-racial-differences-police-use-force.

72. Lee P. Brown, "Community Policing: A Practical Guide for Police Officials," *Perspectives on Policing,* September 1989, https://www.ncjrs.gov/pdffiles1/nij/118001.pdf.

73. Brandi Grissom, "Study: Prosecutors Did Not Face Discipline for Misconduct in Cases," *Texas Tribune*, March 29, 2012, http://www.texastribune.org/2012/03/29/study-prosecutors-not-disciplined-misconduct.

74. Matt Ferner. "Prosecutors Are Almost Never Disciplined for Misconduct," *Huffington Post*, February 11, 2016, http://www.huffingtonpost.com/entry/prosecutor-misconduct-justice_us_56bce00fe4b0c3c55050748a.

75. Jon Herskovitz, "Former Texas Prosecutor Disbarred for Sending Innocent Man to Death Row," *Reuters*, February 8, 2016, 69, http://www.reuters.com/article/texas-prosecutor-idUSL2N15N253; Texas Appleseed and Texas Defender Service, *Towards More Transparent Justice: The Michael Morton Act's First Year* (Austin: Texas Appleseed and Texas Defender Service, 2015), http://texasdefender.org /wp-content/uploads/Towards_More_Transparent_Justice.pdf.

76. Tex. Code of Crim. Proc. Ann. Sec. 39.14 (2013).

Index